Why do you need this new edition?

This edition of *LB Brief* differs from the previous edition in countless ways. Here are five that make the book indispensable:

1 More help with college reading and writing ▪ A chapter on **academic writing** explains the key academic skill of synthesizing your own and others' views as you write in response to texts and images. ▪ **Nine student papers** illustrate the varieties of college papers you may be asked to write. ▪ Material on **text-message and e-mail shortcuts** gives tips for editing them in your academic writing.

2 More help with research writing ▪ Material on **finding and evaluating sources** covers all kinds of print and electronic sources and shows how to distinguish reliable and unreliable sources. ▪ A **research-paper-in-progress** on the environment follows one student's research and writing process, making it easy to see what's expected of you.

3 Up-to-date, more accessible help with citing sources ▪ Detailed explanations and highlighted examples present **the most recent revisions of MLA and APA documentation styles** and show how to document a wide range of print and electronic sources. ▪ **Annotated sample sources** show how to find and format bibliographic information in articles, books, and Web sites.

4 New help with the writing process ▪ A **student work-in-progress** on globalization and jobs illustrates how the writing process can serve you in college work.

5 Access to *MyCompLab* ▪ *LB Brief* is even more useful when you combine it with *MyCompLab,* a Web gateway to resources on grammar, writing, and research developed specifically for writers.

PEARSON

PEARSON
mycomplab

Become a better writer and researcher—and get better grades in all your courses—with *MyCompLab*!

COMPOSING

Compose, revise, and edit all your work in this easy-to-use space that functions like the most popular word-processing programs. Write, store, and manage all your work in one place.

WRITER'S TOOLKIT

Find help in this array of grammar, writing, and research tools that accompanies the Composing space. The Toolkit includes sample student papers, access to live tutoring from Pearson Tutor Services, a bibliography builder from Noodlebib, and much more!

RESOURCES

● Access instruction,
multimedia tutorials,
and exercises in the
Resources area to help
you master skills and
get a better grade.

ADDITIONAL FEATURES

Manage all your written ●
work and assignments
online, in one
easy-to-use place.

Monitor your writing
and exercise scores
in the Gradebook area.

Access a Pearson eText of
your handbook—search
it for key terms, take
notes, and more.
*Please note: Your MyCompLab
account comes with
a Pearson eText only if you or
your instructor ordered
the Pearson eText version.*

......● Register for *MyCompLab* today!

Questions? Go to *www.mycomplab.com/help.html*
and click "Student Support."

If this book did not come packaged with an access
code to *MyCompLab*, you can purchase access online
at *www.mycomplab.com/buy-access.html* or ask your bookstore to order an
access card for you.

LB

Brief

The Little, Brown Handbook, *Brief Version*

FOURTH EDITION

JANE E. AARON

Longman

Boston Columbus Indianapolis New York San Francisco Upper Saddle River
Amsterdam Cape Town Dubai London Madrid Milan Munich Paris Montreal Toronto
Delhi Mexico City São Paulo Sydney Hong Kong Seoul Singapore Taipei Tokyo

Executive Editor: Suzanne Phelps Chambers
Editorial Assistant: Erica Schweitzer
Senior Development Editor: Anne Brunell Ehrenworth
Senior Supplements Editor: Donna Campion
Senior Media Producer: Stefanie Liebman
Senior Marketing Manager: Susan Stoudt
Production Manager: Bob Ginsberg
Project Coordination, Text Design, and Electronic Page Makeup:
   Nesbitt Graphics, Inc.
Cover Design Manager: John Callahan
Cover Designer: Kay Petronio
Visual Researcher: Rona Tuccillo
Senior Manufacturing Buyer: Alfred C. Dorsey
Printer and Binder: RR Donnelley/Crawfordsville
Cover Printer: Lehigh Phoenix

For permission to use copyrighted material, grateful acknowledgment is made to the copyright holders on p. 530, which is hereby made part of this copyright page.

Library of Congress Cataloging-in-Publication Data

Aaron, Jane E.
  LB brief : the Little, Brown handbook, brief version / Jane E. Aaron. —
4th ed.
    p. cm.
  ISBN-13: 978-0-205-76276-7
  ISBN-10: 0-205-76276-X
  ISBN-13: 978-0-205-75155-6 (tabbed ed.)
  ISBN-10: 0-205-75155-5 (tabbed ed.)
  1. English language—Grammar—Handbooks, manuals, etc. 2. English
language—Rhetoric—Handbooks, manuals, etc. I. Title.
  PE1112.A22 2010
  808'.042—dc22
                        2009048847

1 2 3 4 5 6 7 8 9 10—DOC—13 12 11 10

Longman
is an imprint of

ISBN-13: 978-0-205-76276-7
ISBN-10:   0-205-76276-X
ISBN-13: 978-0-205-75155-6 (tabbed edition)
ISBN-10:   0-205-75155-5 (tabbed edition)

www.pearsonhighered.com

Preface for Students

LB Brief contains the basic information you'll need for writing in and out of school. Here you can find out how to get ideas, use commas, search the Web, cite sources, write a résumé, and more—all in a convenient, accessible package.

This book is mainly a reference for you to dip into as needs arise. You probably won't read the book all the way through, nor will you use everything it contains: you already know much of the content anyway, whether consciously or not. The trick is to figure out what you *don't* know—taking cues from your own writing experiences and the comments of others—and then to find the answers to your questions in these pages.

Before you begin using this book, you may need to clear your mind of a very common misconception: that writing is only, or even mainly, a matter of correctness. True, any written message will find a more receptive audience if it is correct in grammar, punctuation, and similar matters. But these concerns should come late in the writing process, after you've allowed yourself to discover what you have to say, freeing yourself to make mistakes along the way. As one writer put it, you need to get the clay on the potter's wheel before you can shape it into a bowl, and you need to shape it into a bowl before you can perfect it. So get your clay on the wheel and work with it until it looks like a bowl. Then worry about correctness.

Finding what you need

You have many ways to find what you need in the handbook:

- **Use a directory.** "Frequently Asked Questions" (inside the front cover) provides questions in everyday language that are commonly asked about the book's main topics. "Contents" (inside the back cover) gives a detailed overview of the entire book.
- **Use the glossary.** "Glossary of Usage" (pp. 517–29) clarifies more than 250 words that are often confused or misused.
- **Use the index.** The extensive index lists every topic, term, and problem word or expression mentioned in the book.
- **Use a list.** Two helpful aids fall on the last pages of the book: "CULTURE LANGUAGE Guide" pulls together all the book's material for students using standard American English as a second language or a second dialect. And "Editing Symbols" explains abbreviations often used to mark papers.
- **Use the elements of the page.** As shown on the next page, each page of the handbook tells you what you can find there.

The handbook's page elements

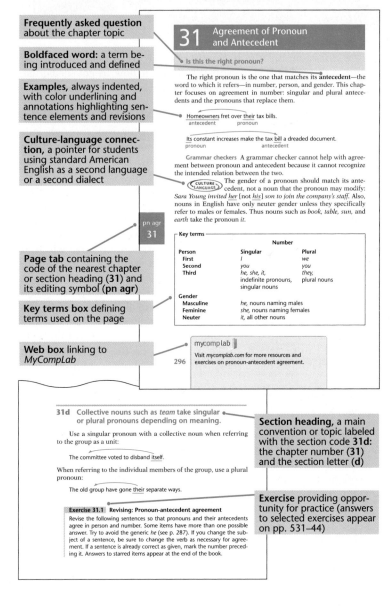

Frequently asked question about the chapter topic

Boldfaced word: a term being introduced and defined

Examples, always indented, with color underlining and annotations highlighting sentence elements and revisions

Culture-language connection, a pointer for students using standard American English as a second language or a second dialect

Page tab containing the code of the nearest chapter or section heading (**31**) and its editing symbol (**pn agr**)

Key terms box defining terms used on the page

Web box linking to *MyCompLab*

Section heading, a main convention or topic labeled with the section code **31d:** the chapter number (**31**) and the section letter (**d**)

Exercise providing opportunity for practice (answers to selected exercises appear on pp. 531–44)

---

31 Agreement of Pronoun and Antecedent

Is this the right pronoun?

The right pronoun is the one that matches its **antecedent**—the word to which it refers—in number, person, and gender. This chapter focuses on agreement in number: singular and plural antecedents and the pronouns that replace them.

Homeowners fret over their tax bills.
antecedent   pronoun

Its constant increases make the tax bill a dreaded document.
pronoun   antecedent

Grammar checkers A grammar checker cannot help with agreement between pronoun and antecedent because it cannot recognize the intended relation between the two.

CULTURE-LANGUAGE The gender of a pronoun should match its antecedent, not a noun that the pronoun may modify: *Sara Young invited her* [not *his*] *son to join the company's staff*. Also, nouns in English have only neuter gender unless they specifically refer to males or females. Thus nouns such as *book, table, sun,* and *earth* take the pronoun *it*.

pn agr 31

Key terms

	Number	
Person	Singular	Plural
First	*I*	*we*
Second	*you*	*you*
Third	*he, she, it,*	*they,*
	indefinite pronouns,	plural nouns
	singular nouns	

Gender		
Masculine	*he,* nouns naming males
Feminine	*she,* nouns naming females
Neuter	*it,* all other nouns

mycomplab
Visit *mycomplab.com* for more resources and exercises on pronoun-antecedent agreement.

296

31d Collective nouns such as *team* take singular or plural pronouns depending on meaning.

Use a singular pronoun with a collective noun when referring to the group as a unit:

The committee voted to disband itself.

When referring to the individual members of the group, use a plural pronoun:

The old group have gone their separate ways.

Exercise 31.1 Revising: Pronoun-antecedent agreement
Revise the following sentences so that pronouns and their antecedents agree in person and number. Some items have more than one possible answer. Try to avoid the generic *he* (see p. 287). If you change the subject of a sentence, be sure to change the verb as necessary for agreement. If a sentence is already correct as given, mark the number preceding it. Answers to starred items appear at the end of the book.

Preface for Instructors

LB Brief provides writers with a reliable, accessible, and affordable reference. Merging the authority of its parent, *The Little, Brown Handbook,* and a concise format, this handbook answers frequently asked questions about the writing process, critical thinking, grammar and style, research writing, and more. With its cross-curricular outlook, easy-to-use format, and assumption of little or no experience with writing or handbooks, *LB Brief* helps students of varying interests and skills.

This new edition improves on the handbook's strengths while keeping pace with the rapid changes in writing and its teaching. In the context of the handbook's many reference functions, the following pages highlight as New the most significant additions and changes.

An introduction to academic writing

The handbook introduces students to the goals and requirements of college writing assignments.

- Nine sample papers, highlighted in "Contents" inside the back cover, illustrate many varieties of college writing, including personal narrative, response to reading, critique, research writing using MLA and APA styles, writing about literature, and essay exams.
- New A reconceived chapter on academic writing shows students how to write in response to texts.
- New Synthesis receives special emphasis wherever students might need help balancing their own and others' views, such as in responding to texts.
- New Expanded advice on avoiding plagiarism shows students at every turn how to acknowledge borrowed material.
- New A greater stress on opposing views in argument includes discussion of Rogerian approaches.
- Part 7 gives students a solid foundation in research writing. Extensive chapters cover documentation and format in MLA and APA styles.

A guide to research writing

With detailed advice and a sample MLA paper, the handbook always attends closely to research writing. The discussion stresses using the library as Web gateway, managing information, evaluating and synthesizing sources, integrating source material, and avoiding plagiarism.

- ■ New A research-paper-in-progress on green consumerism follows a student through the research process and culminates in an annotated paper documented in MLA style.
- ■ New An expanded discussion of evaluating sources illustrates critical criteria with sample articles and Web documents.
- ■ New Many kinds of electronic resources—including blogs, wikis, and multimedia as well as Web documents—receive attention as possible sources that require careful evaluation and documentation.
- ■ New Expanded coverage of paraphrase shows a line-by-line comparison of a research source and a student's paraphrase.
- ■ New The advice for generating primary sources now covers conducting observations and surveys as well as interviews.

A reference for documenting sources

The extensive coverage of MLA and APA documentation styles reflects each style's latest version and includes many examples of electronic sources.

- ■ New MLA style is expanded and completely updated to reflect the 2009 *MLA Handbook for Writers of Research Papers,* Seventh Edition.
- ■ New APA style is updated to reflect the second printing of the 2009 *Publication Manual of the American Psychological Association,* Sixth Edition.
- ■ New Annotated samples of key source types accompany MLA and APA documentation, showing students how to find the bibliographical information needed to cite each type.
- ■ New Highlighting on all documentation models makes authors, titles, dates, and other citation elements easy to grasp.

A guide to the writing process

The handbook takes a concise, practical approach to assessing the writing situation, generating ideas, developing the thesis statement, revising, and other elements of the writing process.

- ■ New A student's work-in-progress on globalization and outsourcing illustrates the stages of the writing process.
- ■ New Coverage of thesis development now includes discussion and examples of explanatory and argumentative thesis statements.
- ■ An extensive chapter on paragraphs provides twenty-five annotated examples.

- An extensive chapter on document design includes help with using illustrations and a section on designing for readers with vision loss.

A reference for usage, grammar, and punctuation

The handbook's core reference material reliably and concisely explains basic concepts and common errors.

- New Advice on avoiding the informalities common to online communication targets nonstandard grammar, punctuation, abbreviations, and spelling.
- Hundreds of examples use color underlining to show clearly both the look of errors and the means of correcting them.
- More than 115 exercise sets give students practice with usage, grammar, punctuation, and mechanics as well as with rhetorical concerns such as thesis statements and paraphrasing. The exercises are in connected discourse, and their subjects come from across the academic curriculum. About half of the exercises are answered in the back of the book.

A guide for culturally and linguistically diverse writers

At notes and sections labeled ⬭CULTURE LANGUAGE⬭, the handbook provides extensive rhetorical and grammatical help for writers whose first language or dialect is not standard American English.

- Fully integrated coverage, instead of a separate section, means that students can find what they need without having to know which problems they do and don't share with native SAE speakers.
- The "⬭CULTURE LANGUAGE⬭ Guide," just before the back endpapers, orients students with advice on mastering SAE and pulls all the integrated coverage together in one place.

A guide to visual literacy

The handbook helps students process visual information and use it effectively in their writing.

- New The discussion of viewing images critically uses fresh and diverse examples to demonstrate identifying and analyzing visual elements.
- New A student's work illustrates the process of analyzing an advertisement.
- Detailed help with preparing or finding illustrations appears in the discussions of document design and research writing.

A uniquely accessible reference

LB Brief opens itself to students, featuring not only a convenient spiral binding but also numerous features designed to help students find what they need and then use what they find.

- "Frequently Asked Questions" provides students with a common-language portal for reaching the handbook's contents. The questions appear inside the front cover and again at the beginning of each chapter.
- The detailed "Contents" appears inside the back cover.
- An unusually direct organization arranges topics in ways that students can easily grasp.
- Rules and other headings use minimal terminology, with examples replacing or supplementing terms.
- "Key terms" boxes define secondary terms used on each page and minimize cross-references.
- Nearly fifty checklist and summary boxes highlight key reference information, such as questions about audience, uses of the comma, and indexes to documentation formats.
- Annotations on both visual and verbal examples connect concepts and illustrations.
- New Highlighting on documentation models distinguishes important elements.
- Dictionary-style headers in the index make it easy to find entries.
- A preface just for students outlines the book's contents, details reference aids, and explains the page layout.

Supplements

Pearson offers a variety of support materials to make teaching easier and to help students improve as writers. The following are geared specifically to *LB Brief.* Visit *pearsonhighered.com* or contact your local Pearson sales representative for more information on these and scores of additional supplements.

- New mycomplab The Web site *MyCompLab* (*mycomplab.com*) combines an online composing space and assessment tools with instruction, multimedia tutorials, and exercises on writing, grammar, and research in a seamless, flexible environment. It provides help for writers in the context of their writing, with functions for instructors' and peers' commentary. Special features include self-paced diagnostics, a personalized study plan, peer review tips, podcasts, an e-portfolio, a bibliography tool, tutoring services, an assignment builder, a grade book, and course-management and evaluative tools created specifically for writing classes. In addition, an e-text of *LB Brief* integrates the many resources of *MyCompLab* into the text.

- **New** Students can subscribe to *LB Brief* as a *CourseSmart* e-textbook. The site includes all of the handbook's content in a format that enables students to search the text, bookmark passages, integrate their notes, and print reading assignments that incorporate lecture notes. For more information, or to subscribe to the *CourseSmart* e-textbook, visit *coursesmart.com*.
- The answer key to *LB Brief* includes answers to all of the book's exercises.
- vango notes *VangoNotes* are study guides in MP3 format that enable students to download handbook information into their own players and then listen to it whenever and wherever they wish. The notes include "need to know" tips for each handbook chapter, practice tests, audio flash cards for learning key concepts and terms, and a rapid review for exams. For more information, visit *VangoNotes.com*.

Acknowledgments

LB Brief stays fresh and useful because instructors talk with the publisher's sales representatives and editors, answer questionnaires, write detailed reviews, and send me personal notes.

For the fourth edition, many instructors earn special thanks for detailed reviews in which they drew on their rich experience to offer insights into the handbook and suggestions for its improvement: Jonathan M. Alexander, Burlington County College; Chris Allen, Piedmont Technical College; Curtis Allen, Ashland University; Greg Barnhisel, Duquesne University; Bridgett Boulton, Truckee Meadows Community College; Mary Dutterer, Howard Community College; Dwonna Naomi Goldstone, Austin Peay State University; Kimberly Hall, Harrisburg Area Community College; Craig Kleinman, City College of San Francisco; D. Erik Neilson, Northern Virginia Community College; William O'seland, Northeastern State University; Susan C. Pesznecker, Portland State University and Clackamas Community College; Karen Rose, Long Beach City College; Deborah Scaggs, Texas A&M International University; Adrianne Treinies Schott, Weatherford College; and Melissa Wilke, Northeast Wisconsin Technical College.

In responding to the ideas of these thoughtful critics, I had the help of several creative people. Mary Dutterer of Howard Community College provided helpful suggestions for updating the CULTURE LANGUAGE notes throughout the handbook. Sylvan Barnet, Tufts University, continued to lend his expertise in the chapter "Reading and Writing about Literature," which is adapted from his *Short Guide to Writing about Literature* and *Introduction to Literature* (with William Burto and William E. Cain). And Carol Hollar-Zwick, sine qua non, served brilliantly as originator, sounding board, critic, coordinator, researcher, producer, and friend.

A superb publishing team helped to make this book. At Longman, editors Suzanne Phelps Chambers and Anne Brunell Ehrenworth offered perceptive insights into instructors' and students' needs, while production editor Bob Ginsberg helped resolve sometimes competing production goals in favor of quality and accuracy. At Nesbitt Graphics, Jerilyn Bockorick freshened the look of the book, and Susan McIntyre performed her usual calm (and calming) miracles of scheduling and management during production. I am grateful to all these collaborators.

1 The Writing Situation

How should I tackle a writing assignment?

Many writers find it helpful to break writing tasks into manageable steps. Such steps are part of the **writing process**—the term for all the activities, mental and physical, that go into creating what eventually becomes a finished piece of work.

There is no one writing process: no two writers proceed in the same way, and even an individual writer adapts his or her process to the task at hand. Still, most experienced writers pass through certain stages that overlap and circle back on one another:

- **Analyzing the writing situation,** especially considering subject, audience, and purpose (this chapter).
- **Invention and planning:** generating ideas, gathering information, focusing on a central theme, and organizing material (Chapters 2–3).
- **Drafting:** expressing and connecting ideas (Chapter 4).
- **Revising and editing:** rethinking and improving structure, content, style, and presentation (Chapter 5).

As you complete varied assignments and try the many techniques included in this book, you will develop your own writing process.

1a Analyze the writing situation.

Any writing you do for others occurs in a **writing situation** that both limits and clarifies your choices. You are communicating within a particular context, about a particular subject, to a particular audience of readers, for a specific reason. You may need to conduct research. You probably face a length requirement and a deadline. And you may be expected to present your work in a certain format.

Analyzing the elements of the writing situation at the very start of a project can tell you much about how to proceed. (For discussion of the following elements, refer to the page numbers given.)

Context (pp. 77–146)

- **What is your writing for?** A course in school? Work? Something else? What are the requirements for writing in this context?
- **Will you present your writing on paper, online, or orally?** What does the presentation method require in preparation time, special skills, and use of technology?

> mycomplab
>
> Visit *mycomplab.com* for more resources and exercises on the writing situation.

- **How much leeway do you have for this writing?** What does the stated or implied assignment tell you?

Subject (pp. 4–6)

- **What does your writing assignment instruct you to write about?** If you don't have a specific assignment, what do you want to write about?
- **What interests you about the subject?** What do you already have ideas about or want to know more about?
- **What does the assignment require you to do with the subject?**

Purpose (pp. 6–7)

- **What aim does your assignment specify?** For instance, does it ask you to explain something or argue a point?
- **Why are you writing?** What do you want your work to accomplish? What effect do you intend it to have on readers?
- **How can you best achieve your purpose?**

Audience (pp. 7–9)

- **Who will read your writing?**
- **What do your readers already know and think about your subject?** Do they have any characteristics—such as educational background, experience in your field, or political views—that could influence their reception of your writing?
- **How should you project yourself in your writing?** What role should you play in relation to readers, and what information should you give? How informal or formal should your writing be?
- **What do you want readers to do or think after they read your writing?**

Research (pp. 374–436)

- **What kinds of evidence will best suit your subject, purpose, and audience?** What combination of facts, examples, and expert opinions will support your ideas?
- **Does your assignment require research?** Will you need to consult sources of information or conduct other research, such as interviews, surveys, or experiments?
- **Even if research is not required, what additional information do you need to develop your subject?** How will you obtain it?
- **What style should you use to cite your sources?** (See pp. 431–33 on documenting sources in the academic disciplines.)

Deadline and length

- **When is the assignment due?** How will you complete the work you have to do in the available time?
- **How long should your writing be?** If no length is assigned, what seems appropriate for your subject, purpose, and audience?

1b

Document design

- **What organization and format does the assignment require?** (See p. 64 on formats in academic disciplines and pp. 132–42 on format in public writing.)
- **How might you use margins, headings, and other elements to achieve your purpose?** (See pp. 66–74.)
- **How might you use graphs, photographs, or other illustrations to support ideas and interest readers?** (See pp. 70–74 on using illustrations in writing.)

Exercise 1.1   Analyzing a writing situation

The following assignment was made in a survey course in psychology. What does the assignment specify and imply about the elements of the writing situation? Given this assignment, how would you answer the questions on the preceding pages and above?

When is psychotherapy most likely to work? That is, what combinations of client, therapist, and theory tend to achieve good results? In your discussion, cite studies supporting your conclusions. Length: 1500 to 1800 words. Post your paper online to me and your discussion group by March 30.

1b   Find an appropriate subject.

A subject for writing has several basic requirements:

- **It should be suitable for the assignment.**
- **It should be neither too general nor too limited for the assigned deadline and paper length.**
- **It should be something you are willing to learn more about, even something you care about.**

When you receive an assignment, study its wording and its implications about your writing situation to guide your choice of subject:

- **What's wanted from you?** Many writing assignments contain words such as *discuss, describe, analyze, report, interpret, explain, define, argue,* or *evaluate*. These words specify the way you are to approach your subject, what kind of thinking is expected of you, and what your general purpose is. (See pp. 6–7.)
- **For whom are you writing?** Many assignments will specify your readers, but sometimes you will have to figure out for yourself who your audience is and what it expects of you. (For more on analyzing your audience, see pp. 7–9.)
- **What kind of research is required?** An assignment may specify the kinds of sources you are expected to consult, and you can use such information to choose your subject. (If you are unsure whether research is required, check with your instructor.)

- **Does the subject need to be narrowed?** To do the subject justice in the length and time required, you'll often need to limit it. (See below.)

Answering these questions about your assignment will help set some boundaries for your choice of subject. Then you can explore your own interests and experiences to narrow the subject so that you can cover it adequately within the space and time assigned. Federal aid to college students could be the subject of a book; the kinds of aid available or why the government should increase aid would be a more appropriate subject for a four-page paper due in a week.

One helpful technique for narrowing a subject is to ask focused questions about it, seeking one that seems appropriate for your assignment and that promises to sustain your interest through the writing process. The following examples illustrate how questioning can scale down broad subjects to specific subjects that are limited and manageable:

Broad subjects	Specific subjects
Social-networking sites	What draws people to these sites? How do the sites alter the ways people interact? What privacy protections should the sites provide for users?
Mrs. Mallard in Kate Chopin's "The Story of an Hour"	What changes does Mrs. Mallard undergo? Why does Mrs. Mallard respond as she does to news of her husband's death? What does the story's irony contribute to the character of Mrs. Mallard?
Lincoln's weaknesses as President	What was Lincoln's most significant error as commander-in-chief of the Union army? Why did Lincoln delay emancipating the slaves? Why did Lincoln have difficulties controlling his cabinet?

Use the following guidelines to narrow broad subjects:

- **Ask as many questions about your broad subject as you can think of.** Make a list.
- **For each question that interests you and fits the assignment, roughly sketch out the main ideas.** Consider how many paragraphs or pages of specific facts, examples, and other details you would need to pin those ideas down. This thinking should give you at least a vague idea of how much work you'd have to do and how long the resulting paper might be.
- **Break a too-broad question down further,** repeating the previous steps.

The Internet can also help you limit a general subject. Browsing a directory such as *BUBL LINK* (*bubl.ac.uk/link*), pursue increasingly narrow categories to find a suitably limited topic.

Exercise 1.2 Narrowing subjects

Choose three of the following broad subjects and, using the techniques above, narrow each one to at least one specific question that can be answered in a three- to four-page paper.

1. Use of cell phones
2. Training of teachers
3. Dance in America
4. The history of women's suffrage
5. Food additives
6. Immigrants in the United States
7. Space exploration
8. African Americans and civil rights
9. Child abuse
10. Successes in cancer research
11. Television evangelism
12. Women writers
13. Campaign finance reform
14. Genetic engineering
15. Trends in popular music

1c Define your purpose.

Your **purpose** in writing is your chief reason for communicating something about your subject to a particular audience of readers. Most writing you do will have one of four main purposes:

- **To entertain readers.**
- **To express your feelings or ideas.**
- **To explain something to readers (exposition).**
- **To persuade readers to accept or act on your opinion (argument).**

These purposes often overlap in a single essay, but usually one predominates. And the dominant purpose will influence your slant on your subject, the details you choose, and even the words you use.

Many writing assignments narrow the purpose by using a signal word, such as the following:

- **Report:** survey, organize, and objectively present the available evidence on the subject.
- **Summarize:** concisely state the main points in a text, argument, theory, or other work.
- **Discuss:** examine the main points, competing views, or implications of the subject.
- **Compare and contrast:** explain the similarities and differences between two subjects. (See also p. 56.)
- **Define:** specify the meaning of a term or a concept—distinctive characteristics, boundaries, and so on. (See also p. 54.)
- **Analyze:** identify the elements of the subject and discuss how they work together. (See also pp. 57–58 and 85–86.)

- **Interpret:** infer the subject's meaning or implications.
- **Evaluate:** judge the quality or significance of the subject, considering pros and cons. (See also pp. 87–88.)
- **Argue:** take a position on the subject and support your position with evidence. (See also pp. 103–17.)

You can conceive of your purpose more specifically, too, in a way that incorporates your particular subject and the outcome you intend:

> To explain how Annie Dillard's "Total Eclipse" builds to its climax so that readers appreciate the author's skill.

> To explain the steps in a new office procedure so that staffers will be able to follow it without difficulty.

> To persuade readers to support the college administration's plan for more required courses.

> To argue against additional regulation of handguns so that readers will perceive the potential disadvantages for themselves and for the nation as a whole.

1d   Consider your audience.

The readers likely to see your work—your **audience**—will often be specified or implied in a writing assignment. When you write an editorial for the student newspaper, your audience consists of fellow students. When you analyze a poem in a literature class, your audience consists of your instructor and perhaps your classmates. The box on page 8 gives questions that can help you define the audience in most writing situations.

Your sense of your audience will influence three key elements of what you write:

- **The specific information you use to gain and keep the attention of readers and guide them to accept your conclusions.** This information may consist of details, facts, examples, and other evidence that make your ideas clear, support your assertions, and suit your readers' needs.
- **The role you choose to play in relation to your readers.** Depending on your purpose, you will want readers to perceive you in a certain way. The possible roles are many and varied—for instance, scholar, storyteller, lecturer, guide, reporter, advocate, inspirer.
- **The tone you use. Tone** in writing is the attitude conveyed by words and sentence structures. Depending on your aims and what you think your readers will expect and respond to, your tone may be formal or informal. The attitude you convey may be serious or light, forceful or calm, irritated or cheerful.

1d

Questions about audience

Identity and expectations

- **Who *are* my readers?**
- **What do my readers expect from the kind of writing I'm doing?** Do they expect features such as a particular organization and format, distinctive kinds of evidence, or a certain style of documenting sources?
- **What do I want readers to know or do after reading my work?** How should I make that clear to them?
- **How should I project myself to my readers?** How formal or informal will they expect me to be? What role and tone should I assume?

Characteristics, knowledge, and attitudes

- **What characteristics of readers are relevant for my subject and purpose?** For instance:

  Age and sex
  Occupation: students, professional colleagues, etc.
  Social or economic role: car buyers, potential employers, etc.
  Economic or educational background
  Ethnic background
  Political, religious, or moral beliefs and values
  Hobbies or activities

- **How will the characteristics of readers influence their attitudes toward my subject?**
- **What do readers already know and *not* know about my topic?** How much do I have to tell them?
- **How should I handle any specialized terms?** Will readers know them? If not, should I define them?
- **What ideas, arguments, or information might surprise, excite, or offend readers?** How should I handle these points?
- **What misconceptions might readers have of my subject and/or my approach to it?** How can I dispel these misconceptions?

Uses and format

- **What will readers do with my writing?** Should I expect them to read every word from the top, to scan for information, or to look for conclusions? Can I help with a summary, headings, illustrations, or other aids? (See pp. 63–75 on document design.)

Your information, role, and tone contribute to your writer's **voice:** your projection of yourself into your writing. Your voice conveys your sense of the world as it applies to the particular writing situation: this subject, this purpose, this audience. Thus voice can vary quite a bit from one writing situation to another, as the following memos illustrate. Both have the same subject and general purpose, but they address different readers.

To coworkers

Ever notice how much paper collects in your trash basket every day? Well, most of it can be recycled with little effort, I promise. Basically, all you need to do is set a bag or box near your desk and deposit wastepaper in it. I know, space is cramped in these little cubicles. But what's a little more crowding when the earth's at stake? . . .

Voice: a peer who is thoughtful, cheerful, and sympathetic

Information: how employees could handle recycling; no mention of costs

Role: colleague

Tone: informal, personal (*Ever notice; Well; you; I know, space is cramped*)

To management

In my four months here, I have observed that all of us throw out baskets of potentially recyclable paper every day. Considering the drain on our forest resources and the pressure on landfills that paper causes, we could make a valuable contribution to the environmental movement by helping to recycle the paper we use. At the company where I worked before, the employees separate clean wastepaper from other trash at their desks. The maintenance staff collects trash in two receptacles, and the trash hauler (the same one we use here) makes separate pickups. I do not know what the hauler charges for handling recyclable material. . . .

Voice: a subordinate who is thoughtful, responsible, and serious

Information: specific reasons; view of company as a whole; reference to another company; problem of cost

Role: employee

Tone: formal, serious (*Considering the drain; forest resources; valuable contribution; no you*)

CULTURE LANGUAGE If English is not your native language, you may not be accustomed to appealing to your readers when you write. In some cultures, for instance, readers may accept a writer's statements with little or no questioning. When writing in English, try to reach out to readers by being accurate, fair, interesting, and clear.

2   Invention

How do writers get ideas?

Writers use a host of techniques to discover ideas for their writing projects, from keeping a journal to making lists to drawing diagrams. There are many such **invention** techniques, but they don't all work for every writer. As you read through this chapter, try a few of the invention strategies that appeal to you. If they don't work, try others.

mycomplab

Visit *mycomplab.com* for more resources and exercises on invention.

2a

Whichever of the invention techniques you use, do your work in writing, not just in your head. Your ideas will then be retrievable, and the very act of writing will lead you to fresh insights.

⟨CULTURE / LANGUAGE⟩ The discovery process encouraged here rewards rapid writing without a lot of thinking beforehand about what you will write or how. If your first language is not standard American English, you may find it helpful initially to do this exploratory writing in your native language or dialect and then to translate the worthwhile material for use in your drafts. This process can be productive, but it is extra work. You may want to try it at first and gradually move to composing in standard American English.

2a Keep a journal.

A **journal** is a diary of ideas kept on paper or on a computer. It gives you a place to record your responses, thoughts, and observations about what you read, see, hear, or experience. It can also provide ideas for writing. Because you write for yourself, you can work out your ideas without the pressure of an audience "out there" who will evaluate logic or organization or correctness. If you write every day, even just for a few minutes, the routine will loosen your writing muscles and improve your confidence.

You can use a journal for varied purposes: perhaps to confide your feelings, explore your responses to movies and other media, practice certain kinds of writing (such as poems or news stories), pursue ideas from your courses, or think critically about what you read. One student, Katy Moreno, used her journal for the last purpose. Her composition instructor had distributed "It's a Flat World, After All," an essay by Thomas L. Friedman about globalization and the job market. The instructor then gave the following assignment, calling for a response to reading:

> In "It's a Flat World, After All," Thomas L. Friedman describes today's global job market, focusing not on manufacturing jobs that have been "outsourced" to overseas workers but on jobs that require a college degree and are no longer immune to outsourcing. Friedman argues that keeping jobs in the United States requires that US students, parents, and educators improve math and science education. As a college student, how do you respond to this analysis of the global market for jobs? Does anything Friedman says cause you to rethink how you will spend your college years or what your major will be?

On first reading the essay, Moreno had found it convincing because Friedman's description of the job market matched her family's experience: her mother had lost her job when it was outsourced to India. After rereading the essay, however, Moreno was not persuaded that more math and science would necessarily improve students' opportunities and preserve their future jobs. She compared Friedman's advice with details she recalled from her mother's experience, and she began to develop a response by writing in her journal:

> Friedman is certainly right that more jobs than we realize are going overseas—that's what happened to Mom's job and we were shocked! But he gives only one way for students like me to compete—take more math and science. At first I thought he's totally right. But then I thought that what he said didn't really explain what happened to Mom—she had lots of math + science + tons of experience, but it was her salary, not better training, that caused her job to be outsourced. An overseas worker would do her job for less money. So she lost her job because of money + because she wasn't a manager. Caught in the middle. I want to major in computer science, but I don't think it's smart to try for the kind of job Mom had—at least not as long as it's so much cheaper for companies to hire workers overseas.

(Further examples of Moreno's writing appear in the next three chapters.)

⟨**CULTURE · LANGUAGE**⟩ A journal can be especially helpful if your first language is not standard American English. You can practice writing to improve your fluency, try out sentence patterns, and experiment with vocabulary words. Equally important, you can experiment with applying what you know from experience to what you read and observe.

2b Observe your surroundings.

Sometimes you can find a good subject—or gather information about a subject—by looking around you, not in the half-conscious way most of us move from place to place in our daily lives but deliberately, all senses alert. On a bus, for instance, are there certain types of passengers? What seems to be on the driver's mind? To get the most from observation, you should have a tablet and pen or pencil handy for notes and sketches. Back at your desk, study your notes and sketches for oddities or patterns that you'd like to explore further.

2c Freewrite.

1 ▪ Writing into a subject

Many writers find subjects or discover ideas by **freewriting**: writing without stopping for a certain amount of time (say, ten minutes) or to a certain length (say, one page). The goal of freewriting is to generate ideas and information from *within* yourself by going around the part of your mind that doesn't want to write or can't think of anything to write. You let words themselves suggest other words. *What* you write is not important; that you *keep* writing is. Don't stop, even if that means repeating the same words until new words come. Don't go back to reread, don't censor ideas that seem dumb or repetitious, and above all don't stop to edit: grammar, punctuation, spelling, and the like are irrelevant at this stage.

If you write on a computer, you can ensure that your freewriting keeps moving forward by turning off your computer's monitor or turning its brightness control all the way down so that the screen is dark. The computer will record what you type but keep it from you and thus prevent you from tinkering with your prose. This **invisible writing** may feel uncomfortable at first, but it can free the mind for very creative results.

CULTURE LANGUAGE Invisible writing can be especially helpful if you are uneasy about writing in standard American English and you tend to worry about errors while writing: the blank computer screen leaves you no choice but to explore ideas without regard for their expression. If you choose to write with the monitor on, concentrate on *what* you want to say, not *how* you're saying it.

2 ▪ Focused freewriting

Focused freewriting is more concentrated: you start with your question about your subject and answer it without stopping for, say, fifteen minutes or one full page. As in all freewriting, you push to bypass mental blocks and self-consciousness, not debating what to say or editing what you've written. With focused freewriting, though, you let the physical act of writing take you into and around your subject.

An example of focused freewriting can be found in Katy Moreno's journal response to Thomas L. Friedman's "It's a Flat World, After All" on the previous page. Because she already had an idea about Friedman's essay, Moreno was able to start there and expand on the idea.

2d Brainstorm.

A method similar to freewriting is **brainstorming**—focusing intently on a subject for a fixed period (say, fifteen minutes), pushing yourself to list every idea and detail that comes to mind. Like freewriting, brainstorming requires turning off your internal editor so that you keep moving ahead. (The technique of invisible writing on a computer, described above, can help you move forward.)

Here is an example of brainstorming by a student, Johanna Abrams, on what a summer job can teach:

summer work teaches—
   how to look busy while doing nothing
   how to avoid the sun in summer
   seriously: discipline, budgeting money, value of money
which job? Burger King cashier? baby-sitter? mail-room clerk?
mail room: how to sort mail into boxes: this is learning??
how to survive getting fired—humiliation, outrage
Mrs. King! the mail-room queen as learning experience
the shock of getting fired: what to tell parents, friends?
Mrs. K was so rigid—dumb procedures
initials instead of names on the mail boxes—confusion!
Mrs. K's anger, resentment: the disadvantages of being smarter than your boss
the odd thing about office work: a world with its own rules for how to act
the pecking order—big chick (Mrs. K) pecks on little chick (me)
a job can beat you down—make you be mean to other people

2e   Draw your ideas.

Many writers find ideas by using **clustering** or **idea mapping**.
Like freewriting and brainstorming, this technique draws on free
association and rapid, unedited work, but it also emphasizes relations among ideas. You start with your subject and radiate outward
from a center point. When an idea occurs, you pursue related ideas
in a branching structure until they seem exhausted. Then you do
the same with other ideas, staying open to links, continuously
branching out or drawing arrows. The following example shows how
a student used clustering to explore writing as a means of disguise:

Clustering or idea mapping

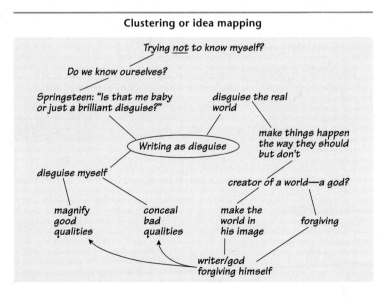

You can use idea-mapping software to draw such diagrams. The software allows you to type your ideas directly into a diagram and then rearrange, delete, and add ideas at any point in the writing process.

2f Ask questions.

Asking yourself a set of questions about your subject—and writing out the answers—can help you look at the topic objectively and see fresh possibilities in it.

1 ▪ Journalist's questions

A journalist with a story to report poses a set of questions:

- **Who was involved?**
- **What happened, and what were the results?**
- **When did it happen?**
- **Where did it happen?**
- **Why did it happen?**
- **How did it happen?**

These questions can also be useful in probing an essay subject, especially when you are telling a story or examining causes and effects.

2 ▪ Questions about patterns

We think about and understand a vast range of subjects through patterns such as narration, classification, and comparison and contrast. Asking questions based on the patterns can help you view your topic from many angles. Sometimes you may want to develop an entire essay using just one pattern.

- **How did it happen?** (Narration)
- **How does it look, sound, feel, smell, taste?** (Description)
- **What are examples of it or reasons for it?** (Illustration or support)
- **What is it? What does it encompass, and what does it exclude?** (Definition)
- **What are its parts or characteristics?** (Division or analysis)
- **What groups or categories can it be sorted into?** (Classification)
- **How is it like, or different from, other things?** (Comparison and contrast)
- **Why did it happen? What results did or could it have?** (Cause-and-effect analysis)
- **How do you do it, or how does it work?** (Process analysis)

For more on these patterns, including paragraph-length examples, see pages 52–58.

3 Thesis and Organization

How does writing take shape?

You'll form rough ideas into writing through two main operations: developing a thesis and organizing the ideas and information that support the thesis. Finding your thesis, or main idea, gives you a focus and direction. Organizing your raw material emphasizes your central concerns and helps you clear away unneeded ideas, spot possible gaps, and energize your topic.

3a Develop a thesis statement.

Your readers will expect your essay to be focused on a main idea, or **thesis.** In your final draft you may express this idea in a **thesis statement,** often at the end of your introduction. You can think of a thesis statement as both a claim about your subject and a promise you make to readers about how you approach the subject. The rest of your essay supports the claim and thus delivers on the promise.

1 ▪ Functions of the thesis statement

As shown in the box below, the thesis statement serves four crucial functions and one optional one.

The thesis statement

- The thesis statement **narrows your subject** to a single, central idea that you want readers to gain from your essay.
- It **claims something specific and significant** about your subject, a claim that requires support.
- It **conveys your purpose,** your reason for writing.
- It **establishes your voice,** suggesting your attitude toward your subject and the role you assume with readers.
- It often concisely **previews the arrangement of ideas,** in which case it can also help you organize your essay.

2 ▪ Evolution of the thesis statement

Your final thesis statement probably will not leap into your head early in the writing process. You may begin with an idea you want to communicate, but you will need to refine that idea to fit the

mycomplab

Visit *mycomplab.com* for more resources and exercises on thesis and organization.

realities of the paper you write. Often you will have to write and rewrite before you come to a conclusion about what you have.

Even though it will change, a sense of your thesis can give you direction as you proceed through the writing process. Try drafting a tentative thesis statement, or conceive of a **thesis question** that can guide you. This question may arise when you try to narrow you subject (p. 5), and it can sharpen as you develop your ideas. Eventually, you'll be able to answer it in your thesis statement.

Following are examples of questions and answering thesis statements. As assertions, the thesis statements each consist of a topic (usually naming the general subject) and a claim about the topic. Notice how each statement also expresses purpose. Statements 1–3 are **explanatory:** the writers mainly want to explain something to readers, such as consumers' choices with online music. Statements 4–6 are **argumentative:** the authors mainly want to convince readers of something, such as that drivers' use of cell phones should be outlawed. Most of the thesis statements you write in college papers will be either explanatory or argumentative.

Thesis question	Explanatory thesis statement
1. What are the advantages of direct distribution of music via the Web?	The music available on the Web gives consumers many more choices than traditional distribution allows. [**Topic:** music available on the Web. **Claim:** gives consumers many more choices.]
2. What steps can prevent juvenile crime?	Juveniles can be diverted from crime by active learning programs, full-time sports, and intervention by mentors and role models. [**Topic:** juveniles. **Claim:** can be diverted from crime in three ways.]
3. Why did Abraham Lincoln delay emancipating the slaves?	Lincoln delayed emancipating any slaves until 1863 because his primary goal was to restore and preserve the Union, with or without slavery. [**Topic:** Lincoln's delay. **Claim:** was caused by his goal of preserving the Union.]

Thesis question	Argumentative thesis statement
4. Why should drivers' use of cell phones be banned?	Drivers' use of cell phones should be outlawed because people who talk and drive at the same time cause accidents. [**Topic:** drivers' use of cell phones. **Claim:** should be outlawed because it causes accidents.]
5. Which college students should be entitled to federal aid?	As an investment in its own economy, the federal government should provide a tuition grant to any college student who qualifies academically. [**Topic:** federal government. **Claim:** should provide a tuition grant to any college student who qualifies academically.]

Thesis question	Argumentative thesis statement
6. Should the state government play a role in moving consumers to hybrid cars?	Each proposal for the state to encourage purchase of hybrid cars—advertising campaigns, trade-in deals, and tax incentives—needlessly involves government in decisions that consumers are already making on their own. [**Topic:** each of three proposals. **Claim:** needlessly involves government in consumer decisions.]

3a

Notice that statements 2 and 6 clearly predict the organization of the essay that will follow.

(CULTURE LANGUAGE) In some cultures it is considered unnecessary or impolite for a writer to have an opinion or to state his or her main idea outright. When writing in standard American English for school or work, you can assume that your readers expect a clear and early idea of what you think.

3 ▪ Revision of the thesis statement

Before you consider your thesis statement final, ask the following questions about it.

▪ **Does the statement make a concise *claim* about your subject?**

Original Toni Morrison won the Nobel Prize in Literature in 1993.

The original sentence states a fact, not a claim about Morrison's work. The following revision states the significance of the prize:

Revised Toni Morrison's 1993 Nobel Prize in Literature, the first awarded to an African American woman, affirms both the strength of her vivid prose style and the importance of her subject matter.

▪ **Is the claim *limited* to a single specific idea?**

Original Diets are dangerous.

The original sentence is so broad that it seems insupportable. The revision limits the kinds of diets and their effects:

Revised Fad diets can be dangerous when they deprive the body of essential nutrients or rely on excessive quantities of potentially harmful foods.

The following original sentence is also too general, whereas the revision specifies differences and their significance:

Original Televised sports are different from live sports.
Revised Although television cannot transmit all the excitement of being in a crowd during a game, its close-ups and slow-motion replays reveal much about the players and the strategy of the game.

- Is the statement *unified* so that its parts clearly relate to each other?

Original   Seat belts can save lives, but carmakers now install air bags.

With two facts linked by *but*, the original sentence moves in two directions, not one. The revision clarifies the relation between the parts and their significance:

Revised   If drivers had used lifesaving seat belts more often, carmakers might not have needed to install air bags.

- Does the statement at least imply your *purpose*?

Original   Educators' motives for using the Internet vary widely.

The original sentence conveys no hint of the writer's reason for exploring the subject. In contrast, the revision implies a purpose of arguing against a mainly financial motivation for using the Internet in education:

Revised   Too often, educators' uses of the Internet seem motivated less by teaching and learning than by making or saving money.

- Does the statement convey your *voice*?

Original   Television viewing can reduce loneliness, cause laughter, and teach children.

The original sentence lacks voice. The revision suggests the writer's attitude toward the subject and the role the writer will assume with readers:

Revised   Despite its many faults, television has at least one strong virtue: it can ease loneliness, spark healthful laughter, and even educate young children by providing voices that supplement our own.

Exercise 3.1   Evaluating thesis statements

Evaluate the following thesis statements, considering whether each one is sufficiently limited, specific, and unified. Also consider whether each is a claim that implies the essay's purpose and conveys the writer's voice. Rewrite the statements as necessary to meet these goals.

1. Aggression usually leads to violence, injury, and even death, and we should use it constructively.
2. The religion of Islam is widely misunderstood in the United States.
3. One evening of a radio talk show amply illustrates both the appeal of such shows and their silliness.
4. Good manners make our society work.
5. The poem is about motherhood.
6. Cell phones are useful for adults who have busy schedules, but they can be harmful for children.

7. I disliked American history in high school, but I like it in college.
8. Drunken drivers, whose perception and coordination are impaired, should receive mandatory suspensions of their licenses.
9. Business is a good major for many students.
10. The state's lenient divorce laws undermine the institution of marriage, which is fundamental to our culture, and they should certainly be made stricter for couples who have children.

3b   Organize your ideas.

Most essays share a basic pattern of introduction (states the subject), body (develops the subject), and conclusion (pulls the essay's ideas together). Introductions and conclusions are discussed on pages 58–62. Within the body, every paragraph develops some aspect of the essay's main idea, or thesis. See pages 37–39 for Katy Moreno's essay, with annotations highlighting the body's pattern of support for the thesis statement.

⟨CULTURE LANGUAGE⟩ If you are not used to reading and writing American academic prose, its pattern of introduction-body-conclusion and the particular schemes discussed here may seem unfamiliar. For instance, instead of introductions that focus quickly on the topic and thesis, you may be used to openings that establish personal connections with readers. And instead of body paragraphs that first emphasize general points and then support those points with specific evidence, you may be used to general statements without support (because writers can assume that readers will supply the evidence themselves) or to evidence without explanation (because writers can assume that readers will infer the general points). When writing American academic prose, you need to take into account readers' expectations for directness and for the statement and support of general points.

1 ▪ The general and the specific

Organizing material for an essay requires that you distinguish general and specific ideas and see the relations between ideas. **General** and **specific** refer to the number of instances or objects included in a group signified by a word. The following "ladder" illustrates a general-to-specific hierarchy:

Most general

↑ life form
| plant
| flowering plant
| rose
↓ Uncle Dan's prize-winning American Beauty rose

Most specific

As you arrange your material, pick out the general ideas and then the specific points that support them. Set aside points that seem irrelevant to your key ideas. On a computer, you can easily experiment with various arrangements of general ideas and supporting information: save the master list, duplicate it, and then use the Cut and Paste functions to move material around.

2 ▪ Schemes for organizing essays

An essay's body paragraphs may be arranged in many ways that are familiar to readers. The choice depends on your subject, purpose, and audience.

- **Spatial:** In describing a person, place, or thing, move through space systematically from a starting point to other features—for instance, top to bottom, near to far, left to right.
- **Chronological:** In recounting a sequence of events, arrange the events as they actually occurred in time, first to last.
- **General to specific:** Begin with an overall discussion of the subject; then fill in details, facts, examples, and other support.
- **Specific to general:** First provide the support; then draw a conclusion from it.
- **Climactic:** Arrange ideas in order of increasing importance to your thesis or increasing interest to the reader.
- **Problem-solution:** First outline a problem that needs solving; then propose a solution.

You can adapt these schemes to the different kinds of writing discussed in Chapters 8–14 of this book. For instance, an argument might take a problem-solution approach, building in the key element of a response to probable objections (see pp. 116–17).

3 ▪ Outlines

It's not essential to craft a detailed outline before you begin drafting an essay; in fact, too detailed a plan could prevent you from discovering ideas while you draft. Still, even a rough scheme can show you patterns of general and specific, suggest proportions, and highlight gaps or overlaps in coverage.

There are several kinds of outlines, some more flexible than others.

Scratch or informal outline

A scratch or informal outline includes key general points and may suggest specific evidence. Here are Katy Moreno's thesis statement and scratch outline on the global job market:

Thesis statement

My mother's experience of having her job outsourced taught a lesson that Thomas L. Friedman overlooks: technical training by itself can be too narrow to produce the communicators and problem solvers needed by contemporary businesses.

Scratch outline

Mom's outsourcing experience
    Excellent tech skills
    Salary too high compared to overseas tech workers
    Lack of planning + communication skills, unlike managers who kept jobs
Well-rounded education to protect vs. outsourcing
    Tech training, as Friedman says
    Also, communication, problem solving, other management skills

A scratch or informal outline may be all you need to begin drafting. Sometimes, though, it may prove too skimpy a guide, and you may want to develop it into a more detailed outline. Katy Moreno used her scratch outline as a base for a detailed formal outline that gave her an even more definite sense of direction (next page).

Tree diagram

In a tree diagram, ideas and details branch out in increasing specificity. Unlike more linear outlines, this diagram can be supplemented and extended indefinitely, so it is easy to alter. From her brainstorming about a summer job (p. 13), Johanna Abrams developed the following thesis statement and the tree diagram below.

Thesis statement

Two months working in a large agency taught me that an office's pecking order should be respected.

Tree diagram

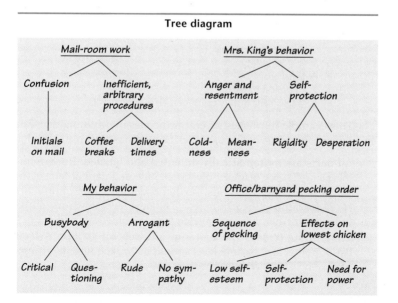

Formal outline

A formal outline not only lays out main ideas and their support but also shows the relative importance of all the essay's elements. On the basis of her scratch outline (previous page), Katy Moreno prepared a detailed formal outline for her essay on the global job market:

Thesis statement

My mother's experience of having her job outsourced taught a lesson that Thomas L. Friedman overlooks: technical training by itself can be too narrow to produce the communicators and problem solvers needed by contemporary businesses.

Formal outline

I.   Summary of Friedman's article
   A. Reasons for outsourcing
      1. Improved technology and access
      2. Well-educated workers
      3. Productive workers
      4. Lower wages
   B. Need for improved technical training in US
II. Mother's experience
   A. Outsourcing of job
      1. Mother's education, experience, performance
      2. Employer's cost savings
   B. Retention of managers' jobs
      1. Planning skills
      2. Communication skills
III. Conclusions about ideal education
   A. Needs of US businesses
      1. Technical skills
      2. Management skills
         a. Communication
         b. Problem solving
         c. Versatility
   B. Personal goals
      1. Technical training
      2. English and history courses for management skills

This example illustrates several principles of outlining that can ensure completeness, balance, and clear relationships:

- **All parts are systematically indented and labeled:** Roman numerals (I, II) for primary divisions; indented capital letters (A, B) for secondary divisions; further indented Arabic numerals (1, 2) for supporting examples. (The next level down would be indented further still and labeled with small letters: a, b.)
- **The outline divides the material into several groups.** A long list of points at the same level should be broken up into groups of closely related points.

- **Topics of equal generality appear in parallel headings,** with the same indention and numbering or lettering.
- **All subdivided headings break into at least two parts.** A topic cannot logically be divided into only one part.
- **All headings are expressed in parallel grammatical form**—in the example, as phrases using nouns plus modifiers. This is a topic outline; in a sentence outline all headings are expressed as full sentences (see pp. 481–82).

Note Because of its structure, a formal outline can be an excellent tool for analyzing a draft before revising it. See page 29.

Unity and coherence

Two qualities of effective writing relate to organization: unity and coherence. When you perceive that someone's writing "flows well," you are probably appreciating these qualities.

To check an outline or draft for **unity,** ask these questions:

- **Is each section relevant to the main idea (thesis) of the essay?**
- **Within main sections, does each example or detail support the principal idea of that section?**

To check your outline or draft for **coherence,** ask the following questions:

- **Do the ideas follow a clear sequence?**
- **Are the parts of the essay logically connected?**
- **Are the connections clear and smooth?**

The following essay illustrates some ways of achieving unity and coherence (highlighted in the annotations).

A Picture of Hyperactivity

A hyperactive committee member can contribute to efficiency. A hyperactive salesperson can contribute to profits. When children are hyperactive, though, people—even parents—may wish they had never been born. A collage of those who must cope with hyperactivity in children is a picture of frustration, anger, and loss.

Introduction establishing subject of essay

Thesis statement

The first part of the collage is the doctors. In their terminology, the word *hyperactivity* has been replaced by *ADHD*, attention-deficit hyperactivity disorder. They apply the term to children who are abnormally or excessively busy. But doctors do not fully understand the problem and thus differ over how to treat it. Some recommend a special diet, others recommend behavior-modifying drugs, and still others, who do not consider ADHD a medical problem, recommend psychotherapy. The result

Paragraph idea, linked to thesis statement

Paragraph developed with evidence supporting its idea

is a merry-go-round of tests, confusion, and frustration for the children and their parents.

Paragraph idea, linked to thesis statement

As the mother of an ADHD child, I can say what the disorder means to the parents who form the second part of the collage. It means worry

Paragraph developed with evidence supporting its idea

that is deep and enduring. It means despair that is a constant companion. It means a mixture of frustration, guilt, and anger. And finally, since there are times when parents' anger goes out of control and threatens the children, it means self-loathing.

Transition

The weight of ADHD, however, does not rest on the doctors and

Paragraph idea, linked to thesis statement

parents. The darkest part of the collage belongs to the children. From early childhood they may be dragged from doctor to doctor, attached to machines, medicated until they feel numb, and tested or discussed by

Paragraph developed with evidence supporting its idea

physicians, teachers, neighbors, and strangers on the street. They may be highly intelligent, but they'll still do poorly in school because of their short attention spans. Their playmates dislike them because of their temper and their unwillingness to follow rules. Even their pets mistrust them because of their erratic behavior. As time goes on, the children see their parents more and more in tears and anger, and they know they are the cause.

Conclusion echoing thesis statement, summarizing, and looking ahead

The collage is complete, and it is dark and somber. *ADHD*, as applied to children, is a term with uncertain, unattractive, and bitter associations. The picture does have one bright spot, however, for inside every ADHD child is a lovely, trusting, calm person waiting to be recognized.

—Linda Devereaux (student)

See also pages 42–51 on unity and coherence in paragraphs.

Exercise 3.2   Organizing ideas

The following list of ideas was extracted by a student from freewriting he did for a brief paper on soccer in the United States. Using his thesis statement as a guide, pick out the general ideas and arrange the relevant specific points under them. In some cases you may have to infer general ideas to cover specific points in the list.

Thesis statement

Although its growth in the United States has been slow and halting, professional soccer may finally be poised to become a major American sport.

List of ideas

In countries of South and Latin America, soccer is the favorite sport.
In the United States the success of a sport depends largely on its ability to attract huge TV audiences.
Soccer was not often presented on US television.
In 2007, the World Cup final was broadcast on ABC and on Spanish-language Univision.

In the past, professional soccer could not get a foothold in the United States because of poor TV coverage and lack of financial backing.

The growing Hispanic population in the United States could help soccer grow as well.

Investors have poured hundreds of millions of dollars into the top US professional league.

Potential fans did not have a chance to see soccer games.

Failures of early start-up leagues made potential backers wary of new ventures.

Recently, the outlook for professional soccer has changed dramatically.

In 2007, the US television audience for the World Cup final was larger than the audience for baseball's World Series.

4 Drafting

What can I do about writer's block?

Writer's block happens to everyone, even the most experienced writers. To confront it, try to think of drafting as an occasion for exploration. Don't expect to transcribe solid thoughts into polished prose: solidity and polish will come with revision and editing. Instead, let the act of writing help you to find and form your meaning.

4a Start writing.

Beginning a draft often takes courage, even for seasoned professionals. Procrastination may actually help if you let ideas simmer at the same time. At some point, though, you'll have to face the blank paper or computer screen. The following techniques can help you begin:

- **Read over what you've already written**—notes, outlines, and so on—and immediately start your draft with whatever comes to mind.
- **Freewrite** (see p. 11).
- **Write scribbles or type nonsense** until usable words start coming.

mycomplab

Visit *mycomplab.com* for more resources and exercises on drafting.

4a

4c

- **Pretend you're writing to a friend about your subject.**
- **Describe an image that represents your subject**—a physical object, a facial expression, two people arguing over something, a giant machine gouging the earth for a mine, whatever.
- **Skip the opening and start in the middle.** Or write the conclusion.
- **Write a paragraph.** Explain what you think your essay will be about when you finish it.
- **Start writing the part that you understand best or feel most strongly about.** Using your outline, divide your essay into chunks—say, one for the introduction, another for the first point, and so on. One of these chunks may call out to be written.

4b   Maintain momentum.

Drafting requires momentum: the forward movement opens you to fresh ideas and connections. To keep moving while drafting, try one or more of these techniques:

- **Set aside enough time for yourself.** For a brief essay, a first draft is likely to take at least an hour or two.
- **Work in a quiet place.**
- **Make yourself comfortable.**
- **If you must stop working, write down what you expect to do next.** Then you can pick up where you stopped with minimal disruption.
- **Be as fluid as possible.** Spontaneity will allow your attitudes toward your subject to surface naturally in your sentences.
- **Keep going.** Skip over sticky spots; leave a blank if you can't find the right word; put alternative ideas or phrasings in brackets so that you can consider them later. If an idea pops out of nowhere but doesn't seem to fit in, quickly jot it down, or write it into the draft and bracket or boldface it for later attention.
- **Resist self-criticism.** Don't worry about your style, grammar, spelling, punctuation, and the like. Don't worry about what your readers will think. These are very important matters, but save them for revision.
- **Use your thesis statement and outline.** They can remind you of your planned purpose, organization, and content. However, if your writing leads you in a direction you find more interesting, then follow.

4c   A sample first draft

Katy Moreno's first-draft response to Thomas L. Friedman's "It's a Flat World, After All" appears on the next two pages. As part of her

4c

assignment, Moreno showed the draft to four classmates whose suggestions for revision appear in the margin of this draft. They used the Comment function of *Microsoft Word*, which allows users to add comments without inserting words into the document's text. (Notice that the classmates ignore errors in grammar and punctuation, concentrating instead on larger issues such as thesis, clarity of ideas, and unity.)

Title?

In "It's a Flat World, After All," Thomas L. Friedman argues that, most US students are not preparing themselves as well as they should to compete in today's economy. Not like students in India, China, and other countries are. The outsourcing of my mother's job proves that Thomas L. Friedman's advice to improve students' technical training is too narrow.

> **Comment [Jared]:** Your mother's job being outsourced is interesting, but your introduction seems rushed.

> **Comment [Rabia]:** The end of your thesis statement is a little unclear—too narrow for what?

Friedman describes a "flat" world where recent technology like the Internet and wireless communication make it possible for college graduates all over the globe, in particular in India and China, to get jobs that once were gotten by graduates of US colleges and universities. He argues that US students need more math and science in order to compete.

> **Comment [Erin]:** Can you include the reasons Friedman gives for overseas students' success?

I came to college with first-hand knowledge of globalization and outsourcing. My mother, who worked for sixteen years in the field of information technology (IT), was laid off six months ago when the company she worked for decided to outsource much of its IT work to a company based in India. My mother majored in computer science, had sixteen years of experience, and her bosses always gave her good reviews. She never expected to be laid off and was surprised when she was. She wasn't laid off because of her background and performance. In fact, my mother had a very strong background in math and science and years of training and job experience. The reason was because her salary and benefits cost the company more than outsourcing her job did. Which hurt my family financially, as you can imagine.

> **Comment [Nathaniel]:** Tighten this paragraph to avoid repetition? Also, how does your mother's experience relate to Friedman and your thesis?

A number of well-paid people in the IT department where my mother worked, namely, IT managers, were not laid off. As my mother explained at the time, they kept their jobs because they were better at planning and they communicated

> **Comment [Erin]:** What were the managers better at planning for?

better, they were better writers and speakers than my mother.

Like my mother, I am more comfortable in front of a computer than I am in front of a group of people. I planned to major in computer science. Since my mother lost her job, though, I have decided to take courses in English and history too, where the classes will require me to do different kinds of work. When I enter the job market, my well-rounded education will make me a more attractive job candidate, and, will help me to be a versatile, productive employee.

Comment [Nathaniel]: Can you be more specific about the kinds of work you'll need to do?

Comment [Rabia]: Can you work this point into your thesis?

We know from our history that Americans have been innovative, hard-working people. We students have educational opportunities to compete in the global economy, but we must use our time in college wisely. As Thomas L. Friedman says, my classmates and I need to be ready for a rapidly changing future. We will have to work hard each day, which means being prepared for class, getting the best grades we can, and making the most of each class. Our futures depend on the decisions we make today.

Comment [Jared]: Conclusion seems to go off in a new direction. Friedman mentions hard work, but it hasn't been your focus before.

Comment [Rabia]: Don't forget your works cited.

5   Revising and Editing

Why and how should I revise?

Revising is an essential task in creating an effective piece of writing. During revision (literally "re-seeing") you shift your focus outward from yourself and your subject toward your readers, concentrating on what will help them respond as you want. Many writers revise in two stages, first viewing the work as a whole, evaluating and improving its overall meaning and structure, and then editing sentences for wording, grammar, punctuation, spelling, and so on.

mycomplab

Visit *mycomplab.com* for more resources and exercises on revising and editing.

For you, as for many writers, overall revision may be more difficult than editing because often you must pull your work apart before you can put it back together and look for sentence-level errors. But knowing that you will edit later also gives you the freedom at first to look beyond the confines of the page or screen to the whole paper.

5a   Revise the essay as a whole.

Your first step in revising your writing should be to examine large-scale issues such as whether your purpose and main idea will be clear to readers and whether the draft fully develops the thesis. In revising, you may need to move, combine, or delete whole paragraphs; rethink major points; or flesh out ideas with details or research.

1 ▪ Reading your work critically

To revise your writing, you have to read it critically, and that means you have to create some distance between your draft and yourself. One of the following techniques may help you see your work objectively:

- **Take a break after finishing the draft.** A few hours may be enough; a whole night or day is preferable.
- **Ask someone to read and react to your draft.** If your instructor encourages collaboration among students, by all means take advantage of the opportunity to hear the responses of others. (See pp. 39–41 for more on collaboration.)
- **Type a handwritten draft.** The act of transcription can reveal gaps in content or problems in structure.
- **Outline your draft.** Highlight the main points supporting the thesis, and write these sentences down separately in outline form. Then examine the outline you've made for logical order, gaps, and digressions. A formal outline can be especially illuminating because of its careful structure (see pp. 22–23).
- **Listen to your draft.** Read the draft out loud to yourself or a friend or classmate, record and listen to it, or have someone read the draft to you.
- **Ease the pressure.** Don't try to re-see everything in your draft at once. Use the checklist on the next page, making a separate pass through the draft for each item.

2 ▪ Revising on a word processor

When you revise on a computer, take a few precautions to avoid losing your work and to keep track of your drafts:

- **Save your work every five to ten minutes.**

Checklist for whole-essay revision

Purpose
What is the essay's purpose? Does it conform to the assignment?

Thesis
What is the thesis of the essay? Where does it become clear? How well does the paper deliver on the commitment of the thesis?

Structure
What are the main points supporting the thesis? (List them.) How does the arrangement of these points contribute to the paper's purpose?

Development
How well do details, examples, and other evidence support each main point? Where, if at all, might readers find support skimpy or have trouble understanding the content?

Voice
How clearly can readers hear your writer's voice? What role will they see you as playing? What tone will they hear? How appropriate is your voice for your subject, purpose, and audience?

Unity
Which, if any, sentences or paragraphs do not contribute to the thesis? Should these digressions be cut, or can they be rewritten to support the thesis?

Coherence
How clearly and smoothly does the paper flow? Where does it seem rough or awkward? Can any transitions be improved?

Title, introduction, conclusion
Does the title reflect the essay's content and purpose? Is it interesting? How well does the introduction engage and focus readers' attention on the thesis of the essay? How effective is the conclusion in providing a sense of completion?

- After doing any major work on a project, create a backup version of the file.
- **Work on a duplicate of your latest draft.** Then the original will remain intact until you're truly finished with it. On the duplicate you can use your word processor's Track Changes function, which shows changes alongside the original text and allows you to accept or reject alterations later.
- **Save each draft under its own file name.** You may need to consult an earlier draft for ideas or phrasings.

3 ▪ Writing a title

The revision stage is a good time to consider a title because attempting to sum up your essay in a phrase can focus your attention sharply on your subject, purpose, and audience.

Here are suggestions for titling an essay:

- ▪ A *descriptive title* **announces the subject clearly and accurately.** Such a title is almost always appropriate and is usually expected for academic writing. Katy Moreno's final title—"Can We Compete? College Education for the Global Economy"—is an example.
- ▪ A *suggestive title* **hints at the subject to arouse curiosity.** Such a title is common in popular magazines and may be appropriate for more informal writing. Moreno might have chosen a suggestive title such as "Training for the New World" or "Education for a Flat World" (echoing Thomas L. Friedman's title).

For more information on essay titles, see pages 362 (capitalizing words in a title), 480 (MLA title format), and 510 (APA title format).

5b   A sample revision

Katy Moreno was satisfied with her first draft: she had her ideas down, and the arrangement seemed logical. Still, from the revision checklist she knew the draft needed work, and her classmates' comments (pp. 27–28) highlighted what she needed to focus on. Following is the first half of her revised draft with marginal annotations highlighting the changes. Moreno used the Track Changes function on her word processor, so that deletions are crossed out and additions are in color.

Descriptive title names topic and forecasts approach.

Can We Compete?
College Education for the Global Economy

~~Title?~~

Expanded introduction draws readers into Moreno's topic, clarifies her point of agreement with Friedman, and states her revised thesis.

Today's students cannot miss news stories about globalization of the economy and outsourcing of jobs, but are students aware of how these trends are affecting the job market? In "It's a Flat World, After All," Thomas L. Friedman argues that most US students are not preparing themselves as well as ~~they should to compete in today's economy. Not like~~ students in India, China, and other countries ~~are.~~ to compete in today's economy, which requires hard-working, productive scientists and engineers. Friedman's argument speaks to me because my mother recently lost her job when it was outsourced to India. But her experience taught a lesson that Friedman overlooks: technical training by itself can be too narrow to produce the communicators and problem solvers needed by contemporary businesses. ~~The outsourcing of my mother's job proves that Thomas L. Friedman's advice to improve students' technical training is too narrow.~~

Friedman describes a "flat" world where recent technology like the Internet and wireless communication makes it possible for college graduates all over the globe~~, in particular~~ to compete for high paying jobs that once belonged to graduates of US colleges and universities. He focuses on workers in India and China~~,~~ who graduate from college with excellent educations in math and science, who are eager for new opportunities, and who are willing to work exceptionally hard, often harder than their American counterparts and, for less money. ~~to get jobs that once were gotten by graduates of US colleges and universities.~~ ~~He~~ Friedman argues that US students must be better prepared academically, especially in ~~need more~~ math and science, so that they can get and keep jobs that will otherwise go overseas. ~~in order to compete.~~

~~I came to college with first hand knowledge of globalization and outsourcing. My mother, who worked for sixteen years in the field of information technology (IT), was laid off six months ago when the company she worked for decided to outsource much of its IT work to a company based in India. My mother~~ At first glance, my mother's experience of losing her job might seem to support the argument of Friedman that better training in math and science is the key to competing in the global job market. Her experience, however, adds dimensions to the globalization story, which Friedman misses. First my mother had the kind of strong background in math and science that Friedman says, today's workers need. She majored in computer science, rose within the information technology (IT) department of a large company, ~~had sixteen years of experience,~~ and her bosses always gave her good performance reviews. Still, when her employer decided to outsource most of its IT work, my mother lost her job. ~~She never expected to be laid off and was surprised when she was. She wasn't laid off because of her background and performance. In fact, my mother had a very strong background in math and science and years of training and job experience.~~ The reason wasn't because her technical skills were inadequate. Instead, her salary and benefits cost the company more than outsourcing her job did. Until wages rise around the globe, jobs like my mother's will be vulnerable. No matter how well you are trained. ~~Which hurt my family financially, as you can imagine.~~

Expanded summary of Friedman's article specifies qualities of overseas workers.

New opening sentences connect to introduction and thesis statement, restating points of agreement and disagreement with Friedman.

Revisions condense long example of mother's experience.

Paragraph's concluding sentences reinforce the point and connect to thesis statement.

5c   Edit the revised draft.

After you've revised your essay so that all the content is in place, then turn to the important work of removing any surface problems that could interfere with a reader's understanding or enjoyment of your ideas.

1 ■ Discovering what needs editing

Try these approaches to spot possible flaws in your work:

- **Take a break.** Even fifteen or twenty minutes can clear your head.
- **If possible, work on a double-spaced paper copy.** Most people find it much harder to spot errors on a screen than on paper.
- **Read the draft slowly, and read what you actually see.** Otherwise, you're likely to read what you intended to write but did not. If you have trouble slowing down, try reading your draft from back to front, sentence by sentence.
- **Listen to the draft.** Read the draft aloud, record the draft and listen to the playback, or use text-to-speech software to create a spoken version. Be alert to awkward rhythms, repetitive sentence patterns, and missing transitions.
- **Have a classmate, friend, or relative read your work.** Make sure you understand and consider the reader's suggestions, even if you decide not take them.
- **Learn from your own experience.** Keep a record of your common problems—certain misspellings, overuse of *there is*, wordy phrases such as *the fact that*, and so on—and check your work against the record. Use a word processor's Find command to locate such problems quickly.
- **Don't rely on a spelling or grammar/style checker to find what needs editing.** See the discussion on pages 35–36.

In your editing, work first for clear and effective sentences that flow smoothly from one to the next. Then check your sentences for correctness. Use the questions in the checklist on the next page to guide your editing.

Following is the third paragraph of Katy Moreno's edited draft. Among other changes, she tightened wording, improved parallelism (with *consistently received*), corrected several comma errors, and repaired the final sentence fragment.

At first glance, my mother's experience of losing her job might seem to support ~~the~~ Friedman's argument ~~of Friedman~~ that better training in math and science is the key to competing in the global job market. However, ~~H~~her experience~~,~~ ~~however,~~ adds dimensions to the globalization story~~, which~~ that Friedman misses.

Checklist for editing

Are my sentences clear?

Do my words and sentences mean what I intend them to mean? Is anything confusing? Check especially for these:

Exact language (pp. 175–83)
Parallelism (pp. 159–61)
Clear modifiers (pp. 281–87)
Clear reference of pronouns (pp. 266–69)
Complete sentences (pp. 288–92)
Sentences separated correctly (pp. 294–98)

Are my sentences effective?

How well do words and sentences engage and hold readers' attention? Where does the writing seem wordy, choppy, or dull? Check especially for these:

Expression of voice (pp. 8–9)
Emphasis of main ideas (pp. 148–58)
Smooth and informative transitions (pp. 49–51)
Variety in sentence length and structure (pp. 163–66)
Appropriate language (pp. 167–74)
Concise sentences (pp. 186–91)

Do my sentences contain errors?

Where do surface errors interfere with the clarity and effectiveness of my sentences? Check especially for these:

- **Spelling errors** (pp. 352–56)
- **Sentence fragments** (pp. 288–92)
- **Comma splices** (pp. 294–98)
- **Verb errors**
  Verb forms, especially *-s* and *-ed* endings, correct forms of irregular verbs, and appropriate helping verbs (pp. 217–33)
  Verb tenses, especially consistency (pp. 234–40)
  Agreement between subjects and verbs, especially when words come between them or the subject is *each, everyone,* or a similar word (pp. 246–52)
- **Pronoun errors**
  Pronoun forms, especially subjective (*he, she, they, who*) vs. objective (*him, her, them, whom*) (pp. 254–60)
  Agreement between pronouns and antecedents, especially when the antecedent contains *or* or the antecedent is *each, everyone, person,* or a similar word (pp. 261–65)
- **Punctuation errors**
  Commas, especially with comma splices (pp. 296–97) and with *and* or *but,* with introductory elements, with nonessential elements, and with series (pp. 310–20)
  Apostrophes in possessives but not plural nouns (*Dave's/witches*) and in contractions but not possessive personal pronouns (*it's/its*) (pp. 333–37)

First, my mother had the kind of strong background in math and science that Friedman says~~,~~ today's workers need. She majored in computer science, rose within the information technology (IT) department of a large company, and consistently received ~~her bosses always gave her~~ good performance reviews. Still, when her employer decided to outsource most of its IT work, my mother lost her job. The reason wasn't ~~because~~that her technical skills were inadequate. Instead, her salary and benefits cost the company more than outsourcing her job did. Until wages rise around the globe, jobs like my mother's will be vulnerable~~,.~~ ~~N~~no matter how well ~~you are~~ a person is trained.

2 ▪ Working with spelling and grammar/style checkers

A spelling checker and a grammar/style checker can be helpful *if* you work within their limitations. The programs miss many problems and may even flag items that are actually correct. Further, they cannot make important decisions about your writing because they know nothing of your subject, your purpose, and your audience. Always use these tools critically:

- **Read your work yourself to ensure that it's clear and error-free.**
- **Consider a checker's suggestions carefully, weighing each one against your intentions.** If you aren't sure whether to accept a checker's suggestion, consult a dictionary, writing handbook, or other source. Your version may be fine.

Using a spelling checker

Your word processor's spelling checker can be a great ally: it will flag words that are spelled incorrectly and will usually suggest alternative spellings that resemble what you've typed. However, this ally also has the potential to undermine you:

- **The checker may flag a word that you've spelled correctly** just because the word does not appear in its dictionary.
- **The checker may suggest incorrect alternatives.** In providing a list of alternative spellings for your word, the checker may highlight the one it considers most likely to be correct. For example, if you misspell *definitely* by typing *definately*, your checker may highlight *defiantly* as the correct option. You need to verify that the alternative suggested by the checker is actually what you intend before selecting it. Consult an online or printed dictionary when you aren't sure of the checker's recommendations (see p. 175).
- **Most important, a spelling checker will not flag words that appear in its dictionary but you have misused.** The jingle shown in the screen shot on the next page has circulated widely as a warning about spelling checkers. (See also p. 357 for an exercise on working with a spelling checker.)

A spelling checker
failed to catch any of
the thirteen errors in
this jingle. Can you
spot them?

> I have a spelling checker,
> It came with my PC;
> It plainly marks four my revue
> Mistakes I cannot sea.
> I've run this poem threw it,
> I'm sure your please too no.
> Its letter perfect in it's weigh,
> My checker tolled me sew.

You can supplement a spelling checker by maintaining a file of your frequent misspellings and then checking for them by selecting Find under the Edit menu. But in the end *the only way to rid your papers of spelling errors is to proofread your papers yourself.* See the next page for proofreading tips. And see Chapter 45 for more advice on spelling.

Using a grammar/style checker

Grammar/style checkers can flag incorrect grammar or punctuation and wordy or awkward sentences. However, these programs can call your attention only to passages that *may* be faulty. They miss many errors because they are not yet capable of analyzing language in all its complexity. (For instance, they can't accurately distinguish a word's part of speech when there are different possibilities, as *light* can be a noun, a verb, or an adjective.) And they often question passages that don't need editing, such as an appropriate passive verb or a deliberate and emphatic use of repetition.

You can customize a grammar/style checker to suit your needs and habits as a writer. (Select Options under the Tools menu.) Most checkers allow you to specify whether to check only grammar or both grammar and style. Some style checkers can be set to the level of writing you intend, such as formal, standard, and informal. (For academic writing choose formal.) You can also instruct the checker to flag specific grammar and style problems that tend to bother you, such as apostrophes in plural nouns, overused passive voice, or a confusion between *its* and *it's*.

5d   Format and proofread the final draft.

After editing your essay, retype or print it one last time. Follow your instructor's directions in formatting your document. Two common formats are discussed and illustrated in this book: Modern Language Association (MLA) on pages 479–81 and American Psychological Association (APA) on pages 509–12. In addition, Chapter 7 treats principles and elements of document design.

Be sure to proofread the final essay several times to spot and correct errors. To increase the accuracy of your proofreading, you may need to experiment with ways to keep yourself from relaxing into the rhythm and the content of your prose. Here are a few tricks, including some used by professional proofreaders:

- **Read printed copy,** even if you will eventually submit the paper electronically. Most people proofread more accurately when reading type on paper than when reading it on a computer screen. (At the same time, don't view the printed copy as necessarily error-free just because it's clean. Clean-looking copy may still harbor errors.)
- **Read the paper aloud,** very slowly, and distinctly pronounce exactly what you see.
- **Place a ruler under each line as you read it.**
- **Read "against copy,"** comparing your final draft one sentence at a time against the edited draft.
- **Ignore content.** To keep the content of your writing from distracting you while you proofread, read the essay backward, end to beginning, examining each sentence as a separate unit. Or, taking advantage of a word processor, isolate each paragraph from its context by printing it on a separate page. (Of course, reassemble the paragraphs before submitting the paper.)

5e   A sample final draft

Katy Moreno's final essay appears on these pages, typed in MLA format except for page numbers. Comments in the margins point out key features of the essay's content.

Katy Moreno

Professor Lacourse

English 110

14 Apr. 2009

Can We Compete?

College Education for the Global Economy

Today's students cannot miss news stories about globalization of the economy and outsourcing of jobs, but are students aware of how these trends are affecting the job market? In "It's a Flat World, After All," Thomas L. Friedman argues that most US students are not preparing themselves as well as students in India, China, and other countries to compete in today's economy, which requires hard-working, productive scientists and engineers. Friedman's argument speaks to me because

Descriptive title

Introduction

my mother lost her job when it was outsourced to India. But her experience taught a lesson that Friedman overlooks: technical training by itself can be too narrow to produce the communicators and problem solvers needed by contemporary businesses.

Friedman describes a "flat" world where recent technology like the Internet and wireless communication makes it possible for college graduates all over the globe to compete for high-paying jobs that once belonged to graduates of US colleges and universities. He focuses on workers in India and China who graduate from college with excellent educations in math and science, who are eager for new opportunities, and who are willing to work exceptionally hard, often harder than their American counterparts, and for less money. Friedman argues that US students must be better prepared academically, especially in math and science, so that they can get and keep jobs that will otherwise go overseas.

At first glance, my mother's experience of losing her job might seem to support Friedman's argument that better training in math and science is the key to competing in the global job market. However, her experience adds dimensions to the globalization story that Friedman misses. First, my mother had the kind of strong background in math and science that Friedman says today's workers need. She majored in computer science, rose within the information technology (IT) department of a large company, and consistently received good performance reviews. Still, when her employer decided to outsource most of its IT work, my mother lost her job. The reason wasn't that her technical skills were inadequate; instead, her salary and benefits cost the company more than outsourcing her job did. Until wages rise around the globe, jobs like my mother's will be vulnerable, no matter how well a person is trained.

The second dimension that Friedman misses is that a number of well-paid people in my mother's IT department, namely, IT managers, were not laid off. As my mother explained at the time, they kept their jobs because they were experienced at figuring out the company's IT needs, planning for changes, researching and proposing solutions, and communicating in writing and speech—skills that her more narrow training and experience had missed. Friedman misses these skills by focusing only on technical training. Without the ability to solve problems creatively and to communicate, people with technical expertise alone may not have enough to save their jobs, as my mother learned.

Like my mother, I am more comfortable in front of a computer than I am in front of a group of people, and I had planned to major in computer

Margin notes (left column):

Thesis statement: basic disagreement with Friedman

Summary of Friedman's article

No source citation for Friedman because paragraph summarizes entire article and mentions Friedman's name

Transition to disagreements with Friedman

First disagreement with Friedman

Examples to support first disagreement

Example to qualify first disagreement

Clarification of first disagreement

Second disagreement with Friedman

Explanation of second disagreement

Conclusion summarizing both disagreements with Friedman

science. Since my mother lost her job, however, I have decided to take courses in English and history as well. Classes in these subjects will require me to read broadly, think critically, research, and communicate ideas in writing—in short, to develop skills that make managers. When I enter the job market, my well-rounded education will make me a more attractive job candidate and will help me to become the kind of forward-thinking manager that US companies will always need to employ here in the US.

> Final point: business needs and author's personal goals

> Explanation of final point

Many jobs that require a college degree are indeed going overseas, as Thomas L. Friedman says, and my classmates and I need to be ready for a rapidly changing future. But rather than focus only on math and science, we need to broaden our academic experiences so that the skills we develop make us not only employable but also indispensable.

> Conclusion recapping points of agreement and disagreement with Friedman and summarizing essay

Work Cited

Friedman, Thomas L. "It's a Flat World, After All." *New York Times Magazine* 3 Apr. 2005: 32-37. Print.

> Work cited in MLA style (see p. 445)

5f   Collaborate on revisions.

In many writing courses students work together on writing, often commenting on each other's work to help with revision. This collaborative writing gives experience in reading written work critically and in reaching others through writing.

Whether you collaborate in person, on paper, or on a computer, you will be more comfortable and helpful and will benefit more from others' comments if you follow a few guidelines:

Commenting on others' writing

- **Be sure you know what the writer is saying.** If necessary, summarize the paper to understand its content. (See pp. 83–85.)
- **Address only your most significant concerns with the work.** Use the revision checklist on page 30 as a guide to what is significant. Unless you have other instructions, ignore mistakes in grammar, punctuation, spelling, and the like. (The temptation to focus on such errors may be especially strong if the writer is less experienced than you are with standard American English.) Emphasizing mistakes will contribute little to the writer's revision.
- **Remember that you are the reader, not the writer.** Don't edit sentences, add details, or otherwise assume responsibility for the paper.
- **Phrase your comments carefully.** Avoid misunderstandings by making sure comments are both clear and respectful. If you are

responding on paper or online, not face to face with the writer, remember that the writer has nothing but your written words to go on. He or she can't ask you for immediate clarification and can't infer your attitudes from gestures, facial expressions, and tone of voice.

- **Be specific.** If something confuses you, say *why*. If you disagree with a conclusion, say *why*.
- **Be supportive as well as honest.** Tell the writer what you like about the paper. Word comments positively: instead of *This paragraph doesn't interest me,* say *You have an interesting detail here that I almost missed.* Question the writer in a way that emphasizes the effect of the work on you, the reader: *This paragraph confuses me because. . . .* And avoid measuring the work against a set of external standards: *This essay is poorly organized. Your thesis statement is inadequate.*
- **While reading, make your comments in writing.** Even if you will be delivering your comments in person later on, the written record will help you recall what you thought.
- **Link comments to specific parts of a paper.** Especially if you are reading the paper on a computer, be clear about what in the paper each comment relates to. You can embed your comments directly into the paper, distinguishing them with highlighting or color. Or you can use a word processor's Comment function, which annotates documents.

Benefiting from comments on your writing

- **Think of your readers as counselors or coaches.** They can help you see the virtues and flaws in your work and sharpen your awareness of readers' needs.
- **Read or listen to comments closely.**
- **Know what the critic is saying.** If you need more information, ask for it, or consult the appropriate section of this handbook.
- **Don't become defensive.** Letting comments offend you will only erect a barrier to improvement in your writing. As one writing teacher advises, "Leave your ego at the door."
- **Revise your work in response to appropriate comments.** You will learn more from the act of revision than from just thinking about changes.
- **Remember that you are the final authority on your work.** You should be open to suggestions, but you are free to decline advice when you think it is inappropriate.
- **Keep track of both the strengths and the weaknesses others identify.** Then in later assignments you can build on your successes and give special attention to problem areas.

CULTURE LANGUAGE In some cultures, writers do not expect criticism from readers, or readers do not expect to think critically about what they read. If critical responses are uncommon in your native culture, collaboration may at first be uncomfortable for you. As a writer in English, think of a draft or even a final paper as more an exploration of ideas than the last word on your subject; then you may be more receptive to readers' suggestions. As a reader, allow yourself to approach a text skeptically, and know that your tactful questions and suggestions will usually be considered appropriate.

5g Prepare a writing portfolio.

Your writing instructor may ask you to assemble samples of your writing into a portfolio, or folder, once or more during the course. Such a portfolio gives you a chance to consider all your writing over a period and showcase your best work.

Although the requirements for portfolios vary, most instructors are looking for a range of writing that demonstrates your progress and strengths as a writer. You, in turn, see how you have advanced from one assignment to the next, as you've had time for new knowledge to sink in and time for practice. Instructors often allow students to revise papers before placing them in the portfolio, even if the papers have already been submitted earlier. In that case, every paper in the portfolio can benefit from all your learning.

A portfolio assignment will probably also provide guidelines for what to include and how the portfolio will be evaluated. Be sure you understand the purpose of the portfolio and who will read it. For instance, if your composition instructor will be the only reader and his or her guidelines encourage you to show evidence of progress, you might include a paper that took big risks but never entirely succeeded. In contrast, if a committee of instructors will read your work and the guidelines urge you to demonstrate your competence as a writer, you might include only papers that did succeed.

Unless the guidelines specify otherwise, provide error-free copies of your final drafts, label all your samples with your name, and assemble them all in a folder. Add a cover letter or memo that lists the samples, explains why you've included each one, and evaluates your progress as a writer. The self-evaluation involved should be a learning experience for you and will help your readers assess your development as a writer.

6 Paragraphs

Paragraphs give you a means of developing your essay's central idea (its thesis) step by step, point by point. They help your readers distinguish your ideas and follow your organization, and they give readers a breather from long stretches of text. In the body of an essay, you may use paragraphs for any of these purposes:

- **To introduce and give evidence for a main point supporting the thesis.** See pages 15–18 for a discussion of an essay's thesis.
- **Within a group of paragraphs centering on one main point, to develop a key example or other important evidence.**
- **To shift approach**—for instance, from pros to cons, from problem to solution, from questions to answers.
- **To mark movement in a sequence,** such as from one reason or step to another.

This chapter discusses the qualities of an effective body paragraph: the topic sentence and unity (below), coherence (p. 45), and development (p. 52). It describes two special kinds of paragraphs: introductions and conclusions (pp. 59 and 61). And finally it shows how paragraphs can be linked in a unified and coherent essay (p. 62).

CULTURE LANGUAGE Not all cultures share the paragraphing conventions of American academic writing. In some other languages, writing moves differently from English—not from left to right, but from right to left or down rows from top to bottom. Even in languages that move as English does, writers may not use paragraphs at all. Or they may use paragraphs but not state the central ideas or provide transitional expressions to show readers how sentences relate. If your native language is not English and you have difficulty with paragraphs, don't worry about paragraphing during drafting. Instead, during a separate step of revision, divide your text into parts that develop your main points. Mark those parts with indentions.

6a Unify the paragraph around a central idea.

An effective paragraph develops one central idea related to the overall thesis of the paper. Often, the central idea is stated up front

mycomplab

Visit *mycomplab.com* for more resources and exercises on paragraphs.

Checklist for revising paragraphs

- **Is the paragraph unified?** Does it focus on one central idea that is either stated in a **topic sentence** or otherwise apparent? (See opposite and below.)
- **Is the paragraph coherent?** Do the sentences follow a clear sequence? Are the sentences linked as appropriate by parallelism, repetition or restatement, pronouns, consistency, and transitional expressions? (See p. 45.)
- **Is the paragraph developed?** Is the general idea of the paragraph well supported with specific evidence such as details, facts, examples, and reasons? (See p. 52.)

---

in a **topic sentence.** The paragraph is **unified** if the rest of the sentences in the paragraph support the topic sentence, as they do in this example:

> Some people really like chili, apparently, but nobody can agree how the stuff should be made. C. V. Wood, twice winner at Terlingua, uses flank steak, pork chops, chicken, and green chilis. My friend Hughes Rudd of CBS News, who imported five hundred pounds of chili powder into Russia as a condition of accepting employment as Moscow correspondent, favors coarse-ground beef. Isadore Bleckman, the cameraman I must live with on the road, insists upon one-inch cubes of stew beef and puts garlic in his chili, an Illinois affectation. An Indian of my acquaintance, Mr. Fulton Batisse, who eats chili for breakfast when he can, uses buffalo meat and plays an Indian drum while it's cooking. I ask you.
>
> —Charles Kuralt, *Dateline America*

Topic sentence: general statement announcing topic of paragraph

Four specific examples, all providing evidence for general statement

Kuralt's paragraph works because it follows through on its central idea, which is stated in the topic sentence. Each of the next four sentences offers an example of a chili concoction. (In the final sentence Kuralt comments on the examples.)

What if instead Kuralt had written his paragraph as follows? Here the topic of chili preparation is forgotten mid-paragraph, as the sentences digress to describe life in Moscow:

> Some people really like chili, apparently, but nobody can agree how the stuff should be made. C. V. Wood, twice winner at Terlingua, uses flank steak, pork chops, chicken, and green chilis. My friend Hughes Rudd, who imported five hundred pounds of chili powder into Russia as a condition of accepting employment as Moscow correspondent,

Topic sentence: general statement

Two examples supporting statement

favors coarse-ground beef. He had some trouble finding the beef in Moscow, though. He some-times had to scour all the markets and wait in long lines. For any American used to overstocked super-markets and department stores, Russia can be quite a shock.

⎤
⎥ — Digression
⎦

Instead of following through on its topic sentence, the paragraph loses its way.

A central idea must always govern a paragraph's content as if it were standing guard at the opening, but in fact paragraphs often do not begin with a topic sentence. You may want to start with a transi-tion from the previous paragraph, not stating the central idea until the second or third sentence. You may want to give the evidence for your idea first and let it build to a topic sentence at the end, as in this example about the Civil War general William Tecumseh Sherman:

Sherman is considered by some to be the in-ventor of "total war": the first general in human history to carry the logic of war to its ultimate ex-treme, the first to scorch the earth, the first to con-sciously demoralize the hostile civilian population in order to subdue its army, the first to wreck an economy in order to starve its soldiers. He has been called our first "merchant of terror" and seen as the spiritual father of our Vietnam War concepts of "search and destroy," "pacification," "strategic hamlets," and "free-fire zones." As such, he re-mains a cardboard figure of our history: a mon-strous arch-villain to unreconstructed Southerners, and an embarrassment to Northerners.

⎤
⎥
⎥ Information supporting and building to topic sentence
⎦

⎤
⎥ — Topic sentence
⎦

—Adapted from James Reston, Jr., "You Cannot Refine It"

Even when the central idea falls at the end of the paragraph, it must still govern all of the preceding details.

Sometimes you may not state a paragraph's central idea at all, especially in narrative and descriptive writing in which the point becomes clear in the details. But the point must be clear whether it is stated or not.

Exercise 6.1   Revising a paragraph for unity

The following paragraph contains ideas or details that do not support its central idea. Identify the topic sentence in the paragraph, and delete the unrelated material.

In the southern part of the state, some people still live much as they did a century ago. They use coal- or wood-burning stoves for heating and cooking. Their homes do not have electricity or indoor bathrooms or running water. The towns they live in don't receive adequate funding from the state and federal governments, so the schools are poor and in bad shape. Beside most homes there is a garden where fresh vegetables are gathered for canning. Small pastures nearby support livestock, including cattle, pigs, horses, and chickens. Most of the people have cars or trucks, but the vehicles are old and beat-up from traveling on unpaved roads.

Exercise 6.2 Writing a unified paragraph

Develop the following topic sentence into a unified paragraph by using the relevant information in the supporting statements. Delete each statement that does not relate directly to the topic, and then rewrite and combine sentences as appropriate. Place the topic sentence in the position that seems most effective to you.

Topic sentence

Mozart's accomplishments in music seem remarkable even today.

Supporting information

Wolfgang Amadeus Mozart was born in 1756 in Salzburg, Austria.
He began composing music at the age of five.
He lived most of his life in Salzburg and Vienna.
His first concert tour of Europe was at the age of six.
On his first tour he played harpsichord, organ, and violin.
He published numerous compositions before reaching adolescence.
He married in 1782.
Mozart and his wife were both poor managers of money.
They were plagued by debts.
Mozart composed over six hundred musical compositions.
His most notable works are his operas, symphonies, quartets, and piano concertos.
He died at the age of thirty-five.

6b   Make the paragraph coherent.

When a paragraph is **coherent,** readers can see how it holds together: the sentences seem to flow logically and smoothly into one another. Exactly the opposite happens with this paragraph:

The ancient Egyptians were masters of preserving dead people's bodies by making mummies of them. Mummies several thousand years old have been discovered nearly intact. The skin, hair, teeth, finger- and toenails, and facial features of the mummies were evident. It is possible to diagnose the diseases they suffered in life, such as smallpox, arthritis, and nutritional deficiencies. The process was remarkably effective. Sometimes apparent were the fatal afflictions of the dead people: a middle-aged king died from a blow on the head, and polio killed a child king. Mummification consisted of removing the internal organs, applying natural preservatives inside and out, and then wrapping the body in layers of bandages.

— Topic sentence

Sentences related to topic sentence but disconnected from each other

The paragraph is hard to read. The sentences lurch instead of gliding from point to point.

The paragraph as it was actually written appears below. It is much clearer because the writer arranged information differently and also built connections into his sentences so that they would flow smoothly:

- After stating the central idea in a topic sentence, the writer moves to two more specific explanations and illustrates the second with four sentences of examples.
- Circled words repeat or restate key terms or concepts.
- Boxed words link sentences and clarify relationships.
- Underlined phrases are in parallel grammatical form to reflect their parallel content.

The ancient Egyptians were masters of preserving dead people's bodies by making mummies of them. Basically, mummification consisted of removing the internal organs, applying natural preservatives inside and out, and then wrapping the body in layers of bandages. And the process was remarkably effective. Indeed, mummies several thousand years old have been discovered nearly intact. Their skin, hair, teeth, finger- and toenails, and facial features are still evident. Their diseases in life, such as smallpox, arthritis, and nutritional deficiencies, are still diagnosable. Even their fatal afflictions are still apparent: a middle-aged king died from a blow on the head; a child king died from polio.

— Topic sentence

— Explanation 1: what mummification is

— Explanation 2: why the Egyptians were masters

— Specific examples of explanation 2

—Mitchell Rosenbaum (student),
"Lost Arts of the Egyptians"

1 ▪ Paragraph organization

A coherent paragraph organizes information so that readers can easily follow along. These are common paragraph schemes:

- **General to specific:** Sentences downshift from more general statements to more specific ones. (See the paragraph above by Mitchell Rosenbaum.)
- **Climactic:** Sentences increase in drama or interest, building to a climax. (See the paragraph by Lawrence Mayer on the facing page.)
- **Spatial:** Sentences scan a person, place, or object from top to bottom, from side to side, or in some other way that approxi-

mates the way people actually look at things. (See the paragraph by Virginia Woolf on p. 53.)

- **Chronological:** Sentences present events as they occurred in time, earlier to later. (See the paragraph by Kathleen LaFrank on p. 49.)

2 ▪ Parallelism

Parallelism helps tie sentences together. In the paragraph below, the underlined parallel structures of *She* and a verb link all sentences after the first one. Parallelism also appears *within* many of the sentences. Aphra Behn (1640–89) was the first Englishwoman to write professionally.

> In addition to her busy career as a writer, Aphra Behn also found time to briefly marry and spend a little while in debtor's prison. She found time to take up a career as a spy for the English in their war against the Dutch. She made the long and difficult voyage to Suriname [in South America] and became involved in a slave rebellion there. She plunged into political debate at Will's Coffee House and defended her position from the stage of the Drury Lane Theater. She actively argued for women's rights to be educated and to marry whom they pleased, or not at all. She defied the seventeenth-century dictum that ladies must be "modest" and wrote freely about sex.
>
> —Angeline Goreau, "Aphra Behn"

3 ▪ Repetition and restatement

Repeating or restating key words helps make a paragraph coherent and also reminds readers what the topic is. In the following paragraph note the underlined repetition of *sleep* and restatement of *adults:*

> Perhaps the simplest fact about sleep is that individual needs for it vary widely. Most adults sleep between seven and nine hours, but occasionally people turn up who need twelve hours or so, while some rare types can get by on three or four. Rarest of all are those legendary types who require almost no sleep at all; respected researchers have recently studied three such people. One of them—a healthy, happy woman in her seventies—sleeps about an hour every two or three days. The other two are men in early middle age, who get by on a few minutes a night. One of them complains about the daily fifteen minutes or so he's forced to "waste" in sleeping.
>
> —Lawrence A. Mayer,
> "The Confounding Enemy of Sleep"

Key term

parallelism The use of similar grammatical structures for similar elements of meaning within or among sentences: *The book caused a stir in the media* and *aroused debate in Congress*. (See also Chapter 16.)

¶ coh

6b

4 ▪ Pronouns

Because pronouns refer to nouns, they can help relate sentences to each other. In the paragraph on the previous page by Angeline Goreau, *she* works just this way by substituting for *Aphra Behn* in every sentence after the first.

5 ▪ Consistency

Consistency (or the lack of it) occurs primarily in the tense of verbs and in the person and number of nouns and pronouns. Any inconsistencies not required by meaning will interfere with a reader's ability to follow the development of ideas.

In the following paragraphs, inconsistencies appear in the underlined words:

Shifts in tense

In the Hopi religion, water is the driving force. Since the Hopi lived in the Arizona desert, they needed water urgently for drinking, cooking, and irrigating crops. Their complex beliefs are focused in part on gaining the assistance of supernatural forces in obtaining water. Many of the Hopi kachinas, or spirit essences, were directly concerned with clouds, rain, and snow.

Shifts in number

Kachinas represent spiritually the things and events of the real world, such as cumulus clouds, mischief, cornmeal, and even death. A kachina is not worshiped as a god but regarded as an interested friend. They visit the Hopi from December through July in the form of men who dress in kachina costumes and perform dances and other rituals.

Shifts in person

Unlike the man, the Hopi woman does not keep contact with kachinas through costumes and dancing. Instead, one receives a tihu, or small effigy, of a kachina from the man impersonating the kachina. You are more likely to receive a tihu as a girl approaching marriage, though a child or older woman may receive one, too.

┌ Key terms ────────────────────────────

pronoun A word that refers to and functions as a noun, such as *I, you, he, she, it, we, they: The bush had a beehive in it.* (See p. 195.)

tense The form of a verb that indicates the time of its action, such as present (*I run*), past (*I ran*), or future (*I will run*). (See p. 234.)

number The form of a noun, pronoun, or verb that indicates whether it is singular (one) or plural (more than one): *boy, boys.*

person The form of a pronoun that indicates whether the subject is speaking (first person: *I, we*), spoken to (second person: *you*), or spoken about (third person: *he, she, it, they*). All nouns are in the third person.

¶ coh

6b

Grammar checkers A grammar checker cannot help you locate shifts in tense, number, or person among sentences. Shifts are sometimes necessary (as when tenses change to reflect actual differences in time), and even a passage with needless shifts may still consist of sentences that are grammatically correct, as all the sentences are in the preceding examples.

6 ▪ Transitional expressions

Transitional expressions such as *therefore, in contrast,* and *meanwhile* can forge specific connections between sentences. Notice the difference in two versions of the same paragraph:

> Medical science has succeeded in identifying the hundreds of viruses that can cause the common cold. It has discovered the most effective means of prevention. One person transmits the cold viruses to another most often by hand. An infected person covers his mouth to cough. He picks up the telephone. His daughter picks up the telephone. She rubs her eyes. She has a cold. It spreads. To avoid colds, people should wash their hands often and keep their hands away from their faces.

Paragraph is choppy and hard to follow

> Medical science has thus succeeded in identifying the hundreds of viruses that can cause the common cold. It has also discovered the most effective means of prevention. One person transmits the cold virus to another most often by hand. For instance, an infected person covers his mouth to cough. Then he picks up the telephone. Half an hour later, his daughter picks up the same telephone. Immediately afterward, she rubs her eyes. Within a few days, she, too, has a cold. And thus it spreads. To avoid colds, therefore, people should wash their hands often and keep their hands away from their faces.

Transitional expressions (boxed) remove choppiness and spell out relationships

> —Kathleen LaFrank (student),
> "Colds: Myth and Science"

Note that transitional expressions can link paragraphs as well as sentences. In the first sentence of LaFrank's paragraph, the word *thus* signals a connection to an effect discussed in the preceding paragraph. See pages 62–63 for more on such transitions.

The following box lists many transitional expressions by the functions they perform:

Transitional expressions

To add or show sequence

again, also, and, and then, besides, equally important, finally, first, further, furthermore, in addition, in the first place, last, moreover, next, second, still, too

To compare

also, in the same way, likewise, similarly

To contrast

although, and yet, but, but at the same time, despite, even so, even though, for all that, however, in contrast, in spite of, nevertheless, notwithstanding, on the contrary, on the other hand, regardless, still, though, yet

To give examples or intensify

after all, an illustration of, even, for example, for instance, indeed, in fact, it is true, of course, specifically, that is, to illustrate, truly

To indicate place

above, adjacent to, below, elsewhere, farther on, here, near, nearby, on the other side, opposite to, there, to the east, to the left

To indicate time

after a while, afterward, as long as, as soon as, at last, at length, at that time, before, earlier, eventually, formerly, immediately, in the meantime, in the past, lately, later, meanwhile, now, presently, shortly, simultaneously, since, so far, soon, subsequently, suddenly, then, thereafter, until, until now, when

To repeat, summarize, or conclude

all in all, altogether, as has been said, in brief, in conclusion, in other words, in particular, in short, in simpler terms, in summary, on the whole, that is, therefore, to put it differently, to summarize

To show cause or effect

accordingly, as a result, because, consequently, for this purpose, hence, otherwise, since, then, therefore, thereupon, thus, to this end

Note Draw carefully on this list of transitional expressions because the ones in each group are not interchangeable. For instance, *besides, finally,* and *second* may all be used to add information, but each has its own distinct meaning.

〔CULTURE LANGUAGE〕 If transitional expressions are not common in your native language, you may be tempted to compensate when writing in English by adding them to the beginnings of most sentences. But such explicit transitions aren't needed everywhere, and in fact too many can be intrusive and awkward. When inserting transitional expressions, consider the reader's need for a signal: often the connection from sentence to sentence is already clear from the context or can be made clear by relating the content of sentences more closely (see pp. 151–52). When you do need transitional expressions, try varying their positions in your sentences, as illustrated in LaFrank's paragraph on page 49.

¶ coh

6b

Exercise 6.3 **Arranging sentences coherently**

After the topic sentence (sentence 1), the sentences in the student paragraph below have been deliberately scrambled to make the paragraph incoherent. Using the topic sentence and other clues as guides, rearrange the sentences to form a well-organized, coherent unit.

> We hear complaints about the Postal Service all the time, but we 1 should not forget what it does *right*. The total volume of mail delivered 2 by the Postal Service each year makes up almost half the total delivered mail in all the world. Its 70,000 employees handle 140 billion pieces of 3 mail each year. And when was the last time they failed to deliver yours? 4 In fact, on any given day the Postal Service delivers almost as much mail 5 as the rest of the world combined. That huge number means over 2 mil- 6 lion pieces per employee and over 560 per man, woman, and child in the country.

Exercise 6.4 **Analyzing paragraphs for coherence**

Study the paragraphs by Hillary Begas (p. 59) and Freeman Dyson (p. 61) for the authors' use of various devices to achieve coherence. Look especially for organization, parallel structures and ideas, repetition and restatement, pronouns, and transitional expressions.

Exercise 6.5 **Writing a coherent paragraph**

Write a coherent paragraph from the following information, combining and rewriting sentences as necessary. First, begin the paragraph with the topic sentence given and arrange the supporting sentences in a climactic order. Then combine and rewrite the supporting sentences, helping the reader see connections by introducing repetition and restatement, parallelism, pronouns, consistency, and transitional expressions.

Topic sentence

Hypnosis is far superior to drugs for relieving tension.

Supporting information

Hypnosis has none of the dangerous side effects of the drugs that relieve tension.

Tension-relieving drugs can cause weight loss or gain, illness, or even death.

Hypnosis is nonaddicting.

Most of the drugs that relieve tension do foster addiction.

Tension-relieving drugs are expensive.

Hypnosis is inexpensive even for people who have not mastered self-hypnosis.

6c   Develop the central idea.

¶ dev

6c

An effective, well-developed paragraph always provides the specific information that readers need and expect in order to understand you and to stay interested in what you say. Paragraph length can be a rough gauge of development: anything much shorter than 75 to 125 words may leave readers with a sense of incompleteness. Take this example:

> Untruths can serve as a kind of social oil when they smooth connections between people. In preventing confrontation and injured feelings, they allow everyone to go on as before.

General statements needing examples to be clear and convincing

This paragraph lacks development, or completeness. It does not provide enough information for us to evaluate or even care about the writer's assertions. To improve the paragraph, the writer needs to support the general statements with specific examples, as in this revision:

> Untruths can serve as a kind of social oil when they smooth connections between people. Assuring a worried friend that his haircut is flattering, claiming an appointment to avoid an aunt's dinner invitation, pretending interest in an acquaintance's children—these lies may protect the liar, but they also protect the person lied to. In preventing confrontation and injured feelings, the lies allow everyone to go on as before.
> —Joan Lar (student), "The Truth of Lies"

Examples specifying kinds of lies and consequences

To develop or shape a paragraph's central idea, one or more of the following patterns may help. (These patterns may also be used to develop entire essays. See p. 14.)

1 ▪ Narration

Narration retells a significant sequence of events, usually in the order of their occurrence (that is, chronologically). A narrator is concerned not just with the sequence of events but also with their consequence, their importance to the whole.

> Jill's story is typical for "recruits" to religious cults. She was very lonely in college and appreciated the attention of the nice young men and women who lived in a house near campus. They persuaded her to share their meals and then to move in with them. Between intense bombardments of "love," they deprived her of sleep and sometimes threatened to throw her out. Jill became increasingly confused and dependent, losing

Important events in chronological order

touch with any reality besides the one in the group. She dropped out of school and refused to see or communicate with her family. Before long she, too, was preying on lonely college students.

—Hillary Begas (student), "The Love Bombers"

2 ▪ Description

Description details the sensory qualities of a person, scene, thing, or feeling, using concrete and specific words to convey a dominant mood, to illustrate an idea, or to achieve some other purpose. In the following paragraph, almost every word helps to create a picture in the reader's mind:

> The sun struck straight upon the house, making the white walls glare between the dark windows. Their panes, woven thickly with green branches, held circles of impenetrable darkness. Sharp-edged wedges of light lay upon the window-sill and showed inside the room plates with blue rings, cups with curved handles, the bulge of a great bowl, the criss-cross pattern in the rug, and the formidable corners and lines of cabinets and bookcases. Behind their conglomeration hung a zone of shadow in which might be a further shape to be disencumbered of shadow or still denser depths of darkness.
>
> —Virginia Woolf, *The Waves*

Specific record of sensory details

3 ▪ Illustration or support

An idea may be developed with several specific examples, like those used by Charles Kuralt on page 43 and by Joan Lar on the facing page. Or it may be developed with a single extended example, as in this paragraph:

> The language problem that I was attacking loomed larger and larger as I began to learn more. When I would describe in English certain concepts and objects enmeshed in Korean emotion and imagination, I became slowly aware of nuances, of differences between two languages even in simple expression. The remark "Kim entered the house" seems to be simple enough, yet, unless a reader has a clear visual image of a Korean house, his understanding of the sentence is not complete. When a Korean says he is "in the house," he may be in his courtyard, or on his porch, or in his small room! If I wanted to give a specific picture of entering the house in the Western sense, I had to say "room" instead of house—sometimes. I say "sometimes"

Topic sentence (assertion to be illustrated)

Single detailed example

because many Koreans entertain their guests on their porches and still are considered to be hospitable, and in the Korean sense, going into the "room" may be a more intimate act than it would be in the English sense. Such problems!
—Kim Yong Ik, "A Book-Writing Venture"

Sometimes you can develop a paragraph by providing your reasons for stating a general idea. For instance:

There are three reasons, quite apart from scientific considerations, that mankind needs to travel in space. —| Topic sentence

The first reason is the need for garbage disposal: we need to transfer industrial processes into space, so that the earth may remain a green and pleasant place for our grandchildren to live in. The second reason is the need to escape material impoverishment: the resources of this planet are finite, and we shall not forgo forever the abundant solar energy and minerals and living space that are spread out all around us. The third reason is our spiritual need for an open frontier: the ultimate purpose of space travel is to bring to humanity not only scientific discoveries and an occasional spectacular show on television but a real expansion of our spirit. —| Three reasons arranged in order of increasing drama and importance
—Freeman Dyson, "Disturbing the Universe"

4 ▪ Definition

Defining a complicated, abstract, or controversial term often requires extended explanation. The following definition of the word *quality* comes from an essay asserting that "quality in product and effort has become a vanishing element of current civilization." Notice how the writer pins down her meaning by offering examples and by setting up contrasts with nonquality:

In the hope of possibly reducing the hail of censure which is certain to greet this essay (I am thinking of going to Alaska or possibly Patagonia in the week it is published), let me say that quality, as I understand it, means investment of the best skill and effort possible to produce the finest and most admirable result possible. —| General definition

Its presence or absence in some degree characterizes every man-made object, service, skilled or unskilled labor—laying bricks, painting a picture, ironing shirts, practicing medicine, shoemaking, scholarship, writing a book. You do it well or you do it half-well. —| Activities in which quality may figure

Materials are sound and durable or they are sleazy; method is painstaking or whatever is easiest. Quality is achieving or reaching for the highest standard as against being —| Contrast between quality and nonquality

satisfied with the sloppy or fraudulent. It is honesty of purpose as against catering to cheap or sensational sentiment. It does not allow compromise with the second-rate.
—Barbara Tuchman, "The Decline of Quality"

5 ▪ Division or analysis

With division or analysis, you separate something into its elements to understand it better—for instance, you might divide a newspaper into its sections, such as national news, regional news, life-style, and so on. As in the paragraph below, you may also interpret the meaning and significance of the elements you identify.

> The surface realism of the soap opera conjures up an illusion of "liveness." The domestic settings and easygoing rhythms encourage the viewer to believe that the drama, however ridiculous, is simply an extension of daily life. The conversation is so slow that some have called it "radio with pictures." (Advertisers have always assumed that busy housewives would listen, rather than watch.) Conversation is casual and colloquial, as though one were eavesdropping on neighbors. There is plenty of time to "read" the character's face; close-ups establish intimacy. The sets are comfortably familiar: well-lit interiors of living rooms, restaurants, offices, and hospitals. Daytime soaps have little of the glamour of their prime-time relations. The viewer easily imagines that the conversation is taking place in real time.
> —Ruth Rosen, "Search for Yesterday"

Topic and focus: how "liveness" seems an extension of daily life

Elements:
Slow conversation

Casual conversation

Intimate close-ups
Familiar sets

Absence of glamour

Appearance of real time

Analysis is a key skill in critical reading. See pages 85–86.

6 ▪ Classification

When you sort many items into groups, you classify the items to see their relations more clearly. The following paragraph identifies three groups, or classes, of parents:

> In my experience, the parents who hire daytime sitters for their school-age children tend to fall into one of three groups. The first group includes parents who work and want someone to be at home when the children return from school. These parents are looking for an extension of themselves, someone who will give the care they would give if they were at home. The second group includes parents who may be home all day themselves but are too disorganized or too frazzled by their children's demands to handle child care alone. They are looking for an

Topic sentence

Three groups:
Alike in one way (all hire sitters)
No overlap in groups (each has a different attitude)

Classes arranged in order of increasing drama

organizer and helpmate. The third and final group includes parents who do not want to be bothered by their children, whether they are home all day or not. Unlike the parents in the first two groups, who care for their children whenever and however they can, these parents are looking for a permanent substitute for themselves.
—Nancy Whittle (student), "Modern Parenting"

7 ▪ Comparison and contrast

Comparison and contrast may be used separately or together to develop an idea. The following paragraph illustrates one of two common ways of organizing a comparison and contrast: **subject by subject,** first one subject and then the other.

> Consider the differences also in the behavior of rock and classical music audiences. At a rock concert, the audience members yell, whistle, sing along, and stamp their feet. They may even stand during the entire performance. The better the music, the more active they'll be. At a classical concert, in contrast, the better the performance, the more *still* the audience is. Members of the classical audience are so highly disciplined that they refrain from even clearing their throats or coughing. No matter what effect the powerful music has on their intellects and feelings, they sit on their hands.   —Tony Nahm (student), "Rock and Roll Is Here to Stay"

Subjects: rock and classical audiences

Rock audience

Classical audience

The next paragraph illustrates the other common organization: **point by point,** with the two subjects discussed side by side and matched feature for feature:

> Arguing is often equated with fighting, but there are key differences between the two. Participants in an argument approach the subject to find common ground, or points on which both sides agree, while people engaged in a fight usually approach the subject with an "us-versus-them" attitude. Participants in an argument are careful to use respectful, polite language, in contrast to the insults and worse that people in a fight use to get the better of their opponents. Finally, participants in an argument commonly have the goal of reaching a new understanding or larger truth about the subject they're debating, while those in a fight have winning as their only goal.
> —Erica Ito (student), "Is an Argument Always a Fight?"

Subjects: arguing and fighting

Approach to subject: argument, fight

Language: argument, fight

Goal: argument, fight

8 ▪ Cause-and-effect analysis

When you use analysis to explain why something happened or what did or may happen, then you are determining causes or effects. In the following paragraph the author looks at the cause of an effect—Japanese collectivism:

> This *shinkansen* or "bullet train" speeds across the rural areas of Japan giving a quick view of cluster after cluster of farmhouses surrounded by rice paddies. This particular pattern did not develop purely by chance, but as a consequence of the technology peculiar to the growing of rice, the staple of the Japanese diet. The growing of rice requires the construction and maintenance of an irrigation system, something that takes many hands to build. More importantly, the planting and the harvesting of rice can only be done efficiently with the cooperation of twenty or more people. The "bottom line" is that a single family working alone cannot produce enough rice to survive, but a dozen families working together can produce a surplus. Thus the Japanese have had to develop the capacity to work together in harmony, no matter what the forces of disagreement or social disintegration, in order to survive.
> —William Ouchi, *Theory Z*

Effect: pattern of Japanese farming

Causes: Japanese dependence on rice, which requires collective effort

Effect: working in harmony

9 ▪ Process analysis

When you analyze how to do something or how something works, you explain a process. The following example identifies a process, describes the equipment needed, and details the steps in the process:

> As a car owner, you waste money when you pay a mechanic to change the engine oil. The job is not difficult, even if you know little about cars. All you need is a wrench to remove the drain plug, a large, flat pan to collect the draining oil, plastic bottles to dispose of the used oil, and fresh oil. First, warm up the car's engine so that the oil will flow more easily. When the engine is warm, shut it off and remove its oil-filler cap (the owner's manual shows where this cap is). Then locate the drain plug under the engine (again consulting the owner's manual for its location) and place the flat pan under the plug. Remove the plug with the wrench, letting the oil flow into the pan. When the oil stops flowing, replace the plug and, at the engine's filler hole, add the amount and kind of

Process: changing the oil

Equipment needed

Steps in process

fresh oil specified by the owner's manual. Pour the used oil into the plastic bottles and take it to a waste-oil collector, which any garage mechanic can recommend.   —Anthony Andres (student), "Do-It-Yourself Car Care"

Exercise 6.6 Analyzing and revising skimpy paragraphs

The following paragraphs are not well developed. Rewrite one into a well-developed paragraph, supplying your own concrete details or examples to support general statements.

1.   One big difference between successful and unsuccessful teachers is the quality of communication. A successful teacher is sensitive to students' needs and excited by the course subject. In contrast, an unsuccessful teacher seems uninterested in students and bored by the subject.

2.   Gestures are one of our most important means of communication. We use them instead of speech. We use them to supplement the words we speak. And we use them to communicate some feelings or meanings that words cannot adequately express.

Exercise 6.7 Writing with the patterns of development

Write at least three focused, coherent, and well-developed paragraphs, each one developed with a different pattern. Draw on the topics here or choose your own topics.

1. **Narration:** an experience of public speaking, a disappointment, leaving home, waking up
2. **Description:** your room, a crowded or deserted place, a food, an intimidating person
3. **Illustration or support:** study habits, having a headache, the best sports event, usefulness (or uselessness) of a self-help book
4. **Definition:** humor, an adult, fear, authority
5. **Division or analysis:** a television news show, a barn, a Web site, a piece of music
6. **Classification:** factions in a campus controversy, styles of playing poker, types of Web sites, kinds of teachers
7. **Comparison and contrast:** using *Facebook* and watching TV, AM and FM radio announcers, high school and college football, movies on TV and in a theater
8. **Cause-and-effect analysis:** connection between tension and anger, causes of failing a course, connection between credit cards and debt, causes of a serious accident
9. **Process analysis:** preparing for a job interview, setting up a blog, protecting your home from burglars, making a jump shot

6d   Write introductory and concluding paragraphs.

Introductory paragraphs set up your essay, piquing readers' interest in your topic. Concluding paragraphs finish your essay, giving readers a sense of completion.

1 ▪ **Introductions**

An introduction draws readers from their world into your world:

- **It focuses readers' attention on the topic and arouses their curiosity about what you have to say.**
- **It specifies your subject and implies your attitude.**
- **Often it includes your thesis statement** (see p. 15).
- **It is concise and sincere.**

To focus readers' attention, you have a number of options:

Some strategies for introductions

- Ask a question.
- Relate an incident.
- Use a vivid quotation.
- Offer a surprising statistic or other fact.
- State an opinion related to your thesis.
- Provide background.

- Create a visual image that represents your subject.
- Make a historical comparison or contrast.
- Outline a problem or dilemma.
- Define a word central to your subject.
- In some business or technical writing, summarize your paper.

(CULTURE / LANGUAGE) These options for an introduction may not be what you are used to if your native language is not English. In other cultures, readers may seek familiarity or reassurance from an author's introduction, or they may prefer an indirect approach to the subject. In academic and business English, however, writers and readers prefer originality and concise, direct expression.

Effective openings

A very common introduction opens with a statement of the essay's general subject, clarifies or limits the subject in one or more sentences, and then asserts the point of the essay in the thesis statement. Here are two examples:

> Can your home or office computer make you sterile? Can it strike you blind or dumb? The answer is, probably not. Nevertheless, reports of side effects relating to computer use should be examined, especially in the area of birth defects, eye complaints, and postural difficulties. Although little conclusive evidence exists to establish a causal link between computer use and problems of this sort, the circumstantial evidence can be disturbing.   —Thomas Hartmann, "How Dangerous Is Your Computer?"

Subject related to reader's experience

Clarification of subject: bridge to thesis statement

Thesis statement

> The Declaration of Independence is so widely regarded as a statement of American ideals that its origins in practical politics tend to be forgotten. ⎤ — Statement about subject
>
> Thomas Jefferson's draft was intensely debated and then revised in the Continental Congress. Jefferson was disappointed with the result. How- ⎤ — Clarification of subject: bridge to thesis statement
>
> ever, a close reading of both the historical context and the revisions themselves indicates that the Congress improved the document for its intended purpose. ⎤ — Thesis statement
>
> —Ann Weiss (student), "The Editing of the Declaration of Independence"

In much public writing, it's more important to tell readers immediately what your point is than to try to engage them. This introduction to a brief memo quickly outlines a problem and (in the thesis statement) suggests a way to solve it:

> Starting next month, staff vacations will leave our department short-handed. We need to hire two or perhaps three temporary keyboarders to ⎤ — Thesis statement
> maintain our schedules for the month.

Additional examples of effective introductions appear throughout this handbook. See the complete writing samples on pages 23, 37, 101, 118, and 125.

Introduction *don'ts*

When writing and revising your introduction, avoid approaches that are likely to bore readers or make them question your sincerity or control:

- **A vague generality or truth.** Don't extend your reach too wide with a line such as *Throughout human history . . .* or *In today's world. . . .* You may have needed a warm-up paragraph to start drafting, but your readers can do without it.
- **A flat announcement.** Don't start with *The purpose of this essay is . . .* , *In this essay I will . . .* , or any similar presentation of your intention or topic.
- **A reference to the essay's title.** Don't refer to the title of the essay in the first sentence—for example, *This is a big problem* or *This book is about the history of the guitar.*
- *According to Webster. . . .* Don't start by citing a dictionary definition. A definition can be an effective springboard to an essay, but this kind of lead-in has become dull with overuse.
- **An apology.** Don't fault your opinion or your knowledge with *I'm not sure if I'm right, but I think . . .* , *I don't know much about this, but . . .* , or similar lines.

2 ▪ Conclusions

Your conclusion finishes off your essay and tells readers where you think you have brought them. It answers the question "So what?"

Effective conclusions

Usually set off in its own paragraph, the conclusion may consist of a single sentence or a group of sentences. It may take one or more of the following approaches:

Some strategies for conclusions

- Recommend a course of action.
- Summarize the paper.
- Echo the approach of the introduction.
- Restate your thesis and reflect on its implications.
- Strike a note of hope or despair.

- Give a symbolic or powerful fact or other detail.
- Give an especially compelling example.
- Create a visual image that represents your subject.
- Use a quotation.

The following paragraph concludes an essay on the Declaration of Independence (the introduction appears on the facing page):

> The Declaration of Independence has come to be a statement of this nation's political philosophy, but that was not its purpose in 1776. Jefferson's passionate expression had to bow to the goals of the Congress as a whole to forge unity among the colonies and to win the support of foreign nations.
>
> —Ann Weiss (student), "The Editing of the Declaration of Independence"

Echo of introduction: contrast between past and present

Restatement and elaboration of thesis

In the next paragraph the author concludes an essay on environmental protection with a call for action:

> Until we get the answers [about the effects of pollutants], I think we had better keep on building power plants and growing food with the help of fertilizers and such insect-controlling chemicals as we now have. The risks are well known, thanks to the environmentalists. If they had not created a widespread public awareness of the ecological crisis, we wouldn't stand a chance. But such awareness by itself is not enough. Flaming manifestos and prophecies of doom are no longer much help, and a search for scapegoats

Summary and opinion

Call for action

can only make matters worse. The time for sen-
sations and manifestos is about over. Now we
need rigorous analysis, united effort and very hard
work.   —Peter F. Drucker,
                "How Best to Protect the Environment"

Conclusions to avoid

Several kinds of conclusions rarely work well:

- **A repeat of the introduction.** Don't simply replay your introduction. The conclusion should capture what the paragraphs of
  the body have added to the introduction.
- **A new direction.** Don't introduce a subject different from the
  one your essay has been about.
- **A sweeping generalization.** Don't conclude more than you reasonably can from the evidence you have presented. If your essay is about your frustrating experience trying to clear a parking
  ticket, you cannot reasonably conclude that *all* local police
  forces are too tied up in red tape to serve the people.
- **An apology.** Don't cast doubt on your essay. Don't say, *Even
  though I'm no expert* or *This may not be convincing, but I believe
  it's true* or anything similar. Rather, to win your readers' confidence, display confidence.

6e   Link paragraphs within an essay.

Though you may draft paragraphs or groups of paragraphs
almost as mini-essays, you will eventually need to stitch them together into a logical, larger whole. The techniques for linking paragraphs mirror those for linking sentences within paragraphs:

- **Make sure each paragraph contributes to your thesis.**
- **Arrange the paragraphs in a clear, logical order.** See pages
  19–24 for advice on organization.
- **Create links between paragraphs.** Use repetition and restatement to stress and connect key terms, and use transitional expressions and transitional sentences to indicate sequence, direction, contrast, and other relationships.

The essay "A Picture of Hyperactivity" on pages 23–24 illustrates the first two of these techniques. The following passages from
the essay illustrate the third technique, with (circled) repetitions and
restatements, boxed transitional expressions, and transitional sentences noted in annotations.

Introduction establishing
subject and stating thesis

A (hyperactive) committee member can contribute to
efficiency. A (hyperactive) salesperson can contribute to

profits. When children are hyperactive, though, people—
even parents—may wish they had never been born. A
collage of those who must cope with hyperactivity in
children is a picture of frustration, anger, and loss.

Thesis statement

The first part of the collage is the doctors. In their
terminology, the word hyperactivity has been replaced by
ADHD, attention-deficit hyperactivity disorder. They apply
the term to children who are abnormally or excessively
busy. . . .

Transitional topic sen-
tence relating to thesis
statement

As the mother of an ADHD child, I can say what the
disorder means to the parents who form the second part of
the collage. . . .

Transitional topic sen-
tence relating to thesis
statement

The weight of ADHD, however, does not rest on the
doctors and parents. The darkest part of the collage belongs
to the children. . . .

Transitional sentence

Topic sentence relating
to thesis statement

The collage is complete, and it is dark and somber.
ADHD, as applied to children, is a term with uncertain,
unattractive, and bitter associations. The picture does have
one bright spot, however, for inside every ADHD child is a
lovely, trusting, calm person waiting to be recognized.

Transitional sentence into
conclusion, restating thesis statement

7   Document Design

What makes documents clear and attractive?

Page margins, paragraph breaks, headings, illustrations, and
other elements of design can clarify and further the purpose of a
document. An appropriate, clear, and pleasing design will not transform poor writing, but it will make strong writing even more effective.

This chapter looks at the principles and elements of design that
can help you effectively present various academic documents. See
Chapter 13 for tips on designing public documents.

mycomplab

Visit *mycomplab.com* for more resources as well as
exercises on document design.

7a Format academic papers appropriately for each discipline.

Many academic disciplines prefer specific formats for students' papers. This book details two such formats:

- MLA, used in English, foreign languages, and other humanities (pp. 479–81).
- APA, used in the social sciences and some natural and applied sciences (pp. 509–12).

Other academic formats can be found in the style guides listed on page 432.

The design guidelines in this chapter extend the range of elements and options covered by most academic styles. Your instructors may want you to adhere strictly to a particular style or may allow some latitude in design. Ask them for their preferences.

Original design

Runs title and subtitle together. Does not distinguish title from text.

Crowds the page with minimal margins.

Downplays paragraph breaks with small indentions.

Buries statistics in a paragraph. Obscures relationships with non-parallel wording.

Does not introduce the figure, leaving readers to infer its meaning and purpose.

Overemphasizes the figure with large size and excessive white space.

Presents the figure undynamically, flat on.

Does not caption the figure to explain what it shows, offering only a figure number and a partial text explanation.

Generation Online: College Students and the Internet

College life once meant classrooms of students listening to teachers or groups of students talking over lunch in the union. But the reality today is more complex: students interact with their peers and professors by computer as much as face to face. As these students graduate and enter the workforce, all of society will be affected by their experience.

According to the Pew Internet Research Center (2008), today's college students are practiced computer and Internet users. The Pew Center reports that 24 percent of students in college today started using computers between ages five and eight. By age eighteen all students were using computers. Almost all college students, 92 percent, rely on the Internet, with 66 percent of students using more than one e-mail address. Computer ownership among this group is also very high: 85 percent have purchased or have been given at least one computer.

Students are eager to tap into the Internet's benefits and convenience.

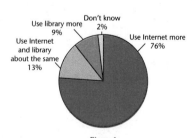

Figure 1

The Internet has eclipsed the library as the site of college students' research, as shown in Figure 1 from the Pew report. In fact, a mere 9 percent of students

7b   Work with the principles of document design.

Most of the principles of design respond to the ways we read. White space, for instance, relieves our eyes and helps to lead us through a document. Groupings or lists help to show relationships. Type sizes, images, and color add variety and help to emphasize important elements.

The sample documents on these two pages illustrate quite different ways of presenting a report for a marketing course. Even at a glance, the second document is easier to scan and read. It uses white space, groups similar elements, uses bullets and fonts for emphasis, and integrates the chart more successfully.

As you design your own documents, think about your purpose, the expectations of your readers, and how readers will move through your document. Also consider the general principles listed on the next page, noting that they overlap and support one another.

Revised design

Generation Online:
College Students and the Internet

College life once meant classrooms of students listening to teachers or groups of students talking over lunch in the union. But the reality today is more complex: students interact with their peers and professors by computer as much as face to face. As these students graduate and enter the workforce, all of society will be affected by their experience.

According to the Pew Internet Research Center (2008), today's college students are practiced computer users and Internet users.

- They started young: 24 percent were using computers between ages five and eight, and all were using them by age eighteen.
- They rely on the Internet: 92 percent have used the network, and 66 percent use more than one e-mail address.
- They own computers: 85 percent have purchased or have been given at least one computer.

Students are eager to tap into the Internet's benefits and convenience. Figure 1, from the Pew report, shows that the Internet has eclipsed the library as the site of college students' research. In fact, a mere 9 percent of students reported using the library more than the Internet as a starting point for research.

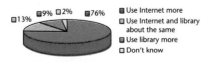

□13%   □9% □2%   ■76%   ■ Use Internet more
□ Use Internet and library about the same
□ Use library more
□ Don't know

Figure 1. College students' use of the Internet and the library for research

> Distinguishes title from subtitle and both from text.
>
> Provides adequate margins.
>
> Emphasizes paragraph breaks with white space.
>
> Groups statistics in a bulleted list set off with white space. Uses parallel wording for parallel information.
>
> Introduces the figure to indicate its meaning and purpose.
>
> Reduces white space around the figure.
>
> Presents the figure to emphasize the most significant segment.
>
> Captions the figure so that it can be read independently from the text.

- **Conduct readers through the document.** Establish flow, a pattern for the eye to follow, with headings, lists, and other elements.
- **Use white space to ease crowding and focus readers' attention.** Provide ample margins, and give breathing room to headings, lists, and other elements. Even the space indicating new paragraphs (indentions or blank lines) gives readers a break and shows that ideas are divided into manageable chunks.
- **Group information to show relationships.** Use headings (like those in this chapter) and lists (like the one you're reading) to convey the similarities and differences among parts of a document.
- **Emphasize important elements.** Establish hierarchies of information with type fonts and sizes, headings, indentions, color, boxes, and white space. In this book, for example, the importance of headings is clear from their size and color and from the presence or absence of decorative devices, such as the rule above 7c below.
- **Standardize to create and fulfill expectations.** Help direct readers through a document by, for instance, using the same size and color for all headings at the same level of importance. Standardizing also reduces clutter, making it easier for readers to determine the significance of the parts.

7c Use the elements of design appropriately for your content and purpose.

Applying the preceding design principles involves margins, text, lists, headings, color, and illustrations. You won't use all these elements for every project, however, and in many academic writing situations you will be required to follow a prescribed format. If you are addressing readers who have vision loss, consider the additional guidelines on pages 75–76.

1 ▪ Margins

Margins at the top, bottom, and sides of a page help to prevent the page from overwhelming readers with unpleasant crowding. Most academic and business documents use a minimum one-inch margin on all sides.

2 ▪ Text

A document must be readable. You can make text readable by attending to line spacing, type fonts and sizes, highlighting, word spacing, and line breaks.

Line spacing

Most academic documents are double-spaced, with an initial indention for paragraphs. Single-spaced exceptions may include documents written for business courses (see Chapter 13) and writing you post on the Web (see p. 74).

Type sizes and fonts

For academic and business documents, choose a type size of 10 or 12 points, as in these samples:

10-point Times New Roman
12-point Times New Roman

These fonts and the one you're reading have **serifs**—the small lines that finish the letters. Serif fonts are suitable for formal writing and are often easier to read on paper. **Sans serif** fonts (*sans* means "without" in French) include the one below, found on many word processors:

10-point Arial   **12-point Arial**

Sans serif fonts can be easier to read on a computer screen and are clearer on paper for readers with some vision loss (see p. 75).

Note Avoid decorative fonts in academic writing, where letter forms should be conventional and regular.

Highlighting

Within a document's text, *italic*, **boldface,** <u>underlined</u>, or even color type can emphasize key words or sentences. Underlining is rarest these days, having been replaced by italics. Academic writing sometimes uses boldface to give strong emphasis—for instance, to a term being defined—and sometimes uses color for headings and illustrations. (See p. 69 for more on color in document design.)

No matter what your writing situation, use highlighting selectively to complement your meaning, not merely to decorate your work. Many readers consider type embellishments to be distracting.

Word spacing

In most writing situations, follow these guidelines for spacing within and between words:

- **Leave one space between words.**
- **Leave one space after all punctuation, with these exceptions:**

Dash (two hyphens or the so-called em-dash on a computer)	book--its	book—its
Hyphen	one-half	
Apostrophe within a word	book's	

| Two or more adjacent marks | book.") |
| Opening quotation mark, parenthesis, or bracket | ("book   [book |

- **Leave one space before and after an ellipsis mark.** In the examples below, ellipsis marks indicate omissions within a sentence and at the end of a sentence. See pages 346–47 for additional examples.

book . . . in   book. . . . The

Line breaks

Your word processor will generally insert appropriate breaks between lines of continuous text: it will not, for instance, automatically begin a line with a comma or period, and it will not end a line with an opening parenthesis or bracket. However, you may have to prevent it from breaking a two-hyphen dash or a three-dot ellipsis mark by spacing to push the beginning of each mark to the next line.

When you instruct it to do so (usually under the Tools menu), your word processor will also automatically hyphenate words to prevent very short lines. If you must decide yourself where to break words, follow the guidelines on page 358.

3 ▪ Lists

Lists give visual reinforcement to the relations between like items—for example, the steps in a process or the elements of a proposal. A list is easier to read than a paragraph and adds white space to the page.

When wording a list, work for parallelism among items—for instance, all complete sentences or all phrases (see also p. 161). Set the list with space above and below and with numbering or bullets (centered dots or other devices, like those used in the following list about headings).

4 ▪ Headings

Headings are signposts: they direct the reader's attention by focusing the eye on a document's most significant content. Most academic documents use headings functionally to divide text, orient readers, and create emphasis. A short paper may not need headings at all. For longer papers, follow these guidelines:

- **Use one, two, or three levels of headings** depending on the needs of your material and the length of your document. Some level of heading every two or so pages will help keep readers on track.
- **Create an outline of your document** to plan where headings should go. Use the first level of heading for the main points

(and sections) of your document. Use a second and perhaps a third level of heading to mark subsections of supporting information.

- **Keep headings as short as possible** while making them specific about the material that follows.
- **Word headings consistently**—for instance, all questions (*What Is the Scientific Method?*), all phrases with *-ing* words (*Understanding the Scientific Method*), or all phrases with nouns (*The Scientific Method*).
- **Indicate the relative importance of headings** with type size, positioning, and highlighting, such as capital letters, underlining, or boldface.

First-Level Heading

Second-Level Heading

Third-Level Heading

Generally, you can use the same type font and size for headings as for the text.

- **Double- or triple-space around headings.**
- **Don't break a page immediately after a heading.** Push the heading to the next page.

Note Document format in psychology and some other social sciences requires a particular treatment of headings. See pages 511–14 for illustrations.

5 ▪ Color

With a computer and a color printer, you can produce documents that use color for bullets, headings, borders, boxes, illustrations, and other elements. Ask your instructor whether color is appropriate in your documents. If you do use it in academic documents, follow these guidelines:

- **Print text in black,** not red, blue, or another color.
- **Make sure that color headings are dark enough to be readable.**
- **Stick to the same color for all headings at the same level**—for instance, red for main headings, black for secondary headings.
- **Use color for bullets, lines, and other nontext elements.** But use no more than a few colors to keep pages clean.
- **Use color to distinguish the parts of illustrations**—the segments of charts, the lines of graphs, and the parts of diagrams. Use only as many colors as you need to make your illustrations clear.

See also pages 75–76 on the use of color for readers who have vision loss.

7d   Use illustrations appropriately for the writing situation.

An illustration can often make a point for you more efficiently than words can. Tables present data. Figures (such as graphs and charts) usually recast data in visual form. Diagrams, drawings, photographs, and other images can explain processes, represent what something looks like, or add emphasis.

In most academic writing, illustrations directly reinforce and amplify the text. Follow these guidelines:

- **Focus on a purpose for each illustration**—a reason for including it and a point you want it to make. Otherwise, readers may find it irrelevant or confusing.
- **Provide a source note for someone else's independent material**—whether you are borrowing data or reproducing an entire illustration (see p. 428). Each discipline has a slightly different style for such source notes: those in the illustrations on the next several pages reflect MLA style for English and some other humanities.
- **Number figures, photographs, and other images together:** Figure 1, Figure 2, and so on.
- **Number and label tables separately:** Table 1, Table 2, and so on.
- **Refer to each illustration in your text**—for instance, "See fig. 2." Place the reference at the point(s) in the text where readers will benefit by consulting the illustration.
- **Determine the placement of illustrations.** The social sciences and some other disciplines require each illustration to fall on a page by itself immediately after the text reference to it (see p. 512). You may want to follow this rule in other situations as well if you have a large number of illustrations. Otherwise, you can embed them in your text pages just after you refer to them. When embedding illustrations, consider where they will help but not distract readers.

1 ▪ Tables

Tables usually present raw data, making complex information accessible to readers. The data may show how variables relate to one another, how variables change over time, or how two or more groups compare and contrast. The following table emphasizes the last function.

des

7d

Table

A self-explanatory title falls above the table. Self-explanatory headings label horizontal rows and vertical columns.	The layout of rows and columns is clear: headings align with their data, and numbers align vertically down columns.

Table 1

Public- and private-school enrollment of US students age five and older, 2006

	Number of students	Percentage in public school	Percentage in private school
All students	74,220,937	83.2	16.8
Kindergarten	4,012,680	86.0	14.0
Grades 1-4	15,758,734	88.8	11.2
Grades 5-8	16,498,217	89.4	10.6
Grades 9-12	17,500,473	90.5	9.5
College (undergraduate)	17,063,732	77.0	23.0
Graduate and professional school	3,387,101	59.8	40.2

Source: Data from *2006 American Community Survey*; US Census Bureau, n.d.; Web; 7 Jan. 2009; Table S1404.

2 ▪ Figures

Figures represent data or show concepts visually. They include charts, graphs, diagrams, and photographs.

Pie charts

Pie charts show the relations among the parts of a whole. The whole totals 100 percent, and each pie slice is proportional in size to its share of the whole. Use a pie chart when shares, not the underlying data, are your focus.

Pie chart

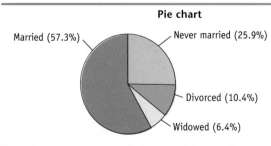

Married (57.3%)   Never married (25.9%)

Divorced (10.4%)

Widowed (6.4%)

Color distinguishes segments of the chart. Use distinct shades of gray, black, and white if your paper will not be read in color.

Segment percentages total 100.

Every segment is clearly labeled. You can also use a key, as in the chart on p. 65.

Self-explanatory caption falls below the chart.

Fig. 1. Marital status in 2008 of adults age eighteen and over. Data from *Current Population Survey: 2008 Social and Economic Supplement*; US Census Bureau, Jan. 2009; Web; 2 Feb. 2009.

Bar charts

Bar charts compare groups or time periods on a measure such as quantity or frequency. Use a bar chart when relative size is your focus. Be sure to start with a zero point in the lower left corner so that the values on the vertical axis are clear.

Bar chart

Vertical scale shows and clearly labels the values being measured. Zero point clarifies values.

Horizontal scale shows and clearly labels the groups being compared.

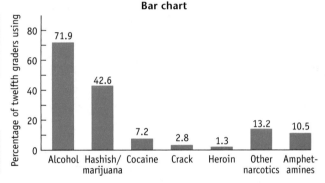

Self-explanatory caption falls below the chart.

Fig. 2. Lifetime prevalence of use of alcohol and other drugs among twelfth graders in 2008. Data from *Monitoring the Future: A Continuing Study of American Youth*; U of Michigan, 11 Dec. 2008; Web; 10 Aug. 2009.

Line graphs

Line graphs show change over time in one or more subjects. They are an economical and highly visual way to compare many

Line graph

Vertical scale shows and clearly labels the values being measured. Zero point clarifies values.

Color and labels distinguish the subjects being compared. Use dotted and dashed black lines if your paper will not be read in color.

Horizontal scale shows and clearly labels the range of dates.

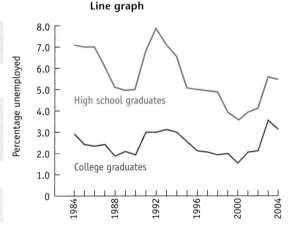

Self-explanatory caption falls below the graph.

Fig. 3. Unemployment rates of high school graduates and college graduates, 1984-2004. Data from Antony Davies; *The Economics of College Tuition*; Mercatus Center, George Mason U, 3 Mar. 2005; Web; 26 June 2009.

points of data. Be sure to start with a zero point in the lower left corner so that the values on the vertical axis are clear.

Diagrams

Diagrams show concepts visually, such as the structure of an organization or the way something works or looks. Often, diagrams show what can't be described economically in words.

Diagram

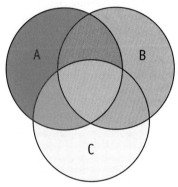

Diagram makes concept comprehensible.

Fig. 4. A Venn diagram, showing all possible relations among individuals or groups A, B, and C. From "Venn Diagram"; *Wikipedia*; Wikimedia, 24 Mar. 2009; Web; 5 Apr. 2009.

Self-explanatory caption falls below the diagram.

Photographs and other images

Sometimes you may focus an entire paper on analyzing an image such as a photograph, painting, or advertisement. But most

---

Photograph

Photograph shows subject more economically and dramatically than words could.

Fig. 5. View of Saturn from the *Cassini* spacecraft, showing the planet and its rings. From *Cassini-Huygens: Mission to Saturn and Titan*; US Natl. Atmospheric and Space Administration, Jet Propulsion Laboratory, 24 Feb. 2005; Web; 26 Apr. 2009.

Self-explanatory caption falls below the image.

commonly you'll use images to add substance to ideas or to enliven them. You might clarify a psychology paper with a photograph from a key experiment, add information to an analysis of a novel with a drawing of the author, or illustrate one side of an argument with a cartoon. Images grab readers' attention, so in academic writing use them carefully to explain or reinforce your writing.

Note When using an image prepared by someone else—for instance, a photograph downloaded from the Web—you must verify that the source permits reproduction of the image before you use it. In most documents but especially academic papers, you must also fully cite the source of any borrowed image. See pages 430–31 on copyright issues with Internet sources.

7e Consider design when writing for the Web.

Most of the preceding design guidelines apply to online writing as well, except that the text is often single-spaced for readability on screen.

1 ▪ Online papers

Some instructors may ask you to post your papers to a Web site or blog. You can usually compose an online paper on your computer and then either upload the paper directly or first use the Save As HTML function to translate the paper into a Web page. (HTML is the most common Web language.) Your word processor should allow you to modify some of the elements of an HTML document, or you can open the document in an HTML editor.

Paper submitted on the Web

White background providing strong contrast

Standard font and single spacing for readability

Menu providing links to major sections in the paper

Heading marking major section

ReadingWorks
Springfield Veterans Administration Hospital

Making a Difference: A Service-Learning Project
Alex Ramirez

Illiteracy or low literacy skills among military veterans is a pervasive problem in Springfield County and around the US. Many veterans do not have the literacy skills to find high-paying jobs needed to own a home and support a family. The literacy center at Springfield VA Hospital, where I volunteer as a tutor and completed my service-learning project, aims to provide the education these veterans need to improve their literacy skills.

Literacy rates among military veterans
Tutoring at ReadingWorks
Preparing documents and a Web site for ReadingWorks

Literacy Rates Among Military Veterans
Most military veterans have basic literacy skills; very few cannot read or

2 ■ Original Web sites

When you create an original Web site, be aware that readers generally alternate between skimming pages for highlights and focusing intently on sections of text. To facilitate this kind of reading, you'll want to design a site that's clear and easy to navigate, as shown in the screen shot below.

Original Web site

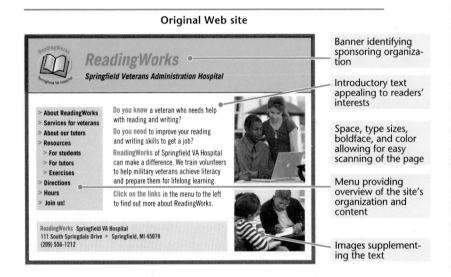

Banner identifying sponsoring organization

Introductory text appealing to readers' interests

Space, type sizes, boldface, and color allowing for easy scanning of the page

Menu providing overview of the site's organization and content

Images supplementing the text

7f   Consider readers with vision loss.

Your audience may include readers who have low vision, problems with color perception, or difficulties processing visual information. If so, consider adapting your design to meet these readers' needs. Here are a few pointers:

- **Use large type fonts.** Most guidelines call for 14 points or larger.
- **Use standard type fonts.** Many people with low vision find it easier to read sans serif fonts such as Arial than serif fonts (see p. 67). Avoid decorative fonts with unusual flourishes, even in headings.
- **Avoid words in all-capital letters.**
- **Avoid relying on color alone to distinguish elements.** Label elements, and distinguish them by position or size.
- **Use red and green selectively.** To readers who are red-green colorblind, these colors will appear in shades of gray, yellow, or blue.

- **Use contrasting colors.** To make colors distinct, choose them from opposite sides of the color spectrum—violet and yellow, for instance, or orange and blue.
- **Use only light colors for tints behind type.** Make the type itself black or a very dark color.

8 Critical Thinking and Reading

Why and how should I think and read critically?

Throughout college and beyond, you will be expected to think and read critically—that is, to question, test, and build on what others say and what you yourself think. In daily life, critical thinking helps you figure out why things happen to you or what your experiences mean. In school and at work, critical thinking sharpens your ability to learn and to perform. It helps you understand which ideas are useful, fair, and wise—and which are not.

Note Critical thinking plays a large role in research writing. See pages 399–410 on evaluating print and online sources and pages 410–12 on synthesizing sources.

crit
8a

8a Use techniques of critical reading.

In college and work, much of your critical thinking will focus on written texts (a short story, a journal article, a blog) or on visual objects (a photograph, a chart, a film). Like all subjects worthy of critical consideration, such works operate on at least three levels: (1) what the creator actually says or shows, (2) what the creator does not say or show but builds into the work (intentionally or not), and (3) what you think. Discovering each level of the work, even if it is visual, involves four main steps: previewing the material, reading actively, summarizing, and forming a critical response.

CULTURE LANGUAGE The idea of reading critically may require you to make some adjustments if readers in your native culture tend to seek understanding or agreement more than engagement in what they read. Readers of English use texts for all kinds of reasons, including pleasure, reinforcement, and information. But they also read skeptically, critically, to see the author's motives, test their own ideas, and arrive at new knowledge.

1 ▪ Previewing the material

When you're reading a work of literature, such as a short story or a poem, it's often best just to plunge right in. But for critical reading of other works, it's worthwhile to skim before reading word for word, forming expectations and even some preliminary questions. The preview will make your reading more informed and fruitful.

---

mycomplab

Visit *mycomplab.com* for more resources and exercises on critical thinking and reading.

- **Gauge length and level.** Is the material brief and straightforward so that you can read it in one sitting, or does it require more time?

- **Check the facts of publication.** Does the date of publication suggest currency or datedness? Does the publisher or publication specialize in scholarly articles, popular books, or something else? For a Web publication, who or what sponsors the site—an individual? a nonprofit organization? a government body? a college or university?

- **Look for content cues.** What do the title, introduction, headings, illustrations, conclusion, and other features tell you about the topic, the author's approach, and the main ideas?

- **Learn about the author.** Does a biography tell you about the author's publications, interests, biases, and reputation in the field? If there is no biography, what can you gather about the author from his or her words? Use a Web search to trace unfamiliar authors.

- **Consider your preliminary response.** What do you already know about the topic? What questions do you have about either the topic or the author's approach to it? What biases of your own—for instance, curiosity, boredom, or an outlook similar or opposed to the author—might influence your reading of the work?

crit
8a

> **Exercise 8.1**   **Previewing an essay**
>
> Following is an essay by Thomas Sowell, an economist, newspaper columnist, and author of many books on economics, politics, and education. The essay was first published in the 1990s, but its subject remains current. Preview the essay using the preceding guidelines, and then read it once or twice, until you think you understand what the author is saying. Note your questions and reactions in writing.

Student Loans

The first lesson of economics is scarcity: There is never enough of 1 anything to fully satisfy all those who want it.

The first lesson of politics is to disregard the first lesson of econom- 2 ics. When politicians discover some group that is being vocal about not having as much as they want, the "solution" is to give them more. Where do politicians get this "more"? They rob Peter to pay Paul.

After a while, of course, they discover that Peter doesn't have 3 enough. Bursting with compassion, politicians rush to the rescue. Needless to say, they do not admit that robbing Peter to pay Paul was a dumb idea in the first place. On the contrary, they now rob Tom, Dick, and Harry to help Peter.

The latest chapter in this long-running saga is that politicians have 4 now suddenly discovered that many college students graduate heavily in debt. To politicians it follows, as the night follows the day, that the government should come to their rescue with the taxpayers' money.

How big is this crushing burden of college students' debt that we 5
hear so much about from politicians and media deep thinkers? For those
students who graduate from public colleges owing money, the debt averages a little under $7000. For those who graduate from private col-
leges owing money, the average debt is a little under $9000.

Buying a very modestly priced automobile involves more debt than 6
that. And a car loan has to be paid off faster than the ten years that college graduates get to repay their student loans. Moreover, you have to
keep buying cars every several years, while one college education lasts a
lifetime.

College graduates of course earn higher incomes than other peo- 7
ple. Why, then, should we panic at the thought that they have to repay
loans for the education which gave them their opportunities? Even graduates with relatively modest incomes pay less than 10 percent of their
annual salary on the loan the first year—with declining percentages in
future years, as their pay increases.

Political hysteria and media hype may focus on the low-income stu- 8
dent with a huge debt. That is where you get your heart-rending stories—
even if they are not all that typical. In reality, the soaring student loans of
the past decade have resulted from allowing high-income people to borrow under government programs.

Before 1978, college loans were available through government pro- 9
grams only to students whose family income was below some cut-off
level. That cut-off level was about double the national average income,
but at least it kept out the Rockefellers and the Vanderbilts. But, in an era
of "compassion," Congress took off even those limits.

That opened the floodgates. No matter how rich you were, it still 10
paid to borrow money through the government at low interest rates.
The money you had set aside for your children's education could be in-
vested somewhere else, at higher interest rates. Then, when the student
loan became due, parents could pay it off with the money they had set
aside—pocketing the difference in interest rates.

To politicians and the media, however, the rapidly growing loans 11
showed what a great "need" there was. The fact that many students
welshed when time came to repay their loans showed how "crushing"
their burden of debt must be. In reality, those who welsh typically
have smaller loans, but have dropped out of college before finishing.
People who are irresponsible in one way are often irresponsible in other
ways.

No small amount of the deterioration of college standards has been 12
due to the increasingly easy availability of college to people who are not
very serious about getting an education. College is not a bad place to
hang out for a few years, if you have nothing better to do, and if someone else is paying for it. Its costs are staggering, but the taxpayers carry
much of that burden, not only for state universities and city colleges, but
also to an increasing extent even for "private" institutions.

Numerous government subsidies and loan programs make it possible 13
for many people to use vast amounts of society's resources at low cost to
themselves. Whether in money terms or in real terms, federal aid to higher
education has increased several hundred percent since 1970. That has en-

abled colleges to raise their tuition by leaps and bounds and enabled professors to be paid more and more for doing less and less teaching.

Naturally all these beneficiaries are going to create hype and hysteria to keep more of the taxpayers' money coming in. But we would be fools to keep on writing blank checks for them.   14

When you weigh the cost of things, in economics that's called "trade-offs." In politics, it's called "mean-spirited." Apparently, if we just took a different attitude, scarcity would go away.   15

—Thomas Sowell

2 ▪ Reading

crit

8a

Reading is itself more than a one-step process. You want to understand the first level on which the text operates—what the author actually says—and begin to form your impressions.

First reading

The first time through new material, read as steadily and smoothly as possible, trying to get the gist of what the author is saying.

- **Read in a place where you can concentrate.** Choose a quiet environment away from distractions such as music or talking.
- **Give yourself time.** Rushing yourself or worrying about something else you have to do will prevent you from grasping what you read.
- **Try to enjoy the work.** Seek connections between it and what you already know. Appreciate new information, interesting relationships, forceful writing, humor, good examples.
- **Make notes sparingly during this first reading.** Mark major stumbling blocks—such as a paragraph you don't understand—so that you can try to resolve them before rereading.

(**CULTURE LANGUAGE**) If English is not your first language and you come across unfamiliar words during a first reading, don't look them up until you are finished. Stopping while reading can distract you from seeing the author's overall meaning. Instead, try to guess the meanings of unfamiliar words from their contexts, circle them, and look them up later.

Rereading

After the first reading, plan on at least one other. This time read *slowly*. Your main concern should be to grasp the content and how it is constructed. That means rereading a paragraph if you didn't get the point or using a dictionary to look up words you don't know.

Use your pen, pencil, or keyboard freely to highlight and distill the text:

- **Distinguish main ideas from supporting ideas.** Look for the central idea, or thesis, for the main idea of each paragraph or section, and for the evidence supporting ideas.
- **Learn key terms.** Understand both their meanings and their applications.
- **Discern the connections among ideas.** Be sure you see why the author moves from point A to point B to point C and how those points relate to support the central idea. It often helps to outline the text or to summarize it (see opposite).

crit
8a

- **Distinguish between facts and opinions.** Especially when reading an argument, tease apart the facts from the author's opinions that may or may not be based on facts. (See pp. 104–05 for more on facts and opinions.)
- **Add your own comments.** In the margins or separately, note links to other readings or to class discussions, questions to explore further, possible topics for your writing, points you find especially strong or weak.

An example of critical reading

The following samples show how a student, Charlene Robinson, approached "Student Loans." After her first reading, Robinson went through Sowell's text more slowly and added her comments and questions. Here are the first four paragraphs with her annotations:

> The first lesson of economics is scarcity: There is never enough of anything to fully satisfy all those who want it.   *fact*
>
> The first lesson of politics is to disregard the first lesson of economics. When politicians discover some group that is being vocal about not having as much as they want, the "solution" is to give them more. Where do politicians get this "more"? They rob Peter to pay Paul.   *opinion—basic contradiction between economics and politics*   *← biblical reference?*
>
> After a while, of course, they discover that Peter doesn't have enough. Bursting with compassion, politicians rush to the rescue. Needless to say, they do not admit that robbing Peter to pay Paul was a dumb idea in the first place. On the contrary, they now rob Tom, Dick, and Harry to help Peter.   *ironic and dismissive language*
>
> The latest chapter in this long-running saga is that politicians have now suddenly discovered that many college students graduate heavily in debt. To politicians it follows, as the night follows day, that the government should come to their rescue with the taxpayers' money.   *politicians = fools? or irresponsible?*

After reading the text, Robinson wrote about it in the journal she kept on her computer. She divided the journal into two columns, one each for the text and her responses. Here is the portion pertaining to the paragraphs above:

Text	Responses
Economics teaches lessons (1), and politics (politicians) and economics are at odds.	Is economics truer or more reliable than politics? More scientific?
Politicians don't accept econ. limits—always trying to satisfy "vocal" voters by giving them more of what they want (2).	Politicians do spend tax money, but do they always disregard economics? Evidence?
"Robbing Peter to pay Paul" (2)— the Bible (the Apostles)?	
Politicians support student-loan program with taxpayer refunds bec. of "vocal" voters (2-4): another ex. of not accepting econ. limits.	I support the loan program, too. Are politicians being irresponsible when they do? (Dismissive language underlined on copy.)

crit
8a

You should try to answer the questions about meaning that you raise in your annotations and your journal, and that may take another reading or some digging in other sources, such as dictionaries and encyclopedias. Recording in your journal what you think the author means will help you build an understanding of the text, and a focused attempt to summarize will help even more (see below). Such efforts will resolve any confusion you feel, or they will give you the confidence to say that your confusion is the fault of the author, not the reader.

Exercise 8.2   Reading

Read Sowell's essay on pages 79–81 at least twice, until you think you understand what the author is saying. Either on these pages or separately, note your questions and reactions in writing, as student writer Charlene Robinson did for the first four paragraphs. Look up any words you don't know, and try to answer your questions. You might want to discuss the essay with your classmates as well.

---

3 ▪ Summarizing

A good way to master the content of a text and to see its strengths and weaknesses is to **summarize** it: distill it to its main points, in your own words. The following box gives a method of summarizing:

Writing a summary

- ▪ **Understand the meaning.** Look up words or concepts you don't know so that you understand the author's sentences and how they relate to one another.
- ▪ **Understand the organization.** Work through the text to identify its sections—single paragraphs or groups of paragraphs focused on a single topic. To understand how parts of a work relate to one another, try drawing a tree diagram or creating an outline (pp. 21–23).

(continued)

Writing a summary
(continued)

- **Distill each section.** Write a one- or two-sentence summary of each section you identify. Focus on the main point of the section, omitting examples, facts, and other supporting evidence.
- **State the main idea.** Write a sentence or two capturing the author's central idea.
- **Support the main idea.** Write a full paragraph (or more, if needed) that begins with the central idea and supports it with the sentences that summarize sections of the work. The paragraph should concisely and accurately state the thrust of the entire work.
- ***Use your own words.*** By writing, you re-create the meaning of the work in a way that makes sense for you.

Summarizing even a passage of text can be tricky. Below is one attempt to summarize the following material from an introductory biology textbook.

Original text

   As astronomers study newly discovered planets orbiting distant stars, they hope to find evidence of water on these far-off celestial bodies, for water is the substance that makes possible life as we know it here on Earth. All organisms familiar to us are made mostly of water and live in an environment dominated by water. They require water more than any other substance. Human beings, for example, can survive for quite a few weeks without food, but only a week or so without water. Molecules of water participate in many chemical reactions necessary to sustain life. Most cells are surrounded by water, and cells themselves are about 70–95% water. Three-quarters of Earth's surface is submerged in water. Although most of this water is in liquid form, water is also present on Earth as ice and vapor. Water is the only common substance to exist in the natural environment in all three physical states of matter: solid, liquid, and gas.
                    —Neil A. Campbell and Jane B. Reece, *Biology*

Draft summary

Astronomers look for water in outer space because life depends on it. It is the most common substance on Earth and in living cells, and it can be a liquid, a solid (ice), or a gas (vapor).

This summary accurately restates ideas in the original, but it does not pare the passage to its essence. The work of astronomers and the three physical states of water add color and texture to the original, but they are asides to the key concept that water sustains life because of its role in life. The following revision narrows the summary to this concept:

Revised summary

Water is the most essential support for life, the dominant substance on Earth and in living cells and a component of life-sustaining chemical processes.

When Charlene Robinson summarized Thomas Sowell's "Student Loans," she first drafted this sentence about paragraphs 1–4:

Draft summary

As much as politicians would like to satisfy voters by giving them everything they ask for, the government cannot afford a student loan program.

Reading the sentence and Sowell's paragraphs, Robinson saw that this draft misread the text by asserting that the government cannot afford student loans. She realized that Sowell's point is more complicated than that and rewrote her summary:

Revised summary

As their support of the government's student loan program illustrates, politicians ignore the economic reality that using resources to benefit one group (students in debt) involves taking the resources from another group (taxpayers).

Notes Using your own words when writing a summary not only helps you understand the meaning but also constitutes the first step in avoiding plagiarism. The second step is to cite the source when you use it in something written for others. See pages 431–33.

Do not count on the AutoSummarize function on your word processor for summarizing texts that you may have copied onto your computer. The summaries are rarely accurate, and you will not gain the experience of interacting with the texts on your own.

Exercise 8.3 Summarizing

Start where the preceding summary of Thomas Sowell's essay ends (at paragraph 5) to summarize the entire essay. Your summary, in your own words, should not exceed one paragraph. (For additional exercises in summarizing, see pp. 418–19.)

8b Form a critical response.

Once you've grasped the content of what you're reading—what the author says—then you can turn to understanding what the author does not say outright but suggests or implies or even lets slip. At this stage you are concerned with the purpose or intention of the author and with how he or she carries it out.

Critical thinking and reading consist of four overlapping operations: analyzing, interpreting, synthesizing, and (often) evaluating.

Analyzing

Analysis is the separation of something into its parts or elements, the better to understand it. To see these elements in what you are reading, begin with a question that reflects your purpose in analyzing the text: why you're curious about it or what you're trying to make out of it. This question will serve as a kind of lens that high-lights some features and not others.

Analyzing Thomas Sowell's "Student Loans" (pp. 79–81), you might ask one of these questions:

Questions for analysis	Elements
What is Sowell's attitude toward politicians?	References to politicians: content, words, tone
How does Sowell support assertions about the loan program's costs?	Support: evidence, such as statistics and examples

Interpreting

Identifying the elements of something is only the beginning: you also need to interpret the meaning or significance of the elements and of the whole. Interpretation usually requires you to infer the author's **assumptions**—that is, opinions or beliefs about what is or what could or should be. (*Infer* means to draw a conclusion based on evidence.)

Assumptions are pervasive: we all adhere to certain values, beliefs, and opinions. But assumptions are not always stated outright. Speakers and writers may judge that their audience already understands and accepts their assumptions; they may not even be aware of their assumptions; or they may deliberately refrain from stating their assumptions for fear that the audience will disagree. That is why your job as a critical thinker is to interpret what the assumptions are.

Thomas Sowell's "Student Loans" is based on certain assumptions, some obvious, some not. If you were analyzing Sowell's attitude toward politicians, as suggested earlier, you would focus on his statements about them. Sowell says that they "disregard the first lesson of economics" (paragraph 2), which implies that they ignore important principles (knowing that Sowell is an economist himself makes this a reasonable assumption on your part). Sowell also says that politicians "rob Peter to pay Paul," are "[b]ursting with compassion," "do not admit . . . a dumb idea," are characters in a "long-running saga," and arrive at the solution of spending taxes "as the night follows the day"—that is, inevitably (paragraphs 2–4). From these statements and others, you can infer the following:

> Sowell assumes that politicians become compassionate when a cause is loud and popular, not necessarily just, and they act irresponsibly by trying to solve the problem with other people's (taxpayers') money.

Synthesizing

If you stopped at analysis and interpretation, critical thinking and reading might leave you with a pile of elements and possible meanings but no vision of the whole. With **synthesis** you make connections among parts *or* among wholes. You use your perspective—your knowledge and beliefs—to create a new whole by drawing conclusions about relationships and implications.

A key component of academic reading and writing, synthesis receives attention in the next chapter (pp. 95–96) and then in the context of research writing (pp. 410–12). Sometimes you'll respond directly to a text, as in the following statement about Thomas Sowell's essay "Student Loans," which connects Sowell's assumptions about politicians to a larger idea also implied by the essay:

crit
8b

> Sowell's view that politicians are irresponsible with taxpayers' money reflects his overall opinion that the laws of economics, not politics, should drive government.

Often synthesis will take you outside the text to the surroundings. The following questions can help you investigate the context of a work:

- **How does the work compare with works by others?** For instance, how have other writers responded to Sowell's views on student loans?
- **How does the work fit into the context of other works by the same author or group?** How do Sowell's views on student loans typify, or not, the author's other writing on political and economic issues?
- **What cultural, economic, or political forces influence the work?** What other examples might Sowell have given to illustrate his view that economics, not politics, should determine government spending?
- **What historical forces influence the work?** How has the indebtedness of college students changed over the past four decades?

Evaluating

Critical reading and writing often end at synthesis: you form and explain your understanding of what the work says and doesn't say. If you are also expected to **evaluate** the work, however, you will go further to judge its quality and significance. You may be evaluating a source you've discovered in research (see pp. 399–410), or you may be completing an assignment to state and defend a judgment, a statement such as *Thomas Sowell does not summon the evidence to support his case.* You can read Charlene Robinson's critical analysis of Thomas Sowell's "Student Loans" on pages 101–03.

Evaluation takes a certain amount of confidence. You may think that you lack the expertise to cast judgment on another's work, especially if the work is difficult or the author well known. True, the more informed you are, the better a critical reader you are. But conscientious reading and analysis will give you the internal authority to judge a work *as it stands* and *as it seems to you*, against your own unique bundle of experiences, observations, and attitudes.

Exercise 8.4   Reading an essay critically

Reread Thomas Sowell's "Student Loans" (pp. 79–81) to form your own critical response to it. Focus on any elements suggested by your questions about the text: possibilities are assumptions, evidence, organization, use of language, tone, vision of education or students. Be sure to write while reading and thinking; your notes will help your analysis and enhance your creativity, and they will be essential for writing about the selection. (See Exercise 9.2, p. 103.)

8c   View images critically.

Every day we are bombarded with images—pictures on billboards, commercials on television, graphs and charts in newspapers and textbooks, to name just a few examples. Most images slide by without our noticing them, or so we think. But images, sometimes even more than text, can influence us covertly. Their creators have purposes, some worthy, some not, and understanding those purposes requires critical reading. The method parallels that in the previous section for reading text critically: preview, read for comprehension, analyze, interpret, synthesize, and (often) evaluate.

1 ▪ Previewing an image

Your first step in exploring an image is to form initial impressions of the work's origin and purpose and to note distinctive features. This previewing process is like the one for previewing a text (pp. 78–79):

- **What do you see?** What is most striking about the image? What is its subject? What is the gist of any text or symbols? What is the overall effect of the image?
- **What are the facts of publication?** Where did you first see the image? Do you think the image was created especially for that location or for others as well? What can you tell about when the image was created?
- **What do you know about the person or group that created the image?** For instance, was the creator an artist, scholar, news organization, or corporation? What seems to have been the creator's purpose?
- **What is your preliminary response?** What about the image interests, confuses, or disturbs you? Are the form, style, and subject familiar or unfamiliar? How might your knowledge, experiences, and values influence your reception of the image?

If possible, print a copy of the image or scan it into your reading journal, and write comments in the image margins or separately.

2 ▪ Reading an image

Reading an image requires the same level of concentration as reading a text. The illustration below shows the notes that a student, Matthew Greene, made while reading an advertisement.

Try to answer the following questions about the image. If some answers aren't clear at this point, skip the question until later.

- ▪ **What is the purpose of the image?** Is it mainly explanatory, conveying information, or is it argumentative, trying to convince readers of something or persuade them to act? What information or point of view does it seem intended to get across?
- ▪ **Who is the intended audience for the image?** What does the source of the image, including its publication facts, tell about the image creator's expectations for readers' knowledge, interests,

crit

8c

Annotation of an image

Advertisement for *BoostUp.org,* 2007

and attitudes? What do the features of the image itself add to your impression?

- **What do any words or symbols add to the image?** Whether located on the image or outside it (such as in a caption), do words or symbols add information, focus your attention, or alter your impression of the image?
- **What people, places, things, or action does the image show?** Does the image tell a story? Do its characters or other features tap into your knowledge, or are they unfamiliar?
- **What is the form of the image?** Is it a photograph, advertisement, painting, graph, diagram, cartoon, or something else? How do its content and apparent purpose and audience relate to its form?

3 ■ Analyzing an image

Elements for analysis

As when analyzing a written work, you analyze an image by identifying its elements. The image elements you might consider appear in the following box. Keep in mind that an image is a visual *composition* whose every element likely reflects a deliberate effort to communicate. Still, few images include all the elements, and you can narrow the list further by posing a question about the image you are reading, as illustrated on the next page.

Elements of images

- **Emphasis:** Most images pull your eyes to certain features: a graph line moving sharply upward, a provocative figure, bright color, thick lines, and so on. The cropping of a photograph or the date range in a chart will also reflect what the image creator considers important.
- **Narration:** Most images tell stories, whether in a sequence (a TV commercial or a graph showing changes over time) or at a single moment (a photograph, a painting, or a pie chart). Sometimes dialog or a title or caption contributes to the story.
- **Point of view:** The image creator influences responses by taking account of both the viewer's physical relation to the image subject—for instance, whether it is seen head-on or from above—and the viewer's assumed attitude toward the subject.
- **Arrangement:** Patterns among colors or forms, figures in the foreground and background, and elements that are juxtaposed or set apart contribute to the image's meaning and effect.
- **Color:** An image's colors can direct the viewer's attention and convey the creator's attitude toward the subject. Color may also suggest a mood, an era, a cultural connection, or another frame in which to view the image.

- **Characterization:** The figures and objects in an image have certain qualities—sympathetic or not, desirable or not, and so on. Their characteristics reflect the roles they play in the image's story.
- **Context:** The source of an image or the background in an image affects its meaning, whether it is a graph from a scholarly journal or a photo of a car on a sunny beach.
- **Tension:** Images often communicate a problem or seize attention with features that seem wrong, such as misspelled or misaligned words, distorted figures, or controversial relations between characters.
- **Allusions:** An **allusion** is a reference to something the audience is likely to recognize and respond to. Examples include a cultural symbol such as a dollar sign, a mythological figure such as a unicorn, or a familiar movie character such as Darth Vader from *Star Wars*.

crit

8c

Question for analysis

You can focus your analysis of elements by framing your main interest in the image as a question. Matthew Greene posed this question about the *BoostUp.org* ad on page 89: *Does the ad move readers to learn more about* BoostUp.org *and how they can help teens to graduate?* The question led Greene to focus on certain elements of the ad:

Image elements	Responses
Emphasis	The ad's emptiness and placement of Kody at the far left puts primary emphasis on the boy's isolation. Danny R.'s message receives secondary emphasis.
Narration	The taped-on message suggests a story and connection between Kody and Danny R. Danny R. might be a friend, relative, or mentor. Based on the direct appeal in the word bubble at the bottom, it appears that Danny R. is trying to help Kody graduate by offering to help him with schoolwork.
Arrangement	The ad places Danny R. and Kody together on the left side of the page, with Danny's message a bright spot on the dull landscape. The appeal to help Kody graduate is subtle and set on its own—the last thing readers look at. It also pulls the elements together so that the ad makes sense.
Characterization	Kody is a sympathetic figure, a lonely-looking teen who would probably benefit from the help Danny R. is offering through *BoostUp.org*.

Sample image for analysis

The following image gives you a chance to analyze elements of a photograph. Try to answer the questions in the annotations.

crit
8c

Elements in a photograph

Emphasis: What is the focus of the photograph? What are your eyes drawn to?

Characterization: What does the man seem to be feeling? Consider especially his mouth and eyes.

Narration: What story or stories might the photograph tell?

Arrangement: What is interesting about the arrangement of elements?

Color: The photograph was created in black and white. What does this presentation contribute to the image? How might the image differ in full color?

Allusion: What symbol do you see? What meaning does it give to the photograph?

Photograph by Steve Simon

4 ▪ Interpreting an image

The strategies for interpreting an image parallel those for interpreting a written text (p. 86). In this process you look more deeply at the elements, considering them in relation to the image creator's likely assumptions and intentions. You aim to draw reasonable inferences about the image creator's assumptions to explain *why* the image looks as it does. Consider this inference about the *BoostUp .org* advertisement on page 89:

> The creators of the *BoostUp.org* ad assume that readers want students to graduate from high school.

This statement is supported by the ad's text: the word bubble connecting to the *BoostUp.org* logo specifically says, "Help Kody graduate at *BoostUp.org.*"

5 ▪ Synthesizing ideas about an image

As discussed on pages 86–87, with synthesis you take analysis and interpretation a step further to consider how a work's elements and underlying assumptions relate and what the overall message is. You may also expand your synthesis to view the whole image in a larger context: How does the work fit into the context of other works? What cultural, economic, political, or historical forces influence the work?

Placing an image in its context often requires research. For instance, to learn more about the assumptions underlying the *BoostUp.org* advertisement and the goals of the larger ad campaign, Matthew Greene visited the Web sites of *BoostUp.org* and the Ad Council, one of the ad's sponsors. The following entry from his reading journal synthesizes this research and his own ideas about the ad:

crit

8c

> The *BoostUp.org* magazine ad that features Kody is part of a larger campaign designed to raise public awareness about high school dropouts and encourage pubic support to help teens stay in school. Sponsored by the US Army and the nonprofit Ad Council, *BoostUp.org* profiles high school seniors who are at risk of dropping out and asks individuals to write the students personal messages of support. Ads like "Kody" are the first point of contact between the public and the teens, but they don't by themselves actually help the teens. For that, readers need to visit *BoostUp.org*. Thus the ad's elements work together like pieces of a puzzle, with the solution to be found only on the Web site.

6 ▪ Evaluating an image

If your critical reading moves on to evaluation, you'll form judgments about the quality and significance of the image: Is the message of the image accurate and fair, or is it distorted and biased? Can you support, refute, or extend the message? Does the image achieve its apparent purpose, and is the purpose worthwhile? How does the image affect you?

You can read Matthew Greene's response to the *BoostUp.org* advertisement by following the links in the e-book version of this handbook at *mycomplab.com*.

Exercise 8.5 **Viewing an image critically**

Review the list of visual elements on pages 90–91 and then take another close look at the *BoostUp.org* advertisement on page 89 or the photograph opposite. Using the guidelines on the preceding pages, draw your own conclusions about one of the images. Write while reading and thinking to help yourself concentrate and develop ideas. A writing suggestion based on this activity appears in Exercise 9.3, page 103.

9 Academic Writing

What's expected of writing in academic situations?

When you write in college, you work within a community of teachers and students who have specific aims and expectations. The basic aim of this community—whether in English, psychology, biology, or some other discipline—is to contribute to and build knowledge through questioning, research, and communication. The differences among disciplines lie mainly in the kinds of questions asked, the kinds of research done to find the answers, and the **genres,** or types of writing, used to communicate the answers, such as case studies, research reports, literary analyses, and reviews of others' writings.

Whatever the discipline, academic writing often asks you to respond to others' work (below) and requires you to analyze each writing situation for your purpose (p. 96), audience (96), structure and content (97), and language (98).

9a Write in response to texts.

Academic knowledge building depends on reading, analyzing, and expanding on the work of others. Thus many academic writing assignments require you to respond to one or more texts—not only to written products such as short stories and journal articles but also to visual communications such as images, charts, films, and advertisements. As you form a response to a text, you will synthesize, or integrate, its ideas and information with yours to come to your own conclusions.

Note A common academic assignment, the research paper, expects you to consult and respond to multiple texts in order to support and extend your ideas. See Chapters 51–55. This section focuses on responding directly to a single text, but the skills involved apply to research writing as well.

1 ▪ Deciding how to respond

When an assignment asks you to respond directly to a text, you might take one of the following approaches. (Note that the word *author* refers to a photographer, painter, or other creator as well as to a writer.)

---

mycomplab

Visit *mycomplab.com* for more resources and exercises on academic writing.

- **Agree with and extend the author's ideas,** exploring related ideas and providing additional examples.
- **Agree with the author on some points but disagree on others.**
- **Disagree with the author on one or more main points.**
- **Explain how the author achieves a particular effect,** such as evoking a historical period or balancing opposing views.
- **Analyze the overall effectiveness of a text**—for example, how well a writer supports a thesis with convincing evidence or whether an advertisement succeeds in its unstated purpose.

2 ▪ Forming a response

9a

You will likely have an immediate response to at least some of the texts you analyze: you may agree or disagree strongly with what the author is saying. But for some other responses, you may need time and thought to determine what the author is saying and what you think about it.

Whatever your assignment, your first task is to examine the text thoroughly so that you're sure you understand what the author says outright and also assumes or implies. Use the process of critical reading described in the previous chapter to take notes on the text, summarize it, and develop a critical response. Then, as you write, use the following tips to convey your response to readers.

Responding to a text

- **Make sure your writing has a point**—a central idea, or thesis, that focuses your response. (For more on developing a thesis, see pp. 15–18.)
- **Include a very brief summary if readers may be unfamiliar with your subject.** But remember that your job is not just to report what the text says or what an image shows; it is to *respond* to the work from your own critical perspective. (For more on summary, see pp. 83–85.)
- **Center each paragraph on an idea of your own that supports your thesis.** Generally, state the idea outright, in your own voice.
- **Support the paragraph idea with evidence from the text**—quotations, paraphrases, details, and examples.
- **Conclude each paragraph with your interpretation of the evidence.** As a general rule, avoid ending paragraphs with source evidence; instead, end with at least a sentence that explains what the evidence shows.

---

3 ▪ Emphasizing synthesis in your response

Following the suggestions in the preceding box will lead you to show readers the synthesis you achieved by thinking critically about the text. That is, you integrate your perspective with that of the author in order to support a conclusion of your own about the work.

A key to synthesis is deciding how to present evidence from your reading and observation in your writing. Especially when you are writing about a relatively unfamiliar subject, you may be tempted to let a text or other source do the talking for you through extensive summary or quotations. However, readers of your academic writing will expect to see you managing ideas and information to make your points. Thus a typical paragraph of text-based writing should open with your own idea, give evidence from the text, and conclude with your interpretation of the evidence. You can see examples of this paragraph pattern in the second through fourth paragraphs of the paper at the end of this chapter (pp. 101–02).

9c

Note Effective synthesis requires careful handling of evidence from the text (quotations and paraphrases) so that it meshes smoothly into your sentences yet is clearly distinct from your own ideas. See pages 419–23 on integrating borrowed material.

9b Determine your purpose.

For most academic writing, your general purpose will be mainly explanatory or mainly argumentative. That is, you will aim to clarify your subject so that readers understand it as you do, or you will aim to gain readers' agreement with a debatable idea about the subject. (See p. 6 for more on general purposes and pp. 103–20 for more on argument.)

Your specific purpose—including your subject and how you hope readers will respond—depends on the kind of writing you're doing. For instance, in a literature review for a biology class, you want readers to understand the research area you're covering, the recent contributions made by researchers, the issues needing further research, and the sources you consulted. Not coincidentally, these topics correspond to the major sections of a literature review. In following the standard format, you both help to define your purpose and begin to meet the discipline's (and thus your instructor's) expectations.

Your specific purpose will be more complex as well. You take a course to learn about a subject and the ways experts think about it. Your writing, in return, contributes to the discipline through the knowledge you uncover and the lens of your perspective. At the same time, as a student you want to demonstrate your competence with research, evidence, format, and other requirements of the discipline.

9c Analyze your audience.

Many academic writing assignments will specify or assume an educated audience or an academic audience. Such readers look for writing that is clear, balanced, well organized, and well reasoned, among other qualities discussed in the next section. Other assignments will specify or assume an audience of experts on your subject, readers who look in addition for writing that meets the subject's requirements for claims and evidence, organization, language, format, and other qualities.

Of course, much of your academic writing will have only one reader besides you: the instructor of the course for which you are writing. Instructors fill two main roles as readers:

- **They represent the audience you are addressing.** They may actually be members of the audience, as when you address academic readers or subject experts. Or they may imagine themselves as members of your audience—reading, for instance, as if they sat on the city council. In either case, they're interested in how effectively you write for the audience.
- **They serve as coaches,** guiding you toward achieving the goals of the course and, more broadly, toward the academic aims of building and communicating knowledge.

9d

Like everyone else, instructors have preferences and peeves, but you'll waste time and energy trying to anticipate them. Do attend to written and spoken directions for assignments, of course. But otherwise view your instructors as representatives of the community you are writing for. Their responses will be guided by the community's aims and expectations and by a desire to teach you about them.

9d Choose the structure and content.

Many academic writing assignments will at least imply how you should organize your paper and even how you should develop your ideas. Like the literature review mentioned opposite, the type of paper required will break into discrete parts, each with its own requirements for content.

No matter what type of paper an assignment specifies, the broad academic aims of building and exchanging knowledge determine features that are common across disciplines. Follow these general guidelines for your academic writing, supplementing them as indicated with others elsewhere in this book:

- **Develop a thesis**—a central idea or claim to which everything in the paper clearly relates. Usually, state your thesis near the beginning of the paper. (For more on theses, see pp. 15–18.)
- **Support the thesis with evidence,** drawn usually from research and sometimes from your own experience. The kinds of evidence will depend on the discipline you're writing in and the type of paper you're doing.
- **Synthesize.** Put your sources to work for you by thinking critically about them. Integrate them into your own perspective

using your own voice. (For more on synthesis, see pp. 95–96 and pp. 410–12 in the discussion of research writing.)

- **Acknowledge sources fully, including online sources.** *Not* acknowledging sources undermines the knowledge-sharing foundation of academic writing and constitutes plagiarism, which can be punishable (see pp. 424–31). For a list of disciplines' style guides, see page 432. For documentation guidelines and samples, see Chapters 56 (MLA) and 57 (APA).

- **Organize clearly within the framework of the type of writing you're doing.** Develop your ideas as simply and directly as your purpose and content allow. Clearly relate sentences, paragraphs, and sections so that readers always know where they are in the paper's development.

CULTURE LANGUAGE These features are far from universal. In other cultures, for instance, academic writers are not expected to acknowledge others' ideas and establish their own credibility by providing citations for their sources. Recognizing differences between practices in your native culture and in the United States can help you adapt to US academic writing. Use the preceding list as a checklist for your own papers.

9e   Use academic language.

American academic writing relies on a dialect called standard American English. The dialect is also used in business, the professions, government, the media, and other sites of social and economic power where people of diverse backgrounds must communicate with one another. It is "standard" not because it is better than other forms of English but because it is accepted as the common language, much as the dollar bill is accepted as the common currency.

In writing, standard American English varies a great deal, from the formality of an academic research report to the more relaxed language of this handbook to informal e-mails between coworkers in a company. Even in academic writing, standard American English allows much room for the writer's own tone and voice, as these passages on the same topic show:

More formal

Using the technique of "color engineering," manufacturers and advertisers can heighten the interest of consumers in a product by adding color that does not contribute to the utility of the product but appeals more to emotions. In one example from the 1920s, manufacturers of fountain pens, which had previously been made of hard black rubber, dramatically increased sales simply by producing the pens in bright colors.

Two complicated sentences, one explaining the technique and one giving the example

Drawn-out phrasing, such as *interest of consumers* instead of *consumers' interest*

Formal vocabulary, such as *heighten, contribute,* and *utility*

Less formal

A touch of "color engineering" can sharpen the emotional appeal of a product or its ad. New color can boost sales even when the color serves no use. In the 1920s, for example, fountain-pen makers introduced brightly colored pens along with the familiar ones of hard black rubber. Sales shot up.

> Four sentences, two each for explaining the technique and giving the example
>
> More informal phrasing, such as *Sales shot up*
>
> More informal vocabulary, such as *touch, boost,* and *ad*

As different as they are, both examples illustrate several common features of academic language:

9e

- **It follows the conventions of standard American English for grammar and usage.** These conventions are described in guides to the dialect, such as this handbook.

- **It uses a standard vocabulary,** not one that only some groups understand, such as slang, an ethnic or regional dialect, or another language. (See pp. 168 and 169–70 for more on specialized vocabularies.)

- **It avoids the informalities of everyday speech, texting, and instant messaging.** These informalities include incomplete sentences, slang, no capital letters, and shortened spellings (*u* for *you, b4* for *before, thru* for *through,* and so on). (See pp. 168–69 for more on these forms.)

- **It generally uses the third person** (*he, she, it, they*)**.** The first person (*I, we*) is sometimes appropriate to express personal opinions or invite readers to think along, but not with a strongly explanatory purpose (*I discovered that "color engineering" can heighten . . .*). The second person (*you*) is appropriate only in addressing readers directly, as in this handbook. Even then, *you* may seem too chummy, particularly if it appears (or is understood) in conversational expressions such as *You know what I mean* or (*You*) *Don't get me wrong.* (For more on *you,* see p. 268.)

- **It is authoritative and neutral.** In the preceding examples, the writers express themselves confidently, not timidly (as in *One possible example of color engineering that might be considered in this case is . . .*). They also refrain from hostility (*Advertisers will stop at nothing to achieve their goals*) and enthusiasm (*Color engineering is genius at work*).

At first, the diverse demands of academic writing may leave you groping for an appropriate voice. In an effort to sound fresh and confident, you may write too casually, as if speaking to friends and family:

Too casual

"Color engineering" is a great way to get at consumers' feelings. . . . When the guys jazzed up the color, sales shot through the roof.

In an effort to sound "academic," you may produce wordy and awkward sentences:

> **Wordy and awkward**
>
> The emotions of consumers can be made more engaged by the technique known as "color engineering." . . . A very large increase in the sales of fountain pens was achieved by the manufacturers of the pens as a result of this color enhancement technique. [The passive voice in this example, such as *increase . . . was achieved* instead of *the manufacturers achieved*, adds to its wordiness and indirection. See pp. 244–45 for more on verb voice.]

9f

A cure for writing too informally or too stiffly is to read academic writing so that the language and style become familiar and to edit your writing (see pp. 33–36).

(CULTURE LANGUAGE) If your first language is not English or is an English dialect besides standard American, you know well the power of communicating with others who share your language. Learning to write standard American English in no way requires you to abandon your first language. Like most multilingual people, you are probably already adept at switching between languages as the situation demands—speaking one way with your relatives, say, and another way with an employer. As you practice academic writing, you'll develop the same flexibility with it.

Exercise 9.1 Using academic language

Revise the following paragraph to make the language more academic while keeping the factual information the same. Possible revisions of starred sentences appear at the back of the book.

> *If you buy into the stereotype of girls chatting away on their cell phones, you should think again. *One of the major wireless companies surveyed 1021 cell phone owners for a period of five years and—surprise!—reported that guys talk on cell phones more than girls do. In fact, guys were way ahead of girls, using an average of 571 minutes a month compared to 424 for girls. That's 35 percent more time on the phone! The survey also asked about conversations on home phones, and while girls still beat the field, the guys are catching up.

9f A sample critical response

The following essay illustrates a common academic assignment, a critical response to, or **critique** of, a text. In the essay, Charlene Robinson responds to Thomas Sowell's essay "Student Loans" (pp. 79–81). Robinson arrived at her response, an argument, through the process of critical reading outlined in the previous chapter and then by gathering and organizing her ideas, developing a thesis about Sowell's text that synthesized his ideas and hers, and drafting and revising until she believed she had supported her thesis with sufficient evidence from her own experience and from Sowell's text.

Robinson did not assume that her readers would see the same things in Sowell's essay or share her views, so her essay offers evidence of Sowell's ideas in the form of direct quotations, summaries, and paraphrases (restatements in her own words). Robinson documents these borrowings from Sowell using the style of the Modern Language Association (MLA): the numbers in parentheses are page numbers in the book containing Sowell's essay, listed at the end as a "work cited." (See Chapter 56 for more on MLA style.)

Note Critical writing is *not* summarizing. Robinson summarized Sowell's text to clarify it for herself (p. 85), and she briefly summarizes Sowell's argument in her introduction. But her critical writing goes beyond summary to bring her perspective to Sowell's work.

9f

Weighing the Costs

In the essay "Student Loans," the economist Thomas Sowell challenges the US government's student-loan program for three main reasons: a scarce resource (taxpayers' money) goes to many undeserving students, a high number of recipients fail to repay their loans, and the easy availability of money has led to both lower academic standards and higher college tuitions. Sowell wants his readers to "weigh the costs of things" (133) in order to see, as he does, that the loan program should not receive so much government funding. But does he provide the evidence of cost and other problems to lead the reader to agree with him? The answer is no, because hard evidence is less common than debatable and unsupported assumptions about students, scarcity, and the value of education.

Sowell's portrait of student-loan recipients is questionable. It is based on averages, some statistical and some not, but averages are often deceptive. For example, Sowell cites college graduates' low average debt of $7,000 to $9,000 (131) without acknowledging the fact that many students' debt is much higher or giving the full range of statistics. Similarly, Sowell dismisses "heart-rending stories" of "the low-income student with a huge debt" as "not at all typical" (132), yet he invents his own exaggerated version of the typical loan recipient: an affluent slacker ("Rockefellers" and "Vanderbilts") for whom college is a "place to hang out for a few years" sponging off the government, while his or her parents clear a profit from making use of the loan program (132). Although such students (and parents) may well exist, are they really typical? Sowell does not offer any data one way or the other—for instance, how many loan recipients come from each income group, what percentage of loan funds go to each group, how many loan recipients

Annotations (right margin):

Introduction

Summary of Sowell's essay

Robinson's critical question

Thesis statement

First main point

Evidence for first point: paraphrases and quotations from Sowell's text

Evidence for first point: Sowell's omissions

receive significant help from their parents, and how many receive none. Together, Sowell's statements and omissions cast doubt on the argument that students don't need or deserve the loans.

Another set of assumptions in the essay has to do with "scarcity": "There is never enough of anything to fully satisfy all those who want it," Sowell says (131). This statement appeals to readers' common sense, but the "lesson" of scarcity does not necessarily apply to the student-loan program. Sowell omits many important figures needed to prove that the nation's resources are too scarce to support the program, such as the total cost of the program, its percentage of the total education budget and the total federal budget, and its cost compared to the cost of defense, Medicare, and other expensive programs. Moreover, Sowell does not mention the interest paid by loan recipients, even though the interest must offset some of the costs of running the program and covering unpaid loans. Thus his argument that there isn't enough money to run the student loan program is unconvincing.

The most fundamental and most debatable assumption underlying Sowell's essay is that higher education is a kind of commodity that not everyone is entitled to. In order to diminish the importance of graduates' average debt from education loans, Sowell claims that a car loan will probably be higher (131). This comparison between education and an automobile implies that the two are somehow equal as products and that an affordable higher education is no more a right than a new car is. Sowell also condemns the "irresponsible" students who drop out of school and "the increasingly easy availability of college to people who are not very serious about getting an education" (132). But he overlooks the value of encouraging education, including the education of those who don't finish college or who aren't scholars. For many in the United States, education has a greater value than that of a mere commodity like a car. And even from an economic perspective such as Sowell's, the cost to society of an uneducated public needs to be taken into account. By failing to give education its due, Sowell undermines his argument at its core.

Sowell writes with conviction, and his concerns are valid: high taxes, waste, unfairness, declining educational standards, obtrusive government. However, the essay's flaws make it unlikely that Sowell could convince readers who do not already agree with him. He does not support his portrait of the typical loan recipient, he fails to demonstrate a lack of resources for the loan program, and he neglects the special nature of education compared to other services and prod-

---

Margin annotations:

Conclusion of first point: Robinson's interpretation

Transition to second main point

Second main point

Evidence for second point: Sowell's omissions

Conclusion of second point: Robinson's interpretation

Third main point

Evidence for third point: paraphrases and quotations from Sowell's text

Evidence for third point: Sowell's omissions

Conclusion of third point: Robinson's interpretation

Conclusion

Acknowledgment of Sowell's concerns

Summary of three main points

ucts. Sowell may have the evidence to back up his assumptions, but by omitting it he himself does not truly weigh the costs of the loan program.

Return to theme of introduction: weighing costs

Work Cited

Sowell, Thomas. "Student Loans." *Is Reality Optional? and Other Essays.* Stanford: Hoover, 1993. 131-33. Print.

Work cited in MLA style (p. 445)

—Charlene Robinson (student)

Exercise 9.2 Writing critically about a text

Write an essay based on your own critical reading of Thomas Sowell's "Student Loans" (Exercise 8.4, p. 88). Your critique may be entirely different from Charlene Robinson's, or you may develop some of the same points. If there are similarities, they should be expressed and supported in your own way, in the context of your own critical perspective.

Exercise 9.3 Writing critically about an image

Write an essay based on your critical reading of the *BoostUp.org* advertisement on page 89 or the photograph on page 92 (Exercise 8.5, p. 93).

arg
10

10 Writing Arguments

How do I make a case for an idea?

Making a case for an idea involves opening readers' minds to your opinion, changing readers' own opinions, or moving readers to action. The method is called **argument:** forming and stating an opinion about a debatable issue, gathering and providing support for your idea, organizing logically, expressing yourself reasonably, and acknowledging views different from your own.

CULTURE LANGUAGE The ways of conceiving and writing arguments described here may be initially uncomfortable to you if your native culture approaches such writing differently. In some cultures, for example, a writer is expected to begin indirectly, to avoid asserting his or her opinion outright, to rely for evidence on appeals to tradition, or to establish a compromise rather than argue a position. In American academic and business settings, writers do show respect for readers and their opinions, but the persuasive purpose favors clear statement of an opinion, evidence gathered from many sources, and a direct and concise argument for the opinion.

mycomplab

Visit *mycomplab.com* for more resources and exercises on argument.

10a Use the elements of argument.

In one common view, an argument has four main elements: a subject, claims, evidence, and assumptions. (The last three are adapted from the work of the British philosopher Stephen Toulmin.)

1 ▪ The subject

arg
10a

An argument starts with a subject and often with an opinion about the subject as well—that is, an idea that makes you want to write about the subject. For instance, you might think that your school should do more for energy conservation or that the school's chemistry laboratory is a disgrace. (If you don't have a subject or you aren't sure what you think about it, try some of the invention techniques discussed on pp. 10–14.)

Your initial opinion should meet several requirements:

- **It can be disputed:** reasonable people can disagree over it.
- **It *will* be disputed:** it is controversial.
- **It is narrow enough to argue in the space and time available.**

On the flip side of these requirements, some subjects will not work as the starting place of argument because they concern indisputable facts, such as the functions of the human liver; personal preferences or beliefs, such as a moral commitment to vegetarianism; or ideas that few would disagree with, such as the virtues of a secure home.

> ### Exercise 10.1   Testing argument subjects
> Analyze each subject below to determine whether it is appropriate for argument. Explain your reasoning in each case.
>
> 1. Granting of athletic scholarships
> 2. Care of automobile tires
> 3. Censoring the Web sites of hate groups
> 4. History of the town park
> 5. Housing for the homeless
> 6. Billboards in urban residential areas or in rural areas
> 7. Animal testing for cosmetics research
> 8. Cats versus dogs as pets
> 9. Ten steps in recycling wastepaper
> 10. Benefits of being a parent

2 ▪ Claims

Claims are statements that require support. In an argument you develop your subject into a central claim or **thesis,** asserted outright as the **thesis statement** (p. 15). This central claim is what the argument is about.

A thesis statement is always an **opinion**—that is, a judgment based on facts and arguable on the basis of facts. It may be one of the following:

- **A claim about past or present reality:**

  In both its space and its equipment, the college's chemistry laboratory is outdated.

  Academic cheating increases with students' economic insecurity.

- **A claim of value:**

  The new room fees are unjustified given the condition of the dormitories.

  Computer music pirates undermine the system that encourages the very creation of music.

- **A recommendation for a course of action,** often a solution to a perceived problem:

  The college's outdated chemistry laboratory should be replaced incrementally over the next five years.

  Schools and businesses can help to resolve the region's traffic congestion by implementing car pools and rewarding participants.

The backbone of an argument consists of specific claims that support the thesis statement. These may also be statements of opinion, or they may fall into one of two other categories:

- **Statements of** *fact,* including facts that are generally known or are verifiable (such as the cost of tuition at your school) and those that can be inferred from verifiable facts (such as the monetary value of a college education).
- **Statements of** *belief,* or convictions based on personal faith or values, such as *The primary goal of government should be to provide equality of opportunity for all.* Although seemingly arguable, a statement of belief is not based on facts and so cannot be contested on the basis of facts.

> **Exercise 10.2   Conceiving a thesis statement**
> Narrow each arguable subject in Exercise 10.1 to a specific opinion, and draft a tentative thesis statement for each. Make each thesis statement a claim about a past or present reality, a claim of value, or a recommendation for a course of action.

3 ■ Evidence

You show the validity of your claims by supporting them with **evidence.** To support the claim above that the chemistry lab is outdated, you might provide the present lab's age, an inventory of facilities and equipment, contrasting examples of up-to-date equipment, and the testimony of chemistry professors.

There are several kinds of evidence:

- **Facts,** statements whose truth can be verified or inferred: *Poland is slightly smaller than New Mexico.*
- **Statistics,** facts expressed as numbers: *Of those polled, 22 percent prefer a flat tax.*
- **Examples,** specific instances of the point being made: *Many groups, such as the elderly and the disabled, would benefit from this policy.*
- **Expert opinions,** the judgments formed by authorities on the subject based on their own examination of the facts: *Affirmative action is necessary to right past injustices, a point argued by Howard Glickstein, a past director of the US Commission on Civil Rights.*
- **Appeals to readers' beliefs or needs**, statements that ask readers to accept a claim in part because it states something they already accept as true without evidence: *The shabby, antiquated chemistry lab shames the school, making it seem a second-rate institution.*

Evidence must be reliable to be convincing. Ask these questions about your evidence:

- **Is it accurate**—trustworthy, exact, and undistorted?
- **Is it relevant**—authoritative, pertinent, and current?
- **Is it representative**—true to its context, neither under- nor overrepresenting any element of the sample it's drawn from?
- **Is it adequate**—plentiful and specific?

4 ▪ Assumptions

An **assumption** is an opinion, a principle, or a belief that ties evidence to claims: the assumption explains why a particular piece of evidence is relevant to a particular claim. For instance:

> **Claim:** The college's chemistry laboratory is outdated.
> **Evidence** (in part): The testimony of chemistry professors.
> **Assumption:** Chemistry professors are the most capable of evaluating the present lab's quality.

Assumptions are not flaws in arguments but necessities: we all acquire beliefs and opinions that shape our views of the world. Interpreting a work's assumptions is a significant part of critical reading (see p. 86), and discovering your own assumptions is a significant part of argumentative critical writing. If your readers do not share your assumptions or if they perceive that you are not forthright about your biases, they will be less receptive to your argument. (See the following discussion of reasonableness.)

10b   Write reasonably.

To establish common ground between you and your readers, your argument must be reasonable. Readers expect logical thinking, appropriate appeals, fairness toward the opposition, and, combining all of these, writing that is free of fallacies.

1 ▪ Logical thinking

The thesis of your argument is a conclusion you reach by reasoning about evidence. Two processes of reasoning, induction and deduction, are familiar to you even if you aren't familiar with their names.

Induction

When you're about to buy a used car, you consult friends, relatives, and consumer guides before deciding what kind of car to buy. Using **induction,** or **inductive reasoning,** you make specific observations about cars (your evidence) and you induce, or infer, a **generalization** that Car X is most reliable. The generalization is a claim supported by your observations.

You might also use inductive reasoning in a term paper on print advertising:

> **Evidence:** Advertisements in newspapers and magazines.
> **Evidence:** Comments by advertisers and publishers.
> **Evidence:** Data on the effectiveness of advertising.
> **Generalization or claim:** Print remains the most cost-effective medium for advertising.

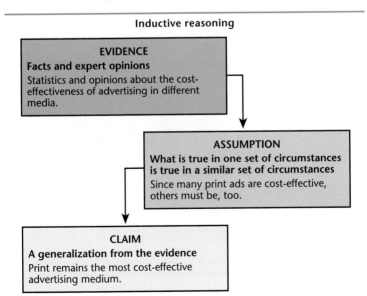

Inductive reasoning

EVIDENCE
Facts and expert opinions
Statistics and opinions about the cost-effectiveness of advertising in different media.

ASSUMPTION
What is true in one set of circumstances is true in a similar set of circumstances
Since many print ads are cost-effective, others must be, too.

CLAIM
A generalization from the evidence
Print remains the most cost-effective advertising medium.

Inductive reasoning builds from the evidence to the claim, with the assumptions connecting evidence to claim. (See the diagram on the previous page.) In this way, induction creates new knowledge from what is already known.

When you reason inductively, you connect your evidence to your generalization by assuming that what is true in one set of circumstances (the ads you look at) is true in a similar set of circumstances (other ads). The more evidence you accumulate, the more probable it is that your generalization is true. Note, however, that absolute certainty is not possible. At some point you must *assume* that your evidence justifies your generalization, for yourself and your readers. Most errors in inductive reasoning involve oversimplifying either the evidence or the generalization. See pages 113–16 on fallacies.

arg
10b

Deduction

You use **deduction,** or **deductive reasoning,** when you proceed from your generalization that Car X is the most reliable used car to your own specific circumstances (you want to buy a used car) to the conclusion that you should buy a Car X. In deduction your assumption is a generalization, principle, or belief that you think is true. You apply it to the evidence (new information) in order to arrive at your claim (the conclusion you draw). The diagram below corresponds to the one on the previous page for induction, picking up the example of print advertising.

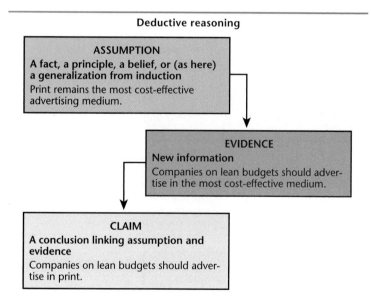

Deductive reasoning

ASSUMPTION
**A fact, a principle, a belief, or (as here)
a generalization from induction**
Print remains the most cost-effective
advertising medium.

EVIDENCE
New information
Companies on lean budgets should adver-
tise in the most cost-effective medium.

CLAIM
**A conclusion linking assumption and
evidence**
Companies on lean budgets should adver-
tise in print.

The conventional way of displaying a deductive argument is in a **syllogism**. If you want the school administration to postpone new room fees for one dormitory, your deductive argument might be expressed in the following syllogism:

> **Premise:** The administration should not raise fees on dorm rooms in poor condition. [A generalization or belief that you assume to be true.]
> **Premise:** The rooms in Polk Hall are in poor condition. [New information: a specific case of the first premise.]
> **Conclusion:** The administration should not raise fees on the rooms in Polk Hall. [Your claim.]

arg

10b

As long as the premises of a syllogism are true, the conclusion derives logically and certainly from them.

The force of deductive reasoning depends on the reliability of the premises and the care taken to apply them in drawing conclusions. The reasoning process is **valid** if the premises lead logically to the conclusion. It is **true** if the premises are believable. Sometimes the reasoning is true but *not* valid:

> **Premise:** The administration should not raise fees on dorm rooms in bad condition.
> **Premise:** Polk Hall is a dormitory.
> **Conclusion:** The administration should not raise fees on the rooms in Polk Hall.

Both premises may be true, but the first does not *necessarily* apply to the second, so the conclusion is invalid. Sometimes, too, the reasoning is valid but *not* true:

> **Premise:** All college administrations are indifferent to students' needs.
> **Premise:** The administration of Valley College is a college administration.
> **Premise:** The administration of Valley College is indifferent to students' needs.

This syllogism is valid but useless: the first premise is an untrue assumption, so the entire argument is untrue. Invalid and untrue syllogisms underlie many of the logical fallacies discussed on pages 113–16.

A particular hazard of deductive reasoning is the **unstated premise**: the basic assumption linking evidence and conclusion is not stated but implied. Here the unstated premise is believable and the argument is reasonable:

> Ms. Stein has worked with drug addicts for fifteen years, so she knows a great deal about their problems. [Unstated premise: Anyone who has worked fifteen years with drug addicts knows about their problems.]

But when the unstated premise is wrong or unfounded, the argument is false. For example:

> Since Jane Lightbow is a senator, she must receive money illegally from lobbyists. [Unstated premise: All senators receive money illegally from lobbyists.]

2 ▪ Appeals

Rational and emotional appeals

In most arguments you will combine **rational appeals** to readers' capacities for logical reasoning with **emotional appeals** to readers' beliefs and feelings. In the following example, the second sentence makes a rational appeal (to the logic of financial gain), and the third sentence makes an emotional appeal (to the sense of fairness and open-mindedness):

> Advertising should show more physically challenged people. The millions of Americans with disabilities have considerable buying power, yet so far advertisers have made little or no attempt to tap that power. Furthermore, by keeping people with disabilities out of the mainstream depicted in ads, advertisers encourage widespread prejudice against disability, prejudice that frightens and demeans those who hold it.

For an emotional appeal to be successful, it must be appropriate for the audience and the argument:

- **It must not misjudge readers' actual feelings.**
- **It must not raise emotional issues that are irrelevant to the claims and the evidence.** See page 114 for a discussion of specific inappropriate appeals, such as bandwagon and ad hominem.

Ethical appeal

A third kind of approach to readers, the **ethical appeal,** is the sense you give of being a competent, fair person who is worth heeding. A rational appeal and an appropriate emotional appeal contribute to your ethical appeal, and so does your acknowledging opposing views (see opposite). An argument that is concisely written and correct in grammar, spelling, and other matters will underscore your competence. In addition, a sincere and even tone will assure readers that you are balanced and want to reason with them.

A sincere and even tone need not exclude language with emotional appeal—words such as *frightens* and *demeans* at the end of the example above about advertising. But avoid certain forms of expression that will mark you as unfair:

- **Insulting words** such as *idiotic* or *fascist.*
- **Biased language** such as *fags* or *broads.* (See pp. 171–73.)
- **Sarcasm**—for instance, using the phrase *What a brilliant idea* to indicate contempt for the idea and its originator.
- **Exclamation points**! They'll make you sound shrill!

3 ▪ Acknowledgment of opposing views

A good test of your fairness in argument is how you handle possible objections. Assuming your thesis is indeed arguable, then others can marshal their own evidence to support a different view or views. By dealing squarely with these opposing views, you show yourself to be honest and fair. You strengthen your ethical appeal and thus your entire argument.

Before or while you draft your essay, list for yourself all the opposing views you can think of. You'll find them in your research, by talking to friends and classmates, and by critically thinking about your own ideas. You can also look for a range of views in an online discussion that deals with your subject. Two places to start are the *Yahoo!* archive of discussion groups at *groups.yahoo.com* and the *Google* blog directory at *blogsearch.google.com*.

arg
10b

A common way to handle opposing views is to state them, refute those you can, grant the validity of others, and demonstrate why, despite their validity, the opposing views are less compelling than your own. A somewhat different approach, developed by the psychologist Carl Rogers, emphasizes the search for common ground. In a **Rogerian argument** you start by showing that you understand readers' views and by establishing points on which you and readers agree and disagree. Creating a connection in this way can be especially helpful when you expect readers to resist your argument, because it encourages them to hear you out as you develop your claims.

Exercise 10.3 **Reasoning inductively**

Study the facts below and then evaluate each of the numbered conclusions. Which of the generalizations are reasonable given the evidence, and which are not? Why? Answers to starred items appear at the back of the book.

In 2007 each American household viewed an average of 101 hours and 54 minutes of television.

Each individual viewed an average of 37 hours and 44 minutes per week.

Those viewing the most television per week (51 hours and 18 minutes) were women over age 65.

Those viewing the least television per week (25 hours and 45 minutes) were teens, ages 12 to 17.

Households earning under $30,000 a year watched an average of 104 hours and 22 minutes a week.

Households earning more than $60,000 a year watched an average of 97 hours and 38 minutes a week.

*1. Households with incomes under $30,000 tend to watch more television than average.

*2. Women watch more television than men.

3. Nonaffluent people watch less television than affluent people.
4. Women over age 65 tend to watch more television than average.
5. Children watch less television than critics generally assume.

Exercise 10.4 Reasoning deductively

Convert each of the following statements into a syllogism. (You may have to state unstated assumptions.) Use the syllogism to evaluate both the validity and the truth of the statement. Answers to starred items appear at the back of the book.

Example:

DiSantis is a banker, so he does not care about the poor.

Premise: Bankers do not care about the poor.
Premise: DiSantis is a banker.
Conclusion: Therefore, DiSantis does not care about the poor.

The statement is untrue because the first premise is untrue.

*1. The mayor opposed pollution controls when he was president of a manufacturing company, so he may not support new controls or vigorously enforce existing ones.
*2. Information on corporate Web sites is unreliable because the sites are sponsored by for-profit entities.
3. Schroeder is a good artist because she trained at Parsons, like many other good artists.
4. Wealthy athletes who use their resources to help others deserve our particular appreciation.
5. Jimson is clearly a sexist because she has hired only one woman.

Exercise 10.5 Identifying appeals

Identify each passage below as primarily a rational appeal or primarily an emotional appeal. Which passages make a strong ethical appeal as well? Answers to starred items appear at the back of the book.

*1. The Web may contribute to the global tendency toward breadth rather than depth of knowledge. Using those most essential of skills—pointing and clicking—our brightest minds may now never even hear of, much less read, the works of Aristotle, Shakespeare, and Darwin.
*2. Thus the data collected by these researchers indicate that a mandatory sentence for illegal possession of handguns may lead to reduction in handgun purchases.
3. Most broadcasters worry that further government regulation of television programming could breed censorship—certainly, an undesirable outcome. Yet most broadcasters also accept that children's television is a fair target for regulation.
4. Anyone who cherishes life in all its diversity could not help being appalled by the mistreatment of laboratory animals. The so-called scientists who run the labs are misguided.
5. Many experts in constitutional law have warned that the rule violates the right to free speech. Yet other experts have viewed the rule, however regretfully, as necessary for the good of the community as a whole.

4 ▪ Fallacies

Fallacies—errors in argument—either evade the issue of the argument or treat the argument as if it were much simpler than it is.

Evasions

An effective argument squarely faces the central issue or question it addresses. An ineffective argument may dodge the issue in one of the following ways:

▪ **Begging the question:** treating an opinion that is open to question as if it were already proved or disproved. In essence, the writer begs readers to accept his or her claim from the start.

The college library's expenses should be reduced by cutting subscriptions to useless periodicals. [Begged questions: Are some of the library's periodicals useless? Useless to whom?]

The fact is that political financing is too corrupt to be reformed. [Begged questions: How corrupt is political financing? Does corruption, even if extensive, put the system beyond reform?]

▪ **Non sequitur** (Latin: "It does not follow"): linking two or more ideas that are not necessarily connected.

She uses a wheelchair, so she must be unhappy. [The second clause does not follow from the first.]

Kathleen Newsome has my vote for mayor because she has the best-run campaign organization. [Shouldn't one's vote be based on the candidate's qualities, not the campaign's organization?]

▪ **Red herring:** introducing an irrelevant issue intended to distract readers from the relevant issues. (A red herring is a kind of fish that might be used to distract a dog from a scent.)

A campus speech code is essential to protect students, who already have enough problems coping with rising tuition. [Tuition costs and speech codes are different subjects. What protections do students need that a speech code will provide?]

Instead of developing a campus speech code that will infringe on students' First Amendment rights, administrators should be figuring out how to prevent another tuition increase. [Again, tuition costs and speech codes are different subjects. How would the code infringe on rights?]

▪ **False authority:** citing as an expert someone whose expertise is doubtful or nonexistent.

Jason Bing, a recognized expert in corporate finance, maintains that pharmaceutical companies do not test their products thoroughly enough. [Bing's expertise in corporate finance bears no apparent relation to the testing of pharmaceuticals.]

According to Helen Liebowitz, the Food and Drug Administration has approved sixty dangerous drugs in the last two years alone. [Who is Helen Liebowitz? On what authority does she make this claim?]

- **Appeal to readers' fear or pity:** substituting emotions for reasoning.

By electing Susan Clark to the city council, you will prevent the city's economic collapse. [Trades on people's fears. Can Clark singlehandedly prevent economic collapse? Is collapse even likely?]

She should not have to pay taxes because she is an aged widow with no friends or relatives. [Appeals to people's pity. Should age and loneliness, rather than income, determine a person's tax obligation?]

- **Snob appeal:** inviting readers to accept an assertion in order to be identified with others they admire.

Tiger Woods has an account at Big City Bank, and so should you. [A celebrity's endorsement does not guarantee the worth of a product, a service, an idea, or anything else.]

- **Bandwagon:** inviting readers to accept a claim because everyone else does.

As everyone knows, marijuana use leads to heroin addiction. [What is the evidence?]

- **Ad populum** (Latin: "to the people"): asking readers to accept a conclusion based on shared values or even prejudices and nothing else.

Any truly patriotic American will support the President's action. [But why is the action worth taking?]

- **Ad hominem** (Latin: "to the man"): attacking the qualities of the people holding an opposing view rather than the substance of the view itself.

One of the scientists has been treated for emotional problems, so his pessimism about nuclear waste merits no attention. [Do the scientist's previous emotional problems invalidate his current views?]

Oversimplifications

In a vain attempt to create something neatly convincing, an ineffective argument may conceal or ignore complexities in one of the following ways:

- **Hasty generalization:** making a claim on the basis of inadequate evidence.

It is disturbing that several of the youths who shot up schools were users of violent video games. Obviously, these games can breed violence, and they should be banned. [A few cases do not establish the relation between the games and violent behavior. Most youths who play violent video games do not behave violently.]

From the way it handled this complaint, we can assume that the consumer protection office has little intention of protecting consumers. [One experience with the office does not demonstrate its intention or overall performance.]

- **Sweeping generalization:** making an insupportable statement. Many sweeping generalizations are **absolute statements** involving words such as *all, always, never,* and *no one* that allow no exceptions. Others are **stereotypes,** conventional and oversimplified characterizations of a group of people:

People who live in cities are unfriendly.
Californians are fad-crazy.
Women are emotional.
Men can't express their feelings.

(See also pp. 171–73 on sexist and other biased language.)

- **Reductive fallacy:** oversimplifying (reducing) the relation between causes and effects.

Poverty causes crime. [If so, then why do people who are not poor commit crimes? And why aren't all poor people criminals?]

The better a school's athletic facilities are, the worse its academic programs are. [The sentence assumes a direct cause-and-effect link between athletics and scholarship.]

- **Post hoc fallacy** (from Latin *post hoc, ergo propter hoc,* meaning "after this, therefore because of this"): assuming that because *A* preceded *B,* then *A* must have caused *B.*

In the two months since he took office, Mayor Holcomb has allowed crime in the city to increase 12 percent. [The increase in crime is probably attributable to conditions existing before Holcomb took office.]

The town council erred in permitting the adult bookstore to open, for shortly afterward two women were assaulted. [It cannot be assumed without evidence that the women's assailants visited or were influenced by the bookstore.]

- **Either/or fallacy:** assuming that a complicated question has only two answers—one good and one bad, both good, or both bad.

City police officers are either brutal or corrupt. [Most city police officers are neither.]

Either we permit mandatory drug testing in the workplace or productivity will continue to decline. [Productivity is not necessarily dependent on drug testing.]

- **False analogy:** assuming that because two things are alike in one respect, they are *necessarily* alike in other respects as well. Analogy can be useful in argument when the similarities are reasonable. For instance, the "war on drugs" equates a battle against a foe with a program to eradicate (or at least reduce) sales and use of illegal drugs: both involve an enemy, a desired goal, officials in uniform, and other features. But the following passage takes this analogy to a false extreme:

> To win the war on drugs, we must wage more of a military-style operation. Prisoners of war are locked up without the benefit of a trial by jury, and drug dealers should be, too. Soldiers shoot their enemy on sight, and officials who encounter big drug operators should be allowed to shoot them, too. Military traitors may be executed, and corrupt law enforcers could be, too.

Exercise 10.6 Identifying and revising fallacies

Identify at least one fallacy illustrated by each of the following sentences. Then revise the sentence to make it more reasonable. Possible answers to starred items appear at the back of the book.

*1. A successful marriage demands a maturity that no one under twenty-five possesses.
*2. Students' persistent complaints about the grading system prove that it is unfair.
*3. The United States got involved in World War II because the Japanese bombed Pearl Harbor.
*4. People watch television because they are too lazy to talk or read or because they want mindless escape from their lives.
*5. Racial tension is bound to occur when people with different backgrounds are forced to live side by side.
6. Emerging nations should not be allowed to use nuclear technology for creating energy because eventually they will use it to wage war.
7. Mountain climbing has more lasting effects than many people think: my cousin blacked out three times after he climbed Pikes Peak.
8. Failing to promote democracy throughout the Middle East will lose the region forever to American influence.
9. She admits to being an atheist, so how could she be a good philosophy teacher?
10. Teenagers are too young to be encouraged to use contraceptives.

10c Organize your argument effectively.

All arguments include the same parts:

- The *introduction* establishes the significance of the subject and provides background. The introduction generally includes the thesis statement, but the statement may come later if you think readers will have difficulty accepting it before they see at least some support. (See pp. 59–60 for more on introductions.)
- The *body* states and develops the claims supporting the thesis, with each claim taking one or more paragraphs.

- The *response to opposing views* details and addresses those views, either demonstrating your argument's greater strengths or conceding the opponents' points.
- The *conclusion* completes the argument, restating the thesis, summarizing the supporting claims, and making a final appeal to readers. (See pp. 61–62 for more on conclusions.)

The structure of the body and the response to opposing views depends on your subject, purpose, audience, and form of reasoning. Here are several possible arrangements:

arg
10d

A common scheme	A variation
Claim 1 and evidence	Claim 1 and evidence
Claim 2 and evidence	Response to opposing views
Claim X and evidence	Claim 2 and evidence
Response to opposing views	Response to opposing views
	Claim X and evidence
	Response to opposing views

The Rogerian scheme	The problem-solution scheme
Common ground and concession to opposing views	The problem: claims and evidence
Claim 1 and evidence	The solution: claims and evidence
Claim 2 and evidence	Response to opposing views
Claim X and evidence	

10d   A sample argument

Craig Holbrook, a student, wrote an argument in response to the following assignment:

> Select an issue that can be argued, that you care about, and that you know something about through experience, reading, Web surfing, and so on. As you plan and draft your argument, keep the following in mind:
>
> Narrow and shape your subject into a specific thesis statement.
> Gather and use evidence to support your claim.
> Be aware of assumptions you are making.
> Present your claims and evidence reasonably, attempting to establish common ground with your readers.
> Acknowledge and try to refute opposing views.
> Organize your argument paper straightforwardly and appropriately for your purpose.
> The paper should be 900–1200 words in length.

Holbrook's response to this assignment illustrates the principles discussed in this chapter. Note especially the structure, the relation of claims and supporting evidence, the kinds of appeals the author makes, and the ways he addresses opposing views.

TV Can Be Good for You

Introduction

Identification of pre-
vailing view

Thesis statement
qualifying prevailing
view with three claims

Television wastes time, pollutes minds, destroys brain cells, and turns some viewers into murderers. Thus runs the prevailing talk about the medium, supported by serious research as well as simple belief. However, television can have strong virtues, too: it can ease loneliness, spark healthful laughter, and even educate young children by providing voices that supplement those of real people.

Background for
claim 1: effects of
loneliness

Almost everyone who has lived alone understands the curse of silence, when the only sound is the buzz of unhappiness or anxiety inside one's own head. Although people of all ages who live alone can experience intense loneliness, the elderly are especially

Evidence for effects of
loneliness

vulnerable to solitude. For example, they may suffer increased confusion or depression when left alone for long periods but then rebound when they have steady companionship (Bondevik and Skogstad 329-30).

Evidence for effects of
television on loneliness

A study of elderly men and women in New Zealand found that television can actually serve as a companion by assuming "the role of social contact with the wider world," reducing "feelings of isolation and loneliness because it directs viewers' attention away

Statement of claim 1

from themselves" ("Television Programming"). Thus television's voices can provide comfort because they distract from a focus on being alone.

Background for
claim 2: effects of
laughter

The absence of real voices can be most damaging when it means a lack of laughter. Here, too, research shows that television can have a positive effect on health. Laughter is one

Evidence for effects of
laughter

of the most powerful calming forces available to human beings, proven in many studies to reduce heart rate, lower blood pressure, and ease other stress-related ailments (Burroughs, Mahoney,

Evidence for comedy
on television

and Lippman 172; Griffiths 18). Television offers plenty of laughter: the recent listings for a single Friday night included more than twenty comedy programs running on the networks and on basic cable.

Evidence for effects of
laughter in response to
television

A study reported in a health magazine found that laughter inspired by television and video is as healthful as the laughter generated by live comedy. Volunteers laughing at a video comedy routine "showed significant improvements in several immune functions, such as natural killer-cell activity" (Laliberte 78). Further, the effects of the comedy were so profound that "merely anticipating watching a funny video improved mood, depression, and anger as much as two days beforehand" (Laliberte 79). Even for people with plenty of companionship, television's voices can have healthful effects by causing laughter.

> Statement of claim 2

Television also provides information about the world. This service can be helpful to everyone but especially to children, whose natural curiosity can exhaust the knowledge and patience of their parents and caretakers. While the TV may be baby-sitting children, it can also enrich them. For example, educational programs such as those on the Discovery Channel, the Disney Channel, and PBS offer a steady stream of information at various cognitive levels. Even many cartoons, which are generally dismissed as mindless or worse, familiarize children with the material of literature, including strong characters enacting classic narratives.

> Background for claim 3: educational effects
>
> Evidence for educational programming on television

Three researchers conducting a review of studies involving children and television found that TV can inspire imaginative play, which psychologists describe as important for children's cognitive development (Thakkar, Garrison, and Christakis 2028). In the studies reviewed, children who watched *Mister Rogers' Neighborhood*, a show that emphasized make-believe, demonstrated significant increases in imaginative play (2029). Thus high-quality educational programming can both inform young viewers and improve their cognitive development.

> Evidence for educational effects of television on children
>
> Statement of claim 3

The value of television voices should not be oversold. For one thing, almost everyone agrees that too much TV does no one any good and may cause much harm. Many studies show that excessive TV watching increases violent behavior, especially in children, and can cause, rather than ease, other antisocial behaviors (Reeks 114; Walsh 34). In addition, human beings require the give and take of actual interaction. Steven Pinker, an expert in children's language acquisition, warns that children cannot develop language properly by watching television. They need to interact with actual speakers who respond directly to their needs (282). Television voices are not real voices and in the end can do only limited good.

> Anticipation of objection: harm of television
>
> Anticipation of objection: need for actual interaction
>
> Qualification of claims in response to objections

But even limited good is something, especially for those who are lonely or neglected. Television is not an entirely positive force, but neither is it an entirely negative one. Its voices stand by to provide company, laughter, and information whenever they're needed.

> Conclusion

Works cited in MLA
style (see p. 445)

Works Cited

Bondevik, Margareth, and Anders Skogstad. "The Oldest Old, ADL,
    Social Network, and Loneliness." *Western Journal of Nursing
    Research* 20.3 (1998): 325-43. Print.

Burroughs, W. Jeffrey, Diana L. Mahoney, and Louis G. Lippman.
    "Attributes of Health-Promoting Laughter: Cross-Generational
    Comparison." *Journal of Psychology* 136.2 (2004): 171-81.
    Print.

Griffiths, Joan. "The Mirthful Brain." *Omni* Aug. 1996: 18-19. Print.

Laliberte, Richard W. "The Benefits of Laughter." *Shape* Sept. 2003:
    78-79. Print.

Pinker, Steven. *The Language Instinct: How the Mind Creates
    Language*. New York: Harper, 1994. Print.

Reeks, Anne. "Kids and TV: A Guide." *Parenting* Apr. 2005: 110-15.
    Print.

"Television Programming for Older People: Summary Research Re-
    port." *NZ on Air*. NZ on Air, 25 July 2004. Web. 15 Oct. 2008.

Thakkar, Rupin R., Michelle M. Garrison, and Dimitri A. Christakis.
    "A Systematic Review for the Effects of Television Viewing by
    Infants and Preschoolers." *Pediatrics* 18.5 (2006): 2025-31.
    Web. 12 Oct. 2008.

Walsh, Teri. "Too Much TV Linked to Depression." *Prevention* Feb.
    2001: 34-36. Print.

—Craig Holbrook (student)

11 Reading and Writing about Literature

By Sylvan Barnet

What's involved in analyzing a story, poem, or other literary work?

Writers of literature—stories, novels, poems, and plays—are concerned with presenting human experience concretely, with giving a sense of the feel of life rather than telling about it. Reading

mycomplab

Visit *mycomplab.com* for more resources as well as exercises on reading and writing about literature.

and writing about literature thus require extremely close attention to the feel of the words. For instance, the word *woods* in Robert Frost's "Stopping by Woods on a Snowy Evening" has a rural, folksy quality that *forest* doesn't have, and many such small distinctions contribute to the poem's effect.

When you read literature, you interpret distinctions like these, forming an idea of the work. When you write about literature, you state your idea as your thesis, and you support the thesis with evidence from the work. (See pp. 15–18 for more on thesis statements.)

Note Writing about literature is not merely summarizing literature. Your thesis is a claim about the meaning or effect of the literary work, not a statement of its plot. And your paper is a demonstration of your thesis, not a retelling of the work's changes or events.

11b

11a Write while reading literature.

You will become more engaged in reading literature if you write while you read. If you own the book you're reading, don't hesitate to underline or highlight passages that especially interest you. Don't hesitate to annotate the margins, indicating your pleasures, displeasures, and uncertainties with remarks such as *Nice detail* or *Do we need this long description?* or *Not believable.* If you don't own the book, make these notes on separate sheets or on your computer.

An effective way to interact with a text is to keep a **reading journal.** A journal is not a diary in which you record your doings; instead, it is a place to develop and store your reflections on what you read, such as an answer to a question you may have posed in the margin of the text or a response to something said in class. You may, for instance, want to reflect on why your opinion is so different from that of another student. You may even make an entry in the form of a letter to the author or from one character to another. (See pp. 10–11 for more on journal keeping.)

11b Read literature critically.

Reading literature critically involves interacting with a text, not in order to make negative judgments but in order to understand the work and evaluate its significance or quality. Such interaction is not passive, like scanning a newspaper or watching television. Instead, it is a process of engagement, of diving into the words themselves.

1 ▪ Meaning in literature

In analyzing any literary work, you face right off the question of *meaning.* Readers disagree all the time over the meanings of works of literature, partly because literature *shows* rather than *tells:* it gives concrete images of imagined human experiences, but it usually does not say how we ought to understand the images. Further, readers bring different experiences to their reading and thus understand images differently. In writing about literature, then, we can offer only our *interpretation* of the meaning rather than *the* meaning. Still, most people agree that there are limits to interpretation: it must be supported by evidence that a reasonable person finds at least plausible if not totally convincing.

2 ▪ Questions for literary analysis

One reason interpretations of meaning differ is that readers approach literary works differently, focusing on certain elements and interpreting those elements distinctively. For instance, historical or cultural criticism considers the effect of the author's context on a work, feminist or gender criticism focuses on the representation of gender in a work, and reader-response criticism stresses the effect of a work on its readers.

This chapter emphasizes so-called formalist criticism, which sees a literary work primarily as something to be understood in itself. This critical framework engages the reader immediately in the work of literature, without requiring extensive historical or cultural background, and it introduces the conventional elements of literature that all critical approaches discuss, even though they view the elements differently. The list below poses questions for each element that can help you think constructively and imaginatively about what you read.

- *Plot:* **the relationships and patterns of events.** Even a poem has a plot—for instance, a change in mood from grief to resignation.

  What actions happen?
  What conflicts occur?
  How do the events connect to each other and to the whole?

- *Characters:* **the people the author creates,** including the narrator of a story or the speaker of a poem.

  Who are the principal people in the work?
  How do they interact?
  What do their actions, words, and thoughts reveal about their personalities and the personalities of others?
  Do the characters stay the same, or do they change? Why?

- *Point of view:* **the perspective or attitude of the speaker in a poem or the voice who tells a story.** The point of view may be **first person** (a participant, using *I*) or **third person** (an outsider, using *he, she, it, they*). A first-person narrator may be a major or a minor character in the narrative and may be **reliable** or **unreliable** (unable to report events wholly or accurately). A third-person narrator may be **omniscient** (knows what goes on in all characters' minds), **limited** (knows what goes on in the mind of only one or two characters), or **objective** (knows only what is external to the characters).

Who is the narrator (or the speaker of a poem)?
How does the narrator's point of view affect the narrative?

- *Tone:* **the narrator's or speaker's attitude,** perceived through the words (for instance, joyful, bitter, or confident).

  What tone (or tones) do you hear? If there is a change, how do you account for it?
  Is there an ironic contrast between the narrator's tone (for instance, confidence) and what you take to be the author's attitude (for instance, pity for human overconfidence)?

11b

- *Imagery:* **word pictures or details involving the senses of sight, sound, touch, smell, taste.**

  What images does the writer use? What senses do they draw on?
  What patterns are evident in the images (for instance, religious or commercial images)?
  What is the significance of the imagery?

- *Symbolism:* **concrete things standing for larger and more abstract ideas.** For instance, the American flag may symbolize freedom, or a dead flower may symbolize mortality.

  What symbols does the author use? What do they seem to signify?
  How does the symbolism relate to the theme of the work?

- *Setting:* **the place where the action happens.**

  What does the locale contribute to the work?
  Are scene shifts significant?

- *Form:* **the shape or structure of the work.**

  What *is* the form? (For example, a story might divide sharply in the middle, moving from happiness to sorrow.)
  What parts of the work does the form emphasize, and why?

- *Themes:* **the main ideas about human experience suggested by the work as a whole.** A theme is neither a plot (what happens) nor a subject (such as mourning or marriage). Rather it is what the author says with that plot about that subject.

  Can you state each theme in a sentence? Avoid mentioning specific characters or actions; instead, write an observation applicable to humanity in general. For instance, you might state the following about Gwendolyn Brooks's poem "The Bean Eaters" (p. 125): *People can live contentedly despite old age and poverty.*

Do certain words, passages of dialog or description, or situations seem to represent a theme most clearly?

How do the work's elements combine to develop a theme?

- *Appeal:* **the degree to which the work pleases you.**

What do you especially like or dislike about the work? Why?

Do you think your responses are unique, or would they be common to most readers? Why?

11c   A sample literary analysis

A poem and a student paper on the work appear on the next three pages. The student develops a thesis about the poem, supporting his main idea with quotations, paraphrases, and summaries from the poem, a primary source. The student also draws sparingly on secondary sources (other critics' views), which further support his own views.

Note the following features of the student's paper:

- **The writer does not merely summarize the literary work.** He summarizes briefly to make his meaning clear, but his essay consists mostly of his own analysis.
- **The writer uses many quotations from the literary work.** The quotations provide evidence for the writer's ideas and let readers hear the voice of the work.
- **The writer integrates quotations smoothly into his own sentences.** See pages 419–23.
- **The writer uses the present tense of verbs** (*Brooks emphasizes; They live alone*) to describe both the poet's work and the action in the work.

Key terms

quotation An exact repetition of an author's words, placed in quotation marks. (See also pp. 339, 417–18.)

paraphrase A restatement of an author's words, closely following the author's line of thought but using different words and sentence structures. (See also pp. 415–17.)

summary A condensation of an extended passage into a sentence or more. (See also pp. 83–85, 414–15.)

primary source A firsthand account: for instance, a historical document, a work of literature, or your own observations. (See also p. 378.)

secondary source A report on or analysis of other sources, often primary ones: for instance, a historian's account of a battle or a critic's view of a poem. (See also p. 378.)

For the format of a literature paper, consult several other sections of this handbook:

- **Use MLA document format** for treatment of margins, quotations, and other elements (pp. 479–81).
- **Cite sources in MLA style:** parenthetical text citations and a list of works cited (pp. 437–78).
- **Indicate any editing of quotations.** Use ellipsis marks (. . .) to indicate deletions from quotations (pp. 345–47). Use brackets to indicate additions to or changes in quotations (p. 348).

Poem

11c

Gwendolyn Brooks

The Bean Eaters

They eat beans mostly, this old yellow pair.
Dinner is a casual affair.
Plain chipware on a plain and creaking wood,
Tin flatware.

Two who are Mostly Good.   5
Two who have lived their day,
But keep on putting on their clothes
And putting things away.

And remembering . . .
Remembering, with twinklings and twinges,   10
As they lean over the beans in their rented back room that
    is full of beads and receipts and dolls and cloths,
    tobacco crumbs, vases and fringes.

An essay on poetry (with secondary sources)

Note The parenthetical citations in the following essay refer either to lines of Brooks's poem or to pages in the secondary sources cited at the end of the essay. We know which is which from the context and from the word *line* in the first citation in the second paragraph.

Kenneth Scheff
Professor MacGregor
English 101A
7 April 2009

Marking Time versus Enduring in
Gwendolyn Brooks's "The Bean Eaters"

Gwendolyn Brooks's poem "The Bean Eaters" runs only eleven lines. It is written in plain language about very plain people. Yet its meaning is ambiguous. One critic, George E. Kent, says the old couple who eat beans "have had their day and exist now as time-markers" (141). However, another critic, D. H. Melhem, perceives not so much time marking as "endurance" in the old couple (123). The reader must decide whether this poem is a despairing picture of old age or a more positive portrait.

"The Bean Eaters" describes an "old yellow pair" who "eat beans mostly" (line 1) off "Plain chipware" (3) with "Tin flatware" (4) in "their rented back room" (11). Clearly, they are poor. They live alone, not with friends or relatives—children or grandchildren are not mentioned—but with memories and a few possessions (9-11). They are "Mostly Good" (5), words Brooks capitalizes at the end of a line, perhaps to stress the old people's adherence to traditional values as well as their lack of saintliness. They are unexceptional.

The isolated routine of the couple's life is something Brooks draws attention to with a separate stanza:

> Two who are Mostly Good.
> Two who have lived their day,
> But keep on putting on their clothes
> And putting things away. (5-8)

Brooks emphasizes how isolated the couple is by repeating "Two who." Then she emphasizes how routine their life is by repeating "putting."

A pessimistic reading of this poem seems justified. The critic Harry B. Shaw reads the lines just quoted as perhaps despairing: "they are putting things away as if winding down an operation and readying for withdrawal from activity" (80). However, Shaw observes, the word *But* also indicates that the couple resist slipping away, that they intend to hold on (80). This dual meaning is at the heart of Brooks's poem: the old people live a meager existence, yes, but their will, their self-control, and their connection with another person—their essential humanity—are unharmed.

The truly positive nature of the poem is revealed in the last stanza. In Brooks's words, the old people remember with some "twinges" perhaps, but also with "twinklings" (10), a cheerful image. As Melhem says, these people are "strong in mutual affection and shared memories" (123). And the final line, which is much longer than all the rest and which catalogs the evidence of the couple's long life together, is almost musically affirmative: "As they lean over the beans in their rented back room that is full of beads and receipts and dolls and cloths, tobacco crumbs, vases and fringes" (11).

What these people have is not much, but it is something.

[New page.]

Works Cited

Brooks, Gwendolyn. "The Bean Eaters." *An Introduction to Literature: Fiction, Poetry, and Drama.* Ed. Sylvan Barnet, William Burto, and William E. Cain. 15th ed. New York: Longman, 2008. 922. Print.

Kent, George E. *A Life of Gwendolyn Brooks*. Lexington: UP of Kentucky, 1990. Print.

Melhem, D. H. *Gwendolyn Brooks: Poetry and the Heroic Voice*. Lexington: UP of Kentucky, 1987. Print.

Shaw, Harry B. *Gwendolyn Brooks*. Boston: Twayne, 1980. Print. Twayne's United States Authors Ser. 395.

12 Taking Essay Exams

How can I write successful essay exams?

Essay exams test your knowledge of a subject as well as your ability to think critically about what you have learned. Doing well on essay exams involves thorough preparation (below) and then, as you take the exam, planning your time and answer (p. 128), drafting an appropriate response (p. 129), and rereading (p. 129).

12a Prepare for the exam.

To do well on an essay exam, you will need to understand the course content, not only the facts but also the interpretation of them and the relations between them.

- **Take careful lecture notes.**
- **Thoughtfully, critically read the assigned texts or articles.**
- **Review regularly.** Give the material time to sink in and stimulate your thinking.
- **Create summaries.** Recast others' ideas in your own words, and extract the meaning from notes and texts. (See pp. 134–35 for instructions on summarizing.)
- **Prepare notes or outlines to reorganize the course material around key topics or issues.** One technique is to create and answer likely essay questions. For instance, in a short-story course you might locate a theme running through all the stories you have read by a certain author or from a certain period. In a psychology course you might outline various theorists' views of what

mycomplab ▌

Visit *mycomplab.com* for more resources as well as exercises on taking essay exams.

causes a disorder such as schizophrenia. Working through such topics can help you anticipate questions, master the material, and estimate your time during the actual exam.

12b Plan your time and your answer.

When you first receive an exam, take a few minutes to get your bearings and plan an approach. The time spent will not be wasted.

- **Read the exam all the way through at least once.** Don't start answering any questions until you've seen them all.
- **Weigh the questions.** Determine which questions seem most important, which ones are going to be most difficult for you, and approximately how much time you'll need for each question. (Your instructor may help by assigning a point value to each question as a guide to its importance or by suggesting an amount of time for you to spend on each question.)

Planning continues when you turn to an individual essay question. Resist the temptation to rush right into an answer without some planning: a few minutes can save you time later and help you produce a stronger essay.

- **Read the question at least twice.** You will be more likely to stick to the question and answer it fully.
- **Examine the words in the question and consider their implications.** Look especially for words such as *describe, define, explain, summarize, analyze, evaluate,* and *interpret,* each of which requires a different kind of response. Here, for example, is an essay question whose key term is *explain:*

Question

Given humans' natural and historical curiosity about themselves, why did a scientific discipline of anthropology not arise until the 20th century? Explain, citing specific details.

Consult discussions of such terms on pages 6–7 and 52–57.

- **Make a brief outline of the main ideas you want to cover.** Use the back of the exam sheet or booklet for scratch paper. In the following brief outline, a student planned her answer to the anthropology question above.

Outline

1. Unscientific motivations behind 19th-c anthro.

   Imperialist/colonialist govts.
   Practical goals
   Nonobjective and unscientific (Herodotus, Cushing)

2. 19th-c ethnocentricity (vs. cultural relativism)

3. 19th-c anthro. = object collecting

    20th-c shift from museum to univ.

    Anthro. becomes acad. disc. and professional (Boas, Malinowski)

- **Write a thesis statement for your essay that responds directly to the question and represents your view of the topic.** (If you are unsure of how to write a thesis statement, see pp. 15–18.) Include key phrases that you can expand with supporting evidence for your view. The thesis statement for the anthropology exam concisely previews a three-part answer to the question:

Thesis statement

Anthropology did not emerge as a scientific discipline until the 20th century because of the practical and political motivations behind 19th-century ethnographic studies, the ethnocentric bias of Western researchers, and a conception of culture that was strictly material.

12d

12c   Draft the essay.

An essay exam does not require a smooth and inviting opening. Instead, begin by stating your thesis immediately and giving an overview of the rest of your essay. Such a capsule version of your answer tells your reader (and grader) generally how much command you have and also how you plan to develop your answer. It also gets you off to a good start.

Develop the essay itself as you would develop any piece of sound academic writing:

- **Observe the methods, terms, or other special requirements of the discipline in which you are writing.**
- **Support your thesis statement with solid generalizations,** each one perhaps the topic sentence of a paragraph.
- **Support each generalization with specific, relevant evidence.**

If you observe a few *don't*s as well, your essay will have more substance:

- **Avoid filling out the essay by repeating yourself.**
- **Avoid other kinds of wordiness that pad and confuse,** whether intentionally or not. (See pp. 186–91.)
- **Avoid resorting to purely subjective feelings.** Keep focused on analysis or whatever is asked of you. (It may help to abolish the word *I* from the essay.)

12d   Reread the essay.

The time limit on an essay examination does not allow for the careful rethinking and revision you would give an essay or research paper. You need to write clearly and concisely the first time. But try to leave yourself a few minutes after finishing the entire exam for rereading the essay (or essays) and doing touch-ups.

- **Correct mistakes:** illegible passages, misspellings, grammatical errors, and accidental omissions.
- **Verify that your thesis is accurate**—that it is, in fact, what you ended up writing about.
- **Ensure that you have supported all your generalizations.** Cross out irrelevant ideas and details, and add any information that now seems important. (Write on another page, if necessary, keying each addition to the page on which it belongs.)

12e

12e Sample essay exams

The following essays illustrate a successful and an unsuccessful answer to the sample essay question on page 128 about anthropology. Both answers were written in the allotted time of forty minutes. Marginal comments on each essay highlight their effective and ineffective elements.

Successful essay answer

Introduction stating thesis

Direct answer to question and preview of three-part response

Anthropology did not emerge as a scientific discipline until the 20th century because of the practical and political motivations behind 19th-century ethnographic studies, the ethnocentric bias of Western researchers, and a conception of culture that was strictly material.

First main point: practical aims

Example

Example

Before the 20th century, ethnographic studies were almost always used for practical goals. The study of human culture can be traced back at least as far as Herodotus's investigations of the Mediterranean peoples. Herodotus was like many pre-20th-century "anthropologists" in that he was employed by a government that needed information about its neighbors, just as the colonial nations in the 19th century needed information about their newly conquered subjects. The early politically motivated ethnographic studies that the colonial nations sponsored tended to be isolated projects, and they aimed less to advance general knowledge than to solve a specific problem. Frank Hamilton Cushing, who was employed by the American government to study the Zuni tribe of New Mexico, and who is considered one of the pioneers of anthropology, didn't even publish his findings. The political and practical aims of anthropologists and the nature of their research prevented their work from being a scholarly discipline in its own right.

Second main point: ethnocentricity

Anthropologists of the 19th century also fell short of the standards of objectivity needed for truly scientific study. This partly had to do with anthropologists' close connection to imperialist governments. But even independent researchers were hampered by the prevailing assumption that Western cultures were inherently superior. While the modern anthropologist believes that a culture must be studied in terms of its own values, early ethnographers were ethno-centric: they judged "primitive" cultures by their own "civilized" values. "Primitive" peoples were seen as uninteresting in their own right. The reasons to study them, ultimately, were to satisfy curiosity, to exploit them, or to prove their inferiority. There was even some debate as to whether so-called savage peoples were human.

Finally, the 19th century tended to conceive of culture in narrow, material terms, often reducing it to a collection of artifacts. When not working for a government, early ethnographers usually worked for a museum. The enormous collections of exotica still found in many museums today are the legacy of this 19th-century object-oriented conception of anthropology, which ignored the myths, symbols, and rituals the objects related to. It was only when the museum tradition was broadened to include all aspects of a culture that anthropology could come into existence as a scientific discipline. When anthropologists like Franz Boas and Bronislaw Malinowski began to publish their findings for others to read and criticize and began to move from the museum to the university, the discipline gained stature and momentum.

Third main point (with transition Finally): focus on objects

Examples

In brief, anthropology required a whole series of ideological shifts to become modern. Once it broke free of its purely practical bent, the cultural prejudices of its practitioners, and the narrow conception that limited it to a collection of objects, anthropology could grow into a science.

Conclusion, restating thesis supported by essay

Unsuccessful essay answer

The discipline of anthropology, the study of humans and their cultures, actually began in the early 20th century and was strengthened by the Darwinian revolution, but the discipline did not begin to take shape until people like Franz Boas and Alfred Kroeber began doing scientific research among nonindustrialized cultures. (Boas, who was born in Germany but emigrated to the US, is the father of the idea of historical particularism.)

Introduction, not answering question

No thesis statement or sense of direction

Irrelevant information

Since the dawn of time, humans have always had a natural curiosity about themselves. Art and literature have always reflected this need to understand human emotions, thought, and behavior. Anthropology is yet another reflection of this need. Anthropologists have a different way of looking at human societies than artists or writers. Whereas the latter paint an individualistic, impressionistic portrait of the world they see, anthropologists study cultures systematically, scientifically. They are thus closer to biologists. They are social scientists, with the emphasis on both words.

Cliché added to language of question without answering question

Wheel spinning, positioning contemporary anthropology as a scientific discipline

Another reason why anthropology did not develop until the 20th century is that people in the past did not travel very much. The expansion of the automobile and the airplane has played a major role in the expansion of the discipline.

Not Another reason but the first reason given

Assertion without support

Cushing's important work among the Zuni Indians in New Mexico is a good example of the transition between 19th-century and 20th-century approaches to anthropology. Cushing was one of the first to develop the method of participant observation. Instead of merely coming in as an outsider, taking notes, and leaving,

Next three paragraphs: discussion of pioneers showing familiarity with their work but not answering question

Cushing actually lived among the Zuni, dressing like them and following their customs. In this way, he was able to build a relationship of trust with his informants, learning much more than someone who would have been seen as an outsider.

Franz Boas, as mentioned earlier, was another anthropology pioneer. A German immigrant, Boas proposed the idea of historical particularism as a response to the prevailing theory of cultural evolution. Cultural evolution is the idea that cultures gradually evolve toward higher levels of efficiency and complexity. Historical particularism is the idea that every culture is unique and develops differently. Boas developed his theory to counter those who believed in cultural evolution. Working with the Kwakiutl Indians, he was also one of the first anthropologists to use a native assistant to help him gain access to the culture under study.

Padding with repetition

Irrelevant information

A third pioneer in anthropology was Malinowski, who developed a theory of functionalism—that culture responds to biological, psychological, and other needs. Malinowski's work is extremely important and still influential today.

Vague assertion without support

Anthropologists have made great contributions to society over the course of the past century. One can only hope that they will continue the great strides they have made, building on the past to contribute to a bright new future.

Irrelevant and empty conclusion

13 Public Writing

How can I communicate effectively in business, community work, and other situations outside of school?

Writing to members of the public outside of school resembles academic writing in many ways. It usually involves the same basic writing process, discussed on pages 2–41: assessing the writing situation, developing what you want to say, freely working out your meaning in a draft, and editing and revising so that your writing will achieve your purpose with readers. It often involves research, as discussed on pages 374–433. And it involves the standards of conciseness, appropriate and exact language, and correct grammar and usage discussed in Chapters 15–50.

But public writing has its own conventions, too, depending on what you're writing and why. This chapter covers several types of public writing: business letters and résumés (opposite), memos (p. 137), e-mail (p. 138), and newsletters and other documents for community work (p. 140).

mycomplab

Visit *mycomplab.com* for more resources as well as exercises on public writing.

CULTURE LANGUAGE Public writing in the United States, especially business writing, favors efficiency and may seem abrupt or impolite compared with such writing in your native culture. For instance, a business letter elsewhere may be expected to begin with polite questions about the addressee or with compliments for the addressee's company, whereas US business letters are expected to get right to the point.

13a   Use established formats for business letters and résumés.

When you write for business, you are addressing busy people who want to see quickly why you are writing and how they should respond to you. Follow these general guidelines:

- **State your purpose right at the start.**
- **Be straightforward, clear, concise, objective, and courteous.**
- **Observe conventions of grammar and usage,** which make your writing clear and impress your reader with your care.

1 ▪ Business letter format

For any business letter, use either unlined white paper measuring 8½″ × 11″ or what is called letterhead stationery with your address printed at the top of the sheet. Type the letter single-spaced (with double spacing between elements) on only one side of a sheet. A common business-letter form is illustrated on the next page:

- **The *return-address heading* gives your address and the date.** Do not include your name. If you are using stationery with a printed heading, you need only give the date.
- **The *inside address* shows the name, title, and complete address of the person you are writing to.**
- **The *salutation* greets the addressee.** Whenever possible, address your letter to a specific person. (Call the company or department to ask whom to address.) If you can't find a person's name, then use a job title (*Dear Human Resources Manager, Dear Customer Service Manager*) or use a general salutation (*Dear Smythe Shoes*). Use *Ms.* as the title for a woman when she has no other title, when you don't know how she prefers to be addressed, or when you know that she prefers *Ms.*
- **The *body* contains the substance.** Instead of indenting the first line of each paragraph, insert an extra line of space between paragraphs.
- **The *close* should reflect the level of formality in the salutation:** *Respectfully, Cordially, Yours truly,* and *Sincerely* are more formal closes; *Regards* and *Best wishes* are less formal.

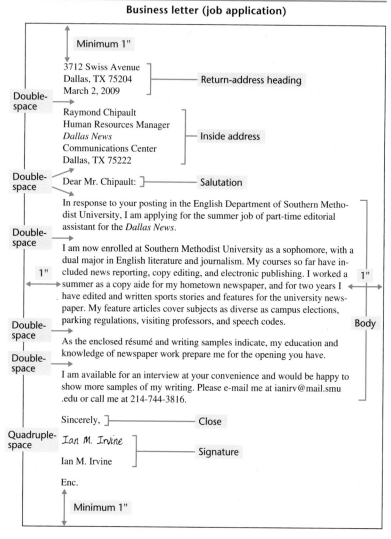

Business letter (job application)

Minimum 1"

3712 Swiss Avenue
Dallas, TX 75204 ——— Return-address heading
March 2, 2009

Double-space

Raymond Chipault
Human Resources Manager
Dallas News ——— Inside address
Communications Center
Dallas, TX 75222

Double-space

Dear Mr. Chipault: ——— Salutation

Double-space

In response to your posting in the English Department of Southern Methodist University, I am applying for the summer job of part-time editorial assistant for the *Dallas News*.

Double-space

1"

I am now enrolled at Southern Methodist University as a sophomore, with a dual major in English literature and journalism. My courses so far have included news reporting, copy editing, and electronic publishing. I worked a summer as a copy aide for my hometown newspaper, and for two years I have edited and written sports stories and features for the university newspaper. My feature articles cover subjects as diverse as campus elections, parking regulations, visiting professors, and speech codes.

1"

Body

Double-space

As the enclosed résumé and writing samples indicate, my education and knowledge of newspaper work prepare me for the opening you have.

Double-space

I am available for an interview at your convenience and would be happy to show more samples of my writing. Please e-mail me at ianirv@mail.smu.edu or call me at 214-744-3816.

Sincerely, ——— Close

Quadruple-space

Ian M. Irvine

Ian M. Irvine ——— Signature

Enc.

Minimum 1"

- **The *signature* has two parts:** your name typed four lines below the close, and your handwritten signature in the space between. Give your name as you sign checks and other documents.
- **Include any additional information below the signature,** such as *Enc.* (indicating an enclosure with the letter) or *cc: Margaret Zusky* (indicating that a copy is being sent to the person named).

Use an envelope that will accommodate the letter once it is folded horizontally in thirds. The envelope should show your name and address in the upper left corner and the addressee's name, title, and address in the center. For easy machine reading, the United States Postal Service recommends all capital letters and no punctuation (spaces separate the elements on a line), as in this address:

RAYMOND CHIPAULT
HUMAN RESOURCES MANAGER
DALLAS NEWS
COMMUNICATIONS CENTER
DALLAS TX 75222-0188

2 ▪ Job-application letter

13a

The sample on the facing page illustrates the key features of a job-application letter:

- **Interpret your résumé for the particular job.** Don't detail your entire résumé, reciting your job history. Instead, highlight and reshape only the relevant parts.
- **Announce at the outset what job you seek and how you heard about it.**
- **Include any special reason you have for applying,** such as a specific career goal.
- **Summarize your qualifications for this particular job,** including relevant facts about education and employment history and emphasizing notable accomplishments. Mention that additional information appears in an accompanying résumé.
- **Describe your availability.** At the end of the letter, mention that you are free for an interview at the convenience of the addressee, or specify when you will be available (for instance, when your current job or classes leave you free, or when you could travel to the employer's city).

3 ▪ Résumé

The résumé that accompanies your letter of application should provide information in table format so that a potential employer can quickly evaluate your qualifications. The résumé should include your name and address, your career objective, your education and employment history, any special skills you have or awards you've received, and information about how to obtain your references. All the information should fit on one uncrowded page unless your education and experience are extensive. See the sample on the next page for writing and formatting guidelines for a résumé that you submit in print.

Employers may ask for an electronic version of your résumé so that they can add it to a database of applicants. The employers may scan your printed résumé to convert it to an electronic file, which they can then store in an appropriate database, or they may request that you embed your résumé in an e-mail message. To produce a

Résumé (print)

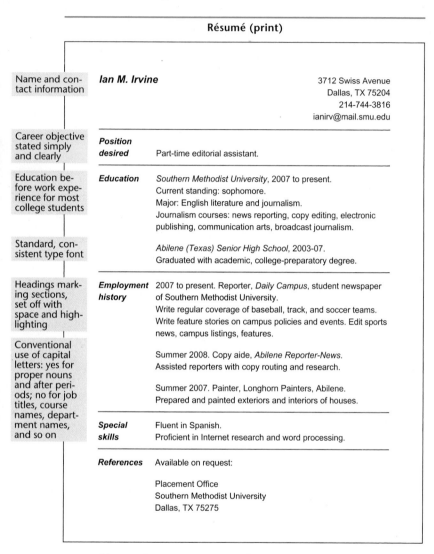

Name and contact information	**Ian M. Irvine**	3712 Swiss Avenue Dallas, TX 75204 214-744-3816 ianirv@mail.smu.edu
Career objective stated simply and clearly	**Position desired**	Part-time editorial assistant.
Education before work experience for most college students	**Education**	*Southern Methodist University*, 2007 to present. Current standing: sophomore. Major: English literature and journalism. Journalism courses: news reporting, copy editing, electronic publishing, communication arts, broadcast journalism.
Standard, consistent type font		*Abilene (Texas) Senior High School*, 2003-07. Graduated with academic, college-preparatory degree.
Headings marking sections, set off with space and highlighting	**Employment history**	2007 to present. Reporter, *Daily Campus*, student newspaper of Southern Methodist University. Write regular coverage of baseball, track, and soccer teams. Write feature stories on campus policies and events. Edit sports news, campus listings, features.
Conventional use of capital letters: yes for proper nouns and after periods; no for job titles, course names, department names, and so on		Summer 2008. Copy aide, *Abilene Reporter-News*. Assisted reporters with copy routing and research. Summer 2007. Painter, Longhorn Painters, Abilene. Prepared and painted exteriors and interiors of houses.
	Special skills	Fluent in Spanish. Proficient in Internet research and word processing.
	References	Available on request: Placement Office Southern Methodist University Dallas, TX 75275

scannable or electronic résumé, follow the guidelines below and consult the sample opposite.

- **Keep the design simple for accurate scanning or electronic transmittal.** Avoid images, unusual type, more than one column, vertical or horizontal lines, italics, and underlining.
- **Use concise, specific words to describe your skills and experience.** The employer's computer may use keywords (often nouns) to identify the résumés of suitable job candidates, and you want to ensure that your résumé includes the appropriate keywords. Name your specific skills—for example, the com-

Résumé (scannable or electronic)

Ian M. Irvine
3712 Swiss Avenue
Dallas, TX 75204
214-744-3816
ianirv@mail.smu.edu

Accurate key-
words, allowing
the employer to
place the ré-
sumé into an
appropriate
database

KEYWORDS: Editor, editorial assistant, publishing, electronic publishing.

OBJECTIVE
Part-time editorial assistant.

EDUCATION
Southern Methodist University, 2007 to present.
Major: English literature and journalism.
Journalism courses: news reporting, copy editing, electronic publishing,
communication arts, broadcast journalism.

Abilene (Texas) Senior High School, 2003-07.
Academic, college preparatory degree.

Simple design,
avoiding un-
usual type,
italics, multiple
columns, deco-
rative lines, and
images

EMPLOYMENT HISTORY
Reporter, Daily Campus, Southern Methodist University, 2007 to present.
Writer of articles for student newspaper on sports teams, campus policies,
and local events. Editor of sports news, campus listings, and features.

Standard font
easily read by
scanners

Copy aide, Abilene Reporter-News, Abilene, summer 2008.
Assistant to reporters, routing copy and doing research.

Every line align-
ing at left
margin

Painter, Longhorn Painters, Abilene, summer 2007.
Preparation and painting of exteriors and interiors of houses.

SPECIAL SKILLS
Fluent in Spanish.
Proficient in Internet research and word processing.

REFERENCES
Available on request:
Placement Office
Southern Methodist University
Dallas, TX 75275

puter programs you can operate—and write concretely with
words like *manager* (not *person with responsibility for*) and
reporter (not *staff member who reports*). Look for likely keywords in the employer's description of the job you seek.

13b Write focused memos.

Business memorandums (memos, for short) address people
within the same organization. Most memos deal briefly with a specific topic, such as an answer to a question or an evaluation.

Both the form and the structure of a memo are designed to get to the point and dispose of it quickly (see the sample below). State your reason for writing in the first sentence. Devote the first paragraph to a concise presentation of your answer, conclusion, or evaluation. In the rest of the memo explain your reasoning or evidence. Use headings or lists as appropriate to highlight key information.

Business memo

Heading: company's name, addressee's name, writer's name and initials, date, and subject description

Bigelow Wax Company

TO: Aileen Rosen, Director of Sales
FROM: Patricia Phillips, Territory 12   *PP*
DATE: November 17, 2009
SUBJECT: 2009 sales of Quick Wax in Territory 12

Body: single-spaced with double spacing between paragraphs; paragraphs not indented

Since it was introduced in January 2009, Quick Wax has been unsuccessful in Territory 12 and has not affected the sales of our Easy Shine. Discussions with customers and my own analysis of Quick Wax suggest three reasons for its failure to compete with our product.

1. Quick Wax has not received the promotion necessary for a new product. Advertising—primarily on radio—has been sporadic and has not developed a clear, consistent image for the product. In addition, the Quick Wax sales representative in Territory 12 is new and inexperienced; he is not known to customers, and his sales pitch (which I once overheard) is weak. As far as I can tell, his efforts are not supported by phone calls or mailings from his home office.

2. When Quick Wax does make it to the store shelves, buyers do not choose it over our product. Though priced competitively with our product, Quick Wax is poorly packaged. The container seems smaller than ours, though in fact it holds the same eight ounces. The lettering on the Quick Wax package (red on blue) is difficult to read, in contrast to the white-on-green lettering on the Easy Shine package.

3. Our special purchase offers and my increased efforts to serve existing customers have had the intended effect of keeping customers satisfied with our product and reducing their inclination to stock something new.

People receiving copies

Copies: L. Mendes, Director of Marketing
          J. MacGregor, Customer Service Manager

13c   Write effective e-mail.

E-mail has a wide range of uses, from corresponding with relatives and friends to collaborating with classmates to presenting a business proposal. Sometimes, as when e-mailing a friend or a classmate, you can write quickly and casually, not worrying much about how the message reads. But when e-mailing people you don't know well and want to impress, you should apply the same care as you would to a business letter. That is, consider your audience and purpose in choosing both content and tone; focus on a central idea; organize effectively; and write concisely, clearly, and accurately. A crafted message like the one below is more likely to achieve the intended purpose.

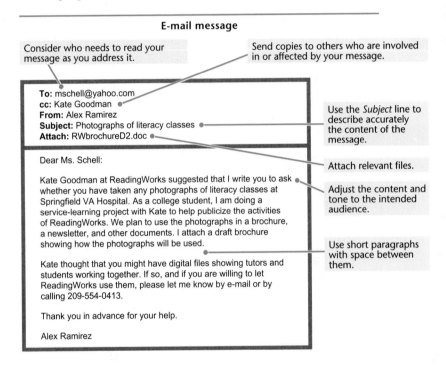

E-mail message

Consider who needs to read your message as you address it.

Send copies to others who are involved in or affected by your message.

To: mschell@yahoo.com
cc: Kate Goodman
From: Alex Ramirez
Subject: Photographs of literacy classes
Attach: RWbrochureD2.doc

Use the *Subject* line to describe accurately the content of the message.

Dear Ms. Schell:

Kate Goodman at ReadingWorks suggested that I write you to ask whether you have taken any photographs of literacy classes at Springfield VA Hospital. As a college student, I am doing a service-learning project with Kate to help publicize the activities of ReadingWorks. We plan to use the photographs in a brochure, a newsletter, and other documents. I attach a draft brochure showing how the photographs will be used.

Kate thought that you might have digital files showing tutors and students working together. If so, and if you are willing to let ReadingWorks use them, please let me know by e-mail or by calling 209-554-0413.

Thank you in advance for your help.

Alex Ramirez

Attach relevant files.

Adjust the content and tone to the intended audience.

Use short paragraphs with space between them.

Addressing messages

- **Avoid spamming.** With a few keystrokes, you can broadcast a message to many recipients at once—all the students in a course, say, or all the participants in a discussion group. Occasionally you may indeed have a worthwhile idea or important information that everyone on the list will want to know. But flooding whole lists with irrelevant messages—called spamming—is rude and irritating.
- **Avoid sending frivolous messages to all the members of a group.** Instead of dashing off "I agree" and distributing the two-word message widely, put some time into composing a thoughtful response and send it only to those who will be interested.

Composing messages

- **Use names.** In the body of your message, address your reader(s) by name if possible and sign off with your own name and information on how to contact you. Your own name is especially important if your e-mail address does not spell it out.
- **Pay careful attention to tone.** Refrain from **flaming,** or attacking, correspondents. Don't use all-capital letters, which SHOUT. And use irony or sarcasm only cautiously: in the absence of facial expressions, they can lead to misunderstandings. To indicate irony and emotions, you can use **emoticons,** such as the smiley :-). These sideways faces made up of punctuation can easily be overused, though, and should not substitute for thoughtfully worded opinions.
- **Avoid saying anything in e-mail that you would not say face to face or in a printed document such as a letter or memo.** E-mail can usually be retrieved from the server, and in business and academic settings it may well be retrieved in disputes over contracts, grades, and other matters.

Reading and responding to messages

- **Be a forgiving reader.** Avoid nitpicking over spelling or other surface errors. And because attitudes are sometimes difficult to convey, give authors an initial benefit of the doubt: a writer who at first seems hostile may simply have tried too hard to be concise; a writer who at first seems unserious may simply have failed at injecting humor into a worthwhile message.
- **Consider who will read your response.** The Reply function will automatically address the person who wrote you, whereas the Reply All function will address others who may have been sent copies of the original message. Before you send the message, choose the readers who need to see the message.
- **Respect others' privacy.** Forward messages only with permission or only if you know that the author of the message won't mind. If you add more recipients to your response, make sure not to pass on previous private messages by mistake.
- **Avoid participating in flame "wars,"** overheated dialogs that contribute little or no information or understanding. If a war breaks out in a group discussion, ignore it: don't rush to defend someone who is being attacked, and don't respond even if you are under attack yourself.

13d

13d Create effective documents when writing for community work.

At some point in your life, you're likely to volunteer for a community organization such as a soup kitchen, a daycare center, or a literacy program. Many college courses involve service learning, in which you do such volunteer work, write about the experience for your course, and write *for* the organization you're helping.

The writing you do for a community group may range from flyers to grant proposals. The newsletter below was prepared for ReadingWorks, a literacy program. Two guidelines in particular can help you prepare effective projects:

- **Craft each document for its purpose and audience.** You are trying to achieve a specific aim with your readers, and the approach and tone you use will influence their responses. If, for

---

Newsletter

ReadingWorks

Springfield Veterans Administration Hospital   **SUMMER 2009**

From the director

Can you help? With more and more learners in the ReadingWorks program, we need more and more tutors. You may know people who would be interested in participating in the program, if only they knew about it.

Those of you who have been tutoring VA patients in reading and writing know both the great need you fulfill and the great benefits you bring to the students. New tutors need no special skills—we'll provide the training—only patience and an interest in helping others.

We've scheduled an orientation meeting for Friday, September 11, at 6:30 PM. Please come and bring a friend who is willing to contribute a couple of hours a week to our work.

Thanks,
Kate Goodman

FIRST ANNUAL AWARDS DINNER

A festive night for students and tutors

The first annual Reading-Works Awards Dinner on May 22nd was a great success. Springfield's own Golden Fork provided tasty food and Amber Allen supplied lively music. The students decorated Suite 42 on the theme of books and reading. In all, 127 people attended.

The highlight of the night was the awards ceremony. Nine students, recommended by their tutors, received certificates recognizing their efforts and special accomplishments in learning to read and write:

Ramon Berva
Edward Byar
David Dunbar
Tony Garnier
Chris Guigni
Akili Haynes
Josh Livingston
Alex Obeld
B. J. Resnansky

In addition, nine tutors received certificates commemorating five years of service to ReadingWorks:

Anita Crumpton
Felix Cruz-Rivera
Bette Elgen

Kayleah Bortoluzzi
Harriotte Henderson
Ben Obiso
Meggie Puente
Max Smith
Sara Villante

Congratulations to all!

PTSD: New Guidelines

Most of us are working with veterans who have been diagnosed with post-traumatic stress disorder. Because this disorder is often complicated by alcoholism, depression, anxiety, and other problems, the National Center for PTSD has issued some guidelines for helping PTSD patients in ways that reduce their stress.

- The hospital must know your tutoring schedule, and you need to sign in and out before and after each tutoring session.

- To protect patients' privacy, meet them only in designated visiting and tutoring areas, never in their rooms.

- Treat patients with dignity and respect, even when (as sometimes happens) they grow frustrated and angry. Seek help from a nurse or orderly if you need it.

Side annotations:

Multicolumn format allowing room for headings, articles, and other elements on a single page

Two-column heading emphasizing the main article

Elements helping readers skim for highlights: spacing, varied font sizes, lines, and a bulleted list

Color focusing readers' attention on banner, headlines, and table of contents

Lively but uncluttered overall appearance

Box in the first column highlighting table of contents

example, you are writing letters to local businesses to raise funds for a homeless shelter, bring to mind the person or people who will read your letter. How can you best persuade those readers to donate money?

- **Expect to work with others.** Much public writing is the work of more than one person. Even if you draft the document on your own, others will review the content, tone, and design. Such collaboration is rewarding, but it sometimes requires patience and goodwill. See pages 39–41 for advice on collaborating.

See also pages 133–35 and 137–38 on letters and memos and pages 144–45 on *PowerPoint* presentations.

14a

14 Making Oral Presentations

How can I speak effectively to a group?

Oral presentation is partly writing, involving the same consideration of subject, audience, and purpose. Yet speechmaking and writing also differ, notably in that a listener cannot stop to rehear a section the way a reader can reread. Effective speakers use organization, voice, body language, and other techniques to help their audience listen.

14a Consider purpose and audience.

The most important step in developing an oral presentation is to identify your purpose: what do you want your audience to know or do as a result of your speech? In school and work settings, you're likely to be speaking for the same reasons that you write: to explain something to listeners or to persuade listeners to accept your opinion or take an action. See pages 6–7 for more on these purposes.

Adapting to your audience is a critical task in public speaking as well as in writing. You'll want to consider the questions about audience on page 8. But a listening audience requires additional considerations as well:

- **Why is your audience assembled?** Listeners who are required to attend may be more difficult to interest and motivate than

mycomplab

Visit *mycomplab.com* for more resources as well as exercises on oral presentations.

listeners who attend because they want to hear you and your ideas.

- **How large is your audience?** With a small group you can be informal. If you are speaking to a hundred or more people, you may need a public address system, a lectern, special lighting, and audiovisual equipment.
- **Where will you speak?** Your approach should match the setting—more casual for a small classroom, more formal for an auditorium.
- **How long are you scheduled to speak?** Whatever your time limit, stick to it. Audiences lose patience when speeches run longer than expected.

14b

14b Organize the presentation.

Give your oral presentation a recognizable shape so that listeners can see how ideas and details relate to each other.

The introduction

The beginning of an oral presentation should try to accomplish three goals:

- **Gain the audience's attention and interest.** Begin with a question, an unusual example or statistic, or a short, relevant story.
- **Put yourself in the speech.** Demonstrate your expertise, experience, or concern to gain the interest and trust of your audience.
- **Introduce and preview your topic and purpose.** By the time your introduction is over, listeners should know what your subject is and the direction you'll take to develop your ideas.

Your introduction should prepare your audience for your main points but not give them away. Think of it as a sneak preview of your speech, not the place for an apology such as *I wish I'd had more time to prepare . . .* or a dull statement such as *My speech is about. . . .*

Supporting material

Just as you do when writing, you should use facts, statistics, examples, and expert opinions to support the main points of your oral presentation. In addition, you can make your points more memorable with vivid description, well-chosen quotations, true or fictional stories, and analogies.

The conclusion

You want your conclusion to be clear, of course, but you also want it to be memorable. Remind listeners of how your topic and main idea connect to their needs and interests. If your speech was motivational, tap an emotion that matches your message. If your speech was informational, give some tips on how to remember important details.

14c Deliver the presentation.

Methods of delivery

You can deliver an oral presentation in several ways:

- **Impromptu, without preparation:** Make a presentation without planning exactly what you will say. Impromptu speaking requires confidence and excellent general preparation.
- **Extemporaneously:** Prepare notes to glance at but not read from. This method allows you to look and sound natural while ensuring that you don't forget anything.
- **Speaking from a text:** Read aloud from a written presentation. You won't lose your way, but you may lose your audience. Avoid reading for an entire presentation.
- **Speaking from memory:** Deliver a prepared presentation without notes. You can look at your audience every minute, but the stress of retrieving the next words may make you seem tense and unresponsive.

Vocal delivery

The sound of your voice will influence how listeners receive you. Rehearse your presentation several times until you are confident that you are speaking loudly, slowly, and clearly enough for your audience to understand you.

Physical delivery

You are more than your spoken words when you make an oral presentation. If you are able, stand up to deliver your presentation, turning your body toward one side of the room and then the other, stepping out from behind any lectern or desk, and gesturing as appropriate. Above all, make eye contact with your audience as you speak. Looking directly in your listeners' eyes conveys your honesty, your confidence, and your control of the material.

Visual aids

You can supplement an oral presentation with visual aids such as posters, models, slides, or videos.

- **Use visual aids to underscore your points.** Short lists of key ideas, illustrations such as graphs or photographs, or objects such as models can make your presentation more interesting and memorable. But use visual aids judiciously: a battery of illustrations or objects will bury your message rather than amplify it.

- **Coordinate visual aids with your message.** Time each visual to reinforce a point you're making. Tell listeners what they're looking at. Give them enough viewing time so that they don't mind turning their attention back to you.

- **Show visual aids only while they're needed.** To regain your audience's attention, remove or turn off any aid as soon as you have finished with it.

Many speakers use *PowerPoint* or other software to project main points, key images, video, or other elements. To use *PowerPoint* or other software effectively, follow the guidelines in the samples below and the tips on the next page.

PowerPoint slides

First slide, introducing the project and presentation

Simple, consistent slide design focusing viewers' attention on information, not *PowerPoint* features

Later slide, using brief, bulleted points to be explained by the speaker

Photographs reinforcing the project's activities

- **Don't put your whole presentation on screen.** Select key points, and distill them to as few words as possible. Think of the slides as quick, easy-to-remember summaries.
- **Use a simple design.** Avoid turning your presentation into a show about the software's many capabilities.
- **Use a consistent design.** For optimal flow through the presentation, each slide should be formatted similarly.
- **Add only relevant illustrations.** Avoid loading the presentation with mere decoration.

Practice

14c

Take time to rehearse your presentation out loud, with the notes you will be using. Gauge your performance by making an audio- or videotape of yourself or by practicing in front of a mirror. Practicing out loud will also tell you if your presentation is running too long or too short.

If you plan to use visual aids, you'll need to practice with them, too. Your goal is to eliminate hitches (upside-down slides, missing charts) and to weave the visuals seamlessly into your presentation.

Stage fright

Many people report that speaking in front of an audience is their number-one fear. Even many experienced and polished speakers have some anxiety about delivering an oral presentation, but they use this nervous energy to their advantage, letting it propel them into working hard on each presentation. Several techniques can help you reduce anxiety:

- **Use simple relaxation exercises.** Deep breathing or tensing and relaxing your stomach muscles can ease some of the physical symptoms of speech anxiety—stomachache, rapid heartbeat, and shaky hands, legs, and voice.
- **Think positively.** Instead of worrying about the mistakes you might make, concentrate on how well you've prepared and practiced your presentation and how significant your ideas are.
- **Don't avoid opportunities to speak in public.** Practice and experience build speaking skills and offer the best insurance for success.

15 Emphasis

When you speak, your tone of voice, facial expressions, and even hand gestures work with your words and sentences to convey your meaning. When you write, your words and sentences must do that work alone. To write exactly what you mean, edit to emphasize the main ideas in your sentences by attending to your subjects and verbs (below), using sentence beginnings and endings (p. 151), coordinating equally important ideas (p. 153), and subordinating less important ideas (p. 156). In addition, emphatic writing is concise writing, the subject of Chapter 20.

Grammar checkers A grammar checker may spot some problems with emphasis, such as nouns made from verbs, passive voice, wordy phrases, and long sentences that may also be flabby and unemphatic. However, no checker can help you identify the important ideas in your sentences or tell you whether those ideas receive appropriate emphasis for your meaning.

emph
15a

15a Use subjects and verbs for key actors and actions.

The heart of every sentence is its subject, which usually names the actor, and its predicate verb, which usually specifies the subject's action: *Children* [subject] *grow* [verb]. When these elements do not identify the key actor and action in the sentence, readers must find that information elsewhere and the sentence may be wordy and unemphatic.

In the next sentences, the subjects and verbs are underlined.

> Unemphatic   The <u>intention</u> of the company <u>was</u> to expand its work-force. A <u>proposal</u> <u>was</u> also <u>made</u> to diversify the backgrounds and abilities of employees.

These sentences are unemphatic because their key ideas do not appear in their subjects and verbs. Revised as shown on the facing page, the sentences are not only clearer but more concise.

┌ **Key terms** ─────────────────────────────
subject Who or what a sentence is about: *Birds fly*. (See p. 202.)

predicate The part of a sentence containing a verb that asserts something about the subject: *Birds fly*. (See p. 202.)
└─────────────────────────────────────

> mycomplab
>
> Visit *mycomplab.com* for more resources and exercises on emphasis.

| Revised | The <u>company intended</u> to expand its workforce. <u>It</u> also <u>proposed</u> to diversify the backgrounds and abilities of employees. |

The constructions discussed below and on the next page usually drain meaning from a sentence's subject and verb.

Nouns made from verbs

Nouns made from verbs can obscure the key actions of sentences and add words. These nouns include *intention* (from *intend*), *proposal* (from *propose*), *decision* (from *decide*), *expectation* (from *expect*), *persistence* (from *persist*), *argument* (from *argue*), and *inclusion* (from *include*).

| Unemphatic | After the company made a <u>decision</u> to hire more workers with disabilities, its next step was the <u>construction</u> of wheelchair ramps and other facilities. |
| Revised | After the company <u>decided</u> to hire more workers with disabilities, it next <u>constructed</u> wheelchair ramps and other facilities. |

emph

15a

Weak verbs

Weak verbs, such as *made* and *was* in the unemphatic sentence above, tend to stall sentences just where they should be moving and often bury key actions:

| Unemphatic | The company <u>is</u> now the leader among businesses in complying with the 1990 disabilities act. Its officers <u>make</u> frequent speeches on the act to business groups. |
| Revised | The company now <u>leads</u> other businesses in complying with the 1990 disabilities act. Its officers frequently <u>speak</u> on the act to business groups. |

Forms of *be, have,* and *make* are often weak, but don't try to eliminate every use of them: *be* and *have* are essential as helping verbs (*is going, has written*); *be* links subjects and words describing them (*Planes are noisy*); and *have* and *make* have independent meanings (among them "possess" and "force," respectively). But do consider replacing forms of *be, have,* and *make* when one of the words after the verb could be made into a strong verb itself, as in the following examples.

> **Key terms**
>
> **noun** A word that names a person, thing, quality, place, or idea: *student, desk, happiness, city, democracy.* (See p. 194.)
>
> **helping verb** A verb used with another verb to convey time, obligation, and other meanings: *was drilling, would have been drilling.* (See p. 197.)

Unemphatic	Emphatic
was influential	influenced
have a preference	prefer
had the appearance	appeared, seemed
made a claim	claimed

Passive voice

Verbs in the passive voice state actions received by, not performed by, their subjects. Thus the passive de-emphasizes the true actor of the sentence, sometimes omitting it entirely. Generally, prefer the active voice, in which the subject performs the action.

Unemphatic	The 1990 law is seen by most businesses as fair, but the costs of complying have sometimes been objected to.
Revised	Most businesses see the 1990 law as fair, but some have objected to the costs of complying.

See also pages 244–45 for appropriate uses of the passive voice and for help editing it.

emph
15a

Exercise 15.1   Revising: Emphasis of subjects and verbs

Rewrite the following sentences so that their subjects and verbs identify their key actors and actions. Answers to starred items appear at the end of the book.

Example:

The issue of students making a competition over grades is a reason why their focus on learning may be lost.

Students who compete over grades may lose their focus on learning.

*1. The work of many heroes was crucial in helping to emancipate the slaves.

*2. The contribution of Harriet Tubman, an escaped slave herself, included the guidance of hundreds of other slaves to freedom on the Underground Railroad.

3. A return to slavery was risked by Tubman or possibly death.
4. During the Civil War she was also a carrier of information from the South to the North.
5. After the war, needy former slaves were helped by Tubman's raising of money.

Key terms

passive voice The verb form when the subject names the *receiver* of the verb's action: *The house was destroyed by the tornado.*

active voice The verb form when the subject names the *performer* of the verb's action: *The tornado destroyed the house.*

15b   Use sentence beginnings and endings.

Readers automatically seek a writer's principal meaning in the main clause of a sentence—essentially, in the subject that names the actor and the predicate verb that usually specifies the action (see p. 148). Thus you can help readers understand your intended meaning by controlling the information in your subjects and the relation of the main clause to any modifiers attached to it.

Old and new information

Generally, readers expect the beginning of a sentence to contain information that they already know or that you have already introduced. They then look to the ending for new information. In the unemphatic passage below, the second and third sentences both begin with new topics, while the old topics appear at the ends of the sentences. The pattern of the passage is A→B. C→B. D→A.

> Unemphatic   Education often means controversy these days, with rising costs and constant complaints about its inadequacies. But the value of schooling should not be obscured by the controversy. The single best means of economic advancement, despite its shortcomings, remains education.

emph

15b

In the more emphatic revision below, old information begins each sentence and new information ends the sentence. The passage follows the pattern A→B. B→C. A→D.

> Revised   Education often means controversy these days, with rising costs and constant complaints about its inadequacies. But the controversy should not obscure the value of schooling. Education remains, despite its shortcomings, the single best means of economic advancement.

Key terms

main clause A word group that can stand alone as a sentence, containing a subject and a predicate and not beginning with a subordinating word: *The books were expensive.* (See p. 213.)

modifier A word or word group that describes another word or word group—for example, *sweet* candy, *running in the park.* (See pp. 198 and 270.)

Cumulative and periodic sentences

You can call attention to information by placing it first or last in a sentence, reserving the middle for incidentals:

Unemphatic	Education remains the single best means of economic advancement, despite its shortcomings. [Emphasizes shortcomings.]
Revised	Despite its shortcomings, education remains the single best means of economic advancement. [Emphasizes advancement more than shortcomings.]
Revised	Education remains, despite its shortcomings, the single best means of economic advancement. [De-emphasizes shortcomings.]

A sentence that begins with the main clause and then adds modifiers is called **cumulative** because it accumulates information as it proceeds:

Cumulative	Education has no equal in opening minds, instilling values, and creating opportunities.
Cumulative	Most of the Great American Desert is made up of bare rock, rugged cliffs, mesas, canyons, mountains, separated from one another by broad flat basins covered with sun-baked mud and alkali, supporting a sparse and measured growth of sagebrush or creosote or saltbush, depending on location and elevation. —Edward Abbey

The opposite kind of sentence, called **periodic,** saves the main clause until just before the end (the period) of the sentence. Everything before the main clause points toward it:

Periodic	In opening minds, instilling values, and creating opportunities, education has no equal.
Periodic	With people from all over the world—Korean doctors, Jamaican cricket players, Vietnamese engineers, Indian restaurant owners—the American mosaic is continually changing.

The periodic sentence creates suspense by reserving important information for the end. But readers should already have an idea of the sentence's subject—because it appeared in the preceding sentence—so that they know what the opening modifiers describe.

emph

15b

Exercise 15.2   Sentence combining: Beginnings and endings

Locate the main idea in each numbered group of sentences. Then combine each group into a single sentence that emphasizes that idea by placing it at the beginning or the end. For sentences 2–5, determine the position of the main idea by considering its relation to the previous sentences: if the main idea picks up a topic that's already been introduced, place it at the beginning; if it adds new information, place it at the end. Possible answers to starred items appear at the end of the book.

Example:

The storm blew roofs off buildings. It caused extensive damage. It knocked down many trees. It severed power lines.

Main idea at beginning: <u>The storm caused extensive damage</u>, blowing roofs off buildings, knocking down many trees, and severing power lines.

Main idea at end: Blowing roofs off buildings, knocking down many trees, and severing power lines, <u>the storm caused extensive damage</u>.

*1. Pat Taylor strode into the room. The room was packed. He greeted students called "Taylor's Kids." He nodded to their parents and teachers.

*2. This was a wealthy Louisiana oilman. He had promised his "Kids" free college educations. He was determined to make higher education available to all qualified but disadvantaged students.

3. The students welcomed Taylor. Their voices joined in singing. They sang "You Are the Wind Beneath My Wings." Their faces beamed with hope. Their eyes flashed with self-confidence.

4. The students had thought a college education was beyond their dreams. It seemed too costly. It seemed too demanding.

5. Taylor had to ease the costs and the demands of getting to college. He created a bold plan. The plan consisted of scholarships, tutoring, and counseling.

coord

15c

15c   Use coordination to relate equal ideas.

Use **coordination** to show that two or more elements in a sentence are equally important in meaning and thus to clarify the relation between them:

- **Link two main clauses with a comma and a coordinating conjunction,** such as *and* or *but*.

  ⎯⎯ equally important ⎯⎯→

  Independence Hall in Philadelphia is now restored, <u>but</u> fifty years ago it was in bad shape.

- **Link two main clauses with a semicolon alone or with a semicolon and a conjunctive adverb,** such as *however*.

  ⎯⎯ equally important ⎯⎯→

  The building was standing; <u>however,</u> it suffered from decay.

- **Within clauses, link words and phrases with a coordinating conjunction,** such as *and* or *or*.

equally
important
The people and officials of the nation were indifferent to Indepen-
equally important
dence Hall or took it for granted.

- **Link main clauses, words, or phrases with a correlative conjunction,** such as *not only . . . but also.*

equally important
People not only took the building for granted but also neglected it.

For the punctuation of coordinate elements, see pages 311 (comma and coordinating conjunction), 324 (coordinating conjunction alone), and 327–28 (semicolon alone or with a conjunctive adverb).

Grammar checkers Grammar and style checkers may spot some errors in punctuating coordinated elements, and they can flag long sentences that may contain excessive coordination. But otherwise they provide little help with coordination because they cannot recognize the relations among ideas in sentences.

coord

15c

1 ▪ Coordinating to smooth sentences

Coordination shows the equality between elements, as illustrated above. At the same time as it clarifies meaning, it can also help smooth choppy sentences like these:

| Choppy sentences | We should not rely so heavily on oil. Coal and uranium are also overused. We have a substantial energy resource in the moving waters of our rivers. Smaller streams add to the total volume of water. The resource renews itself. Coal and oil are irreplaceable. Uranium is also irreplaceable. The cost of water does not increase much over time. The costs of coal, oil, and uranium rise dramatically. |

The following revision groups coal, oil, and uranium and clearly opposes them to water (the connecting words are underlined):

| Ideas coordinated | We should not rely so heavily on coal, oil, and uranium, for we have a substantial energy resource in the moving waters of our rivers and streams. Coal, oil, and uranium are irreplaceable and thus subject to dramatic cost increases; water, however, is self-renewing and more stable in cost. |

Key terms

coordinating conjunctions *And, but, or, nor,* and sometimes *for, so, yet.* (See p. 200.)

conjunctive adverbs Modifiers that describe the relation of the ideas in two clauses, such as *hence, however, indeed,* and *thus.* (See p. 297.)

correlative conjunctions Pairs of connecting words, such as *both . . . and, either . . . or, not only . . . but also.* (See p. 200.)

2 ■ Coordinating effectively

Use coordination only to express the *equality* of ideas or details. A string of coordinated elements—especially main clauses—implies that all points are equally important:

Excessive coordination	The weeks leading up to the resignation of President Nixon were eventful, and the Supreme Court and the Congress closed in on him, and the Senate Judiciary Committee voted to begin impeachment proceedings, and finally the President resigned on August 9, 1974.

Such a passage needs editing to stress the important points in the main clauses (underlined below) and to de-emphasize the less important information:

Revised	The weeks leading up to the resignation of President Nixon were eventful, as the Supreme Court and the Congress closed in on him and the Senate Judiciary Committee voted to begin impeachment proceedings. Finally, the President resigned on August 9, 1974.

coord
15c

Even within a single sentence, coordination should express a logical equality between ideas:

Faulty	John Stuart Mill was a nineteenth-century utilitarian, and he believed that actions should be judged by their usefulness or by the happiness they cause. [The two clauses are not separate and equal: the second expands on the first by explaining what a utilitarian such as Mill believed.]
Revised	John Stuart Mill, a nineteenth-century utilitarian, believed that actions should be judged by their usefulness or by the happiness they cause.

Exercise 15.3   Revising: Excessive or faulty coordination

Revise the following sentences to eliminate excessive or faulty coordination by adding or subordinating information or by forming more than one sentence. Each item has more than one answer. Possible answers to starred items appear at the end of the book.

Example:

My dog barks, and I have to move out of my apartment.

Because my dog's barking disturbs my neighbors, I have to move out of my apartment.

*1. Often soldiers admired their commanding officers, and they gave them nicknames, and these names frequently contained the word *old,* but not all of the commanders were old.

*2. General Thomas "Stonewall" Jackson was also called "Old Jack," and he was not yet forty years old.

3. Another Southern general in the Civil War was called "Old Pete," and his full name was James Longstreet.

4. The Union general Henry W. Halleck had a reputation as a good military strategist, and he was an expert on the work of a French military authority, Henri Jomini, and Halleck was called "Old Brains."

5. General William Henry Harrison won the Battle of Tippecanoe, and he received the nickname "Old Tippecanoe," and he used the name in his presidential campaign slogan, "Tippecanoe and Tyler, Too," and he won the election in 1840, but he died of pneumonia a month after taking office.

15d   Use subordination to emphasize ideas.

Use **subordination** to indicate that some elements in a sentence are less important than others for your meaning. Usually, the main idea appears in the main clause, and supporting details appear in subordinate structures:

- Use a subordinate clause beginning with *although, because, if, until, who* (*whom*), *that, which,* or another subordinating word:

```
                                              more important
     ┌── less important (subordinate clause) ──┐  ┌─(main clause)─┐
     Although production costs have declined, they are still high.
```

```
                       less important
              ┌────────(subordinate clause)────────┐
     Costs, which include labor and facilities, are difficult to control.
     └──────────more important (main clause)────────→
```

- Use a phrase:

```
           less important              more important
     ┌────────(phrase)────────┐  ┌────────(main clause)────────┐
     Despite some decline, production costs are still high.
```

```
              ┌──less important (phrase)──┐
     Costs, including labor and facilities, are difficult to control.
     └─────── more important (main clause)──→
```

- Use a single word:

Declining costs have not matched prices.
Labor costs are difficult to control.

For punctuating subordinate elements, see pages 313–14 (comma with introductory elements) and 315–19 (commas with interrupting elements).

> **Key terms**
>
> **subordinate clause** A word group that contains a subject and a predicate, begins with a subordinating word such as *because* or *who,* and is not a question: *Words can do damage when they hurt feelings.* (See p. 213.)
>
> **phrase** A word group that lacks a subject or predicate or both: *Words can do damage by hurting feelings.* (See p. 210.)

sub
15d

Grammar checkers A grammar checker may spot some errors in punctuating subordinated elements, and it can usually flag long sentences that may contain excessive subordination. But otherwise a checker can provide little help with subordination because it cannot recognize the relations among ideas in sentences.

1 ▪ Subordinating to distinguish important ideas

A string of main clauses can make everything in a passage seem equally important:

String of main clauses	Computer prices have dropped, and production costs have dropped more slowly, and computer manufacturers have struggled, for their profits have been shrinking.

Emphasis comes from keeping the important information in the main clause (underlined) and subordinating less important details:

Revised	Because production costs have dropped more slowly than prices, computer manufacturers have struggled with shrinking profits.

sub
15d

2 ▪ Subordinating effectively

In subordinating elements within a sentence, be careful to keep relationships clear:

▪ **Subordinate only the less important information in the sentence.** Faulty subordination reverses the dependent relation that the reader expects:

Faulty	Ms. Angelo was in her first year of teaching, although she was a better instructor than others with many years of experience. [The sentence suggests that Angelo's inexperience is the main idea, whereas the writer meant to stress her skill *despite* her inexperience.]
Revised	Although Ms. Angelo was in her first year of teaching, she was a better instructor than others with many years of experience.

▪ **Avoid crowding loosely related details into one long sentence.**

Overloaded	The boats that were moored at the dock when the hurricane, which was one of the worst in three decades, struck were ripped from their moorings, because the owners had not been adequately prepared, since the weather service had predicted that the storm would blow out to sea, as storms do at this time of year.
Revised	Struck by one of the worst hurricanes in three decades, the boats at the dock were ripped from their moorings. The owners were unprepared because the weather service had said that hurricanes at this time of year blow out to sea.

- Avoid a dangling modifier—that is, a modifier that doesn't relate sensibly to the rest of the sentence. (See pp. 286–87.)

Dangling modifier	Driving through the region, the destruction from the storm was everywhere.
Revised	Driving through the region, we saw destruction from the storm everywhere.

Exercise 15.4   Revising: Faulty or excessive subordination

Revise the following sentences to eliminate faulty or excessive subordination and to achieve appropriate emphasis. Possible answers to starred items appear at the end of the book.

Example:

Terrified to return home, he had driven his mother's car into a cornfield.

Having driven his mother's car into a cornfield, he was terrified to return home.

sub

15d

*1. Genaro González is a successful writer, which means that his stories and novels have been published to critical acclaim.
*2. He loves to write, although he has also earned a doctorate in psychology.
3. His first story, which reflects his growing consciousness of his Aztec heritage and place in the world, is titled "Un Hijo del Sol."
4. González, who writes equally well in English and Spanish, received a large fellowship that enabled him to take a leave of absence from the University of Texas–Pan American, where he teaches psychology, so that he could write without worrying about an income.
5. González wrote the first version of "Un Hijo del Sol" while he was a sophomore at Pan American, which is in the Rio Grande valley of southern Texas, which González calls "el Valle" in the story.

Exercise 15.5   Revising: Coordination and subordination

The following paragraph consists entirely of simple sentences. Use coordination and subordination to combine sentences in the way you think most effective to emphasize main ideas. Possible answers to starred sentences appear at the end of the book.

   *Sir Walter Raleigh personified the Elizabethan Age. *That was the period of Elizabeth I's rule of England. *The period occurred in the last half of the sixteenth century. *Raleigh was a courtier and poet. *He was also an explorer and entrepreneur. *Supposedly, he gained Queen Elizabeth's favor. *He did this by throwing his cloak beneath her feet at the right moment. *She was just about to step over a puddle. There is no evidence for this story. It does illustrate Raleigh's dramatic and dynamic personality. His energy drew others to him. He was one of Elizabeth's favorites. She supported him. She also dispensed favors to him. However, he lost his queen's goodwill. Without her permission he seduced one of her maids of honor. He eventually married the maid of honor. Elizabeth died. Then her successor imprisoned Raleigh in the Tower of London. Her successor was James I. The king falsely charged Raleigh with treason. Raleigh was released after thirteen years. He was arrested again two years later on the old treason charges. At the age of sixty-six he was beheaded.

16 Parallelism

How can I make connections plain within sentences?

When ideas within sentences have the same function and importance, you can show their connection using parallelism, or parallel structure, as shown in the following example:

The air is dirtied by <u>factories belching smoke</u> and <u>cars spewing exhaust</u>.

//
16a

With **parallelism,** you use the same grammatical forms to express equally important ideas. In the example above, the two underlined phrases have the same function and importance (two sources of air pollution), so they also have the same grammatical construction.

Grammar checkers A grammar checker cannot recognize faulty parallelism because it cannot recognize the relations among ideas.

16a   Use parallelism with *and, but, or, nor, yet.*

The coordinating conjunctions *and, but, or, nor,* and *yet* always signal a need for parallelism, as shown in the following examples.

The industrial base was <u>shifting</u> and <u>shrinking</u>. [Parallel words.]

Politicians rarely <u>acknowledged the problem</u> or <u>proposed alternatives</u>. [Parallel phrases.]

Industrial workers were understandably disturbed <u>that they were losing their jobs</u> and <u>that no one seemed to care</u>. [Parallel clauses.]

> ┌─ **Key term** ─────────────────────────────
> **coordinating conjunctions** Words that connect elements of the same kind and importance: *and, but, or, nor,* and sometimes *for, so, yet.* (See p. 200.)

> **mycomplab**
>
> Visit *mycomplab.com* for more resources and exercises on parallelism.

When sentence elements linked by coordinating conjunctions are not parallel in structure, the sentence is awkward and distracting:

Nonparallel   The reasons steel companies kept losing money were <u>that their plants were inefficient</u>, <u>high labor costs</u>, and <u>foreign competition was increasing</u>.

Revised   The reasons steel companies kept losing money were <u>inefficient plants</u>, <u>high labor costs</u>, and <u>increasing foreign competition</u>.

Nonparallel   Success was difficult even for efficient companies because <u>of the shift away from all manufacturing in the United States</u> and <u>the fact that steel production was shifting toward emerging nations</u>.

Revised   Success was difficult even for efficient companies because <u>of the shift away from all manufacturing in the United States</u> and <u>toward steel production in emerging nations</u>.

All the words required by idiom or grammar must be stated in compound constructions (see also p. 185):

Faulty   Given training, workers can acquire the <u>skills</u> and <u>interest</u> in other jobs. [Idiom dictates different prepositions with *skills* and *interest*.]

Revised   Given training, workers can acquire the skills <u>for</u> and interest in other jobs.

16b   Use parallelism with *both . . . and, not . . . but,* or another correlative conjunction.

Correlative conjunctions stress equality and balance between elements. Parallelism confirms the equality.

It is not <u>a tax bill</u> but <u>a tax relief bill</u>, providing relief not <u>for the needy</u> but <u>for the greedy</u>.   —Franklin Delano Roosevelt

With correlative conjunctions, the element after the second connector must match the element after the first connector:

Nonparallel   Huck Finn learns not only <u>that human beings have an enormous capacity for folly</u> but also <u>enormous dignity</u>. [The first element includes *that human beings have;* the second element does not.]

┌─ Key term ───
correlative conjunctions Pairs of words that connect elements of the same kind and importance, such as *both . . . and, either . . . or, neither . . . nor, not . . . but, not only . . . but also.* (See p. 200.)
└──

Revised   Huck Finn learns that human beings have not only an
               enormous capacity for folly but also enormous dignity.
               [Repositioning *that human beings have* makes the two ele-
               ments parallel.]

16c   Use parallelism in comparisons.

Parallelism confirms the likeness or difference between two elements being compared using *than* or *as.*

Nonparallel   Huck Finn proves less a bad boy than to be an indepen-
               dent spirit. In the end he is every bit as determined in re-
               jecting help as he is to leave for "the territory."
Revised   Huck Finn proves less a bad boy than an independent
               spirit. In the end he is every bit as determined to reject
               help as he is to leave for "the territory."

(See also pp. 273–74 on making comparisons logical.)

16d   Use parallelism in lists, headings, and outlines.

//
16d

The items in a list or outline are coordinate and should be parallel. Parallelism is essential in the headings that divide a paper into
sections (see p. 69) and in a formal topic outline (see pp. 22–23).

Nonparallel	Revised
Changes in Renaissance England	Changes in Renaissance England
1. Extension of trade routes	1. Extension of trade routes
2. Merchant class became more powerful	2. Increased power of the merchant class
3. The death of feudalism	3. Death of feudalism
4. Upsurging of the arts	4. Upsurge of the arts
5. Religious quarrels began	5. Rise of religious quarrels

Exercise 16.1   Revising: Parallelism

Revise the following sentences to create parallelism wherever it is required for grammar and coherence. Add or delete words or rephrase as
necessary. Answers to starred items appear at the end of the book.

Example:

After emptying her bag, searching the apartment, and she called
the library, Jennifer realized she had lost the book.

After emptying her bag, searching the apartment, and calling the library, Jennifer realized she had lost the book.

*1.   The ancient Greeks celebrated four athletic contests: the Olympic
      Games at Olympia, the Isthmian Games were held near Corinth, at

Delphi the Pythian Games, and the Nemean Games were sponsored by the people of Cleonae.
* 2. Each day the games consisted of either athletic events or holding ceremonies and sacrifices to the gods.
* 3. In the years between the games, competitors were taught wrestling, javelin throwing, and how to box.
* 4. Competitors participated in running sprints, spectacular chariot and horse races, and running long distances while wearing full armor.
* 5. The purpose of such events was developing physical strength, demonstrating skill and endurance, and to sharpen the skills needed for war.

6. Events were held for both men and for boys.
7. At the Olympic Games the spectators cheered their favorites to victory, attended sacrifices to the gods, and they feasted on the meat not burned in offerings.
8. The athletes competed less to achieve great wealth than for gaining honor both for themselves and their cities.
9. Of course, exceptional athletes received financial support from patrons, poems and statues by admiring artists, and they even got lavish living quarters from their sponsoring cities.
10. With the medal counts and flag ceremonies, today's Olympians sometimes seem to be proving their countries' superiority more than to demonstrate individual talent.

//
16

Exercise 16.2 Sentence combining: Parallelism

Combine each of the following groups of sentences into one concise sentence that uses parallel structure for parallel elements. You will have to add, delete, change, and rearrange words. Each item has more than one possible answer. Answers to starred items appear at the end of the book.

Example:

The new process works smoothly. It is efficient, too.
The new process works smoothly and <u>efficiently</u>.

* 1. People can develop post-traumatic stress disorder (PTSD). They develop it after experiencing a dangerous situation. They will also have felt fear for their survival.
* 2. The disorder can be triggered by a wide variety of events. Combat is a typical cause. Similarly, natural disasters can result in PTSD. Some people experience PTSD after a hostage situation.

3. PTSD can occur immediately after the stressful incident. Or it may not appear until many years later.
4. Sometimes people with PTSD will act irrationally. Moreover, they often become angry.
5. Other symptoms include dreaming that one is reliving the experience. They include hallucinating that one is back in the terrifying place. In another symptom one imagines that strangers are actually one's former torturers.

17 Variety and Details

Writing that is interesting as well as clear has at least two features: the sentences vary in length and structure, and they are well textured with details.

Grammar checkers Some grammar checkers will flag long sentences, and you can check for appropriate variety in a series of such sentences. But generally these programs cannot help you see where variety may be needed because they cannot recognize the relative importance and complexity of your ideas. Nor can they suggest where you should add details.

17a Vary sentence length.

In most contemporary writing, sentences tend to vary from about ten to about forty words, with an average between fifteen and twenty-five words. If your sentences are all at one extreme or the other, your readers may have difficulty focusing on main ideas and seeing the relations among them.

- **Long sentences.** If most of your sentences contain thirty-five words or more, your main ideas may not stand out from the details that support them. To give the main ideas more emphasis, separate them from the details by breaking them out into their own shorter, simpler sentences.
- **Short sentences.** If most of your sentences contain fewer than ten or fifteen words, all your ideas may seem equally important and the links between them may not be clear. Try combining sentences with coordination (p. 153) and subordination (p. 156) to show relationships and stress main ideas over supporting information.

17b Vary sentence structure.

A passage will be monotonous if all its sentences follow the same pattern, like soldiers marching in a parade. To vary structure, try subordination, sentence combining, varying sentence beginnings, and varying word order.

var
17b

mycomplab

Visit *mycomplab.com* for more resources and exercises on variety and details.

1 ▪ Subordination

A string of main clauses in simple or compound sentences can be especially plodding:

> Monotonous   The moon is now drifting away from the earth. It moves away at the rate of about one inch a year. This movement is lengthening our days. They increase a thousandth of a second every century. Forty-seven of our present days will someday make up a month. We might eventually lose the moon altogether. Such great planetary movement rightly concerns astronomers, but it need not worry us. It will take 50 million years.

Enliven such writing—and make the main ideas stand out—by expressing the less important information in subordinate clauses and phrases. In the following revision, underlining indicates subordinate structures that used to be main clauses.

> Revised   The moon is now drifting away from the earth <u>about one inch a year</u>. <u>At a thousandth of a second every century,</u> this movement is lengthening our days. Forty-seven of our present days will someday make up a month, <u>if we don't eventually lose the moon altogether</u>. Such great planetary movement rightly concerns astronomers, but it need not worry us. It will take 50 million years.

var

17b

2 ▪ Sentence combining

As the preceding example shows, subordinating to achieve variety often involves combining short, choppy sentences into longer units that link related information and stress main ideas. Here is another example of such sentence combining:

> Monotonous   Astronomy may seem a remote science. It may seem to have little to do with people's daily lives. Many astronomers find otherwise. They see their science as soothing. It gives perspective to everyday routines and problems.

┌ Key terms ──────────────────────────

main clause A word group that can stand alone as a sentence because it contains a subject and a predicate and does not begin with a subordinating word: *Tourism is an industry. It brings in over $2 billion a year.* (See p. 213.)

subordinate clause A word group that contains a subject and a predicate, begins with a subordinating word such as *because* or *who,* and is not a question: *Tourism is an industry <u>that brings in over $2 billion a year</u>.* (See p. 213.)

phrase A word group that lacks a subject or a predicate or both: *Tourism is an industry <u>valued at over $2 billion a year</u>.* (See p. 210.)

Combining five sentences into one, the revision is both clearer and easier to read. Underlining highlights the changes:

Revised   Astronomy may seem a remote science having little to do with people's daily lives, but many astronomers find their science soothing because it gives perspective to everyday routines and problems.

3 ▪ Varying sentence beginnings

An English sentence often begins with its subject, which generally captures old information from a preceding sentence (see p. 151):

The defendant's lawyer was determined to break the prosecution's witness. He relentlessly cross-examined the stubborn witness for a week.

However, an unbroken sequence of sentences beginning with the subject quickly becomes monotonous:

Monotonous   The defendant's lawyer was determined to break the prosecution's witness. He relentlessly cross-examined the witness for a week. The witness had expected to be dismissed within an hour and was visibly irritated. She did not cooperate. She was reprimanded by the judge.

var
17b

Beginning some of these sentences with other expressions improves readability and clarity:

Revised   The defendant's lawyer was determined to break the prosecution's witness. For a week he relentlessly cross-examined the witness. Expecting to be dismissed within an hour, the witness was visibly irritated. She did not cooperate. Indeed, she was reprimanded by the judge.

The underlined expressions represent the most common choices for varying sentence beginnings:

- **Adverb modifiers,** such as *For a week* (modifies the verb *cross-examined*).
- **Adjective modifiers,** such as *Expecting to be dismissed within an hour* (modifies *witness*).
- **Transitional expressions,** such as *Indeed*. (See the box on p. 50 for a list.)

┌─ **Key terms** ───
adverb A word or word group that describes a verb, an adjective, another adverb, or a whole sentence: *dressed sharply, clearly unhappy, soaring from the mountain*. (See p. 198.)

adjective A word or word group that describes a noun or pronoun: *sweet smile, certain someone*. (See p. 198.)
└──

CULTURE LANGUAGE In standard American English, placing certain adverb modifiers at the beginning of a sentence requires you to change the normal subject-verb order as well. The
most common of these modifiers are negatives, including *seldom,
rarely, in no case, not since,* and *not until.*

                                   verb
                adverb   subject   phrase
Faulty   Seldom a witness has held the stand so long.

                          helping   main
              adverb verb subject   verb
Revised   Seldom has a witness held the stand so long.

4 ▪ Varying word order

Occasionally, you can vary a sentence and emphasize it at the
same time by inverting the usual order of parts:

> A dozen witnesses testified for the prosecution, and the defense attorney
> barely questioned eleven of them. The twelfth, however, he grilled. [Nor-
> mal word order: *He grilled the twelfth, however.*]

17c

Inverted sentences used without need are artificial. Use them only
when emphasis demands.

17c Add details.

Relevant details such as facts and examples create the texture
and life that keep readers awake and help them grasp your meaning. Notice the difference in the following two examples.

Flat   Constructed after World War II, Levittown, New York, con-
             sisted of thousands of houses in two basic styles. Over the
             decades, residents have altered the houses so dramatically
             that the original styles are often unrecognizable.

Detailed Constructed on potato fields after World War II, Levittown,
             New York, consisted of more than seventeen thousand
             houses in Cape Cod and ranch styles. Over the decades, resi-
             dents have added expansive front porches, punched dormer
             windows through roofs, converted garages to sun porches,
             and otherwise altered the houses so dramatically that the
             original styles are often unrecognizable.

Note The details in the revised passage are effective because
they relate to the writer's point and make that point clearer. Details
that don't support and clarify your points will likely distract or annoy readers.

Exercise 17.1 **Revising: Variety**

The following paragraph consists entirely of simple sentences that begin
with their subjects. Use the techniques discussed in this chapter to vary

the sentences. Delete, add, change, and rearrange words to make the paragraph more readable and to make important ideas stand out clearly. Answers to starred sentences appear at the end of the book.

*The Italian volcano Vesuvius had been dormant for many years. *It then exploded on August 24 in the year AD 79. *The ash, pumice, and mud from the volcano buried two busy towns. *Herculaneum is one. *The more famous is Pompeii. Both towns lay undiscovered for many centuries. Herculaneum and Pompeii were discovered in 1709 and 1748, respectively. The excavation of Pompeii was the more systematic. It was the occasion for initiating modern methods of conservation and restoration. Herculaneum was simply looted of its more valuable finds. It was then left to disintegrate. Pompeii appears much as it did before the eruption. A luxurious house opens onto a lush central garden. An election poster decorates a wall. A dining table is set for breakfast.

18   Appropriate and Exact Words

appr
18a

Is this the right word?

The choice of the "right" word depends partly on whether the word is appropriate for your writing situation (below) and partly on whether it expresses your meaning exactly (p. 175).

18a   Choose appropriate words.

Appropriate words suit your writing situation—your subject, purpose, and audience. In most college and career writing you should rely on what's called **standard American English,** the dialect of English normally expected and used in schools, businesses, government, and the communications media. (For more on its role in academic writing, see pp. 98–100.)

The vocabulary of written standard English is huge, allowing you to express an infinite range of ideas and feelings. However, it does exclude words that only some groups of people use, understand, or find inoffensive. It also excludes words and expressions that are commonly spoken but are too imprecise for writing. Whenever you doubt a word's status, consult a dictionary (see p. 175). A

mycomplab

Visit *mycomplab.com* for more resources and exercises on appropriate and exact words.

label such as *nonstandard, slang,* or *colloquial* tells you that the word is not generally appropriate in academic or business writing.

Grammar checkers A grammar checker can be set to flag potentially inappropriate words, such as nonstandard language, slang, colloquialisms, and gender-specific terms (*manmade, mailman*). However, the checker can flag only words listed in its dictionary of questionable words. For example, a checker flagged *businessman* as potentially sexist in *A successful businessman puts clients first,* but the checker did not flag *his* in *A successful businessperson listens to his clients.* If you use a checker to review your language, you'll need to determine whether a flagged word is or is not appropriate for your writing situation.

1 ▪ Nonstandard dialect

appr

18a

Like many countries, the United States includes scores of regional, social, or ethnic groups with their own distinct **dialects,** or versions of English. Standard American English is one of those dialects, and so are African American English, Appalachian English, Creole, and the English of coastal Maine. All the dialects of English share many features, but each also has its own vocabulary, pronunciation, and grammar.

If you speak a dialect of English besides standard American English, be careful about using your dialect in situations where standard English is the norm, such as in academic or business writing. Dialects are not wrong in themselves, but forms imported from one dialect into another may still be perceived as unclear or incorrect. When you know standard English is expected in your writing, edit to eliminate expressions in your dialect that you know (or have been told) differ from standard English. These expressions may include *theirselves, hisn, them books,* and others labeled *nonstandard* by a dictionary. They may also include certain verb forms, as discussed on pages 222–28. For help identifying and editing nonstandard language, see the "CULTURE LANGUAGE Guide" just before the back endpapers of this book.

Your participation in the community of standard American English does not require you to abandon your own dialect. You may want to use it in writing you do for yourself, such as journals, notes, and drafts, which should be composed as freely as possible. You may want to quote it in an academic paper, as when analyzing or reporting conversation in dialect. And, of course, you will want to use it with others who speak it.

2 ▪ Shortcuts of online communication

Rapid communication by e-mail and text or instant messaging encourages some informalities that are inappropriate for academic writing. If you use these media frequently, you may need to proof-read your academic papers especially to identify and revise errors such as the following:

- **Sentence fragments.** Make sure every sentence has a subject and a predicate. Avoid fragments such as *Observing the results* or *After the meeting.* (See pp. 288–92.)
- **Missing punctuation.** Between and within sentences, use standard punctuation marks. Check especially for missing commas within sentences and missing apostrophes in possessives and contractions. (See pp. 310–23 and 333–38.)
- **Missing capital letters.** Use capital letters at the beginnings of sentences, for proper nouns and adjectives, and in titles. (See pp. 360–63.)
- **Nonstandard abbreviations and spellings.** Avoid forms such as *2* for *to* or *too, b4* for *before, bc* for *because, ur* for *you are* or *you're,* and *+* or *&* for *and.* (See pp. 352–56 and 367–69.)

3 ▪ Slang

appr
18a

Slang is the language used by a group, such as musicians or computer programmers, to reflect common experiences and to make technical references efficient. The following example is from an essay on the slang of "skaters" (skateboarders):

> Curtis slashed ultra-punk crunchers on his longboard, while the Rube-man flailed his usual Gumbyness on tweaked frontsides and lofty fakie ollies.
> —Miles Orkin, "Mucho Slingage by the Pool"

Among those who understand it, slang may be vivid and forceful. It often occurs in dialog, and an occasional slang expression can enliven an informal essay. But most slang is too flippant and imprecise for effective communication, and it is generally inappropriate for college or business writing. Notice the gain in seriousness and precision achieved in the following revision:

Slang   Many students start out <u>pretty together</u> but then <u>get weird</u>.

Revised   Many students start out <u>with clear goals</u> but then <u>lose their direction</u>.

4 ▪ Colloquial language

Colloquial language is the everyday spoken language, including expressions such as *get together, go crazy,* and *do the dirty work.*

When you write informally to friends and family, colloquial language can help you achieve the casual, relaxed effect of conversation. In academic and career writing, however, colloquial language is not precise enough to convey meaning exactly. You may drop an occasional colloquial expression into otherwise formal writing to achieve a desired effect, but generally avoid any words and expressions labeled *informal* or *colloquial* in your dictionary.

Colloquial	According to a Native American myth, the Great Creator <u>had a dog hanging around with him</u> when he created the earth.
Revised	According to a Native American myth, the Great Creator <u>was accompanied by a dog</u> when he created the earth.

5 ▪ Technical words

All disciplines and professions rely on specialized language that allows the members to communicate precisely and efficiently with each other. Chemists, for instance, have their *phosphatides,* and literary critics have their *motifs* and *subtexts.* Without explanation, technical words are meaningless to nonspecialists. When you are writing for nonspecialists, avoid unnecessary technical terms and carefully define terms you must use.

6 ▪ Indirect and pretentious writing

Small, plain, and direct words are almost always preferable to big, showy, or evasive words. Take special care to avoid euphemisms, double-talk, and pretentious writing.

A **euphemism** is a presumably inoffensive word that a writer or speaker substitutes for a word deemed potentially offensive or too blunt, such as *passed away* for *died, misspeak* for *lie,* or *remains* for *corpse.* Use euphemisms only when you know that blunt, truthful words would needlessly hurt or offend members of your audience.

A kind of euphemism that deliberately evades the truth is **double-talk** (also called **doublespeak** or **weasel words**): language intended to confuse or to be misunderstood. Today double-talk is unfortunately common in politics and advertising—the *revenue enhancement* that is really a tax, the *peace-keeping function* that is really war making, the *biodegradable* bags that last decades. Double-talk has no place in honest writing.

Euphemism and sometimes double-talk seem to keep company with **pretentious writing,** fancy language that is more elaborate than its subject requires. Choose your words for their exactness and economy. The big, ornate word may be tempting, but pass it up. Your readers will be grateful.

Pretentious	To perpetuate our endeavor of providing funds for our elderly citizens as we do at the present moment, we will face the exigency of enhanced contributions from all our citizens.
Revised	We cannot continue to fund Social Security and Medicare for the elderly unless we raise taxes.

7 ▪ Sexist and other biased language

Even when we do not mean it to, our language can reflect and perpetuate hurtful prejudices toward groups of people. Such biased language can be obvious—words such as *nigger, honky, mick, kike, fag, dyke,* and *broad.* But it can also be subtle, generalizing about groups in ways that may be familiar but that are also inaccurate or unfair.

Biased language reflects poorly on the user, not on the person or persons whom it mischaracterizes or insults. Unbiased language does not submit to false generalizations. It treats people respectfully as individuals and labels groups as they wish to be labeled.

Stereotypes of race, ethnicity, religion, age, and other characteristics

A **stereotype** is a generalization based on poor evidence, a kind of formula for understanding and judging people simply because of their membership in a group:

Men are uncommunicative.
Women are emotional.
Liberals want to raise taxes.
Conservatives are affluent.

appr
18a

At best, stereotypes betray a noncritical writer, one who is not thinking beyond notions received from others. In your writing, be alert for statements that characterize whole groups of people.

Stereotype	Elderly drivers should have their licenses limited to daytime driving only. [Asserts that all elderly people are poor night drivers.]
Revised	Drivers with impaired night vision should have their licenses limited to daytime driving only.

Some stereotypes have become part of the language, but they are still potentially offensive:

Stereotype	The administrators <u>are too blind</u> to see the need for a new gymnasium. [Equates vision loss and lack of understanding.]
Revised	The administrators <u>do not understand</u> the need for a new gymnasium.

Sexist language

Among the most subtle and persistent biased language is that expressing narrow ideas about men's and women's roles, position, and value in society. Like other stereotypes, this **sexist language** can wound or irritate readers, and it indicates the writer's thoughtlessness or unfairness. The following box suggests some ways of eliminating sexist language.

Eliminating sexist language

■ **Avoid demeaning and patronizing language:**

Sexist   Dr. Keith Kim and Lydia Hawkins coauthored the article.

Revised   Dr. Keith Kim and Dr. Lydia Hawkins coauthored the article.

Revised   Keith Kim and Lydia Hawkins coauthored the article.

Sexist   Ladies are entering almost every occupation formerly filled by men.

Revised   Women are entering almost every occupation formerly filled by men.

■ **Avoid occupational or social stereotypes:**

Sexist   The considerate doctor commends a nurse when she provides his patients with good care.

Revised   The considerate doctor commends a nurse who provides good care for patients.

Sexist   The grocery shopper should save her coupons.

Revised   Grocery shoppers should save their coupons.

■ **Avoid referring needlessly to gender:**

Sexist   Marie Curie, a woman chemist, discovered radium.

Revised   Marie Curie, a chemist, discovered radium.

Sexist   The patients were tended by a male nurse.

Revised   The patients were tended by a nurse.

However, don't overcorrect by avoiding appropriate references to gender: *Pregnant women* [not *people*] *should avoid drinking alcohol.*

■ **Avoid using *man* or words containing *man* to refer to all human beings.** Here are a few alternatives:

businessman	businessperson
chairman	chair, chairperson
congressman	representative, congressperson, legislator
craftsman	craftsperson, artisan
layman	layperson
mankind	humankind, humanity, human beings, humans
manmade	handmade, manufactured, synthetic, artificial
manpower	personnel, human resources
policeman	police officer
salesman	salesperson

Sexist   Man has not reached the limits of social justice.

Revised   Humankind [or Humanity] has not reached the limits of social justice.

Sexist   The furniture consists of manmade materials.

Revised   The furniture consists of synthetic materials.

appr
18a

■ **Avoid the generic *he*, the male pronoun used to refer to both genders.** (See also pp. 262–64.)

Sexist   The newborn child explores his world.

Revised   Newborn children explore their world. [Use the plural for the pronoun and the word it refers to.]

Revised   The newborn child explores the world. [Avoid the pronoun altogether.]

Revised   The newborn child explores his or her world. [Substitute male and female pronouns.]

Use the last option sparingly—only once in a group of sentences and only to stress the singular individual.

(CULTURE LANGUAGE) Forms of address vary widely from culture to culture. In some cultures, for instance, one shows respect by referring to all older women as if they were married, using the equivalent of *Mrs.* Usage in the United States is changing toward making no assumptions about marital status, rank, or other characteristics—for instance, addressing a woman as *Ms.* unless she is known to prefer *Mrs.* or *Miss.*

appr
18a

Appropriate labels

We often need to label groups: *swimmers, politicians, mothers, Christians, Westerners, students.* But labels can be shorthand stereotypes, slighting the person labeled and ignoring the preferences of the group members themselves. Although sometimes dismissed as "political correctness," showing sensitivity about labels hurts no one and helps gain your readers' trust and respect.

■ **Avoid labels that (intentionally or not) disparage the person or group you refer to.** A person with emotional problems is not a *mental patient.* A person with cancer is not a *cancer victim.* A person using a wheelchair is not *wheelchair-bound.*

■ **Use names for racial, ethnic, and other groups that reflect the preferences of each group's members,** or at least many of them. Examples of current preferences include *African American* or *black, latino/latina* (for Americans and American immigrants of Spanish-speaking descent), and *people with disabilities* (rather than *the disabled* or *the handicapped*). But labels change often. To learn how a group's members wish to be labeled, ask them directly, attend to usage in reputable periodicals, or check a recent dictionary.

■ **Identify a person's group only when it is relevant to the point you're making.** Consider the context of the label: Is it a necessary piece of information? If not, don't use it.

A helpful reference is *Guidelines for Bias-Free Writing,* by Marilyn Schwartz and the Task Force on Bias-Free Language of the Association of American University Presses.

appr
18a

Exercise 18.1 Revising: Appropriate words

Rewrite the following sentences as needed for standard American English, focusing on inappropriate slang, technical or pretentious language, and biased language. Consult a dictionary to determine whether particular words are appropriate and to find suitable substitutes. Answers to starred items appear at the end of the book.

Example:

If negotiators get hyper during contract discussions, they may mess up chances for a settlement.

If negotiators become excited or upset during contract discussions, they may harm chances for a settlement.

*1. Acquired immune deficiency syndrome (AIDS) is a major deal all over the world.

*2. The disease gets around primarily by sexual intercourse, exchange of bodily fluids, shared needles, and blood transfusions.

*3. Those who think the disease is limited to homos, druggies, and foreigners are quite mistaken.

*4. Stats suggest that in the United States one in every five hundred college kids carries the HIV virus that causes AIDS.

*5. A person with HIV or full-blown AIDS does not deserve to be subjected to exclusionary behavior or callousness on the part of his fellow citizens. Instead, he has the necessity for all the compassion, medical care, and financial assistance due those who are in the extremity of illness.

6. An HIV or AIDS victim often sees a team of doctors or a single doctor with a specialized practice.

7. The doctor may help his patients by obtaining social services for them as well as by providing medical care.

8. The HIV or AIDS sufferer who loses his job may need public assistance.

9. For someone who is very ill, a home-care nurse may be necessary. She can administer medications and make the sick person as comfortable as possible.

10. Some people with HIV or AIDS have insurance, but others lack the dough for premiums.

Exercise 18.2 Revising: Sexist language

Revise the following sentences to eliminate sexist language. If you change a singular noun or pronoun to plural, be sure to make any needed changes in verbs or other pronouns. Answers to starred items appear at the end of the book.

Example:

The career placement officer at most colleges and universities spends part of his time advising students how to write successful résumés.

Career placement officers at most colleges and universities spend part of their time advising students how to write successful résumés.

*1. When a person applies for a job, he should represent himself with the best possible résumé.

*2. A person applying for a job as a mailman should appear to be honest and responsible.

*3. A girl applying for a position as an in-home nurse should also represent herself as honest and responsible.

*4. Of course, she should also have a background of capable nursing.

*5. The businessman who is scanning a stack of résumés will, of necessity, read them all quickly.

6. The person who wants his résumé to stand out will make sure it highlights his best points.

7. The Web designer will highlight his experience with computers.

8. Volunteer work may be appropriate, too, such as being chairman of a student organization.

9. If the student has been secretary for a campus organization, she could include that volunteer experience in her résumé.

10. If the applicant writing a résumé would keep in mind the man who will be reading it, he might know better what he should include.

exact
18b

18b   Choose exact words.

To write clearly and effectively, you will want to find the words that fit your meaning exactly and convey your attitude precisely.

Grammar checkers A grammar checker can provide some help with inexact language. For instance, you can set it to flag commonly confused words (such as *continuous/continual*), misused prepositions in idioms (such as *accuse for* instead of *accuse of*), and clichés. But a checker can't help you at all with appropriate connotation, excessive abstraction, or other problems discussed in this section.

1 ▪ Word meanings and synonyms

For writing exactly, a dictionary is essential and a thesaurus can be helpful.

Desk dictionaries

A desk dictionary defines about 150,000 to 200,000 words and provides pronunciation, grammatical functions, etymology (word history), and other information. A sample from *Merriam-Webster's Collegiate Dictionary* appears on the next page.

Good desk dictionaries, in addition to *Merriam-Webster's*, include the *American Heritage College Dictionary*, the *Random House Webster's College Dictionary*, and *Webster's New World Dictionary*. Most of these are available in both print and electronic form (CD-ROM or online). In addition, several Web sites provide online dictionaries or links to online dictionaries.

Dictionary entry for *reckon*

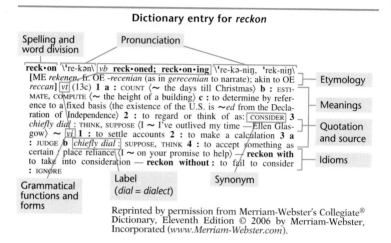

Spelling and word division

Pronunciation

Etymology

Meanings

Quotation and source

Idioms

Grammatical functions and forms

Label
(dial = dialect)

Synonym

Reprinted by permission from Merriam-Webster's Collegiate® Dictionary, Eleventh Edition © 2006 by Merriam-Webster, Incorporated (*www.Merriam-Webster.com*).

exact

18b

CULTURE LANGUAGE If English is not your native language, you proba-bly should own a dictionary prepared especially for students using English as a second language (ESL). Such a diction-ary contains special information on prepositions, count versus non-count nouns, and many other matters. Reliable ESL dictionaries include *COBUILD English Language Dictionary, Longman Dictionary of Contemporary English,* and *Oxford Advanced Learner's Dictionary.*

Thesauruses

To find a word with the exact shade of meaning you intend, you may want to consult a thesaurus, or book of **synonyms**—words with approximately the same meaning. A reference such as *Roget's International Thesaurus* lists most imaginable synonyms for thousands of words. The word *news,* for instance, has half a page of synonyms, including *tidings, dispatch, gossip,* and *journalism.*

Because a thesaurus aims to open up possibilities, its lists of synonyms include approximate as well as precise matches. The the-saurus does not define synonyms or distinguish among them, how-ever, so you need a dictionary to discover exact meanings. In general, don't use a word from a thesaurus—even one you like the sound of—until you are sure of its appropriateness for your meaning.

Note Your word processor may include a thesaurus, making it easy to look up synonyms and insert the chosen word into your text. But still you should consult a dictionary unless you are certain of the word's meaning and appropriateness.

2 ▪ The right word for your meaning

All words have one or more basic meanings, called **denota-tions**—the meanings listed in the dictionary, without reference to emotional associations. If readers are to understand you, you must use words according to their established meanings.

- **Consult a dictionary whenever you are unsure of a word's meaning.**
- **Distinguish between similar-sounding words that have widely different denotations:**

Inexact   Older people often suffer infirmaries [places for the sick].

Exact   Older people often suffer infirmities [disabilities].

Some words, called **homonyms,** sound exactly alike but differ in meaning: for example, *principal/principle* or *rain/reign/rein.* (See pp. 352–53 for a list of commonly confused homonyms.)

- **Distinguish between words with related but distinct meanings:**

Inexact   Television commercials continuously [unceasingly] interrupt programming.

Exact   Television commercials continually [regularly] interrupt programming.

In addition to their emotion-free meanings, many words carry related meanings that evoke specific feelings. These **connotations** can shape readers' responses and are thus a powerful tool for writers. The following word pairs have related denotations but very different connotations:

pride: sense of self-worth
vanity: excessive regard for oneself

firm: steady, unchanging, unyielding
stubborn: unreasonable, bullheaded

lasting: long-lived, enduring
endless: without limit, eternal

enthusiasm: excitement
mania: excessive interest or desire

A dictionary can help you track down words with the exact connotations you want. Besides providing meanings, your dictionary may also list and distinguish synonyms to guide your choices. A thesaurus can also help if you use it carefully, as discussed opposite.

exact

18b

Exercise 18.3   Revising: Denotation

In the following sentences, revise any underlined word that is used incorrectly. Consult a dictionary if you are uncertain of a word's precise meaning. Answers to starred items appear at the end of the book.

Example:

Sam and Dave are going to Bermuda and Hauppage, respectfully, for spring vacation.

Sam and Dave are going to Bermuda and Hauppage, <u>respectively</u>, for spring vacation.

*1. Maxine Hong Kingston was <u>rewarded</u> many prizes for her first two books, *The Woman Warrior* and *China Men.*
*2. Kingston <u>sites</u> her mother's tales about ancestors and ancient Chinese customs as the sources of these memoirs.
*3. Two of Kingston's <u>progeny</u>, her great-grandfathers, are focal points of *China Men.*
*4. Both men led rebellions against <u>suppressive</u> employers: a sugarcane farmer and a railroad-construction <u>engineer</u>.
*5. In her childhood Kingston was greatly <u>effected</u> by her mother's tale about a pregnant aunt who was <u>ostracized</u> by villagers.
  6. The aunt gained <u>avengeance</u> by drowning herself in the village's water supply.
  7. Kingston decided to make her nameless relative <u>infamous</u> by giving her <u>immortality</u> in *The Woman Warrior.*
  8. Kingston's novel *Tripmaster Monkey* has been called the <u>premier</u> novel about the 1960s.
  9. Her characters <u>embody</u> the <u>principles</u> that led to her own protest against the Vietnam War.
 10. Kingston's innovative books <u>infer</u> her opposition to racism and sexism both in the China of the past and in the United States of the present.

exact
18b

Exercise 18.4   Considering the connotations of words

Fill in the blank in each sentence below with the most appropriate word from the list in parentheses. Consult a dictionary to be sure of your choice. Answers to starred items appear at the end of the book.

> *Example:*
>
> Channel 5 _____ Oshu the winner before the polls closed. (*advertised, declared, broadcast, promulgated*)
>
> Channel 5 <u>declared</u> Oshu the winner before the polls closed.

*1. AIDS is a serious health _____. (*problem, worry, difficulty, plight*)
*2. Once the virus has entered the blood system, it _____ T-cells. (*murders, destroys, slaughters, executes*)
  3. The _____ of T-cells is to combat infections. (*ambition, function, aim, goal*)
  4. Without enough T-cells, the body is nearly _____ against infections. (*defenseless, hopeless, desperate*)
  5. To prevent exposure to the disease, one should be especially _____ in sexual relationships. (*chary, circumspect, cautious, calculating*)

3 ▪ Concrete and specific words

Clear, exact writing balances abstract and general words, which outline ideas and objects, with concrete and specific words, which sharpen and solidify.

- **Abstract words** name ideas: *beauty, inflation, management, culture, liberal.* **Concrete words** name qualities and things we can know by our five senses of sight, hearing, touch, taste, and smell: *sleek, humming, rough, salty, musty.*
- **General words** name classes or groups of things, such as *buildings, weather,* or *birds,* and include all the varieties of the class. **Specific words** limit a general class, such as *buildings,* by naming one of its varieties, such as *skyscraper* or *my house on Emerald Street.*

Abstract and general words are useful in the broad statements that set the course for your writing:

The wild horse in America has a <u>romantic</u> history.

<u>Relations</u> between the sexes today are more <u>relaxed</u> than they were in the past.

But such statements need development with concrete and specific detail. Detail can turn a vague sentence into an exact one:

Vague   The size of his hands made his smallness real. [How big were his hands? How small was he?]

Exact   Not until I saw his delicate, doll-like hands did I realize that he stood a full head shorter than most other men.

exact
18b

Note If you write on a computer, you can use its Find function to help you find and revise abstract and general words that you tend to overuse. Examples of such words include *nice, interesting, things, very, good, a lot, a little,* and *some.*

Exercise 18.5   Revising: Concrete and specific words

Make the following paragraph vivid by expanding the sentences with appropriate details of your own choosing. Substitute concrete and specific words for the abstract and general ones that are underlined.

I remember <u>clearly</u> how <u>awful</u> I felt the first time I <u>attended</u> Mrs. Murphy's second-grade class. I had <u>recently</u> moved from a <u>small</u> town in Missouri to a <u>crowded</u> suburb of Chicago. My new school looked <u>big</u> from the outside and seemed <u>dark</u> inside as I <u>walked</u> down the <u>long</u> corridor toward the classroom. The class was <u>noisy</u> as I neared the door; but when I <u>entered</u>, <u>everyone</u> became <u>quiet</u> and <u>looked</u> at me. I felt <u>uncomfortable</u> and <u>wanted</u> a place to hide. However, in a <u>loud</u> voice Mrs. Murphy <u>directed</u> me to the front of the room to introduce myself.

---

4 ▪ Idioms

Idioms are expressions in any language that do not fit the rules for meaning or grammar—for instance, *put up with, plug away at, make off with.*

Idioms that involve prepositions can be especially confusing for both native and nonnative speakers of English. Some idioms with prepositions are listed in the following box. (More appear on pp. 232–33.)

Idioms with prepositions

abide by a rule
    in a place or state
according to
accords with
accuse of a crime
accustomed to
adapt from a source
    to a situation
afraid of
agree on a plan
    to a proposal
    with a person
angry with
aware of
based on
capable of
certain of
charge for a purchase
    with a crime
concur in an opinion
    with a person
contend for a principle
    with a person
dependent on
differ about or over a question
    from in some quality
    with a person
disappointed by or in a person
    in or with a thing
familiar with

identical with or to
impatient for a raise
    with a person
independent of
infer from
inferior to
involved in a task
    with a person
oblivious of or to one's surroundings
    of something forgotten
occupied by a person
    in study
    with a thing
opposed to
part from a person
    with a possession
prior to
proud of
related to
rewarded by the judge
    for something done
    with a gift
similar to
superior to
wait at a place
    for a train, a person
    in a room
    on a customer

---

exact
18b

CULTURE LANGUAGE If you are learning standard American English, you are justified in stumbling over its prepositions: their meanings can shift depending on context, and they have many idiomatic uses. In mastering English prepositions, you probably can't avoid memorization. But you can help yourself by memorizing related groups, such as *at/in/on* and *for/since*.

At, in, or *on* in expressions of time

- Use *at* before actual clock time: *at 8:30.*
- Use *in* before a month, year, century, or period: *in April, in 2007, in the twenty-first century, in the next month.*
- Use *on* before a day or date: *on Tuesday, on August 3, on Labor Day.*

At, in, or *on* in expressions of place

- Use *at* before a specific place or address: *at the school, at 511 Iris Street.*
- Use *in* before a place with limits or before a city, state, country, or continent: *in the house, in a box, in Oklahoma City, in China, in Asia.*
- Use *on* to mean "supported by" or "touching the surface of": *on the table, on Iris Street, on page 150.*

For or *since* in expressions of time

- Use *for* before a period of time: *for an hour, for two years.*
- Use *since* before a specific point in time: *since 1999, since Friday.*

exact

18b

A dictionary of English as a second language is the best source for the meanings of prepositions; see the suggestions on page 176.

Exercise 18.6   Using prepositions in idioms

In the sentences below, insert the preposition that correctly completes each idiom. Consult the box on the previous page or a dictionary as needed. Answers to starred items appear at the end of the book.

Example:

I disagree _____ many feminists who say women should not be homemakers.

I disagree <u>with</u> many feminists who say women should not be homemakers.

*1. Children are waiting longer to become independent _____ their parents.

*2. According _____ US Census data for young adults ages eighteen to twenty-four, 57 percent of men and 47 percent of women live full-time with their parents.

 3. Some of these adult children are dependent _____ their parents financially.

 4. In other cases, the parents charge their children _____ housing, food, and other living expenses.

 5. Many adult children are financially capable _____ living independently but prefer to save money rather than contend _____ high housing costs.

Exercise 18.7   Using prepositions in idioms   (CULTURE LANGUAGE)

Complete the following sentences by filling in the blanks with the appropriate prepositions from this list: *at, by, for, from, in, of, on, to, with.* Answers to starred items appear at the end of the book.

Example:

The most recent amendment to the US Constitution, ratified _____ May 18, 1992, was first proposed _____ 1789.

The most recent amendment to the US Constitution, ratified <u>on</u> May 18, 1992, was first proposed <u>in</u> 1789.

*1. The Eighteenth Amendment _____ the Constitution _____ the United States was ratified _____ 1919.

*2. It prohibited the "manufacture, sale, or transportation _____ intoxicating liquors."

3. It was adopted _____ response _____ a nationwide crusade _____ temperance groups.

4. The amendment did not prevent Americans _____ drinking, and the sale _____ alcoholic beverages was taken over _____ organized crime.

5. Wide-scale smuggling and bootlegging came _____ the demand _____ liquor.

exact
18b

5 ▪ Figurative language

Figurative language (or a **figure of speech**) departs from the literal meanings of words, usually by comparing very different ideas or objects:

Literal   As I try to write, I can think of nothing to say.
Figurative   As I try to write, <u>my mind is a slab of black slate</u>.

Imaginatively and carefully used, figurative language can capture meaning more precisely and emotionally than literal language. Here is a figure of speech at work in technical writing (paraphrasing the physicist Edward Andrade):

The molecules in a liquid move continuously like couples on an overcrowded dance floor, jostling each other.

The two most common figures of speech are the simile and the metaphor. Both compare two things of different classes, often one abstract and the other concrete. A **simile** makes the comparison explicit and usually begins with *like* or *as*:

Whenever we grow, we tend to feel it, <u>as</u> a young seed must feel the weight and inertia of the earth when it seeks to break out of its shell on its way to becoming a plant.   —Alice Walker

A **metaphor** claims that the two things are identical, omitting such words as *like* and *as*:

A school is a hopper into which children are heaved while they are young and tender; therein they are pressed into certain standard shapes and covered from head to heels with official rubber stamps.

—H. L. Mencken

Successful figurative language is fresh and unstrained, calling attention not to itself but to the writer's meaning. Be wary of mixed metaphors, which combine two or more incompatible figures:

Mixed   Various thorny problems that we try to sweep under the rug continue to bob up all the same.

Improved   Various thorny problems that we try to weed out continue to thrive all the same.

Exercise 18.8   Using figurative language

Invent appropriate similes or metaphors of your own to describe each scene or quality below, and use the figure in a sentence.

Example:

The attraction of a lake on a hot day
The small waves like fingers beckoned us irresistibly.

1. The sound of a kindergarten classroom
2. People waiting in line to buy tickets to a rock concert
3. The politeness of strangers meeting for the first time
4. A streetlight seen through dense fog
5. The effect of watching television for ten hours straight

exact

18b

6 ▪ Trite expressions

Trite expressions, or **clichés,** are phrases so old and so often repeated that they have become stale. They include the following:

add insult to injury	needle in a haystack
better late than never	point with pride
crushing blow	pride and joy
easier said than done	ripe old age
face the music	rude awakening
few and far between	sadder but wiser
green with envy	shoulder the burden
hard as a rock	shoulder to cry on
heavy as lead	sneaking suspicion
hit the nail on the head	stand in awe
hour of need	thin as a rail
ladder of success	tried and true
moving experience	wise as an owl

To edit clichés, listen to your writing for any expressions that you have heard or used before. You can also try using a style checker, which may flag clichés. When you find a cliché, substitute fresh words of your own or restate the idea in plain language.

Exercise 18.9   Revising: Trite expressions

Revise the following sentences to eliminate trite expressions. Answers to starred items appear at the end of the book.

> *Example:*
>
> The basketball team had almost seized victory, but it faced the test of truth in the last quarter of the game.
>
> The basketball team <u>seemed about to win</u>, but the <u>real test</u> came in the last quarter of the game.

*1. The disastrous consequences of the war have shaken the small nation to its roots.

*2. Prices for food have shot sky high, and citizens have sneaking suspicions that others are making a killing on the black market.

*3. Medical supplies are so few and far between that even civilians who are as sick as dogs cannot get treatment.

*4. With most men fighting or injured or killed, women have had to bite the bullet and bear the men's burden in farming and manufacturing.

*5. Last but not least, the war's heavy drain on the nation's pocketbook has left the economy in shambles.

6. Our reliance on foreign oil to support our driving habit has hit record highs in recent years.

7. Gas-guzzling vehicles are responsible for part of the increase.

8. In the future, we may have to bite the bullet and use public transportation or drive only fuel-efficient cars.

9. Both solutions are easier said than done.

10. But it stands to reason that we cannot go on using the world's oil reserves at such a rapid rate.

19   Completeness

Are all needed words in place?

Sometimes, omitting even a little word like *of* or *in* can make a sentence unclear. In editing, check your sentences to be sure you've included all the words they need. For additional help with complete sentences, see Chapter 35 on sentence fragments.

---

mycomplab

Visit *mycomplab.com* for more resources on complete sentences.

Grammar checkers A grammar checker will not flag most kinds of incomplete sentences discussed in this chapter.

19a Write complete compounds.

You may omit words from a compound construction when the omission will not confuse readers:

> Environmentalists have hopes for alternative fuels and [for] public transportation.
>
> Some cars will run on electricity, some [will run] on ethanol, and some [will run] on hydrogen.

Such omissions are possible only when the words omitted are common to all the parts of a compound construction. When the parts differ in any way, all words must be included in all parts.

> One new hybrid car <u>gets</u> eighty miles per gallon; some old cars <u>get</u> as little as five miles per gallon. [One verb is singular, the other plural.]
>
> Environmentalists believe <u>in</u> and work <u>for</u> fuel conservation. [Idiom requires different prepositions with *believe* and *work*.]

inc
19b

19b Add needed words.

In haste or carelessness, do not omit small words that are needed for clarity:

Incomplete	Regular payroll deductions are a type painless savings. You hardly notice missing amounts, and after period of years the contributions can add a large total.
Revised	Regular payroll deductions are a type <u>of</u> painless savings. You hardly notice <u>the</u> missing amounts, and after <u>a</u> period of years the contributions can add <u>up to</u> a large total.

Attentive proofreading is the only insurance against this kind of omission. *Proofread all your papers carefully.* See pages 36–37 for suggestions.

CULTURE LANGUAGE If your native language is not English, you may have difficulty knowing when to use the English articles *a, an,* and *the.* For guidelines on using articles, see pages 276–79.

┌─ **Key term** ───

compound construction Two or more elements (words, phrases, clauses) that are equal in importance and that function as a unit: *Rain fell, and streams overflowed* (clauses); *dogs and cats* (words).

Exercise 19.1 Revising: Completeness

Add words to the following sentences so that the sentences are complete and clear. Possible answers to starred items appear at the end of the book.

Example:

The fruit this plant is edible.
The fruit of this plant is edible.

*1. The first ice cream, eaten China in about 2000 BC, was lumpier than modern ice cream.

*2. The Chinese made their ice cream of milk, spices, and overcooked rice and packed in snow to solidify.

3. In the fourteenth century ice milk and fruit ices appeared in Italy and the tables of the wealthy.

4. At her wedding in 1533 to the king of France, Catherine de Médicis offered several flavors fruit ices.

5. Modern sherbets resemble her ices; modern ice cream her soft dessert of thick, sweetened cream.

20 Conciseness

Have I deleted all unneeded words?

Unnecessary words pad your sentences without adding to your meaning, and they can make your writing unclear. You want to make every word count. Bear in mind, however, that detail and originality should not be cut with needless words. Rather, the length of the expression should be appropriate to the thought.

You may find yourself writing wordily when you are unsure of your subject or when your thoughts are tangled. It's fine, even necessary, to stumble and grope while drafting. But straighten out your ideas and aim for conciseness during revision and editing.

Grammar checkers Any grammar checker will identify at least some wordy structures, such as repeated words, weak verbs, and passive voice. No checker can identify all wordy structures, however, nor can it say whether the structure is appropriate for your ideas.

CULTURE LANGUAGE Wordiness is not a problem of incorrect grammar. A sentence may be perfectly grammatical but still contain unneeded words that make it unclear or awkward.

---

mycomplab

Visit *mycomplab.com* for more resources and exercises on writing concisely.

Ways to achieve conciseness

Wordy (87 words)

The highly pressured <u>nature</u> of critical-care
nursing <u>is due to the fact that</u> the patients
have life-threatening illnesses. Critical-care
nurses must <u>have possession</u> of steady nerves
to <u>care for patients who are critically ill and</u>
<u>very sick.</u> The nurses must also have posses-
sion of interpersonal skills. They must also
have medical skills. <u>It is considered by most</u>
<u>health-care professionals</u> that these nurses
are essential <u>if</u> there is to be improvement of
<u>patients</u> who are now in critical care from that
status to the status of intermediate care.

- Focus on subject and verb, and cut or shorten empty words and phrases.
- Avoid nouns made from verbs.
- Cut unneeded repetition.
- Combine sentences.
- Change passive voice to active voice.
- Eliminate *there is* constructions.
- Cut unneeded repetition, and reduce clauses and phrases.

con

20a

Concise (37 words)

Critical-care nursing is highly pressured because the patients have life-
threatening illnesses. Critical-care nurses must possess steady nerves and
interpersonal and medical skills. Most health-care professionals consider
these nurses essential if patients are to improve to intermediate care.

20a Focus on the subject and verb.

Using the subjects and verbs of your sentences for the key actors and actions will reduce words and emphasize important ideas.
(See pp. 148–50 for more on this topic.)

Wordy   The <u>reason</u> why most of the country shifts to daylight saving
time <u>is</u> that winter days are much shorter than summer days.

Concise   Most of the <u>country</u> <u>shifts</u> to daylight saving time because
winter days are much shorter than summer days.

Focusing on subjects and verbs will also help you avoid several
other causes of wordiness discussed further on pages 148–50:

Nouns made from verbs

Wordy   The <u>occurrence</u> of the winter solstice, the shortest day of the
year, <u>is</u> an event taking place about December 22.

Concise   The winter <u>solstice</u>, the shortest day of the year, <u>occurs</u> about
December 22.

Weak verbs

Wordy   The earth's axis has a tilt as the planet is in orbit around the sun so that the northern and southern hemispheres are alternately in alignment toward the sun.

Concise   The earth's axis tilts as the planet orbits around the sun so that the northern and southern hemispheres alternately align toward the sun.

Passive voice

Wordy   During its winter the northern hemisphere is tilted farthest away from the sun, so the nights are made longer and the days are made shorter.

Concise   During its winter the northern hemisphere tilts away from the sun, which makes the nights longer and the days shorter.

See also pages 244–45 on changing the passive voice to the active voice, as in the example above.

20b Cut empty words.

Empty words walk in place, gaining little or nothing in meaning. Many of them can be cut entirely. The following are just a few examples.

all things considered	in a manner of speaking
as far as I'm concerned	in my opinion
for all intents and purposes	last but not least
for the most part	more or less

Other empty words can also be cut, usually along with some of the words around them:

area	element	kind	situation
aspect	factor	manner	thing
case	field	nature	type

Still others can be reduced from several words to a single word:

For	Substitute
at all times	always
at the present time	now, yet
because of the fact that	because
by virtue of the fact that	because
due to the fact that	because
for the purpose of	for

Key terms

passive voice The verb form when the subject names the *receiver* of the verb's action: *The house was destroyed by the tornado.* (See p. 244.)

active voice The verb form when the subject names the *performer* of the verb's action: *The tornado destroyed the house.* (See p. 244.)

For	Substitute
in order to	to
in the event that	if
in the final analysis	finally

Cutting or reducing such words and phrases will make your writing move faster and work harder:

Wordy   <u>In my opinion</u>, the council's proposal to improve the city center is inadequate, <u>all things considered</u>.

Concise   The council's proposal to improve the city center is inadequate.

20c   Cut unneeded repetition.

Deliberate repetition and restatement can make writing more coherent by linking sentences (see p. 47). But unnecessary repetition weakens sentences:

Wordy   Many <u>unskilled</u> workers <u>without training in a particular job</u> are unemployed <u>and do not have any work</u>.

Concise   Many unskilled workers are unemployed.

con
20d

Be especially alert to phrases that say the same thing twice. In the examples below, the unneeded words are underlined:

circle <u>around</u>	important [basic] essentials
consensus <u>of opinion</u>	puzzling <u>in nature</u>
cooperate <u>together</u>	repeat <u>again</u>
<u>final</u> completion	return <u>again</u>
<u>frank and</u> honest exchange	square [round] <u>in shape</u>
the future <u>to come</u>	<u>surrounding</u> circumstances

(CULTURE LANGUAGE) The preceding phrases are redundant because the main word already implies the underlined word or words. A dictionary will tell you what meanings a word implies. *Assassinate*, for instance, means "murder someone well known," so the following sentence is redundant: *Julius Caesar was <u>assassinated and killed</u> in 44 BCE.*

20d   Tighten clauses and phrases.

Modifiers can be expanded or contracted depending on the emphasis you want to achieve. (Generally, the longer a construction, the more emphasis it has.) When editing your sentences, consider whether any modifiers can be reduced without loss of emphasis or clarity.

> ┌ **Key term** ──────────────────────
> **modifier** A word or word group that limits or qualifies another word: *slippery* road. (See p. 270.)

Wordy	The Channel Tunnel, which runs between Britain and France, bores through a bed of solid chalk that is twenty-three miles across.
Concise	The Channel Tunnel between Britain and France bores through twenty-three miles of solid chalk.

20e   Revise *there is* or *it is* constructions.

You can postpone the sentence subject with the words *there* and *it*: *There are three points made in the text. It was not fair that only seniors could vote.* These **expletive constructions** can be useful to emphasize the subject (as when introducing it for the first time) or to indicate a change in direction. But often they just add words and weaken sentences:

Wordy	There were delays and cost overruns that plagued construction of the Channel Tunnel. It had been the expectation of investors that they would see earnings soon after there were trains passing through the tunnel, but profits took years to materialize.
Concise	Delays and cost overruns plagued construction of the Channel Tunnel. Investors had expected to see earnings soon after trains began passing through the tunnel, but profits took years to materialize.

> **CULTURE LANGUAGE** When you must use an expletive construction, be careful to include *there* or *it*. Only commands and some questions can begin with verbs.

20f   Combine sentences.

Often the information in two or more sentences can be combined into one tight sentence:

Wordy	An unexpected problem with the Channel Tunnel is stowaways. The stowaways are mostly illegal immigrants. They are trying to smuggle themselves into England. They cling to train roofs and undercarriages.
Concise	An unexpected problem with the Channel Tunnel is stowaways, mostly illegal immigrants who are trying to smuggle themselves into England by clinging to train roofs and undercarriages.

(See also pp. 164–65 on combining sentences to achieve variety.)

20g   Avoid jargon.

Jargon can refer to the special vocabulary of any discipline or profession (see p. 170). But it has also come to describe vague, inflated language that is overcomplicated, even incomprehensible. When it comes from government or business, we call it **bureaucratese.**

Jargon   The necessity for individuals to become separate entities in their own right may impel children to engage in open rebelliousness against parental authority or against sibling influence, with resultant bewilderment of those being rebelled against.

Translation   Children's natural desire to become themselves may make them rebel against bewildered parents or siblings.

Exercise 20.1   Revising: Writing concisely

Make the following sentences more concise. Combine sentences when doing so reduces wordiness. Answers to starred items appear at the end of the book.

Example:

It is thought by some people that there is gain from exercise only when it involves pain.

Some people think that gain comes from exercise only with pain.

*1. If sore muscles after exercising are a problem for you, there are some measures that can be taken by you to ease the discomfort.
*2. First, the immediate application of cold will help to reduce inflammation.
*3. Blood vessels are constricted by cold. Blood is kept away from the injured muscles.
*4. It is advisable to avoid heat for the first day.
*5. The application of heat within the first twenty-four hours can cause an increase in muscle soreness and stiffness.

6. There are two ways the application of cold can be made: you can take a cold shower or use an ice pack.
7. Inflammation of muscles can also be reduced with aspirin, ibuprofen, or another anti-inflammatory medication.
8. There is the idea that muscle soreness can be worsened by power lifting.
9. While healing is occurring, you need to take it easy.
10. A day or two after overdoing exercise, it is advisable for you to get some light exercise and gentle massage.

Exercise 20.2   Revising: Conciseness

Make the following paragraph as concise as possible. Be merciless. Answers to starred sentences appear at the end of the book.

*At the end of a lengthy line of reasoning, he came to the conclusion that the situation with carcinogens [cancer-causing substances] should be regarded as similar to the situation with the automobile. *Instead of giving in to an irrational fear of cancer, we should consider all aspects of the problem in a balanced and dispassionate frame of mind, making a total of the benefits received from potential carcinogens

con

20g

(plastics, pesticides, and other similar products) and measuring said total against the damage done by such products. This is the nature of most discussions about the automobile. Instead of responding irrationally to the visual, aural, and air pollution caused by automobiles, we have decided to live with them (while simultaneously working to improve on them) for the benefits brought to society as a whole.

PART 4

Sentence Parts and Patterns

BASIC GRAMMAR

Grammar describes how language works, and understanding it can help you create clear and accurate sentences. This section explains the kinds of words in sentences (Chapter 21) and how to build basic sentences (22), expand them (23), and classify them (24).

Grammar checkers A grammar checker can both offer assistance and cause problems as you compose sentences. Look for the cautions and tips for using such checkers in this and the next two parts of this book. For more information about grammar checkers, see pages 35–36.

21 Parts of Speech

What are the kinds of words, and how do they work?

All English words fall into eight groups, or **parts of speech,** such as nouns, verbs, adjectives, and adverbs. A word's part of speech determines its form and its position in a sentence. The same word may even serve as different parts of speech in different sentences, as these examples show:

gram
21a

> The government sent _aid_ to the city. [_Aid_ is a noun.]
> Governments _aid_ citizens. [_Aid_ is a verb.]

The _function_ of a word in a sentence always determines its part of speech in that sentence.

21a Learn to recognize nouns.

Nouns name. They may name a person (_Helen Mirren, Jesse Jackson, astronaut_), a thing (_chair, book, Mt. Rainier_), a quality (_pain, mystery, simplicity_), a place (_city, Washington, ocean, Red Sea_), or an idea (_reality, peace, success_).

The forms of nouns depend partly on where they fit in certain groups, such as the ones following. As the examples indicate, the same noun may appear in more than one group.

mycomplab

Visit _mycomplab.com_ for more resources and exercises on the parts of speech

- **Common nouns** name general classes of things and do not begin with capital letters: *earthquake, citizen, earth, fortitude, army.*
- **Proper nouns** name specific people, places, and things and begin with capital letters: *Angelina Jolie, Washington Monument, El Paso, US Congress.*
- **Count nouns** name things considered countable in English. Most add *-s* or *-es* to distinguish between singular (one) and plural (more than one): *citizen, citizens; city, cities.* Some count nouns form irregular plurals: *woman, women; child, children.*
- **Noncount nouns** name things that aren't considered countable in English (*earth, sugar*), or they name qualities (*chaos, fortitude*). Noncount nouns do not form plurals.
- **Collective nouns** are singular in form but name groups: *army, family, herd, US Congress.*

In addition, most nouns form the **possessive** by adding *-'s* to show ownership (*Nadia's books, citizen's rights*), source (*Auden's poems*), and some other relationships.

21b Learn to recognize pronouns.

Most **pronouns** substitute for nouns and function in sentences as nouns do: *Susanne Ling enlisted in the Navy when she graduated.*

Pronouns fall into several subclasses depending on their form or function:

- **Personal pronouns** refer to a specific individual or to individuals: *I, you, he, she, it, we,* and *they.*
- **Indefinite pronouns,** such as *everybody* and *some,* do not substitute for any specific nouns, though they function as nouns (*Everybody speaks*).
- **Relative pronouns**—*who, whoever, which, that*—relate groups of words to nouns or other pronouns (*The book that won is a novel*).
- **Interrogative pronouns,** such as *who, which,* and *what,* introduce questions (*Who will contribute?*).
- **Demonstrative pronouns,** including *this, that,* and *such,* identify or point to nouns (*This is the problem*).
- **Intensive pronouns**—a personal pronoun plus *-self* or *-selves* (*himself, ourselves*)—emphasize a noun or other pronoun (*He himself asked that question*).
- **Reflexive pronouns** have the same form as intensive pronouns but indicate that the sentence subject also receives the action of the verb (*They injured themselves*).

The personal pronouns *I, he, she, we,* and *they* and the relative pronouns *who* and *whoever* change form depending on their function in the sentence. (See Chapter 30.)

gram
21b

21c   Learn to recognize verbs.

Verbs express an action (*bring, change, grow, consider*), an occurrence (*become, happen, occur*), or a state of being (*be, seem, remain*).

1 ▪ Forms of verbs

Verbs have five distinctive forms. If the form can change as described here, the word is a verb:

▪ The **plain form** is the dictionary form of the verb. When the subject is a plural noun or the pronoun *I, we, you,* or *they,* the plain form indicates action that occurs in the present, occurs habitually, or is generally true.

> A few artists <u>live</u> in town today.
> They <u>hold</u> classes downtown.

▪ The **-s form** ends in *-s* or *-es.* When the subject is a singular noun, a pronoun such as *everyone,* or the personal pronoun *he, she,* or *it,* the *-s* form indicates action that occurs in the present, occurs habitually, or is generally true.

> The artist <u>lives</u> in town today.
> She <u>holds</u> classes downtown.

▪ The **past-tense form** indicates that the action of the verb occurred before now. It usually adds *-d* or *-ed* to the plain form, although most irregular verbs create it in different ways (see pp. 218–20).

> Many artists <u>lived</u> in town before this year.
> They <u>held</u> classes downtown. [Irregular verb.]

▪ The **past participle** is usually the same as the past-tense form, except in most irregular verbs. It combines with forms of *have* or *be* (*has* <u>*climbed*</u>, *was* <u>*created*</u>), or by itself it modifies nouns and pronouns (*the* <u>*sliced*</u> *apples*).

> Artists have <u>lived</u> in town for decades.
> They have <u>held</u> classes downtown. [Irregular verb.]

▪ The **present participle** adds *-ing* to the verb's plain form. It combines with forms of *be* (*is* <u>*buying*</u>), modifies nouns and pronouns (*the* <u>*boiling*</u> *water*), or functions as a noun (<u>*Running*</u> *exhausts me*).

> A few artists are <u>living</u> in town today.
> They are <u>holding</u> classes downtown.

The verb *be* has eight forms rather than the five forms of most other verbs:

Plain form	be		
Present participle	being		
Past participle	been		

	I	*he, she, it*	*we, you, they*
Present tense	am	is	are
Past tense	was	was	were

2 ▪ Helping verbs

Some verb forms combine with **helping verbs** to indicate time, possibility, obligation, necessity, and other kinds of meaning: *can run*, *was sleeping*, *had been working*. In these **verb phrases** *run*, *sleeping*, and *working* are **main verbs**—they carry the principal meaning.

	Verb phrase	
	Helping	*Main*
Artists	can	train others to draw.
The techniques	have	changed little.

The most common helping verbs are listed in the box below. See pages 224–28 for more on helping verbs.

Common helping verbs

Forms of *be:* be, am, is, are, was, were, been, being
Forms of *have:* have, has, had, having
Forms of *do:* do, does, did

be able to	could	may	ought to	used to
be supposed to	had better	might	shall	will
can	have to	must	should	would

> **Exercise 21.1** **Identifying nouns, pronouns, and verbs**
>
> Identify the words that function as nouns (N), pronouns (P), and verbs (V) in the following sentences. Answers to starred items appear at the end of the book.
>
> *Example:*
>
>   N   N   V   N
>
> Ancestors of the gingko tree lived 175 to 200 million years ago.
>
> *1. The gingko tree, which is one of the world's oldest trees, is large and picturesque.
> *2. Gingko trees may grow to over a hundred feet in height.
> *3. Their leaves look like fans and are about three inches wide.
> *4. The leaves turn yellow in the fall.
> *5. Because it tolerates smoke, low temperatures, and low rainfall, the gingko appears in many cities.

6. A shortcoming, however, is the foul odor of its fruit.
7. Inside the fruit is a large white seed, which some people value as food.
8. The fruit often does not appear until the tree is twenty years old.
9. The tree's name means "apricot" in the Japanese language.
10. Originally, the gingko grew only in China, but it has now spread throughout the world.

21d Learn to recognize adjectives and adverbs.

Adjectives describe or modify nouns and pronouns. They specify which one, what quality, or how many.

old   city   generous   one   two   pears
adjective noun   adjective pronoun   adjective noun

Adverbs describe or modify verbs, adjectives, other adverbs, and whole groups of words. They specify when, where, how, and to what extent.

nearly destroyed   too quickly
adverb   verb   adverb adverb

very generous   Unfortunately, taxes will rise.
adverb adjective   adverb   word group

An *-ly* ending often signals an adverb, but not always: *friendly* is an adjective; *never* is an adverb. The only way to tell whether a word is an adjective or an adverb is to determine what it modifies.

Adjectives and adverbs appear in three forms: **positive** (*green, angrily*), **comparative** (*greener, more angrily*), and **superlative** (*greenest, most angrily*).

See Chapter 33 for more on adjectives and adverbs.

> **Exercise 21.2 Identifying adjectives and adverbs**
> Identify the adjectives (ADJ) and adverbs (ADV) in the following sentences. Mark *a, an,* and *the* as adjectives. Answers to starred items appear at the end of the book.
>
> *Example:*
>
>   ADV
> Stress can hit people when they least expect it.
>
> *1. You can reduce stress by making a few simple changes.
> *2. Get up fifteen minutes earlier than you ordinarily do.
> *3. Eat a healthy breakfast, and eat it slowly so that you enjoy it.
> *4. Do your more unpleasant tasks early in the day.
> *5. Every day, do at least one thing you really enjoy.
>
> 6. If waiting in lines is stressful for you, carry a book or magazine when you know you'll have to wait.
> 7. Make promises sparingly and keep them faithfully.

8. Plan ahead to prevent the most stressful situations.
9. For example, carry spare keys so you won't be locked out of your car or house.
10. See a doctor and a dentist regularly.

21e Learn to recognize connecting words: Prepositions and conjunctions.

Connecting words are mostly small words that link parts of sentences. They never change form.

1 ▪ Prepositions

Prepositions form nouns or pronouns (plus any modifiers) into word groups called **prepositional phrases:** *about* love, *down the stairs*. These phrases usually serve as modifiers in sentences, as in *The plants trailed down the stairs*. (See also p. 210.)

Common prepositions

about	before	except for	of	throughout
above	behind	excepting	off	till
according to	below	for	on	to
across	beneath	from	onto	toward
after	beside	in	on top of	under
against	between	in addition to	out	underneath
along	beyond	inside	out of	unlike
along with	by	inside of	outside	until
among	concerning	in spite of	over	up
around	despite	instead of	past	upon
as	down	into	regarding	up to
aside from	due to	like	round	with
at	during	near	since	within
because of	except	next to	through	without

CULTURE LANGUAGE The meanings and uses of English prepositions can be difficult to master. See pages 179–81 for a discussion of prepositions in idioms such as *proud of* and *angry with*. See pages 231–33 for uses of prepositions in two-word verbs such as *look after* and *look up*.

2 ▪ Subordinating conjunctions

Subordinating conjunctions form sentences into word groups called **subordinate clauses,** such as *when the meeting ended*. These clauses serve as parts of sentences: *Everyone was relieved when the meeting ended*. (See pp. 213–14 for more on subordinate clauses.)

gram
21e

Common subordinating conjunctions

after	even if	rather than	until
although	even though	since	when
as	if	so that	whenever
as if	if only	than	where
as long as	in order that	that	whereas
as though	now that	though	wherever
because	once	till	whether
before	provided	unless	while

> **CULTURE-LANGUAGE** Subordinating conjunctions convey meaning without help from other function words, such as the coordinating conjunctions *and, but, for,* or *so:*

Faulty <u>Even though</u> the parents are illiterate, <u>but</u> their children may read well. [*Even though* and *but* have the same meaning, so both are not needed.]

Revised <u>Even though</u> the parents are illiterate, their children may read well.

3 ▪ Coordinating and correlative conjunctions

Coordinating and correlative conjunctions connect words or word groups of the same kind, such as nouns, adjectives, or sentences.

Coordinating conjunctions consist of a single word:

Coordinating conjunctions

and	nor	for	yet
but	or	so	

Biofeedback <u>or</u> simple relaxation can relieve headaches.
Relaxation works well, <u>and</u> it is inexpensive.

Correlative conjunctions are combinations of coordinating conjunctions and other words:

Common correlative conjunctions

both . . . and	neither . . . nor
not only . . . but also	whether . . . or
not . . . but	as . . . as
either . . . or	

Both biofeedback <u>and</u> relaxation can relieve headaches.

The headache sufferer learns <u>not only</u> to recognize the causes of headaches <u>but also</u> to control those causes.

Exercise 21.3 Adding connecting words

Fill each blank in the following sentences with the appropriate connecting word: a preposition, a subordinating conjunction, or a coordinating conjunction. Consult the lists on the previous two pages if you need help. Answers to starred items appear at the end of the book.

> *Example:*
>
> A Trojan priest warned, "Beware _____ Greeks bearing gifts."
> (*preposition*)
>
> A Trojan priest warned, "Beware <u>of</u> Greeks bearing gifts."

*1. Just about everyone has heard the story _____ the Trojan Horse. (*preposition*)
*2. This incident happened at the city of Troy _____ was planned by the Greeks. (*coordinating conjunction*)
*3. The Greeks built a huge wooden horse _____ a hollow space big enough to hold many men. (*preposition*)
*4. At night, they rolled the horse to the gate of Troy _____ left it there filled with soldiers. (*coordinating conjunction*)
*5. _____ the morning, the Trojans were surprised to see the enormous horse. (*preposition*)
 6. They were amazed _____ they saw that the Greeks were gone. (*subordinating conjunction*)
 7. _____ they were curious to examine this gift from the Greeks, they dragged the horse into the city and left it outside the temple. (*subordinating conjunction*)
 8. In the middle of the night, the hidden Greeks emerged _____ the horse and began setting fires all over town. (*preposition*)
 9. _____ the Trojan soldiers awoke and came out of their houses, the Greeks killed them one by one. (*subordinating conjunction*)
10. By the next morning, the Trojan men were dead _____ the women were slaves to the Greeks. (*coordinating conjunction*)

gram
21f

21f   Learn to recognize interjections.

Interjections express feeling or command attention. They are rarely used in academic or business writing.

Oh, the meeting went fine.
They won seven thousand dollars! <u>Wow</u>!

22 The Sentence

What makes a sentence a sentence?

The essential elements of any sentence are the subject and the predicate. Usually naming an actor and an action, the subject and predicate together form a complete thought.

22a Learn to recognize subjects and predicates.

Most sentences make statements. First the **subject** names something; then the **predicate** makes an assertion about the subject or describes an action by the subject.

Subject	Predicate
Art	thrives.

The **simple subject** consists of one or more nouns or pronouns, whereas the **complete subject** also includes any modifiers. The **simple predicate** consists of one or more verbs, whereas the **complete predicate** adds any words needed to complete the meaning of the verb plus any modifiers.

Sometimes, as in the short example *Art thrives,* the simple and complete subject and predicate are the same. More often, they are different:

In the second example, the simple subject and simple predicate are both **compound:** in each, two words joined by a coordinating conjunction (*and*) serve the same function.

CULTURE LANGUAGE The subject of an English sentence may be a noun (*art*) or a pronoun that refers to the noun (*it*), but not both. (See p. 304.)

Faulty	Some <u>art</u> <u>it</u> stirs controversy.
Revised	Some <u>art</u> stirs controversy.

---

mycomplab

Visit *mycomplab.com* for more resources and exercises on the sentence.

gram
22a

Tests to find subjects and predicates

The tests below use the following example:

Art that makes it into museums has often survived controversy.

Identify the subject.

- **Ask *who* or *what* is acting or being described in the sentence.**

  Complete subject   art that makes it into museums

- **Isolate the simple subject by deleting modifiers**—words or word groups that don't name the actor of the sentence but give information about it. In the example, the word group *that makes it into museums* does not name the actor but modifies it.

  Simple subject   art

Identify the predicate.

- **Ask what the sentence asserts about the subject:** what is its action, or what state is it in? In the example, the assertion about *art* is that it *has often survived controversy.*

  Complete predicate   has often survived controversy

- **Isolate the verb, the simple predicate, by changing the time of the subject's action.** The simple predicate is the word or words that change as a result.

  Example   Art . . . has often survived controversy.
  Present   Art . . . often <u>survives</u> controversy.
  Future   Art . . . <u>will</u> often <u>survive</u> controversy.
  Simple predicate   has survived

gram

22a

Note If a sentence contains a word group such as *that makes it into museums* or *because viewers agree about its quality,* you may be tempted to mark the subject and verb in the word group as the subject and verb of the sentence. But these word groups are subordinate clauses, made into modifiers by the words they begin with: *that* and *because.* See pages 213–14 for more on subordinate clauses.

Exercise 22.1 Identifying subjects and predicates

In the following sentences, insert a line between the complete subject and the complete predicate. Underline each simple subject once and each simple predicate twice. Answers to starred items appear at the end of the book.

Example:

The <u>pony</u>, the light <u>horse</u>, and the draft <u>horse</u> | <u><u>are</u></u> the three main types of domestic horses.

*1. The horse has a long history of service to humanity but today is mainly a show and sport animal.

   *2. A member of the genus *Equus,* the domestic horse shares its lineage with the ass and the zebra.

   *3. The domestic horse and its relatives are all plains-dwelling herd animals.

   *4. The modern horse evolved in North America.

   *5. It migrated to other parts of the world and then became extinct in the Americas.

   6. The Spaniards reintroduced the domestic horse to the Americas.

   7. North American wild horses are actually descended from escaped domestic horses.

   8. An average-sized adult horse may require twenty-six pounds or more of pasture feed or hay per day.

   9. According to records, North Americans hunted and domesticated horses as early as four to five thousand years ago.

  10. The earliest ancestor of the modern horse may have been eohippus, approximately 55 million years ago.

22b   Learn the basic predicate patterns.

English sentences usually follow one of five patterns, each differing in the complete predicate (the verb and any words following it).

CULTURE LANGUAGE   Word order in English sentences may not correspond to word order in the sentences of your native language or dialect. English, for instance, strongly prefers subject first, then verb, then any other words, whereas some other languages prefer the verb first.

Pattern 1: The earth trembled.

In the simplest pattern the predicate consists only of an **intransitive verb,** a verb that does not require a following word to complete its meaning.

Subject	Predicate
	Intransitive verb
The earth	trembled.
The hospital	may close.

Pattern 2: The earthquake destroyed the city.

In pattern 2 the verb is followed by a **direct object,** a noun or pronoun that identifies who or what receives the action of the verb. A verb that requires a direct object to complete its meaning is called **transitive.**

Subject	Predicate	
	Transitive verb	*Direct object*
The earthquake	destroyed	the city.
Education	opens	doors.

CULTURE LANGUAGE Only transitive verbs can be used in the passive voice: *The city was destroyed.* Your dictionary will indicate whether a verb is transitive or intransitive. For some verbs (*begin, learn, read, write,* and others), it will indicate both uses.

Pattern 3: The result was chaos.

In pattern 3 the verb is followed by a **subject complement,** a word that renames or describes the subject. A verb in this pattern is called a **linking verb** because it links its subject to the description following. The linking verbs include *be, seem, appear, become, grow, remain, stay, prove, feel, look, smell, sound,* and *taste.* Subject complements are usually nouns or adjectives.

Subject	Predicate	
	Linking verb	*Subject complement*
The result	was	chaos.
The man	became	an accountant.

Pattern 4: The government sent the city aid.

In pattern 4 the verb is followed by a direct object and an **indirect object,** a word identifying to or for whom the action of the verb is performed. The direct object and indirect object refer to different things, people, or places.

Subject	Predicate		
	Transitive verb	*Indirect object*	*Direct object*
The government	sent	the city	aid.
One company	offered	its employees	bonuses.

A number of verbs can take indirect objects, including *allow, bring, buy, deny, find, get, give, leave, make, offer, pay, read, sell, send, show, teach,* and *write.*

CULTURE LANGUAGE Some verbs are never followed by an indirect object—*admit, announce, demonstrate, explain, introduce, mention, prove, recommend, say,* and some others. However, the direct objects of these verbs may be followed by *to* or *for* and a noun or pronoun that specifies to or for whom the action was done: *The manual explains the new procedure to workers. A video demonstrates the procedure for us.*

gram
22b

Key term

passive voice The verb form when the subject names the receiver of the verb's action: *Layoffs were expected by the employees.* In the **active voice** the subject names the actor: *The employees expected layoffs.* (See pp. 207–08.)

Pattern 5: The citizens considered the earthquake a disaster.

In pattern 5 the verb is followed by a direct object and an **object complement,** a word that renames or describes the direct object. Object complements may be nouns or adjectives.

Subject	Predicate		
	Transitive verb	*Direct object*	*Object complement*
The citizens	considered	the earthquake	a disaster.
Success	makes	some people	nervous.

Exercise 22.2 Identifying sentence parts

In the following sentences identify the subject (S) and verb (V) as well as any direct objects (DO), indirect objects (IO), subject complements (SC), or object complements (OC). Answers to starred items appear at the end of the book.

> *Example:*
>   S   V   V   DO
> Crime statistics can cause surprise.

*1. The number of serious crimes in the United States decreased.
*2. A decline in serious crimes occurred each year.
*3. The Crime Index measures serious crime.
*4. The FBI invented the index.
*5. The four serious violent crimes are murder, robbery, forcible rape, and aggravated assault.
  6. The Crime Index calls auto theft, burglary, arson, and larceny-theft the four serious crimes against property.
  7. The Crime Index gives the FBI a measure of crime.
  8. The index shows trends in crimes and criminals.
  9. The nation's largest cities showed the largest decline in crime.
10. However, crime actually increased in smaller cities, proving that the decline in crime is unrepresentative of the nation.

22c Learn alternative sentence patterns.

Most English sentences first name the actor in the subject and then assert something about the actor in the predicate. But four kinds of sentences alter this basic pattern.

1 ▪ Questions

The following are the most common ways of forming questions from statements. Remember to end a question with a question mark (p. 309).

▪ **Move the verb or a part of it to the beginning of the question.** These questions may be answered yes or no. The verb may be a form of *be:*

The rate is high. Is the rate high?

Or the verb may consist of a helping verb and a main verb. Then move the helping verb—or the first helping verb if there's more than one—to the front of the question:

Rates can rise. Can rates rise?
Rates have been rising. Have rates been rising?

- **Start the question with a form of *do*, and use the plain form of the verb.** In this type of question, the verb must consist of only one word and cannot be a form of *be*. The question can be answered yes or no.

  Interest rates rose. Did interest rates rise?

- **Add a question word to the beginning of a yes-or-no question.** The question words are *how, what, who, when, where, which,* and *why*. These questions require explanatory answers.

  Did rates rise today? Why did rates rise today?
  Is the rate high? Why is the rate high?

- **Add *who, what,* or *which* to the beginning of a question as the subject.** Then the subject-verb order remains the same as in a statement:

  Something is the answer. What is the answer?
  Someone can answer. Who can answer?

2 ▪ Commands

Construct a command simply by deleting the subject of the sentence, *you*:

Think of options. Eat your spinach.
Watch the news. Leave me alone.

3 ▪ Passive sentences

In the basic subject-predicate pattern, the subject performs the action of the verb. The verb is in the **active voice**:

     active
subject verb object
Kyong wrote the paper.

┌─ **Key terms** ───
helping verb A verb such as *can, may, be, have,* or *do* that forms a verb phrase with another verb to show time, permission, and other meanings. (See p. 197.)

main verb The verb that carries the principal meaning in a verb phrase: *has walked, could be happening.* (See p. 197.)

plain form The dictionary form of the verb: *You forget.* (See p. 196.)
└───

gram

22c

In the **passive voice,** the subject *receives* the action of the verb:

                       passive
        subject   verb
The paper was written by Kyong.

In the passive voice, the object of the active verb (*paper*) becomes the subject of the passive verb.

Passive verbs always consist of a form of *be* plus the past participle of the main verb (*paper was written, absences were excused*). The actual actor (the person or thing performing the action of the verb) may be expressed in a phrase (as in the example above: *by Kyong*) or may be omitted entirely if it is unknown or unimportant: *The house was flooded.*

For more on the formation and uses of the passive voice, see pages 244–45.

4 ▪ Sentences with postponed subjects

Two kinds of sentences state the subject after the predicate. In one, the normal word order reverses for emphasis:

The cause of the problem lies here. [Normal order.]
Here lies the cause of the problem. [Reversed order.]

The second kind of sentence starts with *there* or *it* and postpones the subject:

        verb   subject
There will be eighteen people at the meeting. [Normal order: *Eighteen people will be at the meeting.*]

        verb   subject
It was surprising that Marinetti was nominated. [Normal order: *That Marinetti was nominated was surprising.*]

The words *there* and *it* in such sentences are **expletives.** Their only function is to postpone the sentence subject. Expletive sentences do have their uses (see p. 190), but they are often just wordy.

    ⟨CULTURE LANGUAGE⟩ When you use an expletive construction, be careful to include *there* or *it.* Only commands and some questions can begin with verbs (see the previous page).

Faulty   No one predicted the nomination. Were no polls showing Marinetti ahead.

Revised   No one predicted the nomination. There were no polls showing Marinetti ahead.

Exercise 22.3   Rewriting passives and expletives

Rewrite each passive sentence as active, and rewrite each expletive construction to restore normal subject-predicate order. Answers to the starred items appear at the end of the book. For additional exercises with the passive voice and with expletives, see pages 150, 191, and 245–46.

Example:

All the trees in the park were planted by the city.
The city planted all the trees in the park.

*1. The screenplay for *Monster's Ball* was cowritten by Milo Addica and Will Rokos.
*2. The film was directed by Marc Foster.
 3. There was only one performance in the movie that received an Academy Award.
 4. It was Halle Berry who won the award for best actress.
 5. Berry was congratulated by the press for being the first African American to win the award.

23   Phrases and Subordinate Clauses

How do word groups work within sentences?

Word groups within sentences serve as modifiers (adjectives or adverbs) or as nouns. Most word groups are one of the following:

- **A phrase,** which lacks either a subject or a predicate or both: *fearing an accident; in a panic.*
- **A subordinate clause,** which contains a subject and a predicate (like a sentence) but begins with a subordinating word: *when prices rise; whoever laughs.*

Because they function as parts of speech (adjectives, adverbs, or nouns), phrases and subordinate clauses cannot stand alone as complete sentences (see Chapter 35 on sentence fragments).

gram
23

┌─ **Key terms** ───

subject The part of a word group that names who or what performs the action: *The moon rises* (main clause); *the moon rising* (phrase). (See p. 202.)

predicate The part of a word group containing a verb that asserts something about the subject: *On some days the moon rises* (main clause) *before the sun sets* (subordinate clause). (See p. 202.)

└───

┌───
│ mycomplab
│
│ Visit *mycomplab.com* for more resources and
│ exercises on phrases and subordinate clauses.
└───

23a   Learn to recognize phrases.

1 ▪ Prepositional phrases

A **prepositional phrase** consists of a preposition plus a noun, pronoun, or word group serving as a noun, called the **object of the preposition.** Prepositions include *about, at, by, for, to, under,* and *with.* A fuller list appears on page 199.

Preposition	Object
of	spaghetti
on	the surface
with	great satisfaction
upon	entering the room
from	where you are standing

Prepositional phrases usually function as adjectives or adverbs, adding details and making sentences more interesting for readers. An adjective phrase usually falls immediately after the word it modifies, but an adverb phrase need not.

Life on a raft was an opportunity for adventure.
noun adjective   noun   adjective phrase
     phrase

Huck Finn rode the raft by choice.
           verb   adverb phrase

With his companion, Jim, Huck met many types of people.
     adverb phrase   verb   noun adjective
                                                   phrase

2 ▪ Verbal phrases

Certain forms of verbs, called **verbals,** can serve as modifiers or nouns. Often these verbals appear with their own modifiers and objects in **verbal phrases.**

Note Verbals cannot serve alone as predicates in sentences. *The sun <u>rises</u> over the dump* is a sentence; *The sun <u>rising</u> over the dump* is a sentence fragment. (See pp. 289–90.)

Participial phrases

A **participle** is a verb form ending in *-ing* (*walking*) or, often, *-d* or *-ed* (*walked*). (See p. 196 for more on these forms.) Participles and participial phrases serve as adjectives. They usually fall just before or after the word they modify.

Strolling shoppers fill the malls.
adjective   noun

They make selections determined by personal taste.
                noun   adjective phrase

Note With irregular verbs, the past participle may have a different ending—for instance, *hidden funds*. (See p. 218.)

⟨CULTURE LANGUAGE⟩ For verbs expressing feeling, the present and past participles have different meanings: *It was a boring lecture. The bored students slept*. (See pp. 275–76.)

Gerund phrases

A **gerund** is the *-ing* form of a verb when it serves as a noun. Gerunds and gerund phrases replace nouns and can do whatever nouns can do.

sentence
subject
Shopping satisfies personal needs.
noun

object of
┌──preposition──┐
Malls are good at creating such needs.
noun phrase

Infinitive phrases

An **infinitive** is the plain form of a verb plus *to: to hide*. Infinitives and infinitive phrases serve as adjectives, adverbs, or nouns. A noun or noun phrase replaces a noun:

sentence
┌──subject──┐ ┌──────subject complement──────┐
To design a mall is to create an artificial environment.
noun phrase   noun phrase

An adverb or adverb phrase modifies a verb, adjective, other adverb, or entire word group and may fall near or away from the word it modifies:

To achieve this goal, designers emphasize the familiar.
adverb phrase   verb

Malls are designed to make shoppers feel safe.
verb   adverb phrase

An adjective or adjective phrase modifies a noun or pronoun and usually falls immediately after the word it modifies:

The environment supports the impulse to shop.
noun adjective

⟨CULTURE LANGUAGE⟩ Infinitives and gerunds may follow some verbs and not others and may differ in meaning after a verb: *The cowboy stopped to sing. The cowboy stopped singing*. (See pp. 229–31.)

3 ▪ Absolute phrases

An **absolute phrase** consists of a noun or pronoun and a participle, plus any modifiers. It modifies the rest of its sentence and may fall in more than one place in the sentence.

gram

23a

Their own place established, many ethnic groups are making way for
    absolute phrase
new arrivals.

Unlike a participial phrase, an absolute phrase always contains a noun that serves as its subject:

Learning English, many immigrants discover American culture.
participial phrase

Immigrants having learned English, their opportunities widen.
        absolute phrase

4 ▪ Appositive phrases

An **appositive** is usually a noun that renames another noun. An appositive phrase includes modifiers as well. Both appositives and appositive phrases usually fall immediately after the nouns they rename.

Bizen ware, a dark stoneware, is produced in Japan.
noun   appositive phrase

Appositives and appositive phrases sometimes begin with *that is, such as, for example,* or *in other words.*

Bizen ware is used in the Japanese tea ceremony, that is, the Zen Bud-
                    noun   appositive phrase
dhist observance that links meditation and art.

Exercise 23.1   Identifying phrases

In each sentence below, identify every verbal and appositive and every verbal, appositive, prepositional, and absolute phrase. All the sentences include at least two such words or phrases. Answers to starred items appear at the end of the book.

Example:
                    ———participial phrase———
Modern English contains words borrowed from many sources.
                        └prepositional phrase┘

*1. With its many synonyms, or words with similar meanings, English can make choosing the right word a difficult task.
*2. Borrowing words from other languages such as French and Latin, English acquired an unusual number of synonyms.
*3. Having so many choices, how does a writer decide between *motherly* and *maternal* or among *womanly, feminine,* and *female?*
*4. Some people prefer longer and more ornate words to avoid the flatness of short words.
*5. During the Renaissance a heated debate occurred between the Latinists, favoring Latin words, and the Saxonists, preferring Anglo-Saxon words derived from Germanic roots.
  6. Students in writing classes are often told to choose the shorter word, generally an Anglo-Saxon derivative.

7. Better advice, wrote William Hazlitt, is the principle of choosing "the best word in common use."
8. Keeping this principle in mind, a writer would choose either *womanly,* the Anglo-Saxon word, or *feminine,* a French derivative, according to meaning and situation.
9. Synonyms rarely have exactly the same meaning, usage having created subtle but real differences over time.
10. The Old English word *handbook,* for example, has a slightly different meaning from the French derivative *manual,* a close synonym.

23b   Learn to recognize subordinate clauses.

A **clause** is any group of words that contains both a subject and a predicate. There are two kinds of clauses, and the distinction between them is important:

- A **main clause** makes a complete statement and can stand alone as a sentence: *The sky darkened.*
- A **subordinate clause** is just like a main clause *except* that it begins with a subordinating word: *when the sky darkened; whoever calls.* The subordinating word reduces the clause from a complete statement to a single part of speech: an adjective, adverb, or noun.

Note A subordinate clause punctuated as a sentence is a sentence fragment. (See pp. 289–91.)

Adjective clauses

An **adjective clause** modifies a noun or pronoun. It usually begins with the relative pronoun *who, whom, whose, which,* or *that* but may also begin with *where, when,* or *why.* The clause ordinarily falls immediately after the word it modifies.

Parents who cannot read may have bad memories of school.
noun   adjective clause

Children whom the schools fail sometimes have illiterate parents.
noun   adjective clause

One school, which is open year-round, helps parents learn to read.
noun   adjective clause

The school is in a city where the illiteracy rate is high.
noun   adjective clause

gram
23b

In the first three examples, the relative pronouns *who, whom,* and *which* refer to the nouns modified by the clause (*Parents, Children, school*). The relative pronoun serves as the subject of its clause (*who cannot read, which is open year-round*) or as an object (*whom the schools fail*). In the last example, *where* substitutes for *in which* (*a city in which the illiteracy rate is high*).

See pages 315–17 for advice on punctuating adjective clauses.

Adverb clauses

An **adverb clause** modifies a verb, an adjective, another adverb, or a whole word group. It always begins with a subordinating conjunction, such as *after, although, because, even though, how, if, until, when,* or *while.* (See p. 200 for a fuller list.) The clause may fall in more than one place in its sentence (but see pp. 282–83 for limitations).

The school began teaching parents when adult illiteracy gained na-
verb   adverb clause
tional attention.

At first the program was not as successful as its founders had hoped.
                              adjective   adverb clause

Because it was directed at people who could not read, advertising had
             adverb clause   main clause
to be inventive.

Noun clauses

A **noun clause** replaces a noun in a sentence and serves as a subject, object, or complement. It begins with *that, what, whatever, who, whom, whoever, whomever, when, where, whether, why,* or *how.*

─────── sentence subject ───────
Whether the program would succeed depended on door-to-door adver-
             noun clause
tising.

─────── object of verb ───────
Teachers explained in person how the program would work.
                              noun clause

─────── sentence subject ───────
Whoever seemed slightly interested was invited to an open meeting.
      noun clause

─────── object of preposition ───────
A few parents were anxious about what their children would think.
                              noun clause

─────── subject complement ───────
The children's needs were what the parents asked most about.
                              noun clause

> **Key terms**
>
> **object** A noun, pronoun, or word group that receives the action of or is influenced by a transitive verb, a verbal, or a preposition. An object may be a *direct object,* an *indirect object,* or an *object of a preposition.* (See pp. 204–05 and 210.)
>
> **complement** A word or word group that completes the sense of a subject, an object, or a verb. (See pp. 205 and 206.)

Exercise 23.2 Identifying clauses

Underline the subordinate clauses in the following sentences. Then identify each one as adjective (ADJ), adverb (ADV), or noun (N) by determining how it functions in its sentence. Answers to starred items appear at the end of the book.

Example:

N

Whoever follows the Koran refers to God as *Allah,* the Arabic word for his name.

* 1. The Prophet Muhammad, who was the founder of Islam, was born about 570 CE in the city of Mecca.
* 2. He grew up in the care of his grandfather and an uncle because both of his parents had died.
* 3. His family was part of a powerful Arab tribe that lived in western Arabia.
* 4. When Muhammad was about forty years old, he had a vision while he was in a cave outside Mecca.
* 5. He believed that God had selected him to be the prophet of a true religion for the Arab people.
  6. Throughout his life he continued to have revelations, which have been written in the Koran.
  7. The Koran is the sacred book of Muslims, who as adherents of Islam view Muhammad as God's messenger.
  8. When he no longer had the support of the clans of Mecca, Muhammad and his followers moved to Medina.
  9. There they established an organized Muslim community that sometimes clashed with the Meccans and with Jewish clans.
 10. Throughout his life Muhammad continued as the religious, political, and military leader of Islam as it spread in Asia and Africa.

24 Sentence Types

How can classifying sentences help me construct them?

Understanding the ways of structuring sentences can be helpful for managing the flow and emphasis of information. One useful classification identifies four sentence types: simple, compound, complex, and compound-complex.

mycomplab

Visit *mycomplab.com* for more resources and exercises on sentence types.

24a Learn to recognize simple sentences.

A **simple sentence** consists of a single main clause and no subordinate clause:

```
┌──────────main clause──────────┐
Last summer was unusually hot.
```

```
┌──────────────────main clause────────────────────────┐
The summer made many farmers leave the area for good or reduced
──────────────────────
them to bare existence.
```

24b Learn to recognize compound sentences.

A **compound sentence** consists of two or more main clauses and no subordinate clause.

```
┌──main clause──┐       ┌──────main clause──────┐
Last July was hot, but August was even hotter.
```

```
┌──────────main clause──────────┐       ┌──────────main clause──────────┐
The hot sun scorched the earth, and the lack of rain killed many crops.
```

24c Learn to recognize complex sentences.

A **complex sentence** consists of one main clause and one or more subordinate clauses:

```
┌──main clause──┐ ┌──────────subordinate clause──────────┐
Rain finally came, although many had left the area by then.
```

```
┌──────────────main clause──────────────┐ ┌─subordinate clause─
Those who remained were able to start anew because the govern-
            subordinate clause
─────────────────────────
ment came to their aid.
```

gram
24d

24d Learn to recognize compound-complex sentences.

A **compound-complex sentence** has the characteristics of both the compound sentence (two or more main clauses) and the complex sentence (at least one subordinate clause):

```
┌──────────subordinate clause──────────┐ ┌──────main clause──────┐
When government aid finally came, many people had already been
──────────────────────┐       ┌──────main clause──────┐
reduced to poverty and others had been forced to move.
```

Exercise 24.1 Identifying sentence structures

Mark the main clauses and subordinate clauses in the following sentences. Then identify each sentence as simple, compound, complex, or compound-complex. Answers to starred items appear at the end of the book.

Example:

┌──────────────main clause──────────────┐ ┌─subordinate clause─┐
The human voice is produced in the larynx, which has two bands
called vocal chords. [Complex.]

*1. Our world has many sounds, but they all have one thing in common.
*2. The one thing that all sounds share is that they are produced by vibrations.
*3. The vibrations make the air move in waves, and these sound waves travel to the ear.
*4. When sound waves enter the ear, the auditory nerves convey them to the brain, and the brain interprets them.
*5. Sound waves can also travel through other material, such as water and even the solid earth.

6. Some sounds are pleasant, and others, which we call noise, are not.
7. Most noises are produced by irregular vibrations at irregular intervals; an example is the barking of a dog.
8. Sounds have frequency and pitch.
9. When an object vibrates rapidly, it produces high-frequency, high-pitched sounds.
10. People can hear sounds over a wide range of frequencies, but dogs, cats, and many other animals can hear high frequencies that humans cannot.

─── VERBS ───

Verbs express actions, conditions, and states of being. The basic uses and forms of verbs are described on pages 196–97. This section explains and solves the most common problems with verbs' forms (Chapter 25), tenses (26), mood (27), and voice (28) and shows how to make verbs match their subjects (29).

25 Verb Forms

What's wrong with *throwed* and *have went*?

Throwed and *have went* are forms of the verbs *throw* and *go* that are considered incorrect in standard American English. (The standard forms are *threw* or *thrown* and *have gone*.) Errors like these in

> mycomplab ▌
>
> Visit *mycomplab.com* for more resources and exercises on verb forms.

verb forms can frustrate or confuse readers who expect standard English.

This chapter focuses on the verb forms most likely to cause difficulty: irregular verbs (below), *-s* and *-ed* endings (p. 222), helping verbs (p. 224), verbs followed by *-ing* or *to* words (p. 229), and two-word verbs (p. 231).

25a   Use the correct forms of *sing/sang/sung* and other irregular verbs.

Most verbs are **regular**: they form their past tense and past participle by adding *-d* or *-ed* to the plain form:

Plain form	Past tense	Past participle
live	lived	lived
act	acted	acted

About two hundred English verbs are **irregular**: they form their past tense and past participle in some irregular way. Check a dictionary under the verb's plain form if you have any doubt about its other forms. If the verb is irregular, the dictionary will list the plain form, the past tense, and the past participle in that order (*go, went, gone*). If the dictionary gives only two forms (as in *think, thought*), then the past tense and the past participle are the same.

Common irregular verbs

Plain form	Past tense	Past participle
arise	arose	arisen
be	was, were	been
become	became	become
begin	began	begun
bend	bent	bent
bite	bit	bitten, bit
blow	blew	blown
break	broke	broken

Key terms

plain form The dictionary form of the verb: *I walk*. *You forget*. (See p. 196.)

past-tense form The verb form indicating action that occurred in the past: *I walked*. *You forgot*. (See p. 196.)

past participle The verb form used with *have, has,* or *had: I have walked*. It may also serve as a modifier: *This is a forgotten book*. (See p. 196.)

Plain form	Past tense	Past participle
bring	brought	brought
build	built	built
burst	burst	burst
buy	bought	bought
catch	caught	caught
choose	chose	chosen
come	came	come
cut	cut	cut
dig	dug	dug
dive	dived, dove	dived
do	did	done
draw	drew	drawn
dream	dreamed, dreamt	dreamed, dreamt
drink	drank	drunk
drive	drove	driven
eat	ate	eaten
fall	fell	fallen
find	found	found
fly	flew	flown
forget	forgot	forgotten, forgot
freeze	froze	frozen
get	got	got, gotten
give	gave	given
go	went	gone
grow	grew	grown
hang (suspend)	hung	hung
hang (execute)	hanged	hanged
have	had	had
hear	heard	heard
hide	hid	hidden
hold	held	held
hurt	hurt	hurt
keep	kept	kept
know	knew	known
lay	laid	laid
lead	led	led
leave	left	left
let	let	let
lie	lay	lain

vb
25a

(continued)

Common irregular verbs

(continued)

Plain form	Past tense	Past participle
lose	lost	lost
pay	paid	paid
ride	rode	ridden
ring	rang	rung
rise	rose	risen
run	ran	run
say	said	said
see	saw	seen
set	set	set
shake	shook	shaken
shrink	shrank, shrunk	shrunk, shrunken
sing	sang, sung	sung
sink	sank, sunk	sunk
sit	sat	sat
sleep	slept	slept
speak	spoke	spoken
stand	stood	stood
steal	stole	stolen
swim	swam	swum
swing	swung	swung
take	took	taken
throw	threw	thrown
wear	wore	worn
write	wrote	written

vb

25a

Grammar checkers A grammar checker may flag incorrect forms of irregular verbs, but it may also fail to do so. For example, a checker flagged *The runner stealed second base* (*stole* is correct) but not *The runner had steal second base* (*stolen* is correct). When in doubt about the forms of irregular verbs, refer to the preceding list or consult a dictionary.

CULTURE LANGUAGE Some English dialects use distinctive verb forms that differ from those of standard American English: for instance, *drug* for *dragged*, *growed* for *grew*, *come* for *came*, or *went* for *gone*. In situations requiring standard American English, use the forms in the preceding list or in a dictionary.

Exercise 25.1 **Using irregular verbs**

For each irregular verb in brackets, supply either the past tense or the past participle, as appropriate, and identify the form you used. Answers to starred items appear at the end of the book.

> *Example:*
> Though we had [hide] the cash box, it was [steal].
> Though we had <u>hidden</u> the cash box, it was <u>stolen</u>. [Two past participles.]

*1. The world population has [grow] by two-thirds of a billion people in less than a decade.

*2. Recently it [break] the 6 billion mark.

*3. Experts have [draw] pictures of a crowded future.

*4. They predict that the world population may have [slide] up to as much as 10 billion by the year 2050.

*5. Though the food supply [rise] in the last decade, the share to each person [fall].

6. At the same time the water supply, which had actually [become] healthier in the twentieth century, [sink] in size and quality.

7. The number of species on earth [shrink] by 20 percent.

8. Changes in land use [run] nomads and subsistence farmers off the land.

9. Yet all has not been [lose].

10. Recently human beings have [begin] to heed these and other problems and to explore how technology can be [drive] to help the earth and all its populations.

11. Some new techniques for waste processing have [prove] effective.

12. Crop management has [take] some pressure off lands with poor soil, allowing their owners to produce food.

13. Genetic engineering could replenish food supplies that have [shrink].

14. Population control has [find] adherents all over the world.

15. Many endangered species have been [give] room to thrive.

vb

25b

25b Distinguish between *sit* and *set, lie* and *lay,* and *rise* and *raise.*

The forms of *sit* and *set, lie* and *lay,* and *rise* and *raise* are easy to confuse.

Plain form	Past tense	Past participle
sit	sat	sat
set	set	set
lie	lay	lain
lay	laid	laid
rise	rose	risen
raise	raised	raised

In each of these confusing pairs, one verb is intransitive (it does not take an object) and one is transitive (it does take an object). (See p. 204 for more on this distinction.)

Intransitive

The patients <u>lie</u> in their hospital beds. [*Lie* means "recline" and takes no object.]

Visitors <u>sit</u> with them. [*Sit* means "be seated" or "be located" and takes no object.]

Patients' temperatures <u>rise</u>. [*Rise* means "increase" or "get up" and takes no object.]

Transitive

Orderlies <u>lay</u> the dinner trays on tables. [*Lay* means "place" and takes an object, here *trays*.]

Orderlies <u>set</u> the trays down. [*Set* means "place" and takes an object, here *trays*.]

Nursing aides <u>raise</u> the shades. [*Raise* means "lift" or "bring up" and takes an object, here *shades*.]

Exercise 25.2   **Distinguishing between** *sit/set, lie/lay, rise/raise*

Choose the correct verb from the pair given in brackets. Then supply the past tense or past participle, as appropriate. Answers to starred items appear at the end of the book.

> *Example:*
>
> After I washed all the windows, I [<u>lie</u>, lay] down the squeegee and then I [<u>sit</u>, set] the table.
>
> After I washed all the windows, I <u>laid</u> down the squeegee and then I <u>set</u> the table.

*1. Yesterday afternoon the child [<u>lie</u>, lay] down for a nap.
*2. The child has been [<u>rise</u>, raise] by her grandparents.

 3. Most days her grandfather has [<u>sit</u>, set] with her, reading her stories.
 4. She has [<u>rise</u>, raise] at dawn most mornings.
 5. Her toys were [<u>lie</u>, lay] on the floor.

25c Use the *-s* and *-ed* forms of the verb when they are required.

Speakers of some English dialects and nonnative speakers of English sometimes omit the *-s* and *-ed* verb endings when they are required in standard American English.

Grammar checkers A grammar checker will flag many omitted *-s* and *-ed* endings from verbs, as in *he ask* and *was ask*. But it will miss many omissions, too.

1 ▪ Required -s ending

Use the -s form of a verb when *both* of these situations hold:

- **The subject is a singular noun (*boy*), an indefinite pronoun (*everyone*), or *he, she,* or *it*.** These subjects are **third person,** used when someone or something is being spoken about.
- **The verb's action occurs in the present.**

The letter asks [not ask] for a quick response.
Delay costs [not cost] money.

Be especially careful with the -s forms of *be* (*is*), *have* (*has*), and *do* (*does, doesn't*). These forms should always be used to indicate present time with third-person singular subjects.

The company is [not be] late in responding.
It has [not have] problems.
It doesn't [not don't] have the needed data.
The contract does [not do] depend on the response.

In addition, *be* has the -s form *was* in the past tense with *I* and third-person singular subjects:

The company was [not were] in trouble before.

Except for the past-tense *I was, I, you,* and plural subjects do *not* take the -s form of verbs:

I am [not is] a student.
You are [not is] also a student.
They are [not is] students, too.

vb

25c

2 ▪ Required -ed or -d ending

The -ed or -d verb form is required in *any* of these situations:

- **The verb's action occurred in the past:**

The company asked [not ask] for more time.

- **The verb form functions as a modifier:**

The data concerned [not concern] should be retrievable.

- **The verb form combines with a form of *be* or *have*:**

The company is supposed [not suppose] to be the best.
It has developed [not develop] an excellent reputation.

Watch especially for a needed -ed or -d ending when it isn't pronounced clearly in speech, as in *asked, discussed, mixed, supposed, walked,* and *used.*

Exercise 25.3   Using *-s* and *-ed* verb endings

Supply the correct form of each verb in brackets. Be careful to include *-s* and *-ed* (or *-d*) endings where they are needed for standard English. Answers to starred items appear at the end of the book.

Example:

Unfortunately, the roof on our new house already [leak].
Unfortunately, the roof on our new house already <u>leaks</u>.

*1. A teacher sometimes [ask] too much of a student.
*2. In high school I was once [punish] for being sick.
*3. I had [miss] a week of school because of a serious case of the flu.
*4. I [realize] that I would fail a test unless I had a chance to make up the class work.
*5. I [discuss] the problem with the teacher.

  6. He said I was [suppose] to make up the work while I was sick.
  7. At that I [walk] out of the class.
  8. I [receive] a failing grade then, but it did not change my attitude.
  9. I [work] harder in the courses that have more understanding teachers.
10. Today I still balk when a teacher [make] unreasonable demands or [expect] miracles.

25d   Use helping verbs with main verbs appropriately.

vb
25d

Helping verbs combine with main verbs in verb phrases: *The line should have been cut. Who was calling?*

Grammar checkers A grammar checker will often spot omitted helping verbs and incorrect main verbs with helping verbs, but sometimes it will not. A checker flagged *Many been fortunate* but overlooked *The conference will be occurred.*

1 ▪ Required helping verbs

Standard American English requires helping verbs in certain situations:

▪ **The main verb ends in *-ing*:**

Researchers <u>are</u> conducting fieldwork all over the world. [Not <u>Researchers conducting</u>. . . .]

Key terms

helping verb A verb such as *can, may, be, have,* or *do* that forms a verb phrase with another verb to show time, permission, and other meanings. (See p. 197.)

main verb The verb that carries the principal meaning in a verb phrase: *has <u>walked</u>, could be <u>happening</u>.* (See p. 197.)

verb phrase A helping verb plus a main verb: *would speak.* (See p. 196.)

▪ **The main verb is *been* or *be*:**

Many <u>have</u> been fortunate in their discoveries. [Not <u>Many been</u>. . . .]
Some <u>could</u> be real-life Indiana Joneses. [Not <u>Some be</u>. . . .]

▪ **The main verb is a past participle,** such as *talked, begun,* or *thrown*:

Their discoveries <u>were</u> covered in newspapers and magazines. [Not <u>Their discoveries covered</u>. . . .]
The researchers <u>have</u> given interviews on TV. [Not <u>The researchers given</u>. . . .]

The omission of a helping verb may create an incomplete sentence, or **sentence fragment,** because a present participle (*conducting*), an irregular past participle (*been*), or the infinitive *be* cannot stand alone as the only verb in a sentence (see pp. 289–90). To work as sentence verbs, these verb forms need helping verbs.

2 ▪ Combination of helping verb + main verb

Helping verbs and main verbs combine into verb phrases in specific ways.

Note The main verb in a verb phrase (the one carrying the main meaning) does not change to show a change in subject or time: *she has <u>sung</u>, you had <u>sung</u>.* Only the helping verb may change.

Form of *be* + present participle

The progressive tenses indicate action in progress. Create them with *be, am, is, are, was, were,* or *been* followed by the main verb's present participle, as in the following example.

She <u>is working</u> on a new book.

vb

25d

Be and *been* require additional helping verbs to form the progressive tenses:

can	might	should ⎫	have ⎫
could	must	will ⎬ <u>be</u> working	has ⎬ <u>been</u> working
may	shall	would ⎭	had ⎭

┌ Key terms ───────────────────────────

past participle The *-d* or *-ed* form of a regular verb: *hedged, walked.* Most irregular verbs have distinctive past participles: *eaten, swum.* (See p. 196.)

present participle The *-ing* form of the verb: *flying, writing.* (See p. 196.)

progressive tenses Verb tenses expressing action in progress—for instance, *I am flying* (present progressive), *I was flying* (past progressive), *I will be flying* (future progressive). (See pp. 236–37.)

When forming the progressive tenses, be sure to use the *-ing* form of the main verb:

Faulty   Her ideas are <u>grow</u> more complex. She is <u>developed</u> a new approach to ethics.

Revised   Her ideas are <u>growing</u> more complex. She is <u>developing</u> a new approach to ethics.

Form of *be* + past participle

The passive voice of the verb indicates that the subject *receives* the action of the verb. Create the passive voice with *be, am, is, are, was, were, being,* or *been* followed by the past participle of a transitive verb:

Her latest book <u>was completed</u> in four months.

Be, being, and *been* require additional helping verbs to form the passive voice:

have ⎱
has ⎰ <u>been</u> completed   am was ⎱
had   is   were ⎰ <u>being</u> completed
                 are

will <u>be</u> completed

Be sure to use the main verb's past participle for the passive voice:

Faulty   Her next book will be <u>publish</u> soon.
Revised   Her next book will be <u>published</u> soon.

Note Only transitive verbs may form the passive voice:

Faulty   A philosophy conference <u>will be occurred</u> in the same week. [*Occur* is not a transitive verb.]

Revised   A philosophy conference <u>will occur</u> in the same week.

See pages 244–45 for advice on when to use and when to avoid the passive voice.

Forms of *have*

Four forms of *have* serve as helping verbs: *have, has, had, having.* One of these forms plus the main verb's past participle creates

---

Key terms

passive voice The verb form when the subject names the receiver of the verb's action: *An essay <u>was written</u> by every student.* (See pp. 207–08.)

transitive verb A verb that requires an object to complete its meaning: *Every student <u>completed</u> an essay* (*essay* is the object of *completed*). (See p. 204.)

one of the perfect tenses, those expressing action completed before another specific time or action:

Some students <u>have complained</u> about the laboratory.
Others <u>had complained</u> before.

Will and other helping verbs sometimes accompany forms of *have* in the perfect tenses:

Several more students <u>will have complained</u> by the end of the week.

Forms of *do*

Do, does, and *did* have three uses as helping verbs, always with the plain form of the main verb:

- **To pose a question:** *How <u>did</u> the trial <u>end</u>?*
- **To emphasize the main verb:** *It <u>did end</u> eventually.*
- **To negate the main verb, along with *not* or *never*:** *The judge <u>did not withdraw</u>.*

Be sure to use the main verb's plain form with any form of *do*:

Faulty   The judge did <u>remained</u> in court.
Revised   The judge did <u>remain</u> in court.

Modals

The modal helping verbs include *can, may, should, would,* and several two- and three-word combinations, such as *have to* and *be supposed to.* (See p. 197 for a list of helping verbs.)

Modals convey various meanings, with these being most common:

- **Ability:** *can, could, be able to*

The equipment <u>can detect</u> small vibrations. [Present.]

The equipment <u>could detect</u> small vibrations. [Past.]

The equipment <u>is able to detect</u> small vibrations. [Present. Past: *was able to.* Future: *will be able to.*]

- **Possibility:** *could, may, might; could/may/might have* + past participle

The equipment <u>could fail</u>. [Present.]
The equipment <u>may fail</u>. [Present or future.]
The equipment <u>might fail</u>. [Present or future.]
The equipment <u>may have failed</u>. [Past.]

vb

25d

┌─ **Key term** ─────────────────────────────
perfect tenses Verb tenses expressing an action completed before another specific time or action: *We have eaten* (present perfect), *We had eaten* (past perfect), *We will have eaten* (future perfect). (See p. 236.)

■ **Necessity or obligation:** *must, have to, be supposed to*

The lab <u>must purchase</u> a backup. [Present or future.]
The lab <u>has to purchase</u> a backup. [Present or future. Past: *had to.*]
The lab <u>will have to purchase</u> a backup. [Future.]
The lab <u>is supposed to purchase</u> a backup. [Present. Past: *was supposed to.*]

■ **Permission:** *may, can, could*

The lab <u>may spend</u> the money. [Present or future.]
The lab <u>can spend</u> the money. [Present or future.]
The lab <u>could spend</u> the money. [Present or future, more tentative.]
The lab <u>could have spent</u> the money. [Past.]

■ **Intention:** *will, shall, would*

The lab <u>will spend</u> the money. [Future.]

<u>Shall</u> we <u>offer</u> advice? [Future. Use *shall* for questions requesting opinion or consent.]

We <u>would have offered</u> advice. [Past.]

■ **Request:** *could, can, would*

Could [or <u>Can</u> or <u>Would</u>] you please <u>obtain</u> a bid? [Present or future.]

■ **Advisability:** *should, had better, ought to; should have* + past participle

You <u>should obtain</u> three bids. [Present or future.]
You <u>had better obtain</u> three bids. [Present or future.]
You <u>ought to obtain</u> three bids. [Present or future.]
You <u>should have obtained</u> three bids. [Past.]

■ **Past habit:** *would, used to*

In years past we <u>would obtain</u> five bids.
We <u>used to obtain</u> five bids.

Exercise 25.4   Using helping verbs

Add helping verbs to the following sentences where they are needed for standard American English. Answers to starred items appear at the end of the book.

> *Example:*
> The school be opened to shelter storm victims.
> The school <u>will</u> be opened to shelter storm victims.

*1. Each year thousands of new readers been discovering Agatha Christie's mysteries.
*2. The books written by a prim woman who had worked as a nurse during World War I.
3. Christie never expected that her play *The Mousetrap* be performed for decades.

4. During her life Christie always complaining about movie versions of her stories.
5. Readers of her stories been delighted to be baffled by her.

Exercise 25.5   Revising: Helping verbs plus main verbs

Revise the following sentences so that helping verbs and main verbs are used correctly. If a sentence is correct as given, mark the number preceding it. Answers to starred items appear at the end of the book.

Example:

The college testing service has test as many as five hundred students at one time.

The college testing service has <u>tested</u> as many as five hundred students at one time.

*1. A report from the Bureau of the Census has confirm a widening gap between rich and poor.

*2. As suspected, the percentage of people below the poverty level did increased over the last decade.

3. More than 17 percent of the population is make 5 percent of all the income.

4. About 1 percent of the population will keeping an average of $500,000 apiece after taxes.

5. The other 99 percent all together will retain about $300,000.

25e   Use a gerund or an infinitive after a verb as appropriate.

Gerunds and infinitives may follow certain verbs but not others. And sometimes the use of a gerund or infinitive with the same verb changes the meaning of the verb.

Grammar checkers A grammar checker will spot some but not all errors in matching gerunds or infinitives with verbs. For example, a checker flagged *I adore <u>to shop</u>* but not *I practice <u>to swim</u>* or *I promise <u>helping</u> out*. Use the lists given here and a dictionary of English as a second language to determine whether an infinitive or a gerund is appropriate. (See p. 176 for a list of ESL dictionaries.)

1 ▪ Either gerund or infinitive

A gerund or an infinitive may come after the following verbs with no significant difference in meaning.

┌─ **Key terms** ─────────────────────────

gerund The *-ing* form of the verb used as a noun: *Smoking is unhealthful.* (See p. 211.)

infinitive The plain form of the verb usually preceded by *to: to smoke.* An infinitive may serve as an adjective, adverb, or noun. (See p. 211.)

begin	continue	intend	prefer
can't bear	hate	like	start
can't stand	hesitate	love	

The pump began <u>working</u>. The pump began <u>to work</u>.

2 ▪ Meaning change with gerund or infinitive

With four verbs, a gerund has quite a different meaning from an infinitive:

forget	stop
remember	try

The engineer stopped <u>eating</u>. [He no longer ate.]
The engineer stopped <u>to eat</u>. [He stopped in order to eat.]

3 ▪ Gerund, not infinitive

Do not use an infinitive after these verbs:

admit	discuss	mind	recollect
adore	dislike	miss	resent
appreciate	enjoy	postpone	resist
avoid	escape	practice	risk
consider	finish	put off	suggest
deny	imagine	quit	tolerate
detest	keep	recall	understand

Faulty   He finished <u>to eat</u> lunch.
Revised   He finished <u>eating</u> lunch.

vb

25e

4 ▪ Infinitive, not gerund

Do not use a gerund after these verbs:

agree	claim	manage	promise
appear	consent	mean	refuse
arrange	decide	offer	say
ask	expect	plan	wait
assent	have	prepare	want
beg	hope	pretend	wish

Faulty   He decided <u>checking</u> the pump.
Revised   He decided <u>to check</u> the pump.

5 ▪ Noun or pronoun + infinitive

Some verbs may be followed by an infinitive alone or by a noun or pronoun and an infinitive. The presence of a noun or pronoun changes the meaning.

ask	dare	need	wish
beg	expect	promise	would like
choose	help	want	

He expected to watch.
He expected his workers to watch.

Some verbs *must* be followed by a noun or pronoun before an
infinitive:

admonish	encourage	oblige	require
advise	forbid	order	teach
allow	force	permit	tell
cause	hire	persuade	train
challenge	instruct	remind	urge
command	invite	request	warn
convince			

He instructed his workers to watch.

Do not use *to* before the infinitive when it follows one of the
next verbs and a noun or pronoun:

feel	make ("force")
have	see
hear	watch
let	

He let his workers learn by observation.

Exercise 25.6 Revising: Verbs plus gerunds
or infinitives

Revise the following sentences so that gerunds or infinitives are used correctly with verbs. Mark the number preceding any sentence that is already
correct. Answers to starred items appear at the end of the book.

Example:

A politician cannot avoid to alienate some voters.
A politician cannot avoid alienating some voters.

*1. A program called HELP Wanted tries to encourage citizens take ac-
   tion on behalf of American competitiveness.
*2. Officials working on this program hope improving education for
   work.
 3. American businesses find that some workers need learning to read.
 4. In the next ten years the United States expects facing a shortage of
   350,000 scientists.
 5. HELP Wanted suggests creating a media campaign.

25f Use the appropriate particles with
two-word verbs.

Standard American English includes some verbs that consist of
two words: the verb itself and a **particle**, a preposition or adverb
that affects the meaning of the verb. For example:

vb
25f

Look up the answer. [Research the answer.]
Look over the answer. [Examine the answer.]

The meanings of these two-word verbs are often quite different from the meanings of the individual words that make them up. (There are some three-word verbs, too, such as *look out for, put up with,* and *run out of.*)

A dictionary of English as a second language will define two-word verbs for you and say whether the verbs may be separated in a sentence, as explained below. (See p. 176 for a list of ESL dictionaries.) A grammar checker will recognize few if any misuses of two-word verbs.

Note Many two-word verbs are more common in speech than in more formal academic or public writing. For formal writing, consider using *research* instead of *look up, examine* or *inspect* instead of *look over.*

1 ▪ Inseparable two-word verbs

Verbs and particles that may not be separated by any other words include the following:

catch on	go over	play around	stay away
come across	grow up	run into	stay up
get along	keep on	run out of	take care of
give in	look into	speak up	turn up at

Faulty   Children <u>grow</u> quickly <u>up</u>.
Revised   Children <u>grow up</u> quickly.

2 ▪ Separable two-word verbs

Most two-word verbs that take direct objects may be separated by the object.

Parents <u>help out</u> their children.
Parents <u>help</u> their children <u>out</u>.

If the direct object is a pronoun, the pronoun *must* separate the verb from the particle.

Faulty   Parents <u>help out</u> them.
Revised   Parents <u>help</u> them <u>out</u>.

> ┌─ **Key terms** ─────────────────────────────
>
> **preposition** A word such as *about, for,* or *to* that takes a noun or pronoun as its object: <u>at</u> *the house,* <u>in</u> *the woods.* (See p. 199 for a list of prepositions.)
>
> **adverb** A word that modifies a verb (*went* <u>down</u>), adjective (<u>very</u> *pretty*), another adverb (<u>too</u> *sweetly*), or a whole word group (<u>Eventually</u>, *the fire died*). (See p. 198.)

vb

25f

The separable two-word verbs include the following:

bring up	give back	make up	throw out
call off	hand in	point out	try on
call up	hand out	put away	try out
drop off	help out	put back	turn down
fill out	leave out	put off	turn on
fill up	look over	take out	turn up
give away	look up	take over	wrap up

Exercise 25.7 Revising: Verbs plus particles

The two- and three-word verbs in the sentences below are underlined. Some are correct as given, and some are not because they should or should not be separated by other words. Revise the verbs and other words that are incorrect. Consult the preceding lists or an ESL dictionary if necessary to determine which verbs are separable. Answers to starred items appear at the end of the book.

> *Example:*
>
> Hollywood producers never seem to come up with entirely new plots, but they also never run new ways out of to present old ones.
>
> Hollywood producers never seem to come up with [correct] entirely new plots, but they also never run out of new ways to present old ones.

*1. American movies treat everything from going out with someone to making up an ethnic identity, but few people look their significance into.

*2. While some viewers stay away from topical films, others turn at the theater up simply because a movie has sparked debate.

3. Some movies attracted rowdy spectators, and the theaters had to throw out them.

4. Filmmakers have always been eager to point their influence out to the public.

5. Everyone agrees that filmmakers will keep creating controversy on, if only because it can fill up theaters.

26 Verb Tenses

Walked and *had walked* illustrate different **tenses** of the verb *to walk*. That is, they show the action of the verb to be occurring at different times, one (*had walked*) before the other (*walked*) and both before the present. The box opposite gives the tense forms for a regular verb. (Irregular verbs have some different forms. See pp. 218–20.)

Grammar checkers A grammar checker can provide little help with incorrect verb tenses and tense sequences because correctness usually depends on meaning.

CULTURE LANGUAGE In standard American English, a verb conveys time and sequence through its form. In some other languages and English dialects, various markers besides verb form may indicate the time of a verb. For instance, in African American dialect *I be attending class on Friday* means that the speaker attends class every Friday. But to someone who doesn't know the dialect, the sentence could mean last Friday, this Friday, or every Friday. In standard American English, the intended meaning is indicated by verb tense: *I attended class on Friday. I will attend class on Friday. I attend class on Friday.*

26a Observe the special uses of the present tense (*sing*).

The present tense has several distinctive uses.

Action occurring now

She understands the problem.
We define the problem differently.

Habitual or recurring action

Banks regularly undergo audits.
The audits monitor the banks' activities.

A general truth

The mills of the gods grind slowly.
The earth is round.

Discussion of literature, film, and so on

Huckleberry Finn has adventures we all envy.
In that article the author examines several causes of crime.

---

mycomplab

Visit *mycomplab.com* for more resources and exercises on verb tenses.

Tenses of a regular verb (active voice)

Present Action that is occurring now, occurs habitually, or is generally true

Simple present Plain form or -*s* form

I walk.
You/we/they walk.
He/she/it walks.

Present progressive *Am, is,* or *are* plus -*ing* form

I am walking.
You/we/they are walking.
He/she/it is walking.

Past Action that occurred before now

Simple past Past-tense form (-*d* or -*ed*)

I/he/she/it walked.
You/we/they walked.

Past progressive *Was* or *were* plus -*ing* form

I/he/she/it was walking.
You/we/they were walking.

Future Action that will occur in the future

Simple future Plain form plus *will*

I/you/he/she/it/we/they will walk.

Future progressive *Will be* plus -*ing* form

I/you/he/she/it/we/they will be walking.

Present perfect Action that began in the past and is linked to the present

Present perfect *Have* or *has* plus past participle (-*d* or -*ed*)

I/you/we/they have walked.
He/she/it has walked.

Present perfect progressive *Have been* or *has been* plus -*ing* form

I/you/we/they have been walking.
He/she/it has been walking.

Past perfect Action that was completed before another past action

Past perfect *Had* plus past participle (-*d* or -*ed*)

I/you/he/she/it/we/they had walked.

Past perfect progressive *Had been* plus -*ing* form

I/you/he/she/it/we/they had been walking.

Future perfect Action that will be completed before another future action

Future perfect *Will have* plus past participle (-*d* or -*ed*)

I/you/he/she/it/we/they will have walked.

Future perfect progressive *Will have been* plus -*ing* form

I/you/he/she/it/we/they will have been walking.

t

26a

Future time

Next week we <u>draft</u> a new budget.
Funding <u>ends</u> in less than a year.

The present tense shows future time with expressions like those in the examples above: *next week, in less than a year.*

26b   Observe the uses of the perfect tenses (*have/had/will have sung*).

The **perfect tenses** consist of a form of *have* plus the verb's past participle (*closed, hidden*). They indicate an action that is completed before another specific time or action. The present perfect tense also indicates action that is begun in the past and continued into the present.

present perfect
The dancer <u>has performed</u> here only once. [The action is completed at the time of the statement.]

present perfect
Critics <u>have written</u> about the performance ever since. [The action began in the past and continues now.]

past perfect
The dancer <u>had trained</u> in Asia before his performance. [The action was completed before another past action.]

future perfect
He <u>will have danced</u> here again by the end of the year. [The action begins now or in the future and will be completed by a specific time in the future.]

CULTURE LANGUAGE   With the present perfect tense, the words *since* and *for* are followed by different information. After *since,* give a specific point in time: *The play has run <u>since 1989.</u>* After *for,* give a span of time: *It has run <u>for decades.</u>*

26c   Observe the uses of the progressive tenses (*is/was/will be singing*).

The **progressive tenses** indicate continuing (therefore progressive) action. They consist of a form of *be* plus the verb's *-ing* form (present participle). (The words *be* and *been* must be combined with other helping verbs. See p. 225.)

present progressive
The team <u>is improving.</u>

past progressive
Last year the team <u>was losing.</u>

future progressive
The owners will be watching for signs of improvement.

present perfect progressive
Sports writers have been expecting an upturn.

past perfect progressive
New players had been performing well.

future perfect progressive
If the season goes badly, fans will have been watching their team lose for ten years straight.

Note Verbs that express unchanging states (especially mental states) rather than physical actions do not usually appear in the progressive tenses. These verbs include *adore, appear, believe, belong, care, hate, have, hear, know, like, love, mean, need, own, prefer, remember, see, sound, taste, think, understand,* and *want.*

| Faulty | She is wanting to study ethics. |
| Revised | She wants to study ethics. |

26d Keep tenses consistent.

Within a sentence, the tenses of verbs and verb forms need not be identical as long as they reflect actual changes in time: *Ramon will graduate from college thirty years after his father arrived in America.* In speech we often shift tenses even when they don't reflect changes in time. But in writing, such needless shifts in tense will confuse or distract readers:

Inconsistent	Immediately after Booth shot Lincoln, Major Rathbone threw himself upon the assassin. But Booth pulls a knife and plunges it into the major's arm.
Revised	Immediately after Booth shot Lincoln, Major Rathbone threw himself upon the assassin. But Booth pulled a knife and plunged it into the major's arm.
Inconsistent	The main character in the novel suffers psychologically because he has a clubfoot, but he eventually triumphed over his disability.
Revised	The main character in the novel suffers psychologically because he has a clubfoot, but he eventually triumphs over his disability. [Use the present tense when discussing the content of literature, film, and so on.]

t
26d

Exercise 26.1 Revising: Consistent past tense
In the following paragraph, change the tenses of the verbs as needed to maintain consistent simple past tense. Answers to the starred sentences appear at the end of the book.

*The 1960 presidential race between Richard Nixon and John F. Kennedy was the first to feature a televised debate. *Despite his extensive political experience, Nixon perspires heavily and looks haggard and uneasy in front of the camera. *By contrast, Kennedy was projecting cool poise and providing crisp answers that made him seem fit for the office of President. The public responded positively to Kennedy's image. His poll ratings shoot up immediately, while Nixon's take a corresponding drop. Kennedy won the election by a close 118,564 votes.

Exercise 26.2 Revising: Consistent present tense

In the paragraph below, change the tenses of the verbs as needed to maintain consistent simple present tense. Answers to the starred sentences appear at the end of the book.

*E. B. White's famous children's novel *Charlotte's Web* is a wonderful story of friendship and loyalty. *Charlotte, the wise and motherly spider, decided to save her friend Wilbur, the young and childlike pig, from being butchered by his owner. *She made a plan to weave words into her web that described Wilbur. She first weaves "Some Pig" and later presented "Terrific," "Radiant," and "Humble." Her plan succeeded beautifully. She fools the humans into believing that Wilbur was a pig unlike any other, and Wilbur lived.

26e Use the appropriate sequence of verb tenses.

The **sequence of tenses** is the relation between the verb tense in a main clause and the verb tense in a subordinate clause. The tenses often differ to reflect differences in relative time:

Ramon's father arrived in the United States thirty years ago, after he had married, and now Ramon has decided that he will return to his father's homeland.

English tense sequence can be tricky for native speakers and especially challenging for nonnative speakers. The main difficulties are discussed on the following pages.

1 ▪ Past or past perfect tense in main clause

When the verb in the main clause is in the past or past perfect tense, the verb in the subordinate clause must also be past or past perfect.

> **Key terms**
>
> **main clause** A word group that can stand alone as a sentence because it contains a subject and a predicate and does not begin with a subordinating word: *Books are valuable.* (See p. 213.)
>
> **subordinate clause** A word group that contains a subject and a predicate, begins with a subordinating word such as *because* or *who,* and is not a question: *Books are valuable when they enlighten.* (See p. 213.)

t seq
26e

main clause: subordinate clause:
      past   past
The researchers <u>discovered</u> that people <u>varied</u> widely in their knowledge of public events.

main clause: subordinate clause:
      past   past perfect
The variation <u>occurred</u> because respondents <u>had been born</u> in different decades.

main clause: subordinate clause:
   past perfect   past
None of them <u>had been born</u> when Eisenhower <u>was</u> President.

Exception Always use the present tense for a general truth, such as *The earth is round:*

main clause: subordinate clause:
      past   present
Most <u>understood</u> that popular Presidents <u>are</u> not necessarily good Presidents.

2 ▪ Conditional sentences

A **conditional sentence** states a factual relation between cause and effect, makes a prediction, or speculates about what might happen. Such a sentence usually consists of a subordinate clause beginning with *if*, *when*, or *unless* and a main clause stating the result. The three kinds of conditional sentences use distinctive verbs.

Factual relation

For statements asserting that something always or usually happens whenever something else happens, use the present tense in both clauses:

subordinate clause: main clause:
      present   present
When a voter <u>casts</u> a ballot, he or she <u>has</u> complete privacy.

If the linked events occurred in the past, use the past tense in both clauses:

subordinate clause: main clause:
      past   past
When voters <u>registered</u> in some states, they <u>had</u> to pay a poll tax.

Prediction

For a prediction, generally use the present tense in the subordinate clause and the future tense in the main clause:

subordinate clause: main clause:
      present   future
Unless citizens <u>regain</u> faith in politics, they <u>will</u> not <u>vote</u>.

Sometimes the verb in the main clause consists of *may, can, should,* or *might* plus the verb's plain form: *If citizens <u>regain</u> faith, they <u>may</u> <u>vote</u>.*

t seq

26e

Speculation

Speculations are mainly of two kinds, each with its own verb pattern. For events that are possible in the present but unlikely, use the past tense in the subordinate clause and *would, could,* or *might* plus the verb's plain form in the main clause:

> subordinate clause: main clause:
> past   *would* + verb
> If voters had more confidence, they would vote more often.

Use *were* instead of *was* when the subject is *I, he, she, it,* or a singular noun. (See pp. 242–43 for more on this distinctive verb form.)

> subordinate clause: main clause:
> past   *would* + verb
> If the voter were more confident, he or she would vote more often.

For events that are impossible now, that are contrary to fact, use the same forms as above (including the distinctive *were* when applicable):

> subordinate clause: main clause:
> past   *might* + verb
> If Lincoln were alive, he might inspire confidence.

For events that were impossible in the past, use the past perfect tense in the subordinate clause and *would, could,* or *might* plus the present perfect tense in the main clause:

> subordinate clause: main clause:
> past perfect   *might* + present perfect
> If Lincoln had lived past the Civil War, he might have helped stabilize the country.

t seq

26e

Example 26.3   Adjusting tense sequence: Past or past perfect tense

The tenses in each sentence below are in correct sequence. Change the tense of one verb as instructed. Then change the tenses of other verbs as needed to restore correct sequence. Some items have more than one possible answer. Answers to starred items appear at the end of the book.

Example:

Delgado will call when he reaches his destination. (*Change will call to called.*)

Delgado called when he reached [or had reached] his destination.

*1. Diaries that Adolf Hitler is supposed to have written have surfaced in Germany. (*Change have surfaced to had surfaced.*)

*2. Many people believe that the diaries are authentic because a well-known historian has declared them so. (*Change believe to believed.*)

3. However, the historian's evaluation has been questioned by other authorities, who call the diaries forgeries. (*Change has been questioned to was questioned.*)

4. They claim, among other things, that the paper is not old enough to have been used by Hitler. (*Change claim to claimed.*)
5. Eventually, the doubters will win the debate because they have the best evidence. (*Change will win to won.*)

Exercise 26.4 Revising: Tense sequence with conditional sentences

Supply the appropriate tense for each verb in brackets below. Answers to starred items appear at the end of the book.

Example:

If Babe Ruth or Jim Thorpe [be] athletes today, they [remind] us that even sports heroes must contend with a harsh reality.

If Babe Ruth or Jim Thorpe were athletes today, they might [or could or would] remind us that even sports heroes must contend with a harsh reality.

*1. When an athlete [turn] professional, he or she commits to a grueling regimen of mental and physical training.
*2. If athletes [be] less committed, they [disappoint] teammates, fans, and themselves.
*3. If professional athletes [be] very lucky, they may play until age forty.
*4. Unless an athlete achieves celebrity status, he or she [have] few employment choices after retirement.
*5. If professional sports [be] less risky, athletes [have] longer careers and more choices after retirement.
 6. If you think you [be] exposed to the flu in the winter, you [get] a flu shot.
 7. If you are allergic to eggs, you [have] an allergic reaction to the flu shot.
 8. If you get the flu after having a flu shot, your illness [be] milder.
 9. If you had had a flu shot last year, you [avoid] the illness.
 10. If you [be] not so afraid of shots, you [will] get a flu shot every year.

vb
27

27 Verb Mood

When is it right to say *he were?*

The odd-sounding construction *he were* illustrates a particular **mood** of the verb *is*, a particular attitude on the writer's or speaker's part toward what he or she is saying. In the sentence *I wish he were going*, the *were* reinforces the writer's expression of a desire.

---

mycomplab

Visit *mycomplab.com* for more resources and exercises on verb mood.

English verbs express three possible moods. The **indicative mood** states a fact or opinion or asks a question: *The theater needs help. Can you help the theater?* The **imperative mood** expresses a command or gives a direction, and it omits the subject of the sentence, *you: Help the theater.* The more complicated **subjunctive mood** expresses wishes, suggestions, and other attitudes, using *he were* and other distinctive verb forms described below.

Grammar checkers A grammar checker may spot some simple errors in the subjunctive mood, but it may miss others. For example, a checker flagged *I wish I was home* (should be *were home*) but not *If I had a hammer, I will hammer in the morning* (should be *would hammer*).

27a Use the subjunctive verb forms appropriately, as in *I wish I were.*

The subjunctive mood expresses a suggestion, requirement, or desire, or it states a condition that is contrary to fact (that is, imaginary or hypothetical).

- **Verbs such as *ask, insist, urge, require, recommend,* and *suggest* indicate request or requirement.** They often precede a subordinate clause beginning with *that* and containing the substance of the request or requirement. For all subjects, the verb in the *that* clause is the plain form:

  plain form
  Rules require that every donation be mailed.

- **Contrary-to-fact clauses state imaginary or hypothetical conditions and usually begin with *if* or *unless* or follow *wish.*** For present contrary-to-fact clauses, use the verb's past-tense form (for *be,* use the past-tense form *were*):

  past   past
  If the theater were in better shape and had more money, its future would be assured.

  past
  I wish I were able to donate money.

  For past contrary-to-fact clauses, use the verb's past perfect form (*had* + past participle):

  past perfect
  The theater would be better funded if it had been better managed last year.

  Note Do not use the helping verb *would* or *could* in a contrary-to-fact clause beginning with *if:*

| Not | Many people would have helped if they <u>would have</u> known. |
| But | Many people would have helped if they <u>had</u> known. |

See also page 240 for more on verb tenses in contrary-to-fact sentences like these.

27b Keep mood consistent.

Shifts in mood within a sentence or among related sentences can be confusing. Such shifts occur most frequently in directions.

| Inconsistent | <u>Cook</u> the mixture slowly, and <u>you should stir</u> it until the sugar is dissolved. [Mood shifts from imperative to indicative.] |
| Revised | <u>Cook</u> the mixture slowly, and <u>stir</u> it until the sugar is dissolved. [Consistently imperative.] |

Exercise 27.1   Revising: Subjunctive mood

Revise the following sentences with appropriate subjunctive verb forms. Answers to starred items appear at the end of the book.

Example:

I would help the old man if I was able to reach him.
I would help the old man if I <u>were</u> able to reach him.

* 1. If John Hawkins would have known of all the dangerous side effects of smoking tobacco, would he have introduced the dried plant to England in 1565?

* 2. Hawkins noted that if a Florida Indian man was to travel for several days, he would have smoked tobacco to satisfy his hunger and thirst.

3. Early tobacco growers feared that their product would not gain acceptance unless it was perceived as healthful.

4. To prevent fires, in 1646 the General Court of Massachusetts passed a law requiring that colonists smoked tobacco only if they were five miles from any town.

5. To prevent decadence, in 1647 Connecticut passed a law mandating that one's smoking of tobacco was limited to once a day in one's own home.

vb
27b

28 Verb Voice

**Which is better: *The book was written by her*
or *She wrote the book?***

Generally, you should prefer the **active voice** of *She wrote the book*, in which the subject (*She*) performs the action of the verb (*wrote*). In the **passive voice** of *The book was written by her*, the subject (*book*) receives the action of the verb (*was written*) and the actual actor appears in a trailing phrase (*by her*). (Naming the actual actor is optional in the passive voice.) The passive voice does have its uses (see below), but the active voice is usually more direct and concise.

⟨**CULTURE LANGUAGE**⟩ A passive verb always consists of a form of *be* plus the past participle of the main verb: *rents are controlled, people were inspired*. Other helping verbs must also be used with the words *be, being,* and *been*: *rents have been controlled, people would have been inspired*. Only a transitive verb (one that takes an object) may be used in the passive voice. (See p. 204.)

28a Prefer the active voice. Use the passive voice when the actor is unknown or unimportant.

pass
28a

The active voice is usually clearer, more concise, and more forthright than the passive voice.

Weak passive	The library is used by both students and teachers for studying and research, and the plan to expand it has been praised by many.
Strong active	Both students and teachers use the library for studying and research, and many have praised the plan to expand it.

The passive voice is useful in two situations: when the actor is unknown and when the actor is unimportant or less important than the object of the action.

> The Internet was established in 1969 by the US Department of Defense. The network has been extended internationally to governments, universities, corporations, and private individuals. [In the first sentence the writer wishes to stress the Internet rather than the Department of Defense. In the second sentence the actor is too complicated to name.]

> After the solution had been cooled to 10°C, the acid was added. [The person who cooled and added, perhaps the writer, is less important than

Active and passive voice

Active voice   The subject acts.

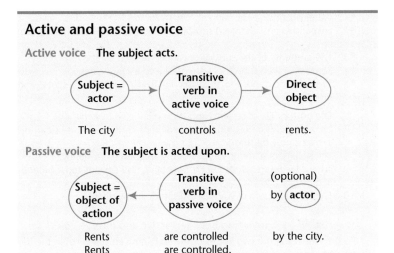

The city   controls   rents.

Passive voice   The subject is acted upon.

Rents   are controlled   by the city.
Rents   are controlled.

the facts that the solution was cooled and acid was added. Passive sentences are common in scientific writing.]

Grammar checkers Most grammar checkers can be set to spot the passive voice. But they can't distinguish between inappropriate passive voice and appropriate passive voice, such as when the actor is unknown.

pass
28b

28b   Keep voice consistent.

Shifts in voice that involve shifts in subject are usually unnecessary and confusing.

Inconsistent	Internet blogs cover an enormous range of topics. Opportunities for people to discuss pet issues are provided on these sites.
Revised	Internet blogs cover an enormous range of topics and provide opportunities for people to discuss pet issues.

A shift in voice is appropriate when it helps focus the reader's attention on a single subject, as in *The candidate campaigned vigorously and was nominated on the first ballot.*

Exercise 28.1   Revising: Using the active voice

Rewrite each of the following passive sentences into the active voice, adding a subject as necessary. Possible answers to starred items appear at the end of the book.

Example:

Contaminants are removed from water by treatment plants.
Treatment plants remove contaminants from water.

*1. Water quality is determined by many factors.
*2. Suspended and dissolved substances are contained in all natural waters.
*3. The amounts of the substances are controlled by the environment.
*4. Some dissolved substances are produced by pesticides.
*5. Sediment is deposited in water by fields, livestock feedlots, and other sources.
  6. The bottom life of streams and lakes is affected by sediment.
  7. Light penetration is reduced by sediment, and bottom-dwelling organisms may be smothered.
  8. The quality of water in city systems is measured frequently.
  9. If legal levels are exceeded by pollutants, the citizens must be notified by city officials.
 10. The chlorine taste of water is disliked by many people.

Exercise 28.2 Converting between active and passive voices

To practice using the two voices of the verb, convert the verbs in the following sentences from active to passive or from passive to active. (In converting from passive to active, you may need to add a subject.) Which version of the sentence seems more effective and why? Answers to starred items appear at the end of the book.

> *Example:*
> The aspiring actor was discovered in a nightclub.
> A talent <u>scout</u> <u>discovered</u> the actor in a nightclub.

*1. When the Eiffel Tower was built in 1889, it was thought by the French to be ugly.
*2. At the time, many people still resisted industrial technology.
  3. The tower's naked steel construction typified this technology.
  4. Beautiful ornament was expected to grace fine buildings.
  5. Further, a structure without solid walls could not even be called a building.

---

29   Agreement of Subject and Verb

Does the verb of this sentence match the subject?

A verb and its subject should match, or **agree**, in number and person: a singular subject takes a singular verb, and a plural subject takes a plural verb, as in the following examples.

> mycomplab
>
> Visit *mycomplab.com* for more resources and exercises on subject-verb agreement.

Daniel Inouye was the first Japanese American in Congress.
    subject   verb

More Japanese Americans live in Hawaii and California than elsewhere.
        subject   verb

Most problems of subject-verb agreement arise when endings are omitted from subjects or verbs or when the relation between sentence parts is uncertain. This chapter covers these tricky situations.

Grammar checkers A grammar checker will catch many simple errors in subject-verb agreement, such as *Addie and John is late*, and some more complicated errors, such as *Is Margaret and Tom going with us?* (should be *are* in both cases). But a checker failed to flag *The old group has gone their separate ways* (should be *have*) and offered a wrong correction for *The old group have gone their separate ways,* which is already correct.

29a   The *-s* and *-es* endings work differently for nouns and verbs.

An *-s* or *-es* ending does opposite things to nouns and verbs: it usually makes a noun *plural,* but it always makes a present-tense verb *singular.* Thus a singular-noun subject will not end in *-s,* but its verb will. A plural-noun subject will end in *-s,* but its verb will not. Between them, subject and verb use only one *-s* ending.

Singular subject	Plural subject
The boy plays.	The boys play.
The bird soars.	The birds soar.

The only exceptions to these rules involve the nouns that form irregular plurals, such as *child/children, woman/women.* The irregular plural still requires a plural verb: *The children play. The women read.*

(CULTURE LANGUAGE) If your first language or dialect is not standard American English, subject-verb agreement may be problematic, especially for the following reasons.

vb agr

29a

Key terms

	Number	
Person	**Singular**	**Plural**
First	I eat.	We eat.
Second	You eat.	You eat.
Third	He/she/it eats.	They eat.
	The bird eats.	Birds eat.

- **Some English dialects follow different rules for subject-verb agreement,** such as omitting the *-s* ending for singular verbs or using the *-s* ending for plural verbs.

Nonstandard	The <u>voter resist</u> change.
Standard	The <u>voter resists</u> change.
Standard	The <u>voters resist</u> change.

The verb *be* changes spelling for singular and plural in both present and past tense. (See also p. 197.)

| Nonstandard | Taxes <u>is</u> high. They <u>was</u> raised just last year. |
| Standard | Taxes <u>are</u> high. They <u>were</u> raised just last year. |

Have also has a distinctive *-s* form, *has*:

| Nonstandard | The new tax <u>have</u> little chance of passing. |
| Standard | The new tax <u>has</u> little chance of passing. |

- **Some other languages change all parts of verb phrases to match their subjects.** In English verb phrases, however, only the helping verbs *be, have,* and *do* change for different subjects. The modal helping verbs—*can, may, should, will,* and others—do not change:

| Nonstandard | The <u>tax mays</u> pass next year. |
| Standard | The <u>tax may</u> pass next year. |

The main verb in a verb phrase also does not change for different subjects:

| Nonstandard | The <u>tax</u> may <u>passes</u> next year. |
| Standard | The <u>tax</u> may <u>pass</u> next year. |

vb agr
29b

29b Subject and verb should agree even when other words come between them.

The catalog of course requirements often <u>baffles</u> [not <u>baffle</u>] students.

The requirements stated in the catalog <u>are</u> [not <u>is</u>] unclear.

Key terms

verb phrase A combination of helping verb and main verb: *will be singing, has opened, would run.* (See p. 197.)

helping verb A verb such as *be, have,* and *can* that combines with another verb to show time, permission, and other meanings: *will be singing, has opened, would run.* (See p. 197.)

main verb The verb that carries the principal meaning in a verb phrase: *will be <u>singing</u>, has <u>opened</u>, would <u>run</u>.* (See p. 197.)

Note Phrases beginning with *as well as, together with, along with,* and *in addition to* do not change the number of the subject:

The president, as well as the deans, has [not have] agreed to revise the catalog.

29c Subjects joined by *and* usually take plural verbs.

Frost and Roethke were contemporaries.

Exceptions When the parts of the subject form a single idea or refer to a single person or thing, they take a singular verb:

Avocado and bean sprouts is a California sandwich.

When a compound subject is preceded by the adjective *each* or *every,* the verb is usually singular:

Each man, woman, and child has a right to be heard.

29d When parts of a subject are joined by *or* or *nor,* the verb agrees with the nearer part.

Either the painter or the carpenter knows the cost.

The cabinets or the bookcases are too costly.

When one part of the subject is singular and the other plural, avoid awkwardness by placing the plural part closer to the verb so that the verb is plural:

Awkward   Neither the owners nor the contractor agrees.

Revised   Neither the contractor nor the owners agree.

vb agr
29e

29e With *everyone* and other indefinite pronouns, use a singular or plural verb as appropriate.

Most indefinite pronouns are singular in meaning (they refer to a single unspecified person or thing), and they take a singular verb:

Something smells.   Neither is right.

Four indefinite pronouns are always plural in meaning: *both, few, many, several.*

Both are correct.   Several were invited.

Six indefinite pronouns may be either singular or plural in meaning: *all, any, more, most, none, some.* The verb with one of these pronouns depends on what the pronoun refers to:

All of the money is reserved for emergencies. [*All* refers to *money*.]

All of the funds are reserved for emergencies. [*All* refers to *funds*.]

None may be singular even when referring to a plural word, especially to emphasize the meaning "not one": *None* [*Not one*] *of the animals has a home.*

 See page 280 for the distinction between *few* ("not many") and *a few* ("some").

29f   Collective nouns such as *team* take singular or plural verbs depending on meaning.

Use a singular verb with a collective noun when the group acts as a unit:

The team has won five of the last six meets.

But when the group's members act separately, not together, use a plural verb:

The old team have gone their separate ways.

The collective noun *number* may be singular or plural. Preceded by *a*, it is plural; preceded by *the*, it is singular:

A number of people are in debt.

Key terms

indefinite pronoun A pronoun that does not refer to a specific person or thing:

Singular			*Singular or plural*	*Plural*
anybody	everyone	nothing	all	both
anyone	everything	one	any	few
anything	much	somebody	more	many
each	neither	someone	most	several
either	nobody	something	none	
everybody	no one		some	

collective noun A noun with singular form that names a group of individuals or things—for instance, *army, audience, committee, crowd, family, group, team.*

The number of people in debt is very large.

CULTURE LANGUAGE Some noncount nouns (nouns that don't form plurals) are collective nouns because they name groups: for instance, *furniture, clothing, mail.* These noncount nouns usually take singular verbs: *Mail arrives daily.* But some of these nouns take plural verbs, including *clergy, military, people, police,* and any collective noun that comes from an adjective, such as *the poor, the rich, the young, the elderly.* If you mean one representative of the group, use a singular noun such as *police officer* or *poor person.*

29g   *Who, which,* and *that* take verbs that agree with their antecedents.

When used as subjects, *who, which,* and *that* refer to another word in the sentence, called the **antecedent**. The verb agrees with the antecedent:

Mayor Garber ought to listen to the people who work for her.

Bardini is the only aide who has her ear.

Agreement problems often occur with *who* and *that* when the sentence includes *one of the* or *the only one of the*:

Bardini is one of the aides who work unpaid. [Of the aides who work unpaid, Bardini is one.]

Bardini is the only one of the aides who knows the community. [Of the aides, only one, Bardini, knows the community.]

CULTURE LANGUAGE In phrases beginning with *one of the*, be sure the noun is plural: *Bardini is one of the aides* [not *aide*] *who work unpaid.*

vb agr
29h

29h   *News* and other singular nouns ending in -s take singular verbs.

Singular nouns ending in -s include *athletics, economics, linguistics, mathematics, measles, mumps, news, physics, politics,* and *statistics,* as well as place names such as *Athens, Wales,* and *United States.*

After so long a wait, the news has to be good.

Statistics is required of psychology majors.

A few of these words also take plural verbs, but only when they describe individual items rather than whole bodies of activity or knowledge: *The statistics prove him wrong.*

Measurements and figures ending in *-s* may also be singular when the quantity they refer to is a unit:

Three years is a long time to wait.

Three-fourths of the library consists of reference books.

29i The verb agrees with the subject even when it precedes the subject.

The verb precedes the subject mainly in questions and in constructions beginning with *there* or *here* and a form of *be*:

Is voting a right or a privilege?

Are a right and a privilege the same thing?

There are differences between them.

29j *Is, are,* and other linking verbs agree with their subjects, not subject complements.

vb agr
29k

Make a linking verb agree with its subject, usually the first element in the sentence, not with the noun or pronoun serving as a subject complement.

The child's sole support is her court-appointed guardians.

Her court-appointed guardians are the child's sole support.

29k Use singular verbs with titles and with words being defined.

Hakada Associates is a new firm.

Key terms

linking verb A verb that connects or equates the subject and subject complement: for example, *seem, become, appear,* and forms of *be*. (See p. 205.)

subject complement A word that describes or renames the subject: *They became chemists*. (See p. 205.)

Dream Days remains a favorite book.

Folks is a down-home word for *people*.

Exercise 29.1 Revising: Subject-verb agreement

Revise the verbs in the following sentences as needed to make subjects and verbs agree in number. If the sentence is already correct as given, mark the number preceding it. Answers to starred items appear at the end of the book.

Example:

Each of the job applicants type sixty words per minute.
Each of the job applicants <u>types</u> sixty words per minute.

*1. Weinstein & Associates are a consulting firm that try to make businesspeople laugh.

*2. Statistics from recent research suggests that humor relieves stress.

*3. Reduced stress in businesses in turn reduce illness and absenteeism.

*4. Reduced stress can also reduce friction within an employee group, which then work together more productively.

*5. In special conferences held by one consultant, each of the participants practice making others laugh.

6. "Isn't there enough laughs within you to spread the wealth?" the consultant asks his students.

7. The consultant quotes Casey Stengel's rule that the best way to keep your management job is to separate the underlings who hate you from the ones who have not decided how they feel.

8. Such self-deprecating comments in public is uncommon among business managers, the consultant says.

9. Each of the managers in a typical firm take the work much too seriously.

10. The humorous boss often feels like the only one of the managers who have other things in mind besides profits.

11. One consultant to many companies suggest cultivating office humor with practical jokes such as a rubber fish in the water cooler.

12. When a manager or employees regularly posts cartoons on the bulletin board, office spirit usually picks up.

13. When someone who has seemed too easily distracted is entrusted with updating the cartoons, his or her concentration often improves.

14. In the face of levity, the former sourpuss becomes one of those who hides bad temper.

15. Every one of the consultants caution, however, that humor has no place in life-affecting corporate situations such as employee layoffs.

vb agr

29k

Exercise 29.2 Adjusting for subject-verb agreement

Rewrite the following paragraphs to change the underlined words from plural to singular. (You will sometimes need to add *a* or *the* for the singular, as in the example.) Then change verbs as necessary so that they agree with their new subjects. Answers to the first paragraph appear at the end of the book.

Example:

Siberian tigers are an endangered subspecies.
The Siberian tiger is an endangered subspecies.

    *Siberian tigers are the largest living cats in the world, much bigger than their relative the Bengal tiger. *They grow to a length of nine to twelve feet, including their tails, and to a height of about three and a half feet. *They can weigh over six hundred pounds. *These carnivorous hunters live in northern China and Korea as well as in Siberia. *During the long winter of this Arctic climate, the yellowish striped coats get a little lighter in order to blend with the snow-covered landscape. *The coats also grow quite thick because the tigers have to withstand temperatures as low as –50°F.
    Siberian tigers sometimes have to travel great distances to find food. They need about twenty pounds of food a day because of their size and the cold climate, but when they have fresh food they may eat as much as a hundred pounds at one time. They hunt mainly deer, boars, and even bears, plus smaller prey such as fish and rabbits. They pounce on their prey and grab them by the back of the neck. Animals that are not killed immediately are thrown to the ground and suffocated with a bite to the throat. Then the tigers feast.

———————— PRONOUNS ————————

   Pronouns—words such as *she* and *who* that refer to nouns—merit special care because all their meaning comes from the other words they refer to. This section discusses pronoun case (Chapter 30), matching pronouns and the words they refer to (31), and making sure pronouns refer clearly to their nouns (32).

30   Pronoun Case

Is it *she and I* or *her and me*? Is it *who* or *whom*?

   Choosing the right **case** of a pronoun—the right form, such as *she* or *her*—requires understanding how the pronoun functions in its sentence.

mycomplab

Visit *mycomplab.com* for more resources and exercises on pronoun case.

- The **subjective case** indicates that the pronoun is a subject or subject complement.
- The **objective case** indicates that the pronoun is an object of a verb or preposition.
- The **possessive case** indicates that the pronoun owns or is the source of a noun in the sentence.

Subjective	Objective	Possessive
I	me	my, mine
you	you	your, yours
he	him	his
she	her	her, hers
it	it	its
we	us	our, ours
you	you	your, yours
they	them	their, theirs
who	whom	whose
whoever	whomever	—

Grammar checkers A grammar checker may flag some problems with pronoun case, but it will also miss many. For instance, one checker spotted the error in *We asked whom would come* (should be *who*), but it overlooked *We dreaded them coming* (should be *their*).

CULTURE LANGUAGE In standard American English, *-self* pronouns do not change form to show function. Their only forms are *myself, yourself, himself, herself, itself, ourselves, yourselves, themselves.* Avoid nonstandard forms such as *hisself, ourself,* and *theirselves.*

case

30a

30a   Distinguish between compound subjects and compound objects: *she and I* vs. *her and me.*

Compound subjects or objects—those consisting of two or more nouns or pronouns—have the same case forms as they would if one noun or pronoun stood alone.

> **Key terms**
>
> **subject** Who or what a sentence is about: *Biologists often study animals. They often work in laboratories.* (See p. 202.)
>
> **subject complement** A word or words that rename or describe the sentence subject: *The best biologists are she and Scoggins.* (See p. 205.)
>
> **object of verb** The receiver of the verb's action (**direct object**): *Many biologists study animals. The animals teach them.* Or the person or thing the action is performed for (**indirect object**): *Some biologists give animals homes. The animals give them pleasure.* (See pp. 204–05.)
>
> **object of preposition** The word linked by *with, for,* or another preposition to the rest of the sentence: *Many biologists work in a laboratory. For them the lab often provides a second home.* (See p. 210.)

compound
subject

<u>She and Novick</u> discussed the proposal.

compound
object

The proposal disappointed <u>her and him</u>.

If you are in doubt about the correct form, try the test below.

A test for case forms in compound constructions

1. **Identify a compound construction** (one connected by *and, but, or, nor*):

   [He, Him] and [I, me] won the prize.
   The prize went to [he, him] and [I, me].

2. **Write a separate sentence for each part of the compound:**

   [He, Him] won the prize. [I, Me] won the prize.
   The prize went to [he, him]. The prize went to [I, me].

3. **Choose the pronouns that sound correct:**

   <u>He</u> won the prize. <u>I</u> won the prize. [Subjective.]
   The prize went to <u>him</u>. The prize went to <u>me</u>. [Objective.]

4. **Put the separate sentences back together:**

   <u>He and I</u> won the prize.
   The prize went to <u>him and me</u>.

case
30b

30b   **Use the subjective case for subject complements:**
It was she.

After a linking verb, a pronoun renaming the subject (a subject complement) should be in the subjective case:

subject
complement

The ones who care most are <u>she and Novick</u>.

subject
complement

It was <u>they</u> whom the mayor appointed.

┌─ **Key term** ─────────────────────────────────────
linking verb A verb, such as a form of *be,* that connects a subject and a word that renames or describes the subject (subject complement): *They are biologists.* (See p. 205.)
└───

If this construction sounds stilted to you, use the more natural order: *She and Novick are the ones who care most. The mayor appointed them.*

Exercise 30.1   Choosing between subjective and objective pronouns

From the pairs in brackets, select the appropriate subjective or objective pronoun(s) for each of the following sentences. Answers to starred items appear at the end of the book.

Example:

"Between you and [I, me]," the seller said, "this deal is a steal."
"Between you and me," the seller said, "this deal is a steal."

*1. Jody and [I, me] had been hunting for jobs.
*2. The best employees at our old company were [she, her] and [I, me], so [we, us] expected to find jobs quickly.

3. Between [she, her] and [I, me] the job search had lasted two months, and still it had barely begun.
4. Slowly, [she, her] and [I, me] stopped sharing leads.
5. It was obvious that Jody and [I, me] could not be as friendly as [we, us] had been.

30c   The use of *who* vs. *whom* depends on the pronoun's function in its clause.

1 ■ Questions

At the beginning of a question, use *who* for a subject and *whom* for an object:

subject⟶
Who wrote the policy?

object ⟵
Whom does it affect?

To find the correct case of *who* in a question, follow the steps below:

1. **Pose the question:**

   [Who, Whom] makes that decision?
   [Who, Whom] does one ask?

2. **Answer the question, using a personal pronoun.** Choose the pronoun that sounds correct, and note its case:

   [She, Her] makes that decision. She makes that decision. [Subjective.]
   One asks [she, her]. One asks her. [Objective.]

3. **Use the same case (*who* or *whom*) in the question:**

   Who makes that decision? [Subjective.]
   Whom does one ask? [Objective.]

2 ▪ Subordinate clauses

In a subordinate clause, use *who* or *whoever* for a subject, *whom* or *whomever* for an object.

subject ⟍
Give old clothes to <u>whoever</u> needs them.

object ⟵———
I don't know <u>whom</u> the mayor appointed.

To determine which form to use, try the test below:

1. **Locate the subordinate clause:**

   Few people know [<u>who</u>, whom] they should ask.
   They are unsure [<u>who</u>, whom] makes the decision.

2. **Rewrite the subordinate clause as a separate sentence, substituting a personal pronoun for *who, whom*.** Choose the pronoun that sounds correct, and note its case:

   They should ask [<u>she</u>, her]. They should ask <u>her</u>. [Objective.]

   [<u>She</u>, her] usually makes the decision. <u>She</u> usually makes the decision. [Subjective.]

3. **Use the same case (*who* or *whom*) in the subordinate clause:**

   Few people know <u>whom</u> they should ask. [Objective.]
   They are unsure <u>who</u> makes the decision. [Subjective.]

case

30c

Note Don't let expressions such as *I think* and *she says* mislead you into using *whom* rather than *who* for the subject of a clause.

subject⟍
He is the one <u>who</u> I think is best qualified.

To choose between *who* and *whom* in such constructions, delete the interrupting phrase so that you can see the true relation between parts: *He is the one <u>who</u> is best qualified.*

Exercise 30.2 Choosing between *who* and *whom*
From the pairs in brackets, select the appropriate form of the pronoun in each of the following sentences. Answers to starred items appear at the end of the book.

Example:

My mother asked me [<u>who</u>, whom] I was meeting.
My mother asked me <u>whom</u> I was meeting.

┌─ **Key term** ─────────────────────────────────
subordinate clause A word group that contains a subject and a predicate and also begins with a subordinating word, such as *who, whom,* or *because.* (See p. 213.)

*1. The school administrators suspended Jurgen, [who, whom] they suspected of setting the fire.

*2. Jurgen had been complaining to other custodians, [who, whom] reported him.

*3. He constantly complained of unfair treatment from [whoever, whomever] happened to be passing in the halls, including pupils.

*4. "[Who, Whom] here has heard Mr. Jurgen's complaints?" the police asked.

*5. "[Who, Whom] did he complain most about?"

6. His coworkers agreed that Jurgen seemed less upset with the staff or students, most of [who, whom] he did not even know, than with the building itself.

7. "He took out his aggression on the building," claimed one coworker [who, whom] often witnessed Jurgen's behavior.

8. "He cursed and kicked the walls and [whoever, whomever] he saw nearby."

9. The coworker thought that Jurgen might have imagined people [who, whom] instructed him to behave the way he did.

10. "He's someone [who, whom] other people can't get next to," said the coworker.

30d   Use the appropriate case in other constructions.

1 ▪ *We* or *us* with a noun

The choice of *we* or *us* before a noun depends on the use of the noun:

object of
preposition
Freezing weather is welcomed by us skaters.

subject
We skaters welcome freezing weather.

2 ▪ Pronoun in an appositive

In an appositive the case of a pronoun depends on the function of the word the appositive describes or identifies:

appositive
identifies object
The class elected two representatives, DeShawn and me.

appositive
identifies subject
Two representatives, DeShawn and I, were elected.

Key term

appositive A noun or noun substitute that renames another noun immediately before it. (See p. 212.)

3 ▪ Pronoun after *than* or *as*

When a pronoun follows *than* or *as* in a comparison, the case of the pronoun indicates what words may have been omitted. A subjective pronoun must be the subject of the omitted verb:

subject

Some critics like Glass more than <u>he</u> [does].

An objective pronoun must be the object of the omitted verb:

object

Some critics like Glass more than [they like] <u>him</u>.

4 ▪ Subject and object of infinitive

Both the object *and* the subject of an infinitive are in the objective case:

subject
of infinitive

The school asked <u>him</u> to speak.

object
of infinitive

Students chose to invite <u>him</u>.

5 ▪ Case before a gerund

Ordinarily, use the possessive form of a pronoun or noun immediately before a gerund:

The coach disapproved of <u>their</u> lifting weights.

The <u>coach's</u> disapproving was a surprise.

case

30d

Exercise 30.3   Revising: Pronoun case

Revise all inappropriate case forms in the sentences below. If a sentence is already correct as given, mark the number preceding it. Answers to starred items appear at the end of the book.

Example:

Convincing we veterans to vote yes will be difficult.
Convincing <u>us</u> veterans to vote yes will be difficult.

*1. Written four thousand years ago, *The Epic of Gilgamesh* tells of a bored king who his people thought was too harsh.
*2. Gilgamesh found a source of entertainment when he met Enkidu, a wild man who had lived with the animals in the mountains.
*3. Him and Gilgamesh wrestled to see whom was more powerful.
*4. After hours of struggle, Enkidu admitted that Gilgamesh was stronger than he.

┌─ **Key terms** ──────────────────────────────

infinitive The plain form of the verb plus *to: to run.* (See p. 211.)

gerund The *-ing* form of a verb used as a noun: *Running is fun.* (See p. 211.)

*5. The friendship of the two strong men was sealed by them fighting.

6. Gilgamesh said, "Between you and I, mighty deeds will be accomplished, and our fame will be everlasting."

7. Among their glorious acts, Enkidu and him defeated a giant bull, Humbaba, and cut down the bull's cedar forests.

8. Their bringing back cedar logs to Gilgamesh's treeless land won great praise from the people.

9. When Enkidu died, Gilgamesh mourned his death, realizing that no one had been a better friend than him.

10. When Gilgamesh himself died many years later, his people raised a monument praising Enkidu and he for their friendship and their mighty deeds of courage.

31 Agreement of Pronoun and Antecedent

Is this the right pronoun?

The right pronoun is the one that matches its **antecedent**—the word to which it refers—in number, person, and gender. This chapter focuses on agreement in number: singular and plural antecedents and the pronouns that replace them.

Homeowners fret over their tax bills.
    antecedent   pronoun

Its constant increases make the tax bill a dreaded document.
 pronoun   antecedent

pn agr

31

┌─ **Key terms** ─────────────────────────────────────

	Number	
Person	**Singular**	**Plural**
First	*I*	*we*
Second	*you*	*you*
Third	*he, she, it,*	*they,*
	indefinite pronouns,	plural nouns
	singular nouns	
Gender		
Masculine	*he,* nouns naming males	
Feminine	*she,* nouns naming females	
Neuter	*it,* all other nouns	

└──

mycomplab

Visit *mycomplab.com* for more resources and exercises on pronoun-antecedent agreement.

Grammar checkers A grammar checker cannot help with agreement between pronoun and antecedent because it cannot recognize the intended relation between the two.

⟨CULTURE LANGUAGE⟩ The gender of a pronoun should match its antecedent, not a noun that the pronoun may modify: *Sara Young invited her* [not *his*] *son to join the company's staff.* Also, nouns in English have only neuter gender unless they specifically refer to males or females. Thus nouns such as *book, table, sun,* and *earth* take the pronoun *it.*

31a   Antecedents joined by *and* usually take plural pronouns.

Mr. Bartos and I cannot settle our dispute.

The dean and my adviser have offered their help.

Exceptions When the compound antecedent refers to a single idea, person, or thing, then the pronoun is singular:

My friend and adviser offered her help.

When the compound antecedent follows *each* or *every,* the pronoun is singular:

Every girl and woman took her seat.

31b   When parts of an antecedent are joined by *or* or *nor,* the pronoun agrees with the nearer part.

Tenants or owners must present their grievances.

Either the tenant or the owner will have her way.

When one subject is plural and the other singular, the sentence will be awkward unless you put the plural subject second:

Awkward   Neither the tenants nor the owner has yet made her case.
Revised   Neither the owner nor the tenants have yet made their case.

31c   With *everyone, person,* and other indefinite words, use a singular or plural pronoun as appropriate.

Most indefinite pronouns and all generic nouns are singular in meaning. When they serve as antecedents, they take singular pronouns:

pn agr
31c

Each of the animal shelters in the region has its population of homeless pets.
indefinite
pronoun

Every worker in our shelter cares for his or her favorite animal.
generic
noun

Four indefinite pronouns are plural in meaning: *both, few, many, several.* As antecedents, they take plural pronouns:

Many of the animals show affection for their caretakers.

Six indefinite pronouns may be singular or plural in meaning: *all, any, more, most, none, some.* As antecedents, they take singular pronouns if they refer to singular words, plural pronouns if they refer to plural words:

Most of the shelter's equipment was donated by its original owner. [*Most* refers to *equipment.*]

Most of the veterinarians donate their time. [*Most* refers to *veterinarians.*]

None may be singular even when referring to a plural word, especially to emphasize the meaning "not one": *None* [*Not one*] *of the shelters has increased its capacity.*

Most agreement problems arise with the singular indefinite words. We often use these words to mean something like "many" or "all" rather than "one" and then refer to them with plural pronouns, as in *Everyone has their own locker* or *A person can padlock their locker.* Often, too, we mean indefinite words to include both masculine and feminine genders and thus resort to *they* instead of the **generic** *he*—the masculine pronoun referring to both genders, as in

pn agr

31c

⌐ Key terms ─────────────────────

indefinite pronoun A noun that does not refer to a specific person or thing:

			Singular or plural	*Plural*
Singular				
anybody	everyone	nothing	all	both
anyone	everything	one	any	few
anything	much	somebody	more	many
each	neither	someone	most	several
either	nobody	something	none	
everybody	no one		some	

generic noun A singular noun such as *person, individual,* or *student* when it refers to a typical member of a group, not to a particular individual: *The individual has rights.*

Everyone deserves his privacy. (For more on the generic *he*, which many readers view as sexist, see p. 173.)

Although some experts accept *they, them,* and *their* with singular indefinite words, most do not, and many teachers and employers regard the plural as incorrect. To be safe, work for agreement between singular indefinite words and the pronouns that refer to them. You have several options:

Ways to correct agreement with indefinite words

■ **Change the indefinite word to a plural, and use a plural pronoun to match:**

Faulty   Every athlete deserves their privacy.
Revised   Athletes deserve their privacy.

■ **Rewrite the sentence to omit the pronoun:**

Faulty   Everyone is entitled to their own locker.
Revised   Everyone is entitled to a locker.

■ **Use *he or she* (*him or her, his or her*) to refer to the indefinite word:**

Faulty   Now everyone has their private space.
Revised   Now everyone has his or her private space.

However, used more than once in several sentences, *he or she* quickly becomes awkward. (Many readers do not accept the alternative *he/she*.) In most cases, using the plural or omitting the pronoun will not only correct agreement problems but also create more readable sentences.

31d Collective nouns such as *team* take singular or plural pronouns depending on meaning.

Use a singular pronoun with a collective noun when referring to the group as a unit:

The committee voted to disband itself.

When referring to the individual members of the group, use a plural pronoun:

The old team have gone their separate ways.

┌─ **Key term** ───
collective noun A noun with singular form that names a group of individuals or things—for instance, *army, audience, committee, crowd, family, group, team.*

CULTURE
LANGUAGE

In standard American English, collective nouns that are noncount nouns (they don't form plurals) usually take singular pronouns: *The mail sits in its own basket.* A few noncount nouns take plural pronouns, including *clergy, military, police, the rich,* and *the poor: The police support their unions.*

Exercise 31.1 Revising: Pronoun-antecedent agreement

Revise the following sentences so that pronouns and their antecedents agree in person and number. Some items have more than one possible answer. Try to avoid the generic *he* (see pp. 263–64). If you change the subject of a sentence, be sure to change the verb as necessary for agreement. If a sentence is already correct as given, mark the number preceding it. Answers to starred items appear at the end of the book.

Example:

Each of the Boudreaus' children brought their laundry home at Thanksgiving.

<u>All</u> of the Boudreaus' children brought their laundry home at Thanksgiving. *Or:* Each of the Boudreaus' children brought <u>laundry</u> home at Thanksgiving. *Or:* Each of the Boudreaus' children brought <u>his or her</u> laundry home at Thanksgiving.

*1. Each girl raised in a Mexican American family in the Rio Grande Valley of Texas hopes that one day they will be given a *quinceañera* party for their fifteenth birthday.

*2. Such celebrations are very expensive because it entails a religious service followed by a huge party.

*3. A girl's immediate family, unless they are wealthy, cannot afford the party by themselves.

*4. The parents will ask each close friend or relative if they can help with the preparations.

*5. Surrounded by her family and attended by her friends and their escorts, the *quinceañera* is introduced as a young woman eligible for Mexican American society.

6. Almost any child will quickly astound observers with their capabilities.

7. Despite their extensive research and experience, neither child psychologists nor parents have yet figured out how children become who they are.

8. Of course, the family has a tremendous influence on the development of a child in their midst.

9. Each member of the immediate family exerts their own unique pull on the child.

10. Other relatives, teachers, and friends also can affect the child's view of the world and of themselves.

11. The workings of genetics also strongly influence the child, but it may never be fully understood.

12. The psychology community cannot agree in its views of whether nurture or nature is more important in a child's development.

13. Another debated issue is whether the child's emotional development or their intellectual development is more central.

14. Just about everyone has their strong opinion on these issues, often backed up by evidence.
15. Neither the popular press nor scholarly journals devote much of their space to the wholeness of the child.

32   Reference of Pronoun to Antecedent

Is it clear what this pronoun refers to?

A pronoun should refer clearly to its **antecedent,** the noun or nouns it refers to. Otherwise, readers will have difficulty grasping the pronoun's meaning. In editing your writing, make sure that each pronoun refers to an obvious, close, and specific antecedent.

Grammar checkers A grammar checker cannot recognize unclear pronoun reference. For instance, a checker did not flag any of the confusing examples on the next page.

CULTURE LANGUAGE In standard American English, a pronoun needs a clear antecedent nearby, but don't use both a pronoun and its antecedent as the subject of the same clause: *Jim* [not *Jim he*] *told Mark to go alone.* (See also pp. 303–04.)

ref

32a

32a   Make a pronoun refer clearly to one antecedent.

When either of two nouns can be a pronoun's antecedent, the reference will not be clear.

Confusing   Emily Dickinson is sometimes compared with Jane Austen, but <u>she</u> was quite different.

Revise such a sentence in one of two ways:

- **Replace the pronoun with the appropriate noun.**

  Clear   Emily Dickinson is sometimes compared with Jane Austen, but <u>Dickinson</u> [or <u>Austen</u>] was quite different.

- **Avoid repetition by rewriting the sentence.** If you use the pronoun, make sure it has only one possible antecedent.

---

mycomplab

Visit *mycomplab.com* for more resources and exercises on pronoun reference.

Clear	Despite occasional comparison, Emily Dickinson and Jane Austen were quite different.
Clear	Though sometimes compared with <u>her</u>, Emily Dickinson was quite different from Jane Austen.

32b   Place a pronoun close enough to its antecedent to ensure clarity.

A clause beginning with *who, which,* or *that* should generally fall immediately after the word to which it refers:

Confusing	Jody found a dress in the attic <u>that</u> her aunt had worn.
Clear	In the attic Jody found a <u>dress</u> <u>that</u> her aunt had worn.

32c   Make a pronoun refer to a specific antecedent, not an implied one.

A pronoun should refer to a specific noun or other pronoun. A reader can only guess at the meaning of a pronoun when its antecedent is implied by the context, not stated outright.

1 ▪ Vague *this, that, which,* or *it*

This, that, which, or *it* should refer to a specific noun, not to a whole word group expressing an idea or situation.

Confusing	The faculty agreed on changing the requirements, but it took time.
Clear	The faculty agreed on changing the requirements, but <u>the agreement</u> took time.
Clear	The faculty agreed on changing the requirements, but <u>the change</u> took time.
Confusing	The British knew little of the American countryside, and they had no experience with the colonists' guerrilla tactics. This gave the colonists an advantage.
Clear	The British knew little of the American countryside, and they had no experience with the colonists' guerrilla tactics. This <u>ignorance and inexperience</u> gave the colonists an advantage.

2 ▪ Indefinite antecedents with *it* and *they*

It and *they* should have definite noun antecedents. Rewrite the sentence if the antecedent is missing.

Confusing	In Chapter 4 of this book it describes the early flights of the Wright brothers.
Clear	Chapter 4 of this book describes the early flights of the Wright brothers.
Confusing	Even in TV reality shows, they present a false picture of life.
Clear	Even TV reality shows present a false picture of life.
Clear	Even in TV reality shows, the producers present a false picture of life.

3 ▪ Implied nouns

A noun may be implied in some other word or phrase, such as an adjective (*happiness* implied in *happy*), a verb (*driver* implied in *drive*), or a possessive (*mother* implied in *mother's*). But a pronoun cannot refer clearly to an implied noun, only to a specific, stated one.

Confusing	Cohen's report brought her a lawsuit.
Clear	Cohen was sued over her report.
Confusing	Her reports on psychological development generally go unnoticed outside it.
Clear	Her reports on psychological development generally go unnoticed outside the field.

32d   Use *you* only to mean "you, the reader."

In all but very formal writing, *you* is acceptable when the meaning is clearly "you, the reader." But the context must be appropriate for such a meaning:

| Inappropriate | In the fourteenth century you had to struggle simply to survive. |
| Revised | In the fourteenth century one [or a person] had to struggle simply to survive. |

Writers sometimes drift into *you* because *one, a person,* or a similar indefinite word can be difficult to sustain. Sentence after sentence, the indefinite word may sound stuffy, and it requires *he* or *he or she* for pronoun-antecedent agreement (see pp. 264–66). To avoid these problems, try using plural nouns and pronouns:

| Original | In the fourteenth century one had to struggle simply to survive. |
| Revised | In the fourteenth century people had to struggle simply to survive. |

32e   Keep pronouns consistent.

Within a sentence or a group of related sentences, pronouns should be consistent. Partly, consistency comes from making pronouns and their antecedents agree (see Chapter 31). In addition, the pronouns within a passage should match each other.

Inconsistent   One finds when reading that your concentration improves with practice, so that I now comprehend more in less time.

Revised   I find when reading that my concentration improves with practice, so that I now comprehend more in less time.

Exercise 32.1   Revising: Pronoun reference

Many of the pronouns in the following sentences do not refer to clear, specific, and appropriate antecedents. Revise the sentences as necessary to correct the errors. Answers to starred items appear at the end of the book.

Example:

In Grand Teton National Park they have moose, elk, and trumpeter swans.

Moose, elk, and trumpeter swans live in Grand Teton National Park.

*1. "Life begins at forty" is a cliché many people live by, and this may or may not be true.
*2. Living successfully or not depends on one's definition of it.
*3. When she was forty, Pearl Buck's novel *The Good Earth* won the Pulitzer Prize.
*4. Buck was raised in a missionary family in China, and she wrote about it in her novels.
*5. In *The Good Earth* you have to struggle, but fortitude is rewarded.
  6. Buck received much critical praise and earned over $7 million, but she was very modest about it.
  7. Pearl Buck donated most of her earnings to a foundation for Asian American children that proves her generosity.
  8. In the *Book of Romance* it reserves a chapter for the story of Elizabeth Barrett, who at forty married Robert Browning against her father's wishes.
  9. In the 1840s they did not normally defy their fathers, but Elizabeth was too much in love to obey.
  10. She left a poetic record of her love for Robert, and readers still enjoy reading them.

ref

32e

Exercise 32.2   Revising: Pronoun reference

Revise the following paragraph so that each pronoun refers clearly to a single, specific, and appropriate antecedent. Answers to starred sentences appear at the end of the book.

*In Charlotte Brontë's *Jane Eyre*, she is a shy young woman that takes a job as governess. *Her employer is a rude, brooding man named Rochester. *He lives in a mysterious mansion on the English moors, which contributes an eerie quality to Jane's experience. *Eerier still are the fires, strange noises, and other unexplained happenings in the house; but Rochester refuses to discuss this. Eventually, they fall in love. On the day they are to be married, however, she learns that he has a wife hidden in the house. She is hopelessly insane and violent and must be guarded at all times, which explains his strange behavior. Heartbroken, Jane leaves the moors, and many years pass before they are reunited.

MODIFIERS

Modifiers describe or limit other words in a sentence. They are adjectives, adverbs, or word groups serving as adjectives or adverbs. This section shows you how to identify and solve problems in the forms of modifiers (Chapter 33) and in their relation to the rest of the sentence (Chapter 34).

---

ad
33

33 Adjectives and Adverbs

Should I use *bad* or *badly*?

Choosing between *bad* and *badly* means choosing whether to use an adjective (*bad*) or an adverb (*badly*). The choice depends on how the word functions in its sentence. An **adjective** modifies nouns (*bad weather*) and pronouns (*bad one*). An **adverb** modifies verbs (*The fans behaved badly*), adjectives (*badly wrong*), other adverbs (*not badly*), and whole word groups (*Otherwise, the room was empty*).

Grammar checkers A grammar checker will spot some but not all problems with misused adjectives and adverbs. For instance, a checker flagged *Some children suffer bad* and *Chang was the most wisest person in town* and *Jenny did not feel nothing*. But it did not flag *Educating children good should be everyone's focus*.

---

mycomplab

Visit *mycomplab.com* for more resources and exercises on adjectives and adverbs.

(CULTURE LANGUAGE) In standard American English, an adjective does not change along with the noun it modifies to show plural number: _white_ [not _whites_] _shoes_, _square_ [not _squares_] _spaces_, _better_ [not _betters_] _chances_. Only nouns form plurals.

33a Use adjectives only to modify nouns and pronouns.

Using adjectives instead of adverbs to modify verbs, adverbs, or other adjectives is nonstandard.

Faulty   Educating children good should be everyone's focus.

Revised   Educating children well should be everyone's focus.

Faulty   Some children suffer bad.

Revised   Some children suffer badly.

(CULTURE LANGUAGE) Choosing between _not_ and _no_ can be a challenge. To negate a verb or an adjective, use the adverb _not_:

They are not learning.   They are not stupid.

To negate a noun, use the adjective _no_:

No child should fail to read.

Exercise 33.1 Revising: Adjectives and adverbs

Revise the following sentences to use adjectives and adverbs appropriately. If any sentence is already correct as given, mark the number preceding it. Answers to starred items appear at the end of the book.

Example:

The announcer warned loud and clear that traffic was stopped on the bridge.

The announcer warned loudly and clearly that traffic was stopped on the bridge.

*1. The eighteenth-century essayist Samuel Johnson fared bad in his early life.
*2. Johnson's family was poor, his hearing was bad, and he received little education.
*3. After failing as a schoolmaster, Johnson moved to London, where he did good.
*4. Johnson was taken serious as a critic and dictionary maker.
*5. Johnson was real surprised when he received a pension from King George III.
6. Thinking about his meeting with the king, Johnson felt proudly.
7. Johnson was relieved that he had not behaved badly in the presence of the king.

ad
33a

8. If he had been more diligent, Johnson might have made money quicker.
9. After living cheap for over twenty years, Johnson finally had enough money from the pension to eat and dress good.
10. With the pension, Johnson could spend time writing and live stylish.

33b Use an adjective after a linking verb to modify the subject. Use an adverb to modify a verb.

Some verbs may or may not be linking verbs, depending on their meaning in the sentence. When the word after the verb modifies the subject, the verb is linking and the word should be an adjective: *He looked happy. The milk turned sour.* When the word modifies the verb, however, it should be an adverb: *He looked carefully. The car turned suddenly.*

Two word pairs are especially tricky. One is *bad* and *badly*:

The weather grew bad.
    linking adjective
    verb

She felt bad.
    linking adjective
    verb

Flowers grow badly in such soil.
    verb adverb

The other tricky pair is *good* and *well. Good* serves only as an adjective. *Well* may serve as an adverb with a host of meanings or as an adjective meaning only "fit" or "healthy."

Decker felt well.
    linking adjective
    verb

Her health was good.
    linking adjective
    verb

She trained well.
    verb   adverb

---

ad
33c

33c Use the comparative and superlative forms of adjectives and adverbs appropriately.

Adjectives and adverbs can show degrees of quality or amount with the endings *-er* and *-est* or with the words *more* and *most* or *less* and *least*. Most modifiers have three forms.

> **Key term**
>
> **linking verb** A verb that connects a subject and a word that describes the subject: *They are golfers.* Linking verbs are forms of *be*, the verbs of our five senses (*look, sound, smell, feel, taste*), and *appear, seem, become, grow, turn, prove, remain, stay.* (See p. 205.)

Positive The basic form listed in the dictionary	Comparative A greater or lesser degree of the quality	Superlative The greatest or least degree of the quality
Adjectives		
red	redder	reddest
awful	more/less awful	most/least awful
Adverbs		
soon	sooner	soonest
quickly	more/less quickly	most/least quickly

If sound alone does not tell you whether to use *-er/-est* or *more/most,* consult a dictionary. If the endings can be used, the dictionary will list them. Otherwise, use *more* or *most.*

1 ▪ Irregular adjectives and adverbs

Irregular modifiers change the spelling of their positive form to show comparative and superlative degrees.

Positive	Comparative	Superlative
Adjectives		
good	better	best
bad	worse	worst
little	littler, less	littlest, least
many ⎤		
some ⎬	more	most
much ⎦		
Adverbs		
well	better	best
badly	worse	worst

ad
33c

2 ▪ Double comparisons

A double comparative or double superlative combines the *-er* or *-est* ending with the word *more* or *most.* It is redundant.

Chang was the wisest [not most wisest] person in town.
He was smarter [not more smarter] than anyone else.

3 ▪ Logical comparisons

Absolute modifiers

Some adjectives and adverbs cannot logically be compared— for instance, *perfect, unique, dead, impossible, infinite.* These absolute words can be preceded by adverbs like *nearly* or *almost* that mean "approaching," but they cannot logically be modified by *more* or *most* (as in *most perfect*).

Not   He was the most unique teacher we had.
But   He was a unique teacher.

Completeness

To be logical, a comparison must also be complete in the following ways:

- **The comparison must state a relation fully enough for clarity.**

Unclear	Carmakers worry about their industry more than environmentalists.
Clear	Carmakers worry about their industry more than environmentalists <u>do</u>.
Clear	Carmakers worry about their industry more than <u>they worry about</u> environmentalists.

- **The items being compared should in fact be comparable.**

Illogical	The cost of a hybrid car can be greater than a gasoline-powered car. [Illogically compares a cost and a car.]
Revised	The cost of a hybrid car can be greater than <u>the cost of</u> [or <u>that of</u>] a gasoline-powered car.

See also page 161 on parallelism with comparisons.

Any vs. *any other*

Use *any other* when comparing something with others in the same group. Use *any* when comparing something with others in a different group.

Illogical	Los Angeles is larger than <u>any</u> city in California. [Since Los Angeles is itself a city in California, the sentence seems to say that Los Angeles is larger than itself.]
Revised	Los Angeles is larger than <u>any other</u> city in California.
Illogical	Los Angeles is larger than <u>any other</u> city in Canada. [The cities in Canada constitute a group to which Los Angeles does not belong.]
Revised	Los Angeles is larger than <u>any</u> city in Canada.

ad

33d

33d   Watch for double negatives.

In a **double negative** two negative words such as *no, not, none, barely, hardly,* or *scarcely* cancel each other out. Some double negatives are intentional: for instance, *She was <u>not unhappy</u>* indicates with understatement that she was indeed happy. But most double negatives say the opposite of what is intended: *Jenny did <u>not</u> feel <u>nothing</u>* asserts that Jenny felt other than nothing, or something. For the opposite meaning, one of the negatives must be eliminated (*She felt <u>nothing</u>*) or one of them must be changed to a positive (*She did not feel <u>anything</u>*).

Faulty	The IRS <u>cannot hardly</u> audit all tax returns. <u>None</u> of its audits <u>never</u> touch many cheaters.
Revised	The IRS <u>cannot</u> audit all tax returns. Its audits <u>never</u> touch many cheaters.

Exercise 33.2 Revising: Double negatives

Identify and revise the double negatives in the following sentences. Each error may have more than one correct revision. If a sentence is already correct as given, mark the number preceding it. Answers to starred items appear at the end of the book.

*1. Interest in books about the founding of the United States is not hardly consistent among Americans: it seems to vary with the national mood.

*2. Americans show barely any interest in books about the founders when things are going well in the United States.

3. However, when Americans can't hardly agree on major issues, sales of books about the Revolutionary War era increase.

4. During such periods, one cannot go to no bookstore without seeing several new volumes about John Adams, Thomas Jefferson, and other founders.

5. When Americans feel they don't have nothing in common, their increased interest in the early leaders may reflect a desire for unity.

33e Distinguish between present and past participles as adjectives.

ad
33e

Both present participles and past participles may serve as adjectives: *a burning building, a burned building.* As in the examples, the two participles usually differ in the time they indicate.

But some present and past participles—those derived from verbs expressing feeling—can have altogether different meanings. The present participle modifies something that causes the feeling: *That was a frightening storm* (the storm frightens). The past participle modifies something that experiences the feeling: *They quieted the frightened horses* (the horses feel fright).

The following participles are among those likely to be confused:

amazing/amazed   annoying/annoyed
amusing/amused   astonishing/astonished

┌─ **Key terms** ───────────────────────────────

present participle The *-ing* form of a verb: *flying, writing.* (See p. 196.)

past participle The *-d* or *-ed* form of a regular verb: *slipped, walked.* Most irregular verbs have distinctive past participles, such as *eaten* or *swum.* (See p. 196.)

boring/bored	frustrating/frustrated
confusing/confused	interesting/interested
depressing/depressed	pleasing/pleased
embarrassing/embarrassed	satisfying/satisfied
exciting/excited	shocking/shocked
exhausting/exhausted	surprising/surprised
fascinating/fascinated	tiring/tired
frightening/frightened	worrying/worried

Exercise 33.3 Revising: Present and past participles

Revise the adjectives in the following sentences as needed to distinguish between present and past participles. If a sentence is already correct as given, mark the number preceding it. Answers to starred items appear at the end of the book.

> *Example:*
>
> The subject was embarrassed to many people.
> The subject was <u>embarrassing</u> to many people.

*1. Several critics found Alice Walker's *The Color Purple* to be a fascinated book.

*2. One confused critic wished that Walker had deleted the scenes set in Africa.

3. Another critic argued that although the book contained many depressed episodes, the overall effect was excited.

4. Since other readers found the book annoyed, this critic pointed out its many surprising qualities.

5. In the end most critics agreed that the book was a satisfied novel about the struggles of an African American woman.

det
33f

33f Use *a, an, the,* and other determiners appropriately.

Determiners are special kinds of adjectives that mark nouns because they always precede nouns. Some common determiners are *a, an,* and *the* (called **articles**) and *my, their, whose, this, these, those, one, some,* and *any.*

Native speakers of standard American English can rely on their intuition when using determiners, but speakers of other languages and dialects often have difficulty with them. In standard American English, the use of determiners depends on the context they appear in and the kind of noun they precede:

- A *proper noun* names a particular person, place, or thing and begins with a capital letter: *February, Joe Allen, Red River.* Most proper nouns are not preceded by determiners.

- A *count noun* names something that is countable in English and can form a plural: *girl/girls, apple/apples, child/children.* A singular count noun is always preceded by a determiner; a plural count noun sometimes is.

- **A *noncount noun* names something not usually considered countable in English, and so it does not form a plural.** A noncount noun is sometimes preceded by a determiner. Here is a sample of noncount nouns, sorted into groups by meaning:

Abstractions: confidence, democracy, education, equality, evidence, health, information, intelligence, knowledge, luxury, peace, pollution, research, success, supervision, truth, wealth, work

Food and drink: bread, candy, cereal, flour, meat, milk, salt, water, wine

Emotions: anger, courage, happiness, hate, joy, love, respect, satisfaction

Natural events and substances: air, blood, dirt, gasoline, gold, hair, heat, ice, oil, oxygen, rain, silver, smoke, weather, wood

Groups: clergy, clothing, equipment, furniture, garbage, jewelry, junk, legislation, machinery, mail, military, money, police, vocabulary

Fields of study: accounting, architecture, biology, business, chemistry, engineering, literature, psychology, science

A dictionary of English as a second language will tell you whether a noun is a count noun, a noncount noun, or both. (See p. 176 for recommended dictionaries.)

Note Many nouns are sometimes count nouns and sometimes noncount nouns:

The library has a room for readers. [*Room* is a count noun meaning "walled area."]

The library has room for reading. [*Room* is a noncount noun meaning "space."]

Grammar checkers Partly because the same noun may fall into different groups, a grammar checker is an unreliable guide to missing or misused articles and other determiners. For instance, a checker flagged the omitted *a* before *Scientist* in *Scientist developed new processes;* it did not flag the omitted *a* before *new* in *A scientist developed new process;* and it mistakenly flagged the correctly omitted article *the* before *Vegetation* in *Vegetation suffers from drought.*

1 ■ *A, an,* and *the*

With singular count nouns

A or *an* precedes a singular count noun when the reader does not already know its identity, usually because you have not mentioned it before:

A scientist in our chemistry department developed a process to strengthen metals. [*Scientist* and *process* are being introduced for the first time.]

det
33f

The precedes a singular count noun that has a specific identity for the reader, for one of the following reasons:

- **You have mentioned the noun before:**

  A scientist in our chemistry department developed a process to strengthen metals. The scientist patented the process. [*Scientist* and *process* were identified in the preceding sentence.]

- **You identify the noun immediately before or after you state it:**

  The most productive laboratory is the research center in the chemistry department. [*Most productive* identifies *laboratory*. *In the chemistry department* identifies *research center*. And *chemistry department* is a shared facility—see below.]

- **The noun names something unique—the only one in existence:**

  The sun rises in the east. [*Sun* and *east* are unique.]

- **The noun names an institution or facility that is shared by the community of readers:**

  Many men and women aspire to the presidency. [*Presidency* is a shared institution.]

  The cell phone has changed communication. [*Cell phone* is a shared facility.]

The is not used before a singular noun that names a general category:

Wordsworth's poetry shows his love of nature [not the nature].
General Sherman said that war is hell. [*War* names a general category.]
The war in Iraq has left many wounded. [*War* names a specific war.]

With plural count nouns

A or *an* never precedes a plural noun. *The* does not precede a plural noun that names a general category. *The* does precede a plural noun that names specific representatives of a category.

Men and women are different. [*Men* and *women* name general categories.]
The women formed a team. [*Women* refers to specific people.]

With noncount nouns

A or *an* never precedes a noncount noun. *The* does precede a noncount noun that names specific representatives of a general category.

Vegetation suffers from drought. [*Vegetation* names a general category.]
The vegetation in the park withered or died. [*Vegetation* refers to specific plants.]

det
33f

With proper nouns

A or *an* never precedes a proper noun. *The* generally does not precede proper nouns.

Garcia lives in Boulder.

There are exceptions, however. For instance, we generally use *the* before plural proper nouns (*the Murphys, the Boston Celtics*) and before the names of groups and organizations (*the Department of Justice, the Sierra Club*), ships (*the* Lusitania), oceans (*the Pacific*), mountain ranges (*the Alps*), regions (the *Middle East*), rivers (*the Mississippi*), and some countries (*the United States, the Netherlands*).

2 ▪ Other determiners

The uses of English determiners besides articles also depend on context and kind of noun. The following determiners may be used as indicated with singular count nouns, plural count nouns, or noncount nouns.

With any kind of noun (singular count, plural count, noncount)
my, our, your, his, her, its, their, possessive nouns (*boy's, boys'*)
whose, which(ever), what(ever)
some, any, the other
no

Their account is overdrawn. [Singular count.]
Their funds are low. [Plural count.]
Their money is running out. [Noncount.]

Only with singular nouns (count and noncount)
this, that

This account has some money. [Count.]
That information may help. [Noncount.]

Only with noncount nouns and plural count nouns
most, enough, other, such, all, all of the, a lot of

Most funds are committed. [Plural count.]
Most money is needed elsewhere. [Noncount.]

Only with singular count nouns
one, every, each, either, neither, another

One car must be sold. [Singular count.]

Only with plural count nouns
these, those
both, many, few, a few, fewer, fewest, several
two, three, and so forth

Two cars are unnecessary. [Plural count.]

det
33f

Note *Few* means "not many" or "not enough." *A few* means "some" or "a small but sufficient quantity."

Few committee members came to the meeting.
A few members can keep the committee going.

Do not use *much* with a plural count noun.

Many [not much] members want to help.

Only with noncount nouns
much, more, little, a little, less, least, a large amount of

Less luxury is in order. [Noncount.]

Note *Little* means "not many" or "not enough." *A little* means "some" or "a small but sufficient quantity."

Little time remains before the conference.
The members need a little help from their colleagues.

Do not use *many* with a noncount noun.

Much [not many] work remains.

Exercise 33.4 Revising: Articles ⟨CULTURE-LANGUAGE⟩

For each blank, indicate whether *a, an, the,* or no article should be inserted. Answers to starred sentences appear at the end of the book.

> *Example:*
> On our bicycle trip across _____ country, we carried _____ map and plenty of _____ food and _____ water.
> On our bicycle trip across the country, we carried a map and plenty of food and water.

*From _____ native American Indians who migrated from _____ Asia 20,000 years ago to _____ new arrivals who now come by _____ planes, _____ United States is _____ nation of foreigners. *It is _____ country of immigrants who are all living under _____ single flag.
*Back in _____ seventeenth and eighteenth centuries, at least 75 percent of the population came from _____ England. *However, between 1820 and 1975 more than 38 million immigrants came to this country from elsewhere in _____ Europe. Many children of _____ immigrants were self-conscious and denied their heritage; many even refused to learn _____ native language of their parents and grandparents. They tried to "Americanize" themselves. The so-called Melting Pot theory of _____ social change stressed _____ importance of blending everyone together into _____ kind of stew. Each nationality would contribute its own flavor, but _____ final stew would be something called "American."
This Melting Pot theory was never completely successful. In the last half of the twentieth century, _____ ethnic revival changed _____

metaphor. Many people now see _____ American society as _____ mosaic. Americans are once again proud of their heritage, and _____ ethnic differences make _____ mosaic colorful and interesting.

Exercise 33.5 Revising: Adjectives and adverbs

Revise the sentences below to correct errors in the use of adjectives and adverbs. If a sentence is already correct as given, mark the number preceding it. Answers to starred items appear at the end of the book.

Example:
Sports fans always feel happily when their team wins.
Sports fans always feel <u>happy</u> when their team wins.

*1. Americans often argue about which professional sport is better: basketball, football, or baseball.
*2. Basketball fans contend that their sport offers more action because the players are constant running and shooting.
*3. Because it is played indoors in relative small arenas, basketball allows fans to be more closer to the action than the other sports do.
*4. Football fanatics say they don't hardly stop yelling once the game begins.
*5. They cheer when their team executes a real complicated play good.
6. They roar more louder when the defense stops the opponents in a goal-line stand.
7. They yell loudest when a fullback crashes in for a score.
8. In contrast, the supporters of baseball believe that it might be the most perfect sport.
9. It combines the one-on-one duel of pitcher and batter struggling valiant with the tight teamwork of double and triple plays.
10. Because the game is played slow and careful, fans can analyze and discuss the manager's strategy.

mm
34

34 Misplaced and Dangling Modifiers

Where can a modifier go in a sentence? When does a modifier dangle?

A modifier needs to relate clearly to the word it describes, and that need limits its possible positions in a sentence. A **misplaced modifier** does not relate to the intended word (see the next page). A **dangling modifier** does not relate sensibly to anything in the sentence (see p. 286).

mycomplab

Visit *mycomplab.com* for more resources and exercises on misplaced and dangling modifiers.

Grammar checkers A grammar checker cannot recognize most problems with modifiers. For instance, a checker failed to flag the misplaced modifiers in *Gasoline high prices affect usually car sales* or the dangling modifier in *The vandalism was visible passing the building.*

34a   Reposition misplaced modifiers.

A misplaced modifier falls in the wrong place in a sentence. It is usually awkward or confusing. It may even be unintentionally funny.

1 ▪ Clear placement

Readers tend to link a modifier to the nearest word it could modify. Any other placement can link the modifier to the wrong word.

Confusing   He served steak to the men on paper plates.

Clear   He served the men steak on paper plates.

Confusing   According to the police, many dogs are killed by automobiles and trucks roaming unleashed.

Clear   According to the police, many dogs roaming unleashed are killed by automobiles and trucks.

2 ▪ *Only* and other limiting modifiers

Limiting modifiers include *almost, even, exactly, hardly, just, merely, nearly, only, scarcely,* and *simply.* For clarity, place such a modifier immediately before the word or word group you intend it to limit.

Unclear   The archaeologist only found the skull on her last dig.

Clear   The archaeologist found only the skull on her last dig.

Clear   The archaeologist found the skull only on her last dig.

3 ▪ Adverbs with grammatical units

Adverbs can often move around in sentences, but some will be awkward if they interrupt certain grammatical units.

┌ **Key term** ───────────────────────────────

adverb A word or word group that describes a verb, adjective, other adverb, or whole word group, specifying how, when, where, or to what extent: *quickly see, solid like a boulder.*

- **A long adverb stops the flow from subject to verb:**

subject ┌──── adverb ────┐ verb
Awkward   The city, <u>after the hurricane</u>, began massive rebuilding.

┌──── adverb ────┐ subject verb
Revised   <u>After the hurricane</u>, the city began massive rebuilding.

- **Any adverb is awkward between a verb and its direct object:**

┌── verb ──┐ adverb   object
Awkward   The hurricane had damaged <u>badly</u> many homes in the city.

┌─ verb ─┐   object
Revised   The hurricane had <u>badly</u> damaged many homes in the city.
adverb

- **A *split infinitive*—an adverb placed between *to* and the verb— annoys many readers:**

┌ infinitive ┐
Awkward   The weather service expected temperatures to <u>not</u> rise.

infinitive
Revised   The weather service expected temperatures <u>not</u> to rise.

A split infinitive may sometimes be natural and preferable, though it may still bother some readers:

┌── infinitive ──┐
Several US industries expect to <u>more than</u> triple their use of robots.

Here the split infinitive is more economical than the alternatives, such as *Several US industries expect to increase their use of robots by more than three times.*

- **A long adverb is usually awkward inside a verb phrase:**

helping
verb ┌──── adverb ────┐
Awkward   People who have osteoporosis can, by increasing their daily
──────────────────────────────┐ main verb
intake of calcium and vitamin D, improve their bone density.

┌──────────── adverb ────────────┐
Revised   By increasing their daily intake of calcium and vitamin D,
verb phrase
people who have osteoporosis can improve their bone density.

(CULTURE LANGUAGE) In a question, place a one-word adverb after the first helping verb and subject.

Key terms

direct object The receiver of the verb's action: *The car hit a <u>tree</u>.* (See p. 204.)

infinitive A verb form consisting of *to* plus the verb's plain (or dictionary) form: *to produce, to enjoy.* (See p. 211.)

verb phrase A verb consisting of a helping verb and a main verb that carries the principal meaning: *will have begun, can see.* (See p. 197.)

mm
34a

```
helping                    rest of
verb   subject  adverb  verb phrase
```
Will spacecraft <u>ever</u> be able to leave the solar system?

4 ▪ Other adverb positions ⟨CULTURE LANGUAGE⟩

A few adverbs are subject to special conventions for placement:

▪ **Adverbs of frequency** include *always, never, often, rarely, seldom, sometimes,* and *usually.* They generally appear at the beginning of a sentence, before a one-word verb, or after the helping verb in a verb phrase:

```
helping              main
  verb   adverb      verb
```
Robots have <u>sometimes</u> put humans out of work.

```
adverb              verb phrase
```
<u>Sometimes</u> robots have put humans out of work.

Adverbs of frequency always follow the verb *be*:

```
    verb adverb
```
Robots are <u>often</u> helpful to workers.

▪ **Adverbs of degree** include *absolutely, almost, certainly, completely, definitely, especially, extremely, hardly,* and *only.* They fall just before the word modified (an adjective, another adverb, sometimes a verb):

```
              adverb    adjective
```
Robots have been <u>especially</u> useful in making cars.

▪ **Adverbs of manner** include *badly, beautifully, openly, sweetly, tightly, well,* and others that describe how something is done. They usually fall after the verb:

```
    verb    adverb
```
Robots work <u>smoothly</u> on assembly lines.

▪ **The adverb *not*** changes position depending on what it modifies. When it modifies a verb, place it after the helping verb (or the first helping verb if more than one):

```
helping      main
  verb       verb
```
Robots do <u>not</u> think.

When *not* modifies another adverb or an adjective, place it before the other modifier:

```
            adjective
```
Robots are <u>not</u> sleek machines.

5 ▪ Order of adjectives ⟨CULTURE LANGUAGE⟩

English follows distinctive rules for arranging two or three adjectives before a noun. (A string of more than three adjectives before a noun is rare.) The adjectives follow this order:

Determiner	Opinion	Size or shape	Color	Origin	Material	Noun used as adjective	Noun
many						state	**laws**
	lovely		green	Thai			**birds**
a		square			wooden		**table**
all						business	**reports**
the			blue		litmus		**paper**

See page 320 on punctuating adjectives before a noun.

Exercise 34.1 Revising: Misplaced modifiers

Revise the following sentences so that modifiers clearly and appropriately describe the intended words. Answers to starred items appear at the end of the book.

> *Example:*
> Although at first I feared the sensation of flight, I came to enjoy flying over time.
> Although at first I feared the sensation of flight, <u>over time</u> I came to enjoy flying.

*1. People dominate in our society who are right-handed.
*2. Hand tools, machines, and doors even are designed for right-handed people.
*3. However, nearly 15 percent may be left-handed of the population.
*4. Children often when they begin school prefer one hand or the other.
*5. Parents and teachers should not try to deliberately change a child's preference for the left hand.

6. Women have contributed much to American culture of great value.
7. For example, Elizabeth Pinckney during the colonial era introduced indigo, the source of a valuable blue dye.
8. Emma Willard founded the Troy Female Seminary, the first institution to provide a college-level education for women in 1821.
9. Mary Lyon founded Mount Holyoke Female Seminary as the first true women's college with directors and a campus who would sustain the college even after Lyon's death.
10. *Una* was the first US newspaper, which was founded by Pauline Wright Davis in 1853, that was dedicated to gaining women's rights.
11. Mitchell's Comet was discovered in 1847, which was named for Maria Mitchell.
12. Mitchell was the first American woman astronomer who lived from 1818 to 1889.

mm

34a

┌─ **Key term** ───
adjective A word that describes a noun or pronoun, specifying which one, what quality, or how many: <u>good</u> one, <u>three</u> cars. (See p. 198.)

13. She was a member at Vassar College of the first faculty.
14. She was when elected to the American Academy of Arts and Sciences in 1848 the first woman to join the prestigious organization.
15. Mitchell said that she was persistent rather than especially capable when asked about her many accomplishments.

Exercise 34.2   Revising: Placement of adverbs and adjectives

Revise the following sentences to correct the positions of adverbs or adjectives. Mark the number preceding any sentence that is correct as given. Answers to starred items appear at the end of the book.

Example:

Gasoline high prices affect usually car sales.
<u>High</u> gasoline prices <u>usually</u> affect car sales.

*1. Some years ago Detroit cars often were praised.
*2. Luxury large cars especially were prized.

3. Then a serious oil shortage led drivers to value small foreign cars that got good mileage.
4. When gasoline ample supplies returned, consumers bought again American large cars and trucks.
5. Consumers not were loyal to the big vehicles when gasoline prices dramatically rose.

34b   Relate dangling modifiers to their sentences.

A **dangling modifier** does not sensibly modify anything in its sentence.

Dangling   Passing the building, the vandalism became visible.

Dangling modifiers usually introduce sentences, contain a verb form, and imply but do not name a subject. In the example above, the implied subject is the someone or something passing the building. Readers assume that this implied subject is the same as the subject of the sentence (*vandalism* in the example), but vandalism does not pass buildings. The modifier "dangles" because it does not connect sensibly to the rest of the sentence. Here is another example:

Dangling   Although intact, graffiti covered every inch of the walls and windows. [The walls and windows, not the graffiti, were intact.]

To revise a dangling modifier, you have to rewrite the sentence. (Revising just by moving the modifier will leave it dangling: *The vandalism became visible passing the building.*) Choose a revision method depending on what you want to emphasize in the sentence:

- Rewrite the dangling modifier as a complete clause with its

Identifying and revising dangling modifiers

- **Find a subject.** If the modifier lacks a subject of its own (e.g., *when in diapers*), identify what it describes.
- **Connect the subject and modifier.** Verify that what the modifier describes is in fact the subject of the main clause. If it is not, the modifier is probably dangling:

┌─modifier──┐   subject

Dangling   When in diapers, my mother remarried.

- **Revise as needed.** Revise a dangling modifier (*a*) by recasting it with a subject of its own or (*b*) by changing the subject of the main clause:

Revision *a*   When I was in diapers, my mother remarried.
Revision *b*   When in diapers, I attended my mother's second wedding.

own stated subject and verb. Readers can accept that the new subject and the sentence subject are different.

Dangling   Passing the building, the vandalism became visible.

Revised   As we passed the building, the vandalism became visible.

- **Change the subject of the sentence to a word the modifier properly describes.**

Dangling   Trying to understand the causes, vandalism has been extensively studied.

Revised   Trying to understand the causes, researchers have extensively studied vandalism.

dm
34b

Exercise 34.3 Revising: Dangling modifiers

Revise the following sentences to eliminate any dangling modifiers. Each item has more than one possible answer. If a sentence is already correct as given, mark the number preceding it. Answers to starred items appear at the end of the book.

Example:

Driving north, the vegetation became more sparse.

Driving north, we noticed that the vegetation became more sparse.
Or: As we drove north, the vegetation became more sparse.

*1. After accomplishing many deeds of valor, Andrew Jackson's fame led to his election to the presidency in 1828 and 1832.
*2. At the age of fourteen, both of Jackson's parents died.
*3. To aid the American Revolution, service as a mounted courier was Jackson's choice.

*4. After being struck with a saber by a British officer, Jackson's craggy face bore a scar.

*5. Though not well educated, a successful career as a lawyer and judge proved Jackson's ability.

6. Winning many military battles, the American public believed in Jackson's leadership.

7. Earning the nicknames "Old Hickory" and "Sharp Knife," the War of 1812 established Jackson's military prowess.

8. Losing only six dead and ten wounded, the triumph of the Battle of New Orleans burnished Jackson's reputation.

9. After putting down raiding parties from Florida, Jackson's victories helped pressure Spain to cede that territory.

10. While briefly governor of Florida, the US presidency became Jackson's goal.

SENTENCE FAULTS

A word group punctuated as a sentence will confuse or annoy readers if it lacks needed parts, has too many parts, or has parts that don't fit together.

35 Sentence Fragments

How can I tell if my sentences are complete?

A complete sentence meets three requirements: it has a subject, the subject has a predicate, and it is not merely a subordinate clause

---
Key terms

subject The part of a sentence that names who or what performs the action or makes the assertion of the predicate: _Ducks swim._ (See p. 202.)

predicate The part of a sentence containing a verb that asserts something about the subject: _Ducks swim._ (See p. 202.)

subordinate clause A word group that contains a subject and a predicate, begins with a subordinating word such as _because_ or _who,_ and is not a question: _Ducks can swim when they are young._ A subordinate clause may serve as a modifier or as a noun. (See p. 213.)

---

mycomplab

Visit _mycomplab.com_ for more resources and exercises on sentence fragments.

Complete sentence versus sentence fragment

A complete sentence or main clause

1. contains a subject and a predicate (*The wind blows*)
2. and is not a subordinate clause (beginning with a word such as *because* or *who*).

A sentence fragment

1. lacks a predicate (*The wind blowing*),
2. or lacks a subject (*And blows*),
3. or is a subordinate clause not attached to a complete sentence (*Because the wind blows*).

(a word group beginning with *because, who,* or a similar word). A **sentence fragment,** in contrast, is a word group that looks like a whole sentence with an initial capital letter and a final period or other end punctuation. Although writers occasionally use fragments deliberately and effectively (see p. 292), readers perceive most fragments as serious errors. To prevent sentence fragments, first test each word group punctuated as a sentence to be sure it is complete (below) and then revise as needed (pp. 291–92).

Grammar checkers A grammar checker can spot many but not all sentence fragments, and it may flag sentences that are actually complete, such as *Continue reading.*

35a   Test your sentences for completeness.

frag

35a

A word group punctuated as a sentence should pass *all three* of the following tests. If it does not, it is a fragment and needs revision.

Test 1: Find the predicate.

Look for a verb that can serve as the predicate of a sentence. Some fragments lack any verb at all:

Fragment   Uncountable numbers of sites on the Web.

Revised   Uncountable numbers of sites <u>make up</u> the Web.

Other fragments may include a verb form but not a **finite verb**—one that changes form as shown on the next page. A verbal does not change and cannot serve as a predicate without a helping verb.

┌─ **Key terms** ───
verbal A verb form that can serve as a noun, a modifier, or a part of a predicate, but not alone as the only verb of a sentence: *drawing, to draw, drawn.* (See p. 210.)

helping verb A verb such as *is, were, have, might,* and *could* that combines with various verb forms to indicate time and other kinds of meaning: for instance, <u>were</u> *drawing,* <u>might</u> *draw.* (See p. 197.)

	Finite verbs in complete sentences	Verbals in sentence fragments
Singular	The network <u>grows</u>.	The network <u>growing</u>.
Plural	Networks <u>grow</u>.	Networks <u>growing</u>.

Present	The network <u>grows</u>.	
Past	The network <u>grew</u>.	The network <u>growing</u>.
Future	The network <u>will grow</u>.	

Fragment	The network <u>taking</u> a primary role in communication and commerce.
Revised	The network <u>is taking</u> a primary role in communication and commerce.

CULTURE LANGUAGE Some languages allow forms of *be* to be omitted as helping verbs or linking verbs, but English requires stating forms of *be*:

Fragments	The network growing rapidly. It much larger than once anticipated.
Revised	The network <u>is</u> growing rapidly. It <u>is</u> much larger than once anticipated.

Test 2: Find the subject.

The subject of the sentence will usually come before the predicate. If there is no subject, the word group is probably a fragment:

Fragment	And has enormous popular appeal.
Revised	And <u>the Web</u> has enormous popular appeal.

In one kind of complete sentence, a command, the subject *you* is understood: [*You*] *Experiment with the Web.*

CULTURE LANGUAGE Some languages allow the omission of the sentence subject, especially when it is a pronoun. But in English, except in commands, the subject is stated:

Fragment	Web commerce has expanded dramatically. <u>Has hurt traditional stores.</u>
Revised	Web commerce has expanded dramatically. <u>It</u> has hurt traditional stores.

Test 3: Make sure the clause is not subordinate.

A subordinate clause usually begins with a subordinating word, such as one of those in the following list.

Key term

linking verb A verb that connects a subject and a word that describes the subject: *They <u>are</u> golfers.* Linking verbs are forms of *be*, the verbs of our five senses (*look, sound, smell, feel, taste*), and *appear, seem, become, grow, turn, prove, remain, stay.* (See p. 205.)

Subordinating conjunctions			Relative pronouns
after	provided	until	that
although	since	when	which
as	so that	whenever	who/whom
because	than	where	whoever/whomever
even if	that	whereas	
even though	though	whether	
if	till	while	
once	unless		

Subordinate clauses serve as parts of sentences (nouns or modifiers), not as whole sentences:

Fragment	When the government devised the Internet.
Revised	The government devised the Internet.
Revised	When the government devised the Internet, <u>no expansive computer network existed.</u>

Fragment	The reason that the government devised the Internet. [This fragment is a noun (*reason*) plus its modifier (*that . . . Internet*).]
Revised	The reason that the government devised the Internet <u>was to provide secure links among departments and defense contractors.</u>

Note Questions beginning with *how, what, when, where, which, who, whom, whose,* and *why* are not sentence fragments: *Who was responsible? When did it happen?*

35b   Revise sentence fragments.

frag

35b

Almost all sentence fragments can be corrected in one of the two ways shown in the following box. The choice depends on the importance of the information in the fragment and thus how much you want to stress it.

Revision of sentence fragments

Option 1

Rewrite the fragment as a complete sentence. This revision gives the information in the fragment the same importance as that in other complete sentences.

Fragment	A major improvement in public health occurred with the widespread use of vaccines. <u>Which protected children against life-threatening diseases.</u>
Revised	A major improvement in public health occurred with the widespread use of vaccines. <u>They</u> protected children against life-threatening diseases.

(continued)

Revision of sentence fragments

(continued)

Option 2

Combine the fragment with a main clause. This revision subordinates the information in the fragment to the information in the main clause.

Fragment	The polio vaccine eradicated the disease from most of the globe. The first vaccine to be used widely.
Revised	The polio vaccine, the first to be used widely, eradicated the disease from most of the globe.

35c   Be aware of the acceptable uses of incomplete sentences.

A few word groups lacking the usual subject-predicate combination are incomplete sentences, but they are not fragments because they conform to the expectations of most readers. They include commands (*Move along. Shut the window.*); exclamations (*Oh no!*); questions and answers (*Where next? To Kansas.*); and descriptions in employment résumés (*Weekly volunteer in soup kitchen.*).

Experienced writers sometimes use sentence fragments when they want to achieve a special effect. Such fragments appear more in informal than in formal writing. Unless you are experienced and thoroughly secure in your own writing, however, you should avoid all fragments and concentrate on writing clear, well-formed sentences.

frag

35c

Exercise 35.1   Revising: Sentence fragments

Correct any sentence fragment in the following items either by combining it with a complete sentence or by making it a complete sentence. If an item contains no sentence fragment, mark the number preceding it. Answers to starred items appear at the end of the book.

Example:

Jujitsu is good for self-protection. Because it enables one to overcome an opponent without the use of weapons.

Jujitsu is good for self-protection because it enables one to overcome an opponent without the use of weapons. *Or:* Jujitsu is good for self-protection. It enables one to overcome an opponent without the use of weapons.

*1. Human beings who perfume themselves. They are not much different from other animals.

*2. Animals as varied as insects and dogs release pheromones. Chemicals that signal other animals.

*3. Human beings have a diminished sense of smell. And do not consciously detect most of their own species' pheromones.
*4. The human substitute for pheromones may be perfumes. Most common in ancient times were musk and other fragrances derived from animal oils.
*5. Some sources say that people began using perfume to cover up the smell of burning flesh. During sacrifices to the gods.
6. Perfumes became religious offerings in their own right. Being expensive to make, they were highly prized.
7. The earliest historical documents from the Middle East record the use of fragrances. Not only in religious ceremonies but on the body.
8. In the nineteenth century, chemists began synthesizing perfume oils. Which previously could be made only from natural sources.
9. The most popular animal oil for perfume today is musk. Although some people dislike its heavy, sweet odor.
10. Synthetic musk oil would help conserve a certain species of deer. Whose gland is the source of musk.

Exercise 35.2 Revising: Sentence fragments

Revise the following paragraphs to eliminate sentence fragments by combining them with main clauses or rewriting them as main clauses. Answers to the first paragraph appear at the end of the book.

Example:

Gymnosperms, the most advanced of nonflowering plants. They thrive in diverse environments.

Gymnosperms, the most advanced of nonflowering plants, thrive in diverse environments. *Or:* Gymnosperms are the most advanced of nonflowering plants. They thrive in diverse environments.

frag

35

*People generally avoid eating mushrooms except those they buy in stores. *But in fact many varieties of mushrooms are edible. *Mushrooms are members of a large group of vegetation called nonflowering plants. *Including algae, mosses, ferns, and coniferous trees. *Even the giant redwoods of California. *Most of the nonflowering plants prefer moist environments. *Such as forest floors, fallen timber, and still water. *Mushrooms, for example. *They prefer moist, shady soil. *Algae grow in water.

Most mushrooms, both edible and inedible, are members of a class called basidium fungi. A term referring to their method of reproduction. The basidia produce spores. Which can develop into mushrooms. This classification including the prized meadow mushroom, cultivated commercially, and the amanitas. The amanita group contains both edible and poisonous species. Another familiar group of mushrooms, the puffballs. They are easily identified by their round shape. Their spores are contained under a thick skin. Which eventually ruptures to release the spores. The famous morels are in still another group. These pitted, spongy mushrooms called sac fungi because the spores develop in sacs.

Anyone interested in mushrooms as food should heed the US Public Health Service warning. Not to eat any wild mushrooms unless their identity and edibility are established without a doubt.

Should a new sentence begin here?

The kernel of a sentence is the main clause consisting of a subject and its predicate. To know that one main clause is ending and another is beginning, readers expect one of these signals:

- **A period,** creating two separate sentences:

  The ship was huge⊙ Its mast stood eighty feet high.

- **A comma and a coordinating conjunction,** linking two clauses in one sentence:

  The ship was huge⊚ and its mast stood eighty feet high.

- **A semicolon,** separating two clauses within one sentence:

  The ship was huge⨀ its mast stood eighty feet high.

Readers may be confused if two main clauses run together in a sentence *without* the second or third signal. The result may be a **comma splice,** in which the clauses are joined (or spliced) *only* with a comma:

Comma splice

The ship was huge, its mast stood eighty feet high.

Or the result may be a **fused sentence** (or **run-on sentence**), in which no punctuation or conjunction appears between the clauses:

Fused sentence

The ship was huge its mast stood eighty feet high.

The usual repairs for comma splices and fused sentences are shown in the box opposite and discussed on the following pages.

Grammar checkers A grammar checker can detect many comma splices, but it will miss most fused sentences. For example, a checker flagged *Money is tight, we need to spend carefully* but not *Money is*

Key terms

main clause A word group that can stand alone as a sentence because it contains a subject and a predicate and does not begin with a subordinating word: *A dictionary is essential.*

coordinating conjunction *And, but, or, nor, for, so, yet.* (See p. 200.)

---

mycomplab

Visit *mycomplab.com* for more resources and exercises on comma splices and fused sentences.

tight we need to spend carefully. A checker may also question sentences that are actually correct, such as *Money being tighter now than before, we need to spend carefully.*

Punctuation of two or more main clauses

The following steps can help you identify and revise comma splices and fused sentences.

1. Underline the main clauses in your draft.

<u>Sailors trained on the ship</u>. <u>They learned about wind and sails</u>. <u>Trainees who took the course ranged from high school students to Navy officers</u>. <u>The ship was built in 1910</u>, <u>it had sailed ever since</u>. In almost a century, <u>it had circled the globe forty times</u>. <u>It burned in 2001 its cabins and decks were destroyed</u>.

2. Are consecutive main clauses separated by periods?

If **yes,** OK.
If **no,** go to question 3.

Comma splice   The ship was built in 1910, it had sailed ever since.
Fused sentence   It burned in 2001 its cabins and decks were destroyed.

3. Are consecutive main clauses linked by a comma?

If **yes,** go to question 4.

Comma splice   The ship was built in 1910, it had sailed ever since.

If **no,** go to question 5.

Fused sentence   It burned in 2001 its cabins and decks were destroyed.

4. Does a coordinating conjunction follow the comma between main clauses?

If **yes,** OK.
If **no,** add a coordinating conjunction: *and, but, or, nor, for, so, yet.*

Revised   The ship was built in 1910, and it had sailed ever since.

5. Are consecutive main clauses separated by a semicolon?

If **yes,** OK.
If **no,** add a semicolon.

Revised   It burned in 2001; its cabins and decks were destroyed.

As an alternative to these revision methods, you can also subordinate one clause to another:

Revised   When it burned in 2001, its cabins and decks were destroyed.

cs/fs
36

CULTURE LANGUAGE In standard American English, a sentence may not include more than one main clause unless the clauses are separated by a comma and a coordinating conjunction or by a semicolon. If your native language does not have such a rule or has accustomed you to writing long sentences, you may need to edit your English writing especially for comma splices and fused sentences.

36a Separate main clauses not joined by *and, but,* or another coordinating conjunction.

If your readers point out comma splices or fused sentences in your writing, you're not creating enough separation between main clauses in your sentences. Use one of the following methods to repair the problem.

Separate sentences

Make the clauses into separate sentences when the ideas expressed are only loosely related:

Comma splice	Chemistry has contributed much to our understanding of foods, many foods such as wheat and beans can be produced in the laboratory.
Revised	Chemistry has contributed much to our understanding of foods⊙ Many foods such as wheat and beans can be produced in the laboratory.

CULTURE LANGUAGE Making separate sentences may be the best option if you are used to writing very long sentences in your native language but often write comma splices in English.

Coordinating conjunction

Insert a coordinating conjunction in a comma splice when the ideas in the main clauses are closely related and are equally important:

Comma splice	Some laboratory-grown foods taste good, they are nutritious.
Revised	Some laboratory-grown foods taste good, <u>and</u> they are nutritious.

In a fused sentence insert a comma and a coordinating conjunction:

Fused sentence	Chemists have made much progress they still have a way to go.
Revised	Chemists have made much progress⊙ <u>but</u> they still have a way to go.

Semicolon

Insert a semicolon between clauses if the relation between the ideas is very close and obvious without a conjunction:

Comma splice	Good taste is rare in laboratory-grown vegetables, they are usually bland.
Revised	Good taste is rare in laboratory-grown vegetables; they are usually bland.

Subordination

When one idea is less important than the other, express the less important idea in a subordinate clause:

Comma splice	The vitamins are adequate, the flavor is deficient.
Revised	Even though the vitamins are adequate, the flavor is deficient.

36b   Separate main clauses related by *however, for example*, and so on.

Two groups of words that are not conjunctions describe how one main clause relates to another: **conjunctive adverbs** and other **transitional expressions.** (See p. 50 for a longer list.)

Common conjunctive adverbs and transitional expressions

accordingly	for instance	in the meantime	otherwise
anyway	further	in the past	similarly
as a result	furthermore	likewise	so far
at last	hence	meanwhile	still
at length	however	moreover	that is
besides	incidentally	namely	then
certainly	in contrast	nevertheless	thereafter
consequently	indeed	nonetheless	therefore
even so	in fact	now	thus
finally	in other words	of course	to this end
for all that	in short	on the contrary	undoubtedly
for example	instead	on the whole	until now

cs/fs

36b

When two main clauses are related by a conjunctive adverb or another transitional expression, they must be separated by a period or by a semicolon. The adverb or expression is also generally set off by a comma or commas.

> ┌ **Key term** ──────────────────────────────
> **subordinate clause** A word group that contains a subject and a predicate, begins with a subordinating word such as *because* or *who,* and is not a question: *Ducks can swim when they are young.* A subordinate clause may serve as a modifier or as a noun. (See p. 213.)

Comma splice	Healthcare costs are higher in the United States than in many other countries, <u>consequently</u> health insurance is also more costly.
Revised	Healthcare costs are higher in the United States than in many other countries⊙ Consequently⊙ health insurance is also more costly.
Revised	Healthcare costs are higher in the United States than in many other countries⨀ <u>consequently</u>⊙ health insurance is also more costly.

Conjunctive adverbs and transitional expressions are different from coordinating conjunctions (*and, but,* and so on) and subordinating conjunctions (*although, because,* and so on):

- **Unlike conjunctions, conjunctive adverbs and transitional expressions do not join two clauses into a grammatical unit.** They merely describe the way two clauses relate in meaning.
- **Unlike conjunctions, conjunctive adverbs and transitional expressions can be moved within a clause.** No matter where in the clause an adverb or expression falls, though, the clause must be separated from another main clause by a period or semicolon:

Many Americans refuse to give up unhealthful habits⨀ our medical costs⊙ <u>consequently</u>⊙ are higher than those of many other countries.

Exercise 36.1   Sentence combining to avoid comma splices and fused sentences

Using the method suggested in parentheses, combine each of the following pairs of sentences into one sentence without creating a comma splice or a fused sentence. Answers to starred items appear at the end of the book.

Example:

The sun sank lower in the sky. The colors gradually faded. (*Subordinate one clause to the other.*)

As the sun sank lower in the sky⊙ the colors gradually faded.

*1. Some people think that dinosaurs were the first living vertebrates. Fossils of turtles go back 40 million years further. (*Supply a comma and coordinating conjunction.*)

*2. Most other reptiles exist mainly in tropical regions. Turtles inhabit a variety of environments worldwide. (*Subordinate one clause to the other.*)

*3. Turtles do not have teeth. Their jaws are covered with a sharp, horny sheath. (*Supply a semicolon.*)

*4. Turtles cannot expand their lungs to breathe air. They make adjustments in how space is used within the shell. (*Supply a semicolon and a conjunctive adverb or transitional expression.*)

*5. Some turtles can get oxygen from water. They don't need to breathe air. (*Supply a semicolon and a conjunctive adverb or transitional expression.*)

cs/fs
36b

6. The exact origin of paper money is unknown. It has not survived as coins, shells, and other durable objects have. (*Subordinate one clause to the other.*)

7. Scholars disagree over where paper money originated. Many believe it was first used in Europe. (*Subordinate one clause to the other.*)

8. Perhaps goldsmiths were also bankers. Thus they held the gold of their wealthy customers. (*Supply a semicolon.*)

9. The goldsmiths probably gave customers receipts for their gold. These receipts were then used in trade. (*Supply a comma and coordinating conjunction.*)

10. The goldsmiths were something like modern-day bankers. Their receipts were something like modern-day money. (*Supply a semicolon.*)

11. The goldsmiths became even more like modern-day bankers. They began issuing receipts for more gold than they actually held in their vaults. (*Subordinate one clause to the other.*)

12. Today's bankers owe more to their customers than they actually have in reserve. They keep enough assets on hand to meet reasonable withdrawals. (*Supply a semicolon and a conjunctive adverb or transitional expression.*)

13. In economic crises, bank customers sometimes fear the loss of their money. Consequently, they demand their deposits. (*Supply a semicolon.*)

14. Depositors' demands may exceed a bank's reserves. The bank may collapse. (*Supply a comma and coordinating conjunction.*)

15. The government now regulates banks to protect depositors. Bank failures are less frequent than they once were. (*Supply a semicolon and a conjunctive adverb or transitional expression.*)

Exercise 36.2 Revising: Comma splices and fused sentences

Correct each of the following comma splices or fused sentences in two of the following ways: (1) make separate sentences of the main clauses; (2) insert an appropriate coordinating conjunction or both a comma and a coordinating conjunction between the main clauses; (3) insert a semicolon and a conjunctive adverb or transitional expression between the main clauses; (4) subordinate one clause to another. If an item contains no comma splice or fused sentence, mark the number preceding it. Answers to starred items appear at the end of the book.

Example:

Carolyn still had a headache, she could not get the child-proof cap off the aspirin bottle.

Carolyn still had a headache because she could not get the child-proof cap off the aspirin bottle. (*Subordination.*)

Carolyn still had a headache, for she could not get the child-proof cap off the aspirin bottle. (*Coordinating conjunction.*)

*1. Money has a long history, it goes back at least as far as the earliest records.

*2. Many of the earliest records concern financial transactions, indeed, early history must often be inferred from commercial activity.

cs/fs

36

*3. Every known society has had a system of money, though the objects serving as money have varied widely.

*4. Sometimes the objects have had real value, in modern times their value has been more abstract.

*5. Cattle, fermented beverages, and rare shells have served as money each one had actual value for the society.

6. As money, these objects acquired additional value they represented other goods.

7. Today money may be made of worthless paper, it may even consist of a bit of data in a computer's memory.

8. We think of money as valuable only our common faith in it makes it valuable.

9. That faith is sometimes fragile, consequently, currencies themselves are fragile.

10. Economic crises often shake the belief in money, indeed, such weakened faith helped cause the Great Depression of the 1930s.

11. Throughout history money and religion were closely linked, there was little distinction between government and religion.

12. The head of state and the religious leader were often the same person so that all power rested in one ruler.

13. These powerful leaders decided what objects would serve as money, their backing encouraged public faith in the money.

14. Coins were minted of precious metals the religious overtones of money were then strengthened.

15. People already believed the precious metals to be divine, their use in money intensified its allure.

Exercise 36.3   Revising: Comma splices and fused sentences

Revise each comma splice and fused sentence in the following paragraphs using the technique that seems most appropriate for the meaning. Answers to the first paragraph appear at the end of the book.

*What many call the first genocide of modern times occurred during World War I, the Armenians were deported from their homes in Anatolia, Turkey. *The Turkish government assumed that the Armenians were sympathetic to Russia, with whom the Turks were at war. *Many Armenians died because of the hardships of the journey many were massacred. *The death toll was estimated at between 600,000 and 1 million.

Many of the deported Armenians migrated to Russia, in 1918 they established the Republic of Armenia, they continued to be attacked by Turkey, in 1920 they became the Soviet Republic of Armenia rather than surrender to the Turks. Like other Soviet republics, Armenia became independent in 1991, about 3.4 million Armenians live there now.

The Armenians have a long history of conquest by others. As a people, they formed a centralized state in the seventh century BC then they were ruled by the Persian empire until it was conquered by Alexander the Great. Greek and Roman rule followed, internal clan leadership marked by disunity and strife was next. In AD 640 the country was invaded by the Arabs in the eleventh century it was conquered by the Byzantines and then by the Turks, under whose control it remained until the twentieth century.

37 Mixed Sentences

Tangled sentences often come from **mixed constructions**: the sentences contain parts that do not fit together in either grammar or meaning. Usually the misfit lies in the subject and predicate, so most repairs focus on these essential elements.

Grammar checkers A grammar checker may recognize a simple mixed construction such as *reason is because,* but it will fail to flag most mixed sentences.

37a Match subjects and predicates in meaning.

In a sentence with mixed meaning, the subject is said to do or be something illogical. Such a mixture is sometimes called **faulty predication** because the predicate conflicts with the subject.

1 ▪ Illogical equation with *be*

When a form of *be* connects a subject and a word that describes the subject (a complement), the subject and complement must be logically related:

Mixed A compromise between the city and the country would be the ideal place to live.

Revised A community that offered the best qualities of both city and country would be the ideal place to live.

2 ▪ *Is when, is where*

Definitions require nouns on both sides of *be.* Clauses that define and begin with *when* or *where* are common in speech but should be avoided in writing.

> **Key terms**
>
> **subject** The part of a sentence that names who or what performs the action or makes the assertion of the predicate: *Geese fly.* (See p. 202.)
>
> **predicate** The part of a sentence containing a verb that asserts something about the subject: *Geese fly.* (See p. 202.)

mixed

37a

> mycomplab
>
> Visit *mycomplab.com* for more resources on mixed sentences.

Mixed   An examination is when you are tested on what you know.

Revised   An examination is a test of what you know.

3 ▪ *Reason is because*

The commonly heard construction *reason is because* is redundant since *because* means "for the reason that":

Mixed   The reason the temple requests donations is because the school needs expansion.

Revised   The reason the temple requests donations is that the school needs expansion.

Revised   The temple requests donations because the school needs expansion.

4 ▪ Other mixed meanings

Faulty predications are not confined to sentences with *be*:

Mixed   The use of emission controls was created to reduce air pollution.

Revised   Emission controls were created to reduce air pollution.

37b   Untangle sentences that are mixed in grammar.

mixed

37b

Many mixed sentences start with one grammatical plan or construction but end with a different one:

┌──────── modifier (prepositional phrase)────────┐ verb

Mixed   By paying more attention to impressions than facts leads us to misjudge others.

This mixed sentence makes a prepositional phrase work as the subject of *leads,* but prepositional phrases function as modifiers, not as nouns, and thus not as sentence subjects.

┌──────── modifier (prepositional phrase)────────┐subject

Revised   By paying more attention to impressions than facts, we

verb

misjudge others.

Constructions that use *Just because* clauses as subjects are common in speech but should be avoided in writing:

┌ modifier (subordinate clause)┐┌── verb──┐

Mixed   Just because no one is watching doesn't mean we have license to break the law.

┌modifier (subordinate clause)┐ subject + verb

Revised   Even when no one is watching, we don't have license to break the law.

A mixed sentence is especially likely when you are working on a computer and connect parts of two sentences or rewrite half a sentence but not the other half. A mixed sentence may also occur when you don't make the subject and predicate verb carry the principal meaning. (See p. 148.)

Exercise 37.1   Revising: Mixed sentences

Revise the following sentences so that their parts fit together both in grammar and in meaning. Each item has more than one possible answer. If a sentence is already correct as given, mark the number preceding it. Answers to starred items appear at the end of the book.

Example:

When they found out how expensive pianos are discouraged them.

When they found out how expensive pianos are, <u>they</u> were discouraged them. *Or:* <u>Finding</u> out how expensive pianos are discouraged them.

*1. A hurricane is when the winds in a tropical depression rotate counterclockwise at more than seventy-four miles per hour.

*2. Because hurricanes can destroy so many lives and so much property is why people fear them.

*3. Through high winds, storm surge, floods, and tornadoes is how hurricanes have killed thousands of people.

*4. Storm surge is where the hurricane's winds whip up a tide that spills over seawalls and deluges coastal islands.

*5. The winds themselves are also destructive, uprooting trees and smashing buildings.

6. Many scientists observe that hurricanes in recent years they have become more ferocious and destructive.

7. However, in the last half-century, with improved communication systems and weather satellites have made hurricanes less deadly.

8. The reason is because people have more time to escape.

9. The emphasis on evacuation is in fact the best way for people to avoid a hurricane's force.

10. Simply boarding up a house's windows will not protect a family from wind, water surges, and flying debris.

mixed

37c

37c   State parts of clauses, such as subjects, only once.

In some languages other than English, certain parts of sentences may be repeated. These include the subject in any kind of clause or an object or adverb in an adjective clause. In English, however, these parts are stated only once in a clause.

Key term

clause A group of words containing both a subject and a predicate. (See p. 213.)

---

1 ■ Repetition of subject

You may be tempted to restate a subject as a pronoun before the verb. But the subject needs stating only once in its clause:

Faulty   The liquid it reached a temperature of 180°F.
Revised The liquid reached a temperature of 180°F.

Faulty   Gases in the liquid they escaped.
Revised Gases in the liquid escaped.

2 ■ Repetition in an adjective clause

Adjective clauses begin with *who, whom, whose, which, that, where,* and *when* (see also p. 213). The beginning word replaces another word: the subject (*He is the person who called*), an object of a verb or preposition (*He is the person whom I mentioned*), or a preposition and pronoun (*He knows the office where [in which] the conference will occur*).

Do not state the word being replaced in an adjective clause:

Faulty   The technician whom the test depended on her was burned.
         [*Whom* should replace *her.*]
Revised The technician whom the test depended on was burned.

Adjective clauses beginning with *where* or *when* do not need an adverb such as *there* or *then*:

Faulty   Gases escaped at a moment when the technician was unprepared then.
Revised Gases escaped at a moment when the technician was unprepared.

Note *Whom, which,* and similar words are sometimes omitted but are still understood by the reader. Thus the word being replaced should not be stated:

Faulty   Accidents rarely happen to technicians the lab has trained them. [*Whom* is understood: . . . *technicians whom the lab has trained.*]
Revised Accidents rarely happen to technicians the lab has trained.

Exercise 37.2 Revising: Repeated subjects and other parts

Revise the following sentences to eliminate any unneeded words. If a sentence is already correct as given, mark the number preceding it. Answers to starred items appear at the end of the book.

Example:

Scientists they use special instruments for measuring the age of artifacts.

Scientists use special instruments for measuring the age of artifacts.

---

mixed
37c

*1. Archaeologists and other scientists they can often determine the age of their discoveries by means of radiocarbon dating.

*2. This technique it can be used on any material that once was living.

*3. This technique is based on the fact that all living organisms they contain carbon.

*4. The most common isotope is carbon 12, which it contains six protons and six neutrons.

*5. A few carbon atoms are classified as the isotope carbon 14, where the nucleus consists of six protons and eight neutrons there.

6. Because of the extra neutrons, the carbon 14 atom it is unstable and radioactive.

7. What is significant about the carbon 14 atom is its half-life of 5700 years.

8. Scientists they measure the proportion of carbon 14 to carbon 12 and estimate the age of the specimen.

9. This kind of dating is most accurate when a specimen is between 500 and 50,000 years old then.

10. With younger specimens too little carbon 14 has decayed, and with older ones too little is left that the scientists can measure it.

mixed

37c

PART **5**

Punctuation

38 End Punctuation

What punctuation goes at the end of a sentence?

End a sentence with one of three punctuation marks: a period (.), a question mark (?), or an exclamation point (!).

Grammar checkers A grammar checker may flag missing question marks after direct questions or incorrect combinations of marks (such as a question mark and a period at the end of a sentence), but it cannot do much else.

38a Use a period after most sentences and in many abbreviations.

1 ▪ Statements, mild commands, and indirect questions

Statement

The airline went bankrupt⊙   It no longer flies⊙

Mild command

Think of the possibilities⊙   Please consider others⊙

Indirect question

An **indirect question** reports what someone asked but not in the exact form or words of the original question:

The judge asked why I had been driving with my lights off⊙
No one asked how we got home⊙

CULTURE LANGUAGE In standard American English, an indirect question uses the wording and subject-verb order of a statement: *The reporter asked why the bank failed* [not *why did the bank fail*].

2 ▪ Abbreviations

Use periods with abbreviations that consist of or end in small letters. Otherwise, omit periods from abbreviations.

Dr.	Mr., Mrs.	e.g.	Feb.	ft.
St.	Ms.	i.e.	p.	a.m., p.m.
PhD	BC, AD	USA	IBM	JFK
BA	AM, PM	US	USMC	AIDS

---

mycomplab ▐

Visit *mycomplab.com* for more resources and exercises on end punctuation.

Note When an abbreviation falls at the end of a sentence, use only one period: *My first class is at 8 a.m.⊙*

38b   Use a question mark after a direct question and sometimes to indicate doubt.

1 ▪ Direct questions

Who will follow her⟨?⟩
What is the difference between these two people⟨?⟩

After indirect questions, use a period: *We wondered who would follow her⊙* (See the facing page.)
Questions in a series are each followed by a question mark:

The officer asked how many times the suspect had been arrested. Three times⟨?⟩ Four times⟨?⟩ More than that⟨?⟩

Note A question mark falls inside or outside a closing quotation mark depending on whether it is part of a quoted question or part of the larger sentence. (See also pp. 341–42.)

He asked, "Who will go⟨?"⟩ [Question mark part of the quoted question.]
Did he say, "I will go"⟨?⟩ [Question mark part of the larger sentence, a question.]

2 ▪ Doubt

A question mark within parentheses can indicate doubt about a number or date.

The Greek philosopher Socrates was born in 470 (⟨?⟩) BC and died in 399 BC. [Socrates's birthdate is not known for sure.]

Use sentence structure and words, not a question mark, to express sarcasm or irony.

Not   Stern's friendliness (?) bothered Crane.
But   Stern's <u>insincerity</u> bothered Crane.

. ? !
38c

38c   Use an exclamation point after an emphatic statement, interjection, or command.

No⟨!⟩ We must not lose this election⟨!⟩
Come here immediately⟨!⟩

┌─ **Key term** ─────────────────────────────────
interjection A word that expresses feeling or commands attention, either alone or within a sentence: *Oh! Hey! Wow!* (See p. 201.)

Follow mild interjections and commands with commas or periods, as appropriate: *Oh⊙ call whenever you can⊙*

Use exclamation points sparingly, even in informal writing. Overused, they'll fail to impress readers, and they may make you sound overemphatic.

Note An exclamation point falls inside or outside a closing quotation mark depending on whether it is part of the quotation or part of the larger sentence. (See also pp. 341–42.)

Example 38.1   Revising: End punctuation

Insert appropriate end punctuation (periods, question marks, or exclamation points) where needed in the following paragraph. Answers to the starred lines appear at the end of the book.

* When visitors first arrive in Hawaii, they often encounter an unex-
* pected language barrier Standard English is the language of business
* and government, but many of the people speak Pidgin English Instead
* of an excited "Aloha" the visitors may be greeted with an excited Pid-
* gin "Howzit" or asked if they know "how fo' find one good hotel"
Many Hawaiians question whether Pidgin will hold children back because it prevents communication with *haoles,* or Caucasians, who run businesses Yet many others feel that Pidgin is a last defense of ethnic diversity on the islands To those who want to make Standard English the official language of the state, these Hawaiians may respond, "Just 'cause I speak Pidgin no mean I dumb" They may ask, "Why you no listen" or, in standard English, "Why don't you listen"

---

39   The Comma

What do commas do (and not do)?

The most common punctuation mark within sentences, commas do mainly the following:

- **Separate main clauses linked by *and, but,* and other coordinating conjunctions** (p. 312).
- **Set off most introductory elements** (p. 313).
- **Set off nonessential elements** (p. 315).
- **Separate items in a series** (p. 320).
- **Separate coordinate adjectives** (p. 320).

---

mycomplab

Visit *mycomplab.com* for more resources and exercises on the comma.

Main uses of the comma

- **Separate main clauses linked by a coordinating conjunction** (next page).

The building is finished꜀ but it has no tenants.

- **Set off most introductory elements** (p. 313).

Unfortunately꜀ the only tenant pulled out.

- **Set off nonessential elements** (p. 315).

$$\text{Main clause} \quad \text{꜀} \quad \text{nonessential element} \quad .$$

The empty building symbolizes a weak local economy꜀ which affects everyone.

$$\text{Beginning of main clause} \quad \text{꜀} \quad \text{nonessential element} \quad \text{꜀} \quad \text{end of main clause} \quad .$$

The primary cause꜀ the decline of local industry꜀ is not news.

- **Separate items in a series** (p. 320).

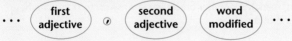

The city needs healthier businesses꜀ new schools꜀ and improved housing.

- **Separate coordinate adjectives** (p. 320).

$$\cdots \quad \text{first adjective} \quad \text{꜀} \quad \text{second adjective} \quad \text{word modified} \quad \cdots$$

A tall꜀ sleek skyscraper is not needed.

39

Other uses of the comma:

Separate parts of dates, addresses, long numbers (p. 321).
Separate quotations and signal phrases (p. 322).

See also page 323 for when *not* to use the comma.

- Separate parts of dates, addresses, place names, and long numbers (p. 321).
- Separate signal phrases and quotations (p. 322).

Commas can be easy to misuse. For guidance on when *not* to use a comma, see page 323.

Grammar checkers A grammar checker will ignore many comma errors. For example, a checker failed to catch the missing commas in *We cooked lasagna spinach and apple pie* and the misused comma in *The travelers were tempted by, the many shops*.

39a   Use a comma before *and, but,* or another coordinating conjunction linking main clauses.

When a coordinating conjunction links words or phrases, do not use a comma: *Dugain plays⌒and sings Irish⌒and English folk songs.* However, *do* use a comma when a coordinating conjunction joins main clauses.

Caffeine can keep coffee drinkers alert⌒ and it may elevate their mood.

Caffeine was once thought to be safe⌒ but now researchers warn of harmful effects.

Coffee drinkers may suffer sleeplessness⌒ for the drug acts as a stimulant to the nervous system.

Note The comma goes *before,* not after, the coordinating conjunction: *Caffeine increases heart rate⌒ and⌒it* [not *and, it*] *constricts blood vessels.*

Exception Some writers omit the comma between main clauses that are very short and closely related in meaning: *Caffeine helps but it also hurts.* If you are in doubt about whether to use the comma in such a sentence, use it. It will always be correct.

> **Exercise 39.1   Punctuating linked main clauses**
> Insert a comma before each coordinating conjunction that links main clauses in the following sentences. If a sentence is already correct as given, mark the number preceding it. Answers to starred items appear at the end of the book.

┌ **Key terms** ───

coordinating conjunctions *And, but, or, nor,* and sometimes *for, so, yet.* (See p. 200.)

main clause A word group that can stand alone as a sentence because it contains a subject and a predicate and does not begin with a subordinating word: *Water freezes at temperatures below 32°F.* (See p. 213.)

^
,
39a

Example:

I would have attended the concert and the reception but I had to baby-sit for my niece.

I would have attended the concert and the reception‸ but I had to baby-sit for my niece.

*1. Parents once automatically gave their children the father's last name‸ but some no longer do.
*2. Parents were once legally required to give their children the father's last name‸but these laws have been contested in court.
*3. Parents may now give their children any last name they choose‸and the arguments for choosing the mother's last name are often strong and convincing.
*4. Parents who choose the mother's last name may do so because they believe that the mother's importance should be recognized‸or because the mother's name is easier to pronounce.
*5. The child's last name may be just the mother's or it may link the mother's and the father's with a hyphen.
6. Sometimes the first and third children will have the mother's last name‸and the second child will have the father's.
7. Occasionally, the mother and father combine parts of their names and a new last name is formed.
8. Critics sometimes point out that unusual names confuse others‸and can create difficulties for children.
9. Children with last names different from their fathers' may feel embarrassed‸ or have identity problems‸ since most children in the United States still bear their fathers' names.
10. Hyphenated names are awkward and difficult to pass on‸ so some observers think they will die out in a generation or two.

39b   Use a comma to set off most introductory elements.

An **introductory element** begins a sentence and modifies a word or words in the main clause that follows. It is usually followed by a comma.

Subordinate clause

Even when identical twins are raised apart‸ they grow up very like each other.

> **Key term**
>
> **subordinate clause** A word group that contains a subject and a predicate, begins with a subordinating word such as *because* or *who*, and is not a question: *When water freezes, crystals form.* (See p. 213.)

Verbal or verbal phrase

Explaining the similarity, some researchers claim that one's genes are one's destiny.

Concerned, other researchers deny the claim.

Prepositional phrase

In a debate that has lasted centuries, scientists use identical twins to argue for or against genetic destiny.

Transitional expression

Of course, scientists can now look directly at the genes themselves to answer questions.

You may omit the comma after a short subordinate clause or prepositional phrase if its omission does not create confusion: *When snow falls the city collapses. By the year 2000 the world population had topped 6 billion.* You may also omit the comma after some transitional expressions when they start sentences: *Thus the debate continues* (see p. 318). However, in both situations the comma is never wrong.

Note Take care to distinguish *-ing* words used as modifiers from *-ing* words used as subjects. The former almost always take a comma; the latter never do.

  ┌────modifier────┐ subject verb
Studying identical twins, geneticists learn about inheritance.

  ┌──────subject──────┐ verb
Studying identical twins helps geneticists learn about inheritance.

> **Exercise 39.2 Punctuating introductory elements**
>
> In the following sentences, insert commas where needed after introductory elements. If a sentence is already correct as given, mark the number preceding it. Answers to starred items appear at the end of the book.
>
> *Example:*
>   After the new library opened the old one became a student union.
>   After the new library opened, the old one became a student union.

39b

> ┌─ **Key terms** ───────────────────────────────
>
> **verbal** A verb form used as an adjective, adverb, or noun. A verbal plus any object or modifier is a **verbal phrase**: *frozen water, ready to freeze, rapid freezing.* (See p. 210.)
>
> **prepositional phrase** A word group consisting of a preposition, such as *for* or *in*, followed by a noun or pronoun plus any modifiers: *in a jar, with a spoon.* (See p. 210.)
>
> **transitional expression** A word or phrase that shows the relationship between sentences: *for example, however, in fact, of course, in contrast.* (See p. 50.)

*1. Veering sharply to the right, a large flock of birds neatly avoids a high wall.
*2. Moving in a fluid mass is typical of flocks of birds and schools of fish.
*3. With the help of complex computer simulations, zoologists are learning more about this movement.
*4. Because it is sudden and apparently well coordinated, the movement of flocks and schools has seemed to be directed by a leader.
*5. Almost incredibly, the group could behave with more intelligence than any individual seemed to possess.
6. However, new studies have discovered that flocks and schools are leaderless.
7. As it turns out, evading danger is really an individual response.
8. When each bird or fish senses a predator, it follows individual rules for fleeing.
9. To keep from colliding with its neighbors, each bird or fish uses other rules for dodging.
10. Multiplied over hundreds of individuals, these responses look as if they have been choreographed.

39c   Use a comma or commas to set off nonessential elements.

Commas around part of a sentence often signal that the element is not necessary to the meaning. This **nonessential element** may modify or rename the word it refers to, but it does not limit the word to a particular individual or group. The meaning of the word would still be clear if the element were deleted:

Nonessential element

The company, which is located in Oklahoma, has an excellent reputation.

(Because it does not restrict meaning, a nonessential element is also called a **nonrestrictive element**.)

In contrast, an **essential** (or **restrictive**) **element** *does* limit the word it refers to: the element cannot be omitted without leaving the meaning too general. Because it is essential, such an element is *not* set off with commas.

Essential element

The company rewards employees who work hard.

Omitting the underlined words would distort the meaning: the company doesn't necessarily reward *all* employees, only the hardworking ones.

The same element in the same sentence may be essential or nonessential depending on your meaning and the context:

A test for nonessential and essential elements

1. **Identify the element:**

   Hai Nguyen <u>who emigrated from Vietnam</u> lives in Denver.
   Those <u>who emigrated with him</u> live elsewhere.

2. **Remove the element.** Does the fundamental meaning of the sentence change?

   Hai Nguyen lives in Denver. **No.**
   Those live elsewhere. **Yes.** [Who are *Those*?]

3. **If *no*, the element is *nonessential* and *should* be set off with punctuation:**

   Hai Nguyen⌒ who emigrated from Vietnam⌒ lives in Denver.

   If *yes*, the element is *essential* and should *not* be set off with punctuation:

   Those⌒who emigrated with him⌒live elsewhere.

Essential

Not all the bands were equally well received, however. The band⌒playing old music⌒held the audience's attention. The other groups created much less excitement. [*Playing old music* distinguishes a particular band from all possible bands, so the information is essential.]

Nonessential

A new band called Fats made its debut on Saturday night. The band⌒playing old music⌒ held the audience's attention. If this performance is typical, the group has a bright future. [*Playing old music* adds information about a band already named and thus already familiar to readers, so the phrase is nonessential.]

Note When a nonessential element falls in the middle of a sentence, be sure to set it off with a pair of commas, one *before* and one *after* the element.

1 ▪ Nonessential phrases and clauses

Most nonessential phrases and subordinate clauses function as adjectives to modify nouns or pronouns. In each of the following examples, the underlined words could be omitted with no loss of clarity.

┌─ **Key terms** ─────────────────────────────

phrase A word group lacking a subject or a verb or both: *in Duluth, carrying water.* (See p. 210.)

subordinate clause A word group that contains a subject and a predicate, begins with a subordinating word such as *who* or *although*, and is not a question: *Samson, <u>who won a gold medal</u>, coaches in Utah.* (See p. 213.)

∧
,
39c

Elizabeth Blackwell was the first woman to graduate from an American medical school◦ in 1849. [Phrase.]

She was a medical pioneer◦ helping to found the first medical college for women. [Phrase.]

She taught at the school◦ which was affiliated with the New York Infirmary. [Clause.]

Blackwell◦ who published books and papers on medicine◦ practiced pediatrics and gynecology. [Clause.]

Note Use *that* only in an essential clause, never in a nonessential clause: . . . *school, which* [not *that*] *was affiliated.* . . . Many writers reserve *which* for nonessential clauses.

2 ▪ Nonessential appositives

Appositives may also be essential or nonessential, depending on meaning and context. A nonessential appositive merely adds information about the word it refers to:

Toni Morrison's fifth novel◦ *Beloved*◦ won the Pulitzer Prize in 1988. [The word *fifth* identifies the novel, so the book's title simply adds a detail.]

In contrast, an essential appositive limits or defines the word it refers to:

Morrison's novel⌒*The Bluest Eye*⌒is about an African American girl who longs for blue eyes. [Morrison has written more than one novel, so the title is essential to identify the intended one.]

3 ▪ Other nonessential elements

Like nonessential modifiers or appositives, many other elements contribute to texture, tone, or overall clarity but are not essential to the meaning. Unlike nonessential modifiers or appositives, these other nonessential elements generally do not refer to any specific word in the sentence.

Note Use a pair of commas—one before, one after—when any of these elements falls in the middle of a sentence.

Absolute phrases

Household recycling having succeeded◦ the city now wants to extend the program to businesses.

Many businesses◦ their profits already squeezed◦ resist recycling.

39c

┌─ **Key terms** ─────────────────────────────

appositive A noun that renames another noun immediately before it: *His wife, Kyra Sedgwick, is also an actor.* (See p. 212.)

absolute phrase A phrase modifying a whole main clause and consisting of a participle and its subject: *Their homework completed, the children watched TV.* (See p. 211.)

Parenthetical and transitional expressions

Generally, set off parenthetical and transitional expressions with commas:

> The world's most celebrated holiday is‸ perhaps surprisingly‸ New Year's Day. [Parenthetical expression.]

> Interestingly‸ Americans have relatively few holidays. [Parenthetical expression.]

> US workers‸ for example‸ receive fewer holidays than European workers do. [Transitional expression.]

(Dashes and parentheses may also set off parenthetical expressions. See pp. 343–44.)

When a transitional expression links main clauses, precede it with a semicolon and follow it with a comma (see p. 327):

> European workers often have long paid vacations‸ indeed‸ they may receive a full month after just a few years with a company.

Exception The conjunctions *and* and *but*, sometimes used as transitional expressions, are never followed by commas (see p. 311). Usage varies with some other transitional expressions, depending on the expression and the writer's judgment. Many writers omit commas with expressions that we read without pauses, such as *also, hence, next, now, then*, and *thus*. The same applies to *therefore* and *instead* when they fall inside or at the ends of clauses.

> US workers‿thus‿put in more work days. But‿the days themselves may be shorter.

> Then‿the total hours worked would come out roughly the same.

Phrases of contrast

> The substance‸ not the style‸ is important.

> Substance‸ unlike style‸ cannot be faked.

Tag questions

> They don't stop to consider others‸ do they?

> Jones should be allowed to vote‸ shouldn't he?

‸
39c

Key terms

parenthetical expression An explanatory or supplemental word or phrase, such as *all things considered, to be frank,* or a brief example or fact. (See p. 345.)

transitional expression A word or phrase that shows the relationship between sentences: *for example, however, in fact.* (See p. 50.)

tag question A question at the end of a statement, consisting of a pronoun, a helping verb, and sometimes *not: It isn't wet, is it?*

Yes and *no*

Yes, the editorial did have a point.

No, that can never be.

Words of direct address

Cody, please bring me the newspaper.

With all due respect, sir, I will not.

Mild interjections

Well, you will never know who did it.

Oh, they forgot all about the baby.

Exercise 39.3   Punctuating essential and nonessential elements

Insert commas in the following sentences to set off nonessential elements, and delete any commas that incorrectly set off essential elements. If a sentence is already correct as given, mark the number preceding it. Answers to starred items appear at the end of the book.

> *Example:*
>
> Elizabeth Blackwell who attended medical school in the 1840s was the first American woman to earn a medical degree.
>
> Elizabeth Blackwell, who attended medical school in the 1840s, was the first American woman to earn a medical degree.

*1. Italians insist that Marco Polo, the thirteenth-century explorer, did not import pasta from China.

*2. Pasta which consists of flour and water and often egg existed in Italy long before Marco Polo left for his travels.

*3. A historian who studied pasta says that it originated in the Middle East in the fifth century.

*4. Most Italians dispute this account although their evidence is shaky.

*5. Wherever it originated, the Italians are now the undisputed masters, in making and cooking pasta.

6. Marcella Hazan, who has written several books on Italian cooking, insists that homemade and hand-rolled pasta is the best.

7. Most cooks buy dried pasta lacking the time to make their own.

8. The finest pasta is made from semolina, a flour from hard durum wheat.

9. Pasta manufacturers choose hard durum wheat, because it makes firmer cooked pasta than common wheat does.

10. Pasta, made from common wheat, gets soggy in boiling water.

39c

┌─ **Key term** ─────────────────────────────────

interjection A word that expresses feeling or commands attention: *Oh, must we?*

39d   Use commas between items in a series.

A **series** consists of three or more items of equal importance. The items may be words, phrases, or clauses.

> Anna Spingle married at the age of seventeen⌒ had three children by twenty-one⌒ and divorced at twenty-two.
> She worked as a cook⌒ a baby-sitter⌒ and a crossing guard.

Some writers omit the comma before the coordinating conjunction in a series (*Breakfast consisted of coffee, eggs⌒and kippers*). But the final comma is never wrong, and it always helps the reader see the last two items as separate.

39e   Use commas between two or more adjectives that equally modify the same word.

Adjectives that equally modify the same word—**coordinate adjectives**—may be separated either by *and* or by a comma.

> Spingle's scratched and dented car is old, but it gets her to work.
> She has dreams of a sleek⌒ shiny car.

Adjectives are not coordinate—and should not be separated by commas—when the one nearer the noun is more closely related to the noun in meaning.

> Spingle's children work at various⌒odd jobs.
> They all expect to go to a nearby⌒community college.

Exercise 39.4   Punctuating series and coordinate adjectives

Insert commas in the following sentences to separate coordinate adjectives or elements in a series. If a sentence is already correct as given, mark the number preceding it. Answers to starred items appear at the end of the book.

Example:

Although quiet by day, the club became a noisy smoky dive at night.

Although quiet by day, the club became a noisy⌒ smoky dive at night.

*1. Shoes with high heels were originally designed to protect feet from mud garbage and animal waste in the streets.
*2. The first known high heels worn strictly for fashion appeared in the sixteenth century.
*3. The heels were worn by men and made of colorful silk fabrics soft suedes or smooth leathers.
*4. High-heeled shoes became popular when the short powerful King Louis XIV of France began wearing them.

Tests for commas with adjectives

1. Identify the adjectives:

She was a faithful sincere friend.
They are dedicated medical students.

2. Can the adjectives be reversed without changing meaning?

She was a sincere faithful friend. *Yes.*
They are medical dedicated students. *No.*

3. Can the word *and* be sensibly inserted between the adjectives?

She was a faithful and sincere friend. *Yes.*
They are dedicated and medical students. *No.*

4. If *yes* to both questions, the adjectives *should* be separated by a comma:

She was a faithful, sincere friend.

5. If *no* to both questions, the adjectives should *not* be separated by a comma:

They are dedicated medical students.

---

*5. Louis's influence was so strong that men and women of the court, priests and cardinals, and even household servants wore high heels.

6. Eventually, only wealthy fashionable French women wore high heels.

⚹ 7. In the seventeenth and eighteenth centuries, French culture represented the one true standard of elegance and refinement.

8. High-heeled shoes for women spread to other courts of Europe, among the Europeans of North America, and to almost all social classes.

9. Now, high heels are common, though depending on the fashion, they range from short squat thick heels to tall skinny spikes.

10. A New York boutique recently showed a pair of purple satin pumps, with tiny jeweled bows and four-inch stiletto heels.

39f

39f   Use commas in dates, addresses, place names, and long numbers.

When they appear within sentences, elements punctuated with a comma also end with a comma, as in the following examples.

Dates

July 4, 1776, is the date the Declaration was signed.
The bombing of Pearl Harbor on Sunday, December 7, 1941, prompted American entry into World War II.

Do not use commas between the parts of a date in inverted order (*15 December 1992*) or in dates consisting of a month or season and a year (*December 1941*).

Addresses and place names

Use the address 220 Cornell Road, Woodside, California 94062, for all correspondence.

Columbus, Ohio, is the location of Ohio State University.

Do not use a comma between a state name and a zip code.

Long numbers

Use the comma to separate the figures in long numbers into groups of three, counting from the right. With numbers of four digits, the comma is optional.

The new assembly plant cost $7,525,000.
A kilometer is 3,281 feet [*or* 3281 feet].

CULTURE LANGUAGE Usage in standard American English differs from that in some other languages, which use a period, not a comma, to separate the figures in long numbers.

39g Use commas with quotations according to standard practice.

The words *she said, he writes,* and so on, identify the source of a quotation. These **signal phrases** should be separated from the quotation by punctuation, usually a comma or commas.

Eleanor Roosevelt said, "You must do the thing you think you cannot do."

"Knowledge is power," wrote Francis Bacon.

"The shore has a dual nature," observes Rachel Carson, "changing with the swing of the tides." [The signal phrase interrupts the quotation at a comma and thus ends with a comma.]

Exceptions Do not use commas with signal phrases in the following situations:

- **Use a semicolon or a period after a signal phrase that interrupts a quotation between main clauses.** The choice depends on the punctuation of the original:

  Not   "That part of my life was over," she wrote, "his words had sealed it shut."

  But   "That part of my life was over," she wrote. "His words had sealed it shut." [*She wrote* interrupts the quotation at a period.]

  Or   "That part of my life was over," she wrote; "his words had sealed it shut." [*She wrote* interrupts the quotation at a semicolon.]

39g

- Omit a comma when a signal phrase follows a quotation ending in an exclamation point or a question mark:

"Claude(!)" Mrs. Harrison called.
"Why must I come home(?)" he asked.

- Use a colon when a complete sentence introduces a quotation:

Her statement was clear(:) "I will not resign."

- Omit commas when a quotation is integrated into your sentence structure, including a quotation introduced by *that*:

James Baldwin insists that◌ "one must never, in one's life, accept . . . injustices as commonplace."
Baldwin thought that the violence of a riot◌ "had been devised as a corrective◌ to his own violence.

- Omit commas with a quoted title unless it is a nonessential appositive:

The Beatles recorded◌ "She Loves You"◌ in the early 1960s.
The Beatles' first huge US hit◌, "She Loves You,"◌ appeared in 1963.

See Exercise 43.1, page 342, for practice with punctuating quotations.

39h Delete commas where they are not required.

Commas can make sentences choppy and even confusing if they are used more often than needed. Following are the most common spots for misused commas.

1 ▪ No comma between subject and verb, verb and object, or preposition and object

Not   The returning <u>soldiers, received</u> a warm welcome. [Separated subject and verb.]

But   The returning <u>soldiers◌received</u> a warm welcome.

Not   They had <u>chosen, to fight</u> for their country <u>despite, the risks.</u> [Separated verb *chosen* and its object; separated preposition *despite* and its object.]

But   They had <u>chosen◌to fight</u> for their country <u>despite◌the risks.</u>

Key term

nonessential appositive A word or words that rename an immediately preceding noun but do not limit or define the noun: *The author's first story, "Biloxi," won a prize.* (See p. 317.)

no ⌃
⸴
39h

2 ▪ No comma in most compound constructions

Compound constructions consisting of two elements almost never require a comma. The only exception is the sentence consisting of two main clauses linked by a coordinating conjunction: *The computer failed, but employees kept working* (see p. 311).

Not   ─────compound subject─────
      Banks, and other financial institutions have helped older people
      ──compound object of preposition──
      with money management, and investment.

But   Banks and other financial institutions have helped older people
      with money management and investment.

Not   ─────compound predicate─────
      One bank created special accounts for older people, and held
      compound object of verb
      classes, and workshops.

But   One bank created special accounts for older people and held
      classes and workshops.

3 ▪ No comma after a conjunction

Not   Parents of adolescents notice increased conflict at puberty,
      and, they complain of bickering.

But   Parents of adolescents notice increased conflict at puberty,
      and they complain of bickering.

Not   Although, other primates leave the family at adolescence, humans
      do not.

But   Although other primates leave the family at adolescence, humans
      do not.

4 ▪ No comma around essential elements

Not   Hawthorne's work, *The Scarlet Letter,* was the first major American
      novel. [The title is essential to distinguish the novel from the rest
      of Hawthorne's work.]

But   Hawthorne's work *The Scarlet Letter* was the first major American
      novel.

Not   The symbols, that Hawthorne uses, have influenced other novel-
      ists. [The clause identifies which symbols were influential.]

no ∧
39h

┌─ **Key terms** ───

compound construction Two or more words, phrases, or clauses connected by a coordinating conjunction, usually *and, but, or, nor: man and woman, old or young, leaking oil and spewing steam.*

conjunction A connecting word such as a **coordinating conjunction** (*and, but, or,* and so on) or a **subordinating conjunction** (*although, because, when,* and so on). (See p. 200.)

But   The symbols that Hawthorne uses have influenced other novelists.

5 ▪ No comma around a series

Commas separate the items *within* a series (p. 320) but do not separate the series from the rest of the sentence.

Not   The skills of, hunting, herding, and agriculture, sustained the Native Americans.

But   The skills of hunting, herding, and agriculture sustained the Native Americans.

6 ▪ No comma before an indirect quotation

Not   The report concluded, that dieting could be more dangerous than overeating.

But   The report concluded that dieting could be more dangerous than overeating.

Exercise 39.5   Revising: Needless and misused commas

Revise the following sentences to eliminate needless or misused commas. If a sentence is already correct as given, mark the number preceding it. Answers to starred items appear at the end of the book.

> *Example:*
> Aquifers can be recharged by rainfall, but, the process is slow.
> Aquifers can be recharged by rainfall, but the process is slow.

*1. Underground aquifers are deep, and sometimes broad layers of water, that are trapped between layers of rock.

*2. Porous rock, or sediment holds the water.

*3. Deep wells drilled through the top layers of solid rock, produce a flow of water.

*4. Such wells are sometimes called, artesian wells.

*5. One of the largest aquifers in North America, the Ogallala aquifer, is named after the Ogallala Indian tribe, which once lived in the region and hunted buffalo there.

6. The Ogallala aquifer underlies a region from western Texas through northern Nebraska, and has a huge capacity of fresh water, that is contained in a layer of sand and gravel.

7. But, the water in the Ogallala is being removed at a rate faster than it is being replaced.

8. Water is pumped from the aquifer for many purposes, such as drinking and other household use, industrial use, and, agricultural use.

9. Scientists estimate that, at the present consumption rate the Ogallala will be depleted in forty years.

no ⌃

39h

┌ **Key term** ───
essential element Limits the word it refers to and thus can't be omitted without leaving the meaning too general. (See p. 315.)
└───

10. Water table levels are receding from six inches to three feet a year, the amount depending on location.

Exercise 39.6 Revising: Commas

Insert commas in the following paragraphs wherever they are needed, and eliminate any misused or needless commas. Answers to the first paragraph appear at the end of the book.

*Ellis Island, New York, reopened for business in 1990, but now the customers are tourists, not immigrants. *This spot, which lies in New York Harbor, was the first American soil seen, or touched by many of the nation's immigrants. *Though other places also served as ports of entry for foreigners, none has the symbolic power of, Ellis Island. *Between its opening in 1892 and its closing in 1954, over 20 million people, about two-thirds of all immigrants, were detained there before taking up their new lives in the United States. *Ellis Island processed over 2000 newcomers a day when immigration was at its peak between 1900 and 1920.

As the end of a long voyage and the introduction to the New World Ellis Island must have left something to be desired. The "huddled masses" as the Statue of Liberty calls them indeed were huddled. New arrivals were herded about, kept standing in lines for hours or days, yelled at and abused. Assigned numbers they submitted their bodies to the pokings and proddings of the silent nurses and doctors, who were charged with ferreting out the slightest sign, of sickness, disability, or insanity. But, millions survived the examination, humiliation and confusion, to take the last short boat ride to New York City, and begin new lives.

40 The Semicolon

When is a semicolon needed?

Use a semicolon (;) to separate equal and balanced sentence elements—usually main clauses (next page) and occasionally items in a series (p. 329).

Grammar checkers A grammar checker can spot a few errors in the use of semicolons. For example, a checker suggested using a semicolon after *perfect* in *The set was perfect, the director had planned every detail*, thus correcting a comma splice. But it missed the incorrect semicolon in *The set was perfect; deserted streets, dark houses, and gloomy mist* (a colon would be correct; see p. 330).

---

mycomplab

Visit *mycomplab.com* for more resources and exercises on the semicolon.

40a Use a semicolon between main clauses not joined by *and, but,* or another coordinating conjunction.

When no coordinating conjunction links two main clauses, the clauses should be separated by a semicolon.

A new ulcer drug arrived on the market with a mixed reputation; doctors find that the drug works but worry about its side effects.

The side effects are not minor; some leave the patient quite uncomfortable or even ill.

Note This rule prevents the errors known as comma splices and fused sentences. (See pp. 296–97.)

40b Use a semicolon between main clauses related by *however, for example,* and so on.

When a conjunctive adverb or another transitional expression relates two main clauses in a single sentence, the clauses should be separated with a semicolon:

An American immigrant, Levi Strauss, invented blue jeans in the 1860s; eventually, his product clothed working men throughout the West.

The position of the semicolon between main clauses never changes, but the conjunctive adverb or transitional expression may move around within the second clause. Wherever the adverb or expression falls, it is usually set off with a comma or commas.

Blue jeans have become fashionable all over the world; however, the American originators still wear more jeans than anyone else.

┌─ Key terms ────────────

main clause A word group that can stand alone as a sentence because it contains a subject and a predicate and does not begin with a subordinating word: *Parks help cities breathe.*

coordinating conjunctions *And, but, or, nor,* and sometimes *for, so, yet.*

conjunctive adverb A modifier that describes the relation of the ideas in two clauses, such as *anyway, besides, consequently, finally, furthermore, hence, however, indeed, instead, meanwhile, moreover, otherwise, still, then, therefore, thus.* (See p. 297.)

transitional expression A word or phrase that shows the relationship between ideas. Transitional expressions include conjunctive adverbs as well as *as a result, at last, even so, for example, in contrast, in fact, in other words, in the meantime, of course, on the whole, until now,* and many other words and phrases. (See p. 50.)

;
40b

Blue jeans have become fashionable all over the world; the American originators, however, still wear more jeans than anyone else.

Blue jeans have become fashionable all over the world; the American originators still wear more jeans than anyone else, however.

Note This rule prevents the errors known as comma splices and fused sentences. (See pp. 297–98.)

Exercise 40.1   Sentence combining: Related main clauses

Combine each of the following sets of sentences into one sentence containing only two main clauses. As indicated in parentheses, connect the clauses with a semicolon alone or with a semicolon plus a conjunctive adverb or transitional expression followed by a comma. You will have to add, delete, change, and rearrange words. Each item has more than one possible answer. Answers to starred items appear at the end of the book.

Example:

The Albanians censored their news. We got little news from them. And what we got was unreliable. (*Therefore and semicolon.*)

The Albanians censored their news; therefore, the little news we got from them was unreliable.

*1. Electronic instruments are prevalent in jazz. They are also prevalent in rock music; They are less common in classical music. (*However and semicolon.*)

*2. Jazz and rock change rapidly. They nourish experimentation. They nourish improvisation. (*Semicolon alone.*)

*3. The notes and instrumentation of traditional classical music were established by a composer. The composer was writing decades or centuries ago; Such music does not change. (*Therefore and semicolon.*)

*4. Contemporary classical music not only can draw on tradition; It can also respond to innovations. These are innovations such as jazz rhythms and electronic sounds. (*Semicolon alone.*)

*5. Much contemporary electronic music is more than just one type of music. It is more than just jazz, rock, or classical; It is a fusion of all three. (*Semicolon alone.*)

6. Most music computers are too expensive for the average consumer. Digital keyboard instruments can be inexpensive. They are widely available. (*However and semicolon.*)

7. Inside the keyboard is a small computer. The computer controls a sound synthesizer; The instrument can both process and produce music. (*Consequently and semicolon.*)

8. The person playing the keyboard presses keys or manipulates other controls; The computer and synthesizer convert these signals. The signals are converted into vibrations and sounds. (*Semicolon alone.*)

9. The inexpensive keyboards can perform only a few functions. To the novice computer musician, the range is exciting. The range includes drum rhythms and simulated instruments. (*Still and semicolon.*)

10. Would-be musicians can orchestrate whole songs. They start from just the melody lines. They need never again play "Chopsticks." (*Semicolon alone.*)

40c Use semicolons between main clauses or series items containing commas.

Normally, commas separate main clauses linked by coordinating conjunctions (*and, but, or, nor*) and separate items in a series. But when the clauses or series items contain commas, a semicolon between them makes the sentence easier to read.

> Lewis and Clark led the men of their party with consummate skill, inspiring and encouraging them, doctoring and caring for them; and they kept voluminous journals. —Page Smith

> The custody case involved Amy Dalton, the child; Ellen and Mark Dalton, the parents; and Ruth and Hal Blum, the grandparents.

40d Delete or replace unneeded semicolons.

Semicolons are often misused in certain constructions that call for other punctuation or no punctuation.

1 ▪ No semicolon between a main clause and subordinate clause or phrase

The semicolon does not separate unequal parts, such as main clauses and subordinate clauses or phrases.

> Not Pygmies are in danger of extinction; because of encroaching development.

> But Pygmies are in danger of extinction because of encroaching development.

> Not According to African authorities; only about 35,000 Pygmies exist today.

> But According to African authorities, only about 35,000 Pygmies exist today.

2 ▪ No semicolon before a series or explanation

Colons and dashes, not semicolons, introduce series, explanations, and so forth. (See pp. 330–31 and 344.)

> Not Teachers have heard all sorts of reasons why students do poorly; psychological problems, family illness, too much work, too little time.

> But Teachers have heard all sorts of reasons why students do poorly: psychological problems, family illness, too much work, too little time.

;
40d

Exercise 40.2 Revising: Semicolons
Insert semicolons in the following paragraph wherever they are needed. Also eliminate any misused or needless semicolons, substituting other

punctuation as appropriate. Answers to starred sentences appear at the end of the book.

*The set, sounds, and actors in the movie captured the essence of horror films. *The set was ideal; dark, deserted streets, trees dipping their branches over the sidewalks, mist hugging the ground and creeping up to meet the trees, looming shadows of unlighted, turreted houses. *The sounds, too, were appropriate, especially terrifying was the hard, hollow sound of footsteps echoing throughout the film. But the best feature of the movie was its actors; all of them tall, pale, and thin to the point of emaciation. With one exception, they were dressed uniformly in gray and had gray hair. The exception was an actress who dressed only in black; as if to set off her pale yellow, nearly white, long hair; the only color in the film. The glinting black eyes of another actor stole almost every scene, indeed, they were the source of the film's mischief.

41 The Colon

What does a colon do?

The colon (:) is mainly a mark of introduction: it signals that the words following it will explain or amplify. It also has several conventional uses, such as in expressions of time.

Grammar checkers Many grammar checkers cannot recognize missing or misused colons and instead simply ignore them.

41a Use a colon before a concluding explanation, series, or appositive and before some quotations.

As an introducer, a colon is always preceded by a complete main clause. It may or may not be followed by a main clause. This is one way the colon differs from the semicolon, which generally separates main clauses only. (See p. 327.)

Explanation

Soul food has a deceptively simple definition: the ethnic cooking of African Americans.

---

mycomplab

Visit *mycomplab.com* for more resources and exercises on the colon.

Sometimes a concluding explanation is preceded by *the following* or *as follows* and a colon:

> A more precise definition might be the following: soul food draws on ingredients, cooking methods, and dishes that originated in Africa, were brought to the New World by slaves, and were modified in the Caribbean and the American South.

Note A complete sentence *after* a colon may begin with a capital letter or a small letter. Just be consistent throughout an essay.

Series

> At least three soul food dishes are familiar to most Americans: fried chicken, barbecued spareribs, and sweet potatoes.

Appositive

> Soul food has one disadvantage: fat.

Namely, that is, and other expressions that introduce appositives *follow* the colon: *Soul food has one disadvantage: namely, fat.*

Quotation

> One soul food chef has a solution: "Soul food doesn't have to be greasy to taste good. Instead of using ham hocks to flavor beans, I use smoked turkey wings. The soulful, smoky taste remains, but without all the fat of pork."

Use a colon before a quotation when the introduction is a complete sentence.

41b Use a colon after the salutation of a business letter, between a title and subtitle, and between divisions of time.

Salutation of business letter
Dear Ms. Burak:

Title and subtitle
Charles Dickens: An Introduction to His Novels

Time
12:26 AM   6:00 PM

41b

┌─ **Key terms** ─────────────────────────────

main clause A word group that can stand alone as a sentence because it contains a subject and a predicate and does not begin with a subordinating word: *Soul food is varied.* (See p. 213.)

appositive A noun or noun substitute that renames another noun immediately before it: *my brother, Jack.* (See p. 212.)

41c Delete or replace unneeded colons.

Use the colon only at the end of a main clause, not in the following situations.

■ **Delete a colon after a verb.**

Not   The best-known soul food dishes <u>are</u>: fried chicken and barbecued spareribs.

But   The best-known soul food dishes <u>are</u>◯fried chicken and barbecued spareribs.

■ **Delete a colon after a preposition.**

Not   Soul food recipes can be found <u>in</u>: mainstream cookbooks as well as specialized references.

But   Soul food recipes can be found <u>in</u>◯mainstream cookbooks as well as specialized references.

■ **Delete a colon after *such as* or *including.***

Not   Many Americans have not tasted delicacies <u>such as</u>: chitlins and black-eyed peas.

But   Many Americans have not tasted delicacies <u>such as</u>◯chitlins and black-eyed peas.

Exercise 41.1 Revising: Colons and semicolons

In the following sentences, use colons or semicolons where they are needed, and delete or replace them where they are incorrect. If a sentence is already correct as given, mark the number preceding it. Answers to starred items appear at the end of the book.

Example:

Mix the ingredients as follows sift the flour and salt together, add the milk, and slowly beat in the egg yolk.

Mix the ingredients as follows◉ sift the flour and salt together, add the milk, and slowly beat in the egg yolk.

* 1. Sunlight is made up of three kinds of radiation⁚visible rays; infrared rays, which we cannot see; and ultraviolet rays, which are also invisible.
* 2. Especially in the ultraviolet range⁻sunlight is harmful to the eyes.
* 3. Ultraviolet rays can damage the retina; furthermore, they can cause cataracts on the lens.

⁝
41c

┌─ **Key term** ───────────────────────────────────

preposition *In, on, outside,* or another word that takes a noun or pronoun as its object: <u>in</u> the house. (See p. 199.)

 * 4. Infrared rays are the longest, measuring 700 nanometers and longer, while ultraviolet rays are the shortest, measuring 400 nanometers and shorter.
 * 5. The lens protects the eye by: absorbing much of the ultraviolet radiation and thus protecting the retina.
   6. By protecting the retina, however, the lens becomes a victim, growing cloudy and blocking vision.
   7. The best way to protect your eyes is to wear hats that shade the face and sunglasses that screen out the ultraviolet rays.
   8. Many sunglass lenses have been designed as ultraviolet screens, many others are extremely ineffective.
   9. If sunglass lenses do not screen out ultraviolet rays and if people can see your eyes through them, they will not protect your eyes, and you will be at risk for cataracts later in life.
  10. People who spend much time outside in the sun; really owe it to themselves to buy a pair of sunglasses that will shield their eyes.

42   The Apostrophe

Where do apostrophes go (and not go)?

The apostrophe (') appears as part of a word to indicate possession (p. 335), the omission of one or more letters (p. 337), and sometimes plural number (p. 337).

Apostrophes are easy to misuse. For safety's sake, check your drafts to be sure that all words ending in *-s* neither omit needed apostrophes nor add unneeded ones.

Grammar checkers A grammar checker usually has mixed results in recognizing apostrophe errors. For instance, it may flag missing apostrophes in contractions (as in *isnt*), but it may not distinguish between *its* and *it's*, *their* and *they're*, *your* and *you're*, *whose* and *who's*. A checker can identify some apostrophe errors in possessives but overlook others, and it may flag correct plurals. Instead of relying on your checker, try using your word processor's Search or Find function to hunt for all words you have ended in *-s*. Then check them to ensure that apostrophes are used correctly.

v
42

mycomplab

Visit *mycomplab.com* for more resources and exercises on the apostrophe.

Uses and misuses of the apostrophe

Uses of the apostrophe

▪ **Use an apostrophe to form the possessives of nouns and indefinite pronouns** (facing page).

Singular	Plural
Ms. Park's	the Parks'
lawyer's	lawyers'
everyone's	two weeks'

▪ **Use an apostrophe to form contractions** (p. 337).

it's a girl	shouldn't
you're	won't

▪ **The apostrophe is optional for plurals of abbreviations, dates, and words or characters named as words** (p. 337).

MAs or MA's	Cs or C's
1960s or 1960's	ifs or if's

Misuses of the apostrophe

▪ **Do not use an apostrophe plus -s to form the possessives of plural nouns** (p. 334). Instead, use an apostrophe alone after the -s that forms the plural.

Not	But
the Kim's car	the Kims' car
boy's fathers	boys' fathers
babie's care	babies' care

▪ **Do not use an apostrophe to form plurals of nouns** (p. 336).

Not	But
book's are	books are
the Freed's	the Freeds

▪ **Do not use an apostrophe with verbs ending in -s** (p. 337).

Not	But
swim's	swims

▪ **Do not use an apostrophe to form the possessives of personal pronouns** (p. 337).

Not	But
it's toes	its toes
your's	yours

√
42

42a   Use the apostrophe to show possession.

A noun or indefinite pronoun shows possession with an apostrophe and, usually, an -s: *the dog's hair, everyone's hope.* (Only personal pronouns such as *hers* and *its* do not use apostrophes for possession.) Remember that the apostrophe or apostrophe-plus-s is an *addition*. Before this addition, always spell the name of the owner or owners without dropping or adding letters.

1 ▪ Singular words: Add -'s.

Bill Boughton's skillful card tricks amaze children.

Anyone's eyes would widen.

Most tricks will pique an adult's curiosity, too.

The -'s ending for singular words pertains also to singular words ending in -s, as the next examples show.

Henry James's novels reward the patient reader.

The business's customers filed suit.

Exception   An apostrophe alone may be added to a singular word ending in -s if another s would make the word difficult to say:

Moses' mother concealed him in the bulrushes.

Joan Rivers' jokes offend many people.

However, the added -s is never wrong (*Moses's, Rivers's*).

2 ▪ Plural words ending in -s: Add -' only.

Workers' incomes have fallen slightly over the past year.

Many students benefit from several years' work after high school.

The Jameses' talents are extraordinary.

Note the difference in the possessives of singular and plural words ending in -s. The singular form usually takes -s: *James's.* The plural takes only the apostrophe: *Jameses'.*

3 ▪ Plural words not ending in -s: Add -'s.

Children's educations are at stake.

We need to attract the media's attention.

⌐ **Key term** ─────────────────────────────

indefinite pronoun   A pronoun that does not refer to a specific person or thing, such as *anyone, no one,* or *something.* (See p. 250.)

4 ▪ Compound words: Add -'s only to the last word.

The brother-in-law's business failed.

Taxes are always somebody else's fault.

5 ▪ Two or more owners: Add -'s depending on possession.

Individual possession

Zimbalé's and Mason's comedy techniques are similar. [Each comedian has his own technique.]

Joint possession

The child recovered despite her mother and father's neglect. [The mother and father were jointly neglectful.]

Exercise 42.1   Forming possessives

Form the possessive of each word or word group in brackets. Answers to starred items appear at the end of the book.

> *Example:*
>
> The [men] blood pressures were higher than the [women].
>
> The men's blood pressures were higher than the women's.

* 1. In the myths of the ancient Greeks, the [goddesses] roles vary widely.
* 2. [Athena] role is to guard the city of Athens.
* 3. [Artemis] function is to care for wild animals and small children.
* 4. [Athena and Artemis] father, Zeus, is the king of the gods.
* 5. Even a single [goddess] responsibilities are often varied.
  6. Over several [centuries] time, Athena changes from a [mariner] goddess to the patron of crafts.
  7. Athena is also concerned with fertility and with [children] well-being.
  8. Athena often changes into [birds] forms.
  9. In [Homer] *Odyssey* she assumes a [sea eagle] form.
  10. In ancient Athens the myths of Athena were part of [everyone] knowledge and life.

42b

42b   Delete or replace any apostrophe in a plural noun, a singular verb, or a possessive personal pronoun.

1 ▪ Plural nouns

The plurals of nouns are generally formed by adding *-s* or *-es*: *boys, families, Joneses*. Don't add an apostrophe to form the plural:

Not   The Jones' controlled the firm's until 2003.

But   The Joneses controlled the firms until 2003.

2 ▪ Singular verbs

Verbs ending in *-s never* take an apostrophe:

Not   The subway break's down less often now.
But   The subway breaks down less often now.

3 ▪ Possessives of personal pronouns

His, hers, its, ours, yours, theirs, and *whose* are possessive forms of *he, she, it, we, you, they,* and *who.* They do not take apostrophes:

Not   The house is her's. It's roof leaks.
But   The house is hers. Its roof leaks.

Don't confuse possessive pronouns with contractions. See the examples below.

42c   Use the apostrophe to form contractions.

A **contraction** replaces one or more letters, numbers, or words with an apostrophe, as in the following examples:

it is	it's	cannot	can't
they are	they're	does not	doesn't
you are	you're	were not	weren't
who is	who's	class of 2009	class of '09

Note Don't confuse contractions with personal pronouns:

Contractions	Personal pronouns
It's a book.	Its cover is green.
They're coming.	Their car broke down.
You're right.	Your idea is good.
Who's coming?	Whose party is it?

42d   The apostrophe is optional to mark plural abbreviations, dates, and words or characters named as words.

42d

You'll sometimes see apostrophes used to form the plurals of abbreviations (BA's), dates (1900's), and words or characters named as words (*but*'s). However, most current style guides recommend against the apostrophe in these cases.

| BAs | PhDs |
| 1990s | 2000s |

The sentence has too many *buts*.
Two *3*s end the zip code.

Note Italicize or underline a word or character named as a word (see p. 365), but not the added *-s*.

Exercise 42.2 Revising: Apostrophes

In the following paragraph, correct any mistakes in the use of apostrophes or any confusion between contractions and possessive personal pronouns. Answers to starred sentences appear at the end of the book.

*People who's online experiences include blogging, Web cams, and social-networking sites are often used to seeing the details of other peoples private lives. *Many are also comfortable sharing they're own opinions, photographs, and videos with family, friend's and even stranger's. *However, they need to realize that employers and even the government can see they're information, too. *Employers commonly put applicants names through social-networking Web sites such as *MySpace* and *Facebook*. Many companies monitor their employees outbound e-mail. People can take steps to protect their personal information by adjusting the privacy settings on their social-networking pages. They can avoid posting photos of themselves that they wouldnt want an employer to see. They can avoid sending personal e-mail while their at work. Its the individuals responsibility to keep certain information private.

---

43 Quotation Marks

How do quotation marks work?

Quotation marks—either double (" ") or single (' ')—mainly enclose direct quotations from speech or writing, enclose certain titles, and highlight words used in a special sense. These are the uses covered in this chapter, along with placing quotation marks before or after other punctuation marks. Additional issues with quotations are discussed elsewhere in this book:

" "
43

- Punctuating *she said* and other signal phrases with quotations (pp. 322–23).
- Altering quotations using the ellipsis mark or brackets (pp. 345–48).

---

mycomplab ▯

Visit *mycomplab.com* for more resources and exercises on quotation marks.

- Quoting sources versus paraphrasing or summarizing them (pp. 414–18).
- Integrating quotations into your text (pp. 419–23).
- Avoiding plagiarism when quoting (pp. 424–31).
- Formatting long prose quotations and poetry quotations in MLA style or in APA style (pp. 480–81 and 512).

Grammar checkers A grammar checker will help you use quotation marks in pairs by flagging a lone mark. It may also look for punctuation inside or outside quotation marks, but it may not detect errors when punctuation should actually fall outside quotation marks.

43a   Use double quotation marks to enclose direct quotations.

A **direct quotation** reports what someone said or wrote, in the exact words of the original:

> "Life," said the psychoanalyst Karen Horney, "remains a very efficient therapist."

When quoting dialog, begin a new paragraph for each speaker.

> "What shall I call you? Your name?" Andrews whispered rapidly, as with a high squeak the latch of the door rose.
> "Elizabeth," she said. "Elizabeth."
> —Graham Greene, *The Man Within*

Note Do not use quotation marks with a direct quotation that is set off from your text. See pages 480–81 and 512 for handling such quotations in MLA and APA styles, respectively. Also do not use quotation marks with an **indirect quotation,** which reports what someone said or wrote but not in the exact words:

> The psychoanalyst Karen Horney claimed that life is a good therapist.

43b   Use single quotation marks to enclose a quotation within a quotation.

> "In formulating any philosophy," Woody Allen writes, "the first consideration must always be: What can we know? Descartes hinted at the problem when he wrote, 'My mind can never know my body, although it has become quite friendly with my leg.'"

Notice that two different quotation marks appear at the end of the sentence—one single (to finish the interior quotation) and one double (to finish the main quotation).

" "

43b

43c   Put quotation marks around the titles of works that are parts of other works.

Use quotation marks to enclose the titles of works that are published or released within larger works. (See the box below.) Use single quotation marks for a quotation within a quoted title, as in the article title and essay title in the box. And enclose all punctuation in the title within the quotation marks, as in the article title.

Titles to be enclosed in quotation marks
Other titles should be italicized or underlined. (See pp. 364–65.)

Song
"The Star-Spangled Banner"

Short story
"The Gift of the Magi"

Short poem
"Mending Wall"

Article in a periodical
"Does 'Scaring' Work?"

Essay
"Joey: A 'Mechanical Boy'"

Page or document on a Web site
"Readers' Page" (on the site *Friends of Prufrock*)

Episode of a television or radio program
"The Mexican Connection" (on *Sixty Minutes*)

Subdivision of a book
"The Mast Head" (Chapter 35 of *Moby-Dick*)

Note Some academic disciplines do not require quotation marks for titles within source citations. See page 495 on the style of the American Psychological Association (APA).

43d   Quotation marks may enclose words being used in a special sense.

On movie sets movable "wild walls" make a one-walled room seem four-walled on film.

Note Use italics or underlining for words you are defining or emphasizing. (See p. 365.)

43e   Delete quotation marks where they are not required.

Title of your paper

Not   "The Death Wish in One Poem by Robert Frost"

But ⟨The Death Wish in One Poem by Robert Frost⟩

Or   The Death Wish in ⟨"Stopping by Woods on a Snowy Evening"⟩

Common nickname

Not   As President, "Jimmy" Carter preferred to use his nickname.

But   As President, ⟨Jimmy⟩ Carter preferred to use his nickname.

Slang or trite expression

Quotation marks will not excuse slang or a trite expression that is inappropriate to your writing. If slang is appropriate, use it without quotation marks.

Not   We should support the President in his "hour of need" rather than "wimp out on him."

But   We should give the President the support he needs rather than turn away like cowards.

43f Place other punctuation marks inside or outside quotation marks according to standard practice.

1 ▪ Commas and periods: Inside quotation marks

Swift uses irony in his essay "A Modest Proposal⟨."⟩

Many first-time readers are shocked to see infants described as "delicious⟨."⟩

"'A Modest Proposal⟨,'"⟩ wrote one critic, "is so outrageous that it cannot be believed⟨."⟩

Exception When a parenthetical source citation immediately follows a quotation, place any period or comma *after* the citation:

One critic calls the essay "outrageous⟨"⟩ (Olms 26)⟨.⟩

Partly because of "the cool calculation of its delivery⟨"⟩ (Olms 27)⟨,⟩ Swift's satire still chills a modern reader.

2 ▪ Colons and semicolons: Outside quotation marks

A few years ago the slogan in elementary education was "learning by playing⟨";⟩ now educators are concerned with teaching basic skills.

We all know the meaning of "basic skills⟨":⟩ reading, writing, and arithmetic.

3 ▪ Dashes, question marks, and exclamation points: Inside quotation marks only if part of the quotation

When a dash, question mark, or exclamation point is part of the quotation, place it *inside* quotation marks. Don't use any other punctuation, such as a period or comma:

"But must you—" Marcia hesitated, afraid of the answer.

"Go away!" I yelled.

Did you say, "Who is she?" [When both your sentence and the quotation would end in a question mark or exclamation point, use only the mark in the quotation.]

When a dash, question mark, or exclamation point applies only to the larger sentence, not to the quotation, place it *outside* quotation marks—again, with no other punctuation:

One evocative line in English poetry—"After many a summer dies the swan"—comes from Alfred, Lord Tennyson.

Who said, "Now cracks a noble heart"?

The woman called me "stupid"!

Exercise 43.1   Revising: Quotation marks

Insert quotation marks as needed in the following paragraph. Answers to starred sentences appear at the end of the book.

*In one class we talked about a passage from I Have a Dream, the speech delivered by Martin Luther King, Jr., on the steps of the Lincoln Memorial on August 28, 1963:

*When the architects of our republic wrote the magnificent words of the Constitution and the Declaration of Independence, they were signing a promissory note to which every American was to fall heir. *This note was a promise that all men would be guaranteed the unalienable rights of life, liberty, and the pursuit of happiness.

*What did Dr. King mean by this statement? the teacher asked. *Perhaps we should define promissory note first. Then she explained that a person who signs such a note agrees to pay a specific sum of money on a particular date or on demand by the holder of the note. One student suggested, Maybe Dr. King meant that the writers of the Constitution and Declaration promised that all people in America should be equal. He and over 200,000 people had gathered in Washington, DC, added another student. Maybe their purpose was to demand payment, to demand those rights for African Americans. The whole discussion was an eye-opener for those of us (including me) who had never considered that those documents make promises that we should expect our country to fulfill.

" "

43f

44 Other Marks

How do writers use the dash, parentheses, the ellipsis mark, brackets, and the slash?

Each of these punctuation marks has distinctive uses:

- **The dash (—) sets off interruptions** (below).
- **Parentheses (( )) enclose some nonessential information and labels for lists within sentences** (p. 344).
- **The ellipsis mark (. . .) indicates an omission from a quotation** (p. 345).
- **Brackets ([ ]) mainly indicate changes in quotations** (p. 348).
- **The slash (/) separates options and lines of poetry** (p. 348).

Grammar checkers A grammar checker may flag a lone parenthesis or bracket so that you can match it with another parenthesis or bracket. But a checker usually will not recognize other misuses of the marks covered in this chapter. Instead, it will simply ignore the marks.

44a Use the dash or dashes to indicate shifts and to set off some sentence elements.

The **dash** is mainly a mark of interruption: it signals a shift, insertion, or break. Form a dash with two hyphens (--), or use the character called an em dash on your word processor. Do not add extra space around or between the hyphens or around the em dash.

Note When an interrupting element starting with a dash falls in the middle of a sentence, be sure to add the closing dash to signal the end of the interruption. See the first example below.

1 ▪ Shifts and hesitations

The novel⊟if one can call it that⊟appeared in 2006.

If the book had a plot⊟but a plot would be conventional.

   "I was worried you might think I had stayed away because I was influenced by⊟" He stopped and lowered his eyes.
   Astonished, Howe said, "Influenced by what?"
   "Well, by⊟" Blackburn hesitated and for an answer pointed to the table.   —Lionel Trilling

> **mycomplab**
>
> Visit *mycomplab.com* for more resources and exercises on the dash, parentheses, the ellipsis mark, brackets, and the slash.

2 ▪ Nonessential elements

Dashes may be used instead of commas to set off and emphasize modifiers, parenthetical expressions, and other nonessential elements:

> Though they are close together—separated by only a few blocks—the two neighborhoods could be in different countries.

Dashes are especially useful when a nonessential element contains punctuation of its own:

> The qualities Monet painted—sunlight, rich shadows, deep colors—abounded near the rivers and gardens he used as subjects.

3 ▪ Introductory series and concluding series and explanations

> Shortness of breath, skin discoloration or the sudden appearance of moles, persistent indigestion, the presence of small lumps—all these may signify cancer. [Introductory series.]
>
> The patient undergoes a battery of tests—CAT scan, bronchoscopy, perhaps even biopsy. [Concluding series.]
>
> Many patients are disturbed by the CAT scan—by the need to keep still for long periods in an exceedingly small space. [Concluding explanation.]

A colon could be used instead of a dash in the last two examples. The dash is more informal.

4 ▪ Overuse

Too many dashes can make writing jumpy or breathy:

Not   In all his life—eighty-seven years—my great-grandfather never allowed his picture to be taken—not even once. He claimed the "black box"—the camera—would steal his soul.

But   In all his eighty-seven years, my great-grandfather did not allow his picture to be taken even once. He claimed the "black box"—the camera—would steal his soul.

( )
44b

44b   Use parentheses to enclose parenthetical expressions and labels for lists within sentences.

Note Parentheses *always* come in pairs, one before and one after the punctuated material.

> ┌─ Key term ───
> **nonessential element** Gives added information but does not limit the word it refers to. (See p. 315.)

1 ▪ Parenthetical expressions

Parenthetical expressions include explanations, facts, digressions, and examples that may be helpful or interesting but are not essential to meaning. Parentheses de-emphasize parenthetical expressions. (Commas emphasize them more and dashes still more.)

> The population of Philadelphia (now about 1.5 million) has declined since 1950.

Note Don't put a comma before a parenthetical expression enclosed in parentheses. Punctuation after the parenthetical expression should be placed outside the closing parenthesis.

> **Not**   The population of Philadelphia compares with that of Phoenix, (just over 1.6 million.)

> **But**   The population of Philadelphia compares with that of Phoenix (just over 1.6 million).

If you enclose a complete sentence in parentheses, capitalize the sentence and place the closing period *inside* the closing parenthesis:

> In general, coaches will tell you that scouts are just guys who can't coach. (But then, so are brain surgeons.)   —Roy Blount

2 ▪ Labels for lists within sentences

> Outside the Middle East, the countries with the largest oil reserves are (1) Venezuela (63 billion barrels), (2) Russia (57 billion barrels), and (3) Mexico (51 billion barrels).

When you set a list off from your text, do not enclose such labels in parentheses.

44c   Use the ellipsis mark to indicate omissions from quotations.

The **ellipsis mark**, consisting of three periods separated by space (. . .), generally indicates an omission from a quotation. The following examples quote from or refer to this passage about environmentalism:

. . .
44c

Original quotation

"At the heart of the environmentalist world view is the conviction that human physical and spiritual health depends on sustaining the planet in a relatively unaltered state. Earth is our home in the full, genetic sense, where humanity and its ancestors existed for all the millions of years of their evolution. Natural ecosystems—forests, coral reefs, marine blue waters—maintain the world exactly as we would wish it to be maintained. When we debase the global environment and extinguish the variety of

life, we are dismantling a support system that is too complex to understand, let alone replace, in the foreseeable future."

—Edward O. Wilson, "Is Humanity Suicidal?"

1. Omission of the middle of a sentence

Wilson writes, "Natural ecosystems . . . maintain the world exactly as we
would wish it to be maintained."

2. Omission of the end of a sentence, without source citation

Wilson writes, "Earth is our home. . . ." [The sentence period, closed up
to the last word, precedes the ellipsis mark.]

3. Omission of the end of a sentence, with source citation

Wilson writes, "Earth is our home . . ." (27). [The sentence period follows the source citation.]

4. Omission of parts of two or more sentences

Wilson writes, "At the heart of the environmentalist world view is the
conviction that human physical and spiritual health depends on sustaining the planet . . . where humanity and its ancestors existed for all the
millions of years of their evolution."

5. Omission of one or more sentences

As Wilson puts it, "At the heart of the environmentalist world view is the
conviction that human physical and spiritual health depends on sustaining the planet in a relatively unaltered state. . . . When we debase the
global environment and extinguish the variety of life, we are dismantling
a support system that is too complex to understand, let alone replace, in
the foreseeable future."

6. Omission from the middle of a sentence through the end of another sentence

"Earth is our home. . . . When we debase the global environment and
extinguish the variety of life, we are dismantling a support system that is
too complex to understand, let alone replace, in the foreseeable future."

7. Omission of the beginning of a sentence, leaving a complete sentence

a. Bracketed capital letter

"[H]uman physical and spiritual health," Wilson writes, "depends on
sustaining the planet in a relatively unaltered state." [No ellipsis mark is
needed because the brackets around the *H* indicate that the letter was
not capitalized originally and thus that the beginning of the sentence
has been omitted.]

b. Small letter

According to Wilson, "human physical and spiritual health depends on
sustaining the planet in a relatively unaltered state." [No ellipsis mark is
needed because the small *h* indicates that the beginning of the sentence
has been omitted.]

c. Capital letter from the original
Hami comments, "⟨. . .⟩Wilson argues eloquently for the environmentalist world view." [An ellipsis mark *is* needed because the quoted part of the sentence begins with a capital letter and it's otherwise not clear that the beginning of the original sentence has been omitted.]

8. Use of a word or phrase
Wilson describes the earth as "our home." [No ellipsis mark needed.]

Note these features of the examples:

- **Use an ellipsis mark when it is not otherwise clear that you have left out material from the source,** as when you omit one or more sentences (examples 5 and 6) or when the words you quote form a complete sentence that is different in the original (examples 1–4 and 7c).
- **You don't need an ellipsis mark when it is obvious that you have omitted something,** such as when a bracketed or small letter indicates omission (examples 7a and 7b) or when a phrase clearly comes from a larger sentence (example 8).
- **Place an ellipsis mark after any sentence period *except* when a parenthetical source citation follows the quotation,** as in example 3. Then the sentence period falls after the citation.

If you omit one or more lines of poetry or paragraphs of prose from a quotation, use a separate line of ellipsis marks across the full width of the quotation to show the omission:

In "Song: Love Armed" from 1676, Aphra Behn contrasts two lovers'
experiences of a romance:

> Love in fantastic triumph sate,
> Whilst bleeding hearts around him flowed,
>
> . . . .
>
> But my poor heart alone is harmed,
> Whilst thine the victor is, and free. (lines 1-2, 15-16)

(See pp. 480–81 for the format of displayed quotations like this one.)

. . .
44c

Exercise 44.1   Using ellipsis marks
Use ellipsis marks and any other needed punctuation to follow the numbered instructions for quoting from the following paragraph. The answer to the starred item appears at the end of the book.

Women in the sixteenth and seventeenth centuries were educated in the home and, in some cases, in boarding schools. Men were educated at home, in grammar schools, and at the universities. The universities were closed to female students. For women, "learning the Bible," as

Elizabeth Joceline puts it, was an impetus to learning to read. To be able to read the Bible in the vernacular was a liberating experience that freed the reader from hearing only the set passages read in the church and interpreted by the church. A Protestant woman was expected to read the scriptures daily, to meditate on them, and to memorize portions of them. In addition, a woman was expected to instruct her entire household in "learning the Bible" by holding instructional and devotional times each day for all household members, including the servants.

—Charlotte F. Otten, *English Women's Voices, 1540–1700*

*1. Quote the fifth sentence, but omit everything from *that freed the reader* to the end.

2. Quote the fifth sentence, but omit the words *was a liberating experience that*.

3. Quote the first and sixth sentences.

44d   Use brackets to indicate changes in quotations.

Brackets have specialized uses in mathematical equations, but their main use for all kinds of writing is to indicate that you have altered a quotation to explain, clarify, or correct it.

"That Texaco station [just outside Chicago] is one of the busiest in the nation," said a company spokesperson.

The word *sic* (Latin for "in this manner") in brackets indicates that an error in the quotation appeared in the original and was not made by you. Do not underline or italicize *sic* in brackets.

According to the newspaper report, "The car slammed thru [sic] the railing and into oncoming traffic."

Do not use *sic* to make fun of a writer or to note errors in a passage that is clearly nonstandard.

44e   Use the slash between options and between lines of poetry run into the text.

/
44e

Option
Some teachers oppose pass/fail courses.

Poetry
Many readers have sensed a reluctant turn away from death in Frost's lines "The woods are lovely, dark and deep, / But I have promises to keep" (13–14).

When separating lines of poetry in this way, leave a space before and after the slash. (See p. 480 for more on quoting poetry.)

Exercise 44.2   Revising: Dashes, parentheses, ellipsis marks, brackets, slashes

Insert dashes, parentheses, ellipsis marks, brackets, or slashes as needed in the following paragraph. In some cases, two or more different marks could be correct. Answers to starred sentences appear at the end of the book.

*"Let all the learned say what they can, 'Tis ready money makes the man." *These two lines of poetry by the Englishman William Somerville 1645–1742 may apply to a current American economic problem. *Non-American investors with "ready money" pour some of it as much as $1.3 trillion in recent years into the United States. *Stocks and bonds, savings deposits, service companies, factories, artworks, political campaigns the investments of foreigners are varied and grow more numerous every day. Proponents of foreign investment argue that it revives industry, strengthens the economy, creates jobs more than 3 million, they say, and encourages free trade among nations. Opponents caution that the risks associated with heavy foreign investment namely decreased profits at home and increased political influence from outside may ultimately weaken the economy. On both sides, it seems, "the learned say, 'Tis ready money makes the man or country." The question is, whose money theirs or ours?

44

Spelling and Mechanics

45 Spelling

You can train yourself to spell better by following this chapter's tips for pinpointing and fixing your spelling problems. But you can improve your spelling instantly by adopting three habits:

- **Carefully proofread all of your writing.**
- **Cultivate a healthy suspicion of your spellings.**
- **Check a dictionary** *every time* **you doubt a spelling.**

Spelling checkers A spelling checker can help you find and track spelling errors in your papers. But its usefulness is limited, mainly because it can't spot the confusion of words with similar spellings, such as *their/they're/there* and *principal/principle*. See pages 35–36 for more on spelling checkers.

45a Anticipate typical spelling problems.

Misspellings often result from misleading pronunciation, different forms of the same word, and the confusion of British and American spellings.

1 ▪ Pronunciation

In English, pronunciation of words is an unreliable guide to their spelling. Pronunciation is especially misleading with **homonyms,** words that are pronounced the same but spelled differently. Some homonyms and near-homonyms appear in the following box.

Words commonly confused

accept (to receive)
except (other than)

affect (to have an influence on)
effect (result)

all ready (prepared)
already (by this time)

allusion (an indirect reference)
illusion (an erroneous belief or
  perception)

ascent (a movement up)
assent (to agree, or an agreement)

bare (unclothed)
bear (to carry, or an animal)

board (a plane of wood)
bored (uninterested)

brake (to stop)
break (to smash)

---

sp
45a

mycomplab

Visit *mycomplab.com* for more resources and exercises on spelling.

buy (to purchase)
by (next to)

capital (the seat of government)
capitol (the building where a
    legislature meets)

cite (to quote an authority)
sight (the ability to see)
site (a place)

desert (to abandon)
dessert (after-dinner course)

discreet (reserved, respectful)
discrete (individual, distinct)

elicit (to draw out)
illicit (illegal or immoral)

eminent (prominent, respected)
imminent (about to occur)

fair (average, or lovely)
fare (a fee for transportation)

forth (forward)
fourth (after *third*)

hear (to perceive by ear)
here (in this place)

heard (past tense of *hear*)
herd (a group of animals)

hole (an opening)
whole (complete)

its (possessive of *it*)
it's (contraction of *it is* or *it has*)

know (to be certain)
no (the opposite of *yes*)

lead (heavy metal)
led (past tense of *lead*)

lessen (to reduce)
lesson (something learned)

meat (flesh)
meet (to encounter, or a
    competition)

passed (past tense of *pass*)
past (after, or a time gone by)

patience (forbearance)
patients (persons under medical
    care)

peace (the absence of war)
piece (a portion of something)

plain (clear)
plane (a carpenter's tool, or an
    airborne vehicle)

presence (the state of being at
    hand)
presents (gifts)

principal (most important, or the
    head of a school)
principle (a basic truth or law)

raise (to lift up)
raze (to tear down)

rain (precipitation)
reign (to rule)
rein (a strap for an animal)

right (correct)
rite (a religious ceremony)
write (to make letters)

road (a surface for driving)
rode (past tense of *ride*)

scene (where an action occurs)
seen (past participle of *see*)

stationary (unmoving)
stationery (writing paper)

their (possessive of *they*)
there (opposite of *here*)
they're (contraction of *they are*)

to (toward)
too (also)
two (following *one*)

waist (the middle of the body)
waste (discarded material)

weak (not strong)
week (Sunday through Saturday)

weather (climate)
whether (*if*, or introducing a
    choice)

which (one of a group)
witch (a sorcerer)

who's (contraction of *who is* or
    who has)
whose (possessive of *who*)

your (possessive of *you*)
you're (contraction of *you are*)

2 ▪ Different forms of the same word

Spellings often differ for the same word's noun and verb forms or noun and adjective forms: for example, *advice* (noun) and *advise* (verb); *height* (noun) and *high* (adjective). Similar changes occur in the parts of some irregular verbs (*know, knew, known*) and the plurals of irregular nouns (*man, men*).

3 ▪ American vs. British spellings

If you learned English outside the United States, you may be accustomed to British rather than American spellings. Here are the chief differences:

American	British
color, humor	colour, humour
theater, center	theatre, centre
canceled, traveled	cancelled, travelled
judgment	judgement
realize, civilize	realise, civilise
connection	connexion

Your dictionary may list both spellings, but it will specially mark the British one with *chiefly Brit* or a similar label.

45b   Follow spelling rules.

1 ▪ *ie* vs. *ei*

To distinguish between *ie* and *ei*, use the familiar jingle:

I before *e*, except after *c*, or when pronounced "ay" as in *neighbor* and *weigh*.

i before *e*	believe	thief	hygiene
ei after *c*	ceiling	conceive	perceive
ei sounded as "ay"	sleigh	eight	beige

Exceptions For some exceptions, remember this sentence:

The weird foreigner neither seizes leisure nor forfeits height.

2 ▪ Final *e*

When adding an ending to a word with a final *e*, drop the *e* if the ending begins with a vowel:

advise + able = advisable   surprise + ing = surprising

Keep the *e* if the ending begins with a consonant:

care + ful = careful   like + ly = likely

Exceptions Retain the *e* after a soft *c* or *g*, to keep the sound of the consonant soft rather than hard: *courageous, changeable.* And drop the *e* before a consonant when the *e* is preceded by another vowel: *argue + ment = argument, true + ly = truly.*

3 ■ Final *y*

When adding an ending to a word with a final *y*, change the *y* to *i* if it follows a consonant:

| beauty, beauties | worry, worried | supply, supplies |

But keep the *y* if it follows a vowel, if it ends a proper name, or if the ending is *-ing*:

| day, days | Minsky, Minskys | cry, crying |

4 ■ Final consonants

When adding an ending to a one-syllable word ending in a consonant, double the final consonant when it follows a single vowel. Otherwise, don't double the consonant.

| slap, slapping | park, parking | pair, paired |

In words of more than one syllable, double the final consonant when it follows a single vowel *and* ends a stressed syllable once the new ending is added. Otherwise, don't double the consonant.

| refer, referring | refer, reference | relent, relented |

5 ■ Prefixes

When adding a prefix, do not drop a letter from or add a letter to the original word:

| unnecessary | disappoint | misspell |

6 ■ Plurals

Most nouns form plurals by adding *s* to the singular form. Add *es* for the plural of nouns ending in *s, sh, ch,* or *x.*

| boy, boys | kiss, kisses | church, churches |

Nouns ending in *o* preceded by a vowel usually form the plural with *s.* Those ending in *o* preceded by a consonant usually form the plural with *es.*

| ratio, ratios | hero, heroes |

Some very common nouns form irregular plurals.

| child, children | woman, women | mouse, mice |

sp
45b

Some English nouns that were originally Italian, Greek, Latin, or French form the plural according to their original language:

analysis, analyses   criterion, criteria   piano, pianos
basis, bases   datum, data   thesis, theses
crisis, crises   medium, media

A few such nouns may form irregular *or* regular plurals: for instance, *index, indices, indexes; curriculum, curricula, curriculums.* The regular plural is more contemporary.

With compound nouns, add *s* to the main word of the compound. Sometimes this main word is not the last word.

city-states   fathers-in-law   passersby

CULTURE LANGUAGE   Noncount nouns do not form plurals, either regularly (with an added *s*) or irregularly. Examples of noncount nouns are *equipment, intelligence,* and *wealth.* See page 277.

Exercise 45.1   Using correct spellings

Select the correct spelling from the choices in brackets, referring as needed to the list of words on pages 352–53, the preceding rules, or a dictionary. Answers to starred items appear at the end of the book.

Example:

The boat [passed, past] us so fast that we rocked violently in [its, it's] wake.

The boat passed us so fast that we rocked violently in its wake.

*1. Science [affects, effects] many [important, importent] aspects of our lives.

*2. Many people have a [pore, poor] understanding of the [role, roll] of scientific breakthroughs in [their, they're] health.

*3. Many people [beleive, believe] that [docters, doctors] are more [responsable, responsible] for [improvements, improvments] in health care than scientists are.

*4. But scientists in the [labratory, laboratory] have made crucial steps in the search for [knowlege, knowledge] about human health and [medecine, medicine].

*5. For example, one scientist [who's, whose] discoveries have [affected, effected] many people is Ulf Von Euler.

6. In the 1950s Von Euler's discovery of certain hormones [lead, led] to the invention of the birth control pill.

7. Von Euler's work was used by John Rock, who [developed, developped] the first birth control pill and influenced family [planing, planning].

8. Von Euler also discovered the [principal, principle] neurotransmitter that controls the heartbeat.

9. Another scientist, Hans Selye, showed what [affect, effect] stress can have on the body.

10. His findings have [lead, led] to methods of [baring, bearing] stress.

Exercise 45.2 **Working with a spelling checker**

Try your computer's spelling checker on the following paragraph. Type the paragraph exactly as it appears below and run it through your spelling checker. Then proofread it to correct the errors missed by the checker. (Hint: There are fourteen errors in all.) Answers to the starred sentences appear at the end of the book.

*The whether effects all of us, though it's affects are different for different people. *Some people love a fare day with warm temperatures and sunshine. *They revel in spending a hole day outside without the threat of rein. Other people prefer dark, rainy daze. They relish the opportunity to slow down and here they're inner thoughts. Most people agree, however, that to much of one kind of whether—reign, sun, snow, or clouds—makes them board.

46 The Hyphen

Where do hyphens go?

Hyphens belong in some compound words and with some prefixes and suffixes. They also divide words at the ends of lines.

46a Use the hyphen in some compound words.

1 ▪ Compound adjectives

When two or more words serve together as a single modifier before a noun, a hyphen forms the modifying words clearly into a unit.

She is a well-known actor.
Some Spanish-speaking students work as translators.

When such a compound adjective follows the noun, the hyphen is unnecessary.

The actor is well known.
Many students are Spanish speaking.

> **Key term**
>
> **compound word** A word expressing a combination of ideas, such as *cross-reference* or *crossroad*.

mycomplab

Visit *mycomplab.com* for more resources and exercises on the hyphen.

hyph
46a

The hyphen is also unnecessary in a compound modifier containing an *-ly* adverb, even before the noun: *clearly defined terms*.

When part of a compound adjective appears only once in two or more parallel compound adjectives, hyphens indicate which words the reader should mentally join with the missing part.

> School-age children should have eight- or nine-o'clock bedtimes.

2 ■ Fractions and compound numbers

Hyphens join the numerator and denominator of fractions: *one-half, three-fourths*. Hyphens also join the parts of the whole numbers *twenty-one* to *ninety-nine*.

3 ■ Prefixes and suffixes

Do not use hyphens with prefixes except as follows:

- **With the prefixes** *self-,* *all-,* **and** *ex-:* *self-control, all-inclusive, ex-student*.
- **With a prefix before a capitalized word:** *un-American*.
- **With a capital letter before a word:** *T-shirt*.
- **To prevent misreading:** *de-emphasize, re-create a story*.

The only suffix that regularly requires a hyphen is *-elect,* as in *president-elect*.

46b Use the hyphen to divide words at the ends of lines.

You can avoid very short lines in your documents by dividing some words between the end of one line and the beginning of the next. You can set a word processor to divide words automatically at appropriate breaks (go to the Tools menu). To divide words manually, follow these guidelines:

- **Divide words only between syllables**—for instance, *win-dows,* not *wi-ndows*. Check a dictionary for correct syllable breaks.
- **Never divide a one-syllable word.**
- **Leave at least two letters on the first line and three on the second line.** If a word cannot be divided to follow this rule (for instance, *a-bus-er*), don't divide it.

If you must break an electronic address—for instance, in a source citation—do so only after a slash or before a period. Do not hyphenate, because readers may perceive any added hyphen as part of the address.

> Not   http://www.library.miami.edu/staff/lmc/soc-
> race.html

But   http://www.library.miami.edu/staff/lmc/
       socrace.html

Or   http://www.library.miami.edu/staff/lmc/socrace
       .html

Exercise 46.1 Using hyphens

Insert hyphens wherever they are needed, and delete them where they are not needed. If a sentence is already correct as given, mark the number preceding it. Answers to starred items appear at the end of the book.

Example:

Elephants have twelve inch long teeth, but they have only four of them.

Elephants have twelve⊝inch⊝long teeth, but they have only four of them.

*1. The African elephant is well known for its size.
*2. Both male and female African elephants can grow to a ten-foot height.
*3. The non African elephants of south central Asia are somewhat smaller.
*4. A fourteen or fifteen year old elephant has reached sexual maturity.
*5. The elephant life span is about sixty five or seventy years.
  6. A newborn elephant calf weighs two to three hundred pounds.
  7. It stands about thirty three inches high.
  8. A two hundred pound, thirty three inch baby is quite a big baby.
  9. Unfortunately, elephants are often killed for their ivory tusks, and partly as a result they are an increasingly-endangered species.
 10. African governments have made tusk and ivory selling illegal.

47   Capital Letters

Is it *South* or *south*?

Although mostly straightforward, the rules for capital letters can sometimes be tricky: it's *South* for a specific geographical region (*I am from the South*) but *south* for a direction (*Birds fly south*).

cap
47

mycomplab

Visit *mycomplab.com* for more resources and exercises on capital letters.

The conventions described in this chapter and a desk dictionary can help you decide whether to capitalize a particular word in most writing. Consult the style guides listed on page 432 for the requirements of particular disciplines.

Grammar checkers   A grammar checker will flag overused capital letters and missing capitals at the beginnings of sentences. It will also spot missing capitals at the beginnings of proper nouns and adjectives—*if* the nouns and adjectives are in the checker's dictionary. For example, a checker caught *christianity* and *europe* but not *china* (for the country) or *Stephen king*.

CULTURE LANGUAGE   Conventions of capitalization vary from language to language. English, for instance, is the only language to capitalize the first-person singular pronoun (*I*), and its practice of capitalizing proper nouns but not most common nouns also distinguishes it from some other languages.

47a   Capitalize the first word of every sentence.

No one expected the outcome.
Will inflation result?
Watch out!

When quoting other writers, you should reproduce the capital letters beginning their sentences or indicate that you have altered the source's capitalization. Whenever possible, integrate the quotation into your own sentence so that its capitalization coincides with yours:

"Psychotherapists often overlook the benefits of self-deception," the author argues.

The author argues that "the benefits of self-deception" are not always recognized by psychotherapists. [Do not capitalize a phrase quoted from inside a sentence.]

If you need to alter the capitalization in the source, indicate the change with brackets.

"[T]he benefits of self-deception" are not always recognized by psychotherapists, the author argues.

The author argues that "[p]sychotherapists often overlook the benefits of self-deception."

Note   Capitalization of questions in a series is optional. Both of the following examples are correct:

Is the population a hundred? Two hundred? More?
Is the population a hundred? two hundred? more?

cap

47a

Also optional is capitalization of the first word in a complete sentence after a colon.

47b Capitalize proper nouns, proper adjectives, and words used as essential parts of proper nouns.

1 ▪ Proper nouns and proper adjectives

Proper nouns name specific persons, places, and things: *Shake-speare, China, World War I*. **Proper adjectives** are formed from some proper nouns: *Shakespearean, Chinese*. Capitalize all proper nouns and proper adjectives but not the articles (*a, an, the*) that precede them.

Proper nouns and adjectives to be capitalized

Specific persons and things

Stephen King	Boulder Dam
Napoleon Bonaparte	the Empire State Building

Specific places and geographical regions

New York City	the Mediterranean Sea
China	the Northeast, the South

But: northeast of the city, going south

Days of the week, months, holidays

Monday	Yom Kippur
May	Christmas

Government offices or departments and institutions

House of Representatives	Polk Municipal Court
Department of Defense	Northeast High School

Political, social, athletic, and other organizations and associations and their members

Democratic Party, Democrats	League of Women Voters
Sierra Club	Boston Celtics
B'nai B'rith	Chicago Symphony Orchestra

Races, nationalities, and their languages

Native American	Germans
African American	Swahili
Caucasian	Italian

But: blacks, whites

Religions, their followers, and terms for the sacred

Christianity, Christians	God
Catholicism, Catholics	Allah
Judaism, Orthodox Jews	the Bible [**but** biblical]
Islam, Muslims	the Koran, the Qur'an

Historical events, documents, periods, movements

the Vietnam War	the Renaissance
the Constitution	the Romantic Movement

cap
47b

2 ▪ Common nouns used as essential parts of proper nouns

Capitalize the common nouns *street, avenue, park, river, ocean, lake, company, college, county,* and *memorial* when they are part of proper nouns naming specific places or institutions:

Main Street	Ford Motor Company
Central Park	Madison College
Mississippi River	George Washington Memorial

3 ▪ Compass directions

Capitalize compass directions only when they name a specific region instead of a general direction:

Students from the West often melt in eastern humidity.

4 ▪ Relationships

Capitalize the names of relationships only when they precede or replace proper names:

Our aunt scolded us for disrespecting Father and Uncle Jake.

5 ▪ Titles with persons' names

Before a person's name, capitalize his or her title. After or apart from the name, do not capitalize the title.

Professor Otto Osborne	Otto Osborne, a professor
Doctor Jane Covington	Jane Covington, a doctor
Governor Ella Moore	Ella Moore, the governor

Note Many writers capitalize a title denoting very high rank even when it follows a name or is used alone: *Ronald Reagan, past President of the United States.*

47c Capitalize most words in titles and subtitles of works.

Within your text, capitalize all the words in a title *except* the following: articles (*a, an, the*); *to* in infinitives; coordinating conjunctions (*and, but,* etc.); and prepositions (*with, between,* etc.). Capitalize even these words when they are the first or last word in a title or when they fall after a colon or semicolon.

"Courtship through the Ages"	*Management: A New Theory*
A Diamond Is Forever	"Once More to the Lake"
"Knowing Whom to Ask"	*An End to Live For*
Learning from Las Vegas	*File under Architecture*

cap

47c

Note The style guides of the academic disciplines have their own rules for capitals in titles. For instance, the preceding guidelines reflect MLA style for English and some other humanities. In contrast, APA style for the social sciences capitalizes only the first word and proper names in book and article titles within source citations (see p. 495).

47d Use capitals according to convention in online communication.

Online messages written in all-capital letters or with no capital letters are difficult to read. Further, messages in all-capital letters may be taken as rude (see also p. 140). Use capital letters according to rules 47a–47c in all your online communication.

Exercise 47.1 **Revising: Capitals**

Edit the following sentences to correct errors in capitalization. Consult a dictionary if you are in doubt. If a sentence is already correct as given, mark the number preceding it. Answers to starred items appear at the end of the book.

> *Example:*
>
> The first book on the reading list is mark twain's *a connecticut yankee in king arthur's court.*
>
> The first book on the reading list is Mark Twain's *A Connecticut Yankee in King Arthur's Court.*

*1. San Antonio, texas, is a thriving city in the southwest.

*2. The city has always offered much to tourists interested in the roots of spanish settlement in the new world.

*3. The alamo is one of five Catholic Missions built by Priests to convert native americans and to maintain spain's claims in the area.

*4. But the alamo is more famous for being the site of an 1836 battle that helped to create the republic of Texas.

*5. Many of the nearby Streets, such as Crockett street, are named for men who died in that Battle.

6. The Hemisfair plaza and the San Antonio river link tourist and convention facilities.

7. Restaurants, Hotels, and shops line the River. the haunting melodies of "Una paloma blanca" and "malagueña" lure passing tourists into Casa rio and other mexican restaurants.

8. The university of Texas at San Antonio has expanded, and a Medical Center lies in the Northwest part of the city.

9. Sea World, on the west side of San Antonio, entertains grandparents, fathers and mothers, and children with the antics of dolphins and seals.

10. The City has attracted high-tech industry, creating a corridor between san antonio and austin.

cap

47d

48 Italics or Underlining

As a work that appears independently—a play—*Hamlet* should be italicized or underlined. (Quotation marks are used for shorter works; see p. 340.) Italic type is used almost universally in academic and business writing, and it is the preferred style of the Modern Language Association (see p. 445). Some instructors recommend underlining, so ask your instructor for his or her preference.

Always use either italics or underlining consistently throughout a document in both text and source citations. If you are using italics, make sure that the italic characters are clearly distinct from the regular type. If you are using underlining and you underline two or more words in a row, underline the space between the words, too: <u>Criminal Statistics: Misuses of Numbers.</u>

Grammar checkers Grammar checkers cannot recognize problems with italics or underlining. Check your work yourself to ensure that you have used highlighting appropriately.

48a Italicize or underline the titles of works that appear independently.

Within your text italicize or underline the titles of works, such as books and periodicals, that are published, released, or produced separately from other works. (See the following box.) Use quotation marks for all other titles.

Titles to be italicized or underlined

Other titles should be placed in quotation marks (see p. 340).

Books
War and Peace
And the Band Played On

Plays
Hamlet
The Phantom of the Opera

Web sites
Friends of Prufrock
Google

Computer software
Microsoft Internet Explorer
Acrobat Reader

Pamphlets
The Truth about Alcoholism

Long musical works
Tchaikovsky's *Swan Lake*
But: Symphony in C

---

ital
48a

mycomplab

Visit *mycomplab.com* for more resources and exercises on italics or underlining.

Television and radio programs	Published speeches
The Shadow	Lincoln's *Gettysburg Address*
NBC Sports Hour	**Movies and videos**
Long poems	*Schindler's List*
Beowulf	*How to Relax*
Paradise Lost	**Works of visual art**
Periodicals	Michelangelo's *David*
Time	the *Mona Lisa*
Philadelphia Inquirer	

Exceptions Legal documents, the Bible, the Koran, and their parts are generally not italicized or underlined:

Not   We studied the *Book of Revelation* in the *Bible.*

But   We studied the Book of Revelation in the Bible.

48b Italicize or underline the names of ships, aircraft, spacecraft, and trains.

Challenger	*Orient Express*	*Queen Mary 2*
Apollo XI	*Montrealer*	*Spirit of St. Louis*

48c Italicize or underline foreign words that are not part of the English language.

Italicize or underline a foreign expression that has not been absorbed into English. A dictionary will say whether a word is still considered foreign to English.

The scientific name for the brown trout is *Salmo trutta.* [The Latin scientific names for plants and animals are always italicized or underlined.]

The Latin *De gustibus non est disputandum* translates roughly as "There's no accounting for taste."

48d Italicize or underline words or characters named as words.

Use italics or underlining to indicate that you are citing a character or word as a word rather than using it for its meaning. Words you are defining fall under this convention.

The word *syzygy* refers to a straight line formed by three celestial bodies, as in the alignment of the earth, sun, and moon.

Some people say *th,* as in *thought,* with a faint *s* or *f* sound.

ital
48d

48e   Occasionally, italics or underlining may be used for emphasis.

Italics or underlining can stress an important word or phrase, especially in reporting how someone said something. But use such emphasis very rarely, or your writing may seem overemotional.

48f   In online communication, use alternatives for italics or underlining.

Some forms of online communication do not allow conventional highlighting such as italics or underlining for the purposes described in this chapter. If you can't use italics or underlining to distinguish book titles and other elements that usually require highlighting, type an underscore before and after the element: *Measurements coincide with those in _Joule's Handbook_.* You can also emphasize words with asterisks before and after: *I *will not* be able to attend.*

Don't use all-capital letters for emphasis; they yell too loudly. (See also p. 140.)

Exercise 48.1   Revising: Italics or underlining

In the following paragraph, circle (1) the words and phrases that need highlighting with italics or underlining and (2) the words and phrases that are highlighted unnecessarily. If a sentence is correct as given, mark the number preceding it. Answers to starred sentences appear at the end of the book.

Example:

Of Hitchcock's movies, Psycho is the scariest.
Of Hitchcock's movies, *Psycho* is the scariest.

*1. Of the many Vietnam veterans who are writers, Oliver Stone is perhaps the most famous for writing and directing the films Platoon and Born on the Fourth of July.

*2. Tim O'Brien has written short stories for Esquire, GQ, and Massachusetts Review.

*3. Going after Cacciato is O'Brien's dreamlike novel about the horrors of combat.

*4. The word Vietnam is technically two words (*Viet* and *Nam*), but most American writers spell it as *one* word.

*5. American writers use words or phrases borrowed from Vietnamese, such as di di mau ("go quickly") or dinky dau ("crazy").

6. Philip Caputo's *gripping* account of his service in Vietnam appears in the book A Rumor of War.

7. Caputo's book was made into a television movie, also titled *A Rumor of War.*

8. David Rabe's plays—including The Basic Training of Pavlo Hummel, Streamers, and Sticks and Bones—depict the effects of the war *not only* on the soldiers *but also* on their families.

9. Called the *poet laureate of the Vietnam war*, Steve Mason has published two collections of poems: Johnny's Song and Warrior for Peace.

10. The Washington Post published *rave* reviews of Veteran's Day, an autobiography by Rod Kane.

49   Abbreviations

Is it *in.* or *inch*? Is it *dr.* or *doctor*?

In academic writing, appropriate abbreviations depend partly on the discipline: *in.* might be a suitable abbreviation in the text of a technical document, but not in a nontechnical document. Appropriate abbreviations also depend on context: *dr.* is okay before a noun (*Dr. Jones*) but not otherwise (*The doctor is in*).

The guidelines in this chapter pertain to the text of a nontechnical document. Consult one of the style guides listed on page 432 for the requirements of the discipline you are writing in.

Usage varies, but writers increasingly omit periods from abbreviations of two or more words written in all-capital letters: *US, BA, USMC*. See page 308 on punctuating abbreviations.

Grammar and spelling checkers A grammar checker may flag some abbreviations, such as *ft.* (for *foot*) and *st.* (for *street*). A spelling checker will flag abbreviations it does not recognize. But neither checker can judge whether an abbreviation is appropriate for your writing situation.

49a   Use standard abbreviations for titles immediately before and after proper names.

Before the name	After the name
Dr. Michael Hsu	Michael Hsu, MD
Mr., Mrs., Ms., Hon.,	DDS, DVM, PhD,
St., Rev., Msgr., Gen.	EdD, OSB, SJ, Sr., Jr.

ab
49a

mycomplab

Visit *mycomplab.com* for more resources and exercises on abbreviations.

Do not use abbreviations such as *Rev., Hon., Prof., Rep., Sen., Dr.,* and *St.* (for *Saint*) unless they appear before a proper name.

49b Familiar abbreviations and acronyms are acceptable in most writing.

An **acronym** is an abbreviation that spells a pronounceable word, such as WHO, NATO, and AIDS. These and other abbreviations using initials are acceptable in most writing as long as they are familiar to readers.

Institutions	LSU, UCLA, TCU
Organizations	CIA, FBI, YMCA, AFL-CIO
Corporations	IBM, CBS, ITT
People	JFK, LBJ, FDR
Countries	US, USA

Note If a name or term (such as *operating room*) appears often in a piece of writing, then its abbreviation (*OR*) can cut down on extra words. Spell out the full term at its first appearance, indicate its abbreviation in parentheses, and then use the abbreviation.

49c Use *BC, BCE, AD, CE, AM, PM, no.,* and *$* only with specific dates and numbers

44 BC	AD 1492	11:26 AM (*or* a.m.)	no. 36 (*or* No. 36)
44 BCE	1492 CE	8:05 PM (*or* p.m.)	$7.41

BC ("before Christ"), BCE ("before the common era"), and CE ("common era") always follow a date. In contrast, AD (*anno Domini,* Latin for "in the year of the Lord") precedes a date.

49d Generally reserve Latin abbreviations for source citations and comments in parentheses.

i.e.	*id est:* that is
cf.	*confer:* compare
e.g.	*exempli gratia:* for example
et al.	*et alii:* and others
etc.	*et cetera:* and so forth
NB	*nota bene:* note well

He said he would be gone a fortnight (i.e., two weeks).
Bloom et al., editors, *Anthology of Light Verse*
Trees, too, are susceptible to disease (e.g., Dutch elm disease).

Some writers avoid these abbreviations in formal writing, even within parentheses.

49e Use *Inc., Bros., Co.,* or *&* (for *and*) only in official names of business firms.

Not   The Santini <u>bros.</u> operate a large moving firm in New York City <u>&</u> environs.

But   The Santini <u>brothers</u> operate a large moving firm in New York City <u>and</u> environs.

Or   Santini <u>Bros.</u> is a large moving firm in New York City <u>and</u> environs.

49f Generally spell out units of measurement and names of places, calendar designations, people, and courses.

In most academic, general, and business writing, the types of words listed below should always be spelled out. (In source citations and technical writing, however, the first three categories are more often abbreviated.)

Units of measurement
The dog is thirty <u>inches</u> [not <u>in.</u>] high.

Geographical names
The publisher is in <u>Massachusetts</u> [not <u>Mass.</u> or <u>MA</u>].

Names of days, months, and holidays
The truce was signed on <u>Tuesday</u> [not <u>Tues.</u>], <u>April</u> [not <u>Apr.</u>] 16.

Names of people
<u>Robert</u> [not <u>Robt.</u>] Frost wrote accessible poems.

Courses of instruction
I'm majoring in <u>political science</u> [not <u>poli. sci.</u>].

Exercise 49.1 Revising: Abbreviations

Revise the following sentences as needed to correct inappropriate use of abbreviations for nontechnical writing. If a sentence is already correct as given, mark the number preceding it. Answers to starred items appear at the end of the book.

> *Example:*
>
> One prof. lectured for five hrs.
> One <u>professor</u> lectured for five <u>hours</u>.

*1. In an issue of *Science* magazine, Dr. Virgil L. Sharpton discusses a theory that could help explain the extinction of dinosaurs.

*2. About 65 mill. yrs. ago, a comet or asteroid crashed into the earth.

*3. The result was a huge crater about 10 km. (6.2 mi.) deep in the Gulf of Mex.

*4. Sharpton's new measurements suggest that the crater is 50 pct. larger than scientists had previously believed.

ab
49f

*5. Indeed, 20-yr.-old drilling cores reveal that the crater is about 186 mi. wide, roughly the size of Conn.

6. The space object was traveling more than 100,000 miles per hour and hit the earth with the impact of 100 to 300 megatons of TNT.

7. On impact, 200,000 cubic km. of rock and soil were vaporized or thrown into the air.

8. That's the equivalent of 2.34 bill. cubic ft. of matter.

9. The impact would have created 400-ft. tidal waves across the Atl. Ocean, temps. higher than 20,000 degs., and powerful earthquakes.

10. Sharpton theorizes that the dust, vapor, and smoke from this impact blocked the sun's rays for mos., cooled the earth, and thus resulted in the death of the dinosaurs.

50 Numbers

Is it *28* or *twenty-eight*?

Expressing numbers in numerals (*28*) or in words (*twenty-eight*) is often a matter of style in a discipline: the technical disciplines more often prefer numerals, and the nontechnical disciplines more often prefer words. All disciplines use many more numerals in source citations than in the document text.

Grammar checkers A grammar checker will flag numerals beginning sentences and can be customized to ignore or to look for numerals. But it can't tell you whether numerals or spelled-out numbers are appropriate for your writing situation.

50a Use numerals according to standard practice in the field you are writing in.

Always use numerals for numbers that require more than two words to spell out.

The leap year has 366 days.
The population of Minot, North Dakota, is about 32,800.

In nontechnical academic writing, spell out numbers of one or two words.

num
50a

mycomplab

Visit *mycomplab.com* for more resources and exercises on numbers.

Twelve nations signed the treaty.

The ball game drew forty-two thousand people. [A hyphenated number may be considered one word.]

In much business writing, use numerals for all numbers over ten: *five reasons, 11 participants*. In technical academic and business writing, such as in science and engineering, use numerals for all numbers over ten, and use numerals for zero through nine when they refer to exact measurements: *2 liters, 1 hour*. (Consult one of the style guides listed on p. 432 for more details.)

Note Use a combination of numerals and words for round numbers over a million: *26 million, 2.45 billion*. And use either all numerals or all words when several numbers appear together in a passage, even if convention would require a mixture.

CULTURE LANGUAGE In standard American English, a comma separates the numerals in long numbers (*26,000*), and a period functions as a decimal point (*2.06*).

50b **Use numerals according to convention for dates, addresses, and other information.**

Days and years		Decimals, percentages, and fractions	
June 18, 1985	AD 12		
456 BC	2010	22.5	3½
		48% (*or* 48 percent)	
The time of day			
9:00 AM	3:45 PM	Scores and statistics	
		21 to 7	a ratio of 8 to 1
Addresses		a mean of 26	
355 Clinton Avenue			
Washington, DC 20036		Pages, chapters, volumes, acts, scenes, lines	
Exact amounts of money		Chapter 9, page 123	
$3.5 million	$4.50	*Hamlet*, act 5, scene 3	

Exceptions Round dollar or cent amounts of only a few words may be expressed in words: *seventeen dollars; sixty cents*. When the word *o'clock* is used for the time of day, also express the number in words: *two o'clock* (not *2 o'clock*).

50c **Spell out numbers that begin sentences.**

For clarity, spell out any number that begins a sentence. If the number requires more than two words, reword the sentence so that the number falls later and can be expressed as a numeral.

Not   3.9 billion people live in Asia.

But   The population of Asia is 3.9 billion.

Exercise 50.1 Revising: Numbers

Revise the following sentences so that numbers are used appropriately for nontechnical writing. If a sentence is already correct as given, mark the number preceding it. Answers to starred items appear at the end of the book.

Example:

Addie paid two hundred and five dollars for used scuba gear.
Addie paid $205 for used scuba gear.

*1. The planet Saturn is nine hundred million miles, or nearly one billion five hundred million kilometers, from the sun.

*2. A year on Saturn equals almost thirty of our years.

*3. Thus, Saturn orbits the sun only two and four-tenths times during the average human life span.

*4. It travels in its orbit at about twenty-one thousand six hundred miles per hour.

*5. 15 to 20 times denser than Earth's core, Saturn's core measures 17,000 miles across.

6. The temperature at Saturn's cloud tops is minus one hundred seventy degrees Fahrenheit.

7. In nineteen hundred thirty-three, astronomers found on Saturn's surface a huge white spot 2 times the size of Earth and 7 times the size of Mercury.

8. Saturn's famous rings reflect almost seventy percent of the sunlight that approaches the planet.

9. The ring system is almost forty thousand miles wide, beginning 8,800 miles from the planet's visible surface and ending forty-seven thousand miles from that surface.

10. The spacecraft *Cassini* traveled more than eight hundred and twenty million miles to explore and photograph Saturn.

PART 7

Research and Documentation

51 Research Strategy

How should I approach and manage a research project?

51a

Like many writers, you may find it helpful to approach research writing as a detective approaches a new case. The mystery is the answer to a question you care about. The search for an answer leads you to consider what others think about your subject, but you do more than simply report their views. You build on them to develop and support your own opinion.

Your investigation will be more productive and enjoyable if you take some steps described in this chapter: plan your work (below); keep a research journal (facing page); find an appropriate subject and research question (p. 376); set goals for your research (p. 377); and keep a working, annotated bibliography (p. 380).

51a Plan the research process.

Research writing is a *writing* process:

- **You work within a particular situation of subject, purpose, audience, and other factors** (see Chapter 1).
- **You gather ideas and information about your subject** (Chapter 2).
- **You focus and arrange your ideas** (Chapter 3).
- **You draft to explore your meaning** (Chapter 4).
- **You revise and edit to develop, shape, and polish** (Chapter 5).

Although the process seems neatly sequential in this list, you know from experience that the stages overlap—that, for instance, you may begin drafting before you've gathered all the information you expect to find, and then while drafting you may discover a source that causes you to rethink your approach. Anticipating the process of research writing can free you to be flexible in your search and open to discoveries.

A thoughtful plan and systematic procedures can help you follow through on the diverse activities of research writing. One step is to make a schedule like the one opposite that apportions the available time to the necessary work. You can estimate that each segment marked off by a horizontal line will occupy *roughly* one-quarter of the total time—for example, a week in a four-week

mycomplab

Visit *mycomplab.com* for more resources as well as exercises on research strategy.

assignment. The most unpredictable segments are the first two, so it's wise to get started early enough to accommodate the unexpected.

Complete
by:

——— 1. Setting a schedule and beginning a research journal (here and below)

——— 2. Finding a researchable subject and question (next page)

——— 3. Setting goals for sources (p. 377)

——— 4. Finding print and electronic sources (p. 382), and making a working, annotated bibliography (p. 380)

——— 5. Evaluating and synthesizing sources (pp. 399, 410)

——— 6. Gathering information from sources (p. 413), often using summary, paraphrase, and direct quotation (p. 414)

——— 7. Taking steps to avoid plagiarism (p. 424)

——— 8. Developing a thesis statement and creating a structure (p. 434)

——— 9. Drafting the paper (p. 435), integrating summaries, paraphrases, and direct quotations into your ideas (p. 419)

——— 10. Revising and editing the paper (p. 435)

——— 11. Citing sources in your text (p. 431)

——— 12. Preparing the list of works cited or references (p. 431)

——— 13. Preparing the final manuscript (p. 436)

——— Final paper due

51b

51b Keep a research journal.

While working on a research project, carry a notebook or a computer with you at all times to use as a **research journal,** a place to record your activities and ideas. (See p. 10 on journal keeping.) In the journal's dated entries, you can write about the sources you consult, the leads you want to pursue, and any difficulties you encounter. Most important, you can record your thoughts about sources, leads, difficulties, new directions, relationships, and anything else that strikes you. The very act of writing in the journal can expand and clarify your thinking.

Note The research journal is the place to track and develop your own ideas. To avoid mixing up your thoughts and those of others, keep separate notes on what your sources actually say, using one of the methods discussed on pages 413–14.

51c   Find a researchable subject and question.

Before reading this section, review the suggestions given in Chapter 1 for finding and narrowing a writing subject (pp. 4–6). Generally, the same procedure applies to writing any kind of research paper. However, selecting and limiting a subject for a research paper can present special opportunities and problems. And before you proceed with your subject, you'll want to transform it into a question that can guide your search for sources.

1 ▪ Appropriate subject

Seek a research subject that interests you and that you care about. (It may be a subject you've already written about without benefit of research.) Starting with your own views will motivate you, and you will be a participant in a dialog when you begin examining sources.

When you settle on a subject, ask the following questions about it. For each requirement, there are corresponding pitfalls.

▪ **Are ample sources of information available on the subject?**

Avoid very recent subjects, such as a newly announced medical discovery or a breaking story in today's newspaper.

▪ **Does the subject encourage research in the kinds and number of sources required by the assignment?**

Avoid (*a*) subjects that depend entirely on personal opinion and experience, such as the virtues of your hobby, and (*b*) subjects that require research in only one source, such as a straight factual biography.

▪ **Will the subject lead you to an objective assessment of sources and to defensible conclusions?**

Avoid subjects that rest entirely on belief or prejudice, such as when human life begins or why women (or men) are superior. Your readers are unlikely to be swayed from their own beliefs.

▪ **Does the subject suit the length of paper assigned and the time given for research and writing?**

Avoid broad subjects that have too many sources to survey adequately, such as a major event in history.

2 ▪ Research question

Asking a question about your subject can give direction to your research by focusing your thinking on a particular approach. To discover your question, consider what about your subject intrigues or perplexes you, what you'd like to know more about. (See below for suggestions on using your own knowledge.)

Try to narrow your research question so that you can answer it in the time and space you have available. The question *How does human activity affect the environment?* is very broad, encompassing issues as diverse as pollution, distribution of resources, climate change, population growth, land use, biodiversity, and the ozone layer. In contrast, the question *How can buying environmentally friendly products help the environment?* or *Should individuals pay a tax on their carbon emissions?* is much narrower. Each question also requires more than a simple *yes* or *no* answer, so that answering, even tentatively, demands thought about pros and cons, causes and effects.

As you read and write, your question will undoubtedly evolve to reflect your increasing knowledge of the subject, and eventually its answer will become your main idea, or thesis statement (see p. 434).

51d

51d Set goals for your sources.

Before you start looking for sources, consider what you already know about your subject and where you are likely to find information on it.

1 ▪ Your own knowledge

Discovering what you already know about your subject will guide you in discovering what you don't know. Take some time to spell out facts you have learned, opinions you have heard or read elsewhere, and of course your own opinions. Use one or more of the discovery techniques discussed in Chapter 2 to explore and develop your ideas: keeping a journal, observing your surroundings, freewriting, brainstorming, clustering, asking questions, and thinking critically.

When you've explored your thoughts, make a list of questions for which you don't have answers, whether factual (*How much do Americans spend on green products?*) or more open-ended (*Are green products worth the higher prices?*). These questions will give you clues about the sources you need to look for first.

2 ▪ Kinds of sources

For many research projects, you'll want to consult a mix of sources, as described on the next two pages. You may start by seeking the outlines of your subject—the range and depth of opinions about it—in reference works and articles in popular periodicals or through a Web search. Then, as you refine your views and your research question, you'll move on to more specialized sources, such as scholarly books and periodicals and your own interviews or surveys. (See pp. 386–99 for more on each kind of source.)

The mix of sources you choose depends heavily on your subject. For example, a paper on green consumerism would require the use of very recent sources because environmentally friendly products are fairly new to the US marketplace. Your mix of sources may also be specified by your instructor or limited by the requirements of your assignment.

51d

Library and Internet sources

The sources available at your library or through its Web site—mainly reference works, periodicals, and books—have two big advantages over most of what you'll find on the open Web: they are cataloged and indexed for easy retrieval; and they are generally reliable, having been screened first by their publishers and then by the library's staff. In contrast, the Internet's retrieval systems are more difficult to use effectively, and Internet sources tend to be less reliable because most do not pass through any screening before being posted. (There are many exceptions, such as online scholarly journals and reference works. But these sources may be available through your library's Web site as well.)

Most instructors expect research writers to consult library sources. But they'll accept Internet sources, too, if you have used them judiciously. Even with its disadvantages, the Internet can be a valuable resource for primary sources, current information, and a diversity of views. For guidelines on evaluating both library and Internet sources, see pages 399–410.

Primary and secondary sources

Use **primary sources** when they are available or are required by your assignment. These sources are firsthand accounts, such as works of literature; historical documents (letters, speeches, and so on); eyewitness reports (including articles by journalists who are on location); reports on experiments or surveys conducted by the writer; and your own interviews, experiments, observations, or correspondence.

Many assignments will allow you to use **secondary sources,** which report and analyze information drawn from other sources, often primary ones. Examples include a reporter's summary of a controversial issue, a historian's account of a battle, a critic's reading of a poem, and a psychologist's evaluation of several studies. Secondary sources may contain helpful summaries and interpretations that direct, support, and extend your own thinking. However, most research-writing assignments expect your own ideas to go beyond those in such sources.

Scholarly and popular sources

The scholarship of acknowledged experts is essential for depth, authority, and specificity. Most instructors expect students to emphasize scholarly sources in research. But the general-interest views and information of popular sources can help you apply more scholarly approaches to daily life.

51d

- **Check the title.** Is it technical, or does it use a general vocabulary?
- **Check the publisher.** Is it a scholarly journal (such as *Education Forum*) or a publisher of scholarly books (such as Harvard University Press), or is it a popular magazine (such as *Time* or *Newsweek*) or a publisher of popular books (such as Little, Brown)?
- **Check the length of periodical articles.** Scholarly articles are generally much longer than magazine and newspaper articles.
- **Check the author.** Have you seen the name elsewhere, which might suggest that the author is an expert?
- **Check the URL.** A Web site's URL, or electronic address, includes an abbreviation that tells you something about the origin of the source: scholarly sites usually end in *edu, org,* or *gov,* while popular sites usually end in *com.* (See pp. 404–05 for more on types of online sources.)

Older and newer sources

Check the publication date. For most subjects a combination of older, established sources (such as books) and current sources (such as newspaper articles, interviews, or Web sites) will provide both background and up-to-date information. Only historical subjects or very current subjects require an emphasis on one extreme or another.

Impartial and biased sources

Seek a range of viewpoints. Sources that attempt to be impartial can offer an overview of your subject and trustworthy facts. Sources with clear biases can offer a diversity of opinion. Of course, to discover bias, you may have to read the source carefully (see pp. 399–410); but you can infer quite a bit just from a bibliographical listing.

- **Check the author.** You may have heard of the author as a respected researcher (thus more likely to be objective) or as a leading proponent of a certain view (less likely to be objective).
- **Check the title.** It may reveal something about point of view. (Consider these contrasting titles: "Go for the Green" and "Green Consumerism and the Struggle for Northern Maine.")

Note Sources you find on the Internet must be approached with particular care. See pages 404–09.

Sources with helpful features

Depending on your topic and how far along your research is, you may want to look for sources with features such as illustrations (which can clarify important concepts), bibliographies (which can direct you to other sources), and indexes (which can help you develop keywords for electronic searches; see p. 384).

51e

51e Keep a working, annotated bibliography.

To track where sources are and what they are, make a **working bibliography,** a file of books, articles, Web sites, and other possibilities. When you have a substantial file—say, ten to thirty sources—you can decide which ones seem most promising and look them up first.

1 ▪ Source information

When you turn in your paper, you will be expected to attach a list of the sources you have used. So that readers can check or follow up on your sources, your list must include all the information needed to find the sources, in a format readers can understand. (See pp. 431–33.) The box opposite shows the information to record for each type of source so that you will not have to retrace your steps later.

Note Whenever possible, record source information in the correct format for the documentation style you will be using. Then you will be less likely to omit needed information or to confuse numbers, dates, and other data when it's time to write your citations. This book describes two styles: MLA (p. 437) and APA (p. 491). For others, consult one of the guides listed on page 432.

2 ▪ Annotations

Creating annotations for a working bibliography converts it from a simple list into a tool for assessing sources. When you discover a possible source, record not only its publication information but also the following:

- **What you know about the content of the source.** Periodical databases and book catalogs generally include abstracts, or summaries, of sources that can help with this part of the annotation.
- **How you think the source may be helpful in your research.** Does it offer expert opinion, statistics, an important example, or a range of views? Does it place your subject in a historical, social, or economic context?

Information for a working bibliography

For books

Library call number
Name(s) of author(s), editor(s),
    translator(s), or others listed
Title and subtitle
Publication data:
  Place of publication
  Publisher's name
  Date of publication
Other important data, such as
    edition or volume number
Medium (print, Web, etc.)

For periodical articles

Name(s) of author(s)
Title and subtitle of article
Title of periodical
Publication data:
  Volume number and issue number
    (if any) in which article appears
  Date of issue
  Page numbers on which article
    appears
Medium (print, Web, etc.)

For electronic sources

Name(s) of author(s)
Title and subtitle of source
Title of Web site, periodical, or
    other larger work
Publication data, such as data
    listed above for a book or arti-
    cle; the publisher or sponsor
of a Web site; and the date of
release, revision, or online
posting
Any publication data for the
    source in another medium
    (print, film, etc.)
Format of online source (Web site
    or page, podcast, e-mail, etc.)
Date you consulted the source
Title of any database used to
    reach the source
Complete URL (but see the note
    below)
Digital Object Identifier, if any
    (for APA style)
Medium (Web, CD-ROM, etc.)

For other sources

Name(s) of author(s), creator(s),
    or others listed, such as a gov-
    ernment department, record-
    ing artist, or photographer
Title of work
Format, such as unpublished
    letter, live performance, or
    photograph
Publication or production data:
  Publication title
  Publisher's or producer's name
  Date of publication, release, or
    production
  Identifying numbers (if any)
Medium (print, typescript, etc.)

Note Documentation styles vary in requiring URLs for citations of electronic sources. For instance, MLA style generally does not require URLs, APA style generally requires just home page URLs, and some other styles always require complete URLs. Even if you don't need the complete URL in your final citation of a source, record it anyway so that you'll be able to track the source down if you want to consult it again. The exception is a source you reach through a library database, because most database URLs can't be used to locate a source.

Taking the time with your annotations can help you discover gaps that may remain in your sources and will later help you decide which sources to pursue in depth. One student annotated a bibliography entry on his computer with a summary and a note on the source features he thought would be most helpful to him:

Entry for an annotated working bibliography

Publication information for source	Gore, Al. *An Inconvenient Truth: The Planetary Emergency of Global Warming and What We Can Do about It.* Emmaus: Rodale, 2006. Print.
Summary of source Ideas on use of source	Book version of the documentary movie supporting Gore's argument that global warming is a serious threat to the planet. Includes summaries of scientific studies, short essays on various subjects, and dozens of images, tables, charts, and graphs. Last chapter offers several suggestions for ways to solve the problem, with an emphasis on changing individual buying habits.

As you become more familiar with your sources, you can use your initial annotated bibliography to record your evaluations of them and more detailed thoughts on how they fit into your research.

52   Finding Sources

How can I locate ideas and information about my research subject?

Your library and a computer connected to the Internet give you access to an almost infinite range of sources. The challenge, of course, is to find the most worthy and appropriate sources for your needs and then to use them effectively. This chapter shows you how to conduct electronic searches (opposite) and take advantage of the print and electronic sources available to you: reference works (p. 386); books (p. 387); periodicals (p. 388); the Web (p. 391); other on-line sources (p. 394); government publications (p. 395); and your own interviews, surveys, and other primary sources (p. 397).

Note As you look for sources, avoid the temptation to seek a "silver bullet"—that is, to locate two or three perfect sources that already say everything you want to say about your subject. Instead

---

mycomplab

Visit *mycomplab.com* for more resources as well as exercises on finding sources.

A tip for researchers

Take advantage of two valuable resources offered by your library:

- **An orientation,** which introduces the library's resources and explains how to reach and use the Web site and the print holdings.
- **Reference librarians,** whose job it is to help you and others navigate the library's resources. Even very experienced researchers often consult reference librarians.

52b

---

of merely repeating others' ideas, read and synthesize many sources so that you develop your own ideas. (For more on synthesis, see pp. 410–12.)

52a Start with your library's Web site.

As you conduct research, the Web will be your gateway to ideas and information. Always start with your library's Web site, not with a public search engine such as *Google*. The library site will lead you to vast resources, including books, periodical articles, and reference works that aren't available on the open Web. More important, every source you find on the library site will have passed through filters to ensure its value. A scholarly journal article, for instance, undergoes at least three successive reviews: subject-matter experts first deem it worth publishing in the journal; then a database vendor deems the journal worth including in the database; and finally your school's librarians deem the database worth subscribing to.

Google and other search engines may seem more user-friendly than the library's Web site and may seem to return plenty of sources for you to work with. Many of the sources may indeed be reliable and relevant to your research, but many more will not be. In the end, a library Web search will be more efficient and more effective than a direct Web search. (For help with evaluating sources from any resource, see pp. 399–410.)

Note Start with the library's Web site, but don't stop there. Many books, periodicals, and other excellent sources are available only on library shelves, not online, and most instructors expect research papers to be built to some extent on these resources. When you spot promising print sources while browsing the library's online databases, make records of them and then look them up at the library.

52b Plan electronic searches.

Searching electronically requires careful planning. Become familiar with the kinds of electronic resources available to you, understand the different search strategies they demand, and take the time to develop **keywords** that name your subject for databases and Web search engines.

1 ▪ Kinds of electronic sources

Your school's library, its Web site, and the open Web offer several kinds of electronic resources that are suitable for academic research:

- **The library's catalog of holdings** is a database that lists all the resources that the library owns or subscribes to: books, journals, magazines, newspapers, reference works, and more. The catalog may also include the holdings of other school libraries nearby or in your state.
- **Online databases** include indexes, bibliographies, and other reference works. They are your main route to articles in periodicals, providing publication information, summaries, and often full text. Your library subscribes to the databases and makes them available through its Web site. (You may also discover databases directly on the Web, but, again, the library is a more productive starting place.)
- **Databases on CD-ROM** include the same information as online databases, but they must be read at a library computer terminal. Increasingly, libraries are moving away from CD-ROMs in favor of online databases.
- **Full-text resources** contain the entire contents of articles, book chapters, even whole books. The library's databases provide access to the full text of many listed sources. In addition, the Web sites of many periodicals and organizations, such as government agencies, offer the full text of articles, reports, and other publications.

2 ▪ Databases vs. the open Web

To develop keywords it helps to understand an important difference in how library databases and the open Web work:

- **A database indexes sources by authors, titles, publication years, and its own subject headings.** The subject headings reflect the database's directory of terms and are assigned by people who have read the sources. You can find these subject headings by using your own keywords until you locate a promising source. The information for the source will list the headings under which the database indexes it and other sources like it. (See p. 391 for an illustration.) You can then use those headings for further searches.
- **A Web search engine seeks your keywords in the titles and texts of sites.** The process is entirely electronic, so the results

depend on how well your keywords describe your subject and anticipate the words used in sources. If you describe your subject too broadly or describe it specifically but don't match the vocabulary in relevant sources, your search will turn up few relevant sources and probably many that aren't relevant.

3 ▪ Keyword refinement

52b

Every database and search engine provides a system that you can use to refine your keywords for a productive search. The basic operations appear in the box below and on the next page, but resources do differ. For instance, some assume that *AND* should link two or more keywords, while others provide options specifying "Must contain all the words," "May contain any of the words," and other equivalents for the operations described in the box. You can learn a search engine's system by consulting the Advanced Search page.

Note You will probably have to use trial and error in developing your keywords, sometimes turning up few or no sources and sometimes turning up thousands of mostly irrelevant sources. But

---

Ways to refine keywords

Most databases and many search engines work with **Boolean operators,** terms or symbols that allow you to expand or limit your keywords and thus your search.

▪ **Use *AND* or + to narrow the search** by including only sources that use all the given words. The keywords *green AND products* request only the sources in the shaded area.

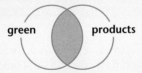

▪ **Use *NOT* or − ("minus") to narrow the search** by excluding irrelevant words. The keywords *green AND products NOT guide* exclude sources that use the word *guide*:

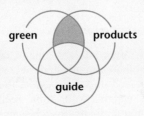

(continued)

Ways to refine keywords
(continued)

- **Use *OR* to broaden the search** by giving alternate keywords. The keywords *green AND products OR goods* allow for sources that use a synonym for *products*:

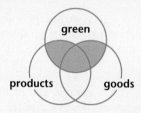

- **Use parentheses or quotation marks to form search phrases.** For instance, *(green products)* requests the exact phrase, not the separate words. Only sources using *green products* would turn up.
- **Use wild cards to permit different versions of the same word.** In *consum**, for instance, the wild card * indicates that sources may include *consume, consumer, consumerism,* and *consumption* as well as *consumptive, consumedly,* and *consummate.* The example suggests that you have to consider all the variations allowed by a wild card and whether it opens up your search too much. If you seek only two or three from many variations, you may be better off using *OR: consumption OR consumerism.* (Note that some systems use *?, :,* or *+* for a wild card instead of **.)
- **Be sure to spell your keywords correctly.** Some search tools will look for close matches or approximations, but correct spelling gives you the best chance of finding relevant sources.

the process is not busywork—far from it. It can teach you a great deal about your subject: how you can or should narrow it, how it is and is not described by others, what others consider interesting or debatable about it, and what the major arguments are.

See pages 393–94 for a sample keyword search of the Web.

52c   Consult reference works.

Reference works, often available online, include encyclopedias, dictionaries, digests, bibliographies, indexes, atlases, almanacs, and handbooks. Your research *must* go beyond these sources, but they can help you decide whether your topic really interests you and whether it meets the requirements for a research paper (p. 376). Preliminary research on reference works can also help you develop keywords for electronic searches and can direct you to more detailed sources on your topic.

You'll find many reference works through your library and directly on the Web. The following lists give general Web references for a range of disciplines.

Internet Public Library (*www.ipl.org*)
Library of Congress (*lcweb.loc.gov*)
LSU Libraries Webliography (*www.lib.lsu.edu/weblio.html*)
World Wide Web Virtual Library (*vlib.org*)

52d

Note The Web-based encyclopedia *Wikipedia* (found at *wikipedia .org*) is one of the largest reference sites on the Internet. Like any encyclopedia, *Wikipedia* can provide background information for research on a topic. But unlike other encyclopedias, *Wikipedia* is a **wiki**, a kind of Web site that can be contributed to or edited by anyone. Ask your instructor whether *Wikipedia* or any other wiki is an acceptable source before you use it. If you do use it, you must carefully evaluate any information you find, using the guidelines on pages 399–410.

52d Consult books.

Your library's book catalog is searchable at a terminal in the library and via the library's Web site. You can search the catalog by author, by title, by your own keywords, or by the headings found in *Library of Congress Subject Headings* (*LCSH*). The screen shot below shows the complete record for a book, including the *LCSH* headings that can be used to find similar sources.

Book catalog full record

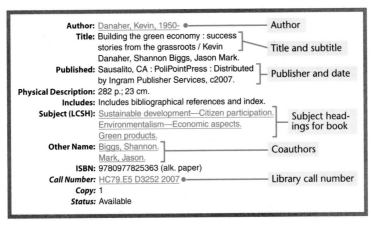

52e   Consult periodicals.

Periodicals include newspapers, academic journals, and magazines, either printed or online. Newspapers are useful for detailed accounts of past and current events. Journals and magazines can be harder to distinguish, but their differences are important. Most college instructors expect students' research to rely more on journals than on magazines.

Journals	Magazines
Examples	
American Anthropologist, Journal of Black Studies, Journal of Chemical Education	*The New Yorker, Time, Rolling Stone, People*
Availability	
Mainly through college and university libraries, either on library shelves or in online databases	Public libraries, newsstands, bookstores, the open Web, and online databases
Purpose	
Advance knowledge in a particular field	Express opinion, inform, or entertain
Authors	
Specialists in the field	May or may not be specialists in their subjects
Readers	
Often specialists in the field	Members of the general public or a subgroup with a particular interest
Source citations	
Source citations always included	Source citations rarely included
Length of articles	
Usually long, ten pages or more	Usually short, fewer than ten pages
Frequency of publication	
Quarterly or less often	Weekly, biweekly, or monthly

1 ▪ Indexes to periodicals

How indexes work

Periodical databases index the articles in journals, magazines, and newspapers. Often these databases include abstracts, or summaries, of the articles, and they may offer the full text of the articles as well. Your library subscribes to many periodical databases and to services that offer multiple databases. Most databases and services will be searchable through the library's Web site.

Note The search engine *Google* is developing *Google Scholar*, a search engine at *scholar.google.com* that seeks out scholarly articles. It is particularly useful for subjects that range across disciplines, for which discipline-specific databases can be too limited. *Google Scholar* can connect to your library's holdings if you tell it to do so under Scholar Preferences. Keep in mind, however, that *Google Scholar*'s searches are not as yet exhaustive. Your library probably subscribes to most of the periodicals searched by *Google Scholar*, so begin there.

52e

Selection of databases

To decide which databases to consult, you'll need to consider what you're looking for:

- **How broadly and deeply should you search?** Periodical databases vary widely in what they index. Some cover many subjects but don't index the full range of periodicals in each subject. (Examples include **EBSCO**'s *Academic Search, ProQuest Research Library,* Gale's *Expanded Academic ASAP,* and *LexisNexis Academic.*) Others databases cover fewer subjects but then include most of the available periodicals. (Examples include *Anthropology Plus, Literature Resource Center,* and *Women's Resource International.*) If your subject ranges across disciplines, then start with a broad database. If your subject focuses on a particular discipline, then start with a narrower database.

- **Which databases most likely include the kinds of resources you need?** The Web sites of most libraries allow you to narrow a database search to a particular discipline. You can then discover each database's focus by checking the description of the database (sometimes labeled "Help" or "Guide") or the list of indexed resources (sometimes labeled "Publications" or "Index"). The description will also tell you the time period the database covers, so you'll know whether you also need to consult older print indexes at the library.

Database searches

When you first search a database, use your own keywords to locate sources. The procedure is illustrated in the three screen shots on the next two pages. Your goal is to find at least one source that seems just right for your subject, so that you can then see what subject headings the database itself uses for such sources. Using one or more of those headings will focus and speed your search.

Note Many databases allow you to limit your search to so-called peer-reviewed or refereed journals—that is, scholarly journals whose articles have been reviewed before publication by experts in the field and then revised by the author. Limiting your search to peer-reviewed journals can help you navigate huge databases that might otherwise return scores of unusable articles.

The use of abstracts

In screen 3 opposite, the full article record shows an **abstract** that summarizes the article. By describing research methods, conclusions, and other information, an abstract can tell you whether you want to pursue an article and thus save you time. However, the abstract cannot replace the actual article. If you want to use the work as a source, you must consult the full text.

52e

---

1. Initial keyword search of a periodical database

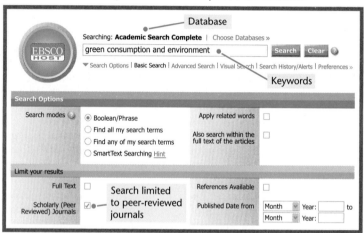

---

2. Partial keyword search results

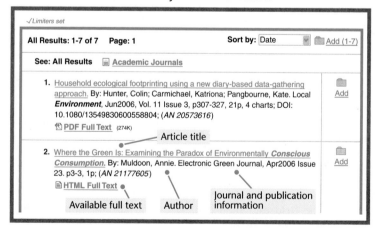

3. Full article record with abstract

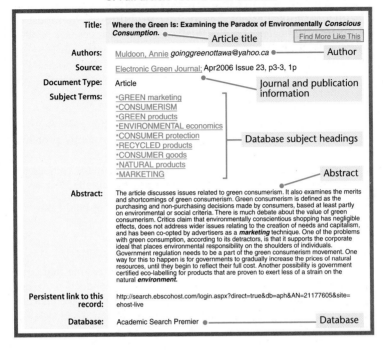

52f

Title:	Where the Green Is: Examining the Paradox of Environmentally *Conscious Consumption.* ●——— Article title [Find More Like This]
Authors:	Muldoon, Annie *goinggreenottawa@yahoo.ca* ●——— Author
Source:	Electronic Green Journal; Apr2006 Issue 23, p3-3, 1p
Document Type:	Article ——— Journal and publication information
Subject Terms:	•GREEN marketing •CONSUMERISM •GREEN products •ENVIRONMENTAL economics •CONSUMER protection ——— Database subject headings •RECYCLED products •CONSUMER goods •NATURAL products •MARKETING ——— Abstract
Abstract:	The article discusses issues related to green consumerism. It also examines the merits and shortcomings of green consumerism. Green consumerism is defined as the purchasing and non-purchasing decisions made by consumers, based at least partly on environmental or social criteria. There is much debate about the value of green consumerism. Critics claim that environmentally conscientious shopping has negligible effects, does not address wider issues relating to the creation of needs and capitalism, and has been co-opted by advertisers as a *marketing* technique. One of the problems with green consumption, according to its detractors, is that it supports the corporate ideal that places environmental responsibility on the shoulders of individuals. Government regulation needs to be a part of the green consumerism movement. One way for this to happen is for governments to gradually increase the prices of natural resources, until they begin to reflect their full cost. Another possibility is government certified eco-labelling for products that are proven to exert less of a strain on the natural *environment.*
Persistent link to this record:	http://search.ebscohost.com/login.aspx?direct=true&db=aph&AN=21177605&site=ehost-live
Database:	Academic Search Premier ●——— Database

2 ▪ Locations of periodicals

If an index listing does not include or link directly to the full text of an article, you'll need to consult the periodical itself. Recent issues of periodicals are probably held in the library's periodical room. Back issues are usually stored elsewhere, either in bound volumes or on film that requires a special machine to read. A librarian will show you how to operate the machine.

52f   Search the Web.

As an academic researcher, you enter the Web in two ways: through your library's Web site, and through public search engines such as *Yahoo!* and *Google.* The library entrance, covered in the preceding sections, is your main path to the books and periodicals that, for most subjects, should make up most of your sources. The public entrance, discussed here, can lead to a wealth of information, but it also has a number of disadvantages:

- **The Web is a wide-open network.** Anyone with the right hardware and software can place information on the Internet, and even a carefully conceived search can turn up sources with widely varying reliability: journal articles, government documents, scholarly data, term papers written by high school students, sales pitches masked as objective reports, wild theories. You must be especially diligent about evaluating Internet sources (see p. 404).

see p. 404

- **The Web changes constantly.** No search engine can keep up with the Web's daily additions and deletions, and a source you find today may be different or gone tomorrow. Generally, you should not put off consulting an online source that you think you may want to use.
- **The Web provides limited information on the past.** Sources dating from before the 1980s or even more recently probably will not appear on the Web.
- **The Web is not all-inclusive.** Most books and many periodicals are available only via the library, not directly via the Web.

Clearly, the Web warrants cautious use. It should not be the only resource you work with.

1 ▪ Search engines

To find sources on the Web, you use a **search engine** that catalogs Web sites in a series of directories and conducts keyword searches (see pp. 385–86). Generally, use a directory when you haven't yet refined your topic or you want a general overview. Use keywords when you have refined your topic and you seek specific information.

see pp. 385–86

Current search engines

The box below lists currently popular search engines. To reach any one of them, enter its address in the Address or Location field of your Web browser.

Web search engines

The features of search engines change often, and new ones appear constantly. For the latest on search engines, see the links collected by *Easy Searcher* at *easysearcher.com*.

Directories that review sites

BUBL Link (*bubl.ac.uk*)
Internet Public Library
   (*ipl.org/div/subject*)

Internet Scout Project
   (*scout.wisc.edu/archives*)
Librarians' Internet Index (*lii.org*)

Search engines

AlltheWeb (*alltheweb.com*)
AltaVista (*altavista.com*)
Ask.com (*ask.com*)
Bing (*bing.com*)
Dogpile (*dogpile.com*)

Google (*google.com*)
Livesearch (*livesearch.com*)
MetaCrawler (*metacrawler.com*)
Yahoo! (*yahoo.com*)

52f

Note For a good range of reliable sources, try out more than a single search engine, perhaps as many as four or five. No search engine can catalog the entire Web—indeed, even the most powerful engine may not include half the sites available at any given time. In addition, most search engines accept paid placements, giving higher billing to sites that pay a fee. These so-called sponsored links are usually marked as such, but they can compromise a search engine's method for arranging sites in response to your keywords.

Search records

Your Web browser includes functions that allow you to keep track of Web sources and your search:

- Use *Favorites* or *Bookmarks* **to save site addresses as links.** Click one of these terms near the top of the browser screen to add a site you want to return to. A favorite or bookmark remains on file until you delete it.
- Use *History* **to locate sites you have visited before.** The browser records visited sites for a certain period, such as a single online session or a week's sessions. (After that period, the history is deleted.) If you forgot to bookmark a site, you can click History or Go to locate your search history and recover the site.

2 ▪ A sample search

The following sample Web search illustrates how the refinement of keywords can narrow a search to emphasize relevant sources. Justin Malik, a student researching the environmental effects of green consumer products, first used the keywords *green consumption* on *Google*. But, as shown on screen 1 below, the search produced more than 3.4 *million* hits, an unusably large number and a sure sign that Malik's keywords needed revision.

1. First *Google* search results

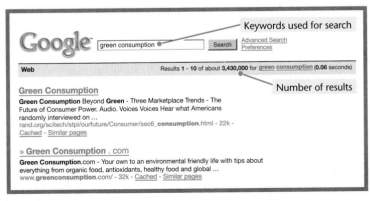

After several tries, Malik arrived at *"green consumption" "environmental issues"* to describe his subject more precisely. He then added *site:.org* to limit the results to nonprofit organizations. Narrowed in this way, Malik's search still produced 387 hits, but this large number included many potential sources on the first few screens, as shown on screen 2 below.

52g

---

2. *Google* results with refined keywords

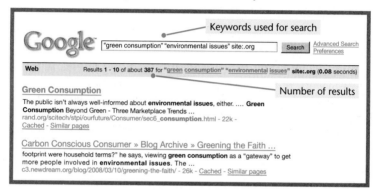

52g   Explore other online sources.

Several online sources can put you directly in touch with experts and others whose ideas and information may inform your research. Because these sources, like Web sites, are unfiltered, you must always evaluate them carefully. (See pp. 409–10.)

1 ▪ Using e-mail

As a research tool, e-mail allows you to communicate with others who are interested in your topic. You might, for instance, carry on an e-mail conversation with a teacher at your school or with other students. Or you might interview an expert in another state to follow up on a scholarly article he or she published. (See pp. 138–40 for more on using e-mail.)

2 ▪ Using blogs

Blogs (Web logs) are personal sites on which an author posts time-stamped comments, generally centering on a common theme, in a format that allows readers to respond to the author and to each other. You can find a directory of blogs at *blogcatalog.com*.

Like all other online media discussed in this section, blogs consulted as potential sources must be evaluated carefully. Some are reliable sources of opinion, news, or evolving scholarship, and many refer to worthy books, articles, Web sites, and other resources. But lots of blogs are little more than outlets for their authors' gripes and prejudices. See pages 409–10 for tips on telling the good from the bad.

3 ▪ Using discussion lists

A **discussion list** (sometimes called a **listserv** or just a **list**) uses e-mail to connect individuals who are interested in a common subject, often with a scholarly or technical focus. By sending a question to an appropriate list, you may be able to reach scores of people who know something about your topic. For an index of discussion lists, see *tile.net/lists*.

Begin research on a discussion list by consulting the list's archive to ensure that the discussion is relevant to your topic and to see whether your question has already been answered. When you write to the list, follow the guidelines for writing e-mail on pages 138–40. And always evaluate messages you receive, following the guidelines on pages 409–10. Although many contributors are reliable experts, almost anyone with an Internet connection can post a message.

4 ▪ Using Web forums and newsgroups

Web forums and newsgroups are more open and less scholarly than discussion lists, so their messages require even more diligent evaluation. **Web forums** allow participants to join a conversation simply by selecting a link on a Web page. For a directory of forums, see *delphiforums.com*. **Newsgroups** are organized under subject headings such as *soc* for social issues and *biz* for business. For a directory of newsgroups, see *groups.google.com*.

52h   Consult government publications.

Government publications provide a vast array of data, compilations, reports, policy statements, public records, and other historical and contemporary information. For US government publications, consult the Government Printing Office's *GPO Access* at *www.gpoaccess.gov*. Also helpful is *Google US Government Search* (*google.com/ig/usgov*) because it returns *.gov* (government) and *.mil* (military) documents and its ranking system emphasizes the most useful documents. Many federal, state, and local government agencies post important publications—legislation, reports, press releases—on their own Web sites. You can find lists of sites for various federal agencies by using the keywords *United States federal government* with a search engine. Use the name of a state, city, or town with *government* for state and local information.

52i   Locate images, audio, and video.

Images, audio, and video can be used as both primary and secondary sources in a research project. A painting, an advertisement, or a video of a speech might be the subject of a paper and thus a primary source. A podcast of a radio interview with an expert on your subject or a college lecture might serve as a secondary source. Because many of these sources are unfiltered—they can be posted by anyone—you must always evaluate them as carefully as you would any source you find on the open Web.

Note You must also cite every image, audio, and video source fully in your paper, just as you cite text sources, with author, title, and publication information. In addition, some sources will require that you seek permission from the copyright holder, either the source itself or a third party such as a photographer or the creator of a video. Permission is especially likely to be required if you are submitting your paper on the public Web. See pages 430–31 for more about online publication.

1 ▪ Images

To find images, you have a number of options:

- **Scout for images while reading sources.** Your sources may include charts, graphs, photographs, and other images that can support your ideas. When you find an image you may want to use, photocopy or download it so you'll have it available later.
- **Create your own images,** such as photographs or charts. See pages 70–74 for examples.
- **Use an image search engine.** *Google, Yahoo!, AlltheWeb,* and some other search engines conduct specialized image searches. They can find scores of images, but the results may be inaccurate or incomplete because the sources surveyed often do not include descriptions of the images. (The engines will search file names and any text accompanying the images.)
- **Use a public image database.** Offering maps, prints, photographs, advertisements, and cartoons, these sites generally conduct accurate searches because their images are filed with information such as a description of the image, the artist's name, and the image's date. Examples include *Ad*Access* (Duke University), *American Memory* (Library of Congress), and *Digital Gallery* (New York Public Library).
- **Use a public image directory.** These sites collect links to image sources. Examples include *Museum Link's Museum of Museums, Popular Culture: Resources for Critical Analysis* (Washington State University), and *Robert B. Haas Family Library: Image Resources* (Yale University).

■ **Use a subscription database.** Your library may subscribe to resources such as *AccuNet/AP Multimedia Archives* (Associated Press), *ARTstor,* and *Grove Art Online.*

Many images you find will be available for free, but some sources do charge a fee for use. Before paying for an image, check with a librarian to see if it is available elsewhere for free.

52j

2 ■ Audio and video

Audio and video, widely available on the Web and on CD-ROM, can provide your readers with the experience of "being there." For example, if you are researching the media response to Martin Luther King's famous "I Have a Dream" speech and you are publishing your paper electronically, you might insert links to the speech and to TV and radio coverage of it.

■ **Audio files** such as podcasts, Webcasts, and CDs record radio programs, interviews, speeches, lectures, and music. They are available on the Web and through your library. Online sources of audio include *American Memory* from the Library of Congress and podcasts at *www.podcastdirectory.com.*
■ **Video files** capture performances, public presentations and speeches, news events, and other activities. They are available on the Web and through your library on DVD. Online sources of video include the Library of Congress's *American Memory*; *YouTube,* which includes commercials, historical footage, current events, and much more (*youtube.com*); and search engines such as *Google* (*video.google.com*).

52j   Generate your own sources.

Academic writing will often require you to conduct primary research for information of your own. For instance, you may need to analyze a poem, conduct an experiment, or interview an expert. Three common forms of primary research are observation, personal interviews, and surveys.

1 ■ Observation

Observation can be an effective way to gather fresh information on your subject. You may observe in a controlled setting—for instance, watching the behavior of children playing in a child-development lab. Or you may observe in a more open setting—for instance, watching the interactions among students at a cafeteria on your campus. Be sure your observation has a well-defined purpose that relates to your research project. Throughout the observation, take careful notes, either on paper or on a handheld computer, and always record the date, time, and location for each session.

2 ■ Personal interviews

An interview can be especially helpful for a research project because it allows you to ask questions precisely geared to your topic. You can conduct an interview in person, over the telephone, or online. A personal interview is preferable if you can arrange it, because you can see the person's expressions and gestures as well as hear his or her tone.

Here are a few guidelines for interviews:

- **Call or write for an appointment.** Tell the person exactly why you are calling, what you want to discuss, and how long you expect the interview to take. Be true to your word on all points.
- **Prepare a list of open-ended questions to ask**—perhaps ten or twelve for a one-hour interview. Plan on doing some research for these questions to discover background on the issues and your subject's published views on the issues.
- **Pay attention to your subject's answers** so that you can ask appropriate follow-up questions. Take care in interpreting answers, especially if you are online and thus can't depend on facial expressions, gestures, and tone of voice to convey the subject's attitudes.
- **Keep thorough notes.** Take notes during an in-person or telephone interview, or record the interview if you have the equipment and your subject agrees. For online interviews, save the discussion in a file of its own.
- **Verify quotations.** Before you quote your subject in your paper, check with him or her to ensure that the quotations are accurate.
- **Send a thank-you note immediately after the interview.** Promise your subject a copy of your finished paper, and send the paper promptly.

3 ■ Surveys

Asking questions of a defined group of people can provide information about respondents' attitudes, behavior, backgrounds, and expectations. Use the following tips to plan and conduct a survey:

- **Decide what you want to find out.** The questions you ask should be dictated by your purpose. Formulating a **hypothesis** about your subject—a generalization that can be tested—will help you refine your purpose.
- **Define your population.** Think about the kinds of people your hypothesis is about—for instance, college men or preschool children. Plan to sample this population so that your findings will be representative.

52j

- **Write your questions.** Surveys may contain closed questions that direct the respondent's answers (checklists and multiple-choice, true/false, or yes/no questions) or open-ended questions that allow brief, descriptive answers. Avoid loaded questions that reveal your own biases or make assumptions about subjects' answers.
- **Test your questions.** Use a few respondents with whom you can discuss the answers. Eliminate or recast questions that respondents find unclear, discomforting, or unanswerable.
- **Tally the results.** Count the actual numbers of answers, including any nonanswers.
- **Seek patterns in the raw data.** Such patterns may confirm or contradict your hypothesis. Revise the hypothesis or conduct additional research if necessary.

53a

53 Working with Sources

How can I use sources critically and effectively?

Research writing is much more than finding sources and reporting their contents. The challenge and interest come from interacting with and synthesizing sources: reading them critically to discover their meanings, judge their relevance and reliability, and create relationships among them; and using them to extend and support your own ideas so that you make your subject your own.

(CULTURE LANGUAGE) Making a subject your own requires thinking critically about sources and developing independent ideas. These goals may at first be uncomfortable for you if your native culture emphasizes understanding and respecting established authority over questioning and enlarging it. The information here will help you work with sources so that you can become an expert in your own right and convincingly convey your expertise to others.

53a   Evaluate sources.

Before you gather ideas and information from your sources, scan them to evaluate what they offer and how you might use them.

mycomplab

Visit *mycomplab.com* for more resources and exercises on working with sources.

53a

Note In evaluating sources, you need to consider how they come to you. The sources you find through the library, both print and online, have been previewed for you by their publishers and by the library's staff. They still require your critical reading, but you can have some confidence in the information they contain. With online sources you reach directly, however, you can't assume similar previewing, so your critical reading must be especially rigorous. Special tips for evaluating Web sites and other online sources appear on pages 404–09.

1 ▪ Relevance and reliability

Not all the sources you find will prove worthwhile: some may be irrelevant to your topic, and others may be unreliable. Gauging the relevance and reliability of sources is the essential task of evaluating them. If you haven't already done so, read this book's Chapter 8 on critical thinking and reading. It provides a foundation for answering the questions in the following box.

Questions for evaluating sources

For online sources, supplement these questions with those on pages 404 and 409.

Relevance

- **Does the source devote some attention to your subject?** Does it focus on your subject or cover it marginally? How does it compare to other sources you've found?
- **Is the source appropriately specialized for your needs?** Check the source's treatment of a topic you know something about, to ensure that it is neither too superficial nor too technical.
- **Is the source up to date enough for your subject?** When was it published? If your subject is current, your sources should be, too.

Reliability

- **Where does the source come from?** Did you find it through your library or directly through the Internet? (If the latter, see pp. 404–09.) Is the source popular or scholarly?
- **Is the author an expert in the field?** Check the author's credentials in a biography (if the source includes one), in a biographical reference, or by a keyword search of the Web.
- **What is the author's bias?** How do the author's ideas relate to those in other sources? What areas does the author emphasize, ignore, or dismiss?
- **Is the source fair, reasonable, and well written?** Does it provide sound reasoning and a fair picture of opposing views? Is the tone calm and objective? Is the source logically organized and error-free?
- **Are the author's claims well supported?** Does the author provide accurate, relevant, representative, and adequate evidence to back up his or her claims? Does the author cite sources, and if so are they reliable?

---

2 ▪ Evaluating library sources

To evaluate sources you find through your library, either in print or on the library's Web site, look at dates, titles, summaries, introductions, headings, author biographies, and any source notes. The following criteria expand on the most important tips in the preceding box. The next two pages show how Justin Malik applied these criteria to two print sources, a magazine article and a journal article, that he consulted while researching green consumerism.

Identify the origin of the source.

Check whether a library source is popular or scholarly. Scholarly sources, such as refereed journals and university press books, are generally deeper and more reliable, though some popular sources, such as firsthand newspaper accounts and books for a general audience, are often appropriate for research projects.

Check the author's expertise.

The authors of scholarly publications tend to be experts whose authority can be verified. Check the source to see whether it contains a biographical note about the author, check a biographical reference, or check the author's name in a keyword search of the Web. Look for other publications by the author and for his or her job and any affiliation, such as teacher at a university, researcher with a nonprofit organization, author of general-interest books, or writer for popular magazines.

Identify the author's bias.

Every author has a point of view that influences the selection and interpretation of evidence. You may be able to learn about an author's bias from biographies or from citation indexes and review indexes, which list references to and reviews of articles and books. But also look at the source itself. How do the author's ideas relate to those in other sources? What areas does the author emphasize, ignore, or dismiss? When you're aware of sources' biases, you can attempt to balance them.

Determine whether the source is fair, reasonable, and well written.

Even a strongly biased work should present solid reasoning and give balanced coverage to opposing views—all in an objective tone. Any source should be organized logically and should be written in clear, error-free sentences. The absence of any of these qualities should raise a warning flag.

Analyze support for the author's claims.

Evidence should be accurate, relevant to the argument, representative of its context, and adequate for the point being made (see pp. 105–06). The author's sources should themselves be reliable.

Evaluating library sources

Opposite are sample pages from two library sources that Justin Malik considered for his paper on green consumerism. Malik evaluated the sources using the questions and guidelines on pages 400–01.

Makower	Jackson
Origin	
Interview with Joel Makower published in *Vegetarian Times*, a popular magazine.	Article by Tim Jackson published in *Journal of Industrial Ecology*, a scholarly journal sponsored by two reputable universities: MIT and Yale.
Author	
Gives Makower's credentials at the beginning of the interview: the author of a book on green products and of a monthly newsletter on green businesses. Quotes another source that calls Makower the "guru of green business practice."	Includes a biography at the end of the article that describes Jackson as a professor at the University of Surrey (UK) and lists his professional activities related to the environment.
Bias	
Describes and promotes green products. Concludes with an endorsement of a for-profit Web site that tracks and sells green products.	Presents multiple views of green consumerism. Argues that a solution to environmental problems will involve green products and less consumption but in different ways than currently proposed.
Reasonableness and writing	
Presents Makower's data and perspective on distinguishing good from bad green products, using conversational writing in an informal presentation.	Presents and cites opposing views objectively, using formal academic writing.
Source citations	
Lacks source citations for claims and data.	Includes more than three pages of source citations, many of scholarly and government sources and all cited within the article.
Assessment	
Probably unreliable: Despite Makower's reputation, the article comes from a nonscholarly source, takes a one-sided approach to consumption, and depends on statistics credited only to Makower.	**Probably reliable:** The article comes from a scholarly journal, the author is an expert in the field, he discusses many views and concedes some, and his source citations confirm evidence from reliable sources.

53a

First and last pages of an interview with Joel Makower, published in *Vegetarian Times*

Largest manufacturer of renewable energy equipment in the United States?	Largest buyer of green energy in the United States?	Largest buyer of fair-trade coffee in the world?
General Electric	**Johnson & Johnson**	**Starbucks**

Sources: Joel Makower

a greater capacity than they did 10 years ago because landfill operators are more sophisticated about composting.

The problem with landfills is that energy and resources used to make the stuff that goes into them. Over 95 percent of the things we buy—disposable cups, single-use water bottles—have a useful life of less than six weeks, and sometimes less than a day. Almost every environmental problem we face is a result of our own wastefulness. We pay a high price for being a consumer society, and not just at the checkout counter.

The promise of green consumerism is that we won't have to do without things we want or need. But that means demanding that manufacturers find better ways to make these things and rewarding the companies that do by buying their products.

q: Who are they?

q: Can we really do much in our own homes?

a: Sure. I live in the house where I grew up. We've made a series of eco-friendly renovations, using wood that is harvested in a sustainable way, paints that don't emit harmful chemicals, energy-efficient appliances and windows. We also asked that the contractors recycle all of the waste from the work they did. Because we live in California, which is a pretty eco-conscious state, contractors got asked to do that quite a lot. But you have to ask. That's what creates a demand for the service.

Being a green consumer isn't just passively selecting the right item at your supermarket. It involves complaining when complaining is warranted, demanding new products and services when they don't exist and buying them when they do. It means taking action.

green-rated products

Alonovo.com—from the Latin *alo novo* for "nurturing change"—is an online eco-shopping service that's associated with Amazon.com. Find a product on Alonovo, and in addition to the description, reviews and price, you'll also see a five-dot rating for the company that produced it. Better still, Alonovo allows you to influence the ratings that products and companies receive by weighting the values most important to you—Healthy Environment, Business Ethics and so forth. Best of all, you can buy products through Alonovo at Amazon prices—but 20 percent of revenues are sent to a nonprofit that you specify. Amazon processes the transaction and ships the goods.

Launched in August 2005, Alonovo [a for-profit company] is one of a number of new services designed to help consumers make smart choices. Similar in concept is idealswork (idealswork.com), which allows you to put more emphasis on a company's animal-welfare policies, for example, than on its concern for workplace equity—or vice versa.

How good will Alonovo be? "It could be one of the most powerful social change tools ever put into consumers' hands."

go for the green

interview by alan pell crawford

buying beer? sneakers? a car? the most eco-conscious companies aren't always the most obvious

---

STATE OF THE DEBATE

Live Better by Consuming Less?

Is There a "Double Dividend" in Sustainable Consumption?

Tim Jackson

First and last pages of an article by Tim Jackson, published in the *Journal of Industrial Ecology*

Keywords

consumer behavior
consumer choice
consumer culture
evolutionary psychology
industrial ecology
symbolic interactionism

... pment Publishing.

UNDP (United Nations Development Programme) 1998. Human development report 1998. Oxford, UK: Oxford University Press.

UNEP (United Nations Environment Programme) 2001. Consumption opportunities: Strategies for change. Paris: UNEP.

Van den Bergh, J. C. J. M., A. Ferrer-i-Carbonell, and G. Munda. 2000. Alternative models of individual behaviour and implications for environmental policy. *Ecological Economics* 32(1): 43–61.

About the Author

Tim Jackson is Professor of Sustainable Development at the Centre for Environmental Strategy (CES) at the University of Surrey, Guildford, United Kingdom. He currently holds a research fellowship in sustainable consumption funded by the Economic and Social Research Council and leads the Ecological Economics Research Group at CES. He is also chair of the Economics Steering Group of the U.K. Sustainable Development Commission and sits on the U.K. Round Table on Sustainable Consumption.

self. This article explores some of these wider debates. In particular, it draws attention to a fundamental disagreement that runs through the literature on consumption and haunts the debate on sustainable consumption: the question of whether, or to what extent, consumption can be taken as "good for us." Some approaches assume that increasing consumption is more or less synonymous with improved well-being the more we consume the better off we are. Others argue, just as vehemently, that the scale of consumption in modern society is both environmentally and psychologically damaging, and that we could reduce consumption significantly without threatening the quality of our lives. The second viewpoint suggests that a kind of "double dividend" is inherent in sustainable consumption: the ability to live better by consuming less and reduce our impact on the environment in the process. In the final analysis, this article argues, such "win-win" solutions may exist but will require a concerted societal effort to realize.

3 ▪ Evaluating Web sites

To a great extent, the same critical reading that helps you evaluate library sources will help you evaluate Web sites that you reach directly. But most Web sites have not undergone prior screening by editors and librarians. On your own, you must distinguish scholarship from corporate promotion, valid data from invented statistics, well-founded opinion from clever propaganda.

53a

The strategy summarized in the box below can help you make such distinctions. On pages 406–07 you can see how Justin Malik applied this strategy to two Web sites that he consulted while researching green consumerism.

Questions for evaluating Web sites

Supplement these questions with those on page 400.

- **What type of site are you viewing?** What does the type lead you to expect about the site's purpose and content?
- **Who is the author or sponsor?** How credible is the person or group responsible for the site?
- **What is the purpose of the site?** What does the site's author or sponsor intend to achieve?
- **What does context tell you?** What do you already know about the site's subject that can inform your evaluation? What kinds of support or other information do the site's links provide?
- **What does presentation tell you?** Is the site's design well thought out and effective? Is the writing clear and error-free?
- **How worthwhile is the content?** Are the site's claims well supported by evidence? Is the evidence from reliable sources? When was the site last updated?

Note   To evaluate a Web document, you'll often need to travel to the site's home page to discover the author or sponsor, date of publication, and other relevant information. The page you're reading may include a link to the home page. If it doesn't, you can find it by editing the URL in the Address or Location field of your browser. Working backward, delete the end of the URL up to the last slash and hit Enter. Repeat this step until you reach the home page. There you may also find a menu option, often labeled "About," that will lead you to a description of the site's author or sponsor.

Determine the type of site.

When you search the Web, you're likely to encounter various types of sites. Although they overlap—a primarily informational site may include scholarship as well—the types can usually be identified by their content and purposes. Here are the main types:

■ **Scholarly sites:** These sites have a knowledge-building interest and include research reports with supporting data and extensive documentation of scholarly sources. The URLs of the sites generally end in *edu* (originating from an educational institution), *org* (a nonprofit organization), or *gov* (a government department or agency). Such sites are more likely to be reliable than the others described below.

53a

■ **Informational sites:** Individuals, nonprofit organizations, corporations, schools, and government bodies all produce sites intended to centralize information on particular subjects. The sites' URLs may end in *edu, org, gov,* or *com* (originating from a commercial organization). Such sites generally do not have the knowledge-building focus of scholarly sites and may omit supporting data and documentation, but they can provide useful information and often include links to scholarly sources. See page 387 on the use of *Wikipedia* and other wikis, which allow anyone to contribute and edit information on the site.

■ **Advocacy sites:** Many sites present the views of individuals or organizations that promote certain policies or actions. Their URLs usually end in *org*, but they may end in *edu* or *com*. Some advocacy sites include serious, well-documented research to support their positions, but others select or distort evidence.

■ **Commercial sites:** Corporations and other businesses maintain Web sites to explain or promote themselves or to sell goods and services. The URLs of commercial sites end in *com*. The information on such a site furthers the sponsor's profit-making purpose, but it can include reliable data.

■ **Personal sites:** The sites maintained by individuals range from diaries of a family's travels to opinions on political issues to reports on evolving scholarship. The sites' URLs usually end in *com* or *edu*. Personal sites are only as reliable as their authors, but some do provide valuable eyewitness accounts, links to worthy sources, and other usable information. A particular kind of personal site, the blog, is discussed on pages 394–95 and 409–10.

Identify the author and sponsor.

A reputable site lists its authors, names the group responsible for the site, and provides information or a link for contacting the author and the sponsor. If none of this information is provided, you should not use the source. If you have only the author's or the sponsor's name, you may be able to discover more in a biographical dictionary, through a keyword search, or in your other sources. Make sure the author and the sponsor have expertise on the subject they're presenting: if an author is a doctor, for instance, what is he or she a doctor of?

(continued on p. 408)

Evaluating Web sites

Opposite are screen shots from two Web sites that Justin Malik considered for his paper on green consumerism. Malik evaluated the sources using the questions in the boxes on pages 400 and 404.

53a

Allianz Knowledge Partnersite

Nature Reports: Climate Change

Author and sponsor

Site sponsor is the Allianz Group, a global insurance company partnering with well-known organizations to provide information on a variety of issues. Author of article is identified as an editor, not a scientist.

Listed authors are scientists, experts on climate change. (Biographies appear at the end of the article.) Site sponsor is the Nature Publishing Group, which also publishes the reputable science journal *Nature.*

Purpose and bias

Educational page on a corporate-sponsored Web site with the self-stated purpose of gathering information about global issues and making it available to an international audience.

Informational site with the self-stated purpose of providing "authoritative, in-depth reporting on climate change and its wider implications for policy, society and the economy." Article expresses bias toward reducing pollution to stop climate change.

Context

One of many sites publishing current information on climate issues.

One of many sites publishing current research on climate issues.

Presentation

Clean, professionally designed site with mostly error-free writing.

Clean, professionally designed site with error-free writing.

Content

Article gives basic information about climate change and provides links to other pages that expand on its claims. Probably because of the intended general (nonscientist) audience, the pages do not include citations of scholarly research.

Article is current (date above the title) and clearly explains the science of climate change with references and links to scholarly sources. Other links connect to hundreds of articles elsewhere on the site about climate-related topics.

Assessment

Probably unreliable: Despite the wealth of information in the article and its links, the material lacks the scholarly source citations necessary for its use as evidence in an academic paper.

Probably reliable: The article has an explicit bias toward stopping climate change, but the site sponsor has a scholarly reputation, the authors are climate-change experts, and the references cite many scholarly and government sources.

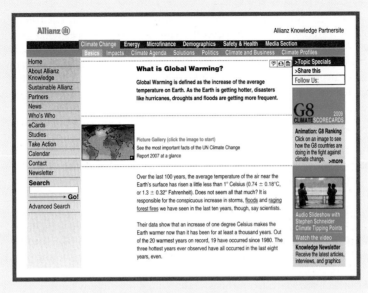

Article published on the Web site *Allianz Knowledge Partnersite*

Article published on the Web site *Nature Reports: Climate Change*

(continued from p. 405)

Gauge purpose and bias.

A Web site's purpose determines what ideas and information it offers. Inferring that purpose tells you how to interpret what you see on the site. If a site is intended to sell a product or an opinion, it will likely emphasize favorable ideas and information while ignoring or even distorting what is unfavorable. In contrast, if a site is intended to build knowledge—for instance, a scholarly project or journal—it will likely acknowledge diverse views and evidence.

Determining the purpose of a site often requires looking beyond the first page and beneath the surface of words and images. To start, read what the site says about itself, usually found on a page labeled "About." Be suspicious of any site that doesn't provide information about itself and its goals.

Consider context.

Your evaluation of a Web site should be informed by considerations outside the site itself. Chief among these is your own knowledge. What do you already know about the site's subject and the prevailing views of it? Where does this site seem to fit into that picture? What can you learn from this site that you don't already know?

In addition, you can follow some of the site's links to see how they support, or don't support, the site's credibility. For instance, links to scholarly sources lend authority to a site—but *only* if the scholarly sources actually relate to and back up the site's claims.

Look at presentation.

Considering both the look of a site and the way it's written can illuminate its intentions and reliability. Are the site's elements all functional and well integrated, or is the site cluttered with irrelevant material and graphics? Does the site seem carefully constructed and well maintained, or is it sloppy? Does the design reflect the apparent purpose of the site, or does it undercut or conceal that purpose in some way? Is the text clearly written, or is it difficult to understand? Is it error-free, or does it contain typos and grammatical errors?

Analyze content.

With information about a site's author, purpose, and context, you're in a position to evaluate its content. Are the ideas and information current, or are they dated? (Check the publication date.) Are they slanted and, if so, in what direction? Are the views and data authoritative, or do you need to balance them—or even reject them? Are claims made on the site supported by evidence drawn from reliable sources? These questions require close reading of both the text and its sources.

4 ■ Evaluating other online sources

Blogs, online discussions, and online images, video, and audio require the same critical scrutiny as Web sites do. Blogs and discussion groups can be sources of reliable data and opinions, but you will also encounter wrong or misleading data and skewed opinions. One podcast may provide an interview with a recognized expert, while another claims authority that it doesn't deserve. A *YouTube* search using "I have a dream" brings up videos of Martin Luther King, Jr., delivering his famous speech as well as videos of people speaking hatefully about King and the speech.

53a

Use the following strategy for evaluating blogs, discussion groups, and multimedia sources:

Questions for evaluating blogs, online discussions, images, video, and audio

Supplement these questions with those on pages 400 and 404.

- **Who is the author or creator?** How credible is he or she?
- **What is the author's or creator's purpose?** What can you tell about why the author or creator is publishing the work?
- **What does the context reveal?** What do other responses to the work, including responses to a blog posting or the other messages in a discussion thread, indicate about the source's balance and reliability?
- **How worthwhile is the content?** Are the claims made by the author or creator supported by evidence? Is the evidence from reliable sources?
- **How does the source compare with other sources?** Do the claims made by the author or creator seem accurate and fair given what you've seen in sources you know to be reliable?

Identify the author or creator.

Checking out the author or creator of a blog, online posting, video file, or podcast can help you judge its reliability. If the author or creator uses a screen name, write directly to him or her requesting full name and credentials. Do not use the source if you don't get a response. Once you know the person's name, you may be able to obtain background information from a keyword search of the Web or a biographical dictionary.

You can also get a sense of the interests and biases of an author or creator by tracking down his or her other publications. For a blog, check whether the author cites or links to other publications. For a discussion-group posting, look for an archive or other feature that allows you to find additional messages by the same author. For multimedia sources, try to gain an overview of the creator's work.

Analyze the author's or creator's purpose.

What can you tell about *why* the author or creator is publishing the work? Look for claims, the use (or lack) of evidence, and the treatment of opposing views. All these convey the person's stand on the subject and general fairness, and they will help you position the source among your other sources.

Consider the context.

Blogs, discussion-group postings, and multimedia sources are often difficult to evaluate in isolation. Looking beyond a particular contribution to the responses of others will give you a sense of how the author or creator is regarded. On a blog, look at the comments others have posted. Do the same with postings, going back to the initial posting in the discussion thread and reading forward.

Analyze content.

A reliable source will offer evidence for claims and sources for evidence. If you don't see such supporting information, ask the author or creator for it. (If he or she fails to respond, don't use the source.) Then verify the sources with your own research: are they reputable?

The tone of writing can also be a clue to its purpose and reliability. Blogs, online discussions, and some podcasts tend to be more informal and often more heated than other kinds of dialog, but look askance at writing that's contemptuous, dismissive, or shrill.

Compare with other sources.

Always consider blogs, postings, and multimedia sources in comparison to other sources so that you can distinguish singular, untested views from more mainstream views that have been subject to verification. Don't assume that a blog author's information and opinions are mainstream just because you see them on other blogs. The technology allows content to be picked up instantly by other blogs, so widespread distribution indicates only popularity, not reliability.

Be wary of blogs or postings that reproduce periodical articles, reports, or other publications. Try to locate the original version of the publication to be sure it has been reproduced fully and accurately, not quoted selectively or distorted. If you can't locate the original version, don't use the publication as a source.

53b   Synthesize sources.

When you begin to locate the differences and similarities among sources, you move into the most significant part of research writing:

forging relationships for your own purpose. This **synthesis** is an essential step in reading sources critically, and it continues through the drafting and revision of a research paper. As you infer connections—say, between one writer's opinions and another's or between two works by the same author—you create new knowledge.

Your synthesis of sources will grow more detailed and sophisticated as you proceed through the process of working with sources described in the balance of this chapter: gathering information from sources (pp. 413–14); deciding whether to summarize, paraphrase, or quote directly from sources (pp. 414–18); and integrating sources into your sentences (pp. 419–23). Unless you are analyzing primary sources such as the works of a poet, at first read your sources quickly and selectively to obtain an overview of your topic and a sense of how the sources approach it. Don't get bogged down in taking detailed notes, but *do* record your ideas about sources in your research journal (p. 375) or your annotated bibliography (p. 380).

53b

Respond to sources.

Write down what your sources make you think. Do you agree or disagree with the author? Do you find his or her views narrow, or do they open up new approaches for you? Is there anything in the source that you need to research further before you can understand it? Does the source prompt questions that you should keep in mind while reading other sources?

Connect sources.

When you notice a link between sources, jot it down. Do two sources differ in their theories or their interpretations of facts? Does one source illuminate another—perhaps commenting or clarifying or supplying additional data? Do two or more sources report studies that support a theory you've read about or an idea of your own?

Heed your own insights.

Apart from ideas prompted by your sources, you are sure to come up with independent thoughts: a conviction, a point of confusion that suddenly becomes clear, a question you haven't seen anyone else ask. These insights may occur at unexpected times, so it's good practice to keep a notebook or computer handy to record them.

Draw your own conclusions.

As your research proceeds, the responses, connections, and insights you form through synthesis will lead you to answer your starting research question with a statement of your thesis (see pp. 433–34). They will also lead you to the main ideas supporting your thesis—conclusions you have drawn from your synthesis of sources, forming the main divisions of your paper.

Use sources to support your conclusions.

Effective synthesis requires careful handling of evidence from sources so that it meshes smoothly into your sentences and yet is clearly distinct from your own ideas. When drafting your paper, make sure that each paragraph focuses on an idea of your own, with the support for the idea coming from your sources. Generally, open each paragraph with your idea, provide evidence from a source or sources with appropriate citations, and close with an interpretation of the evidence. (Avoid ending a paragraph with a source citation; instead, end with your own idea.) In this way, your paper will synthesize others' work into something wholly your own. (For more on structuring paragraphs in academic writing, see p. 95.)

Exercise 53.1   Synthesizing sources

The following three passages address the same issue, the legalization of drugs. What similarities do you see in the authors' ideas? What differences? Write a paragraph of your own in which you use these authors' views as a point of departure for your own view about drug legalization.

Perhaps the most unfortunate victims of drug prohibition laws have been the residents of America's ghettos. These laws have proved largely futile in deterring ghetto-dwellers from becoming drug abusers, but they do account for much of what ghetto residents identify as the drug problem. Aggressive, gun-toting drug dealers often upset law-abiding residents far more than do addicts nodding out in doorways. Meanwhile other residents perceive the drug dealers as heroes and successful role models. They're symbols of success to children who see no other options. At the same time the increasingly harsh criminal penalties imposed on adult drug dealers have led drug traffickers to recruit juveniles. Where once children started dealing drugs only after they had been using them for a few years, today the sequence is often reversed. Many children start using drugs only after working for older drug dealers for a while. Legalization of drugs, like legalization of alcohol in the 1930s, would drive the drug-dealing business off the streets and out of apartment buildings and into government-regulated, tax-paying stores. It also would force many of the gun-toting dealers out of the business and convert others into legitimate businessmen.   —Ethan A. Nadelmann, "Shooting Up"

Statistics argue against legalization. The University of Michigan conducts an annual survey of twelfth graders, asking the students about their drug consumption. In 1980, 56.4 percent of those polled said they had used marijuana in the past twelve months, whereas in 2007 only 41.7 percent had done so. Cocaine use was also reduced in the same period (22.6 percent to 7.8 percent). At the same time, twelve-month use of legally available drugs—alcohol and nicotine-containing cigarettes—remained constant at about 72 percent and 55 percent, respectively. The numbers of illegal drug users haven't declined nearly enough: those teenaged marijuana and cocaine users are still vulnerable to addiction

and even death, and they threaten to infect their impressionable peers. But clearly the prohibition of illegal drugs has helped, while the legal status of alcohol and cigarettes has not made them less popular.
—Sylvia Runkle, "The Case Against Legalization"

I have to laugh at the debate over what to do about the drug problem. Everyone is running around offering solutions—from making drug use a more serious criminal offense to legalizing it. But there isn't a real solution. I know that. I used and abused drugs, and people, and society, for two decades. Nothing worked to get me to stop all that behavior except just plain being sick and tired. Nothing. Not threats, not ten-plus years in prison, not anything that was said to me. I used until I got through. Period. And that's when you'll win the war. When all the dope fiends are done. Not a minute before.
—Michael W. Posey, "I Did Drugs Until They Wore Me Out. Then I Stopped."

53c   Gather information from sources.

You can accomplish a great deal of synthesis while gathering information from your sources. This information gathering is not a mechanical process. Rather, as you read you assess and organize the information in your sources.

Researchers vary in their methods for working with sources, but all methods share the same goals:

- **Keep accurate records of what sources say.** Accuracy helps prevent misrepresentation and plagiarism.
- **Keep accurate records of how to find sources.** These records are essential for retracing steps and for citing sources in the final paper. (See pp. 380–82 on keeping a working bibliography.)
- **Synthesize sources.** Information gathering is a critical process, leading to an understanding of sources, the relationships among them, and their support for your own ideas.

To achieve these goals, you can take handwritten notes, type notes into your computer, annotate photocopies or printouts of sources, or annotate downloaded documents. On any given project, you may use all the methods. Each has advantages and disadvantages.

- **Handwritten notes:** Taking notes by hand is especially useful if you come across a source with no computer or photocopier handy. But handwritten notes can be risky. It's easy to introduce errors as you work from source to note card. And it's possible to copy source language and then later mistake and use it as your own, thus plagiarizing the source. Always take care to make accurate notes and to place big quotation marks around any passage you quote.

- **Notes on computer:** Taking notes on your computer can streamline the path of source to note to paper because you can import the notes into your draft as you write. However, computer notes have the same disadvantages as handwritten notes: the risk of introducing errors and the risk of plagiarizing. As with handwritten notes, strive for accuracy, and use quotation marks for quotations.

- **Photocopies and printouts:** Photocopying from print sources or printing out online sources each has the distinct advantages of convenience and reduction in the risks of error and plagiarism during information gathering. But each method has disadvantages, too. The busywork of copying or printing can distract you from the crucial work of interacting with sources. And you have to make a special effort to annotate copies and printouts with the publication information for sources. If you don't have this information for your final paper, you can't use the source.

- **Downloads:** Researching online, you can usually download full-text articles, Web pages, discussion-group messages, and other materials into your word processor. While drafting, you can import source information from one file into another. Like photocopies and printouts, though, downloads can distract you from interacting with sources and can easily become separated from the publication information you must have in order to use the sources. Even more important, directly importing source material creates a high risk of plagiarism. You must keep clear boundaries between your own ideas and words and those of others.

53d Use summary, paraphrase, and quotation.

Deciding whether to summarize, paraphrase, or quote directly from sources is an important step in synthesizing the sources' ideas and your own. You engage in synthesis when you use your own words to summarize an author's argument or paraphrase a significant example or when you select a significant passage to quote. Choosing summary, paraphrase, or quotation should depend on why you are using a source.

Note Summaries, paraphrases, and quotations all require source citations in your paper. A summary or paraphrase without a source citation or a quotation without quotation marks is plagiarism. (See pp. 424–31 for more on plagiarism.)

1 ▪ Summary

When you **summarize**, you condense an extended idea or argument into a sentence or more in your own words. (See pp. 83–85 for tips.) Summary is most useful when you want to record the gist of an author's idea without the background or supporting evidence.

Following is a passage from a scholarly essay about consumption and its impact on the environment. Then a sample computer note shows a summary of the passage.

Original quotation

Such intuition is even making its way, albeit slowly, into scholarly circles, where recognition is mounting that ever-increasing pressures on ecosystems, life-supporting environmental services, and critical natural cycles are driven not only by the sheer number of resource users and the inefficiencies of their resource use, but also by the patterns of resource use themselves. In global environmental policymaking arenas, it is becoming more and more difficult to ignore the fact that the overdeveloped North must restrain its consumption if it expects the underdeveloped South to embrace a more sustainable trajectory.

—Thomas Princen, Michael Maniates, and Ken Conca,
Confronting Consumption, p. 4

53d

Summary of source

Environmental consequences of consumption

Princen, Maniates, and Conca 4

Overconsumption may be a more significant cause of environmental problems than increasing population is.

---

2 ▪ **Paraphrase**

When you **paraphrase,** you follow much more closely the author's original presentation, but you restate it using your own words and sentence structures. Paraphrase is most useful when you want to present or examine an author's line of reasoning but you don't feel the original words merit direct quotation. Here is a paraphrase of the quotation from *Confronting Consumption.*

Paraphrase of source

Environmental consequences of consumption

Princen, Maniates, and Conca 4

Scholars are coming to believe that consumption is partly to blame for changes in ecosystems, reduction of essential natural resources, and changes in natural cycles. Policy makers increasingly see that wealthy nations have to start consuming less if they want developing nations to adopt practices that reduce pollution and waste. Rising population around the world does cause significant stress on the environment, but consumption is increasing even more rapidly than population.

The preceding paraphrase uses simpler sentences and more common terms than the original passage, in effect translating it as shown below. Only words that lack satisfactory synonyms—such as *ecosystems, natural, cycles,* and *population*—remain the same.

Source authors' words	Paraphrase
Such intuition is even making its way, albeit slowly, into scholarly circles, where recognition is mounting that	Scholars are coming to believe that
ever-increasing pressures on ecosystems, life-supporting environmental services, and critical natural cycles are driven not only by the sheer number of resource users and the inefficiencies of their resource use, but also by the patterns of resource use themselves.	consumption is partly to blame for changes in ecosystems, reduction of essential natural resources, and changes in natural cycles.
In global environmental policy-making arenas, it is becoming more and more difficult to ignore the fact that	Policy makers increasingly see that
overdeveloped countries must restrain their consumption if they expect underdeveloped countries to embrace a more sustainable trajectory.	wealthy nations have to start consuming less if they want developing nations to adopt practices that reduce pollution and waste.
And while global population growth still remains a huge issue in many regions around the world—both rich and poor—	Rising population around the world does cause significant stress on the environment,
per-capita growth in consumption is, for many resources, expanding eight to twelve times faster than population growth.	but consumption is increasing even more rapidly than population.

The paraphrase needs a source citation because it borrows ideas from the source, but it does not need quotation marks. In contrast, an unsuccessful paraphrase—one that plagiarizes—copies the author's words or sentence structures or both *without quotation marks.* (See p. 429 for examples.)

CULTURE
LANGUAGE   If English is your second language and you have difficulty paraphrasing the ideas in sources, try this. Before attempting a paraphrase, read the original passage several times. Then, instead of "translating" line by line, try to state the gist of the passage without looking at it. Check your effort against the original to be sure you have captured the source author's meaning and emphasis without using his or her words and

---

Paraphrasing a source

- **Read the relevant material several times to be sure you understand it.**
- **Restate the source's ideas in your own words and sentence structures.** You need not put down in new words the whole passage or all the details. Select what is relevant to your topic, and restate only that. If complete sentences seem too detailed or cumbersome, use phrases.
- **Be careful not to distort meaning.** Don't change the source's emphasis or omit connecting words, qualifiers, and other material whose absence will confuse you later or cause you to misrepresent the source.

53d

---

sentence structures. If you need a synonym for a word, look it up in a dictionary.

3 ▪ Direct quotation

Your notes from sources may include many quotations, especially if you rely on photocopies, printouts, or downloads. Whether to use a quotation in your draft, instead of a summary or paraphrase, depends on whether the source is primary or secondary and on how important the exact words are:

- **Quote extensively when you are analyzing primary sources**—firsthand accounts such as literary works, eyewitness reports, and historical documents. The quotations will often be both the target of your analysis and the chief support for your ideas.
- **Quote selectively when you are drawing on secondary sources**—reports or analyses of other sources, such as a critic's view of a poem or a historian's synthesis of several eyewitness reports. Favor summaries and paraphrases over quotations, and put every quotation to each test in the following box. Most papers of ten or so pages should not need more than two or three quotations that are longer than a few lines each.

Tests for direct quotations from secondary sources

The author's original satisfies one of these requirements:

- The language is unusually vivid, bold, or inventive.
- The quotation cannot be paraphrased without distortion or loss of meaning.
- The words themselves are at issue in your interpretation.
- The quotation represents and emphasizes a body of opinion or the view of an important expert.
- The quotation emphatically reinforces your own idea.
- The quotation is an illustration such as a graph, diagram, or table.

(continued)

Tests for direct quotations from secondary sources
(continued)

53d

The quotation is as short as possible:

- It includes only material relevant to your point.
- It is edited to eliminate examples and other unneeded material, using brackets and ellipsis marks (pp. 345–48).

When you quote a source, either in your notes or in your draft, take precautions to avoid plagiarism or misrepresentation of the source:

- **Copy the material carefully.** Take down the author's exact wording, spelling, capitalization, and punctuation.
- **Proofread every direct quotation at least twice.**
- **Use quotation marks around the quotation** so that later you won't confuse it with a paraphrase or summary. Be sure to transfer the quotation marks into your draft as well, unless the quotation is long and is set off from your text. For advice on handling long quotations, see pages 480–81 (MLA style) and 512 (APA style).
- **Use brackets** to add words for clarity or to change the capitalization of letters (see pp. 348, 360).
- **Use ellipsis marks** to omit irrelevant material (see pp. 345–47).
- **Cite the source of the quotation in your draft.** See pages 431–33 on documentation.

Exercise 53.2   Summarizing and paraphrasing

Prepare two source notes, one summarizing the entire paragraph below and the other paraphrasing the first four sentences (ending with the word *autonomy*). Use the format for a note illustrated on page 415, omitting only the subject heading.

Federal organization [of the United States] has made it possible for the different states to deal with the same problems in many different ways. One consequence of federalism, then, has been that people are treated differently, by law, from state to state. The great strength of this system is that differences from state to state in cultural preferences, moral standards, and levels of wealth can be accommodated. In contrast to a unitary system in which the central government makes all important decisions (as in France), federalism is a powerful arrangement for maximizing regional freedom and autonomy. The great weakness of our federal system, however, is that people in some states receive less than the best or the most advanced or the least expensive services and policies that government can offer. The federal dilemma does not invite easy solution, for the costs and benefits of the arrangement have tended to balance out.   —Peter K. Eisinger et al., *American Politics*, p. 44

Exercise 53.3 **Combining summary, paraphrase, and direct quotation**

Prepare a source note containing a combination of paraphrase or summary and direct quotation that states the main idea of the passage below. Use the format for a note illustrated on page 415, omitting only the subject heading.

> Most speakers unconsciously duel even during seemingly casual conversations, as can often be observed at social gatherings where they show less concern for exchanging information with other guests than for asserting their own dominance. Their verbal dueling often employs very subtle weapons like mumbling, a hostile act which defeats the listener's desire to understand what the speaker claims he is trying to say (but is really not saying because he is mumbling!). Or the verbal dueler may keep talking after someone has passed out of hearing range—which is often an aggressive challenge to the listener to return and acknowledge the dominance of the speaker.　　—Peter K. Farb, *Word Play*, p. 107

53e

53e Integrate sources into your text.

Integrating source material into your sentences is key to synthesizing others' ideas and information with your own. Evidence drawn from sources should *back up* your conclusions, not *be* your conclusions: you don't want to let your evidence overwhelm your own point of view. The point of research is to investigate and go beyond sources, to interpret them and use them to support your own independent ideas.

Note The examples in this section use the MLA style of source documentation and also present-tense verbs (such as *disagrees*). See pages 422–23 for specific variations in documentation style and verb tense within the academic disciplines. Several other conventions governing quotations are discussed elsewhere in this book:

- Using commas to punctuate signal phrases (pp. 322–23).
- Placing other punctuation marks with quotation marks (pp. 341–42).
- Using brackets and the ellipsis mark to indicate changes in quotations (pp. 345–48).
- Punctuating and placing parenthetical citations (pp. 443–45).
- Formatting long prose quotations and poetry quotations (MLA style, pp. 480–81; APA style, p. 512).

1 ▪ Introduction of borrowed material

Readers will be distracted from your point if borrowed material does not fit into your sentence. In the following passage, the writer has not meshed the structures of her own and her source's sentences:

| Awkward | One editor disagrees with this view and "a good re-porter does not fail to separate opinions from facts" (Lyman 52). |

In the revision below, the writer adds words to integrate the quota-tion into her sentence:

| Revised | One editor disagrees with this view, <u>maintaining that</u> "a good reporter does not fail to separate opinions from facts" (Lyman 52). |

To mesh your own and your source's words, you may some-times need to make a substitution or addition to the quotation, sig-naling your change with brackets:

Words added	"The tabloids [of England] are a journalistic case study in bad reporting," claims Lyman (52).
Verb form changed	A bad reporter, Lyman implies, is one who "[fails] to separate opinions from facts" (52). [The bracketed verb replaces *fail* in the original.]
Capitalization changed	"[T]o separate opinions from facts" is the work of a good reporter (Lyman 52). [In the original, *to* is not capitalized.]
Noun supplied for pronoun	The reliability of a news organization "depends on [reporters'] trustworthiness," says Lyman (52). [The bracketed noun replaces *their* in the original.]

2 ▪ Interpretation of borrowed material

You need to work borrowed material into your sentences so that readers see without effort how it contributes to the points you are making. If you merely dump source material into your paper without explaining how you intend it to be interpreted, readers will have to struggle to understand your sentences and the relationships you are trying to establish. For example, the following passage forces us to figure out for ourselves that the writer's sentence and the quotation state opposite points of view:

| Dumped | Many news editors and reporters maintain that it is im-possible to keep personal opinions from influencing the selection and presentation of facts. "True, news re-porters, like everyone else, form impressions of what they see and hear. However, a good reporter does not fail to separate opinions from facts" (Lyman 52). |

In the revision, the underlined additions tell us how to interpret the quotation:

| Revised | Many news editors and reporters maintain that it is im-possible to keep personal opinions from influencing the selection and presentation of facts. <u>Yet not all au-thorities agree with this view. One editor grants that</u> |

"news reporters, like everyone else, form impressions of what they see and hear." But, he insists, "a good reporter does not fail to separate opinions from facts" (Lyman 52).

Signal phrases

The words *One editor grants* and *he insists* in the preceding revised passage are **signal phrases:** they tell readers who the source is and what to expect in the quotations that follow. Signal phrases usually contain (1) the source author's name (or a substitute for it, such as *One editor* and *he*) and (2) a verb that indicates the source author's attitude or approach to what he or she says.

53e

Some verbs for signal phrases appear below. These verbs are in the present tense, typical of writing in the humanities. In the social and natural sciences, the past tense (*asked*) or present perfect tense (*has asked*) is more common. See page 423.

Author is neutral	Author infers or suggests	Author argues	Author is uneasy or disparaging
comments	analyzes	claims	belittles
describes	asks	contends	bemoans
explains	assesses	defends	complains
illustrates	concludes	holds	condemns
notes	considers	insists	deplores
observes	demonstrates	maintains	deprecates
points out	finds		derides
records	predicts	Author agrees	disagrees
relates	proposes		laments
reports	reveals	admits	warns
says	shows	agrees	
sees	speculates	concedes	
thinks	suggests	concurs	
writes	supposes	grants	

Vary your signal phrases to suit your interpretation of borrowed material and also to keep readers' interest. A signal phrase may precede, interrupt, or follow the borrowed material:

Precedes	Lyman insists that "a good reporter does not fail to separate opinions from facts" (52).
Interrupts	"However," Lyman insists, "a good reporter does not fail to separate opinions from facts" (52).
Follows	"[A] good reporter does not fail to separate opinions from facts," Lyman insists (52).

Background information

You can add information to a signal phrase to inform readers why you are using a source. In most cases, provide the author's name in the text, especially if the author is an expert or readers will recognize the name:

| Author named | Harold Lyman grants that "news reporters, like everyone else, form impressions of what they see and hear." But, Lyman insists, "a good reporter does not fail to separate opinions from facts" (52). |

If the source title contributes information about the author or the context of the quotation, you can provide it in the text:

| Title given | Harold Lyman, in his book *The Conscience of the Journalist*, grants that "news reporters, like everyone else, form impressions of what they see and hear." But, Lyman insists, "a good reporter does not fail to separate opinions from facts" (52). |

If the quoted author's background and experience reinforce or clarify the quotation, you can provide these credentials in the text:

| Credentials given | Harold Lyman, a newspaper editor for more than forty years, grants that "news reporters, like everyone else, form impressions of what they see and hear." But, Lyman insists, "a good reporter does not fail to separate opinions from facts" (52). |

You need not name the author, source, or credentials in your text when you are simply establishing facts or weaving together facts and opinions from varied sources. In the following passage, the information is more important than the source, so the name of the source is confined to a parenthetical acknowledgment:

> To end the abuses of the British, many colonists were urging three actions: forming a united front, seceding from Britain, and taking control of their own international relations (Wills 325–36).

3 ▪ Discipline styles for integrating sources

The preceding guidelines for introducing and interpreting borrowed material apply generally across academic disciplines, but the disciplines do differ in verb tenses and documentation style.

English and some other humanities

Writers in English, foreign languages, and related disciplines use MLA style for documenting sources (see Chapter 56) and generally use the present tense of verbs in signal phrases. In discussing sources other than works of literature, the present perfect tense is also sometimes appropriate:

Lyman insists . . . [present].
Lyman has insisted . . . [present perfect].

In discussing works of literature, use only the present tense to describe both the work of the author and the action in the work:

Kate Chopin builds irony into every turn of "The Story of an Hour." For example, Mrs. Mallard, the central character, finds joy in the death of her husband, whom she loves, because she anticipates "the long procession of years that would belong to her absolutely" (23).

Avoid shifting tenses in writing about literature. You can, for instance, shorten quotations to avoid their past-tense verbs:

| Shift | Her freedom elevates her, so that "she carried herself unwittingly like a goddess of victory" (24). |
| No shift | Her freedom elevates her, so that she walks "unwittingly like a goddess of victory" (24). |

53e

History and other humanities

Writers in history, art history, philosophy, and related disciplines generally use the present tense or present perfect tense of verbs in signal phrases:

Lincoln persisted, as Haworth has noted, in "feeling that events controlled him."[3]

What Miller calls Lincoln's "severe self-doubt"[6] undermined his effectiveness on at least two occasions.

The raised numbers after the quotations are part of the Chicago documentation style, used in history and other disciplines. You can find information on Chicago style and sample student papers documented in Chicago style at *mycomplab.com*.

Social and natural sciences

Writers in the sciences generally use a verb's present tense just for reporting the results of a study (*The data suggest . . .*). Otherwise, they use a verb's past or present perfect tense in a signal phrase, as when introducing an explanation, interpretation, or other commentary. (Thus when you are writing for the sciences generally convert the list of signal-phrase verbs on p. 421 from the present to the past or present perfect tense.)

Lin (2001) has suggested that preschooling may significantly affect children's academic performance not only in elementary school but through high school (pp. 22–23).

In an exhaustive survey of the literature published between 1990 and 2005, Walker (2006) found "no proof, merely a weak correlation, linking place of residence and rate of illness" (p. 121).

These passages conform to APA documentation style, discussed in Chapter 57. APA style, or one quite similar to it, is also used in sociology, education, nursing, biology, and many other social and natural sciences.

Exercise 53.4 Introducing and interpreting borrowed material

Drawing on the ideas in the following paragraph and using examples from your own observations and experiences, write a paragraph about anxiety. Integrate at least one direct quotation and one paraphrase from the following paragraph into your own sentences. In your paragraph identify the author by name and give his credentials: he is a professor of psychiatry and a practicing psychoanalyst.

> There are so many ways in which human beings are different from all the lower forms of animals, and almost all of them make us uniquely susceptible to feelings of anxiousness. Our imagination and reasoning powers facilitate anxiety; the anxious feeling is precipitated not by an absolute impending threat—such as the worry about an examination, a speech, travel—but rather by the symbolic and often unconscious representations. We do not have to be experiencing a potential danger. We can experience something related to it. We can recall, through our incredible memories, the original symbolic sense of vulnerability in childhood and suffer the feeling attached to that. We can even forget the original memory and be stuck with the emotion—which is then compounded by its seemingly irrational quality at this time. It is not just the fear of death which pains us, but the anticipation of it; or the anniversary of a specific death; or a street, a hospital, a time of day, a color, a flower, a symbol associated with death.
>
> —Willard Gaylin, "Feeling Anxious," p. 23

54   Avoiding Plagiarism and Documenting Sources

How can I use sources honestly?

The knowledge building that is the focus of academic writing rests on the honesty of everyone who participates in using and crediting sources, including students. The work of a writer or creator is his or her intellectual property. You and others may borrow the work's ideas and even its words or an image, but you *must* acknowledge that what you borrowed came from someone else.

When you acknowledge sources in your writing, you are doing more than giving credit to the writer or creator the work you consulted. You are also showing what your own writing is based on, which in turn gives you credibility as a researcher and writer. Acknowledging sources creates the trust among scholars, students, writers, and readers that knowledge building requires.

mycomplab

Visit *mycomplab.com* for more resources and exercises on avoiding plagiarism and documenting sources.

Plagiarism (from a Latin word for "kidnapper") is the presentation of someone else's work as your own. Whether deliberate or accidental, plagiarism is a serious offense. It breaks trust, and it undermines or even destroys your credibility as a researcher and writer. In most colleges, a code of academic honesty calls for severe consequences for plagiarism: a reduced or failing grade, suspension from school, or expulsion.

- *Deliberate* plagiarism:
  Copying or downloading a phrase, a sentence, or a longer passage from a source and passing it off as your own by omitting quotation marks and a source citation.
  Summarizing or paraphrasing someone else's ideas without acknowledging your debt in a source citation.
  Handing in as your own work a paper you have bought, copied off the Web, had a friend write, or accepted from another student.

- *Accidental* plagiarism:
  Reading a wide variety of print or Web sources on a subject without taking notes on them, and then not remembering the difference between what you recently learned and what you already knew.
  Forgetting to place quotation marks around another writer's words.
  Carelessly omitting a source citation for a paraphrase.
  Omitting a source citation for another's idea because you are unaware of the need to acknowledge the idea.

The way to avoid plagiarism is to acknowledge your sources by documenting them. This chapter discusses plagiarism and the Internet, shows how to distinguish what doesn't require acknowledgment from what does, and provides an overview of source documentation.

CULTURE · LANGUAGE The concept of intellectual property and thus the rules governing plagiarism are not universal. In some other cultures, for instance, students may be encouraged to copy the words of scholars without acknowledgment in order to demonstrate their mastery of or respect for the scholars' work. In the United States, however, it is plagiarism to copy an author's work without quotation marks and a source citation. If you're unsure about plagiarism after reading this chapter, ask your instructor for advice.

54a   Beware of plagiarism from the Internet.

The Internet has made it easier to plagiarize than ever before, but it has also made plagiarism easier to catch.

Even honest students risk accidental plagiarism by downloading sources and importing portions into their drafts. Dishonest students may take advantage of downloading to steal others' work. They may also use the term-paper businesses on the Web, which offer both ready-made research and complete papers, usually for a fee. **Paying for research or a paper does not make it the buyer's work.** Anyone who submits someone else's work as his or her own is a plagiarist.

Students who plagiarize from the Internet both deprive themselves of an education in honest research and expose themselves to detection. Teachers can use search engines to locate specific phrases or sentences anywhere on the Web, including among scholarly publications, all kinds of Web sites, and term-paper collections. They can search the term-paper sites as easily as students can, looking for similarities with papers they've received. They can also use detection programs such as *Turnitin* that compare students' work with other work anywhere on the Internet, seeking matches as short as a few words.

Some instructors suggest that their students use plagiarism-detection programs to verify that their own work does not include accidental plagiarism, at least not from the Internet.

54b   Know what you need not acknowledge.

1 ▪ Your independent material

Your own observations, thoughts, compilations of facts, or experimental results—expressed in your words and format—do not require acknowledgment. You should describe the basis for your conclusions so that readers can evaluate your thinking, but you need not cite sources for them.

2 ▪ Common knowledge

Common knowledge consists of the standard information on a subject as well as folk literature and commonsense observations.

- **Standard information** includes the major facts of history, such as the dates of Charlemagne's rule as emperor of Rome (800–14). It does *not* include interpretations of facts, such as a historian's opinion that Charlemagne was sometimes needlessly cruel in extending his power.
- **Folk literature,** such as the fairy tale "Snow White," is popularly known and cannot be traced to a particular writer. Literature traceable to a writer is not folk literature, even if it is very familiar.

Checklist for avoiding plagiarism

Type of source

Are you using

- your own independent material,
- common knowledge, or
- someone else's independent material?

You must acknowledge someone else's material.

Quotations

- Do all quotations exactly match their sources? Check them.
- Have you inserted quotation marks around quotations that are run into your text?
- Have you shown omissions with ellipsis marks and additions with brackets?
- Does every quotation have a source citation?

Paraphrases and summaries

- Have you used your own words and sentence structures for every paraphrase and summary? If not, use quotation marks around the original author's words.
- Does every paraphrase and summary have a source citation?

The Web

- Have you obtained any necessary permission to use someone else's material on the Web?

Source citations

- Have you acknowledged every use of someone else's material in each place where you used it?
- Does your list of works cited include all the sources you have used?

- **Commonsense observations** are things most people know, such as that inflation is most troublesome for people with low and fixed incomes. However, an economist's argument about the effects of inflation on Chinese immigrants is *not* a commonsense observation.

  If you do not know a subject well enough to determine whether a piece of information is common knowledge, make a record of the source as you would for any other quotation, paraphrase, or summary. As you read more about the subject, the information may come up in other people's work without any source citation, in which case it is probably common knowledge. But if you are still in doubt when you finish your research, always acknowledge the source.

54c Know what you *must* acknowledge.

You must always acknowledge other people's independent material—that is, any facts or ideas that are not common knowledge or your own. The source may be anything, including a book, an article, a movie, an interview, a microfilmed document, a Web page, a newsgroup posting, or an opinion expressed on the radio. You must acknowledge summaries or paraphrases of ideas or facts as well as quotations of the language and format in which ideas or facts appear: wording, sentence structures, arrangement, and special graphics (such as a diagram). You must acknowledge another's material no matter how you use it, how much of it you use, or how often you use it.

1 ▪ Using copied language: Quotation marks and a source citation

The following example baldly plagiarizes the original quotation from Jessica Mitford's *Kind and Usual Punishment,* page 9. Without quotation marks or a source citation, the example matches Mitford's wording (underlined) and closely parallels her sentence structure:

Original quotation	"The character and mentality of the keepers may be of more importance in understanding prisons than the character and mentality of the kept."
Plagiarism	But the character of prison officials (the keepers) is of more importance in understanding prisons than the character of prisoners (the kept).

To avoid plagiarism, the writer has two options: (1) paraphrase and cite the source (see the revised examples opposite) or (2) use Mitford's actual words *in quotation marks* and *with a source citation* (here, in MLA style):

Revision (quotation)	According to one critic of the penal system, "The character and mentality of the keepers may be of more importance in understanding prisons than the character and mentality of the kept" (Mitford 9).

Even with a source citation and with a different sentence structure, the next example is still plagiarism because it uses some of Mitford's words (underlined) without quotation marks:

Plagiarism	According to one critic of the penal system, the psychology of the kept may say less about prisons than the psychology of the keepers (Mitford 9).
Revision (quotation)	According to one critic of the penal system, the psychology of "the kept" may say less about prisons than the psychology of "the keepers" (Mitford 9).

2 ■ Using paraphrase or summary: Your own words and sentence structure and a source citation

The example below changes the sentence structure of the original Mitford quotation, but it still uses Mitford's words (underlined) without quotation marks and without a source citation:

Plagiarism   In understanding prisons, we should know more about the character and mentality of the keepers than of the kept.

To avoid plagiarism, the writer has two options: (1) use quotation marks and cite the source (opposite) or (2) *use his or her own words* and still *cite the source* (because the idea is Mitford's, not the writer's):

Revision   Mitford holds that we may be able to learn more about
(paraphrase)   prisons from the psychology of the prison officials than from that of the prisoners (9).

Revision   We may understand prisons better if we focus on the
(paraphrase)   personalities and attitudes of the prison workers rather than those of the inmates (Mitford 9).

In the next example, the writer cites Mitford and does not use her words but still plagiarizes her sentence structure:

Plagiarism   One critic of the penal system maintains that the psychology of prison officials may be more informative about prisons than the psychology of prisoners (Mitford 9).

Revision   One critic of the penal system maintains that we may be
(paraphrase)   able to learn less from the psychology of prisoners than from the psychology of prison officials (Mitford 9).

Exercise 54.1   Recognizing plagiarism

The numbered items show various attempts to quote or paraphrase the following passage. Carefully compare each attempt with the original passage. Which attempts are plagiarized, inaccurate, or both, and which are acceptable? Why?

I would agree with the sociologists that psychiatric labeling is dangerous. Society can inflict terrible wounds by discrimination, and by confusing health with disease and disease with badness.
—George E. Vaillant, *Adaptation to Life,* p. 361

1. According to George Vaillant, society often inflicts wounds by using psychiatric labeling, confusing health, disease, and badness (361).
2. According to George Vaillant, "psychiatric labeling [such as 'homosexual' or 'schizophrenic'] is dangerous. Society can inflict terrible wounds by . . . confusing health with disease and disease with badness" (361).
3. According to George Vaillant, when psychiatric labeling discriminates between health and disease or between disease and badness, it can inflict wounds on those labeled (361).

4. Psychiatric labels can badly hurt those labeled, says George Vaillant, because they fail to distinguish among health, illness, and immorality (361).

5. Labels such as "homosexual" and "schizophrenic" can be hurtful when they fail to distinguish among health, illness, and immorality.

6. "I would agree with the sociologists that society can inflict terrible wounds by discrimination, and by confusing health with disease and disease with badness" (Vaillant 361).

54d   Take care with online sources.

Online sources are so accessible and so easy to download into your own documents that it may seem they are freely available, exempting you from the obligation to acknowledge them. They are not. Acknowledging online sources is somewhat trickier than acknowledging print sources, but no less essential. Further, if you are publishing your work online, you need to take account of sources' copyright restrictions as well.

1 ▪ Online sources in an unpublished project

When you use material from an online source in a print or online document to be distributed just to your class, your obligation to cite sources does not change: you must acknowledge someone else's independent material in whatever form you find it. With online sources, that obligation can present additional challenges:

- **Record complete publication information each time you consult an online source.** Online sources may change from one day to the next or even disappear entirely. See page 381 for the information to record, such as the publication date. Without the proper information, you *may not* use the source.
- **Acknowledge linked sites.** If you use not only a Web site but also one or more of its linked sites, you must acknowledge the linked sites as well. One person's use of a second person's work does not release you from the responsibility to cite the second work.
- **Seek the author's permission before using an e-mail message, blog contribution, or discussion-group posting.** Obtaining permission advises the author that his or her ideas are about to be distributed more widely and lets the author verify that you have not misrepresented the ideas.

2 ▪ Print and online sources in a Web composition

When you use material from print or online sources in a composition for the Web, you must not only acknowledge your sources but also take the additional precaution of observing copyright restrictions.

A Web site is a medium of publication just as a book or magazine is and so involves the same responsibility to obtain reprint permission from copyright holders. The exception is a password-protected site (such as a course site), which many copyright holders regard as private. You can find information about copyright holders and permissions on the copyright page of a print publication (following the title page) and on a page labeled something like "Terms of Use" on a Web site. If you don't see an explicit release for student use or publication on private Web sites, assume you must seek permission.

The legal convention of fair use allows an author to reprint a small portion of copyrighted material without obtaining the copyright holder's permission, as long as the author acknowledges the source. The online standards of fair use differ for print and online sources and are not fixed in either case. The guidelines below are conservative:

- **Print sources:** Quote without permission fewer than fifty words from an article or fewer than three hundred words from a book. You'll need the copyright holder's permission to use any longer quotation from an article or book; any quotation at all from a play, poem, or song; and any use of an entire work, such as a photograph, chart, or other illustration.
- **Online sources:** Quote without permission text that represents just a small portion of the whole—say, forty words out of three hundred. Follow the print guidelines above for plays, poems, songs, and illustrations, adding multimedia elements (audio or video clips) to the list of works that require reprint permission for any use.
- **Links:** You may need to seek permission to link your site to another one—for instance, if you rely on the linked site to substantiate your claims or to provide a multimedia element.

54e   Document sources carefully.

Every time you borrow the words, facts, or ideas of others, you must **document** the source—that is, supply a reference (or document) telling readers that you borrowed the material and where you borrowed it from.

Editors and teachers in most academic disciplines require special documentation formats (or styles) in their scholarly journals and in students' papers. All the styles share common features:

- **Citations in the text** signal that material is borrowed and refer readers to detailed information about the sources.
- **Detailed source information,** either in footnotes or at the end of the paper, tells how to locate the sources.

Together, the citations and detailed information allow readers to find each source and the place in it where borrowed material appears.

Aside from these essential similarities, the disciplines' documentation styles differ markedly in citation form, arrangement of source information, and other particulars. Each discipline's style reflects the needs of its practitioners for certain kinds of information presented in certain ways. For instance, the currency of a source is important in the social sciences, where studies build on and correct each other; thus in-text citations in the social sciences include a source's date of publication. In the humanities, however, currency is less important, so in-text citations do not include date of publication.

The disciplines' documentation formats are described in style guides, including those in the box below. This book presents the styles of the *MLA Handbook* and the *Publication Manual of the American Psychological Association*. In addition, at *mycomplab.com* you can find information about *The Chicago Manual of Style* (for the humanities) and *Scientific Style and Format: The CSE Manual for Authors, Editors, and Publishers* (for the natural sciences).

Style guides for documenting sources

Humanities

The Chicago Manual of Style. 15th ed. 2003. (See this book's Web site.)

A Manual for Writers of Research Papers, Theses, and Dissertations, by Kate L. Turabian, 7th ed., rev. Wayne C. Booth, Gregory G. Colomb, and Joseph M. Williams, 2007

MLA Handbook for Writers of Research Papers. 7th ed. 2009. (See pp. 437–78.)

Social sciences

American Anthropological Association. *AAA Style Guide.* 2003. www.aaanet .org/publications/guidelines.cfm.

American Political Science Association. *Style Manual for Political Science.* 2006.

Publication Manual of the American Psychological Association. 6th ed. 2009. (See pp. 491–509.)

American Sociological Association. *ASA Style Guide.* 3rd ed. 2007.

Linguistic Society of America. "LSA Style Sheet." Published every December in *LSA Bulletin.*

A Uniform System of Citation (law). 18th ed. 2005.

Sciences and mathematics

American Chemical Society. *ACS Style Guide: A Manual for Authors and Editors.* 3rd ed. 2006.

American Institute of Physics. *Style Manual for Guidance in the Preparation of Papers.* 4th ed. 1997.

American Medical Association Manual of Style. 10th ed. 2007.

Council of Science Editors. *Scientific Style and Format: The CSE Manual for Authors, Editors, and Publishers.* 7th ed. 2006.

Always ask your instructor which documentation style you should use. If your instructor does not require a particular style, use the one in this book that's appropriate for the discipline you're writing in. Do follow a single system for citing sources so that you provide all the necessary information in a consistent format.

Note Bibliography software—*Zotero, Refworks, Endnote,* and others—can help you format your source citations in the style of your choice. Always ask your instructors if you may use such software for your papers. The programs prompt you for needed information (author's name, book title, and so on) and then arrange, capitalize, and punctuate the information as required by the style. But no program can anticipate all varieties of source information or substitute for your own care and attention in giving your sources accurate and complete acknowledgment in the required form.

55a

55 Writing the Paper

What are the stages of writing research?

Like other kinds of writing, research writing involves focusing on a main idea, organizing ideas, expressing ideas in a draft, revising and editing drafts, and formatting the final paper. Because research writing draws on others' work, however, its stages also require attention to interpreting, integrating, and citing sources.

This chapter complements and extends the detailed discussion of the writing situation and the writing process in Chapters 1–5, which also include many tips for using a computer. If you haven't already done so, read Chapters 1–5 before this one.

55a Focus and organize the paper.

Before you begin using your source notes in a draft, give some thought to your main idea and your organization.

1 ▪ Thesis statement

You began research with a question about your subject (see pp. 376–77). Though that question may have evolved during research, you should be able to answer it once you've consulted most of your sources. Try to state that answer in a **thesis statement,** a claim that narrows your subject to a single idea. Here, for example, are the research question and thesis statement of Justin Malik, whose final paper appears on pages 483–89:

Research question
How can green consumerism help the environment?

Thesis statement
Although green consumerism can help the environment, consumerism itself is the root of some of the most pressing ecological problems we face. To make a real difference, we must consume less.

A precise thesis statement will give you a focus as you organize and draft your paper. For more on thesis statements, see pages 15–18.

2 ▪ Organization

To structure your paper, you'll need to synthesize, or forge relationships among ideas (see pp. 410–12). Here is one approach:

- **Arrange source information in categories.** Each group should correspond to a main section of your paper: a key idea of your own that supports the thesis.
- **Review your research journal** for connections between sources and other thoughts that can help you organize your paper.
- **Look objectively at your categories.** If some are skimpy, with little information, consider whether you should drop the categories or conduct more research to fill them out. If most of your information falls into one or two categories, consider whether they are too broad and should be divided. (If any of this rethinking affects your thesis statement, revise it accordingly.)
- **Within each group, distinguish between the main idea and the supporting ideas and evidence.** Only the support should come from your sources. The main idea should be your own.

See pages 19–23 for more on organizing a paper, including samples of both informal and formal outlines.

55b Draft, revise, and format the paper.

1 ▪ First draft

In drafting your paper, you do not have to proceed methodically from introduction to conclusion. Instead, draft in sections, beginning with the one you feel most confident about. Each section should center on a principal idea contributing to your thesis, a conclusion you have drawn from reading and responding to sources. Start the section by stating the idea; then support it with information, summaries, paraphrases, and quotations from your notes. Remember to insert source information from your notes as well.

- **Weave the sections together with transitions and other signposts.** As the sections of your paper develop, you will see relationships emerging among them. Spell these relationships out, and highlight them with transitions (see pp. 49–50 and 62–63). Headings may be appropriate to highlight your organization and signal direction. These signposts will help create a coherent whole.
- **Track source citations.** As you draft your paper, insert the source of each summary, paraphrase, and quotation in parentheses in the text—for instance, "(Frankel 42)," referring to page 42 in a work by Frankel. If you are conscientious about inserting these notes and carrying them through successive drafts, you will be less likely to plagiarize accidentally and you will have little difficulty documenting your sources in the final paper.

2 ▪ Revision and editing

For a complex project like a research paper, you'll certainly want to revise in at least two stages—first for thesis, structure, and other whole-paper issues, and then for clarity, grammar, and similar sentence-level issues. Chapter 5 supports this two-stage approach with checklists for revision (p. 30) and editing (p. 34). The box below provides additional steps to take when revising a research paper.

Checklist for revising a research paper

Assignment
How does the draft satisfy all of the criteria stated in your instructor's assignment?

Thesis statement
How well does your thesis statement describe your subject and your perspective as they emerged during drafting?

Structure
(Outlining your draft can help you see structure at a glance. See p. 29.)
How consistently does borrowed material illuminate and support—not lead and dominate—your own ideas? How well is the importance of ideas reflected in the emphasis they receive? Will the arrangement of ideas be clear to readers?

Evidence
Where might supporting evidence seem weak or irrelevant to readers?

Reasonableness and clarity
How reasonable will readers find your argument? (See pp. 107–16.) Where do you need to define terms or concepts that readers may not know or may dispute?

55b

3 ▪ Format

The final draft of your paper should conform to the document format recommended by your instructor or by the style guide of the discipline in which you are writing (see pp. 479–81). This book details two common formats: Modern Language Association (pp. 479–81) and American Psychological Association (pp. 509–12).

In any discipline you can use a computer to present your ideas effectively and attractively with readable type fonts, headings, illustrations, and other elements. See pages 66–74 for ideas.

55b

How do I cite sources and format papers in English and other humanities?

English, foreign languages, and some other humanities use the documentation style of the Modern Language Association, detailed in the *MLA Handbook for Writers of Research Papers* (7th ed., 2009). In MLA documentation style, you twice acknowledge the sources of borrowed material:

- In your text, a brief parenthetical citation adjacent to the borrowed material directs readers to a complete list of all the works you cite.
- At the end of your paper, the list of works cited includes complete bibliographical information for every source.

Every entry in the list of works cited has at least one corresponding citation in the text, and every in-text citation has a corresponding entry in the list of works cited.

This chapter describes MLA documentation: writing text citations (below), placing citations (p. 443), using supplementary notes (p. 445), and preparing the list of works cited (p. 445). A detailed discussion of MLA document format (p. 479) and a sample MLA paper (p. 481) conclude the chapter.

MLA
56a

56a Use MLA parenthetical citations in your text.

1 ▪ Citation formats

In-text citations of sources must include just enough information for the reader to locate the following:

- The *source* in your list of works cited.
- The *place* in the source where the borrowed material appears.

For any kind of source, you can usually meet both these requirements by providing the author's last name and (if the source uses them) the page numbers where the material appears. The reader can find the source in your list of works cited and find the borrowed material in the source itself.

The following models illustrate the basic text-citation forms and also forms for more unusual sources, such as those with no

mycomplab ▐

Visit *mycomplab.com* for more resources and
exercises on MLA documentation and format.

MLA parenthetical text citations

1. Author not named in your text *438*
2. Author named in your text *438*
3. A work with two or three authors *439*
4. A work with more than three authors *439*
5. A work by an author of two or more cited works *439*
6. An anonymous work *440*
7. A work with a corporate author *440*
8. A nonprint source *440*
9. A multivolume work *440*
10. An entire work or a work with no page or other reference numbers *441*
11. A work with numbered paragraphs or sections instead of pages *441*
12. An indirect source *441*
13. A literary work *442*
14. The Bible *443*
15. Two or more works in the same citation *443*

named author or no page numbers. See the box above for an index to all the models.

Note Models 1 and 2 show the direct relationship between what you include in your text and what you include in a parenthetical citation. If you do *not* name the author in your text, you include the name in parentheses before the page reference (model 1). If you *do* name the author in your text, you do not include the name in parentheses (model 2).

1. Author not named in your text

When you have not already named the author in your sentence, provide the author's last name and the page number(s), with no punctuation between them, in parentheses.

> One researcher concludes that "women impose a distinctive construction on moral problems, seeing moral dilemmas in terms of conflicting responsibilities" (Gilligan 105-06).

See model 6 for the form to use when the source does not have an author. And see models 10 and 11 for the forms to use when the source does not provide page numbers.

2. Author named in your text

When you have already given the author's name with the material you're citing, do not repeat it in the parenthetical citation. Give just the page number(s).

> Carol Gilligan concludes that "women impose a distinctive construction on moral problems, seeing moral dilemmas in terms of conflicting responsibilities" (105-06).

See model 6 for the form to use when the source does not list an author. And see models 10 and 11 for the forms to use when the source does not provide page numbers.

3. A work with two or three authors

If the source has two or three authors, give all their last names in the text or in the citation. Separate two authors' names with and:

> As Frieden and Sagalyn observe, "The poor and the minorities were the leading victims of highway and renewal programs" (29).

> According to one study, "The poor and the minorities were the leading victims of highway and renewal programs" (Frieden and Sagalyn 29).

With three authors, add commas and also and before the final name:

> The textbook by Wilcox, Ault, and Agee discusses the "ethical dilemmas in public relations practice" (125).

> One textbook discusses the "ethical dilemmas in public relations practice" (Wilcox, Ault, and Agee 125).

4. A work with more than three authors

If the source has more than three authors, you may list all their last names or use only the first author's name followed by et al. (the abbreviation for the Latin *et alii,* "and others"). The choice depends on what you do in your list of works cited (see p. 447).

> Increased competition means that employees of public relations firms may find their loyalty stretched in more than one direction (Cameron et al. 417).

> Increased competition means that employees of public relations firms may find their loyalty stretched in more than one direction (Cameron, Wilcox, Reber, and Shin 417).

5. A work by an author of two or more cited works

If your list of works cited includes two or more works by the same author, then your citation must tell the reader which of the author's works you are referring to. Give the title either in the text or in a parenthetical citation. In a parenthetical citation, give the full title only if it is brief; otherwise, shorten the title to the first one, two, or three main words (excluding *A, An,* or *The*).

> At about age seven, children begin to use appropriate gestures with their stories (Gardner, *Arts* 144-45).

The full title of Gardner's book is *The Arts and Human Development* (see the works-cited entry on p. 447). This shortened title is italicized because the source is a book.

6. An anonymous work

For a work with no named author or editor (whether an individual or an organization), use a full or shortened version of the title, as explained in model 5. In your list of works cited, you alphabetize an anonymous work by the first main word of the title (see p. 450), so the first word of a shortened title should be the same. The following citations refer to an unsigned source titled "The Right to Die." The title appears in quotation marks because the source is a periodical article.

One article notes that a death-row inmate may demand his own execution to achieve a fleeting notoriety ("Right" 16).

"The Right to Die" notes that a death-row inmate may demand execution to achieve a fleeting notoriety (16).

If two or more anonymous works have the same title, distinguish them with additional information in the text citation, such as the publication date.

7. A work with a corporate author

Some works list as author a government body, association, committee, company, or other group. Cite such a work by the organization's name. If the name is long, work it into the text to avoid an intrusive parenthetical citation.

A 2008 report by the Hawaii Department of Education provides evidence of an increase in graduation rates (12).

8. A nonprint source

Cite a nonprint source such as a Web page or a DVD just as you would any other source. If your works-cited entry lists the source under the name of an author or other contributor, use that name in the text citation. The following example cites an authored source that has page numbers.

Business forecasts for the fourth quarter tended to be optimistic (White 4).

If your works-cited entry lists the work under its title, cite the work by title in your text, as explained in model 6. The next example cites an entire work (a film on DVD) and gives the title in the text, so it omits a parenthetical citation (see model 10).

Many decades after its release, *Citizen Kane* is still remarkable for its rich black-and-white photography.

9. A multivolume work

If you consulted only one volume of a multivolume work, your list of works cited will say so (see model 30 on p. 459), and you can treat the volume as you would any book.

If you consulted more than one volume of a multivolume work, give the appropriate volume in your text citation.

> After issuing the Emancipation Proclamation, Lincoln said, "What I did, I did after very full deliberations, and under a very heavy and solemn sense of responsibility" (5: 438).

The number 5 indicates the volume from which the quotation was taken; the number 438 indicates the page number in that volume. When the author's name appears in such a citation, place it before the volume number with no punctuation: (Lincoln 5: 438).

If you are referring generally to an entire volume of a multivolume work and are not citing specific page numbers, add the abbreviation vol. before the volume number as in (vol. 5) or (Lincoln, vol. 5) (note the comma after the author's name). Then readers will not misinterpret the volume number as a page number.

10. An entire work or a work with no page or other reference numbers

When you cite an entire work rather than a part of it, you may omit any page or other reference number. If the work you cite has an author, try to work the author's name into your text. You will not need a parenthetical citation then, but the source still must appear in your list of works cited.

> Boyd deals with the need to acknowledge and come to terms with our fear of nuclear technology.

Use the same format when you cite a specific passage from a work with no page, paragraph, or other reference numbers, such as a Web source.

If the author's name does not appear in your text, put it in a parenthetical citation.

> Almost 20 percent of commercial banks have been audited for the practice (Friis).

11. A work with numbered paragraphs or sections instead of pages

Some electronic sources number each paragraph or section instead of each page. In citing passages in these sources, give the paragraph or section number(s) and distinguish them from page numbers: after the author's name, put a comma, a space, and par. (one paragraph), pars. (more than one paragraph), sec., or secs.

> Twins reared apart report similar feelings (Palfrey, pars. 6-7).

12. An indirect source

When you want to use a quotation that is already in quotation marks—indicating that the author you are reading is quoting someone else—try to find the original source and quote directly from it. If you can't find the original source, then your citation must indicate that your quotation of it is indirect. In the following citation, qtd. in ("quoted in") says that Davino was quoted by Boyd.

> George Davino maintains that "even small children have vivid ideas about nuclear energy" (qtd. in Boyd 22).

The list of works cited then includes only Boyd (the work consulted), not Davino.

13. A literary work

Novels, plays, and poems are often available in many editions, so your instructor may ask you to provide information that will help readers find the passage you cite no matter what edition they consult.

- **Novels:** The page number comes first, followed by a semicolon and then information on the appropriate part or chapter of the work.

  > Toward the end of James's novel, Maggie suddenly feels "the thick breath of the definite—which was the intimate, the immediate, the familiar, as she hadn't had them for so long" (535; pt. 6, ch. 41).

- **Poems that are not divided into parts:** You may omit the page number and supply the line number(s) for the quotation. To prevent confusion with page numbers, precede the numbers with line or lines in the first citation; then use just the numbers.

  > In Shakespeare's Sonnet 73 the speaker identifies with the trees of late autumn, "Bare ruined choirs, where late the sweet birds sang" (line 4). "In me," Shakespeare writes, "thou seest the glowing of such fire / That on the ashes of his youth doth lie . . ." (9-10).

  (See pp. 125–27 for a sample paper on a poem.)

- **Verse plays and poems that are divided into parts:** Omit a page number and cite the appropriate part—act (and scene, if any), canto, book, and so on—plus the line number(s). Use Arabic numerals for parts, including acts and scenes (3.4), unless your instructor specifies Roman numerals (III.iv).

  > Later in Shakespeare's *King Lear* the disguised Edgar says, "The prince of darkness is a gentleman" (3.4.147).

- **Prose plays:** Provide the page number followed by the act and scene, if any. For an example, see the reference to *Death of a Salesman* on page 445.

14. The Bible

When you cite passages of the Bible in parentheses, abbreviate the title of any book longer than four letters—for instance, Gen. (Genesis), 1 Sam. (1 Samuel), Ps. (Psalms), Prov. (Proverbs), Matt. (Matthew), Rom. (Romans). Then give the chapter and verse(s) in Arabic numerals.

> According to the Bible, at Babel God "did . . . confound the language of all the earth" (Gen. 11.9).

15. Two or more works in the same citation

When you refer to more than one work in a single parenthetical citation, separate the references with a semicolon.

> Two recent articles point out that a computer badly used can be less efficient than no computer at all (Gough and Hall 201; Richards 162).

Since long citations in the text can distract the reader, you may choose to cite several or more works in an endnote or footnote rather than in the text. See page 445.

2 ▪ Placement and punctuation of parenthetical citations

The following guidelines will help you place and punctuate text citations to distinguish between your own and your sources' ideas and to make your own text readable. See also pages 419–22 on editing quotations and using signal phrases to integrate source material into your sentences.

Where to place citations

Position text citations to accomplish two goals:

- **Make it clear exactly where your borrowing begins and ends.**
- **Keep the citation as unobtrusive as possible.**

You can accomplish both goals by placing the parenthetical citation at the end of the sentence element containing the borrowed material. This sentence element may be a phrase or a clause, and it may begin, interrupt, or conclude the sentence. Usually, as in the following examples, the element ends with a punctuation mark.

> The inflation rate might climb as high as 30 percent (Kim 164), an increase that could threaten the small nation's stability.

> The inflation rate, which might climb as high as 30 percent (Kim 164), could threaten the small nation's stability.

> The small nation's stability could be threatened by its inflation rate, which, one source predicts, might climb as high as 30 percent (Kim 164).

In the last example the addition of one source predicts clarifies that Kim is responsible only for the inflation-rate prediction, not for the statement about stability.

When your paraphrase or summary of a source runs longer than a sentence, clarify the boundaries by using the author's name in the first sentence and placing the parenthetical citation at the end of the last sentence.

> Juliette Kim studied the effects of acutely high inflation in several South American and African countries since World War II. She discovered that a major change in government accompanied or followed the inflationary period in 56 percent of cases (22-23).

When you cite two or more sources in the same paragraph, position authors' names and parenthetical citations so that readers can see who said what. In the following example, the beginnings and ends of sentences clearly mark the different sources.

> Schools use computers extensively for drill-and-practice exercises, in which students repeat specific skills such as spelling words, using the multiplication facts, or, at a higher level, doing chemistry problems. But many education experts criticize such exercises for boring students and failing to engage their critical thinking and creativity. Jane M. Healy, a noted educational psychologist and teacher, takes issue with "interactive" software for children as well as drill-and-practice software, arguing that "some of the most popular 'educational' software . . . may be damaging to independent thinking, attention, and motivation" (20). Another education expert, Harold Wenglinsky of the Educational Testing Service, found in a well-regarded 1998 study that fourth and eighth graders who used computers frequently, including for drill and practice, actually did worse on tests than their peers who used computers less often (*Does It Compute?* 21). In a later article, Wenglinsky concludes that "the quantity of use matters far less than the quality of use." In schools, he says, high-quality computer work, involving critical thinking, is still rare ("In Search" 17).

How to punctuate citations

Generally place a parenthetical citation *before* any punctuation required by your sentence. If the borrowed material is a quotation, place the citation *between* the closing quotation mark and the punctuation:

> Spelling argues that during the 1970s American automobile manufacturers met consumer needs "as well as could be expected" (26), but not everyone agrees with him.

The exception is a quotation ending in a question mark or exclamation point. Then use the appropriate punctuation inside the closing quotation mark, and follow the quotation with the text citation and a period.

> "Of what use is genius," Emerson asks, "if the organ . . . cannot find a focal distance within the actual horizon of human life?" ("Experience" 60). Mad genius is no genius.

When a citation appears at the end of a quotation set off from the text, place it one space *after* the punctuation ending the quotation. Do not use additional punctuation with the citation or quotation marks around the quotation.

> In Arthur Miller's *Death of a Salesman,* the most poignant defense of Willie Loman comes from his wife, Linda:
>
>> He's not the finest character that ever lived. But he's a human being, and a terrible thing is happening to him. So attention must be paid. He's not to be allowed to fall into his grave like an old dog. Attention, attention must finally be paid to such a person. (56; act 1)

(This citation of a play includes the act number as well as the page number. See p. 442.)

3 ▪ Footnotes or endnotes in special circumstances

Footnotes or endnotes may replace parenthetical citations when you cite several sources at once, when you comment on a source, or when you provide information that does not fit easily in the text. Signal a footnote or endnote in your text with a numeral raised above the appropriate line. Then write a note with the same numeral.

> Text   At least five studies have confirmed these results.[1]

> Note   1. Abbott and Winger 266-68; Casner 27; Hoyenga 78-79; Marino 36; Tripp, Tripp, and Walk 179-83.

In a note, the numeral is not raised, is indented one-half inch, and is followed by a period and a space. If the note appears as a footnote, place it at the bottom of the page on which the citation appears, set it off from the text with quadruple spacing, and single-space the note itself. If the note appears as an endnote, place it in numerical order with the other endnotes on a page between the text and the list of works cited. Double-space all the endnotes.

56b   Prepare an MLA list of works cited.

At the end of your paper, a list titled Works Cited includes all the sources you quoted, paraphrased, or summarized in your paper. (If your instructor asks you to include sources you examined but did not cite, title the list Works Consulted.)

Follow this format for the list of works cited:

- **Arrange your sources in alphabetical order** by the last name of the author. If an author is not given in the source, alphabetize the source by the first main word of the title (excluding *A, An,* or *The*).
- **Type the entire list double-spaced,** both within and between entries.
- **Indent the second and subsequent lines of each entry one-half inch from the left.** Your word processor can format this so-called hanging indent automatically.

MLA works-cited page

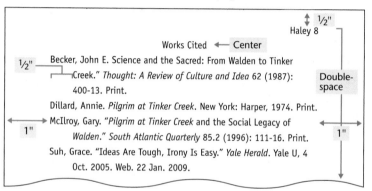

For a complete list of works cited, see the paper by Justin Malik (p. 490).

An index to all the following models appears on pages 448–49. Use your best judgment in adapting the models to your particular sources. If you can't find a model that exactly matches a source you used, locate and follow the closest possible match. You will certainly need to combine formats—for instance, drawing on model 2 ("Two or three authors") and model 10 ("An article in a national newspaper") for a national newspaper article with two authors.

Note MLA style now requires that you give the publication medium for every source you cite, such as print, Web, DVD, or television. For example, if you consulted an article in a print magazine, your works-cited entry should list the medium as Print. If you consulted a book on the Web, your works-cited entry should list the medium as Web. The models here all conform to this standard.

1 ▪ Listing authors

The following models show how to handle authors' names in citing any kind of source.

1. One author

Ehrenreich, Barbara. *Dancing in the Streets: A History of Collective Joy.* New
York: Metropolitan-Holt, 2006. Print.

Give the author's full name—last name first, a comma, first name,
and any middle name or initial. Omit any title, such as *Dr.* or *PhD.*
End the name with a period. If your source lists an editor as author,
see model 22, page 455.

2. Two or three authors

Lifton, Robert Jay, and Greg Mitchell. *Who Owns Death: Capital Punishment,*
the American Conscience, and the End of Executions. New York: Morrow,
2000. Print.

Wilcox, Dennis L., Phillip H. Ault, and Warren K. Agee. *Public Relations: Strate-*
gies and Tactics. 8th ed. New York: Irwin, 2006. Print.

Give the authors' names in the order provided on the title page. Re-
verse the first and last names of the first author *only,* not of any
other authors. Separate two authors' names with a comma and and;
separate three authors' names with commas and with and before the
third name. If your source lists two or three editors as authors, see
model 22, page 455.

3. More than three authors

Cameron, Glen T., Dennis L. Wilcox, Bryan H. Reber, and Jae-Hwa Shin. *Public*
Relations Today: Managing Competition and Conflict. New York: Pearson,
2007. Print.

Cameron, Glen T., et al. *Public Relations Today: Managing Competition and Con-*
flict. New York: Pearson, 2007. Print.

You may, but need not, give all authors' names if the work has more
than three authors. If you do not give all names, provide the name of
the first author only and then add a comma and the abbreviation et al.
(for the Latin *et alii,* meaning "and others"). If your source lists more
than three editors as authors, see model 22, page 455.

4. The same author(s) for two or more works

Gardner, Howard. *The Arts and Human Development.* New York: Wiley, 1973. Print.

---. *Five Minds for the Future.* Boston: Harvard Business School P, 2007. Print.

Give the author's name only in the first entry. For the second and
any subsequent works by the same author, substitute three hyphens
for the author's name, followed by a period. Note that the three hyphens stand for *exactly* the same name or names. If the second
Gardner source were by Gardner and somebody else, both names
would have to be given in full.

(continued on p. 450)

MLA

56b

MLA works-cited models

MLA

56b

(continued from p. 447)

Place an entry or entries using three hyphens immediately after the entry that names the author. Within the set of entries by the same author, arrange the sources alphabetically by the first main word of the title, as with *Arts* and then *Five* in the examples on page 447.

If you cite two or more sources that list as author(s) exactly the same editor(s), follow the hyphens with a comma and ed. or eds. as appropriate. (See model 22, p. 455.)

5. A corporate author

Vault Technologies. *Turnkey Parking Solutions*. Salt Lake City: Mills, 2008. Print.

Corporate authors include institutions, government bodies, companies, and other groups. List the name of the group as author when a source gives only that name and not an individual's name.

6. Author not named (anonymous)

The Dorling Kindersley World Reference Atlas. London: Dorling, 2007. Print.

List a work that names no author—neither an individual nor a group—by its full title. If the work is a book, italicize the title. If the work is a periodical article or other short work, enclose the title in quotation marks:

"Let the Horse Race Begin." *Time* 31 Mar. 2008: 22. Print.

Alphabetize the work by the title's first main word, excluding *A*, *An*, or *The* (*Dorling* in the first example and Let in the second).

2 ▪ Listing periodical print sources

Print periodicals include scholarly journals, newspapers, and magazines that are published at regular intervals (quarterly, monthly, weekly, or daily). To cite more than one author, two or more articles by the same author, a corporate author, or an article with no named author, see models 1–6.

Note The treatment of volume and issue numbers and publication dates varies depending on the kind of periodical being cited, as the models indicate. For the distinction between journals and magazines, see page 388.

Articles in scholarly journals

7. An article in a journal with volume and issue numbers (print)

Bee, Robert. "The Importance of Preserving Paper-Based Artifacts in a Digital Age." *Library Quarterly* 78.2 (2008): 174-94. Print.

The facing page shows the basic format for an article in a print journal and the location of the required information in the journal.

Format for a print journal article

① Bee, Robert. ② "The Importance of Preserving Paper-Based Artifacts in a Digital Age."
③ *Library Quarterly* ④ 78.2 ⑤ (2008): ⑥ 179-94. ⑦ Print.

Journal cover

⑦ **Medium.** Give the medium of the article, Print, followed by a period.

THE
LIBRARY
QVARTERLY

③ **Title of periodical,** in italics. Omit any *A, An,* or *The* from the beginning of the title. Do not end with a period.

④ **Volume and issue numbers,** in Arabic numerals, separated by a period. Do not add a period after the issue number.

⑤ **Year of publication,** in parentheses and followed by a colon.

VOLUME 78 · APRIL 2008 · NUMBER 2

② **Title of article,** in quotation marks. Give the full title and any subtitle, separating them with a colon. End the title with a period inside the final quotation mark.

First page of article

THE IMPORTANCE OF PRESERVING PAPER-BASED ARTIFACTS IN A
DIGITAL AGE

Robert Bee[1]

The preservation of paper-based artifacts is an essential issue for col
agement in academic libraries. In recent years, the library science pr

① **Author.** Give the full name—last name first, a comma, first name, and any middle name or initial. Omit *Dr., PhD,* or any other title. End the name with a period.

[*Library Quarterly*, vol. 78, no. 2, pp. 179–194]
© 2008 by The University of Chicago. All rights reserved.
0024-2519/2008/7802-0002$10.00

179

⑥ **Inclusive page numbers of article,** without "pp." Provide only as many digits in the last number as needed for clarity, usually two.

8. An article in a journal with only issue numbers (print)

Rymhs, Deena. "David Collier's *Surviving Saskatoon* and New Comics." *Canadian
    Literature* 194 (2007): 75-92. Print.

If a scholarly journal numbers only issues, not volumes, give the
issue number alone after the journal title.

9. An abstract of a journal article or a dissertation (print)

Lever, Janet. "Sex Differences in the Games Children Play." *Social Problems*
    23.2 (1996): 478-87. *Psychological Abstracts* 63.5 (1996): item 1431.
    Print.

For an abstract of an article, first provide the publication information for the article, following model 7. Then give the information for
the abstract. If the abstract publisher lists abstracts by item rather
than page number, add item before the number. Add Abstract after the
original publication information if the title of the abstracts journal
does not indicate that your source is an abstract. (See model 65, p.
472, for an example.)

For an abstract appearing in *Dissertation Abstracts* (*DA*) or *Dissertation Abstracts International* (*DAI*), give the author's name and the
title, Diss. (for "Dissertation"), the institution granting the author's degree, the date of the dissertation, and the publication information.

Steciw, Steven K. "Alterations to the Pessac Project of Le Corbusier." Diss.
    U of Cambridge, England, 1986. *DAI* 46.10 (1986): 565C. Print.

See also model 40 on page 462 (entire dissertation), model 63 on
page 472 (abstract on the Web), and model 65 on page 472 (abstract
in an online database).

Note Most instructors expect you to consult and cite full articles, not abstracts. See page 390.

Articles in newspapers

10. An article in a national newspaper (print)

Rohter, Larry. "Is Slam in Danger of Going Soft?" *New York Times* 3 June 2009,
    natl. ed.: C1+. Print.

Give the author, the title of the article, and then the title of the
newspaper as it appears on the first page (but without any *A*, *An*, or
The). Follow the newspaper title with the day, the month, and the
year of publication. (Abbreviate all months except May, June, and
July.) If the newspaper lists an edition at the top of the first page, include it after the date (see natl. ed. above). If the newspaper is divided
into sections that are lettered, provide the section designation before the page number when the newspaper does the same: C1+. (The

plus sign indicates that the article continues on a later page.) If the newspaper is divided into numbered or titled sections, provide the section designation before the colon—for instance, sec. 1: 3 or State and Local sec.: 4+. End with the medium, Print.

11. An article in a local newspaper (print)

Gilbert, Ellen. "Township Passes Barebones Budget." *Town Topics* [Princeton]
    20 May 2009: 1+. Print.

If the city of publication does not appear in the title of a local newspaper, follow the title with the city name, not italicized, in brackets.

Articles in magazines

12. An article in a weekly or biweekly magazine (print)

Mayer, Jane. "The Hard Cases." *New Yorker* 23 Feb. 2009: 38-45. Print.

Give the author, title of the article, and title of the magazine. Follow the magazine title with the day, the month, and the year of publication. (Abbreviate all months except May, June, and July.) Don't place the date in parentheses, and don't provide a volume or issue number. Give the page numbers of the article and the medium, Print.

13. An article in a monthly or bimonthly magazine (print)

Parker, James. "Don't Fear the Reaper." *Atlantic Monthly* Apr. 2009: 36-37.
    Print.

Follow the magazine title with the month and the year of publication. (Abbreviate all months except May, June, and July.) Don't place the date in parentheses, and don't provide a volume or issue number. Give the page numbers of the article and the medium, Print.

Reviews, editorials, letters to the editor, interviews

14. A review (print)

Glasswell, Kathryn, and George Kamberelis. "Drawing and Redrawing the Map
    of Writing Studies." Rev. of *Handbook of Writing Research,* by Charles A.
    MacArthur, Steve Graham, and Jill Fitzgerald. *Reading Research Quarterly*
    42.2 (2007): 304-23. Print.

Rev. is an abbreviation for "Review." The names of the authors of the work being reviewed follow the title of the work, a comma, and by. If the review has no title of its own, then Rev. of and the title of the reviewed work immediately follow the name of the reviewer.

15. An editorial (print)

"A Healthy Tax." Editorial. *New York Times* 3 June 2009, natl. ed.: A22. Print.

For an editorial with no named author, begin with the title and add the word Editorial after the title, as in the example. For an editorial with a named author, start with his or her name and then proceed as in the example.

16. A letter to the editor (print)

Fidrmuc, Jan, and Jarko Fidrmuc. "Language and Trade." Letter. *Economist*
      7 Mar. 2009: 23. Print.

Add the word Letter after the title, if there is one, or after the author's name.

17. An interview (print)

Aloni, Shulamit. Interview. *Palestine-Israel Journal of Politics, Economics, and Culture* 14.4 (2007): 63-68. Print.

Begin with the name of the person interviewed. If the interview does not have a title (as in the example), add Interview after the name. (Replace this description with the title if there is one.) You may also add the name of the interviewer if you know it—for example, Interview by Benson Wright. See model 75 (p. 475) to cite a broadcast interview or an interview you conduct yourself.

MLA
56b

Articles in series or in special issues

18. An article in a series (print)

Kleinfeld, N. R. "Living at an Epicenter of Diabetes, Defiance, and Despair."
      New York Times 10 Jan. 2006, natl. ed.: A1+. Print. Pt. 2 of a series,
      Bad Blood, begun 9 Jan. 2006.

Cite an article in a series following a model on pages 450–53 (scholarly journal, newspaper, or magazine). If you wish, end the entry with a description to indicate that the article is part of a series.

19. An article in a special issue (print)

Rubini, Monica, and Michela Menegatti. "Linguistic Bias in Personnel Selection." *Celebrating Two Decades of Linguistic Bias Research.* Ed. Robbie
      M. Sutton and Karen M. Douglas. Spec. issue of *Journal of Language and Social Psychology* 27.2 (2008): 168-81. Print.

Cite an article in a special issue of a periodical by starting with the author and title of the article. Follow with the title of the special issue, Ed., and the names of the issue's editor(s). Add Spec. issue of before the periodical title. Conclude with publication information, using the appropriate model on pages 450–53 for a journal or magazine.

3 ▪ Listing nonperiodical print sources

Nonperiodical print sources are works that are not published at regular intervals, such as books, government publications, and pamphlets. To cite more than one author, two or more articles by the same author, a corporate author, or a source with no named author, see models 1–6.

Books

20. Basic format for a book (print)

Lahiri, Jhumpa. *Unaccustomed Earth*. New York: Knopf, 2008. Print.

The next page shows the basic format for a book and the location of the required information in the book. When other information is required, put it between the author's name and the title or between the title and the publication information, as in the following models.

21. A second or subsequent edition (print)

Bolinger, Dwight L. *Aspects of Language*. 3rd ed. New York: Harcourt, 1981.
    Print.

For any edition after the first, place the edition number after the title. (If an editor's name follows the title, place the edition number after the name. See model 26.) Use the appropriate designation for editions that are named or dated rather than numbered—for instance, Rev. ed. for "Revised edition."

22. A book with an editor (print)

Holland, Merlin, and Rupert Hart-Davis, eds. *The Complete Letters of Oscar
    Wilde*. New York: Holt, 2000. Print.

Handle editors' names like authors' names (models 1–4), but add a comma and the abbreviation ed. (one editor) or eds. (two or more editors) after the last editor's name.

23. A book with an author and an editor (print)

Mumford, Lewis. *The City in History*. Ed. Donald L. Miller. New York: Pantheon,
    1986. Print.

When citing the work of the author, give his or her name first, and give the editor's name after the title, preceded by Ed. (singular only, meaning "Edited by"). When citing the work of the editor, use model 22 for a book with an editor, adding By and the author's name after the title:

Miller, Donald L., ed. *The City in History*. By Lewis Mumford. New York:
    Pantheon, 1986. Print.

Format for a print book

Lahiri, Jhumpa. *Unaccustomed Earth*. New York: Knopf, 2008. Print.

①②③④⑤⑥

Title page

Unaccustomed Earth

Jhumpa Lahiri

Alfred A. Knopf   New York • Toronto 2008

② **Title**, in italics. Give the full title and any subtitle, separating them with a colon. End the title with a period.

① **Author.** Give the full name—last name first, a comma, first name, and any middle name or initial. Omit *Dr., PhD,* or any other title. End the name with a period.

④ **Publisher's name.** Shorten most publishers' names ("UP" for University Press, "Little" for Little, Brown). Give both imprint and publisher's names when they appear on the title page: e.g., "Vintage-Random" for Vintage Books and Random House.

③ **City of publication.** Precede the publisher's name with its city, followed by a colon. Use only the first city if the title page lists more than one.

⑥ **Medium.** Give the medium of the book, Print, followed by a period.

⑤ **Date of publication.** If the date doesn't appear on the title page, look for it on the next page. End the date with a period.

24. A book with a translator (print)

Alighieri, Dante. *The Inferno*. Trans. John Ciardi. New York: NAL, 1971.
    Print.

When citing the work of the author, as in the preceding example, give his or her name first, and give the translator's name after the title, preceded by Trans. ("Translated by").

When citing the work of the translator, give his or her name first, followed by a comma and trans. Follow the title with By and the author's name:

> Ciardi, John, trans. *The Inferno*. By Dante Alighieri. New York: NAL, 1971.
>   Print.

When a book you cite by author has a translator *and* an editor, give their names in the order used on the book's title page.

25. An anthology (print)

> Kennedy, X. J., and Dana Gioia, eds. *Literature: An Introduction to Fiction,*
>   *Poetry, and Drama*. 11th ed. New York: Longman, 2010. Print.

Cite an entire anthology only when citing the work of the editor or editors or when your instructor permits cross-referencing like that shown in model 27. Give the name of the editor or editors (followed by ed. or eds.) and then the title of the anthology.

26. A selection from an anthology (print)

> Mason, Bobbie Ann. "Shiloh." *Literature: An Introduction to Fiction, Poetry,*
>   *and Drama*. Ed. X. J. Kennedy and Dana Gioia. 11th ed. New York:
>   Longman, 2010. 569-79. Print.

This listing adds the following to the anthology entry in model 25: author of selection, title of selection (in quotation marks), and inclusive page numbers for the selection (without the abbreviation "pp."). If you wish, you may also supply the original date of publication for the work you are citing, after its title. See model 32 on page 459.

If the work you cite comes from a collection of works by one author that has no editor, use the following form:

> Auden, W. H. "Family Ghosts." *The Collected Poetry of W. H. Auden*. New York:
>   Random, 1945. 132-33. Print.

If the work you cite is a scholarly article that was previously printed elsewhere, provide the complete information for the earlier publication of the piece, followed by Rpt. in ("Reprinted in") and the information for the source in which you found the piece:

> Molloy, Francis C. "The Suburban Vision in John O'Hara's Short Stories."
>   *Critique: Studies in Modern Fiction* 25.2 (1984): 101-13. Rpt. in *Short*
>   *Story Criticism: Excerpts from Criticism of the Works of Short Fiction*
>   *Writers*. Ed. David Segal. Vol. 15. Detroit: Gale, 1989. 287-92. Print.

27. Two or more selections from the same anthology (print)

Cisneros, Sandra. "The House on Mango Street." Kennedy and Gioia 518-19.

Kennedy, X. J., and Dana Gioia, eds. *Literature: An Introduction to Fiction,*
Poetry, and Drama. 11th ed. New York: Longman, 2010. Print.

Merwin, W. S. "For the Anniversary of My Death." Kennedy and Gioia 834.

Stevens, Wallace. "Thirteen Ways of Looking at a Blackbird." Kennedy and
Gioia 838-40.

When you are citing more than one selection from the same anthology, your instructor may allow you to avoid repetition by giving the anthology information in full (the Kennedy and Gioia entry) and then simply cross-referencing it in entries for the works you used. Thus the Cisneros, Merwin, and Stevens examples replace full publication information with Kennedy and Gioia and the appropriate pages in that book. Note that each entry appears in its proper alphabetical place among other works cited. Because each entry cross-references the Kennedy anthology, the medium is not required.

28. An article in a reference work (print)

"Reckon." *Merriam-Webster's Collegiate Dictionary.* 11th ed. 2008. Print.

Wenner, Manfred W. "Arabia." *The New Encyclopaedia Britannica: Macropaedia.*
15th ed. 2007. Print.

List an article in a reference work by its title (first example) unless the article is signed (second example). For works with entries arranged alphabetically, you need not include volume or page numbers.

For works that are widely used and often revised, like those above, you may omit the editors' names and all publication information except any edition number, the publication year, and the medium. For works that are specialized—with narrow subjects and audiences—give full publication information:

"Hungarians in America." *The Ethnic Almanac.* Ed. Stephanie Bernardo Johns.
6th ed. New York: Doubleday, 2002. 121-23. Print.

See also models 48 (p. 467) and 68 (p. 473), respectively, to cite reference works appearing on the Web or on a CD-ROM or DVD-ROM.

29. An illustrated book or graphic narrative (print)

Wilson, G. Willow. *Cairo.* Illus. M. K. Perker. New York: Vertigo-DC Comics,
2005. Print.

When citing the work of the writer of a graphic narrative or illustrated book, follow the example above: author's name, title, Illus. ("Illustrated by"), and the illustrator's name. When citing the work of an illustrator, list his or her name first, followed by a comma and illus. ("illustrator"). After the title and By, list the author's name:

Williams, Garth, illus. *Charlotte's Web.* By E. B. White. 1952. New York: Harper,

    1999. Print.

30. A multivolume work (print)

Lincoln, Abraham. *The Collected Works of Abraham Lincoln.* Ed. Roy P. Basler.

    Vol. 5. New Brunswick: Rutgers UP, 1953. Print. 8 vols.

If you use only one volume of a multivolume work, give that volume number before the publication information (Vol. 5 in the preceding example). You may add the total number of volumes at the end of the entry (8 vols. in the example).

If you use two or more volumes of a multivolume work, give the work's total number of volumes before the publication information (8 vols. in the following example). Your text citation will indicate which volume you are citing (see p. 441).

Lincoln, Abraham. *The Collected Works of Abraham Lincoln.* Ed. Roy P. Basler.

    8 vols. New Brunswick: Rutgers UP, 1953. Print.

If you cite a multivolume work published over a period of years, give the inclusive years as the publication date: for instance, Cambridge: Harvard UP, 1978-90.

31. A series (print)

Bergman, Ingmar. *The Seventh Seal.* New York: Simon, 1995. Print. Mod. Film

    Scripts Ser. 12.

Place the name of the series (not quoted or italicized) at the end of the entry, followed by a period, a series number (if any), and another period. Abbreviate common words such as *modern* and *series.*

32. A republished book (print)

James, Henry. *The Bostonians.* 1886. New York: Penguin, 2001. Print.

Republished books include books reissued under new titles and paperbound editions of books originally released in hard covers. Place the original publication date (but not the place of publication or the publisher's name) after the title, and then provide the full publication information for the source you are using. If the book was originally published under a different title, add this title after Rpt. of ("Reprint of") at the end of the entry (after Print) and move the original publication date after the title—for example, Rpt. of *Thomas Hardy: A Life.* 1941.

33. The Bible (print)

The Bible. Print. King James Vers.

The Holy Bible. Trans. Ronald Youngblood et al. Grand Rapids: Zondervan,

    1984. Print. New Intl. Vers.

MLA

56b

When citing a standard version of the Bible (first example), do not italicize the title or the name of the version at the end. You need not provide publication information. For an edition of the Bible (second example), italicize the title, provide editors' and/or translators' names, give full publication information, and add the version name at the end.

34. A book with a title in its title (print)

Eco, Umberto. *Postscript to* The Name of the Rose. Trans. William Weaver. New York: Harcourt, 1983. Print.

When a book's title contains another book title (here *The Name of the Rose*), do not italicize the second title. When a book's title contains a quotation or the title of a work normally placed in quotation marks, keep the quotation marks and italicize both titles: *Critical Response to Henry James's "The Beast in the Jungle."*

35. Published proceedings of a conference (print)

Stimpson, Bill, ed. *AWEA Annual Conference and Exhibition*. Proc. of Amer. Wind Energy Assn. Conf., 3-6 June 2007, New York. Red Hook: Curran, 2008. Print.

To cite the published proceedings of a conference, use a book model—here, an edited book (model 22). Between the title and the publication data, add information about the conference, such as its name, date, and location. You may omit any of this information that already appears in the source title. Treat a particular presentation at the conference like a selection from an anthology (model 26).

36. An introduction, preface, foreword, or afterword (print)

Donaldson, Norman. Introduction. *The Claverings*. By Anthony Trollope. New York: Dover, 1977. vii-xv. Print.

An introduction, foreword, or afterword is often written by someone other than the book's author. When citing such a piece, give its name without quotation marks or italics, as with Introduction above. (If the piece has a title of its own, provide it, in quotation marks, between the name of the author and the name of the book.) Follow the title of the book with By and the book author's name. Give the inclusive page numbers of the part you cite. (In the example above, the small Roman numerals refer to the front matter of the book, before page 1.)

When the author of a preface or introduction is the same as the author of the book, give only the last name after the title:

Gould, Stephen Jay. Prologue. *The Flamingo's Smile: Reflections in Natural History*. By Gould. New York: Norton, 1985. 13-20. Print.

37. A book lacking publication information or pagination (print)

Carle, Eric. *The Very Busy Spider.* New York: Philomel, 1984. N. pag. Print.

Some books are not paginated or do not list a publisher or a place of publication. To cite such a book, provide as much information as you can and indicate the missing information with an abbreviation: n.p. if no publisher or city of publication, n.d. if no publication date, and n. pag. if no page numbers. Capitalize the abbreviation when it falls after a period, as it does in the example.

Other nonperiodical print sources

38. A government publication (print)

Florida. Dept. of Educ. *Teacher's Guide for the Career Cruiser: 2008-09.* Talla-
    hassee: Florida Dept. of Educ., 2008. Print.

United Nations. Dept. of Economic and Social Affairs. *World Youth Report 2007:*
    Young People's Transition to Adulthood—Progress and Challenges. New
    York: United Nations, 2008. Print.

United States. Cong. House. Committee on Agriculture, Nutrition, and Forestry.
    Food and Energy Act of 2007. 110th Cong., 1st sess. Washington: GPO,
    2007. Print.

MLA
56b

If a government publication does not list a person as author or editor, give the appropriate agency as author, as in the above examples.
Provide information in the order illustrated, separating elements
with periods: the name of the government, the name of the agency
(which may be abbreviated), and the title and publication information. For a congressional publication (last example), give the house
and committee involved before the title, and give the number and
session of Congress after the title. In this example, GPO stands for the
US Government Printing Office.

If a government publication lists a person as author or editor,
treat the source as an authored or edited book:

Kim, Jiyul. *Cultural Dimensions of Strategy and Policy.* Carlisle: US Army War
    Coll., Strategic Studies Inst., 2009. Print.

See model 47 (p. 466) to cite a government publication you find
on the Web.

39. A pamphlet or brochure (print)

Understanding Childhood Obesity. Tampa: Obesity Action Coalition, 2008. Print.

Most pamphlets and brochures can be treated as books. In this example, the pamphlet has no listed author, so the title comes first. If
your source has an author, give his or her name first, followed by
the title and publication information.

40. A dissertation (print)

McFaddin, Marie Oliver. *Adaptive Reuse: An Architectural Solution for Poverty and Homelessness.* Diss. U of Maryland, 2007. Ann Arbor: UMI, 2007. Print.

Treat a published dissertation like a book, but after the title insert Diss. ("Dissertation"), the institution granting the degree, and the year.

For an unpublished dissertation, use quotation marks rather than italics for the title and omit publication information.

Wilson, Stuart M. "John Stuart Mill as a Literary Critic." Diss. U of Michigan, 1990. Print.

41. A letter (print)

Buttolph, Mrs. Laura E. Letter to Rev. and Mrs. C. C. Jones. 20 June 1857. *The Children of Pride: A True Story of Georgia and the Civil War.* Ed. Robert Manson Myers. New Haven: Yale UP, 1972. 334-35. Print.

List a published letter under the writer's name. Specify that the source is a letter and to whom it was addressed, and give the date on which it was written. Treat the remaining information as with a selection from an anthology (model 26, p. 457). (See also model 16, p. 454, for the format of a letter to the editor of a periodical.)

For an unpublished letter in the collection of a library or archive, specify the writer, recipient, and date, as for a published letter. Then provide the medium, either MS ("manuscript") or TS ("typescript"). End with the name and location of the archive.

James, Jonathan E. Letter to his sister. 16 Apr. 1970. MS. Jonathan E. James Papers. South Dakota State Archive, Pierre.

For a letter you received, give the name of the writer, note the fact that the letter was sent to you, provide the date of the letter, and add the medium, MS or TS.

Wynne, Ava. Letter to the author. 6 Apr. 2008. MS.

To cite an e-mail message or a discussion-group posting, see models 70–71 (p. 474).

4 ▪ Listing nonperiodical Web sources

This section shows how to cite nonperiodical sources that you find on the Web. These sources may be published only once or occasionally, or they may be updated frequently but not regularly. (Most online magazines and newspapers fall into the latter category. See p. 466.) Some nonperiodical Web sources are available only on the Web (below); others are available in other media as well, such as print or film (pp. 469–70). See models 62–67 (pp. 471–73) to cite a scholarly journal that you find on the Web and any periodical that you find in an online database.

The MLA no longer recommends providing a URL (electronic address) in Web source citations because URLs change frequently and because users can search for documents using search engines. However, do include a URL if your source is hard to find without it, if your source could be confused with another one, or if your instructor requires you to include URLs. See model 61 (p. 470) for the form to use when citing a URL.

Note The *MLA Handbook* does not label its examples of nonperiodical Web sources as particular types. For ease of reference, the following models identify and illustrate the kinds of Web sources you are likely to encounter. If you don't see just what you need, consult the index of models on pages 448–49 for a similar source type whose format you can adapt. If your source does not include all of the information needed for a complete citation, find and list what you can.

Nonperiodical sources available only on the Web

Many nonperiodical Web sources are available only online. The following list, adapted from the *MLA Handbook*, itemizes the possible elements in a nonperiodical Web publication, in order of their appearance in a works-cited entry:

1. **Name of the author or other person responsible for the source,** such as an editor, translator, director, or performer. See models 1–6 (pp. 447 and 450) for the handling of authors' names. For other kinds of contributors, see models 22–24 (editors and translators) and models 74, 76–77, and 83 (directors, performers, and so on).
2. **Title of the cited work.** Use quotation marks for titles of articles, blog entries, and other sources that are parts of larger works. Use italics for books, plays, and other sources that are published independently.
3. **Title of the Web site,** in italics.
4. **Version or edition cited,** if any, following model 21 (p. 455)— for example, *Index of History Periodicals*. 2nd ed.
5. **Publisher or sponsor of the site,** followed by a comma. If you cannot find a publisher or sponsor, use N.p. ("No publisher") instead.
6. **Date of electronic publication, latest revision, or posting.** If no date is available, use n.d. ("no date") instead.
7. **Medium of publication:** Web.
8. **Date of your access:** day, month, year.

For some Web sources, you may want to include information that is not on the preceding list, such as the names of both the writer and the performers on a television show.

42. A short work with a title (Web)

Molella, Arthur. "Cultures of Innovation." *The Lemelson Center for the Study of Invention and Innovation.* Smithsonian Inst., Natl. Museum of Amer. Hist., Spring 2005. Web. 3 Aug. 2009.

See the facing page for an analysis of this entry and the location of the required information on the Web site. If the short work you are citing lacks an author, follow model 6 (p. 450) for an anonymous source, starting the entry with the title of the work:

"Clean Energy 101." *Union of Concerned Scientists: Citizens and Scientists for Environmental Solutions.* Union of Concerned Scientists, 8 Aug. 2008. Web. 11 Mar. 2009.

To cite a short Web source that also appears in another medium (such as print), see models 56–60 (pp. 469–70). To cite an article from a Web journal or from an online database, see models 62–67 (pp. 471–73).

43. A short work without a title (Web)

Crane, Gregory, ed. Home page. *The Perseus Digital Library.* Dept. of Classics, Tufts U, n.d. Web. 21 July 2009.

If you are citing an untitled short work from a Web site, such as the home page of a site or a posting to a blog, insert Home page, Online posting, or another descriptive label in place of the title. Do not use quotation marks or italics for this label.

Note that this source lacks a publication date, indicated by n.d. after the sponsor's name.

44. An entire site (Web)

Cheit, Ross E., ed. *The Recovered Memory Project.* Taubman Center for Public and Amer. Insts., Brown U, July 2007. Web. 8 Oct. 2009.

When citing an entire Web site—for instance, a scholarly project or a foundation site—include the name of the editor, author, or compiler (if available); the title of the site; the sponsor; the date of publication or most recent update; the medium (Web); and your date of access.

If your source lacks a named author or editor, begin with the site title:

Union of Concerned Scientists: Citizens and Scientists for Environmental Solutions. Union of Concerned Scientists, 2009. Web. 2 June 2009.

Format for a short work on the Web

①   ②   ③
Molella, Arthur. "Cultures of Innovation." *The Lemelson Center for the Study of Inven-*
                     ④   ⑤
tion and Innovation. Smithsonian Inst., Natl. Museum of Amer. Hist., Spring
      ⑥   ⑦
2005. Web. 3 Aug. 2009.

Top of page

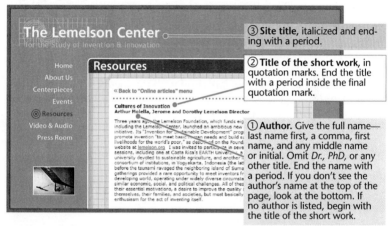

③ **Site title,** italicized and ending with a period.

② **Title of the short work,** in quotation marks. End the title with a period inside the final quotation mark.

① **Author.** Give the full name—last name first, a comma, first name, and any middle name or initial. Omit *Dr., PhD,* or any other title. End the name with a period. If you don't see the author's name at the top of the page, look at the bottom. If no author is listed, begin with the title of the short work.

Bottom of page

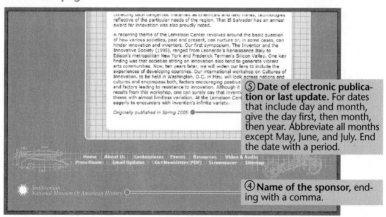

⑤ **Date of electronic publication or last update.** For dates that include day and month, give the day first, then month, then year. Abbreviate all months except May, June, and July. End the date with a period.

④ **Name of the sponsor,** ending with a comma.

⑥ **Medium.** Give the medium of the article, Web, followed by a period.

⑦ **Date of your access.** Give the day first, then month, then year. Abbreviate all months except May, June, and July. End the date with a period.

If your source lacks a sponsor, use the abbreviation N.p. ("No publisher"). If it lacks a publication date, use the abbreviation n.d. The source below lacks both a sponsor and a publication date:

> Corbett, John. *STARN: Scots Teaching and Resource Network*. N.p., n.d. Web. 26 Nov. 2009.

45. An article in a newspaper (Web)

> Campbell, Carol Ann. "Health Outcomes Driving New Hospital Design." *New York Times*. New York Times, 21 May 2009. Web. 8 July 2009.

Even when an online newspaper relates to a printed version, it is treated as a nonperiodical source because the online content changes often and unpredictably. List the author, article title, and newspaper title as in model 10 or 11 (pp. 452–53). Then give the publisher's name and the date. End with the medium of publication (Web) and the date of your access. Use this format to adapt the models for print periodicals if you need to cite a Web newspaper review, editorial, letter to the editor, interview, or article in a series (models 14–18, pp. 453–54).

See model 66 to cite a newspaper article in an online database.

46. An article in a magazine (Web)

> Yabroff, Jennie. "Reenter the Dragon." *Newsweek*. Newsweek, 14 Mar. 2009. Web. 15 Sept. 2009.

Even when an online magazine relates to a printed version, it is treated as a nonperiodical source because the online content changes often and unpredictably. List the author, article title, and magazine title as in model 12 or 13 (p. 453). Then give the publisher's name and the date. End with the medium (Web) and the date of your access. Use this format to adapt the models for print periodicals if you need to cite a Web magazine review, editorial, letter to the editor, interview, or article in a series or special issue (models 14–19, pp. 453–54).

See model 67 to cite a magazine article in an online database.

47. A government publication (Web)

> United States. Dept. of Agriculture. "Inside the Pyramid." *MyPyramid.gov*. US Dept. of Agriculture, n.d. Web. 1 Mar. 2008.

See model 38 for examples of government publications in print. Provide the same information for online publications along with the facts of Web publication. The example above includes the names of the government and department; the title of the source, in quotation marks; the title of the Web site, in italics; the sponsor; n.d. (because there is no publication date); the medium (Web); and the date of access.

48. An article in a reference work (Web)

"Yi Dynasty." *Encyclopaedia Britannica Online*. Encyclopaedia Britannica, 2008.

Web. 7 Apr. 2009.

This source does not list an author, so the entry begins with the title of the article and then proceeds as for other Web sources. If a reference article has an author, place the name before the article title.

For reference works that you find in print or on CD-ROM or DVD-ROM, see models 28 (p. 456) and 68 (p. 473), respectively.

49. An image (Web)

To cite images that are available only on the Web, give the name of the artist or creator, the title of the work, the date of the work (if any), a word describing the type of image (if not otherwise clear from the image or site title), the title of the Web site, the sponsor, the date of the site, the medium (Web), and your date of access. The following examples show a range of possibilities.

A work of visual art:

Simpson, Rick. *Overload*. *Museum of Computer Art*. Museum of Computer Art,

2008. Web. 1 Apr. 2009.

An advertisement:

FreeCreditReport.com. Advertisement. *Facebook*. Facebook, 2009. Web. 6 May

2009.

A map, chart, graph, or diagram:

"Greenhouse Effect." Diagram. *Earthguide*. Scripps Inst. of Oceanography,

2008. Web. 17 July 2009.

See also model 60 (p. 470) to cite an image that appears both on the Web and in another medium; model 73 (p. 475) to cite an image in a digital file; and models 78–82 (pp. 476–77) to cite an image that isn't on the Web.

50. A television or radio program (Web)

Norris, Michele, host. *All Things Considered*. Natl. Public Radio, 6 Apr. 2009.

Web. 21 Apr. 2009.

The Web sites of television and radio networks and programs often include both content that was broadcast as part of a show and content that is unique to the site. Cite either kind of source by its title or by the name of the person whose work you cite. Identify the role of anyone but an author (host in the example). Give the site title, the sponsor, the date, the medium (Web), and the date of your access. You may also cite other contributors (and their roles) after the title, as in model 52.

See also model 74 (p. 475) to cite a television or radio program that isn't on the Web.

51. A video recording (Web)

Green Children Foundation, prod. *The Green Children Visit China*. *YouTube*.

YouTube, 7 Jan. 2008. Web. 28 June 2009.

Cite a video on the Web either by its title or by the name of the person whose work you are citing—in this example, the foundation that produced the video. Identify the role of anyone but an author (prod. in the example). Give the video title, the site title, the sponsor, the date, the medium (Web), and the date of your access. You may also cite other contributors (and their roles) after the title, as in model 52.

See also model 53 to cite a podcast of a video recording; model 59 (p. 470) to cite a video recording or film that appears both on the Web and in another medium (such as DVD); and model 77 (p. 476) to cite a film, DVD, or video recording that isn't on the Web.

52. A sound recording (Web)

Beglarian, Eve. *Five Things*. Perf. Beglarian et al. *Kalvos and Damian*. N.p., 23

Oct. 2001. Web. 8 Mar. 2009.

Cite a musical sound recording by its title or by the name of the person whose work you are citing—in this example, the composer. (If the composer's name comes after the title, precede it with By. See the next example.) The preceding example also gives the work title, the performers of the work, the site title, the sponsor (here unknown, so replaced with N.p.), the date, the medium (Web), and the date of access.

The same format may be used for a spoken-word recording that you find on the Web:

Wasserstein, Wendy, narr. "Afternoon of a Faun." By Wasserstein. *The Borzoi*

Reader Online. Knopf, 2001. Web. 14 Feb. 2009.

See also the next model to cite a sound podcast; model 58 to cite a sound recording that appears both on the Web and in another medium (such as CD); and model 76 (p. 476) to cite a sound recording that isn't on the Web.

53. A podcast (Web)

Simon, Bob. "Exonerated." *60 Minutes*. *CBS News*. CBS News, 4 May 2008.

Web. 6 June 2009.

This podcast from a news program lists the author of a story on the show, the title of the story (in quotation marks), and the program (italicized) as well as the site title, sponsor, date, medium (Web), and access date. If a podcast does not list an author or other creator, begin with the title.

MLA
56b

54. A blog entry (Web)

Marshall, Joshua Micah. "Busted." *Talking Points Memo*. TPM Media, 20 May
2009. Web. 1 June 2009.

For a blog entry, give the author, the title of the entry, the title of the
blog or site, the name of the sponsor (or N.p. if no sponsor is named),
the publication date, the medium (Web), and the date of access. See
model 43 (p. 464) to cite a blog entry without a title.

55. A wiki (Web)

"Podcast." *Wikipedia*. Wikimedia, 30 May 2009. Web. 20 Sept. 2009.

To cite an entry from a wiki, follow the above example: entry title,
site title, sponsor, publication date, medium (Web), and date of access. Begin with the site title if you are citing the entire wiki.

Nonperiodical Web sources also available in print

Some sources you find on the Web may be books, short stories,
and other works that have been scanned from print versions. To
cite such a source, generally provide the information for both original print publication and Web publication. Begin your entry as if
you were citing the print work, consulting models 20–41 for an
appropriate format. Then, instead of giving "Print" as the medium,
provide the title of the Web site you used, any version or edition
number, the medium you used (Web), and the date of your access.

56. A short work with print publication information (Web)

Wheatley, Phillis. "On Virtue." *Poems on Various Subjects, Religious and Moral*.
London, 1773. N. pag. *American Verse Project*. Web. 21 July 2009.

The print information for this poem follows model 26 (p. 457) for a
selection from an anthology, but it omits the publisher's name because the anthology was published before 1900. The print information
ends with N. pag. because the original source has no page numbers.

57. A book with print publication information (Web)

James, Henry. *The Ambassadors*. 1903. New York: Scribner's, 1909. *Oxford Text
Archive*. Web. 5 May 2008.

The print information for this novel follows model 32 (p. 459) for a
republished book, so it includes both the original date of publication (1903) and the publication information for the scanned book.

Nonperiodical Web sources also available in other media

Some images, films, and sound recordings that you find on the
Web may have been published before in other media and then
scanned or digitized for the Web. To cite such a source, generally
provide the information for original publication as well as that for

Web publication. Begin your entry as if you were citing the original, consulting models 74–84 (pp. 475–78) for an appropriate format. Then, instead of giving the original medium of publication, provide the title of the Web site you used, the medium you used (Web), and your date of access.

58. A sound recording with other publication information (Web)

"Rioting in Pittsburgh." CBS Radio, 1968. *Vincent Voice Library*. Web.
7 Dec. 2008.

For Web sound recordings with original publication information, base citations on model 76 (p. 476), adding the information for Web publication.

59. A film or video recording with other publication information (Web)

Coca Cola. Advertisement. Dir. Haskell Wexler. 1971. *American Memory*. Lib. of
Cong. Web. 8 Apr. 2009.

For Web films or videos with original publication information, base citations on model 77 (p. 476), adding the information for Web publication.

60. An image with other publication information (Web)

Pollock, Jackson. *Lavender Mist: Number 1*. 1950. Natl. Gallery of Art, Washington.
WebMuseum. Web. 7 Apr. 2008.

Keefe, Mike. "FAA Inspector in a Quandary." Cartoon. *Denver Post* 5 Apr. 2008.
PoliticalCartoons.com. Web. 7 Apr. 2009.

For Web images with original publication information, base citations on models 78–82 (pp. 476–77), adding the information for Web publication.

Citation of a URL

61. A source requiring citation of the URL

Joss, Rich. "Dispatches from the Ice: The Second Season Begins." *Antarctic
Expeditions*. Smithsonian Natl. Zoo and Friends of the Natl. Zoo, 26 Oct.
2007. Web. 26 Sept. 2008. <http://nationalzoo.si.edu/
ConservationAndScience/AquaticEcosystems/Antarctica/Expedition/
FieldNews>.

Because a URL does not always provide a convenient or usable route to a source, the MLA no longer recommends including URLs in works-cited entries. However, you should include URLs when your instructor requires them. You should also give a URL when readers may not be able to locate a source without one. For example, using a search engine to find "Dispatches from the Ice" (the title in the example) yields more than ten hits, one of which links to the correct site but the wrong document.

If you need to include a URL, ensure accuracy by using Copy and Paste to duplicate it in a file or an e-mail to yourself. In your list of works cited, give the URL after your date of access and a period. Put angle brackets on both ends of the URL, and end with a period. Break URLs *only* after slashes—do not hyphenate.

5 ▪ Listing journals on the Web and periodicals in online databases

This section covers two kinds of periodicals: scholarly journals that you reach directly on the Web (below) and journals, newspapers, and magazines that you reach in online databases (p. 472). Newspapers and magazines that you reach directly on the Web are typically not periodicals (because their content often changes), so they are covered in models 45 and 46 (p. 466).

Citations for Web journals and for periodicals in online databases resemble those for print periodicals, with some changes for the different medium.

Web journals consulted directly

The journals you find directly on the Web may be published only online or may be published in print versions as well. The citation format is the same in either case: begin with an appropriate print model (pp. 450–52), but replace "Print" with Web and add your access date. Because many Web journals are unpaged, you may have to substitute n. pag. for page numbers.

62. An article in a scholarly journal (Web)

Polletta, Francesca. "Just Talk: Public Deliberation after 9/11." *Journal of Public Deliberation* 4.1 (2008): n. pag. Web. 7 Apr. 2009.

Follow model 7 or 8 for a print journal article, listing the author, title of the article, title of the journal (but without *A, An,* or *The*), volume and issue numbers (if both are available), year of publication, and any page numbers. If no page numbers are given, insert n. pag. in their place, as in the example. Conclude with the medium (Web) and the date of access.

Use the same format to adapt the models for print periodicals if you need to cite a Web journal review, editorial, letter to the editor, interview, article in a series, or special issue (models 14–19, pp. 453–54). For a journal article reached in an online database, see model 64.

63. An abstract of a journal article (Web)

Polletta, Francesca. "Just Talk: Public Deliberation after 9/11." *Journal of*
    Public Deliberation 4.1 (2008): n. pag. Abstract. Web. 7 Apr. 2009.

Treat a Web abstract like a Web journal article, but add Abstract between the publication information and the medium. (You may omit
this label if the journal title clearly indicates that the cited work is
an abstract.) See model 65 to cite an abstract in an online database.

Web periodicals consulted in online databases

Many articles in journals, newspapers, and magazines are avail-
able in online databases that you reach through your library's Web
site, such as *Academic Search Complete, ProQuest,* and *Project Muse.*
Follow models 7–19 (pp. 450–54) for print periodicals, but replace
"Print" with the title of the database you consulted, the medium
(Web), and the date of your access.

64. An article in a scholarly journal (online database)

Gorski, Paul C. "Privilege and Repression in the Digital Era: Rethinking the
    Sociopolitics of the Digital Divide." *Race, Gender and Class* 10.4 (2003):
    145-76. *Ethnic NewsWatch.* Web. 23 Apr. 2009.

See the next page for an analysis of this entry and the location of
the required information in the database.

65. An abstract of a journal article (online database)

Gorski, Paul C. "Privilege and Repression in the Digital Era: Rethinking the
    Sociopolitics of the Digital Divide." *Race, Gender and Class* 10.4 (2003):
    145-76. Abstract. *Ethnic NewsWatch.* Web. 23 Apr. 2009.

Treat an abstract in an online database like a journal article in a
database, but add Abstract between the publication information and
the database title. (You may omit this label if the journal title
clearly indicates that the cited work is an abstract.)

66. An article in a newspaper (online database)

Fusilli, Jim. "Music: They're Hip, but Canadian." *Wall Street Journal* 27 May
    2009, eastern ed.: D9+. *ProQuest.* Web. 3 July 2009.

Follow model 10 or 11 (pp. 452–53) for citing author, title of article,
title of newspaper, publication date, edition (if any), and page numbers. Add the database title, the medium (Web), and your date of access.

67. An article in a magazine (online database)

Brown, Kathryn. "The Skinny on the Environment." *Scientific American* Jan.
    2008: 30-37. *Academic Search Premier.* Web. 3 Aug. 2009.

Format for a journal article in an online database

① ②
Gorski, Paul C. "Privilege and Repression in the Digital Era: Rethinking the Socio-

③   ④   ⑤   ⑥
politics of the Digital Divide." *Race, Gender and Class* 10.4 (2003): 145-76.

⑦   ⑧   ⑨
Ethnic NewsWatch. Web. 23 Apr. 2008.

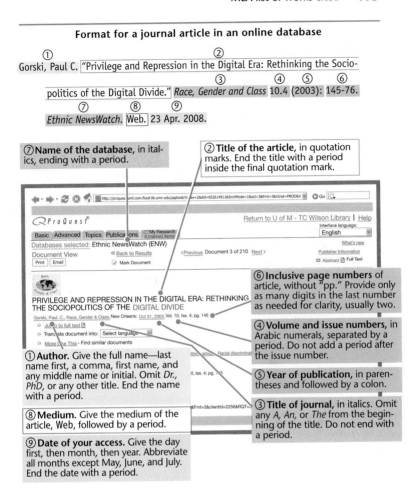

⑦ **Name of the database,** in italics, ending with a period.

② **Title of the article,** in quotation marks. End the title with a period inside the final quotation mark.

⑥ **Inclusive page numbers** of article, without "pp." Provide only as many digits in the last number as needed for clarity, usually two.

④ **Volume and issue numbers,** in Arabic numerals, separated by a period. Do not add a period after the issue number.

① **Author.** Give the full name—last name first, a comma, first name, and any middle name or initial. Omit *Dr.,* *PhD,* or any other title. End the name with a period.

⑤ **Year of publication,** in parentheses and followed by a colon.

⑧ **Medium.** Give the medium of the article, Web, followed by a period.

③ **Title of journal,** in italics. Omit any *A, An,* or *The* from the beginning of the title. Do not end with a period.

⑨ **Date of your access.** Give the day first, then month, then year. Abbreviate all months except May, June, and July. End the date with a period.

Follow model 12 or 13 (p. 453) for citing author, title of article, title of magazine, publication date, and page numbers. Add the title of the database, the medium (Web), and the date of your access.

6 ■ Listing other electronic sources

Publications on CD-ROM or DVD-ROM

68. A nonperiodical CD-ROM or DVD-ROM

Nunberg, Geoffrey. "Usage in the Dictionary." *The American Heritage Dictionary of the English Language.* 4th ed. Boston: Houghton, 2000. CD-ROM.

Single-issue CD-ROMs may be encyclopedias, dictionaries, books, and other resources that are published just once, like print books. Follow models 20–37 for print books (pp. 455–61), but replace "Print" with CD-ROM or DVD-ROM. If the disc has a vendor that differs from the publisher of the work, add the vendor's place of publication, name, and publication date after the medium—for instance, Philadelphia: Soquest, 2006.

See also models 28 (p. 458) and 48 (p. 467) to cite reference works in print and on the Web.

69. A periodical CD-ROM or DVD-ROM

Kolata, Gina. "Gauging Body Mass Index in a Changing Body." *New York Times* 28 June 2005, natl. ed.: D1+. CD-ROM. *New York Times Ondisc.* UMI-ProQuest. Sept. 2005.

Databases on **CD-ROM** or **DVD-ROM** are issued periodically—for instance, every six months or every year. The journals, newspapers, and other publications included in such a database are generally available in print as well, so your works-cited entry should give the information for both formats. Start with information for the print version, following models 7–19 (pp. 450–54). Then replace "Print" with the medium (CD-ROM or DVD-ROM), the database title, the vendor's name (UMI-ProQuest in the example), and the database publication date.

E-mail and discussion-group postings

70. An e-mail message

Greene, Natasha. "Re: Travel to Asia." Message to the author. 27 Mar. 2008. E-mail.

For e-mail, give the writer's name; the title, if any, from the e-mail's subject heading, in quotation marks; Message to the author (or the name of a recipient besides you); the date of the message; and the medium, E-mail. You do not need to include the date of your access.

71. A posting to a discussion group

Williams, Frederick. "Circles as Primitive." *The Math Forum @ Drexel.* Drexel U, 28 Feb. 2008. E-mail.

Cite a posting to a discussion group like a blog entry (model 54, p. 469). This example for a discussion-list posting includes author's name, title of the posting, title of the list, name of the sponsor, date of the posting, and medium (E-mail). If the posting is untitled, give Online posting instead. You need not add the date of your access.

Digital files

You may want to cite a digital file that is not on the Web or on a disc, such as a PDF document, a JPEG image, or an MP3 sound recording that you downloaded onto your computer. Use the appropriate model for your kind of source (for instance, model 79 for a personal photograph), but replace the medium with the file format you're using. If you don't know the file format, use Digital file.

72. A text file (digital)

Berg, John K. "Estimates of Persons Driving While Intoxicated." *Law Enforcement Today* 17 Apr. 2008. PDF file.

Fernandez, Carlos. "Semester in Spain." 2009. *Microsoft Word* file.

73. A media file (digital)

Springsteen, Bruce. "Empty Sky." *The Rising*. Columbia, 2002. MP3 file.

Girls at the pool. Personal photograph by Granger Goetz. 2009. JPEG file.

7 ▪ Listing other print and nonprint sources

The source types covered in this section are not on a computer or, generally, in printed sources. Most of these types have parallel citation formats elsewhere in this chapter when you reach them through electronic and print media. See model 17 (p. 454) to cite an interview in print. See models 49–52 (pp. 467–68) to cite images, television and radio programs, video recordings, and sound recordings that are available only on the Web. See models 58–60 (p. 470) to cite such sources when they are available on the Web and in other media. And see model 73 to cite such sources in digital files.

MLA

56b

74. A television or radio program

"Piece of My Heart." By Stacy McKee. Dir. Mark Tinker. *Grey's Anatomy*. ABC. KGO, San Francisco, 1 May 2008. Television.

Start with the title unless you are citing the work of a person or persons. The example here cites an episode title (in quotation marks) and the names of the episode's writer and director. By and Dir. identify their roles. Then the entry gives the program title (in italics), the name of the network, the call letters and city of the local station, the date, and the medium (Television). If you list individuals who worked on the entire program, put their names after the program title.

75. A personal or broadcast interview

Govek, James. Personal interview. 7 June 2009.

Diaz, Junot. Interview by Terry Gross. *Fresh Air*. National Public Radio. WGBH, Boston, 18 Oct. 2007. Radio.

Begin with the name of the person interviewed. For an interview you conducted, specify Personal interview or the medium (such as Telephone interview or E-mail interview), and then give the date. For an interview you heard or saw, provide the title if any or Interview if there is no title. Add the name of the interviewer if he or she is identified. Then follow an appropriate model for the kind of source (here, a radio program), and end with the medium (here, Radio).

76. A sound recording

Rubenstein, Artur, perf. Piano Concerto no. 2 in B-flat. By Johannes Brahms.
  Cond. Eugene Ormandy. Philadelphia Orch. RCA, 1972. LP.

Springsteen, Bruce. "Empty Sky." *The Rising*. Columbia, 2002. CD.

Begin with the name of the individual whose work you are citing. Unless this person is the composer, identify his or her role, as with perf. ("performer") in the first example. If you're citing a work identified by form, number, and key (first example), do not use quotation marks or italics for the title. If you're citing a song or song lyrics (second example), give the title in quotation marks; then provide the title of the recording in italics. Following the title, identify the composer or author if you haven't already, after By, and name and identify other participants you want to mention. Then provide the manufacturer of the recording, the date of release, and the medium: LP in the first example, CD in the second.

77. A film, DVD, or video recording

A Beautiful Mind. Dir. Ron Howard. Universal, 2001. Film.

Start with the title of the work unless you are citing the work of a person (see the next example). Generally, identify and name the director. You may list other participants (writer, lead performers, and so on) as you judge appropriate. For a film, end with the distributor, date, and medium (Film):

For a DVD or videocassette, include the original release date (if any), the distributor's name and release date, and the medium (DVD or Videocassette):

Balanchine, George, chor. *Serenade*. Perf. San Francisco Ballet. Dir. Hilary
  Bean. 1991. PBS Video, 2006. DVD.

78. A painting, photograph, or other work of visual art

Arnold, Leslie. *Seated Woman*. N.d. Oil on canvas. DeYoung Museum, San Francisco.

Sugimoto, Hiroshi. *Pacific Ocean, Mount Tamalpais*. 1994. Photograph.
  Private collection.

To cite an actual work of art, name the artist and give the title (in italics) and the date of creation (or N.d. if the date is unknown). Then provide the medium of the work (such as Oil on canvas or Photograph) and the name and location of the owner, if known. (Use Private collection if not.)

For a work you see only in a reproduction, provide the complete publication information for the source you used. Omit the medium of the work itself, and replace it with the medium of the re-production (Print in the following example). Omit such information only if you examined the actual work.

Hockney, David. *Place Furstenberg, Paris.* 1985. Coll. Art Gallery, New Paltz. *David Hockney: A Retrospective.* Ed. Maurice Tuchman and Stephanie Barron. Los Angeles: Los Angeles County Museum of Art, 1988. 247. Print.

79. A personal photograph

Common milkweed on Lake Michigan shoreline. Personal photograph by the author. 22 Aug. 2008.

For a personal photograph by you or by someone else, give the sub-ject (without quotation marks or italics), the photographer, and the date. The current edition of the *MLA Handbook* does not cover per-sonal photographs, so this format comes from the previous edition.

80. A map, chart, graph, or diagram

"The Sonoran Desert." Map. *Sonoran Desert: An American Deserts Handbook.* By Rose Houk. Tucson: Western Natl. Parks Assn., 2000. 12. Print.

Unless the creator of an illustration is given on the source, list the illustration by its title. Put the title in quotation marks if it comes from another publication or in italics if it is published indepen-dently. Then add a description (Map, Chart, and so on), the publica-tion information, and the medium (here, Print).

81. A cartoon or comic strip

Trudeau, Garry. "Doonesbury." Comic strip. *San Francisco Chronicle* 11 Aug. 2009: E6. Print.

Cite a cartoon or comic strip with the artist's name, the title (in quo-tation marks), the description Cartoon or Comic strip, the publication information, and the medium (here, Print).

82. An advertisement

Soyjoy. Advertisement. *New Yorker* 1 June 2009: 26. Print.

Cite an advertisement with the name of the product or company ad-vertised, the description Advertisement, the publication information, and the medium (Print, Television, Radio, and so on).

83. A performance

Levine, James, cond. Boston Symphony Orch. Symphony Hall, Boston. 23 Sept. 2009. Performance.

The New Century. By Paul Rudnick. Dir. Nicholas Martin. Mitzi E. Newhouse Theater, New York. 6 May 2008. Performance.

For a live performance, generally base your citation on film citations (model 77). Place the title first (second example) unless you are citing the work of an individual (first example). After the title, provide relevant information about participants as well as the theater, city, and performance date. Conclude with the medium (Performance).

84. A lecture, speech, address, or reading

von Lates, Adrienne. "Visionary Artists from Bosch to Barney." Museum of

    Contemporary Art. MOCA at Goldman Warehouse, Miami. 17 June 2009.

    Address.

Give the speaker's name, the title if any (in quotation marks), the title of the meeting if any, the name of the sponsoring organization, the location of the presentation, and the date. End with a description of the type of presentation (Lecture, Speech, Address, Reading).

Although the MLA does not provide a specific style for citing classroom lectures in your courses, you can adapt the preceding format for this purpose:

Cavanaugh, Carol. Class lecture on teaching mentors. Lesley U. 4 Apr. 2008.

    Lecture.

Exercise 56.1 Writing works-cited entries

Prepare works-cited entries from the following information. Follow the MLA models given in this chapter unless your instructor specifies a different style. Arrange the finished entries in alphabetical order, not numbered. Answers to starred items appear at the back of the book.

*1. An article titled "Use of Third Parties to Collect State and Local Taxes on Internet Sales," appearing in the print periodical *The Pacific Business Journal,* volume 5, issue 2, in 2004. The authors are Malai Zimmerman and Kent Hoover. The article appears on pages 45 through 48 of the journal.

*2. A government publication you consulted on November 12, 2009, on the Web. The author is the Advisory Commission on Electronic Commerce. The commission is an agency of the United States government. The title of the publication is *Report to Congress.* It was published in April 2005.

*3. A Web article with no listed author. The title and sponsor of the Web site is Center on Budget and Policy Priorities. The title of the article is "The Internet Tax Freedom Act and the Digital Divide," and the site is dated September 26, 2007. You consulted the site on November 2, 2009.

*4. An article in the magazine *Forbes,* published November 28, 2007, on pages 56 through 58. The author is Janet Novack. The title is "Point, Click, Pay Tax." You accessed the source through the *ProQuest* database on November 10, 2009.

5. A print book titled *All's Fair in Internet Commerce, or Is It?* by Sally G. Osborne. The book was published in 2004 by Random House in New York.

6. An e-mail interview you conducted with Nora James on November 1, 2009.
7. An article titled "State and Local Sales/Use Tax Simplification," appearing on pages 67 through 80 of a print anthology, *The Sales Tax in the Twenty-first Century*. The anthology is edited by Matthew N. Murray and William F. Fox. The article is by Wayne G. Eggert. The anthology was published in 2004 by Praeger in Westport, Connecticut.

56c   Format the paper in MLA style.

The *MLA Handbook* provides guidelines for a fairly simple document format, with just a few elements. For guidelines on type fonts, headings, lists, illustrations, and other features that MLA style does not specify, see pages 66–74.

The samples below show the formats for the first page and a later page of a paper. For the format of the list of works cited, see page 446.

First page of MLA paper

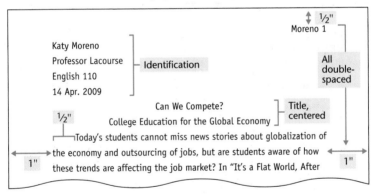

Later page of MLA paper

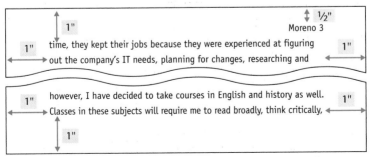

Margins Use minimum one-inch margins on all sides of every page.

Spacing and indentions Double-space throughout. Indent the first lines of paragraphs one-half inch. (See below for indention of poetry and long prose quotations.)

Paging Begin numbering on the first page, and number consecutively through the end (including the list of works cited). Use Arabic numerals (1, 2, 3) positioned in the upper right, about one-half inch from the top. Place your last name before the page number in case the pages later become separated.

Identification and title MLA style does not require a title page for a paper. Instead, give your name, your instructor's name, the course title, and the date on separate lines in the upper left of the first page—one inch from the top of the paper. (See the sample on the previous page.) Double-space between all lines of this identification.

Double-space again, and center the title. Do not highlight the title with italics, underlining, boldface, larger type, or quotation marks. Capitalize the words in the title according to the guidelines on pages 362–63. Double-space the lines of the title and between the title and the text.

Poetry and long prose quotations Treat a single line of poetry like any other quotation, running it into your text and enclosing it in quotation marks. You may run in two or three lines of poetry as well, separating the lines with a slash surrounded by space.

> An example of Robert Frost's incisiveness is in two lines from "Death of the Hired Man": "Home is the place where, when you have to go there / They have to take you in" (119-20).

Always set off from your text a poetry quotation of more than three lines. Use double spacing above and below the quotation and for the quotation itself. Indent the quotation one inch from the left margin. *Do not add quotation marks.*

> Emily Dickinson stripped ideas to their essence, as in this description of "A narrow Fellow in the Grass," a snake:
>
> > I more than once at Noon
> > Have passed, I thought, a Whip lash
> > Unbraiding in the Sun
> > When stopping to secure it
> > It wrinkled, and was gone (12-16)

Also set off a prose quotation of more than four typed lines. (See pp. 417–18 on when to use such long quotations.) Double-space and indent as with the preceding poetry example. *Do not add quotation marks.*

> In the influential *Talley's Corner* from 1967, Elliot Liebow observes that
> "unskilled" construction work requires more skill than is generally assumed:
>> A healthy, sturdy, active man of good intelligence requires from two
>> to four weeks to break in on a construction job. . . . It frequently
>> happens that his foreman or the craftsman he services is not willing
>> to wait that long for him to get into condition or to learn at a
>> glance the difference in size between a rough 2 x 8 and a finished
>> 2 x 10. (62)

Do not use a paragraph indention for a quotation of a single complete paragraph or a part of a paragraph. Use paragraph indentions of one-quarter inch only for a quotation of two or more complete paragraphs.

56d   A sample paper in MLA style

The sample paper beginning on page 483 follows MLA guidelines for overall format, parenthetical citations, and the list of works cited. Marginal annotations highlight features of the paper.

Note Because the sample paper addresses a current topic, many of its sources come from the Internet and do not use page or other reference numbers. Thus the in-text citations of these sources do not give reference numbers. In a paper relying solely on printed journals, books, and other traditional sources, most if not all in-text citations would include page numbers.

A note on outlines

Some instructors ask students to submit an outline of the final paper. For advice on constructing a formal or topic outline, see pages 22–23. Following is an outline of the sample paper, written in complete sentences. Note that the thesis statement precedes either a topic or a sentence outline.

> *Thesis statement:* Although green consumerism can help the environment,
> consumerism itself is the root of some of the most pressing ecological prob-
> lems we face. To make a real difference, we must consume less.
>
> I. Green products claiming to help the environment both appeal to and
>   confuse consumers.
>   A. The market for ecologically sound products is enormous.
>   B. Determining whether or not a product is as green as advertised can
>   be a challenge.

II. Green products don't solve the high rate of consumption that truly threatens the environment.
- A. Overconsumption is a significant cause of three of the most serious environmental problems.
    1. It depletes natural resources.
    2. It contributes to pollution, particularly from the greenhouse gases responsible for global warming.
    3. It produces a huge amount of solid waste.
- B. The availability of greener products has not reduced the environmental effects of consumption.

III. Since buying green products does not reduce consumption, other solutions must be found for environmental problems.
- A. Experts have proposed many far-reaching solutions, but they require concerted government action and could take decades to implement.
- B. For shorter-term solutions, individuals can change their own behavior as consumers.
    1. Precycling may be the greenest behavior that individuals can adopt.
        a. Precycling means avoiding purchase of products that use raw materials and excessive packaging.
        b. More important, precycling means avoiding purchases of new products whenever possible.
    2. For unavoidable purchases, individuals can buy green products and influence businesses to embrace ecological goals.

Justin Malik

Ms. Rossi

English 112-02

18 Mar. 2009

Identification: writer's name, instructor's name, course title, date.

The False Promise of Green Consumerism

Title centered.

They line the aisles of just about any store. They seem to dominate television and print advertising. Chances are that at least a few of them belong to you. From organic jeans to household cleaners to hybrid cars, products advertised as environmentally friendly are readily available and are so popular they're trendy. It's easy to see why Americans are buying these things in record numbers. The new wave of "green" consumer goods makes an almost irresistible promise: we can save the planet by shopping.

Double-space throughout.

Introduction: establishes the issue with examples (first paragraph) and background (second paragraph).

Saving the planet does seem to be urgent. Thanks partly to former Vice President Al Gore, who sounded the alarm in 1992 with *Earth in the Balance* and again in 2006 with *An Inconvenient Truth,* the threat of global warming has become a regular feature in the news media and a recurring theme in popular culture. Unfortunately, as Gore himself points out, climate change is just one of many environmental problems competing for our attention: the rainforests are vanishing, our air and our water are dangerously polluted, alarming numbers of species are facing extinction, and landfills are overflowing (*Earth* 23-28). All the bad news can be overwhelming, and most people feel powerless to halt the damage. Thus it is reassuring that we may be able to help by making small changes in what we buy—but it is not entirely true. Although green consumerism can help the environment, consumerism itself is the root of some of the most pressing ecological problems we face. To make a real difference, we must consume less.

Citation form: no parenthetical citation because author and titles are named in the text and discussion cites entire works.

Citation form: shortened title for one of two works by the same author.

Thesis statement.

Consumers respond well to products they perceive as ecologically sound. Experts estimate that spending on green products already approaches $200 billion a year (Adler et al.). Yet shoppers don't always know whether their purchases are as green as advertised. Claims vary: a product might be labeled as organic, biodegradable, energy efficient, recycled, carbon

Background on green products.

Citation form: source with more than three authors; no page number because source from an online database is unnumbered.

neutral, renewable, or just about anything that sounds environmentally positive. However, none of these terms carries a universally accepted meaning, and no enforceable labeling regulations exist ("It's Not Easy"). Some of the new product options offer clear environmental benefits: for instance, compact fluorescent light bulbs last ten times as long as regular bulbs and draw about a third of the electricity (Gore, *Inconvenient* 306), and paper made from recycled fibers saves many trees. But other "green" products just as clearly do little or nothing to help the environment: a disposable razor made with less plastic is still a disposable razor, destined for a landfill after only a few uses.

Distinguishing truly green products from those that are not so green merely scratches the surface of a much larger issue. The products aren't the problem; it's our high rate of consumption that poses the real threat to the environment. We seek what's newer and better—whether cars, clothes, phones, computers, televisions, shoes, or gadgets—and they all require resources to make, ship, and use them. Political scientists Thomas Princen, Michael Maniates, and Ken Conca maintain that overconsumption is a leading force behind several ecological crises, warning that

> ever-increasing pressures on ecosystems, life-supporting environmental services, and critical natural cycles are driven not only by the sheer number of resource users . . . but also by the patterns of resource use themselves. (4)

Those patterns of resource use are disturbing. In just the second half of the twentieth century, gross world product (the global output of consumer goods) grew at five times the rate of population growth—a difference explained by a huge rise in consumption per person. (See fig. 1.) Such growth might be good for the economy, but it is bad for the environment. As fig. 1 shows, it is accompanied by the depletion of natural resources, increases in the carbon emissions that cause global warming, and increases in the amount of solid waste disposal.

The first negative effect of overconsumption, the depletion of resources, occurs because the manufacture and distrib-

Citation form: shortened title for anonymous source; page number for a one-page source not required.

Citation form: author not named in the text; shortened title for one of two works by the same author. Position of citation clarifies which example comes from the source.

Writer adds his own example. No source citations required.

Environmental effects of consumption (next four paragraphs). Writer synthesizes information from half a dozen sources to develop his own ideas.

Quotation over four lines set off without quotation marks. See pp. 480–81.

Ellipsis mark signals that writer has omitted unneeded material from quotation.

Citation form with displayed quotation: follows sentence period. Authors named in text, so not named in parenthetical citation.

Text refers to and discusses figure.

Malik 3

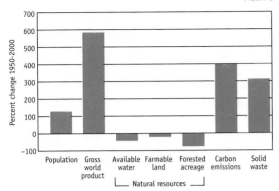

Figure presents numerical data visually.

Fig. 1 Global population, consumption, and environmental impacts, 1950-2000. Data from United Nations Development Programme; *Human Development Report: Changing Today's Consumption Patterns—For Tomorrow's Human Development* (New York: Oxford UP, 1998; print; 4); and from Earth Policy Inst.; "Eco-Economy Indicators"; *Earth Policy Institute*; EPI, Feb. 2008; Web; 6 Mar. 2009.

Figure caption explains the chart and gives complete source information.

ution of any consumer product depends on the use of water, land, and raw materials such as wood, metal, and oil. Paul Hawken, a respected environmentalist, explains that just in the United States "[i]ndustry moves, mines, extracts, shovels, burns, wastes, pumps, and disposes of *4 million pounds of material* in order to provide one average . . . family's needs for a year" (qtd. in DeGraaf, Wann, and Naylor 85; emphasis added). The United Nations Development Programme's 1998 *Human Development Report* (still the most comprehensive study of the environmental impacts of consumerism) warns that many regions in the world don't have enough water, productive soil, or forests to meet the basic needs of their populations (4). More recent data from the Earth Policy Institute show that as manufacturing and per-person consumption continue to rise, the supply of resources needed for survival continues to decline. Thus heavy consumption poses a threat not only to the environment but also to the well-being of the human race.

In addition to using up scarce natural resources, manufacturing and distributing products harms the earth by

Brackets signal capitalization changed to integrate quotation with writer's sentence.

Citation form: source with three authors; "qtd. in" indicates indirect source (Hawken quoted by DeGraaf, Wann, and Naylor); "emphasis added" indicates italics were not in original quotation.

Citation form: corporate author is named in the text, so page number only.

Citation form: no parenthetical citation because author is named in the text and online source has no page or other reference numbers.

spewing pollution into the water, soil, and air. The most

worrisome aspect of that pollution may be its link to global

warming. As Al Gore explains, the energy needed to power

manufacturing and distribution comes primarily from burning

fossil fuels, a process that releases carbon dioxide and other

greenhouse gases into the air. Those gases build up and trap

heat in the earth's atmosphere. The result, most scientists

now believe, is increasing global temperatures that will raise

sea levels, expand deserts, and cause more frequent floods

and hurricanes (*Inconvenient* 26-27, 81, 118-19, 184). As the

preceding bar chart shows, carbon emissions, like production

of consumer goods in general, are rising at rates out of

proportion with population growth. The more we consume, the

more we contribute to global warming.

As harmful as they are, gradual global warming and the

depletion of resources half a world away can be difficult to

comprehend or appreciate. A more immediate environmental

effect of our buying habits can be seen in the volumes of

trash those habits create. The US Environmental Protection

Agency found that in a single year (2006), US residents,

corporations, and institutions produced 251 million tons of

municipal solid waste, amounting to "4.6 pounds per person

per day" (1-2). Nearly a third of that trash came just from the

wrappers, cans, bottles, and boxes used for shipping consumer

goods. Yet the mountains of trash left over from consump-

tion are only a part of the problem. In industrial countries

overall, 90 percent of waste comes not from what gets thrown

out, but from the manufacturing processes of converting nat-

ural resources into consumer products (DeGraaf, Wann, and

Naylor 192). Nearly everything we buy creates waste in pro-

duction, comes in packaging that gets discarded immediately,

and ultimately ends up in landfills that are already overflow-

ing.

Unfortunately, the growing popularity of green products

has not reduced the environmental effects of consumption. A

study conducted by economists Jeff Rubin and Benjamin Tal

for the research firm CIBC World Markets found that while eco-

friendly and energy-efficient products have become more

Marginal notes:

Summary reduces six pages in the source to three sentences. Signal phrase and parenthetical citation mark boundaries of the summary.

Citation form: shortened title for one of two works by the same author; page numbers indicate exact locations of information in source.

Writer's own conclusion from preceding data.

Citation form: author (a US government body) named in text; parenthetical citation lists only source's page numbers.

Citation form: source with three authors; authors not named in text.

Environmental effects of green consumption.

available, "consumption is growing by ever-increasing amounts." The authors give the example of automobiles: in the last generation, cars have become much more energy efficient, but the average American now drives 2500 more miles a year, for a net gain in energy use (4-5). At the same time, per-person waste production in the United States has risen by more than 20 percent (United States 1). Greener products may reduce our cost of consumption and even reduce our guilt about consumption, but they do not reduce consumption and its effects.

> Citation form: authors are named in the text, so page numbers only.

> Citation form: US government source not named in text.

> Writer's own conclusion from preceding data.

If buying green won't solve the problems caused by overconsumption, what will? Politicians, environmentalists, and economists have proposed an array of far-reaching ideas, including creating a financial market for carbon credits and offsets, aggressively taxing consumption and pollution, offering financial incentives for environmentally positive behaviors, and even abandoning market capitalism altogether (Muldoon). However, all of these are "top-down" solutions that require concerted government action. Gaining support for any one of them, putting it into practice, and getting results could take decades. In the meantime, the environment would continue to deteriorate. Clearly, short-term solutions are also essential.

> Solutions to problem of consumption (next three paragraphs).

> Citation form: author's name only, because scholarly article on the Web has no page or other reference numbers.

The most promising short-term solution is for individuals to change their own behavior as consumers. The greenest behavior that individuals can adopt may be precycling, the term widely used for avoiding purchases of products that involve the use of raw materials. Precycling includes choosing eco-friendly products made of recycled or nontoxic materials (such as aluminum-free deodorants and fleece made from soda bottles) and avoiding items wrapped in excessive packaging (such as kitchen tools strapped to cardboard and printer cartridges sealed in plastic clamshells). More important, though, precycling means not buying new things in the first place. Renting and borrowing, when possible, save money and resources; so do keeping possessions in good repair and not replacing them until absolutely necessary. Good-quality used items, from clothing to furniture to electronics, can be obtained for free,

> Paragraph developed from common-knowledge definition and writer's own ideas and examples. None require source citations.

or very cheaply, through online communities like *Craigslist* and *Freecycle,* from thrift stores and yard sales, or by trading with friends and relatives. When consumers choose used goods over new, they can help to reduce demand for manufactured products that waste energy and resources, and they can help to keep unwanted items out of the waste stream.

Avoiding unnecessary purchases brings personal benefits as well. Brenda Lin, an environmental activist, explained in an e-mail interview that frugal living not only saves money but also provides pleasure:

> You'd be amazed at what people throw out or give away: perfectly good computers, oriental rugs, barely used sports equipment, designer clothes, you name it. . . . It's a game for me to find what I need in other people's trash or at Goodwill. You should see the shock on people's faces when I tell them where I got my stuff. I get almost as much enjoyment from that as from saving money and helping the environment at the same time.

Reducing consumption, it turns out, does not have to be a sacrifice; it can actually improve one's life.

For unavoidable purchases like food and light bulbs, buying green can make a difference by influencing corporate decisions. Some ecologists and economists believe that as more shoppers choose earth-friendly products over their traditional counterparts—or boycott products that are clearly harmful to the environment—more manufacturers and retailers will look for ways to limit the environmental effects of their industrial practices and the goods they sell (Gore, *Earth* 193; Muldoon). Indeed, as environmental business consultant Gregory C. Unruh points out in an article for *Harvard Business Review,* several major companies, among them Wal-Mart, Coca-Cola, General Electric, and Nike, have already taken up sustainability initiatives in response to market pressure. In the process, the companies have discovered that environmentally minded practices tend to raise profits and strengthen customer loyalty (111-12). By giving industry solid, bottom-line reasons to embrace ecological goals, consumer demand

Primary source: personal interview by e-mail.

Quotation of over four lines set off without quotation marks. See pp. 480–81.

Ellipsis mark signals omission from quotation.

Citation form: no parenthetical citation because author is named in the text and interview has no page or other reference numbers.

Writer's own conclusion from source.

Benefits of green consumerism.

Citation form: two works in the same citation.

Citation form: author is named in the text, so page numbers only.

for earth-friendly products can magnify the effects of individual action.

    Careful shopping can help the environment, but green doesn't necessarily mean "Go." All consumption depletes resources, increases the likelihood of global warming, and creates waste, so even eco-friendly products must be used in moderation. As individuals, we can each play a small role in helping the environment—and help ourselves at the same time—by not buying anything we don't really need, even if it seems environmentally sound. Reducing our personal impact on the earth is a small price to pay for preserving a livable planet for future generations.

> Conclusion: summary and a call for action.

Works Cited

Adler, Jerry, et al. "The Greening of America." *Newsweek* 14
    Aug. 2006: n. pag. *Master File Premier*. Web. 20 Feb.
    2009.

DeGraaf, John, David Wann, and Thomas H. Naylor. *Affluenza:
    The All-Consuming Epidemic*. San Francisco: Berrett-
    Koehler, 2001. Print.

Earth Policy Inst. "Eco-Economy Indicators." *Earth Policy Insti-
    tute*. EPI, Feb. 2008. Web. 6 Mar. 2009.

Gore, Al. *Earth in the Balance: Ecology and the Human Spirit*.
    Boston: Houghton, 1992. Print.

---. *An Inconvenient Truth: The Planetary Emergency of Global
    Warming and What We Can Do about It*. Emmaus: Rodale,
    2006. Print.

"It's Not Easy Buying Green." *Consumer Reports* Sept. 2007: 9.
    Print.

Lin, Brenda. Message to the author. 7 Mar. 2009. E-mail.

Muldoon, Annie. "Where the Green Is: Examining the Paradox
    of Environmentally Conscious Consumption." *Electronic
    Green Journal* 23 (2006): n. pag. Web. 28 Feb. 2009.

Princen, Thomas, Michael Maniates, and Ken Conca. Introduc-
    tion. *Confronting Consumption*. Ed. Princen, Maniates,
    and Conca. Cambridge: MIT P, 2002. 1-20. Print.

Rubin, Jeff, and Benjamin Tal. "Does Energy Efficiency Save
    Energy?" *StrategEcon*. CIBC World Markets, 27 Nov. 2007.
    Web. 13 Mar. 2009.

United Nations Development Programme. *Human Development
    Report 1998: Changing Today's Consumption Patterns—
    For Tomorrow's Human Development*. New York: Oxford
    UP, 1998. Print.

United States. Environmental Protection Agency. Solid Waste
    and Emergency Response. *Municipal Solid Waste
    Generation, Recycling, and Disposal in the United States:
    Facts and Figures for 2006*. US Environmental Protection
    Agency, Nov. 2007. Web. 4 Feb. 2009.

Unruh, Gregory C. "The Biosphere Rules." *Harvard Business Re-
    view* 86.2 (2008): 111-17. *Business Source Premier*. Web.
    14 Mar. 2009.

Annotations (left margin):
New page, double-spaced. Sources alphabetized by authors' last names.
An unpaged article with more than three authors, from a weekly magazine in an online database.
A print book with three authors.
A short, titled work on a Web site, with a corporate author.
A print book with one author.
Second source by author of two or more cited works: three hyphens replace author's name.
An anonymous article in a print magazine, listed and alphabetized by title.
An e-mail interview.
An article in a Web scholarly journal that numbers only issues and does not use page numbers.
An introduction to a print anthology.
A short, titled work on a Web site, by two authors.
A print book with a corporate author.
A US government source with no named author, so government body given as author.
An article in a scholarly journal that numbers volumes and issues, consulted in an online database.

57 APA Documentation and Format

How do I cite sources and format papers
in the social sciences?

The style guide for psychology and some other social sciences is the *Publication Manual of the American Psychological Association* (6th ed., 2010). The guidelines here reflect the second printing of the *Publication Manual*, which corrected some errors in the first printing. (The corrections are posted on the APA's Web site: *apastyle.org.*)

In APA documentation style, you acknowledge each of your sources twice:

- **In your text, a parenthetical citation near the borrowed material directs readers to a list of all the works you refer to.**
- **At the end of your paper, the list of references includes complete bibliographical information for every source.**

Every entry in the list of references has at least one corresponding citation in the text, and every in-text citation has a corresponding entry in the list of references.

This chapter describes APA text citations (below) and references (p. 494), details APA document format (p. 509), and concludes with a sample APA paper (p. 512).

57a Use APA parenthetical citations in your text.

In APA documentation style, parenthetical citations within the text refer the reader to a list of sources at the end of the text. See below for an index to the models for various kinds of sources.

APA parenthetical text citations

mycomplab

Visit *mycomplab.com* for more resources as well as exercises on APA documentation and format.

1. Author not named in your text

One critic of Milgram's experiments insisted that the subjects "should have been fully informed of the possible effects on them" (Baumrind, 1988, p. 34).

When you do not name the author in your text, place in parentheses the author's last name, the date of the source, and sometimes the page number as explained below. Separate the elements with commas. Position the reference so that it is clear what material is being documented *and* so that the reference fits as smoothly as possible into your sentence structure. (See pp. 443–45 for guidelines.) The following would also be correct:

In the view of one critic of Milgram's experiments (Baumrind, 1988), the subjects "should have been fully informed of the possible effects on them" (p. 34).

Unless none is available, the APA requires a page or other identifying number for a direct quotation (as in the examples above) and recommends an identifying number for a paraphrase. Use an appropriate abbreviation before the number—for instance, p. for *page* and para. for *paragraph*. The identifying number may fall with the author and date (first example) or by itself in a separate pair of parentheses (second example). See also model 11, page 494.

2. Author named in your text

Baumrind (1988) insisted that the subjects in Milgram's study "should have been fully informed of the possible effects on them" (p. 34).

When you use the author's name in the text, do not repeat it in the reference. Place the source date in parentheses after the author's name. Place any page or paragraph reference either after the borrowed material (as in the example) or with the date: (1988, p. 34). If you cite the same source again in the paragraph, you need not repeat the reference as long as it is clear that you are using the same source and the page number (if any) is the same.

3. A work with two authors

Pepinsky and DeStefano (1997) demonstrated that a teacher's language often reveals hidden biases.

One study (Pepinsky & DeStefano, 1997) demonstrated the hidden biases often revealed in a teacher's language.

When given in the text, two authors' names are connected by and. In a parenthetical citation, they are connected by an ampersand, &.

4. A work with three to five authors

Pepinsky, Dunn, Rentl, Corson, and Espenschade (1999) further demonstrated that the gestures of teachers also reveal unspoken attitudes and feelings.

In the first citation of a work with three to five authors, name all the authors. In the second and subsequent references to a work with three to five authors, generally give only the first author's name, followed by et al. (Latin abbreviation for "and others"):

In the work of Pepinsky et al. (1999), the loaded gestures included head shakes and eye contact.

However, two or more sources published in the same year could shorten to the same form—for instance, two references shortening to Pepinsky et al., 1999. In that case, cite the last names of as many authors as you need to distinguish the sources, and then give et al.: for instance, (Pepinsky, Dunn, et al., 1999) and (Pepinsky, Bradley, et al., 1999).

5. A work with six or more authors

One study (Rutter et al., 2003) attempted to explain these geographical differences in adolescent experience.

For six or more authors, even in the first citation of the work, give only the first author's name, followed by et al. If two or more sources published in the same year shorten to the same form, give additional names as explained with model 4.

6. A work with a group author

The students' later work improved significantly (Lenschow Research, 2009).

For a work that lists an institution, agency, corporation, or other group as author, treat the name of the group as if it were one person's name. If the name is long and has a familiar abbreviation, you may use the abbreviation in the second and subsequent citations. For example, you might abbreviate American Psychological Association as APA.

7. A work with no author or an anonymous work

One article ("Right to Die," 1996) noted that a death-row inmate may crave notoriety.

For a work with no named author, use the first two or three words of the title in place of an author's name, excluding an initial *The, A,* or *An.* Italicize book and journal titles, place quotation marks around article titles, and capitalize the significant words in all titles cited in the text. (In the reference list, however, do not use quotation marks for article titles, and capitalize only the first word in all but periodical titles. See p. 495.)

For a work that lists "Anonymous" as the author, use that word in the citation: (Anonymous, 2009).

8. One of two or more works by the same author(s)

At about age seven, most children begin to use appropriate gestures to reinforce their stories (Gardner, 1973a).

When you cite one of two or more works by the same author(s), the date will tell readers which source you mean—as long as your reference list includes only one source published by the author(s) in that year. If your reference list includes two or more works published by the same author(s) *in the same year,* the works should be lettered in the reference list (see p. 498). Then your parenthetical citation should include the appropriate letter with the date: 1973a in the example.

9. Two or more works by different authors

Two studies (Marconi & Hamblen, 1999; Torrence, 2007) found that monthly safety meetings can dramatically reduce workplace injuries.

List the sources in alphabetical order by their authors' names. Insert a semicolon between sources.

10. An indirect source

Supporting data appeared in a study by Chang (as cited in Torrence, 2007).

The phrase as cited in indicates that the reference to Chang's study was found in Torrence. Only Torrence then appears in the list of references.

11. An electronic source

Ferguson and Hawkins (2006) did not anticipate the "evident hostility" of participants (para. 6).

Electronic sources can be cited like printed sources, usually with the author's last name and the publication date. When quoting or paraphrasing electronic sources that number paragraphs instead of pages, provide the paragraph number preceded by para. If the source does not number pages or paragraphs but does include headings, list the heading under which the quotation appears and then (counting paragraphs yourself) the number of the paragraph in which the quotation appears—for example, (Endter & Decker, 2008, Method section, para. 3). When the source does not number pages or paragraphs or provide headings, omit any reference number.

57b Prepare an APA reference list.

In APA style, the in-text parenthetical citations refer to the list of sources at the end of the text. This list, titled References, includes full publication information on every source cited in the paper. The list falls at the end of the paper, numbered in sequence with the preceding pages.

Arrangement Arrange sources alphabetically by the author's last name. If there is no author, alphabetize by the first main word of the title. Do *not* group sources by type (books, journals, and so on).

APA reference list

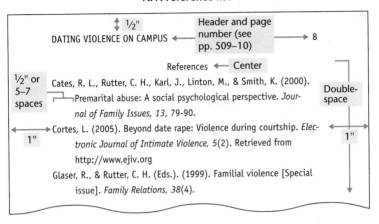

APA reference list

Spacing Double-space everything in the references, as shown in the sample above, unless your instructor requests single spacing. (If you do single-space the entries themselves, always double-space *between* them.)

Indention As illustrated in the sample above, begin each entry at the left margin, and indent the second and subsequent lines five to seven spaces or one-half inch.

Punctuation Separate the parts of the reference (author, date, title, and publication information) with a period and one space. Do not use a final period in references that conclude with a DOI or a URL (see p. 502).

Authors For works with up to seven authors, list all authors with last name first, separating names and parts of names with commas. Use initials for first and middle names. Use an ampersand (&) before the last author's name. See model 3 (next page) for the treatment of eight or more authors.

Publication date Place the publication date in parentheses after the author's or authors' names, followed by a period. Generally this date is the year only, though for some sources (such as magazine and newspaper articles) it includes the month and sometimes the day as well.

Titles In titles of books and articles, capitalize only the first word of the title, the first word of the subtitle, and proper nouns; all other words begin with small letters. In titles of journals, capitalize all significant words. Italicize the titles of books and journals. Do not italicize or use quotation marks around the titles of articles.

City and state of publication For print sources that are not periodicals (such as books or government publications), give the city of publication, a comma, the two-letter postal abbreviation of the state, and a colon. Omit the state if the publisher is a university whose name includes the state name, such as University of Arizona.

Publisher's name For nonperiodical print sources, give the publisher's name after the place of publication and a colon. Use shortened names for many publishers (such as Morrow for William Morrow), and omit "Co.," "Inc.," and "Publishers." However, give full names for associations, corporations, and university presses (such as Harvard University Press), and do not omit "Books" or "Press" from a publisher's name.

Page numbers Use the abbreviation p. or pp. before page numbers in books and in newspapers. Do *not* use the abbreviation for journals and magazines. For inclusive page numbers, include all figures: 667-668.

An index to the following models appears opposite. If you don't see a model listed for the kind of source you used, try to find one that comes close, and provide ample information so that readers can trace the source. Often you will have to combine models to provide the necessary information on a source—for instance, combining "Two to seven authors" (model 2) and "An article in a journal" (model 7) for a journal article with two or more authors.

1 ▪ Listing authors

1. One author

Rodriguez, R. (1982). *A hunger of memory: The education of Richard Rodriguez.*
Boston, MA: Godine.

The initial R. appears instead of the author's first name, even though the author's full first name appears on the source. In this book title, only the first words of the title and subtitle and the proper name are capitalized.

2. Two to seven authors

Nesselroade, J. R., & Baltes, P. B. (1999). *Longitudinal research in behavioral studies.* New York, NY: Academic Press.

Separate authors' names with commas, and use an ampersand (&) before the last author's name.

3. Eight or more authors

Wimple, P. B., Van Eijk, M., Potts, C. A., Hayes, J., Obergau, W. R., Zimmer, S., . . . Smith, H. (2001). *Case studies in moral decision making among adolescents.* San Francisco, CA: Jossey-Bass.

APA references

APA

57b

For a work by eight or more authors, list the first six authors' names, insert an ellipsis mark (three spaced periods), and then give the last author's name.

4. A group author

Lenschow Research. (2009). *Trends in secondary curriculum*. Baltimore, MD: Arrow Books.

For a work with a group author—such as a research group, a government agency, or a corporation—begin the entry with the group name. In the reference list, alphabetize the work as if the first main word (excluding any *The*, *A*, and *An*) were an author's last name.

5. Author not named (anonymous)

Merriam-Webster's collegiate dictionary (11th ed.). (2009). Springfield, MA: Merriam-Webster.

Heroes of the environment. (2009, October 5). *Time, 174*(13), 45-54.

When no author is named, list the work under its title and alphabetize it by the first main word (excluding any *The*, *A*, *An*).

For a work whose author is actually given as "Anonymous," use that word in place of the author's name and alphabetize it as if it were a name:

Anonymous. (2008). *Teaching research, researching teaching.* New York, NY: Alpine Press.

6. Two or more works by the same author(s) published in the same year

Gardner, H. (1973a). *The arts and human development.* New York, NY: Wiley.

Gardner, H. (1973b). *The quest for mind: Piaget, Lévi-Strauss, and the structuralist movement.* New York, NY: Knopf.

When citing two or more works by exactly the same author(s), published in the same year, arrange them alphabetically by the first main word of the title and distinguish the sources by adding a letter to the date. Both the date and the letter are used in citing the source in your text (see pp. 493–94).

When citing two or more works by exactly the same author(s) but *not* published in the same year, arrange the sources in order of their publication dates, earliest first.

2 ▪ Listing print periodicals: Journals, newspapers, magazines

7. An article in a journal (print)

Selwyn, N. (2005). The social processes of learning to use computers. *Social Science Computer Review, 23*, 122-135.

The facing page shows the basic format for a print journal article and the location of the required information in the journal. If the print article has a Digital Object Identifier, add it at the end of the entry. See model 18, page 502.

Note Some journals number the pages of issues consecutively throughout a year, so that each issue after the first begins numbering where the previous issue left off—say, at page 132 or 416. For this kind of journal, give the volume number after the title, as in the

Format for a print journal article

① ② ③ ④
Selwyn, N. (2005). The social processes of learning to use computers. *Social Science*
⑤ ⑥
Computer Review, 23, 122-135.

Journal cover

⑤ **Volume number,** italicized and followed by a comma. See page 500 for when to include the issue number.

SPRING 2005   VOLUME 23   NUMBER 1

② **Year of publication,** in parentheses and followed by a period.

④ **Title of periodical,** in italics. Capitalize all significant words and end with a comma.

SOCIAL
SCIENCE
COMPUTER
REVIEW

③ **Title of article.** Give the full article title and any subtitle, separating them with a colon. Capitalize only the first words of the title and subtitle, and do not place the title in quotation marks.

The Social Processes of Learning to Use Computers

NEIL SELWYN
Cardiff School of Social Sciences

① **Author.** Give the last name first, a comma, the initial of the first name, and any middle initial, following each initial with a period. Omit *Dr., PhD,* or any other title.

The ability to use a computer is assumed to be a cornerstone of effective ci Age, with a range of initiatives and educational provisions being introduc become competent with information technology (IT). Despite such provi and competence have been found to vary widely throughout the general population, and we know little of how different ways of learning to use computers contribute to people's eventual use of IT. Based on data from in-depth interviews with 100 adults in the United Kingdom, this article examines the range and social stratification of formal and informal learning about computers that is taking place, suggesting that formal computer instruction orientated toward the general public may inadvertently widen the digital knowledge gap. In particular, the data highlight the importance of informal learning about IT and of encouraging such learning, especially in the home.

AUTHOR'S NOTE: This article is based on a project funded by the Economic and Social Research Council (R000239518). I would like to thank the other members of the Adults Learning@Home project (Stephen Gorard and John Furlong) as well as the individuals who took part in the in-depth interviews. Correspondence concerning this article may be addressed to Neil Selwyn, School of Social Sciences, Cardiff University, Glamorgan Building, King Edward VII Avenue, Cardiff CF10 3WT, UK; e-mail: selwynnc@cardiff.ac.uk.

122

⑥ **Inclusive page numbers of article,** without "pp." Do not omit any numerals.

preceding example. The page numbers are enough to guide readers to the issue you used. Other journals and most magazines start each issue with page 1. For these journals and magazines, place the issue number (not italicized) in parentheses immediately after the volume number. See model 10 for an example of a volume and issue number.

8. An abstract of a journal article (print)

Emery, R. E. (2006). Marital turmoil: Interpersonal conflict and the children of discord and divorce. *Psychological Bulletin, 92*, 310-330. Abstract obtained from *Psychological Abstracts*, 2006, *69*, Item 1320.

When you cite the abstract of an article rather than the article itself, give full publication information for the article, followed by Abstract obtained from and the information for the collection of abstracts, including title, date, volume and issue numbers, and either page number or other reference number (Item 1320 in the example).

9. An article in a newspaper (print)

Elliott, S. (2009, June 3). Trying to pitch products to the savers. *The New York Times*, p. B3.

Give month *and* day along with year of publication. Use *The* in the newspaper name if the paper itself does. Precede the page number(s) with p. or pp.

10. An article in a magazine (print)

Newton-Small, J. (2009, October 5). Divided loyalties. *Time, 174*(13), 38.

Give the full date of the issue: year, followed by a comma, month, and day (if any). Give all page numbers even when the article appears on discontinuous pages, without "pp." If a magazine has volume and issue numbers, provide both because magazine issues are paginated separately. (See the top of this page.)

11. A review (print)

Dinnage, R. (1987, November 29). Against the master and his men [Review of the book *A mind of her own: The life of Karen Horney,* by S. Quinn]. *The New York Times Book Review*, 10-11.

If the review is not titled, use the bracketed information as the title, keeping the brackets.

3 ▪ Listing print books

12. Basic format for a book (print)

Ehrenreich, B. (2007). *Dancing in the streets: A history of collective joy.* New York, NY: Holt.

Give the author's or authors' names, following models 1–4. Then give the complete title, including any subtitle. Italicize the title, and capitalize only the first words of the title and subtitle. End the entry with the city and state of publication and the publisher's name. (See pp. 495–96 for how to treat these elements.)

13. A book with an editor (print)

Dohrenwend, B. S., & Dohrenwend, B. P. (Eds.). (1999). *Stressful life events: Their nature and effects.* New York, NY: Wiley.

List the editors' names as if they were authors, but follow the last name with (Eds.).—or (Ed.). with only one editor. Note the periods inside and outside the final parenthesis.

14. A book with a translator (print)

Trajan, P. D. (1927). *Psychology of animals* (H. Simone, Trans.). Washington, DC: Halperin.

The name of the translator appears in parentheses after the title, followed by a comma, Trans. and a closing parenthesis, and a final period.

15. A later edition (print)

Bolinger, D. L. (1981). *Aspects of language* (3rd ed.). New York, NY: Harcourt Brace Jovanovich.

The edition number in parentheses follows the title and is followed by a period.

16. A work in more than one volume (print)

Lincoln, A. (1953). *The collected works of Abraham Lincoln* (R. P. Basler, Ed.). (Vol. 5). New Brunswick, NJ: Rutgers University Press.
Lincoln, A. (1953). *The collected works of Abraham Lincoln* (R. P. Basler, Ed.). (Vols. 1-8). New Brunswick, NJ: Rutgers University Press.

The first entry cites a single volume (5) in the eight-volume set. The second cites all eight volumes. Use the abbreviation Vol. or Vols. in parentheses and follow the closing parenthesis with a period. In the absence of an editor's name, the description of volumes would follow the title directly: *The collected works of Abraham Lincoln* (Vol. 5).

17. An article or a chapter in an edited book (print)

Paykel, E. S. (1999). Life stress and psychiatric disorder: Applications of the clinical approach. In B. S. Dohrenwend & B. P. Dohrenwend (Eds.), *Stressful life events: Their nature and effects* (pp. 239-264). New York, NY: Wiley.

Give the publication date of the collection (1999 here) as the publication date of the article or chapter. After the article or chapter title and a period, say In and then provide the editors' names (in normal order), (Eds.) and a comma, the title of the collection, and the page numbers of the article in parentheses.

4 ▪ Listing Web and other electronic sources

In APA style, most electronic references begin as those for print references do: author, date, title. Then you add information on how to retrieve the source, generally giving either a DOI (see model 18) or a URL (see model 19). In addition, note the following:

- ▪ APA does not require your access date if the source is unlikely to change or if it has a publication date or edition or version number. See model 29 for use of an access date.
- ▪ APA does not require a full URL if the source can be located by searching the home page of a Web site. See model 32 for an example of a complete URL.
- ▪ When you need to divide a URL or DOI from one line to the next, APA calls for breaking before punctuation such as a period or slash. (But break after the two slashes in http://.) Do not hyphenate a URL or a DOI.

If you don't see a model for your particular electronic source, consult the index of models on page 497 for a similar source type whose format you can adapt. If your source does not include all of the information needed for a complete citation, find and list what you can.

18. A journal article with a Digital Object Identifier (DOI) (Web)

Cunningham, J. A., & Selby, P. (2007). Relighting cigarettes: How common is
    it? *Nicotine and Tobacco Research, 9*, 621-623. doi:10.1080
    /14622200701239688

The facing page shows the basic format for a periodical article that you access either directly online or through an online database as well as the location of the required information on the source.

Many publishers now assign a Digital Object Identifier (DOI) to journal articles and other documents. A DOI functions as a unique identifier and a link to the text. When a DOI is available, include it instead of a URL or a database name. (The DOI may be evident on the source, or it may be found by clicking on "Article" or "Cross-Ref.") Do not add a period at the end of the DOI.

19. A journal article without a DOI (Web)

Polletta, F. (2008). Just talk: Public deliberation after 9/11. *Journal of Public
    Deliberation, 4*(1). Retrieved from http://services.bepress.com/jpd

Format for a journal article on the Web

① ② ③
Cunningham, J. A., & Selby, P. (2007). Relighting cigarettes: How common is it?
④ ⑤ ⑥ ⑦
Nicotine and Tobacco Research, 9, 621-623. doi:10.1080

/14622200701239688

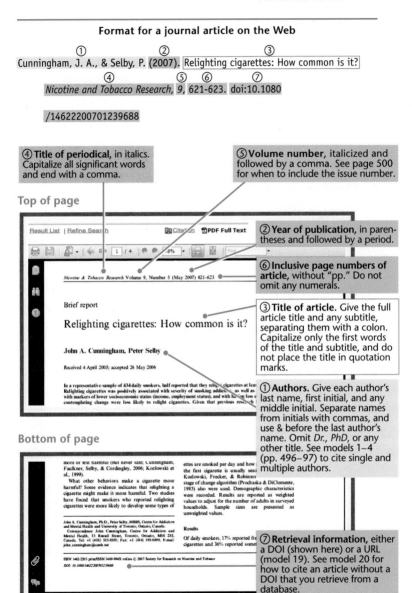

④ **Title of periodical,** in italics. Capitalize all significant words and end with a comma.

⑤ **Volume number,** italicized and followed by a comma. See page 500 for when to include the issue number.

Top of page

② **Year of publication,** in parentheses and followed by a period.

⑥ **Inclusive page numbers** of article, without "pp." Do not omit any numerals.

③ **Title of article.** Give the full article title and any subtitle, separating them with a colon. Capitalize only the first words of the title and subtitle, and do not place the title in quotation marks.

① **Authors.** Give each author's last name, first initial, and any middle initial. Separate names from initials with commas, and use & before the last author's name. Omit *Dr., PhD,* or any other title. See models 1–4 (pp. 496–97) to cite single and multiple authors.

Bottom of page

⑦ **Retrieval information,** either a DOI (shown here) or a URL (model 19). See model 20 for how to cite an article without a DOI that you retrieve from a database.

When a journal article does not have a DOI, give the URL of the journal's home page in a statement beginning Retrieved from. Do not add a period at the end of the URL.

20. A periodical article in an online database (Web)

Rosen, I. M., Maurer, D. M., & Darnall, C. R. (2008). Reducing tobacco use in
adolescents. *American Family Physician, 77,* 483-490. Retrieved from
http://www.aafp.org/online/en/home/publications/journals/afp.html

Generally, do not give the name of the database in which you found
your source, because readers may not be able to find the source the
same way you did. Instead, use a search engine to find the home
page of the periodical and give the home page URL in your retrieval
statement (preceding example).

If you don't find the home page of the periodical, then give the
database name in your retrieval statement, as in this example:

Smith, E. M. (1926, March). Equal rights—internationally! *Life and Labor
Bulletin, 4,* 1-2. Retrieved from Women and Social Movements in the
United States, 1600-2000, database.

21. An abstract of a journal article (Web)

Polletta, F. (2008). Just talk: Public deliberation after 9/11. *Journal of Public
Deliberation, 4*(1). Abstract retrieved from http://services.bepress.com/jpd

22. An article in a newspaper (Web)

Campbell, C. A. (21 May 2009.) Health outcomes driving new hospital design.
The New York Times. Retrieved from http://www.nytimes.com

Give the URL of the newspaper's home page in the retrieval statement. If you found the article in an online database, see model 20.

23. An article in a magazine (Web)

Young, E. (2009, February 21). Sleep well, keep sane. *New Scientist, 201*(26),
34-37. Retrieved from http://www.newscientist.com

Give the URL of the magazine's home page in the retrieval statement. If you found the article in an online database, see model 20.

24. Supplemental periodical content that appears only online (Web)

Gawande, A. (2009, June 1). More is less [Supplemental material]. *The New
Yorker.* Retrieved from http://www.newyorker.com

If you cite material from a periodical's Web site that is not included
in the print version of the publication, add [Supplemental material] after
the title and give the URL of the publication's home page.

25. A review (Web)

Bond, M. (2008, December 18). Does genius breed success? [Review of the
book *Outliers: The story of success*, by M. Gladwell]. *Nature, 456,* 785.
doi:10.1038/456874a

Cite an online review like a print review (model 11, p. 500), concluding with retrieval information (here, a DOI).

26. A report or other material from the Web site of an organization or government (Web)

Ellerman, D., & Joskow, P. L. (2008, May). *The European Union's emissions trading system in perspective.* Retrieved from the Pew Center on Global Climate Change website: http://www.pewclimate.org

Treat the title of an independent Web document like the title of a book. Provide the name of the publishing organization as part of the retrieval statement when the publisher is not listed as the author, as in the preceding example.

If the document you cite is difficult to locate from the organization's home page, give the complete URL in the retrieval statement:

Union of Concerned Scientists. *Clean vehicles.* (2009, April 24). Retrieved from http://www.ucsusa.org/clean_vehicles

If the document you cite is undated, use the abbreviation n.d. in place of the publication date and give the date of your access in the retrieval statement:

U.S. Department of Agriculture. (n.d.). *Inside the Pyramid.* Retrieved April 23, 2009, from http://www.mypyramid.gov

27. A book (Web)

Hernandez, L. M., & Munthali, A. W. (Eds.). (2007). *Training physicians for public health careers.* Retrieved from http://books.nap.edu /catalog.php?record_id=11915

For online books, replace the publisher's city and name with a retrieval statement. See models 14–17 (p. 501) to cite variations in book entries: a translator, a later edition, a book in more than one volume, and an article or a chapter in a book.

28. An article in a reference work (Web)

Perception. (2008). In *Encyclopaedia Britannica Online.* Retrieved from http:// www.britannica.com

APA requires only the home page or index page URL for reference works.

29. An article in a wiki (Web)

Cognitive neuropsychology. (2009, June 15). Retrieved August 3, 2009, from Wikipedia: http://en.wikipedia.org

Give your retrieval date for sources that are likely to change, such as this wiki.

30. A dissertation (Web)

A dissertation in a commercial database:

McFaddin, M. O. (2007). *Adaptive reuse: An architectural solution for poverty and homelessness* (Doctoral dissertation). Available from ProQuest Dissertations and Theses database. (ATT 1378764)

If a dissertation is from a commercial database, give the name of the database in the retrieval statement, followed by the accession or order number in parentheses.

A dissertation in an institutional database:

Chang, J. K. (2003). *Therapeutic intervention in treatment of injuries to the hand and wrist* (Doctoral dissertation). Retrieved from http://medsci .archive.liasu.edu/61724

If a dissertation is from an institution's database, give the URL in the retrieval statement.

See also model 38 (p. 508) for examples of print dissertations.

31. A podcast (Web)

Ferracca, J. (Producer). (2009, June 1). Guerilla gardening [Audio podcast]. *Here on earth: Radio without borders.* Retrieved from http://www.wpr.org /hereonearth

32. A film or video recording (Web)

Green Children Foundation (Producer). (2009). *Hear me now* [Video file]. Retrieved from http://www.youtube.com/watch?v=zN3e7qdQaxY

If the film or video you cite is difficult to locate from the home page of the Web site, give the complete URL in the retrieval statement, as in the example.

33. An image (Web)

United Nations Population Fund (Cartographer). (2005). *Percent of population living on less than $1/day* [Demographic map]. Retrieved from http:// www.unfpa.org

34. A message posted to a blog or discussion group (Web)

Munger, D. (2009, May 9). Does recess really improve classroom behavior? [Web log post]. Retrieved from http://scienceblogs.com/cognitivedaily

Include postings to blogs and discussion groups in your list of references *only* if they are retrievable by others. (The source above is retrievable by a search of the home page URL.) Follow the message title with [Web log post], [Electronic mailing list message], or [Online forum comment]. Include the name of the blog or discussion group in the retrieval statement if it isn't part of the URL.

35. A personal communication (text citation)

At least one member of the research team has expressed reservations about the design of the study (L. Kogod, personal communication, February 6, 2009).

Personal e-mail and other online postings that are not retrievable by others should be cited only in your text, as here, not in your list of references.

5 ▪ Listing other sources

36. A report (print)

Gerald, K. (2003). *Medico-moral problems in obstetric care* (Report No. NP-71). St. Louis, MO: Catholic Hospital Association.

Treat a printed report like a book, but provide any report number in parentheses immediately after the title, with no punctuation between them.

For a report from the Educational Resources Information Center (ERIC), provide the ERIC document number in parentheses at the end of the entry:

Jolson, M. K. (2001). *Music education for preschoolers* (Report No. TC-622). New York, NY: Teachers College, Columbia University. (ERIC Document Reproduction Service No. ED264488)

37. A government publication (print)

Hawaii. Department of Education. (2008). *Kauai district schools, profile 2007-08.* Honolulu, HI: Author.

Stiller, A. (2002). *Historic preservation and tax incentives.* Washington, DC: U.S. Department of the Interior.

If no person is named as the author, list the publication under the name of the sponsoring agency. When the agency is both the author and the publisher, use Author in place of the publisher's name, as in the first example.

For legal materials such as court decisions, laws, and testimony at hearings, the APA recommends formats that correspond to conventional legal citations. The following example of a congressional hearing includes the full title, the number of the Congress, the page number where the hearing transcript starts in the official publication, and the date of the hearing.

APA

57b

> *Medicare payment for outpatient physical and occupational therapy services:*
> *Hearing before the Committee on Ways and Means, House of Representa-*
> *tives,* 110th Cong. 3 (2007).

38. A dissertation (print)

A dissertation abstracted in DAI:

> Steciw, S. K. (1986). Alterations to the Pessac project of Le Corbusier.
> *Dissertation Abstracts International, 46*(6), 565C.

An unpublished dissertation:

> Hernandez, A. J. (2005). *Persistent poverty: Transient work and workers in*
> *today's labor market* (Unpublished doctoral dissertation). University of
> Illinois, Urbana-Champaign.

39. An interview (print)

> Schenker, H. (2007). No peace without third-party intervention [Interview
> with Shulamit Aloni]. *Palestine-Israel Journal of Politics, Economics, and*
> *Culture, 14*(4), 63-68.

List a published interview under the interviewer's name, and provide the title, if any, without italics or quotation marks. If there is
no title, or if the title does not indicate the interview format or the
interviewee (as in the example), add a bracketed explanation. End
with the publication information for the kind of source the interview appears in (here, a journal).

An interview you conduct yourself should not be included in
the list of references. Instead, use an in-text parenthetical citation,
as shown in model 35 (p. 507) for a personal communication.

40. A motion picture

> American Psychological Association (Producer). (2001). *Ethnocultural psy-*
> *chotherapy* [DVD]. Available from http://www.apa.org/videos
> Howard, R. (Director). (2001). *A beautiful mind* [Motion picture]. United
> States: Universal.

Depending on whose work you are citing, begin with the name or
names of the creator, director, producer, or primary contributor, followed by the function in parentheses. (The second example would
begin with the producer's name if you were citing the motion picture
as a whole, not specifically the work of the director.) Add the medium in brackets after the title: [Motion picture] (for film), [DVD], or
[Videocassette]. For a work in wide circulation (second example), give
the country of origin and the studio that released the picture. For a
work that is not widely circulated (first example), give the distributor's address or URL.

41. A musical recording

Springsteen, B. (2002). Empty sky. On *The rising* [CD]. New York, NY: Columbia.

Begin with the name of the writer or composer. (If you cite another artist's recording of the work, provide this information after the title of the work—for example, [Recorded by E. Davila].) Give the medium in brackets ([CD], [LP], and so on). Finish with the city, state, and name of the recording label.

42. A television series or episode

Rhimes, S. (Executive Producer). (2008). *Grey's anatomy* [Television series]. New York, NY: CBS.

McKee S. (Writer), & Tinker, M. (Director). (2009). Sweet surrender [Television series episode]. In S. Rhimes (Executive Producer), *Grey's anatomy*. New York, NY: CBS.

For a television series, begin with the producers' names and identify their function in parentheses. Add [Television series] after the series title, and give the city and name of the network. For an episode, begin with the writer and then the director, identifying the function of each in parentheses, and add [Television series episode] after the episode title. Then provide the series information, beginning with In and the producers' names and function, giving the series title, and ending with the city, state, and name of the network.

57c Format the paper in APA style.

The following guidelines for document format reflect the second printing of the APA *Publication Manual*, 6th edition, which corrected some errors in the first printing. (The corrections are posted on the APA's Web site: *apastyle.org*.)

Note See page 495 for the APA format of a reference list. And see pages 66–74 for guidelines on type fonts, lists, tables and figures, and other elements of document design.

Margins Use one-inch margins on the top, bottom, and both sides.

Spacing and indentions Double-space everywhere. (The only exception is tables and figures, where related data, labels, and other elements may be single-spaced.) Indent paragraphs and displayed quotations one-half inch or five to seven spaces.

Paging Begin numbering on the title page, and number consecutively through the end (including the reference list). Provide a header about one-half inch from the top of every page, as shown in the samples on the next page. The header consists of the page number on the far right and your full or shortened title on the far left. Type the title in all-capital letters. On the title page only, precede the title with the label Running head and a colon. Omit this label on all other pages.

Title page Include the full title, your name, the course title, the instructor's name, and the date. (See below.) Type the title on the top half of the page, followed by the identifying information, all centered horizontally and double-spaced.

APA title page

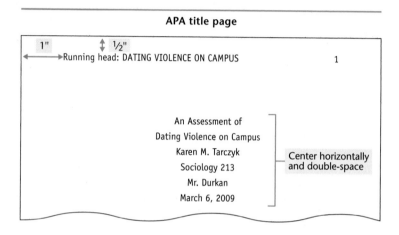

Abstract Summarize (in a maximum of 120 words) your subject, research method, findings, and conclusions. (See below.) Put the abstract on a page by itself.

APA abstract

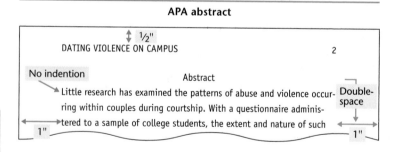

Body Begin with a restatement of the paper's title and then an introduction (not labeled). The introduction concisely presents the problem you researched, your research method, the relevant background (such as related studies), and the purpose of your research.

The next section, labeled **Method**, provides a detailed discussion of how you conducted your research, including a description of

First page of APA body

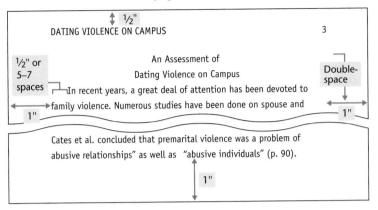

Later page of APA body

the research subjects, any materials or tools you used (such as questionnaires or surveys), and the procedure you followed. In the illustration above, the labels **Method** and **Sample** are first-level and second-level headings, respectively. When you need one, two, or three levels of headings, use the following formats, always double-spacing above and below:

First-Level Heading

Second-Level Heading

    Third-level heading. Run this heading into the text paragraph.

The **Results** section (labeled with a first-level heading) summarizes the data you collected, explains how you analyzed them, and presents them in detail, often in tables, graphs, or charts.

The **Discussion** section (labeled with a first-level heading) interprets the data and presents your conclusions. (When the discussion is brief, you may combine it with the previous section under the heading **Results and Discussion**.)

The **References** section, beginning a new page, includes all your sources. See pages 494–96 for an explanation and sample.

Long quotations Run into your text all quotations of forty words or less, enclosed in quotation marks. For quotations of more than forty words, set them off from your text by indenting all lines one-half inch or five to seven spaces, double-spacing throughout.

> Echoing the opinions of other Europeans at the time, Freud (1961) had a poor view of Americans:
>
> > The Americans are really too bad. . . . Competition is much more pungent with them, not succeeding means civil death to every one, and they have no private resources apart from their profession, no hobby, games, love or other interests of a cultured person. And success means money. (p. 86)

Do not use quotation marks around a quotation displayed in this way.

Illustrations Present data in tables and figures (graphs or charts), as appropriate. (See p. 515 and pp. 71–73 for examples.) Begin each illustration on a separate page. Number each kind of illustration consecutively and separately from the other (Table 1, Table 2, etc., and Figure 1, Figure 2, etc.). Refer to all illustrations in your text—for instance, (see Figure 3). Generally, place illustrations immediately after the text references to them.

57d   A sample paper in APA style.

The following excerpts from a sociology paper illustrate elements of a research paper using the APA style of documentation and format.

[Title page.]
Running head: DATING VIOLENCE ON CAMPUS   1

Header and page number. (See pp. 509–10.)

An Assessment of

Dating Violence on Campus

Karen M. Tarczyk

Sociology 213

Mr. Durkan

March 6, 2009

Double-space all information: title, name, course title, instructor, date.

[New page.]
DATING VIOLENCE ON CAMPUS   2

Abstract

Little research has examined the patterns of abuse and violence occurring within couples during courtship. With a questionnaire administered to a sample of college students, the extent and nature of such abuse and violence were investigated. The results, interpretations, and implications for further research are discussed.

Abstract: summary of subject, research method, conclusions.

Double-space throughout.

[New page.]
DATING VIOLENCE ON CAMPUS   3

An Assessment of

Dating Violence on Campus

In recent years, a great deal of attention has been devoted to family violence. Numerous studies have been done on spouse and child abuse. However, violent behavior occurs in dating relationships as well, yet the problem of dating violence has been relatively ignored by sociological research. It should be examined further since the premarital relationship is one context in which individuals learn and adopt behaviors that surface in marriage.

The sociologist James Makepeace (1989) contended that courtship violence is a "potential mediating link" between violence in one's family of orientation and violence in one's later family of procreation (p. 103). Studying dating behaviors at Bemidji State University in Minnesota, Makepeace reported that one-fifth of the respondents had had at least one encounter with dating violence. He then extended these percentages to students nationwide, suggesting the existence of a major hidden social problem.

Title repeated on first text page.

Introduction: presentation of the problem researched by the writer.

Citation form: author named in the text.

Citation form: page number given for quotation.

More recent research supports Makepeace's. Cates, Rutter, Karl, Linton, and Smith (2000) found that 22.3% of respondents at Oregon State University had been either the victim or the perpetrator of pre-marital violence.

Another study (Cortes, 2005) found that so-called date rape, while much more publicized and discussed, was reported by many fewer woman respondents (2%) than was other violence during courtship (21%).

[The introduction continues.]

All these studies indicate a problem that is being neglected. My objective was to gather data on the extent and nature of premarital violence and to discuss possible interpretations.

Method

Sample

I conducted a survey of 200 students (134 females, 66 males) at a large state university in the northeastern United States. The sample consisted of students enrolled in an introductory sociology course.

[The explanation of method continues.]

The Questionnaire

A questionnaire exploring the personal dynamics of relationships was distributed during regularly scheduled class. Questions were answered anonymously in a 30-minute period. The survey consisted of three sections.

[The explanation of method continues.]

Section 3 required participants to provide information about their current dating relationships. Levels of stress and frustration, communication between partners, and patterns of decision making were examined. These variables were expected to influence the amount of violence in a relationship. The next part of the survey was adopted from Murray Strauss's Conflict Tactics Scales (1992). These scales contain 19 items designed to measure conflict and the means of conflict resolution, including reasoning, verbal aggression, and actual violence. The final page of the questionnaire contained general questions on the couple's use of alcohol, sexual activity, and overall satisfaction with the relationship.

Results

The questionnaire revealed significant levels of verbal aggression and threatened and actual violence among dating couples. A high number of students, 50% (62 of 123 subjects), reported that they had been the victim of verbal abuse, either being insulted or sworn at. In addition, almost 14% of respondents (17 of 123) admitted being threatened with some type of violence, and more than 14% (18 of 123) reported being pushed, grabbed, or shoved. (See Table 1.)

Reference to table.

[The explanation of results continues.]

[Table on a page by itself.]

DATING VIOLENCE ON CAMPUS   6

Table 1

Incidence of Courtship Violence

Table presents data in clear format.

Type of violence	Number of students reporting	Percentage of sample
Insulted or swore	62	50.4
Threatened to hit or throw something	17	13.8
Threw something	8	6.5
Pushed, grabbed, or shoved	18	14.6
Slapped	8	6.5
Kicked, bit, or hit with fist	7	5.7
Hit or tried to hit with something	2	1.6
Threatened with a knife or gun	1	0.8
Used a knife or gun	1	0.8

Discussion

Violence within premarital relationships has been relatively ignored. The results of the present study indicate that abuse and force do occur in dating relationships. Although the percentages are small, so was the sample. Extending them to the entire campus population of 5,000 would mean significant numbers. For example, if the nearly 6% incidence of being kicked, bitten, or hit with a fist is typical, then 300 students might have experienced this type of violence.

"Discussion" section: interpretation of data and presentation of conclusions.

[The discussion continues.]

If the courtship period is characterized by abuse and violence, what accounts for it? The other sections of the survey examined some variables that appear to influence the relationship. Level of stress and frustration, both within the relationship and in the respondent's life, was one such variable. The communication level between partners, both the frequency of discussion and the frequency of agreement, was another.

[The discussion continues.]

The method of analyzing the data in this study, utilizing frequency distributions, provided a clear overview. However, more tests of significance and correlation and a closer look at the social and individual variables affecting the relationship are warranted. The courtship period may set the stage for patterns of married life. It merits more attention.

[New page.]

New page for reference list.

DATING VIOLENCE ON CAMPUS 8

References

An article in a print journal.

Cates, R. L., Rutter, C. H., Karl, J., Linton, M., & Smith, K. (2000). Premarital abuse: A social psychological perspective. *Journal of Family Issues, 13*, 79-90.

An article in an online journal without a Digital Object Identifier.

Cortes, L. (2005). Beyond date rape: Violence during courtship. *Electronic Journal of Intimate Violence, 5*(2). Retrieved from http://www.ejiv.org

Glaser, R., & Rutter, C. H. (Eds.). (1999). Familial violence [Special issue]. *Family Relations, 38*(4).

Makepeace, J. M. (1989). Courtship violence among college students. *Family Relations, 28*(6), 97-103.

A book. ("Tactics Scales" is part of a proper name and so is capitalized.)

Strauss, M. L. (1992). *Conflict Tactics Scales*. New York, NY: Sociological Tests.

Glossary of Usage

This glossary provides notes on words or phrases that often cause problems for writers. The recommendations for standard American English are based on current dictionaries and usage guides. Items labeled **nonstandard** should be avoided in speech and especially in writing. Those labeled **colloquial** and **slang** occur in speech and in some informal writing but are best avoided in the more formal writing usually expected in college and business. (Words and phrases labeled *colloquial* include those labeled by many dictionaries with the equivalent term *informal*.)

Note Two lists in the text supplement this glossary: idioms with prepositions, such as *part from* and *part with* (p. 180); and words that are pronounced the same or similarly but spelled differently, such as *heard* and *herd* (pp. 352–53).

a, an Use *a* before words beginning with consonant sounds, including those spelled with an initial pronounced *h* and those spelled with vowels that are sounded as consonants: *a historian, a one-o'clock class, a university.* Use *an* before words that begin with vowel sounds, including those spelled with an initial silent *h: an organism, an L, an honor.*

The article before an abbreviation depends on how the abbreviation is to be read: *She was once an AEC undersecretary* (*AEC* is to be read as three separate letters). *Many Americans opposed a SALT treaty* (*SALT* is to be read as one word, *salt*).

See also pp. 276–79 on the uses of *a/an* versus *the.*

accept, except *Accept* is a verb meaning "receive." *Except* is usually a preposition or conjunction meaning "but for" or "other than"; when it is used as a verb, it means "leave out." *I can accept all your suggestions except the last one. I'm sorry you excepted my last suggestion from your list.*

advice, advise *Advice* is a noun, and *advise* is a verb: *Take my advice; do as I advise you.*

affect, effect Usually *affect* is a verb, meaning "to influence," and *effect* is a noun, meaning "result": *The drug did not affect his driving; in fact, it seemed to have no effect at all.* But *effect* occasionally is used as a verb meaning "to bring about": *Her efforts effected a change.* And *affect* is used in psychology as a noun meaning "feeling or emotion": *One can infer much about affect from behavior.*

agree to, agree with *Agree to* means "consent to," and *agree with* means "be in accord with": *How can they agree to a treaty when they don't agree with each other about the terms?*

all ready, already *All ready* means "completely prepared," and *already* means "by now" or "before now": *We were all ready to go to the movie, but it had already started.*

all right *All right* is always two words. *Alright* is a common error.

517

all together, altogether   *All together* means "in unison" or "gathered in one place." *Altogether* means "entirely." *It's not altogether true that our family never spends vacations all together.*

allusion, illusion   An *allusion* is an indirect reference, and an *illusion* is a deceptive appearance: *Paul's constant allusions to Shakespeare created the illusion that he was an intellectual.*

almost, most   *Almost* means "nearly"; *most* means "the greater number (or part) of." In formal writing, *most* should not be used as a substitute for *almost: We see each other almost* [not *most*] *every day.*

a lot   *A lot* is always two words, used informally to mean "many." *Alot* is a common misspelling.

among, between   In general, use *among* for relationships involving more than two people or for comparing one thing to a group to which it belongs. *The four of them agreed among themselves that the choice was between New York and Los Angeles.*

amount, number   Use *amount* with a singular noun that names something not countable (a noncount noun): *The amount of food varies.* Use *number* with a plural noun that names more than one of something countable (a plural count noun): *The number of calories must stay the same.*

and/or   *And/or* indicates three options: one or the other or both (*The decision is made by the mayor and/or the council*). If you mean all three options, *and/or* is appropriate. Otherwise, use *and* if you mean both, *or* if you mean either.

ante-, anti-   The prefix *ante-* means "before" (*antedate, antebellum*); *anti-* means "against" (*antiwar, antinuclear*). Before a capital letter or *i*, *anti-* takes a hyphen: *anti-Freudian, anti-isolationist.*

anxious, eager   *Anxious* means "nervous" or "worried" and is usually followed by *about. Eager* means "looking forward" and is usually followed by *to. I've been anxious about getting blisters. I'm eager* [not *anxious*] *to get new running shoes.*

anybody, any body; anyone, any one   *Anybody* and *anyone* are indefinite pronouns; *any body* is a noun modified by *any; any one* is a pronoun or adjective modified by *any. How can anybody communicate with any body of government? Can anyone help Amy? She has more work than any one person can handle.*

any more, anymore   *Any more* means "no more"; *anymore* means "now." Both are used in negative constructions. *He doesn't want any more. She doesn't live here anymore.*

are, is   Use *are* with a plural subject (*books are*), *is* with a singular subject (*book is*).

as   *As* may be vague or ambiguous when it substitutes for *because, since,* or *while: As the researchers asked more questions, their money ran out.* (Does *as* mean "while" or "because"?) *As* should never be used as a substitute for *whether* or *who. I'm not sure whether* [not *as*] *we can make it. That's the man who* [not *as*] *gave me directions.*

Usage

as, like In formal speech and writing, *like* should not introduce a full clause (with a subject and a verb) because it is a preposition. The preferred choice is *as* or *as if*: *The plan succeeded as* [not *like*] *we hoped. It seemed as if* [not *like*] *it might fail. Other plans like it have failed.*

assure, ensure, insure *Assure* means "to promise": *He assured us that we would miss the traffic. Ensure* and *insure* often are used interchangeably to mean "make certain," but some reserve *insure* for matters of legal and financial protection and use *ensure* for more general meanings: *We left early to ensure that we would miss the traffic. It's expensive to insure yourself against floods.*

awful, awfully Strictly speaking, *awful* means "awe-inspiring." As intensifiers meaning "very" or "extremely" (*He tried awfully hard*), *awful* and *awfully* should be avoided in formal speech or writing.

a while, awhile *Awhile* is an adverb; *a while* is an article and a noun. *I will be gone awhile* [not *a while*]. *I will be gone for a while* [not *awhile*].

bad, badly In formal speech and writing, *bad* should be used only as an adjective; the adverb is *badly. He felt bad because his tooth ached badly.* In *He felt bad*, the verb *felt* is a linking verb and the adjective *bad* describes the subject. See also pp. 271–72.

being as, being that Colloquial for *because*, the preferable word in formal speech or writing: *Because* [not *Being as*] *the world is round, Columbus never did fall off the edge.*

beside, besides *Beside* is a preposition meaning "next to." *Besides* is a preposition meaning "except" or "in addition to" as well as an adverb meaning "in addition." *Besides, several other people besides you want to sit beside Dr. Christensen.*

better, had better *Had better* (meaning "ought to") is a verb modified by an adverb. The verb is necessary and should not be omitted: *You had better* [not just *better*] *go.*

between, among See *among, between.*

bring, take Use *bring* only for movement from a farther place to a nearer one and *take* for any other movement. *First take these books to the library for renewal; then take them to Mr. Daniels. Bring them back to me when he's finished.*

but, hardly, scarcely These words are negative in their own right; using *not* with any of them produces a double negative (see pp. 274–75). *We have but* [not *haven't got but*] *an hour before our plane leaves. I could hardly* [not *couldn't hardly*] *make out her face.*

but, however, yet Each of these words is adequate to express contrast. Don't combine them. *He had finished, yet* [not *but yet*] *he continued.*

can, may Strictly, *can* indicates capacity or ability, and *may* indicates permission or possibility: *If I may talk with you a moment, I believe I can solve your problem.*

censor, censure To *censor* is to edit or remove from public view on moral or other grounds; to *censure* is to give a formal scolding. *The* *lieutenant was censured by Major Taylor for censoring the letters her soldiers wrote home from boot camp.*

cite, sight, site   *Cite* is a verb usually meaning "quote," "commend," or "acknowledge": *You must cite your sources. Sight* is both a noun meaning "the ability to see" or "a view" and a verb meaning "perceive" or "observe": *What a sight you see when you sight Venus through a strong telescope. Site* is a noun meaning "place" or "location" or a verb meaning "situate": *The builder sited the house on an unlikely site.*

climatic, climactic   *Climatic* comes from *climate* and refers to the weather: *Recent droughts may indicate a climatic change. Climactic* comes from *climax* and refers to a dramatic high point: *During the climactic duel between Hamlet and Laertes, Gertrude drinks poisoned wine.*

complement, compliment   To *complement* something is to add to, complete, or reinforce it: *Her yellow blouse complemented her black hair.* To *compliment* something is to make a flattering remark about it: *He complimented her on her hair. Complimentary* can also mean "free": *complimentary tickets.*

conscience, conscious   *Conscience* is a noun meaning "a sense of right and wrong"; *conscious* is an adjective meaning "aware" or "awake." *Though I was barely conscious, my conscience nagged me.*

continual, continuous   *Continual* means "constantly recurring": *Most movies on television are continually interrupted by commercials. Continuous* means "unceasing": *Some cable channels present movies continuously without commercials.*

could of   See *have, of.*

credible, creditable, credulous   *Credible* means "believable": *It's a strange story, but it seems credible to me. Creditable* means "deserving of credit" or "worthy": *Steve gave a creditable performance. Credulous* means "gullible": *The credulous Claire believed Tim's lies.* See also *incredible, incredulous.*

criteria   The plural of *criterion* (meaning "standard for judgment"): *Our criteria are strict. The most important criterion is a sense of humor.*

data   The plural of *datum* (meaning "fact"). Though *data* is often used as a singular noun, many readers prefer the plural verb, and it is always correct: *The data fail* [not *fails*] *to support the hypothesis.*

device, devise   *Device* is the noun, and *devise* is the verb: *Can you devise some device for getting his attention?*

different from, different than   *Different from* is preferred: *His purpose is different from mine.* But *different than* is widely accepted when a construction using *from* would be wordy: *I'm a different person now than I used to be* is preferable to *I'm a different person now from the person I used to be.*

differ from, differ with   To *differ from* is to be unlike: *The twins differ from each other only in their hairstyles.* To *differ with* is to disagree with: *I have to differ with you on that point.*

discreet, discrete *Discreet* (noun form *discretion*) means "tactful": *What's a discreet way of telling Maud to be quiet?* *Discrete* (noun form *discreteness*) means "separate and distinct": *Within a computer's memory are millions of discrete bits of information.*

disinterested, uninterested *Disinterested* means "impartial": *We chose Pete, as a disinterested third party, to decide who was right.* *Uninterested* means "bored" or "lacking interest": *Unfortunately, Pete was completely uninterested in the question.*

don't *Don't* is the contraction for *do not,* not for *does not*: *I don't care, you don't care,* and *he doesn't* [not *don't*] *care.*

due to the fact that Wordy for *because.*

eager, anxious See *anxious, eager.*

effect See *affect, effect.*

elicit, illicit *Elicit* is a verb meaning "bring out" or "call forth." *Illicit* is an adjective meaning "unlawful." *The crime elicited an outcry against illicit drugs.*

emigrate, immigrate *Emigrate* means "to leave one place and move to another": *The Chus emigrated from Korea.* *Immigrate* means "to move into a place where one was not born": *They immigrated to the United States.*

ensure See *assure, ensure, insure.*

enthused Used colloquially as an adjective meaning "showing enthusiasm." The preferred adjective is *enthusiastic*: *The coach was enthusiastic* [not *enthused*] *about the team's victory.*

et al., etc. Use *et al.,* the Latin abbreviation for "and other people," only in source citations: *Jones et al.* Avoid *etc.,* the Latin abbreviation for "and other things," in formal writing, and do not use it to refer to people or to substitute for precision, as in *The government provides health care, etc.*

everybody, every body; everyone, every one *Everybody* and *everyone* are indefinite pronouns: *Everybody* [*Everyone*] *knows Tom steals.* *Every one* is a pronoun modified by *every,* and *every body* a noun modified by *every.* Both refer to each thing or person of a specific group and are typically followed by *of*: *The game commissioner has stocked every body of fresh water in the state with fish, and now every one of our rivers is a potential trout stream.*

everyday, every day *Everyday* is an adjective meaning "used daily" or "common"; *every day* is a noun modified by *every*: *Everyday problems tend to arise every day.*

everywheres Nonstandard for *everywhere.*

except See *accept, except.*

except for the fact that Wordy for *except that.*

explicit, implicit *Explicit* means "stated outright": *I left explicit instructions.* *Implicit* means "implied, unstated": *We had an implicit understanding.*

farther, further   *Farther* refers to additional distance (*How much farther is it to the beach?*), and *further* refers to additional time, amount, or other abstract matters (*I don't want to discuss this any further*).

fewer, less   *Fewer* refers to individual countable items (a plural count noun), *less* to general amounts (a noncount noun, always singular). *Skim milk has fewer calories than whole milk. We have less milk left than I thought.*

flaunt, flout   *Flaunt* means "show off": *If you have style, flaunt it. Flout* means "scorn" or "defy": *Hester Prynne flouted convention and paid the price.*

flunk   A colloquial substitute for *fail.*

fun   As an adjective, *fun* is colloquial and should be avoided in most writing: *It was a pleasurable* [not *fun*] *evening.*

further   See *farther, further.*

get   This common verb is used in many slang and colloquial expressions: *get lost, that really gets me, getting on. Get* is easy to overuse: watch out for it in expressions such as *it's getting better* (substitute *improving*) and *we got done* (substitute *finished*).

good, well   *Good* is an adjective, and *well* is nearly always an adverb: *Larry's a good dancer. He and Linda dance well together. Well* is properly used as an adjective only to refer to health: *You look well.* (*You look good*, in contrast, means "Your appearance is pleasing.")

good and   Colloquial for "very": *I was very* [not *good and*] *tired.*

had better   See *better, had better.*

had ought   The *had* is unnecessary and should be omitted: *He ought* [not *had ought*] *to listen to his mother.*

hanged, hung   Though both are past-tense forms of *hang, hanged* is used to refer to executions and *hung* is used for all other meanings: *Tom Dooley was hanged* [not *hung*] *from a white oak tree. I hung* [not *hanged*] *the picture you gave me.*

hardly   See *but, hardly, scarcely.*

have, of   Use *have*, not *of*, after helping verbs such as *could, should, would, may,* and *might: You should have* [not *should of*] *told me.*

he, she; he/she   Convention has allowed the use of *he* to mean "he or she": *After the infant learns to creep, he progresses to crawling.* However, many writers today consider this usage inaccurate and unfair because it seems to exclude females. The construction *he/she*, one substitute for *he*, is awkward and objectionable to most readers. The better choice is to make the pronoun plural, to rephrase, or, sparingly, to use *he or she.* For instance: *After infants learn to creep, they progress to crawling. After learning to creep, the infant progresses to crawling. After the infant learns to creep, he or she progresses to crawling.* See also pp. 173 and 263–64.

herself, himself   See *myself, herself, himself, yourself.*

hisself   Nonstandard for *himself.*

hopefully   *Hopefully* means "with hope": *Freddy waited <u>hopefully</u> for a glimpse of Eliza.* The use of *hopefully* to mean "it is to be hoped," "I hope," or "let's hope" is now very common; but many readers continue to object strongly to the usage, so try to avoid it. *I hope* [not *Hopefully*] *the law will pass.*

idea, ideal   An *idea* is a thought or conception. An *ideal* (noun) is a model of perfection or a goal. *Ideal* should not be used in place of *idea*: *The <u>idea</u>* [not *<u>ideal</u>*] *of the play is that our <u>ideals</u> often sustain us.*

if, whether   Use *whether* rather than *if* when you are expressing an alternative: *<u>If</u> I laugh hard, people can't tell <u>whether</u> I'm crying or not.*

illicit   See *elicit, illicit.*

illusion   See *allusion, illusion.*

immigrate, emigrate   See *emigrate, immigrate.*

implicit   See *explicit, implicit.*

imply, infer   Writers or speakers *imply*, meaning "suggest": *Jim's letter <u>implies</u> he's having a good time.* Readers or listeners *infer*, meaning "conclude": *From Jim's letter I <u>infer</u> he's having a good time.*

incredible, incredulous   *Incredible* means "unbelievable"; *incredulous* means "unbelieving": *When Nancy heard Dennis's <u>incredible</u> story, she was frankly <u>incredulous</u>.* See also *credible, creditable, credulous.*

individual, person, party   *Individual* should refer to a single human being in contrast to a group or should stress uniqueness: *The US Constitution places strong emphasis on the rights of the <u>individual</u>.* For other meanings *person* is preferable: *What <u>person</u>* [not *<u>individual</u>*] *wouldn't want the security promised in that advertisement? Party* means "group" (*Can you seat a <u>party</u> of four for dinner?*) and should not be used to refer to an individual except in legal documents. See also *people, persons.*

infer   See *imply, infer.*

in regards to   Nonstandard for *in regard to, as regards,* or *regarding.*

insure   See *assure, ensure, insure.*

irregardless   Nonstandard for *regardless.*

is, are   See *are, is.*

is because   See *reason is because.*

is when, is where   These are faulty constructions in sentences that define: *Adolescence <u>is a stage</u>* [not *<u>is when a person is</u>*] *between childhood and adulthood. Socialism <u>is a system in which</u>* [not *<u>is where</u>*] *government owns the means of production.* See also p. 301.

its, it's   *Its* is the pronoun *it* in the possessive case: *That plant is losing <u>its</u> leaves. It's* is a contraction for *it is* or *it has*: *<u>It's</u>* [*<u>It is</u>*] *likely to die. <u>It's</u>* [*<u>It has</u>*] *got a fungus.* Many people confuse *it's* and *its* because possessives are most often formed with *-'s*; but the possessive *its*, like *his* and *hers*, never takes an apostrophe.

kind of, sort of, type of   In formal speech and writing, avoid using *kind of* or *sort of* to mean "somewhat": *He was <u>rather</u>* [not *<u>kind of</u>*] *tall.*

Kind, sort, and *type* are singular and take singular modifiers and verbs: *This kind of dog is easily trained.* Agreement errors often occur when these singular nouns are combined with the plural adjectives *these* and *those*: *These kinds* [not *kind*] *of dogs are easily trained. Kind, sort,* and *type* should be followed by *of* but not by *a*: *I don't know what type of* [not *type* or *type of a*] *dog that is.*

Use *kind of, sort of,* or *type of* only when the word *kind, sort,* or *type* is important: *That was a strange* [not *strange sort of*] *statement.*

lay, lie   *Lay* means "put" or "place" and takes a direct object: *We could lay the tablecloth in the sun.* Its main forms are *lay, laid, laid. Lie* means "recline" or "be situated" and does not take an object: *I lie awake at night. The town lies east of the river.* Its main forms are *lie, lay, lain.* (See also p. 221.)

leave, let   *Leave* and *let* are interchangeable only when followed by *alone; leave me alone* is the same as *let me alone.* Otherwise, *leave* means "depart" and *let* means "allow": *Jill would not let Sue leave.*

less   See *fewer, less.*

lie, lay   See *lay, lie.*

like, as   See *as, like.*

like, such as   Strictly, *such as* precedes an example that represents a larger subject, whereas *like* indicates that two subjects are comparable. *Steve has recordings of many great saxophonists such as Ben Webster and Lee Konitz. Steve wants to be a great jazz saxophonist like Ben Webster and Lee Konitz.*

literally   This word means "actually" or "just as the words say," and it should not be used to qualify or intensify expressions whose words are not to be taken at face value. The sentence *He was literally climbing the walls* describes a person behaving like an insect, not a person who is restless or anxious. For the latter meaning, *literally* should be omitted.

lose, loose   *Lose* means "mislay": *Did you lose a brown glove? Loose* means "unrestrained" or "not tight": *Ann's canary got loose. Loose* also can function as a verb meaning "let loose": *They loose the dogs as soon as they spot the bear.*

lots, lots of   Colloquial substitutes for *very many, a great many,* or *much.* Avoid *lots* and *lots of* in college or business writing.

may, can   See *can, may.*

may be, maybe   *May be* is a verb, and *maybe* is an adverb meaning "perhaps": *Tuesday may be a legal holiday. Maybe we won't have classes.*

may of   See *have, of.*

media   *Media* is the plural of *medium* and takes a plural verb: *All the news media are increasingly visual.* The singular verb is common, even in the media, but many readers prefer the plural verb, and it is always correct.

might of   See *have, of.*

moral, morale   As a noun, *moral* means "ethical conclusion" or "lesson": *The moral of the story escapes me. Morale* means "spirit" or "state of mind": *Victory improved the team's morale.*

most, almost   See *almost, most.*

must of   See *have, of.*

myself, herself, himself, yourself   The *-self* pronouns refer to or intensify another word or words: *Paul helped <u>himself</u>; Jill <u>herself</u> said so.* The *-self* pronouns are often used colloquially in place of personal pronouns, but that use should be avoided in formal speech and writing: *No one except <u>me</u>* [not *<u>myself</u>*] *saw the accident. Our delegates will be Susan and <u>you</u>* [not *<u>yourself</u>*]. See also p. 255 on the unchanging forms of the *-self* pronouns in standard American English.

nowheres   Nonstandard for *nowhere.*

number   See *amount, number.*

of, have   See *have, of.*

off of   *Of* is unnecessary. Use *off* or *from* rather than *off of: He jumped <u>off</u>* [or *<u>from</u>*, not *<u>off of</u>*] *the roof.*

OK, O.K., okay   All three spellings are acceptable, but avoid this colloquial term in formal speech and writing.

on the other hand   This transitional expression of contrast should be preceded by its mate, *on the one hand: <u>On the one hand</u>, we hoped for snow. <u>On the other hand</u>, we worried that it would harm the animals.* However, the two combined can be unwieldy, and a simple *but, however, yet,* or *in contrast* often suffices: *We hoped for snow. <u>However,</u> we worried that it would harm the animals.*

owing to the fact that   Wordy for *because.*

party   See *individual, person, party.*

people, persons   In formal usage, *people* refers to a general group: *We the <u>people</u> of the United States. . . . Persons* refers to a collection of individuals: *Will the person or <u>persons</u> who saw the accident please notify. . . .* Except when emphasizing individuals, prefer *people* to *persons.* See also *individual, person, party.*

per   Except in technical writing, an English equivalent is usually preferable to the Latin *per: $10 <u>an</u>* [not *<u>per</u>*] *hour; sent <u>by</u>* [not *<u>per</u>*] *parcel post; requested <u>in</u>* [not *<u>per</u>* or *<u>as per</u>*] *your letter.*

percent (per cent), percentage   Both these terms refer to fractions of one hundred. *Percent* always follows a number (*<u>40 percent</u> of the voters*), and the word should be used instead of the symbol (%) in general writing. *Percentage* stands alone (*the <u>percentage</u> of voters*) or follows an adjective (*a <u>high percentage</u>*).

person   See *individual, person, party.*

persons   See *people, persons.*

phenomena   The plural of *phenomenon* (meaning "perceivable fact" or "unusual occurrence"): *Many <u>phenomena are</u> not recorded. One <u>phenomenon is</u> attracting attention.*

plenty   A colloquial substitute for *very: The reaction occurred <u>very</u>* [not *<u>plenty</u>*] *fast.*

plus   *Plus* is standard as a preposition meaning "in addition to": *His income plus mine is sufficient.* But *plus* is colloquial as a conjunctive adverb: *Our organization is larger than theirs; moreover [not plus], we have more money.*

precede, proceed   The verb *precede* means "come before": *My name precedes yours in the alphabet.* The verb *proceed* means "move on": *We were told to proceed to the waiting room.*

prejudice, prejudiced   *Prejudice* is a noun; *prejudiced* is an adjective. Do not drop the *-d* from *prejudiced*: *I knew that my parents were prejudiced [not prejudice].*

pretty   Overworked as an adverb meaning "rather" or "somewhat": *He was somewhat [not pretty] irked at the suggestion.*

principal, principle   *Principal* is an adjective meaning "foremost" or "major," a noun meaning "chief official," or, in finance, a noun meaning "capital sum." *Principle* is a noun only, meaning "rule" or "axiom." *Her principal reasons for confessing were her principles of right and wrong.*

proceed, precede   See *precede, proceed.*

question of whether, question as to whether   Wordy substitutes for *whether.*

raise, rise   *Raise* means "lift" or "bring up" and takes a direct object: *The Kirks raise cattle.* Its main forms are *raise, raised, raised. Rise* means "get up" and does not take an object: *They must rise at dawn.* Its main forms are *rise, rose, risen.* (See also p. 221.)

real, really   In formal speech and writing, *real* should not be used as an adverb; *really* is the adverb and *real* an adjective. *Popular reaction to the announcement was really [not real] enthusiastic.*

reason is because   This colloquial and redundant expression should be avoided in formal speech and writing. Use a *that* clause after *reason is*: *The reason he is absent is that [not is because] he is sick.* Or: *He is absent because he is sick.* (See also p. 302.)

respectful, respective   *Respectful* means "full of (or showing) respect": *Be respectful of other people. Respective* means "separate": *The French and the Germans occupied their respective trenches.*

rise, raise   See *raise, rise.*

scarcely   See *but, hardly, scarcely.*

sensual, sensuous   *Sensual* suggests sexuality; *sensuous* means "pleasing to the senses." *Stirred by the sensuous scent of meadow grass and flowers, Cheryl and Paul found their thoughts growing increasingly sensual.*

set, sit   *Set* means "put" or "place" and takes a direct object: *He sets the pitcher down.* Its main forms are *set, set, set. Sit* means "be seated" and does not take an object: *She sits on the sofa.* Its main forms are *sit, sat, sat.* (See also p. 221.)

shall, will   *Will* is the future-tense helping verb for all persons: *I will go, you will go, they will go.* The main use of *shall* is for first-person questions requesting an opinion or consent: *Shall I order a pizza? Shall we* *dance? Shall* can also be used for the first person when a formal effect is desired (*I shall expect you around three*), and it is occasionally used with the second or third person to express the speaker's determination (*You shall do as I say*).

should of   See *have, of.*

sight, site, cite   See *cite, sight, site.*

since   *Since* mainly relates to time: *I've been waiting since noon.* But *since* is also often used to mean "because": *Since you ask, I'll tell you.* Revise sentences in which the word could have either meaning, such as *Since I studied physics, I have been planning to major in engineering.*

sit, set   See *set, sit.*

site, cite, sight   See *cite, sight, site.*

so   Avoid using *so* alone or as a vague intensifier: *He was so late. So* needs to be followed by *that* and a clause that states a result: *He was so late that I left without him.*

somebody, some body; someone, some one   *Somebody* and *someone* are indefinite pronouns; *some body* is a noun modified by *some;* and *some one* is a pronoun or an adjective modified by *some. Somebody ought to invent a shampoo that will give hair some body. Someone told Janine she should choose some one plan and stick with it.*

sometime, sometimes, some time   *Sometime* means "at an indefinite time in the future": *Why don't you come up and see me sometime? Sometimes* means "now and then": *I still see my old friend Joe sometimes. Some time* means "a span of time": *I need some time to make the payments.*

somewheres   Nonstandard for *somewhere.*

sort of, sort of a   See *kind of, sort of, type of.*

such   Avoid using *such* as a vague intensifier: *It was such a cold winter. Such* should be followed by *that* and a clause that states a result: *It was such a cold winter that Napoleon's troops had to turn back.*

such as   See *as, like.*

supposed to, used to   In both these expressions, the *-d* is essential: *I used to* [not *use to*] *think so. He's supposed to* [not *suppose to*] *meet us.*

sure   Colloquial when used as an adverb meaning *surely: James Madison sure was right about the need for the Bill of Rights.* If you merely want to be emphatic, use *certainly: Madison certainly was right.* If your goal is to convince a possibly reluctant reader, use *surely: Madison surely was right.*

sure and, sure to; try and, try to   *Sure to* and *try to* are the correct forms: *Be sure to* [not *sure and*] *buy milk. Try to* [not *Try and*] *find some decent tomatoes.*

take, bring   See *bring, take.*

than, then   *Than* is a conjunction used in comparisons, *then* an adverb indicating time: *Holmes knew then that Moriarty was wilier than he had thought.*

that, which   *That* introduces an essential clause: *We should use the lettuce that Susan bought* (*that Susan bought* limits the lettuce to a particular lettuce). *Which* can introduce both essential and nonessential clauses, but many writers reserve *which* only for nonessential clauses: *The leftover lettuce, which is in the refrigerator, would make a good salad* (*which is in the refrigerator* simply provides more information about the lettuce we already know of). Essential clauses (with *that* or *which*) are not set off by commas; nonessential clauses (with *which*) are. See also pp. 315–17.

that, which, who   Use *that* for animals, things, and sometimes collective or anonymous people: *The rocket that failed cost millions. Infants that walk need constant tending.* Use *which* only for animals and things: *The river, which flows south, divides two countries.* Use *who* only for people and for animals with names: *Dorothy is the girl who visits Oz. Her dog, Toto, who accompanies her, gives her courage.*

their, there, they're   *Their* is the possessive form of *they*: *Give them their money.* *There* indicates place (*I saw her standing there*) or functions as an expletive (*There is a hole behind you*). *They're* is a contraction for *they are*: *They're going fast.*

theirselves   Nonstandard for *themselves*.

them   In standard American English, *them* does not serve as an adjective: *Those* [not *Them*] *people want to know.*

then, than   See *than, then*.

these kind, these sort, these type, those kind   See *kind of, sort of, type of*.

this, these   *This* is singular: *this car* or *This is the reason I left.* *These* is plural: *these cars* or *These are not valid reasons.*

thru   A colloquial spelling of *through* that should be avoided in all academic and business writing.

to, too, two   *To* is a preposition; *too* is an adverb meaning "also" or "excessively"; and *two* is a number. *I too have been to Europe two times.*

too   Avoid using *too* as a vague intensifier: *Monkeys are too mean.* When you do use *too*, explain the consequences of the excessive quality: *Monkeys are too mean to make good pets.*

toward, towards   Both are acceptable, though *toward* is preferred. Use one or the other consistently.

try and, try to   See *sure and, sure to; try and, try to*.

type of   See *kind of, sort of, type of*. Don't use *type* without *of*: *It was a family type of* [not *type*] *restaurant.* Or better: *It was a family restaurant.*

uninterested   See *disinterested, uninterested*.

unique   *Unique* means "the only one of its kind" and so cannot sensibly be modified with words such as *very* or *most*: *That was a unique* [not *a very unique* or *the most unique*] *movie.*

usage, use   *Usage* refers to conventions, most often those of a language: *Is "hadn't ought" proper usage?* *Usage* is often misused in place of the noun *use*: *Wise use* [not *usage*] *of insulation can save fuel.*

use, utilize   *Utilize* can be used to mean "make good use of": *Many teachers utilize computers for instruction.* But for all other senses of "place in service" or "employ," prefer *use.*

used to   See *supposed to, used to.*

wait for, wait on   In formal speech and writing, *wait for* means "await" (*I'm waiting for Paul*) and *wait on* means "serve" (*The owner of the store herself waited on us*).

ways   Colloquial as a substitute for *way*: *We have only a little way* [not *ways*] *to go.*

well   See *good, well.*

whether, if   See *if, whether.*

which, that   See *that, which.*

which, who, that   See *that, which, who.*

who, whom   *Who* is the subject of a sentence or clause (*We don't know who will come*). *Whom* is the object of a verb or preposition (*We do not know whom we invited*). (See also pp. 257–58.)

who's, whose   *Who's* is the contraction of *who is* or *who has*: *Who's* [*Who is*] *at the door? Jim is the only one who's* [*who has*] *passed. Whose* is the possessive form of *who*: *Whose book is that?*

will, shall   See *shall, will.*

would be   Often used instead of *is* or *are* to soften statements needlessly: *One example is* [not *would be*] *gun-control laws. Would* can combine with other verbs for the same unassertive effect: *would ask, would seem, would suggest,* and so on.

would have   Avoid this construction in place of *had* in clauses that begin *if* and state a condition contrary to fact: *If the tree had* [not *would have*] *withstood the fire, it would have been the oldest in town.* See also p. 240.

would of   See *have, of.*

you   In all but very formal writing, *you* is generally appropriate as long as it means "you, the reader." In all writing, avoid indefinite uses of *you*, such as *In one ancient tribe your first loyalty was to your parents.* See also p. 268.

your, you're   *Your* is the possessive form of *you*: *Your dinner is ready. You're* is the contraction of *you are*: *You're bound to be late.*

yourself   See *myself, herself, himself, yourself.*

Credits

Answers to Selected Exercises

These pages provide answers to all exercise items and sentences that are labeled with a star (✻) in the book.

Exercise 9.1, p. 100

Possible revision

The stereotype that women talk more on cell phones than men do turns out to be false. In a five-year survey of 1021 cell phone owners, a major wireless company found that men spend 35 percent more time on their phones.

Exercise 10.3, p. 111

1. A reasonable generalization.
2. An unreasonable generalization that cannot be inferred from the evidence.

Exercise 10.4, p. 112

Possible answers

1. **Premise:** Anyone who has opposed pollution controls may continue to do so.
   Premise: The mayor has opposed pollution controls.
   Conclusion: The mayor may continue to do so.
   The statement is valid and true.
2. **Premise:** Corporate Web sites are sponsored by for-profit entities.
   Premise: Information from for-profit entities is unreliable.
   Conclusion: Information on corporate Web sites is unreliable.
   The statement is untrue because the second premise is untrue.

Exercise 10.5, p. 112

Possible answers

1. Primarily emotional appeal. Ethical appeal: knowledgeable, concerned, reasonable (at least in the two uses of *may*), slightly sarcastic (*most essential of skills*).
2. Primarily rational appeal. Ethical appeal: knowledgeable, reasonable.

Exercise 10.6, p. 116

Possible answers

1. Sweeping generalization and begged question.
   A revision: A successful marriage demands a degree of maturity.
2. Hasty generalization and non sequitur.
   A revision: Students' persistent complaints about the unfairness of the grading system should be investigated.
3. Reductive fallacy.
   A revision: The United States got involved in World War II for many complex reasons. The bombing of Pearl Harbor was a triggering incident.
4. Either/or fallacy and hasty generalization.
   A revision: People watch television for many reasons, but some watch because they are too lazy to talk or read or because they want mindless escape from their lives.
5. Reductive fallacy and begged question.
   A revision: Racial tension may occur when people with different backgrounds live side by side.

Exercise 15.1, p. 150

Possible answers

1. Many heroes helped to emancipate the slaves.
2. Harriet Tubman, an escaped slave herself, guided hundreds of other slaves to freedom on the Underground Railroad.

531

Exercise 15.2, p. 153

Possible answers

1. Pat Taylor strode into the packed room, greeting students called "Taylor's Kids" and nodding to their parents and teachers.
2. This wealthy Louisiana oilman had promised his "Kids" free college educations because he was determined to make higher education available to all qualified but disadvantaged students.

Exercise 15.3, p. 155

Possible answers

1. Because soldiers admired their commanding officers, they often gave them nicknames containing the word *old*, even though not all of the commanders were old.
2. General Thomas "Stonewall" Jackson was also called "Old Jack," although he was not yet forty years old.

Exercise 15.4, p. 158

Possible answers

1. Genaro González is a successful writer whose stories and novels have been published to critical acclaim.
2. Although he loves to write, he has also earned a doctorate in psychology.

Exercise 15.5, p. 158

Possible revision

Sir Walter Raleigh personified the Elizabethan Age, the period of Elizabeth I's rule of England, in the last half of the sixteenth century. Raleigh was a courtier, a poet, an explorer, and an entrepreneur. Supposedly, he gained Queen Elizabeth's favor by throwing his cloak beneath her feet at the right moment, just as she was about to step over a puddle.

Exercise 16.1, p. 161

Possible answers

1. The ancient Greeks celebrated four athletic contests: the Olympic Games at Olympia, the Isthmian Games near Corinth, the Pythian Games at Delphi, and the Nemean Games at Cleonae.
2. Each day the games consisted of either athletic events or ceremonies and sacrifices to the gods.
3. In the years between the games, competitors were taught wrestling, javelin throwing, and boxing.
4. Competitors ran sprints, participated in spectacular chariot and horse races, and ran long distances while wearing full armor.
5. The purpose of such events was developing physical strength, demonstrating skill and endurance, and sharpening the skills needed for war.

Exercise 16.2, p. 162

Possible answers

1. People can develop post-traumatic stress disorder (PTSD) after experiencing a dangerous situation and fearing for their survival.
2. The disorder can be triggered by a wide variety of events, such as combat, a natural disaster, or a hostage situation.

Exercise 17.1, p. 167

Possible revision

After being dormant for many years, the Italian volcano Vesuvius exploded on August 24 in the year AD 79. The ash, pumice, and mud from the volcano buried two towns—Herculaneum and the more famous Pompeii—which lay undiscovered until 1709 and 1748, respectively.

Exercise 18.1, p. 174

Possible answers

1. Acquired immune deficiency syndrome (AIDS) is a <u>serious threat</u> all over the world.
2. The disease <u>is transmitted</u> primarily by sexual intercourse, exchange of bodily fluids, shared needles, and blood transfusions.
3. Those who think the disease is limited to <u>homosexuals</u>, <u>drug users</u>, and foreigners are quite mistaken.
4. <u>Statistics</u> suggest that in the United States one in every five hundred college <u>students</u> carries the HIV virus that causes AIDS.
5. <u>People</u> with HIV or full-blown AIDS <u>do</u> not deserve <u>others' exclusion</u> or callousness. Instead, <u>they need</u> all the compassion, medical care, and financial assistance due <u>the seriously ill</u>.

Exercise 18.2, p. 174

Possible answers

1. When <u>people apply</u> for a job, <u>they</u> should represent <u>themselves</u> with the best possible résumé.
2. A person applying for a job as a <u>mail carrier</u> should appear to be honest and responsible.
3. <u>Applicants</u> for a position as an in-home nurse should also represent <u>themselves</u> as honest and responsible.
4. Of course, <u>the applicant</u> should also have a background of capable nursing.
5. The business <u>executive</u> who is scanning a stack of résumés will, of necessity, read them all quickly.

Exercise 18.3, p. 177

1. Maxine Hong Kingston was <u>awarded</u> many prizes for her first two books, *The Woman Warrior* and *China Men*.
2. Kingston <u>cites</u> her mother's tales about ancestors and ancient Chinese customs as the sources of these memoirs.
3. Two of King's <u>progenitors</u>, her great-grandfathers, are focal points of *China Men*.
4. Both men led rebellions against <u>oppressive</u> employers: a sugarcane farmer and a railroad-construction engineer.
5. In her childhood Kingston was greatly <u>affected</u> by her mother's tale about a pregnant aunt who was ostracized by villagers. [*Ostracized* is correct.]

Exercise 18.4, p. 178

1. AIDS is a serious health <u>problem</u>.
2. Once the virus has entered the blood system, it <u>destroys</u> T-cells.

Exercise 18.6, p. 181

1. Children are waiting longer to become independent <u>of</u> their parents.
2. According <u>to</u> US Census data for young adults ages eighteen to twenty-four, 57 percent of men and 47 percent of women live full-time with their parents.

Exercise 18.7, p. 182

1. The Eighteenth Amendment <u>to</u> the Constitution <u>of</u> the United States was ratified <u>in</u> 1919.
2. It prohibited the "manufacture, sale, or transportation <u>of</u> intoxicating liquors."

Exercise 18.9, p. 184

Possible answers

1. The <u>disasters</u> of the war have shaken the small nation <u>severely</u>.
2. Prices for food have <u>risen markedly</u>, and citizens <u>suspect</u> that others are <u>profiting</u> on the black market.
3. Medical supplies are so <u>scarce</u> that even <u>very sick</u> civilians cannot get treatment.
4. With most men fighting or injured or killed, women have had to <u>take men's places</u> in farming and manufacturing.

5. <u>Finally</u>, the war's <u>high cost</u> has <u>destroyed the nation's economy</u>.

Exercise 19.1, p. 186

1. The first ice cream, eaten <u>in</u> China in about 2000 BC, was lumpier than modern ice cream.
2. The Chinese made their ice cream of milk, spices, and overcooked rice and packed <u>it</u> in snow to solidify.

Exercise 20.1, p. 191

Possible answers

1. If sore muscles after exercising are a problem for you, there are some <u>things you can do</u> to ease the discomfort.
2. First, <u>apply cold immediately</u> to reduce inflammation.
3. <u>Cold constricts</u> blood vessels <u>and keeps</u> blood away from the injured muscles.
4. <u>Avoid</u> heat for the first day.
5. <u>Applying</u> heat within the first twenty-four hours <u>can increase</u> muscle soreness and stiffness.

Exercise 20.2, p. 191

Possible answers

    <u>After much thought</u>, he <u>concluded</u> that carcinogens <u>could be treated</u> like automobiles. Instead of giving in to <u>a fear</u> of cancer, we should <u>balance</u> the benefits <u>we receive</u> from potential carcinogens (<u>such as</u> plastic <u>and pesticides</u>) against the damage <u>they do</u>.

Exercise 21.1, p. 197

1. The gingko tree, which is one of the world's oldest trees, is large and picturesque.
2. Gingko trees may grow to over a hundred feet in height.
3. Their leaves look like fans and are about three inches wide.
4. The leaves turn yellow in the fall.
5. Because it tolerates smoke, low temperatures, and low rainfall, the gingko appears in many cities.

Exercise 21.2, p. 198

1. You can reduce stress by making a few simple changes.
2. Get up fifteen minutes earlier than you ordinarily do.
3. Eat a healthy breakfast, and eat it slowly so that you enjoy it.
4. Do your more unpleasant tasks early in the day.
5. Every day, do at least one thing you really enjoy.

Exercise 21.3, p. 201

1. Just about everyone has heard the story <u>of</u> the Trojan Horse.
2. This incident happened at the city of Troy <u>and</u> was planned by the Greeks.
3. The Greeks built a huge wooden horse <u>with</u> a hollow space big enough to hold many men.
4. At night, they rolled the horse to the gate of Troy <u>and</u> left it there filled with soldiers.
5. <u>In</u> the morning, the Trojans were surprised to see the enormous horse.

Exercise 22.1, p. 203

1. The <u>horse</u> / <u>has</u> a long history of service to humanity but today <u>is</u> mainly a show and sport animal.
2. A member of the genus *Equus*, the domestic <u>horse</u> / <u>shares</u> its lineage with the ass and the zebra.
3. The domestic <u>horse</u> and its <u>relatives</u> / <u>are</u> all plains-dwelling herd animals.
4. The modern <u>horse</u> / <u>evolved</u> in North America.
5. <u>It</u> / <u>migrated</u> to other parts of the world and then <u>became</u> extinct in the Americas.

Exercise 22.2, p. 206

1. The number of serious crimes in the United States decreased.
   - S (The number)
   - V (decreased)

2. A decline in serious crimes occurred each year.
   - S (A decline)
   - V (occurred)

3. The Crime Index measures serious crime.
   - S (The Crime Index)
   - V (measures)
   - DO (serious crime)

4. The FBI invented the index.
   - S (The FBI)
   - V (invented)
   - DO (the index)

5. The four serious violent crimes are murder, robbery, forcible rape, and aggravated assault.
   - S (The four serious violent crimes)
   - V (are)
   - SC (murder)
   - SC (robbery)
   - SC (forcible rape)
   - SC (aggravated assault)

Exercise 22.3, p. 208

1. <u>Milo Addica and Will Rokos cowrote</u> the screenplay for *Monster's Ball*.
2. <u>Marc Foster directed</u> the film.

Exercise 23.1, p. 212

1. With its many synonyms, or words with similar meanings, English can make choosing the right word a difficult task.
   - prepositional phrase (With its many synonyms)
   - appositive phrase (or words with similar meanings)
   - prepositional phrase (with similar meanings)
   - participial phrase (choosing the right word)

2. Borrowing words from other languages such as French and Latin, English acquired an unusual number of synonyms.
   - participial phrase (Borrowing words from other languages such as French and Latin)
   - prepositional phrase (from other languages)
   - appositive phrase (such as French and Latin)
   - prepositional phrase (of synonyms)

3. Having so many choices, how does a writer decide between *motherly* and *maternal* or among *womanly*, *feminine*, and *female*?
   - participial phrase (Having so many choices)
   - prepositional phrase (between *motherly* and *maternal*)
   - prepositional phrase (among *womanly*, *feminine*, and *female*)

4. Some people prefer longer and more ornate words to avoid the flatness of short words.
   - infinitive phrase (to avoid the flatness of short words)
   - prepositional phrase (of short words)

5. During the Renaissance a heated debate occurred between the Latinists, favoring Latin words, and the Saxonists, preferring Anglo-Saxon words derived from Germanic roots.
   - prepositional phrase (During the Renaissance)
   - participle (heated)
   - prepositional phrase (between the Latinists)
   - participial phrase (favoring Latin words)
   - participial phrase (preferring Anglo-Saxon words derived)
   - participial phrase (derived from Germanic roots)
   - prepositional phrase (from Germanic roots)

Exercise 23.2, p. 215

1. The Prophet Muhammad, <u>who was the founder of Islam</u>, was born about 570 CE in the city of Mecca.
   - ADJ

2. He grew up in the care of his grandfather and an uncle <u>because both of his parents had died</u>.
   - ADV

3. His family was part of a powerful Arab tribe <u>that lived in western Arabia</u>.
   - ADJ

4. <u>When Muhammad was about forty years old</u>, he had a vision <u>while he was in a cave outside Mecca</u>.
   - ADV
   - ADV

5. He believed <u>that God had selected him to be the prophet of a true religion for the Arab people</u>.
   - N

Exercise 24.1, p. 217

1. Our world has many sounds, but they all have one thing in common. [Compound.]
   - main clause (Our world has many sounds)
   - main clause (they all have one thing in common)

┌─────────────────────── main clause ───────────────────────┐
2. The one thing that all sounds share is that they are produced by vibrations.
   [Complex.] └── subordinate clause ──┘ └──────── subordinate clause ────────┘

┌─────────── main clause ───────────┐   ┌────────── main clause ──────────┐
3. The vibrations make the air move in waves, and these sound waves travel to the ear.
   [Compound.]

   ┌────────── subordinate clause ──────────┐ ┌──────────── main clause ────────────┐
4. When sound waves enter the ear, the auditory nerves convey them to the brain, and
   ┌───── main clause ─────┐
   the brain interprets them. [Complex.]

┌──────────────────── main clause ────────────────────┐
5. Sound waves can also travel through other material, such as water and even the
   solid earth. [Simple.]

Exercise 25.1, p. 221

1. The world population has **grown** by two-thirds of a billion people in less than a decade. [Past participle.]
2. Recently it **broke** the 6 billion mark. [Past tense.]
3. Experts have **drawn** pictures of a crowded future. [Past participle.]
4. They predict that the world population may have **slid** up to as much as 10 billion by the year 2050. [Past participle.]
5. Though the food supply **rose** in the last decade, the share to each person **fell**. [Both past tense.]

Exercise 25.2, p. 222

1. Yesterday afternoon the child **lay** down for a nap.
2. The child has been **raised** by her grandparents.

Exercise 25.3, p. 224

1. A teacher sometimes **asks** too much of a student.
2. In high school I was once **punished** for being sick.
3. I had **missed** a week of school because of a serious case of the flu.
4. I **realized** that I would fail a test unless I had a chance to make up the class work.
5. I **discussed** the problem with the teacher.

Exercise 25.4, p. 228

1. Each year thousands of new readers **have** been discovering Agatha Christie's mysteries.
2. The books **were** written by a prim woman who had worked as a nurse during World War I.

Exercise 25.5, p. 229

1. A report from the Bureau of the Census has **confirmed** a widening gap between rich and poor.
2. As suspected, the percentage of people below the poverty level did **increase** over the last decade.

Exercise 25.6, p. 231

1. A program called HELP Wanted tries to encourage citizens **to** take action on behalf of American competitiveness.
2. Officials working on this program hope **to improve** education for work.

Exercise 25.7, p. 233

1. American movies treat everything from going out with [correct] someone to making up [correct] an ethnic identity, but few people **look into their significance**.
2. While some viewers stay away from [correct] topical films, others **turn up at the theater** simply because a movie has sparked debate.

Exercise 26.1, p. 237

The 1960 presidential race between Richard Nixon and John F. Kennedy was the first to feature a televised debate. [Sentence correct.] Despite his extensive political experience, Nixon perspired heavily and looked haggard and uneasy in front of the camera. By contrast, Kennedy projected cool poise and provided crisp answers that made him seem fit for the office of President.

Exercise 26.2, p. 238

E. B. White's famous children's novel *Charlotte's Web* is a wonderful story of friendship and loyalty. [Sentence correct.] Charlotte, the wise and motherly spider, decides to save her friend Wilbur, the young and childlike pig, from being butchered by his owner. She makes a plan to weave words into her web that describe Wilbur.

Exercise 26.3, p. 240

1. Diaries that Adolf Hitler was supposed to have written had surfaced in Germany.
2. Many people believed that the diaries were authentic because a well-known historian had declared them so.

Exercise 26.4, p. 241

1. When an athlete turns professional, he or she commits to a grueling regimen of mental and physical training.
2. If athletes were less committed, they would disappoint teammates, fans, and themselves.
3. If professional athletes are very lucky, they may play until age forty.
4. Unless an athlete achieves celebrity status, he or she will have few employment choices after retirement.
5. If professional sports were less risky, athletes would have longer careers and more choices after retirement.

Exercise 27.1, p. 243

1. If John Hawkins had known of all the dangerous side effects of smoking tobacco, would he have introduced the dried plant to England in 1565?
2. Hawkins noted that if a Florida Indian man were to travel for several days, he would smoke tobacco to satisfy his hunger and thirst.

Exercise 28.1, p. 245

Possible answers

1. Many factors determine water quality.
2. All natural waters contain suspended and dissolved substances.
3. The environment controls the amounts of the substances.
4. Pesticides produce some dissolved substances.
5. Fields, livestock feedlots, and other sources deposit sediment in water.

Exercise 28.2, p. 246

Possible answers

1. When engineers built the Eiffel Tower in 1889, the French thought it to be ugly.
2. At that time, industrial technology was still resisted by many people.

Exercise 29.1, p. 253

1. Weinstein & Associates is a consulting firm that tries to make businesspeople laugh.
2. Statistics from recent research suggest that humor relieves stress.
3. Reduced stress in businesses in turn reduces illness and absenteeism.
4. Reduced stress can also reduce friction within an employee group, which then works together more productively.
5. In special conferences held by one consultant, each of the participants practices making others laugh.

Exercise 29.2, p. 253

The Siberian tiger is the largest living cat in the world, much bigger than its relative the Bengal tiger. It grows to a length of nine to twelve feet, including its tail, and to a height of about three and a half feet. It can weigh over six hundred pounds. This carnivorous hunter lives in northern China and Korea as well as in Siberia. During the long winter of this Arctic climate, the yellowish striped coat gets a little lighter in order to blend with the snow-covered landscape. The coat also grows quite thick because the tiger has to withstand temperatures as low as −50°F.

Exercise 30.1, p. 257

1. Jody and I had been hunting for jobs.
2. The best employees at our old company were she and I, so we expected to find jobs quickly.

Exercise 30.2, p. 258

1. The school administrators suspended Jurgen, whom they suspected of setting the fire.
2. Jurgen had been complaining to other custodians, who reported him.
3. He constantly complained of unfair treatment from whoever happened to be passing in the halls, including pupils.
4. "Who here has heard Mr. Jurgen's complaints?" the police asked.
5. "Whom did he complain most about?"

Exercise 30.3, p. 260

1. Sentence correct.
2. Sentence correct.
3. He and Gilgamesh wrestled to see who was more powerful.
4. Sentence correct.
5. The friendship of the two strong men was sealed by their fighting.

Exercise 31.1, p. 265

Possible answers

1. Each girl raised in a Mexican American family in the Rio Grande valley of Texas hopes that one day she will be given a *quinceañera* party for her fifteenth birthday.
2. Such a celebration is very expensive because it entails a religious service followed by a huge party. [*Or:* Such celebrations are very expensive because they entail a religious service followed by a huge party.]
3. A girl's immediate family, unless it is wealthy, cannot afford the party by itself.
4. The parents will ask each close friend or relative if he or she can help with the preparations. [*Or:* The parents will ask close friends or relatives if they can help with the preparations.]
5. Sentence correct.

Exercise 32.1, p. 269

Possible answers

1. "Life begins at forty" is a cliché many people live by, and this saying may or may not be true.
2. Living successfully or not depends on one's definition of success.
3. When Pearl Buck was forty, her novel *The Good Earth* won the Pulitzer Prize.
4. Buck was raised in a missionary family in China, which [*or* whom] she wrote about in her novels.
5. In *The Good Earth* the characters have to struggle, but fortitude is rewarded.

Exercise 32.2, p. 269

Possible revision

In Charlotte Brontë's *Jane Eyre*, Jane is a shy young woman who takes a job as governess. Her employer is a rude, brooding man named Rochester. [Sentence correct.] He lives in a mysterious mansion on the English moors, and both the mansion and the moors contribute an eerie quality to Jane's experience. Eerier still are the fires, strange noises, and other unexplained happenings in the house; but Rochester refuses to discuss them.

Exercise 33.1, p. 271

1. The eighteenth-century essayist Samuel Johnson fared badly in his early life.
2. Sentence correct.
3. After failing as a schoolmaster, Johnson moved to London, where he did well.
4. Johnson was taken seriously as a critic and dictionary maker.
5. Johnson was really surprised when he received a pension from King George III.

Exercise 33.2, p. 275

1. Interest in books about the founding of the United States is not [*or* is hardly] consistent among Americans: it seems to vary with the national mood.
2. Sentence correct.

Exercise 33.3, p. 276

1. Several critics found Alice Walker's *The Color Purple* to be a fascinating book.
2. Sentence correct.

Exercise 33.4, p. 280

From the native American Indians who migrated from Asia 20,000 years ago to the new arrivals who now come by planes, the United States is a nation of foreigners. It is a country of immigrants who are all living under a single flag.

Back in the seventeenth and eighteenth centuries, at least 75 percent of the population came from England. However, between 1820 and 1975 more than 38 million immigrants came to this country from elsewhere in Europe.

Exercise 33.5, p. 281

1. Americans often argue about which professional sport is best: basketball, football, or baseball.
2. Basketball fans contend that their sport offers more action because the players are constantly running and shooting.
3. Because it is played indoors in relatively small arenas, basketball allows fans to be closer to the action than the other sports do.
4. Football fanatics say they hardly stop yelling once the game begins.
5. They cheer when their team executes a really complicated play well.

Exercise 34.1, p. 285

1. People who are right-handed dominate in our society.
2. Hand tools, machines, and even doors are designed for right-handed people.
3. However, nearly 15 percent of the population may be left-handed.
4. When they begin school, children often prefer one hand or the other.
5. Parents and teachers should not try deliberately to change a child's preference for the left hand.

Exercise 34.2, p. 286

1. Some years ago Detroit cars were often praised.
2. Large luxury cars were especially prized.

Exercise 34.3, p. 287

Possible answers

1. After Andrew Jackson had accomplished many deeds of valor, his fame led to his election to the presidency in 1828 and 1832.
2. When Jackson was fourteen, both of his parents died.
3. To aid the American Revolution, Jackson chose service as a mounted courier.
4. Sentence correct.
5. Though not well educated, Jackson proved his ability in a successful career as a lawyer and judge.

Exercise 35.1, p. 292

Possible answers

1. Human beings who perfume themselves are not much different from other animals.
2. Animals as varied as insects and dogs release pheromones, chemicals that signal other animals.
3. Human beings have a diminished sense of smell and do not consciously detect most of their own species' pheromones.
4. No sentence fragment.
5. Some sources say that people began using perfume to cover up the smell of burning flesh during sacrifices to the gods.

Exercise 35.2, p. 293

Possible answers

People generally avoid eating mushrooms except those they buy in stores. But in fact many varieties of mushrooms are edible. Mushrooms are members of a large group of vegetation called nonflowering plants⊙ including algae, mosses, ferns, and coniferous trees⊙ even the giant redwoods of California. Most of the nonflowering plants prefer moist environments⌢such as forest floors, fallen timber, and still water. Mushrooms, for example⊙ prefer moist, shady soil. Algae grow in water.

Exercise 36.1, p. 298

Possible answers

1. Some people think that dinosaurs were the first living vertebrates⊙ but fossils of turtles go back 40 million years or further.
2. Although most other reptiles exist mainly in tropical regions⊙ turtles inhabit a variety of environments worldwide.
3. Turtles do not have teeth⊙ their jaws are covered with a sharp, horny sheath.
4. Turtles cannot expand their lungs to breathe air⊙ as a result⊙ they make adjustments in how space is used within the shell.
5. Some turtles can get oxygen from water⊙ therefore⊙ they don't need to breathe air.

Exercise 36.2, p. 299

Possible answers

1. Money has a long history⊙ It goes back at least as far as the earliest records.
   Money has a long history⊙ it goes back at least as far as the earliest records.
2. Many of the earliest records concern financial transactions⊙ Indeed, early history must often be inferred from commercial activity.
   Many of the earliest records concern financial transactions⊙ indeed, early history must often be inferred from commercial activity.
3. Sentence correct.
4. Sometimes the objects have had real value⊙ however⊙ in modern times their value has been more abstract.
   Although sometimes the objects have had real value, in modern times their value has been more abstract.
5. Cattle, fermented beverages, and rare shells have served as money⊙ and each one had actual value for the society.
   Cattle, fermented beverages, and rare shells have served as money⊙ Each one had actual value for the society.

Exercise 36.3, p. 300

Possible answers

What many call the first genocide of modern times occurred during World War I, when the Armenians were deported from their homes in Anatolia, Turkey. The Turkish government assumed that the Armenians were sympathetic to Russia, with whom the Turks were at war. Many Armenians died because of the hardships of the journey, and many were massacred. The death toll was estimated at between 600,000 and 1 million.

Exercise 37.1, p. 303

Possible answers

1. A hurricane occurs when the winds in a tropical depression rotate counterclockwise at more than seventy-four miles per hour.
2. Because hurricanes can destroy so many lives and so much property, people fear them.
3. Through high winds, storm surge, floods, and tornadoes, hurricanes have killed thousands of people.
4. Storm surge occurs when the hurricane's winds whip up a tide that spills over seawalls and deluges coastal islands.
5. Sentence correct.

Exercise 37.2, p. 304

1. Archaeologists and other scientists _can_ often determine the age of their discoveries by means of radiocarbon dating.
2. This technique _can_ be used on any material that once was living.
3. This technique _is_ based on the fact that all living organisms _contain_ carbon.
4. The most common isotope is carbon 12, which _contains_ six protons and six neutrons.
5. A few carbon atoms are classified as the isotope carbon 14, where the nucleus consists of six protons and eight neutrons.

Exercise 38.1, p. 310

When visitors first arrive in Hawaii, they often encounter an unexpected language barrier. Standard English is the language of business and government, but many of the people speak Pidgin English◯ Instead of an excited "Aloha◯" the visitors may be greeted with an excited Pidgin "Howzit◯" or asked if they know "how fo' find one good hotel◯"

Exercise 39.1, p. 312

1. Parents once automatically gave their children the father's last name◯ but some no longer do.
2. Parents were once legally required to give their children the father's last name◯ but these laws have been contested in court.
3. Parents may now give their children any last name they choose◯ and the arguments for choosing the mother's last name are often strong and convincing.
4. Sentence correct.
5. The child's last name may be just the mother's◯ or it may link the mother's and the father's with a hyphen.

Exercise 39.2, p. 314

1. Veering sharply to the right◯ a large flock of birds neatly avoids a high wall.
2. Sentence correct.
3. With the help of complex computer simulations◯ zoologists are learning more about this movement.
4. Because it is sudden and apparently well coordinated◯ the movement of flocks and schools has seemed to be directed by a leader.
5. Almost incredibly◯ the group could behave with more intelligence than any individual seemed to possess.

Exercise 39.3, p. 319

1. Italians insist that Marco Polo◯ the thirteenth-century explorer◯ did not import pasta from China.
2. Pasta◯which consists of flour and water and often egg◯ existed in Italy long before Marco Polo left for his travels.
3. Sentence correct.
4. Most Italians dispute this account◯ although their evidence is shaky.
5. Wherever it originated, the Italians are now the undisputed masters◯in making and cooking pasta.

Exercise 39.4, p. 320

1. Shoes with high heels were originally designed to protect feet from mud◯ garbage◯ and animal waste in the streets.
2. Sentence correct.
3. The heels were worn by men and made of colorful silk fabrics◯ soft suedes◯ or smooth leathers.
4. High-heeled shoes became popular when the short◯ powerful King Louis XIV of France began wearing them.
5. Louis's influence was so strong that men and women of the court◯ priests and cardinals◯ and even household servants wore high heels.

Exercise 39.5, p. 325

1. Underground aquifers are deep and sometimes broad layers of water that are trapped between layers of rock.
2. Porous rock or sediment holds the water.
3. Deep wells drilled through the top layers of solid rock produce a flow of water.
4. Such wells are sometimes called artesian wells.
5. Sentence correct.

Exercise 39.6, p. 326

Ellis Island, New York, reopened for business in 1990, but now the customers are tourists, not immigrants. This spot, which lies in New York Harbor, was the first American soil seen or touched by many of the nation's immigrants. Though other places also served as ports of entry for foreigners, none has the symbolic power of Ellis Island. Between its opening in 1892 and its closing in 1954, over 20 million people, about two-thirds of all immigrants, were detained there before taking up their new lives in the United States. Ellis Island processed over 2000 [*or* 2,000] newcomers a day when immigration was at its peak between 1900 and 1920.

Exercise 40.1, p. 328

Possible answers

1. Electronic instruments are prevalent in jazz and rock music; however, they are less common in classical music.
2. Jazz and rock change rapidly; they nourish experimentation and improvisation.
3. The notes and instrumentation of traditional classical music were established by a composer writing decades or centuries ago; therefore, such music does not change.
4. Contemporary classical music not only can draw on tradition; it can also respond to innovations such as jazz rhythms and electronic sounds.
5. Much contemporary electronic music is more than just jazz, rock, or classical; it is a fusion of all three.

Exercise 40.2, p. 329

The set, sounds, and actors in the movie captured the essence of horror films. The set was ideal: dark, deserted streets; trees dipping their branches over the sidewalks; mist hugging the ground and creeping up to meet the trees; looming shadows of unlighted, turreted houses. The sounds, too, were appropriate; especially terrifying was the hard, hollow sound of footsteps echoing throughout the film.

Exercise 41.1, p. 332

1. Sunlight is made up of three kinds of radiation: visible rays; infrared rays, which we cannot see; and ultraviolet rays, which are also invisible.
2. Especially in the ultraviolet range, sunlight is harmful to the eyes.
3. Ultraviolet rays can damage the retina; furthermore, they can cause cataracts on the lens.
4. Infrared rays are the longest, measuring 700 nanometers and longer, while ultraviolet rays are the shortest, measuring 400 nanometers and shorter.
5. The lens protects the eye by absorbing much of the ultraviolet radiation and thus protecting the retina.

Exercise 42.1, p. 336

1. In the myths of the ancient Greeks, the goddesses' roles vary widely.
2. Athena's role is to guard the city of Athens.
3. Artemis's function is to care for wild animals and small children.
4. Athena and Artemis's father, Zeus, is the king of the gods.
5. Even a single goddess's responsibilities are often varied.

Exercise 42.2, p. 338

People whose online experiences include blogging, Web cams, and social-networking sites are often used to seeing the details of other people's private lives. Many are also comfortable sharing their own opinions, photographs, and videos with family, friends, and even <u>strangers</u>. However, they need to realize that employers and even the government can see <u>their</u> information, too. Employers commonly put <u>applicants'</u> names through social-networking Web sites such as *MySpace* and *Facebook*.

Exercise 43.1, p. 342

In one class we talked about a passage from "I Have a Dream," the speech delivered by Martin Luther King, Jr., on the steps of the Lincoln Memorial on August 28, 1963:

> When the architects of our republic wrote the magnificent words of the Constitution and the Declaration of Independence, they were signing a promissory note to which every American was to fall heir. This note was a promise that all men would be guaranteed the unalienable rights of life, liberty, and the pursuit of happiness.

"What did Dr. King mean by this statement?" the teacher asked. "Perhaps we should define "promissory note" first."

Exercise 44.1, p. 347

1. "To be able to read the Bible in the vernacular was a liberating experience. . . ."

Exercise 44.2, p. 349

"Let all the learned say what they can, / 'Tis ready money makes the man." These two lines of poetry by the Englishman William Somerville (1645–1742) may apply to a current American economic problem. Non-American investors with "ready money" pour some of it—as much as $1.3 trillion in recent years—into the United States. Stocks and bonds, savings deposits, service companies, factories, artworks, political campaigns—the investments of foreigners are varied and grow more numerous every day.

Exercise 45.1, p. 356

1. Science <u>affects</u> many <u>important</u> aspects of our lives.
2. Many people have a <u>poor</u> understanding of the <u>role</u> of scientific breakthroughs in <u>their</u> health.
3. Many people <u>believe</u> that <u>doctors</u> are more <u>responsible</u> for <u>improvements</u> in health care than scientists are.
4. But scientists in the <u>laboratory</u> have made crucial steps in the search for <u>knowledge</u> about human health and <u>medicine</u>.
5. For example, one scientist <u>whose</u> discoveries have <u>affected</u> many people is Ulf Von Euler.

Exercise 45.2, p. 357

The <u>weather</u> <u>affects</u> all of us, though <u>its</u> <u>effects</u> are different for different people. Some people love a <u>fair</u> day with warm <u>temperatures</u> and sunshine. They revel in spending a <u>whole</u> day outside without the threat of <u>rain</u>.

Exercise 46.1, p. 359

1. Sentence correct.
2. Sentence correct.
3. The non-African elephants of south-central Asia are somewhat smaller.
4. A fourteen- or fifteen-year-old elephant has reached sexual maturity.
5. The elephant life span is about sixty-five or seventy years.

Exercise 47.1, p. 363

1. San Antonio, Texas, is a thriving city in the <u>Southwest</u>.
2. The city has always offered much to tourists interested in the roots of Spanish settlement of the <u>New World</u>.
3. The <u>Alamo</u> is one of five Catholic <u>missions</u> built by <u>priests</u> to convert <u>Native</u> <u>Americans</u> and to maintain <u>Spain's</u> claims in the area.
4. But the <u>Alamo</u> is more famous for being the site of an 1836 battle that helped to create the <u>Republic</u> of Texas.
5. Many of the nearby <u>streets</u>, such as Crockett <u>Street</u>, are named for men who died in that <u>battle</u>.

Exercise 48.1, p. 366

1. Of the many Vietnam veterans who are writers, Oliver Stone is perhaps the most famous for writing and directing the films *Platoon* and *Born on the Fourth of July*.
2. Tim O'Brien has written short stories for *Esquire*, *GQ*, and *Massachusetts Review*.
3. *Going after Cacciato* is O'Brien's dreamlike novel about the horrors of combat.
4. The word *Vietnam* is technically two words (*Viet* and *Nam*), but most American writers spell it as one word. [*Viet* and *Nam* were correctly highlighted. Highlighting removed from *one*.]
5. American writers use words or phrases borrowed from Vietnamese, such as *di di mau* ("go quickly") or *dinky dau* ("crazy").

Exercise 49.1, p. 369

1. Sentence correct.
2. About 65 million years ago, a comet or asteroid crashed into the earth.
3. The result was a huge crater about 10 kilometers (6.2 miles) deep in the Gulf of Mexico.
4. Sharpton's new measurements suggest that the crater is 50 percent larger than scientists had previously believed.
5. Indeed, 20-year-old drilling cores reveal that the crater is about 186 miles wide, roughly the size of Connecticut.

Exercise 50.1, p. 372

1. The planet Saturn is 900 million miles, or nearly 1.5 billion kilometers, from the sun.
2. Sentence correct.
3. Thus, Saturn orbits the sun only 2.4 times during the average human life span.
4. It travels in its orbit at about 21,600 miles per hour.
5. Fifteen to twenty times denser than Earth's core, Saturn's core measures seventeen thousand miles across.

Exercise 56.1, p. 478

The entries below follow the order of the exercise and so are not alphabetized.

Zimmerman, Malai, and Kent Hoover. "Use of Third Parties to Collect State and Local Taxes on Internet Sales." *Pacific Business Journal* 5.2 (2004): 45-48. Print.

United States. Advisory Commission on Electronic Commerce. *Report to Congress.* US Advisory Commission on Electronic Commerce, Apr. 2005. Web. 12 Nov. 2009.

"The Internet Tax Freedom Act and the Digital Divide." *Center on Budget and Policy Priorities.* Center on Budget and Policy Priorities, 26 Sept. 2007. Web. 2 Nov. 2009.

Novack, Janet. "Point, Click, Pay Tax." *Forbes* 28 Nov. 2007: 56-58. *Proquest.* Web. 10 Nov. 2009.

Index

Index

Index

Index

Index

Index

Index

Index

Index

Index

Index

Index

Index

Index

Index

Index

Index

Editing Symbols

Boldface numbers and letters refer to chapters and sections of the handbook.

ab	Faulty abbreviation, **49**	⌃ ⌄	Comma, **39**
ad	Misused adjective or adverb, **33**	;	Semicolon, **40**
agr	Error in agreement, **29**, **31**	:	Colon, **41**
ap	Apostrophe needed or misused, **42**	⌄	Apostrophe, **39**
appr	Inappropriate word, **18a**	" "	Quotation marks, **40**
arg	Faulty argument, **10b–d**	— ( ) … [ ] /	Dash, parentheses, ellipsis mark, brackets, slash, **44**
awk	Awkward construction	par, ¶	Start new paragraph, **6**
cap	Use capital letter, **47**	¶ coh	Paragraph not coherent, **6b**
case	Error in case form, **30**	¶ dev	Paragraph not developed, **6c**
cit	Missing source citation or error in form of citation, **54e**	¶ un	Paragraph not unified, **6a**
coh	Coherence lacking, **3b-3**, **6b**	pass	Ineffective passive voice, **28a**
con	Be more concise, **20**	pn agr	Error in pronoun-antecedent agreement, **31**
coord	Coordination needed, **15c**	ref	Error in pronoun reference, **32**
crit	Think or read more critically, **8a–c**	rep	Unnecessary repetition, **20c**
cs	Comma splice, **36**	rev	Revise or proofread, **5**
d	Ineffective diction (word choice), **18**	run-on	Run-on (fused) sentence, **36**
des	Ineffective or incorrect document design, **7**	shift	Inconsistency, **26d**, **27b**, **28b**, **32f**
det	Error in use of determiner, **33f**	sp	Misspelled word, **45**
dm	Dangling modifier, **34b**	spec	Be more specific, **6c**, **18b-2**
emph	Emphasis lacking or faulty, **15**	sub	Subordination needed or faulty, **15d**
exact	Inexact word, **18b**	t	Error in verb tense, **26**
frag	Sentence fragment, **35**	t seq	Error in tense sequence, **26e**
fs	Fused sentence, **36**	trans	Transition needed, **6b-6**
gram	Error in grammar, **21–24**	und	Underline or italicize, **48**
hyph	Error in use of hyphen, **46**	usage	See Glossary of Usage, p. 517
inc	Incomplete construction, **19**	var	Vary sentence structure, **17b**
ital	Italicize or underline, **48**	vb	Error in verb form, **25**
k	Awkward construction	vb agr	Error in subject-verb agreement, **29**
lc	Use lowercase (small) letter, **47**	w	Wordy, **20**
mixed	Mixed construction, **37**	ww	Wrong word, **18b-1**
mm	Misplaced modifier, **34a**	//	Faulty parallelism, **16**
mng	Meaning unclear	#	Separate with a space
no cap	Unnecessary capital letter, **47**	◯	Close up the space
no ⌃	Comma not needed, **39h**	✐	Delete
no ¶	No new paragraph needed, **6**	the	Capitalize, **47**
num	Error in use of numbers, **50**	The	Use a small letter, **47**
p	Error in punctuation, **38–44**	teh	Transpose letters or words
. ? !	Period, question mark, exclamation point, **38**	x	Obvious error
		∧	Something missing, **19**
		??	Document illegible or meaning unclear

589

Throughout this handbook, the symbol ⟨CULTURE LANGUAGE⟩ signals topics for students whose first language or dialect is not standard American English. These topics can be tricky because they arise from rules in standard English that are quite different in other languages and dialects. Many of the topics involve significant cultural assumptions as well.

No matter what your language background, as a college student you are learning the culture of US higher education and the language that is used and shaped by that culture. The process is challenging, even for native speakers of standard American English. It requires not just writing clearly and correctly but also mastering conventions of developing, presenting, and supporting ideas. The challenge is greater if, in addition, you are trying to learn standard American English and are accustomed to other conventions. Several habits can help you succeed:

- **Read.** Besides course assignments, read newspapers, magazines, and books in English. The more you read, the more fluently and accurately you'll write.
- **Write.** Keep a journal in which you practice writing in English every day.
- **Talk and listen.** Take advantage of opportunities to hear and use English.
- **Ask questions.** Your instructors, tutors in the writing lab, and fellow students can clarify assignments and help you identify and solve writing problems.
- **Don't try for perfection.** No one writes perfectly, and the effort to do so can prevent you from expressing yourself fluently. View mistakes not as failures but as opportunities to learn.
- **Revise first; then edit.** Focus on each essay's ideas, support, and organization before attending to grammar and vocabulary. See the revision and editing checklists on pages 30 and 34.
- **Set editing priorities.** Concentrate first on any errors that interfere with clarity, such as problems with word order or subject-verb agreement. The following index can help you identify the topics you need to work on and can lead you to appropriate text discussions. The pages marked * include exercises for self-testing.

Contents

← "Editing Symbols" and "CULTURE LANGUAGE Guide"